contents

PART 4   PRODUCT AND PRICE DECISIONS 239

PART 5　　DISTRIBUTION DECISIONS 329

PART 6   PROMOTION DECISIONS 391

AVAILABLE ONLY ONLINE:

Appendix A: Financial Analysis in Marketing
Appendix B: Sample Marketing Plan
Appendix C: Careers in Marketing

preface

THE IMPORTANCE OF MARKETING TO BUSINESS

The environment of marketing has significantly changed over the last few years. While this revision reflects these changes, the foundational concepts of marketing continue to be important. All business students need to understand how marketing activities and functions are necessary for success. The 8th edition of *Foundations of Marketing* has been revised to provide a complete understanding of marketing by engaging students in decision making. We use active learning through the use of examples, exercises, cases, and MindTap. MindTap is an online personalized teaching experience with relevant assignments that guide students to analyze, apply, and improve thinking, allowing skills and outcomes to be measured with ease.

JamesBrey/Getty Images

Pride and Ferrell *Foundations of Marketing* facilitates students in mastering essential concepts. Therefore, evolving marketing areas such as digital marketing and social networking, marketing ethics and social responsibility, as well as major decision variables related to product, price, distribution, and promotion have received complete revision based on available research and marketing best practices. Examples and boxes have been replaced to be as up-to-date as possible.

We also provide numerous ancillary materials to aid in student comprehension of marketing concepts as well as for increasing instructor resources for teaching this important material. The Mind-Tap materials include building a Marketing Plan, concept check quizzes in the reading, self-assessments, homework assignments, PowerPoint presentations, videos of real companies, role play and group project assignments, flashcards, and more! Additionally, on the instructor companion site, YouTube videos are available for each chapter with worksheets to engage students in applying concepts. Our marketing video case series enables students to learn about how real-world companies address marketing challenges. Our Marketing Plan activities and video program provide students with practical knowledge of the challenges and the planning process of launching a new product. Together these revisions and additional materials will assist students in gaining a full understanding of pertinent marketing practices.

The decline of established ways of shopping is changing the retailing landscape, promotion, and consumer engagement. As consumers change the way they purchase products, department stores such as Macy's are closing stores. About two-thirds of books, music, films, and office supplies are now purchased online. It is not just that consumers are shopping and obtaining product information online, but also that consumer behavior is changing. We have addressed these changes and recognize that it is not just shopping from home. Consumers are increasingly focused on trust, value, and convenience. They are more aware of the best place to obtain products they want.

Specific details of this extensive revision are available in the transition guide in the *Instructor's Resource Manual*. We have also made efforts to improve all teaching ancillaries and student learning tools. PowerPoint presentations continue to be a very popular teaching device, and a special effort has been made to upgrade the PowerPoint program to enhance classroom teaching. The *Instructor's Manual* continues to be a valuable tool updated with engaging in-class activities and projects. The authors and publisher have worked together to provide a comprehensive teaching package and ancillaries that are unsurpassed in the marketplace.

The authors have maintained a hands-on approach to teaching this material and revising the text and its ancillaries. This results in an integrated teaching package and approach that is accurate, sound, and successful in reaching students. The outcome of this involvement fosters trust and confidence in the teaching package and in student learning outcomes. Student feedback regarding this textbook is highly favorable.

WHAT'S NEW TO THIS EDITION?

Our goal is to provide the most up-to-date content possible, including concepts, examples, cases, exercises, and data. Therefore, in this revision there are significant changes that make learning more engaging and interesting to the students. The following information highlights the types of changes that were made in this revision.

- **Foundational content.** Each chapter has been updated with the latest knowledge available related to frameworks, concepts, and academic research. These additions have been seamlessly integrated into the text. Many examples are new and a review of footnotes at the end of the chapters reveals where new content has been added. Most of the other examples have been updated.
- **Opening vignettes: *Marketing Insights*.** All of the chapter-opening vignettes are new. They are written to introduce the general content of each chapter by focusing on actual entrepreneurial companies and how they deal with real-world situations.
- **Boxed features.** Each chapter includes new or updated boxed features that highlight green marketing, marketing entrepreneurs, emerging trends in marketing, or controversial issues in marketing. The majority of the boxed features are new to this edition.
- **New Snapshot features.** All of the Snapshot features are new and engage students by highlighting interesting, up-to-date statistics that link marketing theory to the real world.

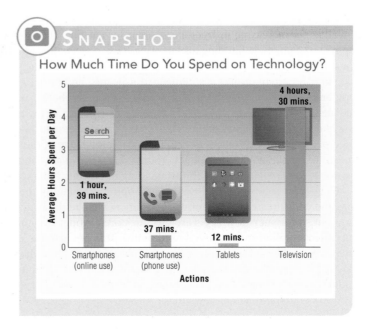

- **New research.** Throughout the text we have updated content with the most recent research that supports the frameworks and best practices for marketing.
- **New illustrations and examples.** New advertisements from well-known firms are employed to illustrate chapter topics. Experiences of real-world companies are used to exemplify marketing concepts and strategies throughout the text. Most examples are new or updated to include digital marketing concepts as well as several new sustainable marketing illustrations.
- **End-of-chapter video cases.** Each chapter contains one video case, profiling firms to illustrate concrete application of marketing concepts and strategies. Some of our video cases are new and others have been revised.
- **YouTube videos.** Each chapter has a YouTube video related to a concept. Student worksheets are available for application. These are all available on the instructor companion site.

FEATURES OF THE BOOK

As with previous editions, this edition of the text provides a comprehensive and practical introduction to marketing that is both easy to teach and to learn. *Foundations of Marketing* continues to be one of the most widely adopted introductory marketing textbooks in the world. We appreciate the confidence that adopters have placed in our textbooks and continue to work hard to make sure that, as in previous editions, this edition keeps pace with changes. The entire text is structured to excite students about the subject and to help them learn completely and efficiently.

- An *organizational model* at the beginning of each part provides a "road map" of the text and a visual tool for understanding the connections among various components.
- *Objectives* at the start of each chapter present concrete expectations about what students are to learn as they read the chapter.
- Every chapter begins with an *opening vignette*. This feature provides an example of the real world of marketing that relates to the topic covered in the chapter. After reading the vignette, the student should be motivated to want to learn more about concepts and strategies that relate to the varying topics. Students will be introduced to such companies as TOMS, Blue Apron, Netflix, Airbnb, and Hyundai.
- The *Emerging Trends* boxes cover such marketing phenomena as the Fair Trade movement, product placement, stores within department stores, and native advertising. Featured companies include Apple, Amazon, and EpiPen.

Promotion
Roper uses country music artist Joe Nichols to promote its western wear.

Roperusa.com

ECONOMIC FORCES — POLITICAL FORCES — DISTRIBUTION — LEGAL AND REGULATORY FORCES — TECHNOLOGY FORCES — SOCIOCULTURAL FORCES — COMPETITIVE FORCES — PRODUCT — PRICE — CUSTOMER — PROMOTION

EMERGING TRENDS IN MARKETING

The Fair Trade Movement Explodes

Fair Trade–certified organizations require factories to meet different conditions. They must pay their workers a minimum wage in the country in which they are employed, with the intention of working toward a "livable wage." A livable wage allows workers to afford basic necessities. Additionally, brands must pay a premium to factory workers. These premiums are placed in a collective bank account and are used for bonuses or to address community needs.

Traditionally, Fair Trade gained attention with commodities like coffee and cocoa. The Fair Trade trend is gaining traction among fashion and home furnishings. Many apparel and home furnishing brands have made a commitment to improve factory conditions. Consumers are embracing Fair Trade

apparel and home goods as well. For instance, during the back-to-school shopping season, Bed, Bath & Beyond quickly sold out of back-to-school supplies labeled as Fair Trade certified. This demonstrates consumers' increased concern for how goods are manufactured.

In particular, Fair Trade certification focuses on improving the labor conditions of factory workers. Although Fair Trade certification costs brands 1 to 5 percent of what companies pay to factories, it is clear that demand is on the rise. Fair Trade apparel and home furnishings have increased fivefold in the past few years, spurring more factories to work toward achieving certification. Marketers monitoring the environment are finding the costs of Fair Trade well worth the benefits.[a]

GOING GREEN

Can Cleaners Be Greener?

Eco-friendly detergents are a major marketing battleground for Procter & Gamble and Unilever, two giants of the laundry industry. Procter & Gamble's detergent brands include Tide and Gain, while Unilever's well-known detergents include Surf and Omo. But in recent years, green brands such as Seventh Generation and Method have nibbled away at the market share of traditional detergents as more consumers switch to eco-friendly products. As a result of these shifts in market share and consumer behavior, both Unilever and Procter & Gamble have revamped their marketing strategies to go greener and maintain momentum in the profitable detergent industry.

Unilever purchased Seventh Generation in 2016, in line with its strategic vision of emphasizing a larger social purpose. This deal brought Unilever

a business unit with a healthy bottom line and an established green reputation. Seventh Generation gained access to Unilever's marketing and manufacturing muscle so it can expand even more rapidly as demand increases.

Meanwhile, Procter & Gamble launched Tide purclean, a green version of its ever-popular Tide detergent. This formula is biobased and produced in a zero-waste factory powered by renewable wind energy, adding to the product's green credentials. Because biobased ingredients aren't yet well known, Procter & Gamble must use its marketing to educate consumers, raise awareness, promote product trial, and encourage repeat purchasing. What's next for Procter & Gamble and Unilever in their high-stakes battle over detergent market share?[a]

- The *Going Green* boxes introduce students to such topics as digital coupons, profiting from recycling, and green energy. Featured companies include Green Eileen, Walmart, Patagonia, and Procter & Gamble.

- The *Digital Marketing* features illustrate how organizations use social media and online marketing. Examples of organizations discussed include Facebook, Starbucks, Domino's, CoverGirl, and ReplyYes.

DIGITAL MARKETING

Digital Marketing Research Leads to Behavioral Advertising

It is no secret that online advertisers track consumer Internet activity and use the information to target ads toward each person's interests and preferences. These efforts used to be largely limited to individual websites tracking their own visitors. Now, however, technology enables the tracking of Internet users across sites. For example, every site with Facebook's "Like" button—as well as every smartphone app installed—sends Facebook information, which it then uses to target ads to its users.

Marketers claim this is a win–win for businesses and consumers. When ads are targeted to each user's behavior, users are more likely to see offerings

in which they have an interest, improving their online experience. Targeted ads are also more efficient for businesses. Some privacy advocates, however, criticize the tracking of Internet users without their consent. Another concern is keeping information secure in a digital environment where hacking attempts are increasing. Privacy advocates therefore argue that behavioral advertising should be strictly regulated. Self-regulation is also an option. Facebook, for instance, now offers an online tool that allows users to opt out of having ads shown to them based on sites they have visited outside the social network.[a]

ENTREPRENEURSHIP IN MARKETING

Blue Bottle Coffee: Not Your Typical Daily Grind

At John Freeman's Blue Bottle Coffee Company, headquartered in Oakland, California, coffee is more than a commodity. Blue Bottle embraces the third-wave movement, a movement that makes premium coffee into an exquisite experience of purity, flavor, and artisanship, similar to wine and cigars. To show that this experience is worth paying for, Blue Bottle has adopted a different marketing style than that of traditional coffee shops or even Starbucks.

For example, the stores of Blue Bottle emphasize the coffee experience above all else. Beverages only come in one size. With the exception of its

Palo Alto location, stores do not have Wi-Fi so as to prevent distraction. Beans for each order are freshly ground and brewed from scratch right in front of the customer. The price: between $4.00 and $7.00 per cup.

While this may seem expensive for the average coffee lover, Blue Bottle shows that its niche target market is those who experience the quality and experience of coffee. Apparently, this market is growing—Blue Bottle has 33 locations worldwide with ongoing expansion plans in the works.[a]

- The *Entrepreneurship in Marketing* feature focuses on the role of entrepreneurship and the need for creativity in developing successful marketing strategies by featuring successful entrepreneurial companies like Blue Bottle Coffee, Instacart, Pad & Quill, Dollar Shave Club, and Tastefully Simple.

- *Key term definitions* appear in the margins to help students build their marketing vocabulary.
- Figures, tables, photographs, advertisements, and Snapshot features increase comprehension and stimulate interest.
- A complete *chapter review* covers the major topics discussed and is organized based upon the chapter objectives.
- The list of key concepts provides another end-of-chapter study aid to expand students' marketing vocabulary.
- *Issues for discussion and review* at the end of each chapter encourage further study and exploration of chapter content
- The Marketing Applications are designed to facilitate students' comprehension of important topics and to enhance their critical thinking skills. Additional application questions have been included to help students quantify and apply marketing strategies. These questions have been developed based on a higher-level of thinking as related to Bloom's taxonomy. The primary purpose of these questions is to guide students from a basic knowledge of marketing concepts to application, analysis, and synthesis of marketing activities. The Marketing Applications appear online.

- The *Developing Your Marketing Plan* feature allows students to explore each chapter topic in relation to developing and implementing a marketing plan.
- Each chapter has an end-of-chapter video case to help students understand the application of chapter concepts. Some examples of companies highlighted in the cases are Ford, Apple Pay, Sephora, Alibaba, and Scripps Networks.
- *Appendices* discuss marketing career opportunities, explore financial analysis in marketing, and present a sample marketing plan. All of these appendices appear online on the instructor and student companion sites and in MindTap.
- A comprehensive *glossary* defines more than 600 important marketing terms.

TEXT ORGANIZATION

We have organized the six parts of *Foundations of Marketing* to give students a theoretical and practical understanding of marketing decision making.

Part 1   Strategic Marketing and Its Environment

In **Chapter 1,** we define marketing and explore several key concepts: customers and target markets, the marketing mix, relationship marketing, the marketing concept, and value-driven marketing. In **Chapter 2,** we look at an overview of strategic marketing topics, such as the strategic planning process; corporate, business-unit, and marketing strategies; the implementation of marketing strategies; performance evaluation of marketing strategies; and the components of the marketing plan. We examine competitive, economic, political, legal and regulatory, technological, and sociocultural forces as well as social responsibility and ethical issues in marketing decisions that can have profound effects on marketing strategies in **Chapter 3.**

Part 2   Marketing Research and Target Markets

In **Chapter 4,** we provide a foundation for analyzing buyers with a look at marketing information systems and the basic steps in the marketing research process. We look at elements that affect buying decisions to better analyze customers' needs and evaluate how specific marketing strategies can satisfy those needs. In **Chapter 5,** we deal with how to select and analyze target markets—one of the major steps in marketing strategy development.

Part 3   Customer Behavior and E-Marketing

We examine consumer buying decision processes and factors that influence buying decisions in **Chapter 6.** In **Chapter 7,** we explore business markets, business customers, the buying center, and the business buying decision process. **Chapter 8** focuses on the actions, involvement, and strategies of marketers that serve international customers. In **Chapter 9,** we discuss digital marketing, social media, and social networking.

Part 4   Product and Price Decisions

In **Chapter 10,** we introduce basic concepts and relationships that must be understood to make effective product decisions as well as branding, packaging, and labeling. We analyze a variety of dimensions regarding product management in **Chapter 11,** including line extensions and product modification, new-product development, product deletions, and the nature, importance, and characteristics of services. In **Chapter 12,** we initially discuss price and non-price competition. Then we analyze the eight stages of the process marketers use to establish prices. We explore a variety of pricing topics such as demand, elasticity, marginal analysis, break-even analysis, the basis for pricing, and pricing strategies.

Part 5   Distribution Decisions

In **Chapter 13,** we look at supply-chain management, marketing channels, and the decisions and activities associated with the physical distribution of products, such as order processing, materials handling, warehousing, inventory management, and transportation. **Chapter 14** explores retailing and wholesaling, including types of retailers and wholesalers, direct marketing and selling, and strategic retailing issues.

Part 6   Promotion Decisions

We discuss integrated marketing communications in **Chapter 15.** The communication process and major promotional methods that can be included in promotion mixes are described. In **Chapter 16,** we analyze the major steps in developing an advertising campaign. We also define public relations and how it can be used. **Chapter 17** deals with personal selling and the role it can play in a firm's promotional efforts. We also explore the general characteristics of sales promotion and describe sales-promotion techniques.

A COMPREHENSIVE INSTRUCTIONAL RESOURCE PACKAGE

For instructors, this edition of *Foundations of Marketing* includes an exceptionally comprehensive package of teaching materials.

Instructor's Manual

The *Instructor's Manual* has been revamped to meet the needs of an engaging classroom environment. It has been updated with diverse and dynamic discussion starters, classroom activities, and group exercises. It includes such tools as:

- Quick Reference Guide to see the available key terms, overview of the learning objectives, and major topics in each chapter
- What's New in Each Chapter?
- Purpose Statement
- Integrated Lecture Outline
- Discussion Starter recommendations that encourage active exploration of the in-text examples
- Class Exercises, Semester Project Activities, and Chapter Quizzes
- Suggested Answers to end-of-chapter exercises, cases, and strategic cases

Test Bank

The test bank provides more than 3,000 test items including true/false, multiple-choice, and essay questions. Each objective test item is accompanied by the correct answer, appropriate Learning Objective, level of difficulty, Bloom's level of thinking, Interdisciplinary Learning Outcomes, and Marketing Disciplinary Learning Outcomes. Cengage Learning Testing Powered by Cognero is a flexible, online system that allows you to:

- Author, edit, and manage test bank content from multiple Cengage Learning solutions
- Create multiple test versions in an instant
- Deliver tests from your LMS, your classroom, or wherever you want

American Marketing Association Professional Certified Marketer®

The American Marketing Association has recently started offering marketing graduates the opportunity of adding the AMA PCM® credentials to their undergraduate or MBA degree, which can serve as a symbol of professional excellence that affirms mastery of marketing knowledge and commitment to quality in the practice of marketing. Certification, which is voluntary, requires passing a rigorous and comprehensive exam and then maintaining your certification through continuing education. Earning your AMA PCM® certification demonstrates to employers, peers, and clients that you:

- Have mastered essential marketing knowledge and practices
- Go the extra mile to stay current in the marketing field
- Follow the highest professional standards

The AMA recommends Pride and Ferrell *Foundations of Marketing* as a suggested resource for AMA PCM® students to utilize as they prepare for taking the AMA PCM® Certification exam, and the text was used as a source to design the course and as a source for suitable examination questions. Now, more than ever, you need to stand out in the marketplace. AMA's Professional Certified Marketer (PCM®) program is the perfect way to showcase your expertise and set yourself apart.

To learn more about the American Marketing Association and the AMA PCM® exam, visit **https://www.ama.org/events-training/Certification/Pages/digital-marketing-certification.aspx**.

PowerPoint Slides

PowerPoint continues to be a very popular teaching device, and a special effort has been made to upgrade the PowerPoint program to enhance classroom teaching. Premium lecture slides, containing such content as advertisements, Web links, and unique graphs and data, have been created to provide instructors with up-to-date, unique content to increase student application and interest.

MindTap for Marketing

MindTap is a personalized teaching experience with relevant assignments that guide students to analyze, apply, and improve thinking, allowing them to measure skills and outcomes with ease.

- Personalized Teaching: Becomes yours with a learning path that is built with key student objectives. Control what students see and when they see it. Use it as-is or match to your syllabus exactly—hide, rearrange, add, and create your own content.
- Guide Students: A unique learning path of relevant readings, multimedia, and activities that move students up the learning taxonomy from basic knowledge and comprehension to analysis and application.
- Promote Better Outcomes: Empower instructors and motivate students with analytics and reports that provide a snapshot of class progress, time in course, and engagement and completion rates.

MINDTAP
From Cengage

FOUNDATIONS OF MARKETING, 8TH EDITION

📁 Part 1: Strategic Marketing and Its Environment (Ch. 1-3)

📁 Part 2: Marketing Research and Target Markets (Ch. 4-5)

📁 Part 3: Customer Behavior and E-Marketing (Ch. 6-9)

📁 Part 4: Product and Price Decisions (Ch. 10-12)

📁 Part 5: Distribution Decisions (Ch. 13-14)

📁 Part 6: Promotion Decisions (Ch. 15-17)

📁 Appendices

Marketing Video Case Series

This series contains videos specifically tied to the video cases found at the end of the book. The videos include information about exciting companies, such as New Belgium Brewing, Sephora, Huy Fong, and Warby Parker.

Authors' Website

The authors also maintain a website at http://prideferrell.net to provide video resources that can be used as supplements and class exercises. The videos have been developed as marketing labs with worksheets for students to use on observing the videos. Some of the videos are accessible through links, and there is also information on where some of the videos can be obtained.

Building a Marketing Plan

New to MindTap in this edition, the marketing plan has been expanded into six parts that walk students through the steps of building a marketing plan as they finish relevant content in the book. These flexible, modular assignments allow you to assign a complete marketing plan in stages—or pick only specific sections to assign. Featuring fill-in-the-blank response fields for quick review of student-provided information and corresponding templates for students to complete and upload, these assignments present a flexible, course-integrated way to give students experience thinking through and building out a marketing plan.

SUPPLEMENTS TO MEET STUDENT NEEDS

The MindTap has been updated with key features to help address your students' needs and engage them in the material. It is the digital learning solution that powers students from memorization to mastery by challenging students to apply what they have learned instead of just recalling the information with activities such as You Make the Decision and Group Project and Role Play video activities. It gives you complete control of your course—to provide engaging content, to challenge every individual, and to build their confidence.

Other MindTap activities include:

- Self-Assessments
- Concept Checks
- Adaptive Test Prep
- Flashcards
- PowerPoint slides
- And more!

YOUR COMMENTS AND SUGGESTIONS ARE VALUED

As authors, our major focus has been on teaching and preparing learning materials for introductory marketing students. We have traveled extensively to work with students and to understand the needs of professors of introductory marketing courses. We both teach introductory marketing courses on a regular basis and test the materials included in this book, test bank, and other ancillary materials to make sure they are effective in the classroom. Bill Pride has recently developed an online principles of marketing course using our book at Texas A&M University.

Through the years, professors and students have sent us many helpful suggestions for improving the text and ancillary components. We invite your comments, questions, and criticisms. We want to do our best to provide materials that enhance the teaching and learning of marketing concepts and strategies. Your suggestions will be sincerely appreciated. Please write us, or e-mail us at **w-pride@tamu.edu** or **ocf0003@auburn.edu**, or call 979-845-5857 (Bill Pride).

acknowledgments

Like most textbooks, this one reflects the ideas of many academicians and practitioners who have contributed to the development of the marketing discipline. We appreciate the opportunity to present their ideas in this book.

   A number of individuals have made helpful comments and recommendations in their reviews of this or earlier editions. We appreciate the generous help of these reviewers:

Zafar U. Ahmed
Lebanese American University

Thomas Ainscough
University of South Florida

Sana Akili
U.S. Department of Commerce

Katrece Albert
Southern University

Joe F. Alexander
Belmont University

Mark I. Alpert
University of Texas at Austin

David M. Ambrose
University of Nebraska

David Andrus
Kansas State University

Linda K. Anglin
Minnesota State University

George Avellano
Central State University

Emin Babakus
University of Memphis

Siva Balasubramanian
Illinois Institute of Technology

Joseph Ballenger
Stephen F. Austin State University

Frank Barber
Cuyahoga Community College

Joseph Barr
Framingham State College

Thomas E. Barry
Southern Methodist University

Richard C. Becherer
University of Tennessee–Chattanooga

Walter H. Beck, Sr.
Reinhardt College

Russell Belk
York University

John Bennett
University of Missouri–Columbia

W. R. Berdine
California State Polytechnic Institute

Karen Berger
Pace University

Stewart W. Bither
Pennsylvania State University

Roger Blackwell
Blackwell Business Advisors

Nancy Bloom
Nassau Community College

Paul N. Bloom
Duke University

James P. Boespflug
Arapahoe Community College

Joseph G. Bonnici
Central Connecticut State University

John Boos
Ohio Wesleyan University

Peter Bortolotti
Johnson & Wales University

Chris D. Bottomley
Ocean County College

Jenell Bramlage
University of Northwestern Ohio

James Brock
Pacific Lutheran University

John R. Brooks, Jr.
Houston Baptist University

John Buckley
Orange County Community College

Pat J. Calabros
University of Texas–Arlington

Linda Calderone
State University of New York College of Technology at Farmingdale

Joseph Cangelosi
University of Central Arkansas

William J. Carner
University of Texas–Austin

Nancy M. Carr
Community College of Philadelphia

James C. Carroll
University of Central Arkansas

Terry M. Chambers
Westminster College

Lawrence Chase
Tompkins Cortland Community College

Larry Chonko
University of Texas at Arlington

Ernest F. Cooke
Loyola College–Baltimore

Robert Copley
University of Louisville

Robert Corey
West Virginia University

Deborah L. Cowles
Virginia Commonwealth University

William L. Cron
Texas Christian University

Gary Cutler
Dyersburg State Community College

Bernice N. Dandridge
Diablo Valley College

Sally Dibb
Open University

Katherine Dillon
Ocean County College

Ralph DiPietro
Montclair State University

Paul Dishman
Utah Valley University

Casey L. Donoho
Northern Arizona University

Todd Donovan
Colorado State University

Kent Drummond
University of Wyoming

Tinus Van Drunen
University Twente (Netherlands)

Robert F. Dwyer
University of Cincinnati

Roland Eyears
Central Ohio Technical College

Cheryl A. Fabrizi
Broome Community College, State University of New York

Kathleen Ferris-Costa
Bridgewater State University

James Finch
University of Wisconsin–La Crosse

Renée Florsheim
Loyola Marymount University

Charles W. Ford
Arkansas State University

John Fraedrich
Southern Illinois University, Carbondale

Terry Gabel
Monmouth College

Robert Garrity
University of Hawaii

Geoffrey L. Gordon
Northern Illinois University

Sharon F. Gregg
Middle Tennessee University

Charles Gross
University of New Hampshire

John Hafer
University of Nebraska at Omaha

David Hansen
Texas Southern University

Richard C. Hansen
Ferris State University

Nancy Hanson-Rasmussen
University of Wisconsin–Eau Claire

Robert R. Harmon
Portland State University

Michael Hartline
Florida State University

Salah S. Hassan
George Washington University

Manoj Hastak
American University

Dean Headley
Wichita State University

Esther Headley
Wichita State University

Debbora Heflin-Bullock
California State Polytechnic University–Pomona

Tony Henthorne
University of Nevada, Las Vegas

Charles L. Hilton
Eastern Kentucky University

Elizabeth C. Hirschman
Rutgers, State University of New Jersey

Charlie Hofacker
Florida State University

Deloris James
Howard University

Ron Johnson
Colorado Mountain College

Theodore F. Jula
Stonehill College

Peter F. Kaminski
Northern Illinois University

Jerome Katrichis
University of Hartford

Garland Keesling
Towson University

James Kellaris
University of Cincinnati

Alvin Kelly
Florida A&M University

Sylvia Keyes
Bridgewater State College

William M. Kincaid, Jr.
Oklahoma State University

Hal Koenig
Oregon State University

Kathleen Krentler
San Diego State University

John Krupa, Jr.
Johnson & Wales University

Barbara Lafferty
University of South Florida

Patricia Laidler
Massasoit Community College

Bernard LaLonde
Ohio State University

Richard A. Lancioni
Temple University

Geoffrey P. Lantos
Stonehill College

Charles L. Lapp
University of Texas at Dallas

Virginia Larson
San Jose State University

John Lavin
Waukesha County Technical Institute

Marilyn Lavin
University of Wisconsin Whitewater

Hugh E. Law
East Tennessee State University

Monle Lee
Indiana University–South Bend

Ron Lennon
University of South Florida–Sarasota-Manatee

Richard C. Leventhal
Ashford University

Marilyn L. Liebrenz-Himes
George Washington University

Terry Loe
Kennesaw State University

Mary Logan
Global University

Paul Londrigan
Mott Community College

Anthony Lucas
Community College of Allegheny County

George Lucas
U.S. Learning, Inc.

William Lundstrom
Cleveland State University

Rhonda Mack
College of Charleston

Stan Madden
Baylor University

Patricia M. Manninen
North Shore Community College

Gerald L. Manning
Des Moines Area Community College

Lalita A. Manrai
University of Delaware

Franklyn Manu
Morgan State University

Allen S. Marber
University of Bridgeport

Gayle J. Marco
Robert Morris College

Carolyn A. Massiah
University of Central Florida

James McAlexander
Oregon State University

Donald McCartney
University of Wisconsin–Green Bay

Jack McNiff
State University of New York College of Technology at Farmington

Lee Meadow
Eastern Illinois University

Jeffrey A. Meier
Fox Valley Technical College

Marilyn Martin Melchiorre
College of Idaho

James Meszaros
County College of Morris

Brian Meyer
Minnesota State University

Martin Meyers
University of Wisconsin–Stevens Point

Stephen J. Miller
Oklahoma State University

Carol Morris-Calder
Loyola Marymount University

David Murphy
Madisonville Community College

Keith Murray
Bryant University

Sue Ellen Neeley
University of Houston–Clear Lake

Carolyn Y. Nicholson
Stetson University

Francis L. Notturno, Sr.
Owens Community College

Terrence V. O'Brien
Northern Illinois University

James R. Ogden
Kutztown University of Pennsylvania

Shannon Ogden
Black River Technical College

Lois Bitner Olson
San Diego State University

Robert S. Owen
Texas A&M University—Texarkana

David P. Paul III
Monmouth University

Terry Paul
Ohio State University

Teresa Pavia
University of Utah

John Perrachione
Truman State University

Lana Podolak
Community College of Beaver County

William Presutti
Duquesne University

Daniel Rajaratnam
University of Texas at Dallas

Mohammed Rawwas
University of Northern Iowa

James D. Reed
Louisiana State University–Shreveport

John Reed
University of New Mexico

William Rhey
Florida Southern College

Glen Riecken
College of Charleston

Ed Riordan
Wayne State University

Bruce Robertson
San Francisco State University

Robert A. Robicheaux
University of Alabama–Birmingham

Linda Rose
Westwood College Online

Bert Rosenbloom
Drexel University

Robert H. Ross
Wichita State University

Tom Rossi
Broome Community College

Vicki Rostedt
The University of Akron

Catherine Roster
University of New Mexico

Don Roy
Middle Tennessee State University

Catherine Ruggieri
St. John's University

Rob Salamida
SUNY Broome Community College

Ronald Schill
Middlebury Institute of International Studies at Monterey

Bodo Schlegelmilch
Vienna University of Economics and Business Administration

Edward Schmitt
Villanova University

Donald Sciglimpaglia
San Diego State University

Stanley Scott
University of Alaska—Anchorage

Beheruz N. Sethna
University of West Georgia

Abhay Shah
Colorado State University—Pueblo

Morris A. Shapero
Eckerd College

Mark Siders
Southern Oregon University

Carolyn F. Siegel
Eastern Kentucky University

Lyndon Simkin
University of Reading

Roberta Slater
Cedar Crest College

Paul J. Solomon
University of South Florida

Sheldon Somerstein
City University of New York

Eric R. Spangenberg
University of Mississippi

Rosann L. Spiro
Indiana University

William Staples
University of Houston–Clear Lake

Carmen Sunda
University of New Orleans

Crina Tarasi
Central Michigan University

Ruth Taylor
Texas State University

Steven A. Taylor
Illinois State University

Ira Teich
Lander College for Men

Debbie Thorne
Texas State University

Sharynn Tomlin
Angelo State University

James Underwood
University of Louisiana–Lafayette

Barbara Unger
Western Washington University

Dale Varble
Indiana State University

Bronis Verhage
Georgia State University

R. "Vish" Viswanathan Iyer
University of Northern Colorado

Kirk Wakefield
Baylor University

Harlan Wallingford
Pace University

Jacquelyn Warwick
Andrews University

James F. Wenthe
Georgia College

Sumner M. White
Massachusetts Bay Community College

Janice Williams
University of Central Oklahoma

Alan R. Wiman
Rider College

John Withey
St. Edwards University

We would like to thank Charlie Hofacker and Michael Hartline, both of Florida State University, for many helpful suggestions and insights in developing the chapter on digital marketing and social networking. Michael Hartline also assisted in the development of the marketing plan outline and provided suggestions throughout the text. In this edition we also appreciate a review and helpful comments from Martin Key for the Digital Marketing chapter. Catherine Roster, University of New Mexico, and Marty Meyers, University of Wisconsin–Stevens Point, provided important assistance in revising "Marketing Research and Information Systems," "Consumer Buying Behavior," and "Digital Marketing and Social Networking."

We thank Gwyn Walters and Kelsey Reddick for their research and editorial assistance in the revision of the chapters. In addition, Kelsey Reddick revised the *Instructor's Manual*. We appreciate the efforts of Marian Wood and Jennifer Sawayda for developing and revising a number of boxed features and cases. We deeply appreciate the assistance of Fatima Wood, Marilyn Ayala, Brenda Aram, Jessica Minks, Jaime Mitash, Clarissa Means, Amy Handlin, and Susan Leshnower for providing editorial technical assistance and support.

We express appreciation for the support and encouragement given to us by our colleagues at Texas A&M University and Auburn University. We are also grateful for the comments and suggestions we received from our own students, student focus groups, and student correspondents who provided feedback through the website.

A number of talented professionals at Cengage Learning and Integra have contributed to the development of this book. We are especially grateful to Erin Joyner, Mike Schenk, Bryan Gambrel, Heather Mooney, Allie Janneck, Jean Buttrom, John Rich, Stephanie Hall, Bethany Casey, Katie Jergens, Tawny Schaad, and Megan Fischer. Their inspiration, patience, support, and friendship are invaluable.

William M. Pride
O. C. Ferrell

about the authors

William M. Pride is Professor of Marketing, Mays Business School, at Texas A&M University. He received his PhD from Louisiana State University. In addition to this text, he is the co-author of Cengage Learning's *Business MindTap* and *Foundations of Business*, market leaders. Dr. Pride has taught Principles of Marketing and other marketing courses for more than 40 years at both the undergraduate and graduate levels.

Dr. Pride's research interests are in advertising, promotion, and distribution channels. His research articles have appeared in major journals in the fields of marketing, such as the *Journal of Marketing,* the *Journal of Marketing Research,* the *Journal of the Academy of Marketing Science,* and the *Journal of Advertising.*

Dr. Pride is a member of the American Marketing Association, Academy of Marketing Science, Society for Marketing Advances, and the Marketing Management Association. He has received the Marketing Fellow Award from the Society for Marketing Advances and the Marketing Innovation Award from the Marketing Management Association. Both of these are lifetime-achievement awards.

O. C. Ferrell is the James T. Pursell Sr. Eminent Scholar in Ethics and Director of the Center for Ethical Organizational Cultures, Auburn University. He served as the Distinguished Professor of Leadership and Ethics at Belmont University and University Distinguished Professor of Marketing in the Anderson School of Management at University of New Mexico. He has also been on the faculties of the University of Wyoming, Colorado State University, University of Memphis, Texas A&M University, Illinois State University, and Southern Illinois University. He received his PhD in Marketing from Louisiana State University.

He is past president of the Academic Council of the American Marketing Association and chaired the American Marketing Association Ethics Committee. Under his leadership, the committee developed the AMA Code of Ethics and the AMA Code of Ethics for Marketing on the Internet. In addition, he is a former member of the Academy of Marketing Science Board of Governors and is a Society of Marketing Advances and Southwestern Marketing Association Fellow and an Academy of Marketing Science Distinguished Fellow. He was the vice president of publications and is president-elect of the Academy of Marketing Science. He was the first recipient of the Marketing Education Innovation Award from the Marketing Management Association. He received a Lifetime Achievement Award from the Macromarketing Society and a special award for service to doctoral students from the Southeast Doctoral Consortium. He received the Harold Berkman Lifetime Service Award from the Academy of Marketing Science and more recently the Cutco/Vector Distinguished Marketing Educator Award.

Dr. Ferrell is the co-author of 20 books and more than 100 published articles and papers. His articles have been published in the *Journal of Marketing Research*, the *Journal of Marketing,* the *Journal of Business Ethics*, the *Journal of Business Research,* the *Journal of the Academy of Marketing Science*, and the *Journal of Public Policy & Marketing,* as well as other journals.

Part 1

Rawpixel/Shutterstock.com

Strategic Marketing and Its Environment

PART 1 introduces the field of marketing and offers a broad perspective from which to explore and analyze various components of the marketing discipline. **CHAPTER 1** defines *marketing* and explores some key concepts, including customers and target markets, the marketing mix, relationship marketing, the marketing concept, and value. **CHAPTER 2** provides an overview of strategic marketing issues such as the effect of organizational resources and opportunities on the planning process; the role of the mission statement; corporate, business-unit, and marketing strategies; and the creation of the marketing plan. These issues are profoundly affected by competitive, economic, political, legal and regulatory, technological, and sociocultural forces in the marketing environment. **CHAPTER 3** deals with these environmental forces, and with the role of social responsibility and ethics in marketing decisions.

chapter 1

Customer-Driven Strategic Marketing

+0.83% First quarter
Jan-Mar

-1.5% Secoud quarter
Apr-Jun

+0.12% [T]ird quarter
[J]l-Sep

THIS YEAR ▼ 32.8876
▲ 42.9841

+83.0

+41.9

+12.0

LEARNING OBJECTIVES

1-1 Define marketing.

1-2 Explain the different variables of the marketing mix.

1-3 Describe how marketing creates value.

1-4 Briefly describe the marketing environment.

1-5 Summarize the marketing concept.

1-6 Identify the importance of building customer relationships.

1-7 Explain why marketing is important to our global economy.

Airbnb: Home Sweet Home

Airbnb has come far in the 10 years it has been in business. The company started when founders Brian Chesky and Joe Gebbia turned their apartment into a bed and breakfast so they could afford to pay rent. The founders had identified an unmet customer need: the desire to stay in less expensive but homier lodgings. They launched the Airbnb website in 2007 to connect travelers to people in the area willing to rent out their couch or extra room. Like Uber, the car-sharing service, Airbnb embraces the sharing economy concept that promotes the renting of underutilized human and physical resources. Airbnb does not own the rooms like Marriott or Hyatt but provides access to the owner's rooms.

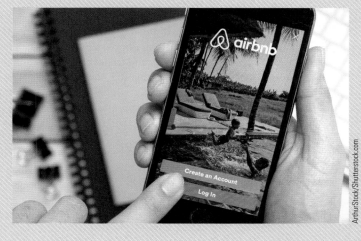

The target market was initially conference attendees but soon expanded to all types of travelers. Today, Airbnb connects travelers to lodgings in 34,000 cities across 191 countries. Those who wish to rent an extra room or house can set their own prices, and Airbnb takes 3 percent of the booking price when the property is rented out. Therefore, Airbnb is facilitating an exchange between a buyer and a seller.

Despite its immense success, Airbnb believes it can create more value for more customers. It began to offer Business Travel on Airbnb to concentrate on corporate clients. Airbnb has signed up hundreds of businesses, including Google and Salesforce.com. It is especially popular among new employees who are being put up by an employer until they find a more permanent location.

Not all stakeholders are happy about Airbnb, however. Some cities and regulators believe Airbnb encourages owners of multiple properties to rent them in the short-term rather than turning them into long-term residences—thus causing a disruption in urban housing. However, Airbnb contends that creating customer value in the form of less expensive lodging for travelers and additional income for renters is a valuable service.[1]

ArthurStock/Shutterstock.com

Airbnb provides access to lodging that is provided by owners of the property. The company facilitates an exchange transaction between the owner of the property and consumers who want to get lodging at a good price and a property often more unique than a traditional hotel. Airbnb creates the relationship that involves pricing and communication as well reducing risks of the transaction to the consumer and owner. However, it is faced with competitors such as VRBO, which provides a lodging access service. Like all organizations, Airbnb must make marketing decisions and create a satisfying exchange relationship.

This chapter introduces the strategic marketing concepts and decisions covered throughout the text. First, we develop a definition of *marketing* and explore each element of the definition in detail. Next, we explore the importance of value-driven marketing. We also introduce the marketing concept and consider several issues associated with its implementation. Additionally, we take a look at the management of customer relationships and relationship marketing. Finally, we examine the importance of marketing in global society.

1-1 DEFINING MARKETING

LO 1-1 Define marketing.

If you ask several people what *marketing* is, you are likely to hear a variety of descriptions. Although many people think marketing is advertising or selling, marketing is much more complex than most people realize. In this book we define **marketing** as the process of creating, pricing, distributing, and promoting goods, services, and ideas to facilitate satisfying exchange relationships with customers and to develop and maintain favorable relationships with stakeholders in a dynamic environment. Our definition is consistent with that of the American Marketing Association (AMA), which defines marketing as "the activity, set of institutions, and processes for creating, communicating, delivering, and exchanging offerings that have value for customers, clients, partners, and society at large."[2]

marketing The process of creating, pricing, distributing, and promoting goods, services, and ideas to facilitate satisfying exchange relationships with customers and to develop and maintain favorable relationships with stakeholders in a dynamic environment

customers The purchasers of organizations' products; the focal point of all marketing activities

FIGURE 1.1   COMPONENTS OF STRATEGIC MARKETING

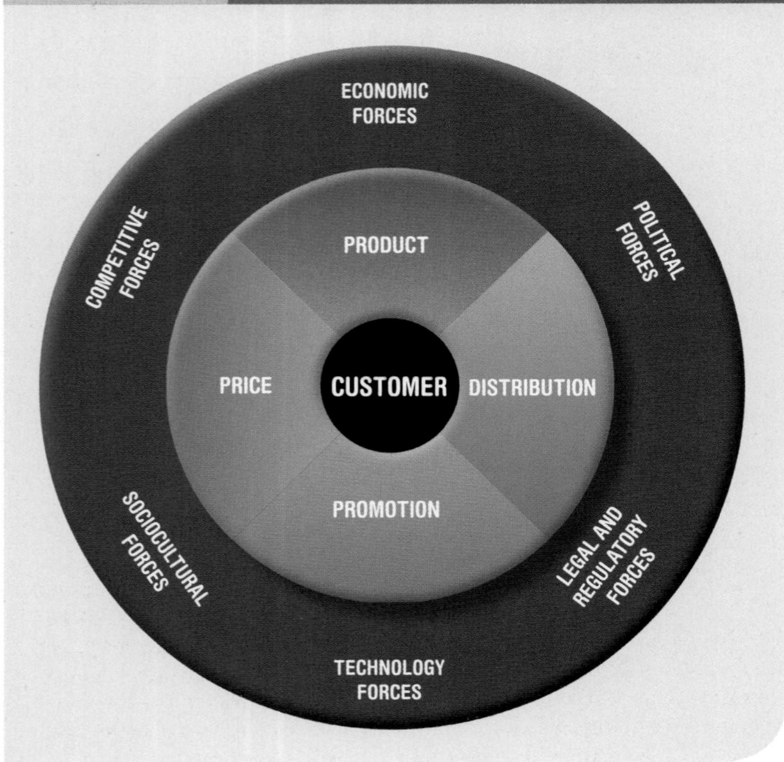

Marketing-mix variables are often viewed as controllable because they can be modified. However, there are limits to how much marketing managers can alter them. Economic conditions, competitive structure, and government regulations may prevent a manager from adjusting the marketing mix frequently or significantly. Making changes in the size, shape, and design of most tangible goods is expensive; therefore, such product features are not altered very often. Services are easier to adjust and, as the Airbnb example illustrates, there could be an opportunity for the consumer to select a service. In addition, promotional campaigns and methods used to communicate with and persuade consumers ordinarily cannot be revised overnight. Changes in the way products are distributed are much easier than in the past due to e-commerce. Pricing may be the easiest marketing-mix variable to change.

1-1a Marketing Focuses on Customers

As the purchasers of the products that organizations develop, price, distribute, and promote, **customers** are the focal point of marketing activities (see Figure 1.1).

Companies define their products not as what they make or produce, but as what they do to satisfy customers. The Walt Disney Company is not in the business of establishing theme parks; it is in the business of entertainment and making people happy. At Disney World, customers are guests and employees are cast members providing a performance and entertainment experience.

The essence of marketing is to develop satisfying exchanges from which both customers and marketers benefit. The customer expects to gain a reward or benefit greater than the costs incurred in a marketing transaction. The marketer expects to gain something of value in return, generally the price charged for the product. Through buyer–seller interaction, a customer develops expectations about the seller's future behavior. To fulfill these expectations, the marketer must deliver on promises made. Over time, this interaction results in relationships between the two parties. Fast-food restaurants such as Wendy's and Subway depend on repeat purchases from satisfied customers—many often live or work a few miles from these restaurants—whereas customer expectations revolve around tasty food, value, and dependable service.

Organizations generally focus their marketing efforts on a specific group of customers, called a **target market**. Looking at the ad for Fresh Step, indoor cat owners who want high-quality products for their pets are their target market.

Marketing managers may define a target market as a vast number of people, or as a relatively small group. Often companies target multiple markets with different products, prices, distribution systems, and promotions for each one. Others focus on a smaller, niche market. For example, Shwood manufactures wooden eye glass frames, which are handcrafted in their Portland, Oregon, workshop. The goal is to allow the wood's personality to come through and not to over-engineer the natural material honed into its frames.[3] Home Depot, on the other hand, targets multiple markets with thousands of product items.

Appealing to Target Markets
Responding to the public's increasing interest in pets, Fresh Step provides a high-quality, effective cat pet litter with a 10-day guarantee.

1-2 MARKETING DEALS WITH PRODUCTS, PRICE, DISTRIBUTION, AND PROMOTION

LO 1-2 Explain the different variables of the marketing mix.

Marketing involves developing and managing a product that will satisfy customer needs. It also requires promotion to help customers learn about the product and determine if it will satisfy their needs. It focuses on communicating availability in the right place and at the right price. Activities are planned, organized, implemented, and controlled to meet the needs of customers within the target market. Marketers refer to four variables—product, pricing, distribution, and promotion—as the **marketing mix**. Marketing creates value through the marketing mix. A primary goal of marketing managers is to create and maintain the right mix of these variables to satisfy customers' needs for a general product type. They decide what type of each variable to use, and how to synchronize the variables. (Note in Figure 1.1 that the marketing mix is built around the customer.) Apple is well known for its implementation of the marketing mix. It constantly engages in research and development to create new or upgraded products. It promotes these products through traditional advertising, social media, and media events. Apple distributes its products through retail stores, AT&T and

target market A specific group of customers on whom an organization focuses its marketing efforts

marketing mix Four marketing variables—product, pricing, distribution, and promotion—that a firm controls to meet the needs of customers within its target market

other service providers, and through the Internet. It provides its products at a premium price to demonstrate their quality and effectiveness.

Marketing managers strive to develop a marketing mix that matches the needs of customers in the target market. For example, Chrome Industries was founded in Boulder, Colorado, to make unique, durable bags for bike messengers. This target market showed such affinity for the product that the company has since expanded with a variety of bags as well as clothing and shoes.[4] Marketing managers must constantly monitor the competition and adapt their product, pricing, distribution, and promotion decisions to create long-term success.

Before marketers can develop a marketing mix, they must collect in-depth, up-to-date information about customer needs. Such information might include data about the age, income, ethnicity, gender, and educational level of people in the target market, their preferences for product features, their attitudes toward competitors' products, and the frequency with which they use the product. Today, marketers have access to a large amount of data about their customers by tracking purchases using social media and other sources. Chrome Industries closely monitors trends to adjust its marketing mix to provide constant functional as well as style changes. Armed with market information, marketing managers are better able to develop a marketing mix that satisfies a specific target market.

Let's look more closely at the decisions and activities related to each marketing-mix variable.

1-2a Product

product A good, a service, or an idea

Successful marketing efforts result in products that become part of everyday life. Consider the satisfaction customers have had over the years from Coca-Cola, Levi's jeans, Visa credit cards, Tylenol pain relievers, and the Microsoft Surface. The product variable of the marketing mix deals with researching customers' needs and wants and designing a product that satisfies them. A **product** can be a good, a service, or an idea. A good is a physical entity you can touch. Oakley sunglasses, Nike running shoes, and Tesla automobiles are all examples of products. A service is the application of human and mechanical efforts to people or objects to provide intangible benefits to customers. Air travel, education, lodging, banking, medical care, and day care are examples of services. Ideas include concepts, philosophies, images, and issues. For instance, a personal trainer, for a fee, helps clients exercise and manage their health and wellness. Other marketers of ideas include political parties, churches, and animal protection groups. Products can also be designed for personal use – consumer product – or for use by businesses. In the advertisement, AT&T and DHL target business markets with their cybersecurity and shipping services.

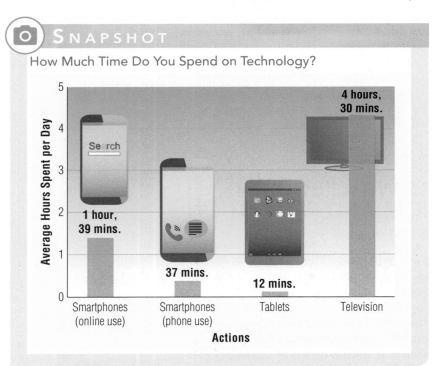

SNAPSHOT

How Much Time Do You Spend on Technology?

Smartphones (online use): 1 hour, 39 mins.
Smartphones (phone use): 37 mins.
Tablets: 12 mins.
Television: 4 hours, 30 mins.

(Y-axis: Average Hours Spent per Day — 0 to 5; X-axis: Actions)

A Nielson study shows that Americans spend 10 hours and 39 minutes "consuming media" each day. This includes handheld devices to computers and entertainment in the form of television and radio.

Source: www.denverpost.com/2016/06/29/media-use-america-11-hours/

Types of Products
AT&T and DHL are both examples of companies that target business markets.

The product variable also involves creating or modifying brand names and packaging, and it may include decisions regarding warranty and repair services. For example, Coca-Cola released a new global design for its products that features the traditional red as the main color. The "one brand" strategy is to create a unified global presence for its flagship soda.

Product variable decisions and related activities are important because they are directly involved with creating products that address customers' needs and wants. Apple continues to upgrade its iPhone using different model numbers such as 5, 6, and 7 to signal new modifications. To maintain an assortment of products that helps an organization achieve its goals, marketers must develop new products, modify existing ones, and eliminate those that no longer satisfy enough buyers or that yield unacceptable profits.

1-2b **Price**

The price charged for a product helps establish its value. A company's established pricing objectives and policies determine its products' prices. Price is a critical component of the marketing mix because customers are concerned about benefits, roles, and costs. Price is an important competitive tool that provides an advantage. Higher prices can be used competitively to establish a product's premium image. Seven For All Mankind jeans and J Brand, for example, have an image of high quality and high price that has given them significant status. Other companies are skilled at providing products at prices lower than their competitors' (consider

Walmart's tagline "Save Money, Live Better"). Amazon uses its vast network of partnerships and cost efficiencies to provide products at low prices. Brick-and-mortar retailers have not been able to offer comparable products at such low prices, providing Amazon with a considerable competitive advantage. Pricing is the most flexible marketing-mix variable and can be changed very quickly. Also, price multiplied by quantity sold establishes revenue, which is the responsibility of the marketing function.

1-2c **Distribution**

To satisfy customers, products must be available at the right time and in appropriate locations. Subway, for example, locates not only in strip malls but also inside Walmart and Home Depot stores, laundromats, churches, and hospitals, as well as inside Goodwill stores, car dealerships, and appliance stores. There are approximately 45,000 Subways worldwide, surpassing McDonald's as the world's largest chain.

In dealing with the distribution variable, a marketing manager makes products available in the quantities desired to as many target market customers as possible, keeping total inventory, transportation, and storage costs as low as possible. A marketing manager also may select and motivate intermediaries (wholesalers and retailers), establish and maintain inventory control procedures, and develop and manage transportation and storage systems. All companies must depend on intermediaries to move their final products to the market. The advent of the Internet and electronic commerce also has dramatically influenced the distribution variable. Companies now can make their products available throughout the world without maintaining facilities in each country. For example, Netflix started in the United States with its DVD by mail service in 1998. Today, because of its Internet presence, Netflix is available in over 190 countries. We examine distribution issues in Chapters 13 and 14.

Promotion
Roper uses country music artist Joe Nichols to promote its western wear.

1-2d **Promotion**

The promotion variable relates to activities used to inform and persuade to create a desired response. Promotion can increase public awareness of the organization and of new or existing products. It can help create a direct response such as accessing a website to order a product. GEICO uses television and radio advertising to encourage people to spend 15 minutes "to save 15% or more on car insurance." GEICO's tagline encourages consumers to call GEICO to save money.

Promotional activities also educate customers about product features. For example, in the western wear advertisement, Roper uses celebrities that appeal to its target market. Promotion can also urge people to take a particular stance on a political or social issue, such as voting, smoking, or drug abuse. For example, the Centers for Disease Control and Prevention (CDC) developed an advertising campaign to deter smoking. The ads were released on television, radio, and billboards. They featured disturbing testimonials from people who have suffered the effects of smoking. The CDC claims that advertisements such as these have had a major impact on convincing smokers to quit.[5]

Promotion can help to sustain interest in established products that have been available for decades, such as Jell-O or Tide detergent. Many companies use websites, apps, or social media to communicate information about themselves and their products. Betty Crocker and Kraft Foods maintain two of the most popular recipe websites.[6]

1-3 MARKETING CREATES VALUE

LO 1-3 Describe how marketing creates value.

Value is an important element of managing long-term customer relationships and implementing the marketing concept. We view **value** as a customer's subjective assessment of benefits relative to costs in determining the worth of a product (customer value = customer benefits – customer costs). Consumers develop a concept of value through the integration of their perceptions of product quality and financial sacrifice.[7] From a company's perspective, there is a trade-off between maintaining the desired value and achieving profit objectives.[8]

Customer benefits include anything a buyer receives in an exchange. Hotels and motels, for example, basically provide a room with a bed and bathroom, but each brand provides a different level of service, amenities, and atmosphere to satisfy its guests. Ramada Inn offers the minimum services necessary to maintain a quality, efficient, low-price overnight accommodation. In contrast, the Ritz-Carlton provides every imaginable service a guest might desire. The hotel even allows its staff members to spend up to $2,000 to settle customer complaints.[9] Airbnb competes with these traditional hotels and motels by providing almost no services other than access to a property at a price the consumer considers a good value. Customers judge which type of accommodation offers the best value according to the benefits they desire and their willingness and ability to pay for the costs associated with the benefits.

Customer costs include anything a buyer must give up to obtain the benefits the product provides. The most obvious cost is the monetary price of the product, but nonmonetary costs can be equally important in a customer's determination of value. Two nonmonetary costs are the time and effort customers expend to find and purchase desired products. To reduce time and effort, a company can increase product availability, thereby making it more convenient for buyers to purchase the firm's products. Another nonmonetary cost is risk, which can be reduced by offering good, basic warranties or extended warranties for an additional charge.[10] One risk-reduction strategy is the offer of a 100 percent satisfaction guarantee. This strategy is increasingly popular in today's catalog/telephone/Internet shopping environment. Zappos, which carries over 1,000 brands of shoes, has a 100 percent satisfaction guarantee, and shoes can be returned for free within 365 days.

The processes people use to determine the value of a product may differ widely. All of us tend to get a feel for the worth of products based on our own expectations and previous experience. We can, for example, compare the value of auto rental, airfare, and computers directly with the value of competing products. We evaluate movies, sporting events, and performances by entertainers on the more subjective basis of personal preferences and emotions. For most purchases, we do not consciously calculate the associated benefits and costs. It becomes an instinctive feeling that General Mills' Cheerios is a good value, or that McDonald's is a good place to take children for a quick lunch. The purchase of an automobile or a mountain bike may have emotional components, but more conscious decision making also may figure in the process of determining value. Consider the advertisement for Orville Redenbacher's popcorn. The ad shows that each bag contains three cups more of popcorn over the competitor brand, Pop Secret, increasing the overall value provided. Perceptions of value regarding more aesthetic products such as flowers are likely to vary greatly because different consumers have different tastes in what they view as aesthetically pleasing.

In developing marketing activities, it is important to recognize that customers receive benefits based on their experiences. For example, many appliance buyers consider services

value A customer's subjective assessment of benefits relative to costs in determining the worth of a product

THE SAME SIZE BAG. **3 CUPS MORE POPCORN.**

3 CUPS MORE
POPCORN PER BAG.

Orville Redenbacher's

Value-Driven Marketing
Orville Redenbacher's popcorn promotes its good value
by providing more popcorn in each bag.

such as fast delivery, ease of installation, technical advice, and training assistance to be important elements of the product. Each marketing activity has its own benefits and costs and must be adapted for its contribution to value.[11] For example, Amazon found that one- and two-day delivery adds value, leading to the development of its Prime Shipping program. Customers also derive benefits from the act of shopping and selecting products. These benefits can be affected by the atmosphere or environment of a store, such as Red Lobster's nautical/seafood theme. Even the ease of navigating a website can have a tremendous impact on perceived value. When the download and streaming music service GhostTunes was developed, co-owner country singer Garth Brooks had to ensure that the site was user-friendly. The site had to make it easy for users to navigate and choose music to stream or download. Unlike iTunes, Brooks wants GhostTunes to allow copyright holders more freedom as to how their music should be sold on the site.[12] Different customers may view different songs or albums on the site as an exceptional value for their own personal satisfaction.

The marketing mix can enhance perceptions of value. A product that demonstrates value usually has a feature or an enhancement that provides benefits. Promotional activities can also create image and prestige characteristics that customers consider in their assessment of a product's value. In some cases, value may be perceived simply as the lowest price. Many customers may not care about the quality of the paper towels they buy; they simply want the cheapest ones for use in cleaning up spills because they plan to throw them in the trash anyway. On the other hand, people looking for the fastest, most convenient way to achieve a goal become insensitive to pricing. For example, many busy customers buy prepared meals in supermarkets to take home and serve quickly, even though these products cost considerably more than meals prepared from scratch. In such cases the products with the greatest convenience may be perceived as having the greatest value. The availability or distribution of products also can enhance their value. Taco Bell wants its Mexican fast food available at any time and any place people are thinking about consuming food. It therefore has introduced Taco Bell products into supermarkets, vending machines, college campuses, and other convenient locations. Thus, the development of an effective marketing strategy requires understanding the needs and desires of customers, designing a marketing mix to satisfy them, and providing the value they want.

1-3a Marketing Builds Relationships with Customers and Other Stakeholders

Marketing also creates value through the building of stakeholder relationships. Individuals and organizations engage in marketing to facilitate **exchanges**, the provision or transfer of goods, services, or ideas in return for something of value. Any product (good, service, or even idea) may be involved in a marketing exchange. We assume only that individuals and organizations expect to gain a reward in excess of the costs incurred.

For an exchange to take place, four conditions must exist. First, two or more individuals, groups, or organizations must participate, and each must possess something of value that the other party desires. Second, the exchange should provide a benefit or satisfaction to both parties involved in the transaction. Third, each party must have confidence in the promise

exchanges The provision or transfer of goods, services, or ideas in return for something of value

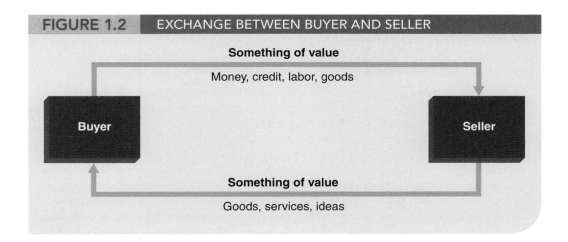

FIGURE 1.2   EXCHANGE BETWEEN BUYER AND SELLER

of the "something of value" held by the other. If you go to a Justin Timberlake or Rihanna concert, for example, you go with the expectation of a great performance. Finally, to build trust, the parties to the exchange must meet expectations.

Figure 1.2 depicts the exchange process. The arrows indicate that the parties communicate that each has something of value available to exchange. An exchange will not necessarily take place just because these conditions exist; marketing activities can occur even without an actual transaction or sale. You may see an ad for a Sub-Zero refrigerator, for instance, but you might never buy the luxury appliance. When an exchange occurs, products are traded for other products or for financial resources.

Marketing activities should attempt to create and maintain satisfying exchange relationships. To maintain an exchange relationship, buyers must be satisfied with the good, service, or idea obtained, and sellers must be satisfied with the financial reward or something else of value received. A dissatisfied customer who lacks trust in the relationship often searches for alternative organizations or products. The customer relationship often endures over an extended time period, and repeat purchases are critical for the firm.

Marketers are concerned with building and maintaining relationships not only with customers but also with relevant stakeholders. Stakeholders include those constituents who have a "stake," or claim, in some aspect of a company's products, operations, markets, industry, and outcomes; these include customers, employees, shareholders, suppliers, governments, communities, competitors, and many others. While engaging in marketing activities, the firm should be proactive and responsive to stakeholder concerns. This engagement has been found to increase financial performance.[13] Therefore, developing and maintaining favorable relations with stakeholders is crucial to the long-term growth of an organization and its products. For example, employees directly influence customer satisfaction, and suppliers are necessary to make quality products. Communities can be a positive contributor to the firm's reputation and in turn they provide an opportunity to make a social and economic contribution. Customers and competitors are often considered to be core stakeholders in developing a marketing strategy.[14]

stakeholders Constituents who have a "stake," or claim, in some aspect of a company's products, operations, markets, industry, and outcomes

Satisfying Stakeholder Needs
This advertisement points out that Nellie's free range eggs satisfy the needs of consumers who are concerned about animal rights and their overall health.

marketing environment
The competitive, economic, political, legal and regulatory, technological, and sociocultural forces that surround the customer and affect the marketing mix

1-4 MARKETING OCCURS IN A DYNAMIC ENVIRONMENT

LO 1-4 Briefly describe the marketing environment.

Marketing activities do not take place in a vacuum. The **marketing environment**, which includes competitive, economic, political, legal and regulatory, technological, and sociocultural forces, surrounds the customer and affects the marketing mix (see Figure 1.1). The effects of these forces on buyers and sellers can be dramatic and difficult to predict. Their impact on value can be extensive, as market changes can easily impact how stakeholders perceive certain products. They can create threats to marketers but also generate opportunities for new products and new methods of reaching customers. For example, popular brands such as Fiat Chrysler, Kellogg's, and Choice Hotels as well as others have found their ads on fake news sites. This resulted from computers placing the ads on a website based on user clicks. While technology facilitates online advertising, it is sometimes uncontrollable.[15]

The forces of the marketing environment affect a marketer's ability to facilitate value-driven marketing exchanges in three general ways. First, they influence customers by affecting their lifestyles, standards of living, and preferences and needs for products. Because a marketing manager tries to develop and adjust the marketing mix to satisfy customers, effects of environmental forces on customers also have an indirect impact on marketing-mix components. Second, marketing environment forces help to determine whether and how a marketing manager can perform certain marketing activities. Third, environmental forces may affect a marketing manager's decisions and actions by influencing buyers' reactions to the firm's marketing mix.

Marketing environment forces can fluctuate quickly and dramatically, which is one reason why marketing is so interesting and challenging. Because these forces are closely interrelated, changes in one may cause changes in others. For example, evidence linking children's consumption of soft drinks and fast foods to health issues has exposed marketers of such products to negative publicity and generated calls for legislation regulating the sale of soft drinks in public schools. Some companies have responded to these concerns by voluntarily reformulating products to make them healthier or by introducing new products. With the popularity of spicy foods, restaurants, including McDonald's, Taco Bell, Subway, Chick-fil-A, Wendy's, Burger King, and Applebee's, as well as others, have introduced Sriracha hot sauce items to their menu.

Changes in the marketing environment produce uncertainty for marketers and at times hurt marketing efforts, but they also create opportunities. For example, when oil prices increase, consumers shift to potential alternative sources of transportation including bikes, buses, light rail, trains, ride sharing, electric and hybrid vehicles, or telecommuting when possible. Marketers who are alert to changes in environmental forces not only can adjust to and influence these changes but can also capitalize on the opportunities such changes provide. Marketing-mix variables—product, price, distribution, and promotion—are factors over which an organization has control; the forces of the environment, however, are subject to far less control. Even though marketers know that they cannot predict changes in the marketing environment with certainty, they must nevertheless plan for them. Because these environmental forces have such a profound effect on marketing activities, we explore each of them in considerable depth in Chapter 3.

1-5 UNDERSTANDING THE MARKETING CONCEPT

LO 1-5 Summarize the marketing concept.

Firms frequently fail to attract customers with what they have to offer because they define their business as "making a product" rather than as "helping potential customers satisfy their needs and wants." On the other hand, Horizon, with their preservative-free snack crackers, satisfies the needs of mothers who want healthy snacks for their children and kids who want snacks that taste good. The advertisement promoting Horizon's snack crackers and cookies is cross promoting a Peanuts movie to enhance the appeal to children. Horizon focuses on promoting how its product can meet the needs of its target market.

According to the **marketing concept**, an organization should try to provide products that satisfy customers' needs through a coordinated set of activities that also allows the organization to achieve its goals. Customer satisfaction is the major focus of the marketing concept. To implement the marketing concept, an organization strives to determine what buyers want and uses this information to develop satisfying products. It focuses on customer analysis, competitor analysis, and integration of the firm's resources to provide customer value and satisfaction, as well as to generate long-term profits.[16] The firm also must continue to alter, adapt, and develop products to keep pace with customers' changing desires and preferences. Howard Schultz, founder and former CEO of Starbucks, demonstrated the company's grasp on the marketing concept by explaining that Starbucks is not a coffee business that serves people, but rather a "people business serving coffee." Starbucks' leadership sees the company as being "in the business of humanity," emphasizing the fact that Starbucks is not only concerned about customers but society as well.[17] Thus, the marketing concept emphasizes that marketing begins and ends with customers. Research has found a positive association between customer satisfaction and shareholder value,[18] and high levels of customer satisfaction also tend to attract and retain high-quality employees and managers.[19]

Implementing the Marketing Concept
Horizon meets the needs of moms and kids with their preservative-free snack crackers.

marketing concept A managerial philosophy that an organization should try to satisfy customers' needs through a coordinated set of activities that also allows the organization to achieve its goals

The marketing concept is not a second definition of marketing. It is a management philosophy guiding an organization's overall activities. This philosophy affects all organizational activities, not just marketing. Production, finance, accounting, human resources, and marketing departments must work together. For example, at Procter & Gamble the marketing function coordinates research and development, distribution, and resource deployment to focus on providing consumer products for households.

The marketing concept is a strategic approach to achieve objectives. A firm that adopts the marketing concept must satisfy not only its customers' objectives but also its own, or it will not stay in business long. The overall objectives of a business might relate to increasing profits, market share, sales, or a combination of all three. The marketing concept stresses that an organization can best achieve these objectives by being customer oriented. Thus, implementing the marketing concept should benefit the organization as well as its customers.

It is important that marketers consider not only their current buyers' needs, but also the long-term needs of society. Striving to satisfy customers' desires by sacrificing society's long-term welfare is unacceptable. For instance, there is significant demand for large SUVs and trucks. However, environmentalists and federal regulators are challenging automakers to produce more fuel-efficient vehicles with increased miles-per-gallon standards. The question that remains is whether or not Americans are willing to give up their spacious SUVs for the good of the environment.

1-5a Evolution of the Marketing Concept

There have always been companies that embraced the marketing concept and focused on the interests of consumers. However, while satisfying consumers is necessary for business success, historically not all firms were successful in implementing this concept. The development of marketing has been divided into three time periods, including production, sales, and market orientation. Although this is an over-simplification, these frameworks help to understand marketing over time.

The Production Orientation

During the second half of the 19th century, the Industrial Revolution was in full swing in the United States. Electricity, rail transportation, division of labor, assembly lines, and mass production made it possible to produce goods more efficiently. With new technology and new ways of using labor, products poured into the marketplace, where demand for manufactured goods was strong. Although mass markets were evolving, firms were developing the ability to produce more products, and competition was becoming more intense.

The Sales Orientation

While sales have always been a prerequisite to making profits, during the first half of the 20th century competition increased, and businesses realized that they would have to focus more on selling products to many buyers. Businesses viewed sales as the major means of increasing profits, and this period came to have a sales orientation. Businesspeople believed that the most important marketing activities were personal selling, advertising, and distribution. Today, some businesses incorrectly equate marketing with a sales orientation, and are still guided by this approach.

The Market Orientation

Although marketing history reveals that some firms have always produced products that consumers desired, by the 1950s, both businesses and academics developed new philosophies and terminology to explain why this approach is necessary for organizational success. This perspective emphasized that marketers first need to determine what customers want and then produce those products, rather than making the products first and then trying to persuade customers that they need them. As more organizations realized the importance of satisfying customers' needs, U.S. businesses entered the marketing era and adopted a market orientation.

ENTREPRENEURSHIP IN MARKETING

Blue Bottle Coffee: Not Your Typical Daily Grind

At John Freeman's Blue Bottle Coffee Company, headquartered in Oakland, California, coffee is more than a commodity. Blue Bottle embraces the third-wave movement, a movement that makes premium coffee into an exquisite experience of purity, flavor, and artisanship, similar to wine and cigars. To show that this experience is worth paying for, Blue Bottle has adopted a different marketing style than that of traditional coffee shops or even Starbucks.

For example, the stores of Blue Bottle emphasize the coffee experience above all else. Beverages only come in one size. With the exception of its Palo Alto location, stores do not have Wi-Fi so as to prevent distraction. Beans for each order are freshly ground and brewed from scratch right in front of the customer. The price: between $4.00 and $7.00 per cup.

While this may seem expensive for the average coffee lover, Blue Bottle shows that its niche target market is those who experience the quality and experience of coffee. Apparently, this market is growing—Blue Bottle has 33 locations worldwide with ongoing expansion plans in the works.[a]

A **market orientation** requires the "organizationwide generation of market intelligence pertaining to current and future customer needs, dissemination of the intelligence across departments, and organizationwide responsiveness to it."[20] Market orientation is linked to new-product innovation by developing a strategic focus to explore and develop new products to serve target markets.[21] For example, with an increasing "green attitude" in this country, consumers like environmentally responsible products offered at fair prices. To meet this demand, Method laundry detergent is eight times more concentrated and can clean 50 loads of laundry from a container the size of a small soft-drink bottle. Top management, marketing managers, nonmarketing managers (those in production, finance, human resources), and customers are all important in developing and carrying out a market orientation. Trust, openness, honoring promises, respect, collaboration, and recognizing the market as the *raison d'etre* are six values required by organizations striving to become more market oriented.[22]

A market orientation should recognize the need to create specific types of value-creating capabilities that enhance organizational performance.[23] For example, a bank needs to use its resources to maximize the desired level of customer service. Also, unless marketing managers provide continuous, customer-focused leadership with minimal interdepartmental conflict, achieving a market orientation will be difficult. Nonmarketing managers must communicate with marketing managers to share information important to understanding the customer. Finally, a market orientation involves being responsive to ever-changing customer needs and wants. Keurig Green Mountain has released successful products such as coffee blends, brewing systems, and Keurig cups because it understands what consumers want. Trying to assess what customers want, which is difficult to begin with, is further complicated by the speed with which fashions and tastes can change. Today, businesses want to satisfy customers and build meaningful, long-term, buyer–seller relationships. Doing so helps a firm boost its financial value.[24]

1-5b Implementing the Marketing Concept

To implement the marketing concept, a market-oriented organization must accept some general conditions, and recognize and deal with several problems. Consequently, the marketing concept has yet to be fully accepted by all businesses.

Management must first establish an information system to discover customers' real needs, and then use the information to create satisfying products. Firms such as Apple Inc., Harley Davidson, and Amazon have excelled in listening to consumers and providing satisfying products. Listening and responding to consumers' frustrations and recommendations is key to implementing the marketing concept.[25] An information system is usually expensive; management must commit money and time for its development and maintenance. Without an adequate information system, however, an organization cannot be market oriented.

To satisfy customers' objectives as well as its own, a company must coordinate all of its activities. This may require restructuring its internal operations, including production, marketing, and other business functions. This requires the firm to adapt to a changing external environment, including changing customer expectations. Companies who monitor the external environment can often predict major changes and adapt successfully. General Mills is focused on removing artificial colors and flavors from its cereals and providing organic food products to adapt to changing consumer demand. With consumer preference rapidly evolving, General Mills is changing to satisfy a growing target market.[26] If marketing is not included in the organization's top-level management, the company could fail to address actual customer needs and desires. Implementing the marketing concept demands the support not only of top management but also of managers and staff at all levels of the organization. At General Mills, CEO Ken Powell provides leadership for a marketing strategy to address a changing market focused on organic and healthful ingredients in foods.

market orientation An organizationwide commitment to researching and responding to customer needs

customer relationship management (CRM) Using information about customers to create marketing strategies that develop and sustain desirable customer relationships

relationship marketing Establishing long-term, mutually satisfying buyer–seller relationships

1-6 CUSTOMER RELATIONSHIP MANAGEMENT

LO 1-6 Identify the importance of building customer relationships.

Customer relationship management (CRM) focuses on using information about customers to create marketing strategies that develop and sustain desirable customer relationships. Achieving the full profit potential of each customer relationship should be the fundamental goal of every marketing strategy. Marketing relationships with customers are the lifeblood of all businesses. At the most basic level, profits can be obtained through relationships in the following ways: (1) by acquiring new customers, (2) by enhancing the profitability of existing customers, and (3) by extending the duration of customer relationships. In addition to retaining customers, companies also should focus on regaining and managing relationships with customers who have abandoned the firm.[27] Implementing the marketing concept means optimizing the exchange relationship, otherwise known as the relationship between a company's financial investment in customer relationships and the return generated by customer loyalty and retention. Firms use e-mail, blogs, phone calls, and consumer loyalty programs as well as social media to build relationships. It costs many times more to acquire a new customer, and a small increase in retention can significantly boost profits.

Maintaining positive relationships with customers is an important goal for marketers. The term **relationship marketing** refers to "long-term, mutually beneficial arrangements in which both the buyer and seller focus on value enhancement through the creation of more satisfying exchanges."[28] Relationship marketing continually deepens the buyer's trust in the company. As the customer's confidence grows, this, in turn, increases the firm's understanding of the customer's needs. Buyers and marketers can thus enter into a close relationship in which both participate in the creation of value.[29] Successful marketers respond to customer needs and strive to increase value to buyers over time. Eventually, this interaction becomes a solid relationship that allows for cooperation and mutual dependency. Southwest Airlines has implemented relationship marketing with the view that customers are its most important stakeholder. The company's mission statement is "dedication to the highest quality Customer Service delivered with a sense of warmth, friendliness, individual pride, and Company Spirit."[30]

Relationship marketing strives to build satisfying exchange relationships between buyers and sellers by gathering useful data at all customer contact points and analyzing that data to better understand customers' needs, desires, and habits. It focuses on building and using databases and leveraging technologies to identify strategies and methods that will maximize the lifetime value of each desirable customer to the company. It is imperative that marketers educate themselves about their customers' expectations if they are to satisfy their needs; customer dissatisfaction will only lead to defection.[31]

To build these long-term customer relationships, marketers are increasingly turning to marketing research and information technology. Organizations try to retain and increase long-term profitability through customer loyalty, which results from increasing customer value. The airline industry is a key player in CRM efforts with its frequent-flyer programs. Frequent-flyer programs enable airlines to track individual information about customers, using databases that can help airlines understand what different customers want and treat customers differently depending on their flying habits.[32] For example, Southwest Airlines' consumer loyalty program offers an opportunity for companions to fly free for frequent flyers. These customer reward programs have become popular in other industries as well, including coffee shops, fast-food restaurants, and movie theaters.

Through the use of Internet-based marketing strategies (e-marketing), companies can personalize customer relationships on a nearly one-on-one basis. The advertising for a wide range of products such as computers, jeans, golf clubs, cosmetics, and greeting cards can be tailored for specific customers. Customer relationship management provides a strategic bridge between information technology and marketing strategies aimed at long-term relationships. This involves finding and retaining customers by using information to improve customer value and satisfaction. At the same time, ensuring customer satisfaction is not a one-way street. Customers contribute to the relationship by their purchase behaviors and their use of resources to maximize customer satisfaction. For example, customers can research and spend experience or examine the product before purchasing it.[33] Ride sharing companies such as Lyft offer $50 to $100 in credits as a promotion to get consumers to experience their service.

1-7 THE IMPORTANCE OF MARKETING IN OUR GLOBAL ECONOMY

LO 1-7 Explain why marketing is important to our global economy.

Our definition of marketing and discussion of marketing activities reveal some obvious reasons why the study of marketing is relevant in today's world. In this section, we look at how marketing affects us as individuals and its role in our increasingly global society.

1-7a Marketing Costs Consume a Sizable Portion of Buyers' Dollars

Many marketing activities are necessary to provide satisfying goods and services. Obviously, these activities cost money. About one-half of a buyer's dollar goes toward marketing costs. If you spend $25 on a new Blu-ray disc, 50 to 60 percent goes toward marketing expenses, including promotion and distribution, as well as profit margins. The production (pressing) of the disc represents about $1.00, or 4 percent of its price. A family with a monthly income of $6,000 that allocates $1,200 to taxes and savings spends about $4,800 for goods and services. On average, $2,400 goes toward marketing activities. If marketing expenses consume that much of your dollar, you should know how this money is being used.

1-7b Marketing Is Used in Nonprofit Organizations

Although the term *marketing* may bring to mind advertising for Coca-Cola, Ford, and AT&T, marketing is also important in organizations working to achieve goals other than ordinary business objectives (such as profit). Government agencies at the federal, state, and local levels engage in marketing activities to fulfill their mission and goals. In addition, universities and colleges engage in marketing activities to recruit new students, as well as to obtain donations from alumni and businesses.

Like the private sector, nonprofit organizations also employ marketing activities to create, price, distribute, and promote programs that benefit particular segments of society. The Red Cross provides disaster relief throughout the world and offers promotional messages to encourage donations to support their efforts. Nonprofits operate just like businesses in that they serve a client base and must create revenue to meet their needs. Marketing activities are necessary to create effective exchange relationships with donors and those served by the nonprofit.

1-7c Marketing Is Important to Businesses and the Economy

Businesses must engage in marketing to survive and grow, and marketing activities are needed to reach customers and provide products. Marketing is the business function responsible for creating revenue to sustain the operations of the organization and provide financial returns to investors. Innovation in operations and products drive business success and customer loyalty. Without businesses creating jobs, making profits, paying taxes, and making donations, nonprofits would not exist.

Marketing activities help to produce the profits that are essential to the survival of individual businesses. Without profits, businesses would find it difficult, if not impossible, to buy rawer

THE POWER OF PRENATAL VITAMINS

Babies of poorly nourished moms may be stillborn, small, or have low birth weights.

Vitamin Angels is a 4-star charity that provides life changing prenatal vitamins to malnourished mothers in the U.S. and around the world. By helping these moms, we can ensure healthy pregnancies, safe deliveries, and adequate breast milk.

vitamin angels'   vitaminangels.org/donate

Vitamin Angels

Implementing the Marketing Concept
Vitamin Angels is a charity focused on providing nutritional supplements for impoverished mothers and children around the world.

materials, hire more employees, attract more capital, and create additional products that, in turn, make more profits. Without profits, marketers cannot continue to provide jobs and contribute to social causes. Charitable foundations, such as Vitamin Angels, serve an important social need. Their focus on supporting the nutritional health of women who are pregnant and nursing produces a very worthwhile outcome through healthier pregnancies and babies. Companies support social causes through their donations and promotional activities. Therefore, marketing helps create a successful economy and contributes to the well-being of society.

1-7d Marketing Fuels Our Global Economy

Marketing is necessary to advance a global economy. Advances in technology, along with falling political and economic barriers and the universal desire for a higher standard of living, have made marketing across national borders commonplace while stimulating global economic growth. As a result of worldwide communications and increased international travel, many global brands have achieved widespread acceptance. Many U.S. firms such as Google, Facebook, and Microsoft have been born global with an international market from the beginning of their existence. At the same time, customers in the United States have greater choices among the products they buy because foreign brands such as Toyota (Japan), Bayer (Germany), and Nestlé (Switzerland) sell alongside U.S. brands such as General Motors, Microsoft, and McDonald's. People around the world watch CNN and MTV on Samsung and Sony televisions they purchased at Walmart. Social media and the Internet now enable businesses of all sizes to reach buyers worldwide. We explore the international markets and opportunities for global marketing in Chapter 8.

1-7e Marketing Knowledge Enhances Consumer Awareness

Besides contributing to the well-being of our global economy, marketing activities help to improve the quality of our lives. In general, consumers have access to more accurate information about products—through websites, social media, and required disclosure—than at any other time in history. Consumers have the opportunity to shop, compare prices, and then return products that do not satisfy their needs. Americans returned products valued at $26 billion out of a total of $3.3 trillion sold in a recent year.[34] Many of these products are sold at retailer's outlet stores, and Amazon has a section on its website for "gently used" products. As you become more knowledgeable, it is possible to improve career options as well as purchasing decisions. Understanding marketing enables us to evaluate corrective measures (such as laws, regulations, and industry guidelines) that could stop unfair, damaging, or unethical marketing practices. Also, knowledge of marketing helps us evaluate public policy toward marketing that could potentially affect economic well-being. Thus, understanding how marketing activities work helps us to be better consumers and increases our ability to maximize value from our purchases.

1-7f Marketing Connects People through Technology

Technology, especially information technology, helps marketers understand and satisfy more customers than ever before. Access to the Internet has changed the daily lives of consumers. While mobile devices, e-mail, and office management systems are almost universally used, these tools are being supplemented by emerging technologies. Facebook, Twitter, and Google are changing the way consumers communicate, learn about products, make purchases, and share their opinions with others. The global spread of mobile devices has enabled marketers and consumers to forge new relationships that challenge how traditional marketing-mix variables are implemented. Evolving software makes it easy to create, store, share, and collaborate.[35]

Marketers have new methods to store, communicate, and share information through advanced platforms that access what has been termed as "big data." We define big data as massive data files that can be obtained from both structured and unstructured databases. Companies such as Salesforce.com use big data to provide customer relationship management services. A new generation of consumers are using social networks and mobile messaging applications rather than word documents and e-mail.[36] Table 1.1 shows some of the most common cell phone activities.

The Internet allows companies to provide tremendous amounts of information about their products to consumers, and to interact with them through e-mail and websites. A consumer shopping for a new car, for example, can access automakers' webpages, configure an ideal vehicle, and get instant feedback on its cost. Consumers can visit Autobytel, Edmund's, and other websites to find professional reviews and obtain comparative pricing information on both new and used cars to help them find the best value. They can also visit a consumer opinion site such as Yelp to read other consumers' reviews of the products. They can then purchase a vehicle online or at a dealership. Many companies employ social media to connect with their customers, using blogs and social networking sites such as Facebook and Twitter. We will discuss digital marketing in more detail in Chapter 9.

1-7g Socially Responsible Marketing: Promoting the Welfare of Customers and Stakeholders

The success of our economic system depends on marketers whose values promote trust and cooperative relationships in which customers and other stakeholders are proactively engaged, and have their concerns addressed through marketing activities. Social responsibility and ethical conduct are part of strategic planning and the implementation of marketing activities. Although some marketers' irresponsible or unethical activities end up on the front pages of *USA Today* or

TABLE 1.1	HOW CONSUMERS USE THEIR SMARTPHONES		
Activity	Cell Phone Owners 18–29	Cell Phone Owners 30–49	Cell Phone Owners 50+
Get directions, recommendations, other info related to your location	95%	94%	82%
Listen to an online radio/music service	87	74	41
Buy a product online	73	67	44
Get sports scores or analysis	52	48	36
Participate in a video call or chat	66	49	27
Watch movies or TV through a paid subscription	52	36	13

Source: Pew Research Center survey conducted July 10–12, 2015. Trend data is from previous Pew Research Center surveys.

green marketing A strategic process involving stakeholder assessment to create meaningful, long-term relationships with customers while maintaining, supporting, and enhancing the natural environment

The Wall Street Journal, most take a responsible approach to developing long-term relationships with customers and other stakeholders. Firms recognize that trust is built on ethical conduct.

In the area of the natural environment, companies are increasingly embracing the notion of **green marketing**, which is a strategic process involving stakeholder assessment to create meaningful, long-term relationships with customers while maintaining, supporting, and enhancing the natural environment. Many firms are reducing energy consumption, developing environmentally friendly packaging, and creating easily recyclable products. *Newsweek* magazine ranks the top "green companies" each year. Recent highly-ranked companies include Hasboro Inc., Nike, Hershey Co., NVIDIA Corp., and Biogen Inc.[37] Such initiatives not only reduce the negative impact that businesses have on the environment but also serve to enhance their reputations as sustainability concerns continue to grow. By addressing concerns about the impact of marketing on society, a firm can contribute to society through socially responsible activities as well as increase its financial performance.

1-7h Marketing Offers Many Exciting Career Prospects

The marketing field offers a variety of interesting and challenging career opportunities throughout the world, such as product development, personal selling, social media management, distribution, pricing, advertising, marketing research, wholesaling, and retailing. All industries have marketing positions, including health care, sports, consumer products, nonprofits, government, as well as agriculture and the oil and gas industry. When unemployment is high, sales positions remain among the most attractive job opportunities. Marketing positions are among the most secure positions because of the need to manage customer relationships. In addition, many individuals working for nonbusiness organizations engage in marketing activities to promote political, educational, cultural, church, civic, and charitable activities. It is a mistake to believe that the only way to contribute to society is to work for a nonprofit. Without businesses, the economic system that supports jobs and contributes to a good standard of living would not exist. Consider that 5 percent of charitable contributions are corporate donations. Many large companies form foundations to serve their communities. Foundations donate 16 percent of all charitable contributions in the United States.[38] Successful businesses provide the resources necessary to sustain nonprofits and governments. Most charitable contributions are from individuals, the majority of whom earned their wealth as entrepreneurs or corporate managers. Therefore, marketing plays a key role in supporting philanthropy. Whether a person earns a living through marketing activities or performs them voluntarily for a nonprofit group, marketing knowledge and skills are valuable personal and professional assets.

GOING GREEN

Walmart's Environmental Initiative: It's Not Easy Being Green

According to Walmart, people across the globe care about sustainability. It estimates that 55 percent of worldwide consumers are willing to pay more for green products. These changes in consumer values have prompted the company to focus on increasing the sustainability of its products and operations.

Walmart partnered with the Sustainability Consortium to develop a green index that measures the sustainability of products. Because it can be difficult for consumers to know if a product is sustainable, the green index increases trust between Walmart and customers by providing them with a way to judge how sustainable its products really are. Today, 1,300 Walmart suppliers use its index.

Sustainability improvements will also help Walmart save costs. It plans to reduce carbon emissions by 18 percent and be powered 50 percent by renewable energy by 2025, with the goal to increase this to 100 percent. This will result in millions of dollars of savings per year. This does not mean that a global sustainability strategy is easy. Different countries value different aspects of sustainability. For instance, in Africa consumers put more emphasis on detergents that do not need much water, while consumers in other countries prefer other green product attributes. Yet it is clear that despite differences, the world's population is placing greater value on sustainable products—and Walmart is ready to meet this demand.[b]

Chapter Review

1-1 Define marketing.

Marketing is the process of creating, pricing, distributing, and promoting goods, services, and ideas to facilitate satisfying exchange relationships with customers and to develop and maintain favorable relationships with stakeholders in a dynamic environment. The essence of marketing is to develop satisfying exchanges from which both customers and marketers benefit. Organizations generally focus their marketing efforts on a specific group of customers called a target market. A target market is the group of customers toward which a company directs a set of marketing efforts.

1-2 Explain the different variables of the marketing mix.

Marketing involves developing and managing a product that will satisfy customer needs, making the product available at the right place and at a price acceptable to customers, and communicating information that helps customers determine if the product will satisfy their needs. These activities—product, price, distribution, and promotion—are known as the marketing mix because marketing managers decide what type of each variable to use and in what amounts. Marketing managers strive to develop a marketing mix that matches the needs of customers in the target market. Before marketers can develop a marketing mix, they must collect in-depth, up-to-date information about customer needs. The product variable of the marketing mix deals with researching customers' needs and wants, and designing a product that satisfies them. A product can be a good, a service, or an idea. The price variable involves decisions and actions associated with establishing pricing policies and determining product prices. In dealing with the distribution variable, a marketing manager tries to make products available in the quantities desired to as many customers as possible. The promotion variable relates to activities used to inform individuals or groups about the organization and its products. These marketing-mix variables are often viewed as controllable because they can be changed, but there are limits to how much they can be altered.

1-3 Describe how marketing creates value.

Individuals and organizations engage in marketing to facilitate exchanges—the provision or transfer of goods, services, and ideas in return for something of value. Four conditions must exist for an exchange to occur. First, two or more individuals, groups, or organizations must participate, and each must possess something of value that the other party desires. Second, the exchange should provide a benefit or satisfaction to both parties involved in the transaction.

Third, each party must have confidence in the promise of the "something of value" held by the other. Finally, to build trust, the parties to the exchange must meet expectations. Marketing activities should attempt to create and maintain satisfying exchange relationships.

1-4 Briefly describe the marketing environment.

The marketing environment, which includes competitive, economic, political, legal and regulatory, technological, and sociocultural forces, surrounds the customer and the marketing mix. These forces can create threats to marketers, but they also generate opportunities for new products and new methods of reaching customers. These forces can fluctuate quickly and dramatically.

1-5 Summarize the marketing concept.

According to the marketing concept, an organization should try to provide products that satisfy customers' needs through a coordinated set of activities that also allows the organization to achieve its goals. Customer satisfaction is the marketing concept's major objective. The philosophy of the marketing concept emerged in the United States during the 1950s, after the production and sales eras. Organizations that develop activities consistent with the marketing concept become market-oriented organizations. To implement the marketing concept, a market-oriented organization must establish an information system to discover customers' needs and use the information to create satisfying products. It must also coordinate all its activities and develop marketing mixes that create value for customers in order to satisfy their needs.

1-6 Identify the importance of building customer relationships.

Relationship marketing involves establishing long-term, mutually satisfying buyer–seller relationships. Customer relationship management (CRM) focuses on using information about customers to create marketing strategies that develop and sustain desirable customer relationships. Managing customer relationships requires identifying patterns of buying behavior and using that information to focus on the most promising and profitable customers. A customer's value over a lifetime represents an intangible asset to a marketer that can be augmented by addressing the customer's varying needs and preferences at different stages in his or her relationship with the firm. Customer lifetime value is a key measurement that forecasts a customer's lifetime economic contribution based on continued-relationship marketing efforts. Knowing a customer's potential lifetime value helps marketers determine how to best allocate resources to marketing strategies to sustain that customer over a lifetime.

1-7 Explain why marketing is important to our global economy.

Marketing is important to our economy in many ways. Marketing costs absorb about half of each buyer's dollar. Marketing activities are performed in both business and nonprofit organizations. Marketing activities help business organizations generate profits, and they help fuel the increasingly global economy. Knowledge of marketing enhances consumer awareness. New technology improves marketers' ability to connect with customers. Socially responsible marketing can promote the welfare of customers and society. Green marketing is a strategic process involving stakeholder assessment to create meaningful, long-term relationships with customers while maintaining, supporting, and enhancing the natural environment. Finally, marketing offers many exciting career opportunities.

 Go to www.cengagebrain.com for resources to help you master the content in this chapter, as well as for materials that will expand your marketing knowledge!

Developing Your Marketing Plan

Successful companies develop strategies for marketing their products. The strategic plan guides the marketer in making many of the detailed decisions about the attributes of the product, its pricing, distribution, and promotional activities. A clear understanding of the foundations of marketing is essential in formulating a strategy and in the development of a specific marketing plan. To guide you in relating the information in this chapter to the development of your marketing plan, consider the following:

1. Discuss how the marketing concept contributes to a company's long-term success.
2. Describe the level of market orientation that currently exists in your company. How will a market orientation contribute to the success of your new product?
3. What benefits will your product provide to the customer? How will these benefits play a role in determining the customer value of your product?

Key Concepts

marketing   4
customers   4
target market   5
marketing mix   5

product   6
value   9
exchanges   10
stakeholders   11

marketing environment   12
marketing concept   13
market orientation   15

customer relationship
   management (CRM)   16
relationship marketing   16
green marketing   20

Issues for Discussion and Review

1. What is *marketing*? How did you define the term before you read this chapter?
2. What is the focus of all marketing activities? Why?
3. What are the four variables of the marketing mix? Why are these elements known as variables?
4. What is value? How can marketers use the marketing mix to enhance the perception of value?
5. What conditions must exist before a marketing exchange can occur? Describe a recent exchange in which you participated.
6. What are the forces in the marketing environment?

How much control does a marketing manager have over these forces?
7. Discuss the basic elements of the marketing concept. Which businesses in your area use this philosophy? Explain why.
8. How can an organization implement the marketing concept?
9. What is customer relationship management? Why is it so important to "manage" this relationship?
10. Why is marketing important in our society? Why should you study marketing?

VIDEO CASE 1
Cruising to Success: The Tale of New Belgium Brewing

In 1991, Jeff Lebesch and Kim Jordan began making Belgian-style ales in their basement. The impetus for the brewery occurred after Lebesch had spent time in Belgium riding throughout the country on his mountain bike. He believed he could manufacture high-quality Belgian beers in America. After spending time in the Colorado Rockies establishing the values and directions of their new company, the two launched New Belgium Brewing (NBB), with Kim Jordan as marketing director. The company's first beer was named Fat Tire in honor of Lebesch's Belgian mountain biking trek. Fat Tire remains one of NBB's most popular ales.

NBB has come far from its humble basement origins. Today, the Fort Collins–based brewery is the fourth-largest craft brewer in the country and eighth-largest brewery in the nation, with products available in 45 states, plus the District of Columbia and British Columbia. Kim Jordan helms the company as one of the few female CEOs of a large beer firm. "This entrepreneurial thing sneaks up on you," Jordan states. "And even after twenty years, I still have those 'pinch me' moments where I think, wow, this is what we've created here together." While total beer sales remain flat, the craft beer industry now maintains a 12 percent market share.

Creating such success required a corporate culture that stressed creativity and an authentic approach to treating all stakeholders with respect. While the New Belgium product is a quality craft beer, just as important to the company is how it treats its 685 employees, the community, and the environment. Each variable of the marketing mix was carefully considered. The company spends a significant amount of time researching and creating its beers, even collaborating with other craft brewers to co-create new products. This collaboration has led to products such as Ranger IPA and Biere de Garde. NBB's culture is focused on making a quality product and satisfying customers. It has even ventured into organic beer with its creation of Mothership Wit Organic Wheat Beer. The company has several product line varieties, including its more popular beers Fat Tire, 1554, Shift, and Sunshine Wheat; seasonal beers such as Pumpkick, Accumulation, and Tour de Fall; and its Lips of Faith line, a series of experimental beers produced in smaller batches, including La Folie and Chocolate Stout.

The distribution variable of the marketing mix was complex at the outset. In her initial role as marketing director, Jordan needed to convince distributors to carry their products. Often, new companies must work hard to convince distributors to carry their brands because distributors are fearful of alienating more established rivals. However, Jordan tirelessly got NBB beer onto store shelves, even

delivering beer in her Toyota station wagon. As a craft brewer, NBB uses a premium pricing strategy. Its products are priced higher than domestic brands such as Coors or Budweiser, and have higher profit margins. The popularity of NBB beers has prompted rivals to develop competitive products such as MillerCoors' Blue Moon Belgian White.

Perhaps the most notable dimension of NBB's marketing mix is promotion. From the beginning, the company based its brand on its core values, including practicing environmental stewardship and forming a participative environment in which all employees can exert their creativity. "For me brand is absolutely everything we are. It's the people here. It's how we interact with one another. And then there's the other piece of that creativity, obviously, which is designing beers," Kim Jordan said. NBB promotion has attempted to portray the company's creativity and its harmony with the natural environment. For instance, one NBB video features a tinkerer repairing a bicycle and riding down the road, while another features NBB "rangers" singing a hip-hop number to promote the company's Ranger IPA ale. The company has also heavily promoted its brand through Facebook and Twitter. This "indie" charm has served to position NBB as a company committed to having fun and being a socially responsible firm.

NBB also markets itself as a company committed to sustainability. Sustainability has been a core value at NBB from day one. The company was the first fully wind-powered brewery in the United States. NBB recycles cardboard boxes, keg caps, office materials, and amber glass. The brewery stores spent barley and hop grains in an on-premise silo and invites local farmers to pick up the grains, free of charge, to feed their pigs. The company also provides employees with a cruiser bicycle after one year of employment so they can bike to work instead of drive.

NBB's popularity allowed it to expand on the East Coast with a brewery in Asheville, North Carolina, that began brewing in 2016. The combination of a unique brand image, strong marketing mix, and an orientation that considers all stakeholders has turned NBB into a multimillion-dollar success.[39]

Questions for Discussion

1. How has New Belgium implemented the marketing concept?
2. What has Kim Jordan done to create success at New Belgium?
3. How does New Belgium's focus on sustainability as a core value contribute to its corporate culture and success?

chapter 2

Planning, Implementing, and Evaluating Marketing Strategies

Rawpixel.com/Shutterstock.com

LEARNING OBJECTIVES

2-1 Explain the strategic planning process.

2-2 Understand the importance of a firm's mission statement and corporate and business-unit strategy.

2-3 Assess how analyzing organizational resources and the marketing environment can help identify opportunities and create competitive advantage.

2-4 Explore how a firm develops marketing objectives and strategies that contribute to overall objectives.

2-5 Identify what is necessary to manage the effective implementation of marketing strategies.

2-6 Describe the four major elements of strategic performance evaluation.

2-7 Discuss the development of a marketing plan.

Blue Apron's Strategic Recipe

Matt Salzberg, Matt Wadiak, and Ilia Papas didn't set out to introduce the country to fairy tale eggplant, yuzu, and pink lemons when they launched Blue Apron in 2012. The unusual produce plays an integral role in the New York-based company's marketing strategy for differentiating itself from its competitors as it gains customers, year after year.

Blue Apron is a meal kit delivery business. Customers log onto the company's website (www.blueapron.com) or use its app to indicate their preferences and order weekly deliveries of boxes filled with just the right ingredients to cook tasty dinners for two or four. All the ingredients are high quality, fresh, and from sustainable sources. In fact, Blue Apron works directly with farmers to ensure sufficient quantities of the fruits and vegetables that add special flavor to the company's seasonal recipes.

The co-founders recognized an opportunity to profit by sending consumers the exact ingredients for each meal, plus step-by-step directions, adding convenience and saving time that would have been spent shopping, as well as eliminating the waste of left-over ingredients. Despite careful planning, the entrepreneurs were surprised by the rapid pace of growth: they exceeded their six-year sales projections in only two years. Today, Blue Apron ships 8 million meals per month and begins planning products a year in advance. As launch time approaches, the firm fine-tunes recipes and ingredients according to current customer preferences and market realities. With competitors crowding in, Blue Apron relies on unique ingredients, supply-chain skills, and sustainability as competitive advantages for continued success.[1]

This Way Up
Perishable
Handle With Care

Blue Apron

**Fresh ingredients
and great recipes**

WWW.BLUEAPRON.COM

Roman Tiraspolsky/Shutterstock.com

strategic marketing management The process of planning, implementing, and evaluating the performance of marketing activities and strategies, both effectively and efficiently

strategic planning The process of establishing an organizational mission and formulating goals, corporate strategy, marketing objectives, marketing strategy, and a marketing plan

Whether it's Blue Apron or Panera, an organization must be able to create customer value and achieve its goals. This occurs through successful strategic marketing management. **Strategic marketing management** is the process of planning, implementing, and evaluating the performance of marketing activities and strategies, both effectively and efficiently. Effectiveness and efficiency are key concepts to understanding strategic marketing management. *Effectiveness* is the degree to which long-term customer relationships help achieve an organization's objectives. *Efficiency* refers to minimizing the resources an organization uses to achieve a specific level of desired customer relationships. Thus, the overall goal of strategic marketing management is to facilitate highly desirable customer relationships while minimizing the costs of doing so.

We begin this chapter with an overview of the strategic planning process and a discussion of the nature of marketing strategy. These elements provide a framework for an analysis of the development, implementation, and evaluation of marketing strategies. We conclude with a discussion of how to create a marketing plan.

2-1 THE STRATEGIC PLANNING PROCESS

LO 2-1 Explain the strategic planning process.

Through the process of **strategic planning**, a company establishes an organizational mission and formulates goals, a corporate strategy, marketing objectives, and a marketing strategy.[2] A market orientation should guide the process of strategic planning to ensure that a concern for customer satisfaction is an integral part of the entire company, leading to the development of successful marketing strategies and planning processes.[3]

Figure 2.1 shows the various components of the strategic planning process, which begins with the establishment or revision of an organization's mission and goals. The corporation

FIGURE 2.1   COMPONENTS OF THE STRATEGIC PLANNING PROCESS

Organizational mission and goals

Corporate and business-unit strategies

Analysis of organization's strengths and weaknesses
Identification of organization's opportunities and threats

Marketing
- Objectives
- Strategy
- Marketing plan

Production
- Objectives
- Strategy
- Production plan

Finance
- Objectives
- Strategy
- Finance plan

Human Resources
- Objectives
- Strategy
- Human resources plan

and individual business units then develop strategies to achieve these goals. The company performs a detailed analysis of its strengths and weaknesses, and identifies opportunities and threats within the external marketing environment. Next, each functional area of the organization (marketing, production, finance, human resources, and so on) establishes its own objectives and develops strategies to achieve them, which must support the organization's overall goals and mission and should be focused on market orientation. In this book, we are most interested in marketing objectives and strategies. We will examine the strategic planning process by taking a closer look at each component, beginning with organizational mission statements and goals.

mission statement A long-term view, or vision, of what the organization wants to become

2-2 ESTABLISHING ORGANIZATIONAL MISSION, GOALS, AND STRATEGIES

LO 2-2 Understand the importance of a firm's mission statement and corporate and business-unit strategy.

The strategic planning process begins with deciding on the firm's organizational mission—its *raison d'etre*—and goals. These give meaning and direction to the organization.

2-2a Developing Organizational Mission and Goals

The goals of any organization should derive from its **mission statement**, a long-term view, or vision, of what the organization wants to become. For example, Facebook's mission, "to give people the power to share and make the world more open and connected," speaks to a desire to transform the way the world communicates.[4]

Mission statements, goals, and objectives must be properly implemented to achieve the desired result. It is advantageous to broadcast them to the public, customers, employees, and other stakeholders so that they know what they may expect from the firm. Slack, a cloud-based team collaboration service, has established this mission: "To make people's working lives simpler, more pleasant, and more productive." This statement drives Slack's strategies and activities, and it is reiterated in every interview given by the firm's CEO. Hiring managers underscore the mission to prospective employees at the beginning of the hiring process, and they strive to find new employees who share that mission and the firm's expressed values. This mission also fosters a culture of inclusion, transparency, direct feedback, learning from mistakes, and continuous improvement, which have helped make Slack the fastest growing workplace software.[5]

An organization's goals and objectives, derived from its mission statement, guide its planning efforts. Goals focus on the end results the organization seeks. Each level of management and department within the firm should have goals that stem from the mission statement and provide direction for the firm's activities.

2-2b Developing Corporate and Business-Unit Strategies

In most organizations, strategic planning begins at the corporate level and proceeds downward to the business-unit and marketing levels. However, organizations are increasingly developing and conducting strategic planning that moves in both directions. When conducting strategic planning, a firm is likely to seek out experts from many levels of the organization to take advantage of in-house expertise and a variety of opinions.

Figure 2.2 shows the relationships between the three planning levels: corporate, business unit, and marketing. Corporate strategy is the broadest level and should be developed with the organization's overall mission in mind. Business-unit strategy should be consistent with the corporate strategy while also serving the unit's needs. Marketing strategy utilizes the marketing mix to develop a message that is consistent with the business-unit

corporate strategy A strategy that determines the means for utilizing resources in the various functional areas to reach the organization's goals

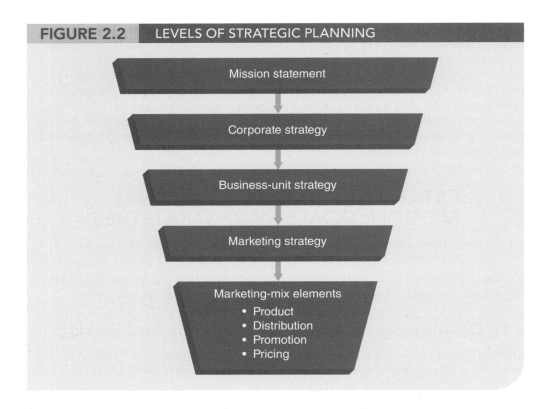

FIGURE 2.2   LEVELS OF STRATEGIC PLANNING

Mission statement

Corporate strategy

Business-unit strategy

Marketing strategy

Marketing-mix elements
- Product
- Distribution
- Promotion
- Pricing

Strategic Marketing
Qualcomm engages in strategic marketing by identifying and analyzing its target market and then developing a marketing mix to meet customers' needs.

and corporate strategies. Consider the advertisement for Qualcomm, which makes telecommunications equipment. Because Qualcomm sells many of its products to telecommunications firms, its marketing strategy emphasizes its continuing innovation in providing faster connections, such as 5G technology. The advertisement includes a neon-like image depicting connected devices such as a car, home, computer, washer, and more to convey how Qualcomm's products link a connected world.

Corporate Strategies

Corporate strategy determines the means for utilizing resources in the functional areas of marketing, production, finance, research and development, and human resources to achieve the organization's goals. A corporate strategy outlines the scope of the business and such considerations as resource deployment, competitive advantages, and overall coordination of functional areas. Top management's level of marketing expertise and ability to deploy resources to address the company's markets can affect sales growth and profitability. Corporate strategy addresses two questions: *Who are our customers?* and *What is our core competency?* The term *corporate* does not apply solely to corporations. In this context, it refers to the top-level (i.e., highest) strategy and is used by organizations of all sizes and types.

Corporate strategy planners are concerned with broad issues such as corporate culture, competition, differentiation, diversification, interrelationships among business units, and environmental and social issues. They attempt to match the resources of the organization with the opportunities and threats in the environment. Real estate firm Re/Max Holdings, for example, capitalized on its knowledge of the real-estate buying process and home buyers' needs to launch a new business, Motto Mortgage. As a mortgage broker, Motto Mortgage brings home buyers looking for financing together with lending institutions looking for customers. Motto Mortgage will help Re/Max franchisees become "one-stop shops" for home buyers.[6] Corporate strategy planners are also concerned with defining and coordinating the scope and role of the company's business units in order to reach the ends desired. The proactive nature of a company's corporate strategy can affect its capacity to innovate.

iStock.com/Leszek Kobusinski

Corporate Strategy
Apple's corporate strategy includes frequent introductions of newly designed, technologically advanced products.

Business-Unit Strategies

After analyzing corporate operations and performance, the next step in strategic planning is to determine the direction of the business and develop strategies for individual business units. A **strategic business unit (SBU)** is a division, product line, or other profit center within the parent company. Nestlé, for example, has SBUs for Pet Care and Beverages. Each SBU sells a distinct set of products to an identifiable group of customers, and each competes with a well-defined set of competitors. The revenues, costs, investments, and strategic plans of an SBU can be separated from those of the parent company and evaluated. SBUs face different market growth rates, opportunities, competition, and profit-making potential. Business strategy should seek to create value for the company's target markets and attain greater performance. Marketing research suggests that this requires implementing appropriate strategic actions and targeting appropriate market segments.[7]

strategic business unit (SBU) A division, product line, or other profit center within the parent company

GOING GREEN

Can Cleaners Be Greener?

Eco-friendly detergents are a major marketing battleground for Procter & Gamble and Unilever, two giants of the laundry industry. Procter & Gamble's detergent brands include Tide and Gain, while Unilever's well-known detergents include Surf and Omo. But in recent years, green brands such as Seventh Generation and Method have nibbled away at the market share of traditional detergents as more consumers switch to eco-friendly products. As a result of these shifts in market share and consumer behavior, both Unilever and Procter & Gamble have revamped their marketing strategies to go greener and maintain momentum in the profitable detergent industry.

Unilever purchased Seventh Generation in 2016, in line with its strategic vision of emphasizing a larger social purpose. This deal brought Unilever a business unit with a healthy bottom line and an established green reputation. Seventh Generation gained access to Unilever's marketing and manufacturing muscle so it can expand even more rapidly as demand increases.

Meanwhile, Procter & Gamble launched Tide purclean, a green version of its ever-popular Tide detergent. This formula is biobased and produced in a zero-waste factory powered by renewable wind energy, adding to the product's green credentials. Because biobased ingredients aren't yet well known, Procter & Gamble must use its marketing to educate consumers, raise awareness, promote product trial, and encourage repeat purchasing. What's next for Procter & Gamble and Unilever in their high-stakes battle over detergent market share?[a]

market A group of individuals and/or organizations that have needs for products in a product class and have the ability, willingness, and authority to purchase those products

market share The percentage of a market that actually buys a specific product from a particular company

market growth/market share matrix A helpful business tool, based on the philosophy that a product's market growth rate and its market share are important considerations in determining its marketing strategy

Strategic planners should recognize the performance capabilities of each SBU and carefully allocate resources among them. Several tools allow a company's planners to classify and visually display its portfolio of SBUs, or even individual products, according to the desirability of markets and the business's relative market share. A **market** is a group of individuals and/or organizations that have needs for products in a product class and have the ability, willingness, and authority to purchase those products. The percentage of a market that actually buys a specific product from a particular company is referred to as that product's (or business unit's) **market share**. Google, for example, has a dominant share of the search engine market in the United States, with nearly 80 percent of desktop searches and nearly 95 percent of mobile searches.[8] Product quality, order of entry into the market, and market share have all been associated with SBU success.[9]

One of the most helpful tools for a marketer is the **market growth/market share matrix**, developed by the Boston Consulting Group (BCG). This approach is based on the philosophy that a product's market growth rate and its market share are important considerations in determining marketing strategy. To develop such a tool, all of the company's SBUs and products are integrated into a single matrix and compared and evaluated to determine appropriate strategies for individual products and overall portfolio strategies. Managers use this model to determine and classify each product's expected future cash contributions and future cash requirements. However, the BCG analytical approach is more of a diagnostic tool than a guide for making strategy prescriptions.

Figure 2.3, which is based on work by the BCG, enables a strategic planner to classify a company's products into four basic types: stars, cash cows, dogs, and question marks. *Stars* are products with a dominant share of the market and good prospects for growth. However, they use more cash than they generate in order to finance growth, add capacity, and increase market share. An example of a star might be Amazon's Fire tablet computers. Although it still trails Apple and Samsung in the tablet industry, Amazon's year over year sales of the inexpensive Fire tablet grew 5,422 percent at a time when the two heavyweights lost market share.[10] *Cash cows* have a dominant share of the market but low prospects for growth. They typically generate more cash than is required to maintain market share. Bounty paper towels represent a cash cow for Procter & Gamble because it is a product that consistently sells well. *Dogs* have a subordinate share of the market and low prospects for growth. Dogs are often found in established markets. The cathode-ray tube television would probably be considered a dog by a company like Panasonic, as most customers prefer flat screens. *Question marks*, sometimes called "problem children," have a small share of a growing market and require a large amount of cash to build market share. The Chevrolet Bolt electric car, for example, is a question mark relative to General Motors' more established gasoline-powered cars and trucks.

The long-term health of an organization depends on having a range of products, some that generate cash (and acceptable profits) and others that use cash to support growth. The major indicators of a firm's overall health are the size and vulnerability of the cash cows, the prospects for the stars, and the number of question marks and dogs. Particular attention should be paid to products that require large cash flows, because most firms cannot afford to sponsor many such products. If resources are spread too thin, the company will be unable to finance promising new product entries or acquisitions. Procter & Gamble, for example, divested a number of units and brands with lower growth or profit potential, including Duracell, Iams, and CoverGirl, in order to focus its resources on its best-performing brands of products.[11]

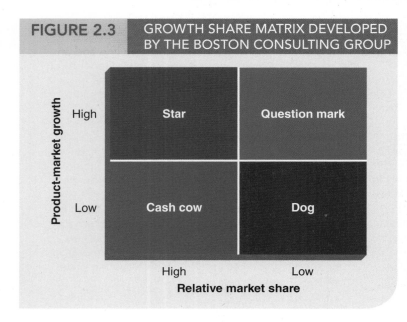

FIGURE 2.3   GROWTH SHARE MATRIX DEVELOPED BY THE BOSTON CONSULTING GROUP

Competitive Growth Strategies

Based on analyses of each product or business unit, a firm may choose one or more competitive strategies. Figure 2.4 shows these competitive strategies on a product-market matrix. The matrix can help in determining growth that can be implemented through marketing strategies.

Market penetration is a strategy of increasing sales in current markets with current products. Coca-Cola, for example, boosted sales due to a promotion that offered soft-drink bottles and cans labeled with hundreds of different personal names, song lyrics, and phrases such as "Friends," "Family," and "BFF." The personalized labels were especially popular with younger consumers, who shared photos of personalized bottles on Instagram along with the hashtag #shareacoke.[12] *Market development*

FIGURE 2.4	COMPETITIVE GROWTH STRATEGIES		

Source: H.I. Ansoff, *New Corporate Strategy* (New York: Wiley, 1988), p. 109.

is a strategy of increasing sales of current products in new markets. Arm & Hammer successfully introduced its baking soda, the firm's basic product, into new markets for use as carpet deodorizer, litter box freshener, laundry detergent, deodorant, and toothpaste. Market development also occurs when a company introduces its products into international markets for the first time.

Product development is a strategy of increasing sales by improving present products or developing new products for current markets. Apple introduced a smartwatch that provides the functionality and style of its iPhone with the wearability of a wristwatch and health benefits of a fitness band. Perhaps the most common example of product development occurs in the automotive industry, in which car manufacturers regularly introduce redesigned or completely new models to their current markets. Finally, *diversification* is a strategy of developing new products to be sold in new markets. Diversification allows firms to make better and wider use of their managerial, technological, and financial resources. Coca-Cola, for example, partnered with a dairy coop to develop Fairlife, a long-life, lactose-free milk product with 50 percent more protein and 50 percent less sugar than conventional milk. The company hopes the premium-priced dairy product—which ultimately will come in whole, reduced fat, skim, and chocolate versions—will boost its presence beyond its traditional soft-drink and water markets to help it survive declining soft-drink sales.[13] Diversification also offers some advantages over single-business firms because it allows firms to spread their risk across a number of markets.

2-3 ASSESSING ORGANIZATIONAL RESOURCES AND OPPORTUNITIES

LO 2-3 Assess how analyzing organizational resources and the marketing environment can help identify opportunities and create competitive advantage.

The next phase of the strategic planning process is an analysis of the marketing environment, including the industry in which the company operates or intends to sell its products. As we will see in Chapter 3, the external marketing environment—which includes competitive, economic, political, legal and regulatory, technological, and sociocultural forces—can threaten an organization and influence its overall goals. These forces affect the amount and type of resources the company can acquire, but also create favorable opportunities that can help an organization achieve its goals and marketing objectives.

Any strategic planning effort must take into account the organization's available financial and human resources and capabilities and how they are likely to change over time, as change may affect the organization's ability to achieve its mission and goals. Adequate resources can help a firm generate customer satisfaction and loyalty, goodwill, and a positive reputation, all of which impact marketing through creating well-known brands and strong financial

Silk

Competitive Advantage
Silk has gained a competitive advantage over milk products because it contains plants, no sugar, and is dairy-free.

core competencies Things a company does extremely well, which sometimes give it an advantage over its competition

market opportunity A combination of circumstances and timing that permits an organization to take action to reach a particular target market

strategic windows Temporary periods of optimal fit between the key requirements of a market and the particular capabilities of a company competing in that market

competitive advantage The result of a company matching a core competency to opportunities it has discovered in the marketplace

SWOT analysis Assessment of an organization's strengths, weaknesses, opportunities, and threats

performance. IBM, Coca-Cola, and Google all benefit from high brand recognition and goodwill. Such strengths also include **core competencies**, things a company does extremely well—sometimes so well that they give the company an advantage over competition.

Analysis of the marketing environment also includes identifying opportunities in the marketplace, which requires a solid understanding of the company's industry. When the right combination of circumstances and timing permits an organization to take action to reach a particular target market, a **market opportunity** exists. For example, Whole Foods saw an opportunity in the $1.5 billion market for meal kits, which come with everything needed for a time-crunched consumer to prepare a healthy home-cooked meal. Whole Foods introduced $20 Purple Carrot meal kits to compete with the very successful Blue Apron and Hello Fresh subscription services that have become popular with Millennial consumers. Purple Carrot kits, however, can be purchased in Whole Foods stores as well as online for home delivery.[14] Such opportunities are often called **strategic windows**, temporary periods of optimal fit between the key requirements of a market and the particular capabilities of a company competing in that market.[15]

When a company matches a core competency to opportunities it has discovered in the marketplace, it is said to have a **competitive advantage**. Some companies possess manufacturing, technical, or marketing skills that they can tie to market opportunities to create a competitive advantage. The advertisement for Silk, for instance, highlights the products' plant-based formulas and their lack of sugar and dairy to create a competitive advantage in the nondairy milk category. The ad prominently displays, "No sugar added. Yes, plants added," over an image of pouring milk to appeal to those adhering to a primarily plant-based diet or trying to avoid added sugar. The images of Silk's cashew, almond, and coconut nondairy milk products show consumers the range of products Silk offers to satisfy their needs and values.

2-3a SWOT Analysis

A SWOT analysis can be helpful for gauging a firm's capabilities and resources relative to its industry. The **SWOT analysis** is used to assess an organization's strengths, weaknesses, opportunities, and threats. It can provide a firm with insights into such factors as timing market entry into a new geographic region or product category. Figure 2.5 depicts the SWOT analysis as a four-cell matrix that shows how marketers must seek to convert weaknesses into strengths and threats into opportunities, and to match internal strengths with external opportunities to develop competitive advantages. Strengths and weaknesses are internal factors that can influence an organization's ability to satisfy target markets. *Strengths* refer to competitive advantages, or core competencies, that give the company an advantage over other firms in meeting the needs of its target markets. *Weaknesses* are limitations a company faces in developing or implementing a marketing strategy. Consider Walmart, a company that was dominant for so long it almost did not need to worry about competitors. However, Amazon, with its low costs and high customer satisfaction, has grown into such a threat that Walmart has been forced to acknowledge it has a serious weakness in online sales and technological innovation. To respond to this threat, Walmart has made numerous acquisitions, such as Jet.com, to help the company improve its online shopping experience and delivery.[16] Marketers must keep in mind that strengths and weaknesses are only meaningful when they help or hinder the company in meeting customer needs and desires.

Opportunities and threats affect all organizations within an industry, market, or geographic region because they exist outside of and independently of the company. *Opportunities* refer to favorable conditions in the environment that could produce rewards for the organization if acted upon. Opportunities are situations that exist but must be exploited for the company to benefit from them. *Threats,* on the other hand, refer to barriers that could prevent the company from reaching its objectives. Opportunities and threats can stem from many sources within the marketing environment. When a competitor's introduction of a new product threatens a company, a firm may require a defensive strategy. If the company can develop and launch a new product that meets or exceeds the competition's offering, it can transform the threat into an opportunity. It is important to use SWOT analysis to explore the internal organization and the marketing environment without judgment, focusing on issues that could lead to the greatest possibilities of success. This means using some resources for open-minded examination rather than looking for information to confirm current beliefs.[17]

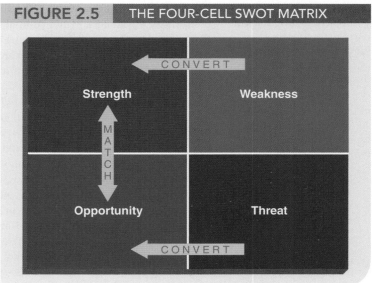

FIGURE 2.5   THE FOUR-CELL SWOT MATRIX

Source: Adapted from Nigel F. Piercy, *Market-Led Strategic Change.* Copyright 1992, Butterworth-Heinemann Ltd., p. 371. Reprinted with permission.

2-3b First-Mover and Late-Mover Advantage

An important factor that marketers must consider when identifying organizational resources and opportunities is whether the firm has the resources to cultivate a first-mover advantage, or is in a position to choose between developing a first-mover or late-mover advantage. A **first-mover advantage** is the ability of an innovative company to achieve long-term competitive advantages by being the first to offer a certain product in the marketplace. Being the first to enter a market helps a company build a reputation as a pioneer and market leader. Amazon and eBay were both first-mover start-ups that remain leaders as they grow and innovate ahead of the competition. For a first mover, the market is, for at least a short period, free of competition as potential competitors work to develop a rival product. Because consumers have no choice initially, being a first mover also helps establish customer brand loyalty in cases when switching to another brand later, when there are more options, may be costly or difficult for the consumer. The first to develop a new product can also protect secrets and technology through patents.

There are risks, however, of being the first to enter a market. Usually, high outlays are associated with creating a new product, including marketing research, product development, production, and marketing—or buyer education—costs. Also, early sales growth may not match predictions if the firm overestimates demand or fails to target marketing efforts properly. The company runs the risk that the product will fail due to market uncertainty, or that the product might not completely meet consumers' expectations or needs.

First-Mover Advantage
Tesla had the first-mover advantage for creating an autonomous vehicle. What advantages will Tesla experience by being first to market?

first-mover advantage
The ability of a company to achieve long-term competitive advantages by being the first to offer an innovative product in the marketplace

late-mover advantage
The ability of later market entrants to achieve long-term competitive advantages by not being the first to offer a product in a marketplace

marketing objective A statement of what is to be accomplished through marketing activities

A **late-mover advantage** is the ability of later market entrants to achieve long-term competitive advantages by not being the first to offer a certain product in a marketplace. Competitors that enter the market later can benefit from the first mover's mistakes, and they have a chance to improve on the product design and marketing strategy. For example, Google Home was not the first smart speaker/home automation device, but Google's technology and experience with voice search along with richer features may give Home a late-mover advantage over first mover Amazon Echo.[18] A late mover is also likely to have lower initial investment costs than the first mover, because the first mover has already developed a distribution infrastructure and educated buyers about the product. By the time a late mover enters the market, there is also more data, and therefore more certainty, about product success.

Being a late mover has disadvantages, too. The company that entered the market first may have patents and other protections on its technology, and trade secrets that prevent the late mover from producing a similar product. If customers who have already purchased the first mover's product believe that switching to the late mover's product will be expensive or time consuming, it may be difficult for the late mover to gain market share.

It is important to note that the timing of entry into the market is crucial. Companies that are relatively quick to enter the market after the first mover generally have a greater chance of building market share and brand loyalty. Companies that enter the market later on, after many other companies have done so, face strong competition and more disadvantages.

2-4 DEVELOPING MARKETING OBJECTIVES AND MARKETING STRATEGIES

LO 2-4 Explore how a firm develops marketing objectives and strategies that contribute to overall objectives.

The next phase in strategic planning is the development of marketing objectives and marketing strategies, which are used to achieve marketing objectives. A **marketing objective** states what is to be accomplished through marketing activities. These objectives can be given in terms of product introduction, product improvement or innovation, sales volume, profitability, market share, pricing, distribution, advertising, or employee training activities. The advertisement for Tropicana, for example, highlights the company's objective to generate new customers and gain a greater share of the orange juice market through a new product appealing to consumers looking to reduce the amount of sugar in their diets. To emphasize that Trop50 has half the sugar of regular orange juice, the ad's primary image is half a bottle of the product. Marketing objectives should be based on a careful study of the SWOT analysis, matching strengths to opportunities, eliminating weaknesses, and minimizing threats.

A marketing objective should possess certain characteristics. First, it should be expressed in clear, simple terms so that all marketing and non-marketing personnel in the company understand exactly what they are trying to achieve. Second, a marketing objective should be measurable, which allows the organization to track progress and compare outcomes against beginning benchmarks. For instance, if Tropicana's objective is to use its new Trop50 product to increase market share by 10 percent in the United States, the company should be able to measure market share changes accurately to ensure that it is making gains toward that objective. Third, it should specify a time frame for its accomplishment, such as six months or one year. Finally, a marketing objective should be consistent with both business-unit and corporate strategies. This ensures that the company's mission is carried out consistently at all levels of the organization by all personnel. Marketing objectives should be achievable and use company

Marketing Objectives
What is Tropicana hoping to achieve with this ad?

Tropicana Products, Inc.

resources effectively, and successful accomplishment should contribute to the overall corporate strategy.

A marketing strategy ensures that the firm has a plan in place to achieve its marketing objectives. A **marketing strategy** is the selection of a target market and the creation of a marketing mix that will satisfy the needs of that target market. A marketing strategy articulates the best use of the company's resources to accomplish its marketing objectives. It also directs resource deployment so as to boost competitive advantage. Marketing strategy is the key variable in strengthening organizational competitiveness.[19]

Marketing strategies may need to be adapted as the environment changes. Some organizations fail to adapt their strategy in response to competition, consumer behavior, or other factors that may create the need for a new, modified strategy.[20] For example, as tablet computers became popular, Microsoft had to adapt its strategy to compete in the market. It did so by developing its Microsoft Surface tablet in response to competition and consumer demand.

marketing strategy A plan of action for identifying and analyzing a target market and developing a marketing mix to meet the needs of that market

2-4a Selecting the Target Market

Selecting an appropriate target market may be the most important decision a company makes in the strategic planning process, as it is key to strategic success. The target market must be chosen before the organization can adapt its marketing mix to meet customers' needs and preferences. If a company selects the wrong target market, all other marketing decisions are likely to be in vain.

Careful and accurate target market selection is crucial to productive marketing efforts. Products, and even whole companies, sometimes fail because marketers misidentify the best target market for their products. Organizations that try to be all things to all people rarely satisfy the needs of any customer group very well. Identification and analysis of a target market provide a foundation on which a company can develop its marketing mix.

When exploring possible target markets, marketing managers evaluate how entry could affect the company's sales, costs, and profits. Marketing information should be organized to facilitate a focus on the chosen target customers. Accounting and information systems, for example, can be used to track revenues and costs by customer (or customer group). Firms should reward managers and employees who focus efforts on profitable customers. Also, they should develop teamwork skills that promote a flexible customer orientation that allows them to adapt to changes in the marketing environment.

Target Market Selection
Are Marriott and the Fairfield Hotels aiming at the same target market?

Marketers should determine whether a selected target market aligns with the company's overall mission and objectives. If it does, they should assess whether the company has the appropriate resources to develop a marketing mix (product, price, distribution, and promotion) that meets the needs of that target market. The size and number of competitors already marketing products in potential target markets are concerns as well. For example, the market for mobile gaming has exploded in recent years. The market has become so competitive that new entrants must carefully evaluate whether their product would be in demand by the target market, or be a genuine improvement over what already exists. This market accounts for 85 percent of all mobile app revenue and is projected to reach $74.6 billion by 2020.[21]

2-4b Creating Marketing Mixes

Using all relevant information available to conduct in-depth research allows a firm to select the most appropriate target market, which is the basis for creating a marketing mix that satisfies the needs of that market. Tesla Motors selected a unique segment of the electric vehicle market and created a marketing mix of new technology that included distribution direct from the manufacturer. It selected promotional methods and price points that suitably reflected the upper end of the electric car market.[22]

An organization should analyze demographic information, customer needs, preferences, and behaviors with respect to product design, pricing, distribution, and promotion. For example, to grow beyond its core Baby Boomer market, Thor Industries developed a new Airstream recreational vehicle to target Millennials. To meet the needs and desires of Millennials, the Airstream Basecamp is smaller, solar powered, and can be towed with a Subaru. The $35,000 Basecamp includes Bluetooth speakers, Italian cabinetry, and a panoramic window for taking in Instagram-ready views.[23]

Marketing-mix decisions should have two additional characteristics: consistency and flexibility. All marketing-mix decisions should be consistent with the business-unit and corporate strategies. Such consistency allows the organization to achieve its objectives on all three levels of planning. Flexibility, on the other hand, permits the organization to alter the marketing mix in response to changes in market conditions, competition, and customer needs. Marketing-strategy flexibility has a positive influence on organizational performance.

Utilizing the marketing mix as a tool set, a company can detail how it will achieve a sustainable competitive advantage. A **sustainable competitive advantage** is one that the competition cannot copy in the foreseeable future. Walmart, for example, maintains a sustainable competitive advantage in groceries over supermarkets because of its highly efficient and low-cost distribution system. This advantage allows Walmart to offer lower prices and has helped it to maintain the largest share of the supermarket business. Maintaining a sustainable competitive advantage requires flexibility in the marketing mix when facing uncertain environments.

2-5 MANAGING MARKETING IMPLEMENTATION

LO 2-5 Identify what is necessary to manage the effective implementation of marketing strategies.

sustainable competitive advantage An advantage that the competition cannot copy

marketing implementation The process of putting marketing strategies into action

Marketing implementation is the process of putting marketing strategies into action. Through planning, marketing managers provide purpose and direction for an organization's marketing efforts and are positioned to implement specific marketing strategies. The effective implementation of all marketing activities depends on a well-organized marketing department that is capable of motivating personnel, communicating effectively, employing strong coordination efforts, and setting reasonable, attainable timetables for activity completion. Managers play a key role in creating desired outcomes through supervisory actions that provide rewards, reduce risks, and recognize behaviors that implement the marketing strategy.[24]

2-5a Organizing the Marketing Unit

The structure and relationships of a marketing unit—including lines of authority and communication that connect and coordinate individuals—strongly affect marketing activities. Companies that truly adopt the marketing concept develop an organizational culture based on a shared set of beliefs that places the customers' needs at the center of decisions about strategy and operations.

Firms must decide whether to centralize or decentralize operations, a choice that directly affects marketing decision making and strategy. In a **centralized organization**, top-level managers delegate little authority to lower levels. In a **decentralized organization**, decision-making authority is delegated as far down the chain of command as possible. In centralized organizations, marketing decisions are made at the top levels. However, centralized decision making may prove ineffective in firms that must respond quickly to fluctuations in customer demand. In these organizations, decentralized authority allows the company to adapt more rapidly to customer needs.

How effectively a company's marketing management can implement marketing strategies also depends on how the marketing unit is organized. Organizing marketing activities to align with the overall strategic marketing approach enhances organizational efficiency and performance. A marketing department should clearly outline the hierarchical relationships between personnel and designate responsibility for performing certain activities and making decisions.

2-5b Coordinating and Communicating

Marketing managers must coordinate diverse employee actions to achieve marketing objectives, and they must work closely with management in many areas, including research and development, production, finance, accounting, and human resources to ensure that marketing activities align with other functions of the firm. They must also coordinate the activities of internal marketing staff with the marketing efforts of external organizations, including advertising agencies, resellers (wholesalers and retailers), researchers, and shippers. Marketing managers can improve coordination by making each employee aware of how his or her job relates to others, and how his or her actions contribute to the achievement of marketing objectives. This requires effective communication and motivation of everyone involved in the marketing process.

Marketing managers must be in clear communication with the firm's upper-level management to ensure that they are aware of the firm's goals and achievements and that marketing activities are consistent with the company's overall goals and strategies. The marketing unit should also take steps to ensure that its activities are in sync with those of other departments, such as finance or human resources. For example, marketing personnel should work with the production staff to design products with features that marketing research indicates customers desire.

It is important that communication flows up, from the front lines of the organization to upper management. Customer-contact employees are in a unique position to understand customers' wants and needs, and pathways should be open for them to communicate this knowledge to marketing managers. In this way, marketing managers can gain access to a rich source of information about what customers require, how products are selling, the effectiveness of marketing activities, and any issues with marketing implementation. Upward communication also allows marketing managers to understand the problems and requirements of lower-level employees—a critical group to keep satisfied, as they are the ones who interface with customers.

Training is a key part of communicating with marketing employees. An effective training program provides employees with a forum to learn and ask questions, and results in employees who are empowered and can be held accountable for their performance. Many firms utilize a formalized, high-tech information system that tracks data and facilitates communication between marketing managers, sales managers, and sales personnel. Information systems expedite communications within and between departments and support activities such as allocating scarce organizational resources, planning, budgeting, sales analyses, performance evaluations, and report preparation.

centralized organization A structure in which top-level managers delegate little authority to lower levels

decentralized organization A structure in which decision-making authority is delegated as far down the chain of command as possible

Recognition
Recognizing outstanding performance is one approach to motivating marketing personnel.

To motivate marketing personnel, managers must address their employees' needs to maintain a high level of workplace satisfaction. Employee motivation and reward programs should be fair, ethical, and well understood by members of the organization. Employee rewards should also be tied to organizational goals. A firm can motivate its workers through a variety of methods, including linking pay to performance, informing workers how their performance affects department and corporate results as well as their own compensation, providing appropriate and competitive compensation, implementing a flexible benefits program, and adopting a participative management approach.

Diversity in the workplace can complicate employee motivational strategies. Different generations and cultures may be motivated by different things; for example, an employee might value autonomy or recognition more than a pay increase. In addition to money and fringe benefits, managers can reward employees with nonfinancial rewards such as prestige or recognition, job autonomy, skill variety, task significance, increased feedback, or even a more relaxed dress code. It is crucial for management to show pride in its workforce and motivate employees to take pride in their company.

2-5c Establishing a Timetable for Implementation

Successful marketing implementation requires that employees know the specific activities for which they are responsible and the timetable for completing them. Establishing an implementation timetable involves several steps: (1) identifying the activities to be performed, (2) determining the time required to complete each activity, (3) separating the activities to be performed in sequence from those to be performed simultaneously, (4) organizing the activities in the proper order, and (5) assigning responsibility for completing each activity to one or more employees, teams, or managers. Completing all implementation activities on schedule requires tight coordination within the marketing unit and among other departments that contribute to marketing activities, such as production. Pinpointing which activities can be performed simultaneously will reduce the total amount of time needed to put a given marketing strategy into practice. Because scheduling is a complicated task, most organizations use sophisticated software to plan the timing of marketing activities.

2-6 EVALUATING MARKETING STRATEGIES

LO 2-6 Describe the four major elements of strategic performance evaluation.

To achieve marketing objectives, marketing managers must evaluate marketing strategies effectively. **Strategic performance evaluation** consists of establishing performance standards, measuring actual performance, comparing actual performance with established standards, and modifying the marketing strategy, if needed.

2-6a Establishing Performance Standards

A **performance standard** is an expected level of performance against which actual performance can be compared. A performance standard might be a 20 percent reduction in customer complaints, a monthly sales quota of $150,000, or a 10 percent increase per month in new-customer accounts. Performance standards are derived from marketing objectives that are set while developing the marketing strategy. By establishing marketing objectives, a firm indicates what its marketing strategy is supposed to accomplish. Marketing objectives

strategic performance evaluation Establishing performance standards, measuring actual performance, comparing actual performance with established standards, and modifying the marketing strategy, if needed

performance standard An expected level of performance against which actual performance can be compared

directly or indirectly set forth performance standards, usually in terms of sales, costs, or communication dimensions, such as brand awareness or product feature recall. Actual performance should be measured in similar terms to facilitate comparisons.

2-6b Analyzing Actual Performance

The principal means by which a marketer can gauge whether a marketing strategy has been effective in achieving objectives is by analyzing the actual performance of the marketing strategy. Consider the advertisement for Milk-Bone Brushing Chews dental chew treats. While measuring the cost of this advertisement is not difficult, evaluating the overall effectiveness of the strategy can be challenging. The advertisement arouses the viewer's interest by featuring a handsome white dog with healthy teeth. The text describes the benefits of using Brushing Chews to clean dogs' teeth, even the hard-to-reach back ones, with its twisted design. To assess the campaign's performance, Milk-Bone managers may compare sales or brand awareness before launching the campaign with those metrics following the campaign to see whether any changes occurred. However, even if marketers discover a change in sales or brand awareness, it can be difficult to determine whether this advertising campaign alone was responsible for the difference, or whether it was the result of a combination of factors. Generally speaking, however, technological advancements have made it easier for firms to analyze actual performance.

Another means of analyzing actual performance is by conducting customer research and surveys. In this section, we focus on two bases—sales and cost—for evaluating the actual performance of marketing strategies.

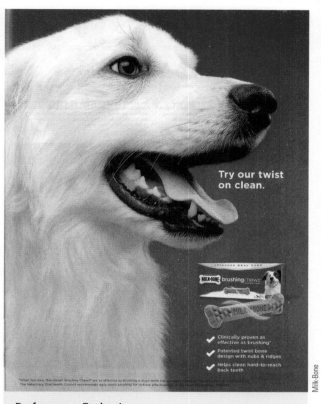

Performance Evaluation
Measuring the cost of an advertising campaign is not difficult. Evaluating the effectiveness of an advertising campaign is challenging.

Sales Analysis

Sales analysis uses sales figures to evaluate a firm's current performance. It is a common method of evaluation because sales data are readily available, at least in aggregate form, and can reflect the target market's reactions to a marketing mix. If sales spike after a particular marketing mix is implemented, marketers can be reasonably certain that the marketing mix was effective at reaching the target audience. Consider the sales spike that McDonald's experienced when it began selling its breakfast menu all day long.[25] Information from sales data alone is not sufficient, however. To provide useful information, marketers must compare current sales data with forecasted sales, industry sales, specific competitors' sales, and the costs incurred from marketing efforts to achieve the sales volume. For example, if Milk-Bone managers forecast $6 million in sales for its Brushing Chews dental chew treats for the next quarter, but actually sell $7 million, marketers may assume that the advertisement had a positive impact on sales.

Although sales may be measured in several ways, the basic unit of measurement is the sales transaction. A sales transaction results in an order for a specified quantity of the organization's product sold under specified terms by a particular salesperson or sales team on a certain date. Organizations should record all information related to a transaction so that they can analyze sales in terms of dollar volume or market share. Firms frequently use dollar volume in their sales analyses because the dollar is a common denominator of sales, costs, and profits. A marketing manager who uses dollar-volume analysis should factor out the effects of price changes, which can skew the numbers by making it seem that more or fewer sales have been made than is the case.

sales analysis Analysis of sales figures to evaluate a firm's performance

ENTREPRENEURSHIP IN MARKETING

Want to Avoid Student Debt? Scholly Can Help

How do entrepreneurs find and assess market opportunities? Christopher Gray started with his own experience. During his junior year of high school in Birmingham, Alabama, Gray spent seven months searching for scholarships to pay his way through college. Eventually, his research and persistence paid off, as he amassed $1.3 million to attend Drexel University in Philadelphia.

Majoring in business at Drexel, Gray was constantly approached by classmates seeking assistance in locating grants and scholarships. That's when the market opportunity came into sharper focus. In his words, "You have students drowning in debt and scholarships that go unawarded" because students simply don't know about them. So Gray decided to build on his knowledge and expertise by founding a business to match students with money, using sophisticated software that analyzes the fit

between an applicant's qualifications and a scholarship's requirements. He developed a website and a smartphone app he called Scholly, priced access at $2.99 per download, and got listed in the Apple App Store.

Gray's big break came when he appeared on the *Shark Tank* television show. Not only did Scholly attract a $40,000 investment, the site received 80,000 visits overnight and the app became an instant best-seller. In the first two years, the Scholly app was downloaded 850,000 times and matched users with $50 million in scholarships. No wonder Gray has been honored as one of *Forbes's* "30 Under 30" businesspeople, named as one of Oprah Winfrey's "SuperSoul 100," and awarded the Smithsonian American Ingenuity Award for Youth Achievement.[b]

A firm's market share is the sales of a product stated as a percentage of total industry sales of competing products. Market share analysis lets a company compare its marketing strategy with competitors' strategies. The primary reason for using market share analysis is to estimate whether sales changes have resulted from the firm's marketing strategy or from uncontrollable environmental forces. When a company's sales volume declines, but its share of the market stays the same, the marketer can assume that industry sales declined because of external factors. However, if a company experiences a decline in both sales and market share, it should consider changing its marketing strategy to make it more effective.

Even though market share analysis can be helpful in evaluating the performance of a marketing strategy, the user must exercise caution when interpreting results. When attributing a sales decline to uncontrollable factors, a marketer must keep in mind that factors in the external marketing environment do not affect all firms equally because firms have varying strategies and objectives. Changes in the strategies of one company can affect the market shares of one or all companies in that industry. Within an industry, the entrance of new firms, the launch of new products by competing firms, or the demise of established products also affect a firm's market share. Market share analysts should attempt to account for these effects. Apple, for example, caused its competitors to reevaluate their marketing strategies when it introduced the iPad, spurring competitor innovation and revised marketing strategies.

Marketing Cost Analysis

Although sales analysis is critical for evaluating the performance of a marketing strategy, it provides only a partial picture. A marketing strategy that successfully generates sales may not be deemed effective if it is extremely costly. A firm must take into account the marketing costs associated with a strategy to gain a complete understanding of its effectiveness at achieving a desired sales level. **Marketing cost analysis** breaks down and classifies costs to determine which are associated with specific marketing efforts. Comparing costs of previous marketing activities with results allows a marketer to better allocate the firm's resources in the future. Marketing cost analysis lets a company evaluate the performance of

marketing cost analysis Analysis of costs to determine which are associated with specific marketing efforts

a marketing strategy by comparing sales achieved and costs sustained. By pinpointing exactly where a company incurs costs, this form of analysis can help isolate profitable or unprofitable customers, products, and geographic areas.

A company that understands and manages costs appropriately has a competitive advantage. A low-cost provider is in a position to engage in aggressive price competition, for example. The Internet offers low-cost marketing options such as e-mail, social media, and viral video. One way to analyze a company's costs is by comparing them with industry averages. Many companies check expenditures on marketing efforts and other operations against average levels for the industry to identify areas in need of improvement. When looking at industry averages, however, a company should take into account its own unique situation. The

SNAPSHOT

How Much Do Companies Spend on Marketing?

Company	Total revenue	Percent of revenue spent on marketing
salesforce.com	$2,170,000,000	53%
Twitter	$614,110,000	44%
Linkedin	$774,410,000	35%
Tempur + Sealy	$619,900,000	21%
Microsoft	$51,810,000,000	18%

Source: Vital, "Content Marketing Strategy: What Percent of Revenue Do Publicly Traded Companies Spend on Marketing and Sales?" Infographic by Sarah Brady, https://vtldesign.com/inbound-marketing/content-marketing-strategy/percent-of-revenue-spent-on-marketing-sales/ (accessed January 13, 2017).

company's costs can differ from the industry average for several reasons, including its marketing objectives, cost structure, geographic location, types of customers, and scale of operations.

Costs can be categorized in different ways when performing marketing cost analysis. One way is to identify costs affected by sales or production volume. Some costs are fixed, meaning they do not change between different units of time, regardless of a company's production or sales volume. Fixed costs are expenses such as rent and employees' salaries, which will not be affected by fluctuations in production or sales. Fixed costs are generally not very illuminating when determining how to utilize marketing funds more effectively. It does little good, for example, to know that a firm spends $80,000 on rent annually. The marketing analyst must conduct additional research to determine that, of the $80,000 spent on rent, $32,000 is spent on facilities associated with marketing efforts.

Some costs are directly attributable to production and sales volume. Known as variable costs, they are stated in terms of a per quantity (or unit) cost. Variable costs include the cost to produce or sell each unit of a specific product, such as the materials and labor, or commissions paid to salespeople when they sell products.

Another way to categorize costs is based on whether or not they can be linked to a specific business function. Costs that can be linked are allocated, using one or several criteria, to the functions that they support. For example, if a firm spends $80,000 to rent space for production, storage, and sales facilities, the total rental cost can be allocated to each of the three functions using a measurement such as square footage. Such costs as interest paid on loans, taxes paid to the government, and the salaries of top management cannot be assigned according to any logical criteria.

2-6c Comparing Actual Performance with Performance Standards and Making Changes, If Needed

When comparing actual performance with established performance standards, a firm may find that it exceeded or failed to meet performance standard benchmarks. When actual performance exceeds performance standards, marketers will likely be satisfied and a marketing strategy will be deemed effective. It is important that a firm seek to gain an understanding of why the strategy was effective, because this information may allow marketers to adjust the strategy tactically to be even more effective.

When actual performance fails to meet performance standards, marketers should seek to understand why the marketing strategy was less effective than expected. For example, perhaps a marketing-mix variable such as price was not ideally suited to the target market, which could result in lower performance. Environmental changes and aggressive competition can also cause a marketing strategy to underperform.

When a marketer finds that a strategy is underperforming expectations, a question sometimes arises as to whether the marketing objective, against which performance is measured, is realistic. After studying the problem, the firm may find that the marketing objective is indeed unrealistic. In this case, marketers must alter the marketing objective to bring it in line with more sensible expectations. It is also possible that the marketing strategy is underfunded, which can result in lower performance.

2-7 CREATING THE MARKETING PLAN

LO 2-7 Discuss the development of a marketing plan.

The strategic planning process ultimately yields a marketing strategy that is the framework for a **marketing plan**, a written document that specifies the marketing activities to be performed to implement and evaluate the organization's marketing strategies. Developing a clear, well-written marketing plan, though time consuming, is important. It provides a uniform marketing vision for the firm and is the basis for internal communications. It delineates marketing responsibilities and tasks, and outlines schedules for implementation. The plan presents objectives and specifies how resources are to be allocated to achieve them. Finally, the marketing plan helps managers monitor and evaluate the performance of a marketing strategy.

A single marketing plan can be developed and applied to the business as a whole, but it is more likely that a company will choose to develop multiple marketing plans, with each relating to a specific brand or product. Multiple marketing plans are part of a larger strategic business plan, and are used to implement specific parts of the overall strategy.

Organizations use many different formats when producing a marketing plan. They may be written for strategic business units, product lines, individual products or brands, or specific markets. The key is to make sure that the marketing plan aligns with corporate and business-unit strategies and is accessible to and shared with all key employees. A marketing plan represents a critical element of a company's overall strategy development. It should reflect the company's culture and be representative of all functional specialists in the firm.

Marketing planning and implementation are closely linked in successful companies. The marketing plan provides a framework to stimulate thinking and provide strategic direction. Implementation is an adaptive response to day-to-day issues, opportunities, and unanticipated situations—for example, an economic slowdown that dampens sales—that cannot be incorporated into marketing plans.

Table 2.1 describes the major elements of a typical marketing plan. Each component builds on the last. The first component is the executive summary, which provides an overview of the entire plan so that readers can quickly identify the key issues and their roles in the planning and implementation processes. The executive summary includes an introduction, an explanation of the major aspects of the plan, and a statement about costs. The next component of the marketing plan is the environmental analysis, which supplies information about the company's current situation with respect to the marketing environment, the target market, and the firm's current objectives and performance. The environmental analysis includes an assessment of all the environmental factors—competitive, economic, political, legal and regulatory, technological, and sociocultural—that can affect marketing activities. The analysis then examines the current needs of the organization's target markets. In the final section of the environmental analysis, the company evaluates its marketing objectives and performance to ensure that objectives are consistent with the

marketing plan A written document that specifies the activities to be performed to implement and control the organization's marketing strategies

TABLE 2.1	COMPONENTS OF THE MARKETING PLAN	
Plan Component	**Component Summary**	**Highlights**
Executive Summary	One- to two-page synopsis of the entire marketing plan	1. Stress key points 2. Include one to three key points that make the company unique
Environmental Analysis	Information about the company's current situation with respect to the marketing environment	1. Assess marketing environment factors 2. Assess target market(s) 3. Assess current marketing objectives and performance
SWOT Analysis	Assessment of the organization's strengths, weaknesses, opportunities, and threats	1. Company strengths 2. Company weaknesses 3. Opportunities in the environment and industry 4. Threats in the environment and industry
Marketing Objectives	Specification of the company's marketing objectives	1. Qualitative measures of what is to be accomplished 2. Quantitative measures of what is to be accomplished
Marketing Strategies	Outline of how the company will achieve its objectives	1. Target market(s) 2. Marketing mix
Marketing Implementation	Outline of how the company will implement its marketing strategies	1. Marketing organization 2. Activities and responsibilities 3. Implementation timetable
Performance Evaluation	Explanation of how the company will evaluate the performance of the implemented plan	1. Performance standards 2. Financial controls 3. Monitoring procedures (audits)

changing marketing environment. The next component of the marketing plan is the SWOT (strengths, weaknesses, opportunities, and threats) analysis, which utilizes the information gathered in the environmental analysis. The marketing objectives section of the marketing plan states what the company wants to accomplish through marketing activities, using the SWOT analysis as a guide to where the firm stands in the market. The marketing strategies component outlines how the firm plans to achieve its marketing objectives and discusses the company's target market selection(s) and marketing mix. The marketing implementation component of the plan outlines how marketing strategies will be executed. The success of a marketing strategy depends on the feasibility of marketing implementation. Finally, the performance evaluation establishes standards for how results will be measured and evaluated, and actions the company should take to reduce the differences between planned and actual performance.

It is important to note that most organizations utilize their own formats and terminology to describe the marketing plan. Every marketing plan is, and should be, unique to the organization for which it was created.

Creating and implementing a marketing plan allows the organization to achieve its marketing objectives and its business-unit and corporate goals. However, a marketing plan is only as good as the information it contains and the effort and creativity that went into its development. Therefore, the importance of having a good marketing information system that generates robust, reliable data cannot be overstated. Equally important is the role of managerial judgment throughout the strategic planning process. While the creation of a marketing plan is an important milestone in strategic planning, it is by no means the final step. To succeed, a company must have a plan that is closely followed yet flexible enough to adapt to the changing marketing environment.

Chapter Review

2-1 Explain the strategic planning process.

Through the process of strategic planning, a company establishes an organizational mission and formulates goals, a corporate strategy, marketing objectives, and a marketing strategy.

2-2 Understand the importance of a firm's mission statement and corporate and business-unit strategy.

An organization's goals should align with its mission statement—a long-term view, or vision, of what the organization wants to become. A well-formulated mission statement gives an organization a clear purpose and direction, distinguishes it from competitors, provides direction for strategic planning, and fosters a focus on customers. An organization's goals, which focus on desired results, guide the remainder of its planning efforts.

Corporate strategy determines the means for utilizing resources in the areas of production, finance, research and development, human resources, and marketing to reach the organization's goals. Business-unit strategy focuses on strategic business units (SBUs)—divisions, product lines, or other profit centers within the parent company used to define areas for consideration in a specific strategic marketing plan. The Boston Consulting Group's market growth/market share matrix integrates a company's products or SBUs into a single, overall matrix for evaluation to determine appropriate strategies for individual products and business units. Based on its analysis, a firm may choose one or more competitive strategies: market penetration, market development, product development, and/or diversification.

2-3 Assess how analyzing organizational resources and the marketing environment can help identify opportunities and create competitive advantage.

The marketing environment, including competitive, economic, political, legal and regulatory, technological, and sociocultural forces, can affect the resources available to a company to create favorable opportunities. Resources may help a firm develop core competencies, which are things that a company does extremely well—sometimes so well that it gives the company an advantage over its competition. When the right combination of circumstances and timing permits an organization to take action toward reaching a particular target market, a market opportunity exists. Strategic windows are temporary periods of optimal fit between the key requirements of a market and the particular capabilities of a company competing in that market. When a company matches a core competency to opportunities in the marketplace, it is said to have a competitive advantage. A marketer can use SWOT (strengths, weaknesses, opportunities, and threats) analysis to assess a firm's ability to achieve a competitive advantage.

If marketers want to understand how the timing of entry into a marketplace can create competitive advantage, they can examine the comparative benefits of first-mover versus late-mover advantages.

2-4 Explore how a firm develops marketing objectives and strategies that contribute to overall objectives.

The next phase of strategic planning involves the development of marketing objectives and strategies. Marketing objectives state what is to be accomplished through marketing activities, and should be consistent with both business-unit and corporate strategies. Marketing strategies, the most detailed and specific of the three levels, are composed of two elements: the selection of a target market and the creation of a marketing mix that will satisfy the needs of the target market. The selection of a target market serves as the basis for the creation of the marketing mix to satisfy the needs of that market. Marketing-mix decisions should also be consistent with business-unit and corporate strategies, and be flexible enough to respond to changes in market conditions, competition, and customer needs. Marketers can alter elements of the marketing mix to accommodate different marketing strategies.

2-5 Identify what is necessary to manage the effective implementation of marketing strategies.

Marketing implementation is the process of putting marketing strategies into action. Through planning, marketing managers provide purpose and direction for an organization's marketing efforts. Marketing managers must understand the problems and elements of marketing implementation before they can undertake specific marketing activities effectively.

The marketing unit must have a coherent internal structure in order to organize direct marketing efforts. In a centralized organization, top-level managers delegate very little authority to lower levels, whereas in decentralized organizations, decision-making authority is delegated as far down the chain of command as possible. Marketing managers must also be able to effectively coordinate the activities of the marketing staff within the firms and integrate those activities with the marketing actions of external organizations that are also involved in implementing the marketing strategies. Proper communication should move down (from top management to lower-level employees) and up (from lower-level employees to top management). Marketing managers learn marketing employees' needs and develop methods to motivate them to help the organization meet its goals.

Finally, successful marketing implementation requires that a timetable be established. Establishment of an implementation timetable involves several steps and ensures that employees know the specific activities for which they are responsible and the timeline for completing each activity. Completing all activities on schedule requires tight coordination among departments. Many organizations use sophisticated software to plan the timing of marketing activities.

2-6 Describe the four major elements of strategic performance evaluation.

Strategic performance evaluation consists of establishing performance standards, analyzing actual performance, comparing actual performance with established standards, and modifying the marketing strategy when needed. When actual performance is compared with performance standards, marketers must determine whether a discrepancy

exists and, if so, whether it requires corrective action such as changing the standard or improving actual performance. Two possible ways to evaluate the actual performance of marketing strategies are sales analysis and marketing cost analysis.

Sales analysis uses sales figures to evaluate a firm's current performance. It is the most common method of evaluation because sales data are a good indication of the target market's reaction to a marketing mix. Marketing cost analysis breaks down and classifies costs to determine which are associated with specific marketing efforts. Marketing cost analysis helps companies decide how to best allocate their marketing resources by identifying profitable or unprofitable customers, products, and geographic areas.

2-7 Discuss the development of a marketing plan.

A key component of marketing planning is the development of a marketing plan, which outlines all the activities necessary to implement marketing strategies. The plan fosters communication among employees, assigns responsibilities and schedules, specifies how resources are to be allocated to achieve objectives, and helps marketing managers monitor and evaluate the performance of a marketing strategy.

 Go to www.cengagebrain.com for resources to help you master the content in this chapter as well as for materials that will expand your marketing knowledge!

Developing Your Marketing Plan

One of the foundations of a successful marketing strategy is a thorough analysis of your company. To make the best decisions about what products to offer, which markets to target, and how to reach target market members, you must recognize your company's strengths and weaknesses. The information collected in this analysis should be referenced when making many of the decisions in your marketing plan. While beginning to develop your plan, the information in this chapter can help you with the following issues:

1. Can you identify the core competencies of your company? Do they currently contribute to a competitive

advantage? If not, what changes could your company make to establish a competitive advantage?
2. Conduct a SWOT analysis of your company to identify its strengths and weaknesses. Continue your analysis to include the business environment, discovering any opportunities that exist or threats that may impact your company.
3. Using the information from your SWOT analysis, have you identified opportunities that are a good match with your company's core competencies? Likewise, have you discovered weaknesses that could be converted to strengths through careful marketing planning?

Key Concepts

strategic marketing
   management   26
strategic planning   26
mission statement   27

corporate strategy   28
strategic business unit
   (SBU)   29
market   30

market share   30
market growth/market
   share matrix   30
core competencies   32

market opportunity   32
strategic windows   32
competitive advantage
   32

Issues for Discussion and Review

1. Identify the major components of strategic planning, and explain how they are interrelated.
2. Explain how an organization can create a competitive advantage at the corporate strategy level and at the business-unit strategy level.
3. What are some issues to consider in analyzing a company's resources and opportunities? How do these issues affect marketing objectives and marketing strategy?
4. What is SWOT analysis, and why is it important?
5. How can an organization make its competitive advantages sustainable over time? How difficult is it to create sustainable competitive advantages?
6. How should organizations set marketing objectives?
7. What are the two major parts of a marketing strategy?
8. When considering the strategic planning process, what factors influence the development of a marketing strategy?
9. Identify and explain the major managerial actions that are part of managing the implementation of marketing strategies.
10. Which element of the strategic planning process plays a major role in the establishment of performance standards? Explain.
11. When assessing actual performance of a marketing strategy, should a marketer perform marketing cost analysis? Why or why not?
12. Identify and explain the major components of a marketing plan.

VIDEO CASE 2
Mi Ola Rides the Marketing Wave

Helena Fogarty got the idea for her start-up bikini manufacturing firm, Mi Ola ("My Wave"), when she learned to surf while on vacation from her fast-paced, New York City fashion career. As much as she enjoyed the fun of riding a wave, she was frustrated with the fit and durability of her swimwear. Based on her experience, Fogarty identified a profitable opportunity to make a business splash with a new line of colorful bikini tops and bottoms designed to look good and to stay in place, in and out of the surf.

Once she founded Mi Ola, Fogarty selected as her target market the segment of women who are active in water sports and seek the benefits of chic swimwear that fits, wears well wash after wash, and protects the skin. For added appeal and differentiation, she decided to manufacture her bikinis domestically and market them as "made in America." Fogarty recognized that her brand was new and unknown, so she planned to use social media and public relations to build awareness and attract the attention of retailers and customers alike. Facebook and Twitter were only the start—she also recognized that the visual qualities of Instagram, Pinterest,

and YouTube would help convey her brand's unique image of fashion and function.

In addition to distributing through traditional retailers, Fogarty wanted to reach her target market directly through e-commerce. Rather than pay models to wear her bikinis, the entrepreneur sought out actual surfers as brand ambassadors and product testers—and asked them for their candid feedback about improving Mi Ola swimwear.

Because Fogarty had worked with top style brands such as Chanel, she understood that the fashion world revolves around the introduction of seasonal clothing collections. To be competitive, she would need to have her products ready during the periods when store buyers typically review new collections and place orders. This meant establishing a strict schedule for each step in her marketing plan, from design to production to distribution and communication. She had to make difficult decisions about how many pieces of each design, in each color and each size, she would pay to manufacture. Her objective was to meet projected demand without having an ocean of unsold inventory left at the end of the season.

Based on several years of introducing multiple swimwear collections, Fogarty has now gained valuable experience with the entire cycle of marketing strategy, planning, implementation, and evaluation. She has a keener sense of how to manage the marketing mix and coordinate marketing activities with all other functions of her growing firm. Each year, she increases the number of styles she offers, and expands fabric color and pattern choices to reflect the latest fashion trends, aiming to encourage repeat purchases by current customers while also bringing in first-time buyers.

Despite feeling some pressure to plan for dramatically higher revenue and sales volume as the business grows, the entrepreneur remains realistic about assessing her resources and opportunities. She keeps a close eye on costs and sales results so she can adjust her marketing plan frequently to account for changes in customer buying habits, competition, and other factors that can affect Mi Ola's marketing performance.[26]

Questions for Discussion

1. How would you describe Mi Ola's strengths, weaknesses, opportunities, and threats?
2. Does Mi Ola have a first-mover or late-mover advantage? Explain your answer.
3. Helena Fogarty talks about being ready to adjust her marketing plan frequently. Should she focus more on possible adjustments to strategy, objectives, implementation, or some combination of these three?

The Marketing Environment, Social Responsibility, and Ethics

mangostock/Shutterstock.com

LEARNING OBJECTIVES

3-1 Summarize why it is important to examine and respond to the marketing environment.

3-2 Explain how competitive factors affect an organization's ability to compete.

3-3 Articulate how economic factors influence a customer's ability and willingness to buy products.

3-4 Identify the types of political forces in the marketing environment.

3-5 Explain how laws, government regulations, and self-regulatory agencies affect marketing activities.

3-6 Describe how new technology impacts marketing and society.

3-7 Outline the sociocultural issues marketers must deal with as they make decisions.

3-8 Define the four dimensions of social responsibility.

3-9 Examine how social responsibility and ethics can be incorporated into strategic planning.

MARKETING INSIGHTS

TOMS: Taking Big Steps to Change Lives

Although TOMS is most famous for its iconic slip-on shoes, the company also sells sunglasses, handbags, coffee accessories, and more. All of its products are tied together in one important way: they are a part of TOMS' One for One model®.

The idea for TOMS came after founder Blake Mycoskie realized that many families across the world could not afford to purchase shoes for their children. Mycoskie decided to develop a business based upon a philanthropic model. For every pair of shoes sold, TOMS donated a pair of shoes to children in need across the world. Demand for TOMS shoes exploded, and after giving away its one millionth pair of shoes the company decided to expand its one-for-one model to restoring vision. For every pair of sunglasses sold, TOMS provides treatment or prescription glasses for those who cannot afford them.

While the one-for-one model has made TOMS famous—and led other firms such as Warby Parker to adopt similar models—it is not without controversy. One major criticism is that simply donating shoes takes business away from local cobblers and is not a long-term solution. In answer to these criticisms, TOMS now tries to source the shoes it donates from local sources. It has also branched out into other areas of investing in communities through product expansion. For instance, the firm uses proceeds from its bags to provide birth kits and safe treatment to more than 25,000 mothers. Additionally, TOMS helps provide safe drinking water to those in need for every coffee accessory sold. Consumers seem to appreciate TOMS' socially responsible focus as the company earns $500 million in annual sales.[1]

Astrid Stawiarz/Getty Images

To succeed in today's highly competitive global marketplace, companies must respond to changes in the marketing environment, particularly changes in customer and public desires and competitors' actions. Increasingly, success also requires that marketers act responsibly and ethically. Because recognizing and responding to changes in the marketing environment are crucial to marketing success, this chapter explores in some detail the forces that contribute to these changes.

The first half of this chapter explores the competitive, economic, political, legal and regulatory, technological, and sociocultural forces that make up the marketing environment. This discussion addresses the importance of scanning and analyzing the marketing environment, as well as how each of these forces influences marketing strategy decisions. The second half of the chapter considers the role of social responsibility and ethics. These increasingly important forces raise several issues that pose threats and present opportunities to marketers, such as the natural environment and consumerism.

3-1 THE MARKETING ENVIRONMENT

LO 3-1 Summarize why it is important to examine and respond to the marketing environment.

The marketing environment consists of external forces that directly or indirectly influence an organization's acquisition of inputs (human, financial, natural resources and raw materials, and information) and creation of outputs (goods, services, or ideas). As indicated in Chapter 1, the marketing environment includes six such forces: competitive, economic, political, legal and regulatory, technological, and sociocultural.

Whether fluctuating rapidly or slowly, environmental forces are always dynamic. Changes in the marketing environment create uncertainty, threats, and opportunities for marketers. For instance, firms providing digital products such as software, music, and movies face many environmental threats as well as opportunities. Advancing technology enables digital delivery of these products, which is an efficient, effective way to reach global markets. Facebook stepped away from the competition with its introduction of Facebook Messenger. The product allows up to six people to see each other live while chatting. There can be up to 50 connected, but only one person can be seen at a time. Facebook Messenger is a distinct improvement over its WhatsApp and competitor's products including Snap Inc.'s Snapchat, Apple's FaceTime, and Google Duo, which allow one-to-one communication.[2] Monitoring the environment is therefore crucial to an organization's survival and the long-term achievement of its goals and competitive strategies.

To monitor changes in the marketing environment effectively, marketers engage in environmental scanning and analysis. **Environmental scanning** is the process of collecting information about forces in the marketing environment. Scanning involves observation; secondary sources such as business, trade, government, and Internet sources; and marketing research. The Internet is a popular scanning tool because it makes data accessible and allows companies to gather needed information quickly. For example, information can be obtained to determine proposed legislation or consumer protection regulations that could affect a firm's operations.

Environmental analysis is the process of assessing and interpreting the information gathered through environmental scanning. A manager evaluates the information for accuracy; tries to resolve inconsistencies in the data; and, if warranted, assigns significance to the findings. By evaluating this information, the manager should be able to identify potential threats and opportunities linked to environmental changes. A threat could be rising interest rates or commodity prices. An opportunity could be increases in consumer income, decreases in the unemployment rate, or a sudden drop in commodity prices. Oil prices dropped more than 40 percent before starting to rise between 2014 and 2017. Lower prices for energy gave consumers more purchasing power during this time.

environmental scanning
The process of collecting information about forces in the marketing environment

environmental analysis
The process of assessing and interpreting information gathered through environmental scanning

Understanding the current state of the marketing environment, and recognizing threats and opportunities arising from changes within it, helps companies with strategic planning. In particular, they help marketing managers assess the performance of current marketing efforts and develop future marketing strategies.

3-1a Responding to the Marketing Environment

Marketing managers take two general approaches to environmental forces: accepting them as uncontrollable or attempting to influence and shape them.[3] An organization that views environmental forces as uncontrollable remains *passive* and *reactive* toward the environment. Instead of trying to influence forces in the environment, its marketing managers adjust current marketing strategies to environmental changes. They approach with caution market opportunities discovered through environmental scanning and analysis. On the other hand, marketing managers who believe that environmental forces can be shaped adopt a more *proactive* approach. If a market opportunity is blocked by environmental constraints, proactive marketing managers may use their political skills to overcome obstacles. For example, a company that aligns itself with social interests should be proactive and disclose its social responsibility activities in order to maintain transparent communication with stakeholders. Amazon, Intel, and Google, for example, have responded to political, legal, and regulatory concerns by communicating the value of their competitive approaches to stakeholders. While they deal with regulatory issues related to privacy, they contend that their products are superior for their customers and benefit society.

A proactive approach can be constructive and bring desired results. To exert influence on environmental forces, marketing managers seek to identify market opportunities or to extract greater benefits relative to costs from existing market opportunities. However, managers must recognize that there are limits on the degree to which environmental forces can be shaped. Although an organization may be able to influence legislation through lobbying—as the movie and music industries are trying to do to stop piracy of their products—it is unlikely that a single organization can significantly change major economic factors such as recessions, interest rates, or commodity prices. Consider the work that Energizer has done to provide the first battery made from recycled batteries and branded as "Ecoadvanced" in the provided ad. Innovation of this type is welcomed by consumers and the public at large.

THE NEWEST THING IN BATTERIES ISN'T 100% NEW.
Introducing *Energizer* EcoAdvanced™

Our *longest-lasting* alkaline is also the **WORLD'S FIRST** AA battery made with **4% RECYCLED BATTERIES.**
that's positiv**energy.**
energizer.com/ecoadvanced

Responding to the Marketing Environment
Energizer innovates in a proactive way by providing the first battery made with recycled batteries.

| 3-2 COMPETITIVE FORCES

LO 3-2 Explain how competitive factors affect an organization's ability to compete.

Few firms, if any, operate free of competition. In fact, for most products, customers have many alternatives from which to choose. For example, the seven best-selling soft drinks are Coca-Cola, Diet Coke, Pepsi-Cola, Mountain Dew, Dr. Pepper, Sprite and Diet Pepsi.[4] In 2016, Diet Coke passed Pepsi-Cola to move into second place in U.S. soft drink popularity. This represents a move to less sugary drinks as consumers have also turned to flavored water, bottled water, and tea. The soft drink market is highly competitive with many alternative products for consumers. The number of firms that supply a product may affect the

Coke/Pepsi Co

Brand Competition
Coke and Pepsi compete head-to-head in the soft-drink market.

competition Other firms that market products that are similar to or can be substituted for a firm's products in the same geographic area

brand competitors Firms that market products with similar features and benefits to the same customers at similar prices

product competitors Firms that compete in the same product class but market products with different features, benefits, and prices

generic competitors Firms that provide very different products that solve the same problem or satisfy the same basic customer need

total budget competitors Firms that compete for the limited financial resources of the same customers

monopoly A competitive structure in which an organization offers a product that has no close substitutes, making that organization the sole source of supply

strength of competition. When just one or a few firms control supply, competitive factors exert a different sort of influence on marketing activities than when many competitors exist.

Broadly speaking, all firms compete with one another for customers' dollars. More practically, however, a marketer generally defines a firm's **competition** as other firms that market products that are similar to or can be substituted for its products in the same geographic area. These competitors can be classified into one of four types. **Brand competitors** market products with similar features and benefits to the same customers at similar prices. For example, a thirsty, calorie-conscious customer may choose a diet soda such as Diet Coke or Diet Pepsi from the soda machine. However, these sodas face competition from other types of beverages such as flavored water like LaCroix. **Product competitors** compete in the same product class but market products with different features, benefits, and prices. The thirsty dieter, for instance, might purchase iced tea, juice, a sports beverage, coconut water, or bottled water instead of a soda. **Generic competitors** provide very different products that solve the same problem or satisfy the same basic customer need. Our dieter, for example, might simply have a glass of water from the kitchen tap to satisfy his or her thirst. **Total budget competitors** compete for the limited financial resources of the same customers.[5] Total budget competitors for Diet Coke, for example, might include gum, a newspaper, and bananas. Although all four types of competition can affect a firm's marketing performance, brand competitors are the most significant because buyers typically see the different products of these firms as direct substitutes for one another. Consequently, marketers tend to concentrate environmental analyses on brand competitors.

When just one or a few firms control supply, competitive factors exert a different form of influence on marketing activities than when many competitors exist. Table 3.1 presents four general types of competitive structures: monopoly, oligopoly, monopolistic competition, and pure competition. A **monopoly** exists when an organization offers a product that has no close substitutes, making that organization the sole source of supply. Because the organization has no competitors, it controls supply of the product completely and, as a single seller, can erect barriers to potential competitors. In reality, many monopolies operating today are local

TABLE 3.1	SELECTED CHARACTERISTICS OF COMPETITIVE STRUCTURES			
Type of Structure	Number of Competitors	Ease of Entry into Market	Product	Example
Monopoly	One	Many barriers	Almost no substitutes	Water utilities
Oligopoly	Few	Some barriers	Homogeneous or differentiated (with real or perceived differences)	UPS, FedEx, United States Postal Service (package delivery)
Monopolistic competition	Many	Few barriers	Product differentiation, with many substitutes	Wrangler, Levi Strauss, Diesel, Lee Jeans (jeans)
Pure competition	Unlimited	No barriers	Homogeneous products	Vegetable farm (sweet corn)

utilities, which are heavily regulated by local, state, or federal agencies. Regulators in a number of countries allege that Google is becoming a digital monopoly. It has almost 80 percent of the Web search-engine market in the United States with Bing's share 10 percent.[6] The European Parliament has suggested that Google is too powerful and should be broken up by unbundling its search engine.[7]

oligopoly A competitive structure in which a few sellers control the supply of a large proportion of a product

An **oligopoly** exists when a few sellers control the supply of a large proportion of a product. In this case, each seller considers the reactions of other sellers to changes in marketing activities. Products facing oligopolistic competition may be homogeneous, such as aluminum, or differentiated, such as package delivery services. The airline industry is an example of an oligopoly. However, even an industry dominated by a few companies must still compete and release promotional materials. Turkish Airlines releases advertising which appeals to consumers' desire to travel abroad for pleasure. The ad depicts very unique scenery, showing that Turkish Airlines can help "Widen your world." **Monopolistic competition** exists when a firm with many potential competitors attempts to develop a marketing strategy to differentiate its product. For example, Wrangler and True Religion have established an advantage for their blue jeans through well-known trademarks, design, advertising, and a reputation for quality. Wrangler is associated with a cowboy image, while True Religion tries to maintain a premium designer image. Although many competing brands of blue jeans are available, these firms have carved out market niches by emphasizing differences in their products, especially style and image. **Pure competition**, if it existed at all, would entail a large number of sellers, none of which could significantly influence price or supply. The closest thing to an example of pure competition is an unregulated farmers' market, where local growers gather to sell their produce. Pure competition is an ideal at one end of the continuum; monopoly is at the other end. Most marketers function in a competitive environment somewhere between these two extremes.

Marketers need to monitor the actions of major competitors to determine what specific strategies competitors are using and how those strategies affect their own. Price is one marketing strategy variable that most competitors monitor. Delta developed a pricing strategy to compete more effectively with discount airlines such as Southwest. Delta offers "basic economy"

Oligopoly
Turkish Airlines operates in an oligopolistic industry.

monopolistic competition
A competitive structure in which a firm has many potential competitors and tries to develop a marketing strategy to differentiate its product

pure competition A market structure characterized by an extremely large number of sellers, none strong enough to significantly influence price or supply

buying power Resources—such as money, goods, and services—that can be traded in an exchange

disposable income After-tax income

discretionary income Disposable income available for spending and saving after an individual has purchased the basic necessities of food, clothing, and shelter

to compete with discount carriers and attract more price sensitive customers. Other airlines are adopting this pricing strategy as well. Iceland Air adds a free stopover in Iceland for flights from the United States to Europe. Iceland Air, as well as discount airlines like Allegiant and Spirit Airlines, have small niche markets and offer unique services to compete with the major airlines. Airlines are an oligopoly because they have relatively few competitors and large market share. This situation has only grown more extreme with airline acquisitions and mergers. Monitoring guides marketers in developing competitive advantages and aids them in adjusting current marketing strategies and planning new ones. When two large companies such as Time Warner Cable and Comcast merge, there is the potential for less competition.

In monitoring competition, it is not enough to analyze available information; the firm must develop a system for gathering ongoing information about competitors. Understanding the market and what customers want, as well as what the competition is providing, will assist in maintaining a market orientation.[8] Information about competitors allows marketing managers to assess the performance of their own marketing efforts and to recognize the strengths and weaknesses in their own marketing strategies. Data about market shares, product movement, sales volume, and expenditure levels can be useful. However, accurate information on these matters is often difficult to obtain. We explore how marketers collect and organize such data in Chapter 4.

3-3 ECONOMIC FORCES

LO 3-3 Articulate how economic factors influence a customer's ability and willingness to buy products.

Economic forces in the marketing environment influence marketers' and customers' decisions and activities alike. In this section, we examine the effects of buying power and willingness to spend, as well as general economic conditions.

3-3a Buying Power and Willingness to Spend

The strength of a person's **buying power** depends on economic conditions and the amount of resources—money, goods, and services that can be traded in an exchange—that enable the individual to make purchases. The major financial sources of buying power are income, credit, and wealth.

For an individual, *income* is the amount of money received through wages, rents, investments, pensions, and subsidy payments for a given period, such as a month or a year. Normally, this money is allocated among taxes, spending for goods and services, and savings. Marketers are most interested in the amount of money left after payment of taxes because this **disposable income** is used for spending or saving. Because disposable income is a ready source of buying power, the total amount available in a nation is important to marketers. Several factors determine the size of total disposable income, including total amount of income—which is affected by wage levels, the rate of unemployment, interest rates, and dividend rates—and the kinds and amount of taxes. Disposable income that is available for spending and saving after an individual has purchased the basic necessities of food, clothing, and shelter is called **discretionary income**. People use discretionary income to purchase entertainment, vacations, automobiles, education, pets, furniture, appliances, and so on. Changes in total discretionary income affect sales of these products, especially automobiles, furniture, large appliances, and other costly durable goods.

Credit is important because it enables people to spend future income now or in the near future. However, credit increases current buying power at the expense of future buying power. Several factors determine whether people acquire, use, or forgo credit. Since the last recession, obtaining a mortgage has become more difficult for consumers due to the number of homeowners who defaulted on their loans. Banks have tightened the requirements for loans. Interest rates affect buyers' decisions to use credit, especially for expensive purchases such as homes, appliances, and automobiles. When interest rates are low, the total cost of automobiles and houses becomes more affordable. In contrast, when interest rates are high, consumers are more likely to delay buying such expensive items. Use of credit is also affected by credit terms such as size of the down payment and amount and number of monthly payments.

Wealth is the accumulation of past income, natural resources, and financial resources. It exists in many forms, including cash, securities, savings accounts, gold, jewelry, and real estate. The significance of wealth to marketers is that as people become wealthier, they gain buying power in three ways: they can use their wealth to make current purchases, generate income, and acquire large amounts of credit. Knowing that Maryland ranks as the richest state and Mississippi the poorest state according to the U.S. Census Bureau would be helpful selling Tesla high-end electric sports cars. High discretionary income individuals are often wealthy and purchase luxury items such as the Graf von Faber-Castell pens shown in the ad. Pens of this type are sought for their unique craftsmanship, quality, and status.

People's **willingness to spend**—their inclination to buy because of expected satisfaction from a product—is related, to some degree, to their ability to buy. That is, people are sometimes more willing to buy if they have the buying power. However, several other elements also influence willingness to spend. Some elements affect specific products; others influence spending in general. A product's price and value influence almost all of us. Cross pens, for example, appeal to customers who are willing to spend more for fine writing instruments even when lower-priced pens are readily available. The amount of satisfaction received from a product already owned also may influence customers' desires to buy other products. Satisfaction depends not only on the quality of the currently owned product but also on numerous psychological and social forces. The American Customer Satisfaction

GRAF VON FABER-CASTELL

COMMITTED TO TRADITION

PLATINUM-PLATED WRITING INSTRUMENTS WITH ORNATE FLUTED BARRELS
IN DARK BROWN GRENADILLA, BLACK MATTE EBONY OR RED-BROWN PERNAMBUCO WOOD.

Graf von Faber-Castell

Discretionary Income
Graf von Faber-Castell makes fine, luxury pens out of platinum, rare woods, and various finishes for high-income individuals.

willingness to spend An inclination to buy because of expected satisfaction from a product, influenced by the ability to buy and numerous psychological and social forces

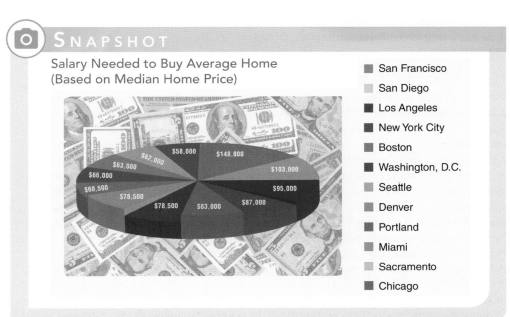

SNAPSHOT

Salary Needed to Buy Average Home
(Based on Median Home Price)

- San Francisco $148,000
- San Diego $103,000
- Los Angeles $95,000
- New York City $87,000
- Boston $83,000
- Washington, D.C. $78,500
- Seattle $78,500
- Denver $68,500
- Portland $66,000
- Miami $63,000
- Sacramento $62,000
- Chicago $58,000

Source: Libby Kane, "Here's the Salary You Have to Earn to Buy a Home in 19 Major US Cities," *Business Insider*, March 3, 2016, www.businessinsider.com/salary-to-buy-a-home-2016-3 (accessed January 17, 2017).

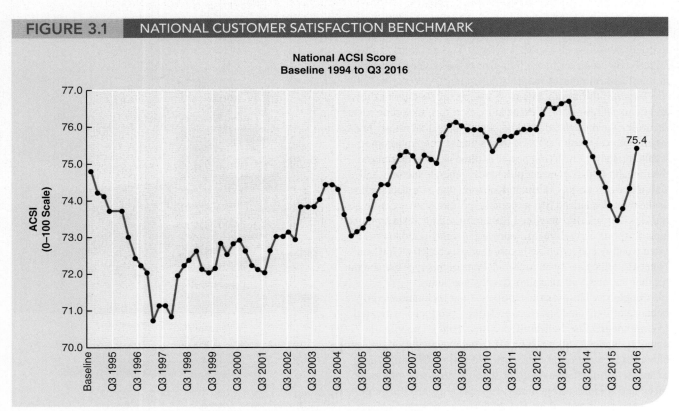

National ACSI Score
Baseline 1994 to Q3 2016

Source: Data from American Customer Satisfaction Index, "U.S. Overall Customer Satisfaction," www.theacsi.org/national-economic-indicator/us-overall -customer-satisfaction (accessed January 11, 2017).

Index, computed by the National Quality Research Center at the University of Michigan (see Figure 3.1), offers an indicator of customer satisfaction with a wide variety of businesses. The American Customer Satisfaction Index helps marketers understand how consumers perceive their industries and businesses. By understanding how satisfied (or dissatisfied) customers are with their business or industry, marketers can take this information and adapt their marketing strategies accordingly.

3-3b **Economic Conditions**

The overall state of the economy fluctuates in all countries. Changes in general economic conditions affect (and are affected by) supply and demand, buying power, willingness to spend, consumer expenditure levels, and the intensity of competitive behavior. Therefore, current economic conditions and changes in the economy have a broad impact on the success of organizations' marketing strategies.

Fluctuations in the economy follow a general pattern, often referred to as the **business cycle**. In the traditional view, the business cycle consists of four stages: prosperity, recession, depression, and recovery. During *prosperity,* unemployment is low, and total income is relatively high. Assuming a low inflation rate, this combination ensures high buying power. During a *recession,* however, unemployment rises, while total buying power declines. Pessimism accompanying a recession often stifles both consumer and business spending. A prolonged recession may become a *depression,* a period in which unemployment is extremely high, wages are very low, total disposable income is at a minimum, and consumers lack confidence in the economy. During *recovery,* the economy moves from depression or recession to prosperity. During this period, high unemployment begins to decline, total disposable income increases, and the economic gloom that reduced consumers' willingness to buy subsides. Both the ability and the willingness to buy increase.

business cycle A pattern of economic fluctuations that has four stages: prosperity, recession, depression, and recovery

The business cycle can enhance the success of marketing strategies. In the prosperity stage, for example, marketers may expand their product offerings to take advantage of increased buying power. They may be able to capture a larger market share by intensifying distribution and promotion efforts. In times of recession or depression, when buying power decreases, many customers may become more price conscious and seek basic, functional products. For example, when buying power decreased during the last recession, purchases of new cars dropped. During the recovery cycle, demand for certain vehicles—such as SUVs and light trucks—soared. However, one reason why these sales were booming could have been the increase in subprime auto loans, or loans provided to individuals with low credit scores.[9]

During economic downturns, a company should focus its efforts on determining precisely what functions buyers want and ensure that these functions are available in its product offerings. Promotional efforts should emphasize value and utility. Some firms make the mistake of drastically reducing their marketing efforts during a recession, harming their ability to compete. The United States and most of the world experienced a period of prosperity in 2004–2007. During this time, household net worth increased by almost 6 percent a year, with rapidly increasing home values, low unemployment, low interest rates, and expanding credit availability. The decision by the government and financial institutions to grant subprime loans (higher-interest loans to people with poor credit ratings) triggered the default of these loans. In 2008, the United States experienced an economic downturn due to higher energy prices, falling home values, increasing unemployment, the financial crisis in the banking industry, and fluctuating currency values. That recession was the longest since the Great Depression of the 1930s and has been called the Great Recession. As the United States was recovering from the Great Recession, Europe and Japan's economies continued to struggle. By 2017, unemployment levels in the United States were back down to 2007 levels. The world economy is so integrated that if one region has an economic problem, it affects all the other countries.[10]

3-4 POLITICAL FORCES

LO 3-4 Identify the types of political forces in the marketing environment.

Political, legal, and regulatory forces of the marketing environment are closely interrelated. Legislation is enacted; legal decisions are interpreted by courts; and regulatory agencies are created and operated, for the most part, by elected or appointed officials. Legislation and regulations (or their lack) reflect the current political outlook. Consequently, the political forces of the marketing environment have the potential to influence marketing decisions and strategies. For instance, after the financial crisis caused a worldwide recession, the government passed the Dodd-Frank Wall Street Reform and Consumer Protection Act of 2010.[11] The legislation established a new Consumer Financial Protection Bureau to protect consumers from deceptive financial practices.[12]

Reactive marketers view political forces as beyond their control and simply adjust to conditions arising from those forces. Some proactive firms, however, seek to influence the political process. In some cases, organizations publicly protest the actions of legislative bodies. More often, organizations help elect to political office individuals who regard them positively. Much of this help takes the form of campaign contributions. Goldman Sachs and AT&T Inc. are examples of companies that have attempted to influence legislation and regulation over a long period of time. For years, legislators and other groups have sought to limit the amount of corporate campaign contributions. In the 2010 case *Citizens United v. Federal Election Commission*, the Supreme Court ruled that the government is not authorized to ban corporate spending in candidate elections.[13] This means that elections can be affected by large corporate donations to candidates. Marketers also can influence the political process through political action committees (PACs), which solicit donations from individuals and then contribute those funds to candidates running for political office.

Companies also can participate in the political process through lobbying to persuade public and/or government officials to favor a particular position. Many companies concerned about the threat of legislation or regulation that may negatively affect their operations employ lobbyists to communicate their concerns to elected officials. For instance, as the U.S. government debates whether to pass stricter laws regulating marketing activities over the Internet, social media firms such as Facebook are employing lobbyists to convey their respective viewpoints regarding the proposed legislation.

3-5 LEGAL AND REGULATORY FORCES

LO 3-5 Explain how laws, government regulations, and self-regulatory agencies affect marketing activities.

A number of federal laws influence marketing decisions and activities. Table 3.2 lists some of the most significant legislation. Regulatory agencies and self-regulatory forces also affect marketing efforts.

TABLE 3.2 — MAJOR FEDERAL LAWS AFFECTING MARKETING DECISIONS

Act (Date Enacted)	Purpose
Procompetitive Legislation	
Sherman Antitrust Act (1890)	Prohibits contracts, combinations, or conspiracies to restrain trade; calls monopolizing or attempting to monopolize a misdemeanor offense.
Clayton Act (1914)	Prohibits specific practices such as price discrimination, exclusive dealer arrangements, and stock acquisitions in which the effect may notably lessen competition or tend to create a monopoly.
Federal Trade Commission Act (1914)	Created the Federal Trade Commission (FTC); also gives the FTC investigatory powers to be used in preventing unfair methods of competition.
Robinson-Patman Act (1936)	Prohibits price discrimination that lessens competition among wholesalers or retailers; prohibits producers from giving disproportionate services of facilities to large buyers.
Wheeler-Lea Act (1938)	Prohibits unfair and deceptive acts and practices, regardless of whether competition is injured; places advertising of foods and drugs under the jurisdiction of the FTC.
Celler-Kefauver Act (1950)	Prohibits any corporation engaged in commerce from acquiring the whole or any part of the stock or other share of the capital assets of another corporation when the effect substantially lessens competition or tends to create a monopoly.
Consumer Goods Pricing Act (1975)	Prohibits the use of price-maintenance agreements among manufacturers and resellers in interstate commerce.
Antitrust Improvements Act (1976)	Requires large corporations to inform federal regulators of prospective mergers or acquisitions so that they can be studied for possible violations of the law.
Consumer Protection Legislation	
Pure Food and Drug Act (1906)	Prohibits the adulteration and mislabeling of food and drug products; established the Food and Drug Administration.
Fair Packaging and Labeling Act (1966)	Makes illegal the unfair or deceptive packaging or labeling of consumer products.
Consumer Product Safety Act (1972)	Established the Consumer Product Safety Commission; protects the public against unreasonable risk of injury and death associated with products.

TABLE 3.2	MAJOR FEDERAL LAWS AFFECTING MARKETING DECISIONS (*continued*)

Act (Date Enacted)	Purpose
Magnuson-Moss Warranty (FTC) Act (1975)	Provides for minimum disclosure standards for written consumer product warranties; defines minimum consent standards for written warranties; allows the FTC to prescribe interpretive rules in policy statements regarding unfair or deceptive practices.
Nutrition Labeling and Education Act (1990)	Prohibits exaggerated health claims and requires all processed foods to contain labels showing nutritional information.
Telephone Consumer Protection Act (1991)	Establishes procedures to avoid unwanted telephone solicitations; limits marketers from using an automated telephone dialing system or an artificial or prerecorded voice.
Children's Online Privacy Protection Act (2000)	Regulates the online collection of personally identifiable information (name, mailing address, e-mail address, hobbies, interests, or information collected through cookies) from children under age 13.
Do Not Call Implementation Act (2003)	Directs the Federal Communications Commission and the FTC to coordinate so that their rules are consistent regarding telemarketing call practices, including the Do Not Call Registry and other lists, as well as call abandonment.
Credit Card Act (2009)	Implements strict rules on credit card companies regarding areas such as issuing credit to youths, terms disclosure, interest rates, and fees.
Dodd-Frank Wall Street Reform and Consumer Protection Act (2010)	Promotes financial reform to increase accountability and transparency in the financial industry, protects consumers from deceptive financial practices, and established the Bureau of Consumer Financial Protection.
Trademark and Copyright Protection Legislation	
Lanham Act (1946)	Provides protections and regulation of brand names, brand marks, trade names, and trademarks.
Trademark Law Revision Act (1988)	Amends the Lanham Act to allow brands not yet introduced to be protected through registration with the Patent and Trademark Office.
Federal Trademark Dilution Act (1995)	Gives trademark owners the right to protect trademarks and requires relinquishment of names that match or parallel existing trademarks.
Digital Millennium Copyright Act (1998)	Refines copyright laws to protect digital versions of copyrighted materials, including music and movies.

3-5a **Regulatory Agencies**

Federal regulatory agencies influence many marketing activities, including product development, pricing, packaging, advertising, personal selling, and distribution. Usually, these bodies have the power to enforce specific laws, as well as some discretion in establishing operating rules and regulations to guide certain types of industry practices.

Of all the federal regulatory units, the **Federal Trade Commission (FTC)** most influences marketing activities. Although the FTC regulates a variety of business practices, it allocates considerable resources to curbing false advertising, misleading pricing, and deceptive packaging and labeling. When it receives a complaint or otherwise has reason to believe that a firm is violating a law, the commission issues a complaint stating that the business is in violation. If a company continues the questionable practice, the FTC can issue a cease-and-desist order demanding that the business halt the activity causing the complaint. The firm can appeal to the federal courts to have the order rescinded. However, the FTC can seek civil penalties in court, up to a maximum penalty of $10,000 a day for each infraction, if a cease-and-desist order is violated. The FTC also assists businesses

Federal Trade Commission (FTC) An agency that regulates a variety of business practices and curbs false advertising, misleading pricing, and deceptive packaging and labeling

Protesting against Business and Government
Protestors carry signs to protest genetically modified food and call for food transparency.

in complying with laws and files lawsuits against those engaging in deceptive marketing practices. For instance, the FTC filed a complaint against AT&T for slowing the speed of data. AT&T would slow data speeds if the customer used too much data during the billing cycle. This "throttling," the FTC alleged, was deceptive to consumers who were promised unlimited data plans.[14]

Unlike the FTC, other regulatory units are limited to dealing with specific products or business activities. For example, the Food and Drug Administration (FDA) enforces regulations prohibiting the sale and distribution of adulterated, misbranded, or hazardous food and drug products. The Consumer Product Safety Commission (CPSC) ensures compliance with the Consumer Product Safety Act and protects the public from unreasonable risk of injury from any consumer product not covered by other regulatory agencies.

In addition, laws have been created to prevent businesses from gaining an unfair advantage through bribery. The U.S. Foreign Corrupt Practices Act (FCPA) prohibits American companies from making illicit payments to foreign officials in order to obtain or keep business. Teva Pharmaceutical Industries has agreed to pay the largest criminal fine against a pharmaceutical company, $519 million, for violating the Foreign Corrupt Practices Act. The largest manufacturer of generic pharmaceuticals violated bribery laws in Ukraine, Mexico, and Russia.[15]

The FCPA does allow for small facilitation ("grease") payments to expedite routine government transactions. However, the passage of the U.K. Bribery Act does not allow for facilitation payments.[16] The U.K. Bribery Act is more encompassing than the FCPA and has significant implications for global business. Under this law companies can be found guilty of bribery even if the bribery did not take place within the United Kingdom, and company officials without explicit knowledge about the misconduct can still be held accountable. The law applies to any business with operations in the United Kingdom.[17] It also can hold companies liable if its joint-venture partners or subsidiaries are found guilty of bribery. However, the U.K. Bribery Law does allow for leniency if the company has an effective compliance program and undergoes periodic ethical assessments.[18] In response to the law, companies have begun to strengthen their compliance programs related to bribery. For instance, Lockheed-Martin publicly changed its internal compliance procedures to ban facilitation payments in adherence to the new law.[19]

State consumer protection laws offer an opportunity for state attorneys general to deal with marketing issues related to fraud and deception. Most states have consumer protection laws that are very general in nature and provide enforcement when new schemes evolve that injure consumers. For example, the New York Consumer Protection Board is very proactive in monitoring consumer protection and providing consumer education. More recently, the New York Consumer Protection Board has taken measures to warn consumers about military identity theft because service members often use their Social Security numbers for identification.[20]

Consumer Credit Card Security
Chipped credit cards represent a more secure shopping process.

3-5b **Self-Regulation**

Various forms of self-regulation that promote cooperation, along with voluntary ethics and social responsibility standards, create accountability and transparency
that go beyond government regulation.[21] In an attempt
to be good corporate citizens and prevent government
intervention, some industries try to regulate themselves.
Several trade associations have also developed self-
regulatory programs. Although these programs are not
a direct outgrowth of laws, many were established to
stop or stall the development of laws and governmental
regulatory groups that would regulate the associations'
marketing practices. Sometimes trade associations establish ethics codes by which their members must abide
or risk censure or exclusion from the association. For
instance, the National Association of Home Builders has
adopted a code of ethics and guiding principles by which
its members must abide. The Direct Selling Association and
the Direct Marketing Association also require compliance with detailed codes of ethics in
order for member organizations to retain their membership.

Better Business Bureau
The Better Business Bureau is a well-known nongovernmental
regulatory group helping settle disputes between consumers
and business.

Perhaps the best-known nongovernmental regulatory group is the **Better Business
Bureau**, a local regulatory agency supported by local businesses. About 112 bureaus help to
settle disputes between consumers and specific businesses in the United States and Canada.
Each bureau also acts to preserve good business practices in a locality, although it usually
lacks strong enforcement tools for dealing with firms that employ questionable practices.
When a firm continues to violate what the Better Business Bureau believes to be good business practices, the bureau warns consumers through local newspapers or broadcast media. If
the offending organization is a Better Business Bureau member, it may be expelled from the
local bureau. Local chapters themselves are also held accountable. In an unusual case, the
BBB expelled the Southern California chapter of the Better Business Bureau, its largest in
the country, because it was involved in a scheme in which member organizations had to pay
to receive high ratings.[22] BBBs have ongoing challenges due to Angie's List, Yelp, and other
Internet sites that allow "grading" of business experiences.

The National Advertising Division (NAD) of the Council of Better Business Bureaus
operates a self-regulatory program that investigates claims regarding alleged deceptive
advertising. For example, NAD recommended that Pursuit of Research LLC stop all
claims that its Nutriiveda dietary supplements provided cures for conditions including
autism, attention deficit disorder, and strokes. NAD did not believe there was enough
evidence to support these health claims.[23] Another self-regulatory entity, the **National
Advertising Review Board (NARB)**, considers cases in which an advertiser challenges
issues raised by NAD about an advertisement. Cases are reviewed by panels drawn from
NARB members representing advertisers, agencies, and the public. A panel of the NARB
has asked that Rust-Oleum stop using the "2X" classification from its Painter's Touch
Ultra Cover product branding. Sherwin Williams brought their concerns to the NARB
challenging their competitors claim that you get twice the coverage in a single application.[24] The NARB, sponsored by the Council of Better Business Bureaus and three advertising trade organizations, has no official enforcement powers. However, if a firm refuses
to comply with its decision, the NARB may publicize the questionable practice and file a
complaint with the FTC.

Self-regulatory programs have several advantages over governmental laws and regulatory agencies. Establishment and implementation are usually less expensive, and guidelines
are generally more realistic, operational, and relevant. In addition, effective self-regulatory
programs reduce the need to expand government bureaucracy. However, these programs
have several limitations. When a trade association creates a set of industry guidelines for

Better Business Bureau
A local, nongovernmen-
tal regulatory agency,
supported by local
businesses, that helps
settle problems between
customers and specific
business firms

**National Advertising
Review Board (NARB)**
A self-regulatory unit
that considers challenges
to issues raised by the
National Advertising
Division (an arm of the
Council of Better Busi-
ness Bureaus) about an
advertisement

its members, nonmember firms do not have to abide by them. Furthermore, many self-regulatory programs lack the tools or authority to enforce guidelines. Finally, guidelines in self-regulatory programs are often less strict than those established by government agencies.

3-6 TECHNOLOGICAL FORCES

LO 3-6 Describe how new technology impacts marketing and society.

The word *technology* brings to mind scientific advances such as self-driving vehicles, drones, virtual home and office communication, lifestyle drugs, radio-frequency identification tags, and more. Such developments make it possible for marketers to operate more efficiently and provide an exciting array of products for consumers. However, even though these innovations are outgrowths of technology, none of them *is* technology. **Technology** is the application of knowledge and tools to solve problems and perform tasks more efficiently.

Technology determines how we, as members of society, satisfy our physiologic needs. In various ways and to varying degrees, eating and drinking habits, sleeping patterns, sexual activities, health care, and work performance are all influenced by both existing technology and advances in technology. Because of the technological revolution in communications, for example, marketers can now reach vast numbers of people more efficiently through a variety of media. Social networks, smartphones, and tablet computers help marketers to interact with customers, make appointments, and handle last-minute orders or cancellations. Approximately 90 percent of Americans have cell phones with 58 percent of males and 42 percent of females having no other phone service.[25] The decrease in landlines is affecting the marketing research and political polling industries.

The growth of information technology (IT) is staggering. IT is changing the lives of consumers across the globe. Not only does it offer lucrative career opportunities, it also provides business opportunities for the entrepreneur. For instance, entrepreneur Marc Bernioff built an entire organization around the cloud computing industry. Today Salesforce.com continues to be listed among the world's most innovative companies.[26] The Internet also improves supply-chain management as it allows manufacturers, distributors, retailers, and other members of the supply chain to collaborate more closely and serve their customers more efficiently.[27] The importance of the Internet will only increase in the future. It is estimated that by the end of the decade, more than 50 billion things, including cars, refrigerators, medical devices, and more, will be hooked up to the Internet infrastructure. South Korea is making significant progress in this pursuit. This phenomenon—known as the Internet of Things—will greatly impact how we do business and live our daily lives.[28] However, it also requires significant investment in security systems to protect these devices from cybercriminals.

Although computers are a staple in American homes, the type of computer has been changing drastically in this past decade. Traditional desktop computers appear to be on the decline. Laptops became immensely popular due to their mobility, but analysts estimate that laptops might be entering the maturity stage of the product life cycle. Conversely, tablet computers such as Apple iPad, Samsung Galaxy, Google Pixel, Sony Xperia, and Microsoft Surface are in the growth stage, but their rate of growth has begun to slow.[29] In response many companies are creating apps specifically made for the iPad and similar devices. The rapidly evolving state of technology requires marketers to keep pace with the latest technological changes.

The effects of technology relate to such characteristics as dynamics, reach, and the self-sustaining nature of technological progress. The *dynamics* of technology involve the constant change that often challenges the structures of social institutions, including social relationships, the legal system, religion, education, business, and leisure. *Reach* refers to the broad nature of technology as it moves through society. Consider the impact of cellular and wireless telephones. The ability to call from almost any location has many benefits, but also negative side effects, including increases in traffic accidents, increased noise

technology The application of knowledge and tools to solve problems and perform tasks more efficiently

pollution, and fears about potential health risks.[30] The *self-sustaining* nature of technology relates to the fact that technology acts as a catalyst to spur even faster development. As new innovations are introduced, they stimulate the need for more advancements to facilitate further development. Apple, for instance, has developed a mobile payment system to make it easy for consumers to pay via their smartphones. This creates significant competition for PayPal, which has struggled to release a successful mobile PayPal app. If PayPal cannot generate consumer interest in its mobile technology, it risks being left behind.[31] Technology initiates a change process that creates new opportunities for new technologies in every industry segment or personal life experience that it touches. At some point, there is even a multiplier effect that causes still greater demand for more change to improve performance.[32] It is important for firms to determine when technology is changing an industry and define the strategic influence of the new technology. For example, wireless devices in use today include digital assistants (Google Home), smartphones, short range wireless devices (Bluetooth), and car keys. To remain competitive, companies must adapt to these technological advances. Through a procedure known as *technology assessment,* managers try to foresee the effects of new products and processes on their firms' operations, on other business organizations, and on society in general. With information obtained through a technology assessment, management tries to estimate whether benefits of adopting a specific technology outweigh costs to the firm and to society at large. The degree to which a business is technologically based also influences its managers' response to technology.

3-7 SOCIOCULTURAL FORCES

LO 3-7 Outline the sociocultural issues marketers must deal with as they make decisions.

Sociocultural forces are the influences in a society and its culture(s) that bring about changes in attitudes, beliefs, norms, customs, and lifestyles. Profoundly affecting how people live, these forces help to determine what, where, how, and when people buy products. Like the other environmental forces, sociocultural forces present marketers with both challenges and opportunities.

sociocultural forces The influences in a society and its culture(s) that change people's attitudes, beliefs, norms, customs, and lifestyles

Changes in a population's demographic characteristics—age, gender, race, ethnicity, marital and parental status, income, and education—have a significant bearing on relationships and individual behavior. These shifts lead to changes in how people live and ultimately in their consumption of products such as food, clothing, housing, transportation, communication, recreation, education, and health services. We'll now look at a few of the changes in demographics and diversity that are affecting marketing activities.

One demographic change affecting the marketplace is the increasing proportion of older consumers. According to the U.S. Census Bureau, not only are people living longer, but, for the first time in history, the number of people over 65 will be higher than the number under 5.[33] Consequently, marketers can expect significant increases in the demand for health-care services, recreation, tourism, retirement housing, and selected skin-care products and a decrease in demand for infant and child services.

The number of singles is also on the rise. Singles currently comprise more than half of American households.[34]

Arina P Habich/Shutterstock.com

Sociocultural Forces
Growing concerns for health, sustainability, and support for local economies is causing many consumers to turn toward locally grown foods. Locally grown foods provide revenues for farmers and reduce carbon emissions because they decrease transportation distances.

Single people have quite different spending patterns than couples and families with children. They are less likely to own homes and thus buy less furniture and fewer appliances. They spend more heavily on convenience foods, restaurants, travel, entertainment, and recreation. In addition, they tend to prefer smaller packages, whereas families often buy bulk goods and products packaged in multiple servings.

About 23 percent of the total population are age 18 or younger; the original Baby Boomers, born between 1946 and 1964, account for about one-quarter of the population.[35] The children of the original Baby Boomers differ from one another radically in terms of race, living arrangements, and socioeconomic class. Thus, the newest baby boom is much more diverse than previous generations. Today, the population of the United States is about 325 million people.

Despite these trends, the United States is facing a baby bust with its lowest fertility rate ever.[36] This means that without immigration, the United States will fail to grow.[37] The U.S. population as a whole experienced the slowest rate of growth in the last decade since the Great Depression. While the birthrate is declining, new immigrants help with population gains.[38] It is estimated that those in the U.S. population that were born in other countries has more than quadrupled since the 1960s, with more than 41 million foreign-born individuals.[39] President Obama also granted temporary legal status to nearly 5 million undocumented immigrants.[40] This represents another noteworthy population trend: the increasingly multicultural nature of U.S. society. By the turn of the 20th century, the U.S. population had shifted from one dominated by whites to one consisting largely of three racial and ethnic groups: whites, blacks, and Hispanics. Pew Research Center projects that by the year 2065, more than 167 million Asians, 137 million Hispanics, and 40 million blacks will call the United States home.[41]

Marketers recognize that these profound changes in the U.S. population bring unique problems and opportunities. For example, Hispanic purchasing power is approximately $1.7 trillion. But a diverse population means a more diverse customer base, and marketing practices must be modified—and diversified—to meet its changing needs. In an effort to target this expanding demographic, Google has launched the domain name .soy for Hispanic consumers. Hispanic brands and companies can now use this domain name to connect with users and other members of the Hispanic community.[42]

Changes in social and cultural values have dramatically influenced people's needs and desires for products. Although these values do not shift overnight, they do change at varying speeds. Marketers try to monitor these changes because knowing this information can equip them to predict changes in consumers' needs for products, at least in the near future.

People today are more concerned about the foods they eat and thus are choosing more low-fat, organic, natural, and healthy products. Marketers have responded with a proliferation of foods, beverages, and exercise products that fit this lifestyle. In addition to the proliferation of new, organic brands, many conventional marketers have introduced organic versions of their products, including General Mills, Heinz, and even Walmart.

The major source of values is the family. Values about the permanence of marriage are changing, but children remain important. Marketers have responded with safer, upscale baby gear and supplies, children's electronics, and family entertainment products. Marketers are also aiming more marketing efforts directly at children because children often play pivotal roles in purchasing decisions. Children and family values are also a factor in the trend toward more eat-out and takeout meals. Busy families generally want to spend less time in the kitchen and more time together enjoying themselves. Beneficiaries of this trend primarily have been fast-food and casual restaurants like McDonald's, Taco Bell, Boston Market, and Applebee's, but most supermarkets have added more ready-to-cook or ready-to-serve meal components to meet the needs of busy customers. Some, like Whole Foods, also offer eat-in cafés.

EMERGING TRENDS IN MARKETING

The Fair Trade Movement Explodes

Fair Trade–certified organizations require factories to meet different conditions. They must pay their workers a minimum wage in the country in which they are employed, with the intention of working toward a "livable wage." A livable wage allows workers to afford basic necessities. Additionally, brands must pay a premium to factory workers. These premiums are placed in a collective bank account and are used for bonuses or to address community needs.

Traditionally, Fair Trade gained attention with commodities like coffee and cocoa. The Fair Trade trend is gaining traction among fashion and home furnishings. Many apparel and home furnishing brands have made a commitment to improve factory conditions. Consumers are embracing Fair Trade apparel and home goods as well. For instance, during the back-to-school shopping season, Bed, Bath & Beyond quickly sold out of back-to-school supplies labeled as Fair Trade certified. This demonstrates consumers' increased concern for how goods are manufactured.

In particular, Fair Trade certification focuses on improving the labor conditions of factory workers. Although Fair Trade certification costs brands 1 to 5 percent of what companies pay to factories, it is clear that demand is on the rise. Fair Trade apparel and home furnishings have increased fivefold in the past few years, spurring more factories to work toward achieving certification. Marketers monitoring the environment are finding the costs of Fair Trade well worth the benefits.[a]

3-8 SOCIAL RESPONSIBILITY AND ETHICS IN MARKETING

LO 3-8 Define the four dimensions of social responsibility.

In marketing, **social responsibility** refers to an organization's obligation to maximize its positive impact and minimize its negative impact on society. Social responsibility thus deals with the total effect on society of all marketing decisions. In marketing, social responsibility includes the managerial processes needed to monitor, satisfy, and even exceed stakeholder expectations and needs. Remember from Chapter 1 that stakeholders are groups that have a "stake," or claim, in some aspect of a company's products, operations, markets, industry, and outcomes. Forbes identifies companies with the best corporate social responsibility (CSR) reputations in the world. At the top of the list, Google, Microsoft, Disney, BMW, and Lego.[43]

Ample evidence demonstrates that ignoring stakeholders' demands for responsible marketing can destroy customers' trust and even prompt government regulations. Irresponsible actions that anger customers, employees, or competitors may not only jeopardize a marketer's financial standing, but have legal repercussions as well. CSR can have a direct, observable effect on both employees and customers. If employees perceive that management and customers support social responsibility activities, they positively identify with the firm. This means social responsibility activities can improve employee performance and customer loyalty to the organization. Socially responsible activities can also generate positive publicity and boost sales. For example, Xerox developed a program called "Xerox Community Involvement" that provides funds to employee teams for local community projects. Xerox Maui worked with the Maui Food Bank in Wailuku to construct shelving units and donated $2,000 for materials. This both creates positive publicity for Xerox and empowers local employee teams to select and work on community projects.[44]

Socially responsible efforts such as Xerox's have a positive impact on local communities; at the same time, they indirectly help the sponsoring organization by attracting goodwill, publicity, and potential customers and employees. Thus, while social responsibility

social responsibility An organization's obligation to maximize its positive impact and minimize its negative impact on society

Social Responsibility
Panera's social responsibility in donating bread to the local community impacts key stakeholders, including customers, employees, and communities.

is certainly a positive concept in itself, most organizations embrace it in the expectation of indirect, long-term benefits.

Socially responsible organizations strive for **marketing citizenship** by adopting a strategic focus for fulfilling the economic, legal, ethical, and philanthropic social responsibilities that their stakeholders expect of them. Companies that consider the diverse perspectives of stakeholders in their daily operations and strategic planning are said to have a *stakeholder orientation,* an important element of corporate citizenship.[45] A stakeholder orientation in marketing goes beyond customers, competitors, and regulators to include understanding and addressing the needs of all stakeholders, including communities and special-interest groups. As a result, organizations are now under pressure to undertake initiatives that demonstrate a balanced perspective on stakeholder interests.[46] Panera has many CSR programs exhibiting its marketing citizenship. One such program is Day-End Dough-Nation. At the end of each day, leftover items are shared with food banks, homeless shelters, and other charitable organizations to help those in need.[47] As Figure 3.2 shows, the economic, legal, ethical, and philanthropic dimensions of social responsibility can be viewed as a pyramid.[48] The economic and legal aspects have long been acknowledged, but ethical and philanthropic issues have gained recognition more recently.

3-8a **Economic Dimension**

At the most basic level, all companies have an economic responsibility to be profitable so that they can provide a return on investment to their owners and investors, create jobs for the community, and contribute goods and services to the economy. How organizations relate to stockholders, employees, competitors, customers, the community, and the natural environment affects the economy.

Marketers also have an economic responsibility to compete fairly. Size frequently gives companies a competitive advantage. Large firms often can generate economies of scale that allow them to put smaller firms out of business. Consequently, small companies and even whole communities may resist the efforts of firms such as Walmart, Home Depot, and Best Buy to open stores in their vicinity. These firms can operate at such low costs that small, local firms often cannot compete. Such issues create concerns about social responsibility for organizations, communities, and consumers.

3-8b **Legal Dimension**

Marketers are expected to obey laws and regulations. The efforts of elected representatives and special-interest groups to promote responsible corporate behavior have resulted in laws and regulations designed to keep U.S. companies' actions within the range of acceptable conduct. Although most cases in the news deal with serious misconduct, not all legal cases are violations of the law. Sometimes, they are an attempt to interpret the law. Laws can be ambiguous, and new situations arise that create a need for courts to interpret whether the situation should be allowed or regulated. For instance, Internet tracking and privacy issues have caused lawmakers to consider whether to develop legislation limiting the types of information marketers can gather over the Internet.

marketing citizenship
The adoption of a strategic focus for fulfilling the economic, legal, ethical, and philanthropic social responsibilities expected by stakeholders

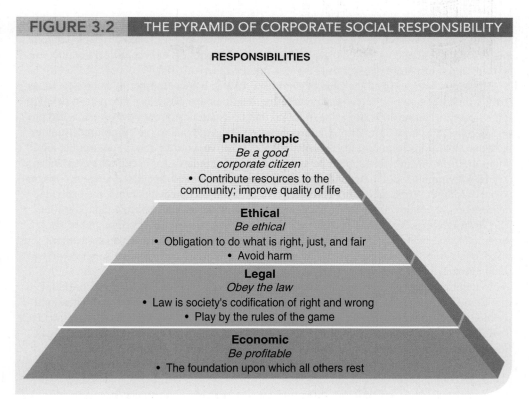

FIGURE 3.2 THE PYRAMID OF CORPORATE SOCIAL RESPONSIBILITY

RESPONSIBILITIES

Philanthropic
*Be a good
corporate citizen*
• Contribute resources to the
community; improve quality of life

Ethical
Be ethical
• Obligation to do what is right, just, and fair
• Avoid harm

Legal
Obey the law
• Law is society's codification of right and wrong
• Play by the rules of the game

Economic
Be profitable
• The foundation upon which all others rest

Source: Adapted from Archie B. Carroll, "The Pyramid of Corporate Social Responsibility: Toward the Moral Management of Organizational Stakeholders," adaptation of Figure 3, p. 42.

When marketers engage in deceptive practices to advance their own interests over those of others, charges of fraud may result. In general, fraud is any purposeful communication that deceives, manipulates, or conceals facts in order to create a false impression. It is considered a crime, and convictions may result in fines, imprisonment, or both. It is estimated by a Certified Fraud Examiners study that the average fraud losses totaled $6.3 billion with the loss per case averaging $2.7 million. While asset misappropriation was the most common type of fraud cited, financial statement fraud resulted in the highest losses.[49]

When customers, interest groups, or businesses become outraged over what they perceive as irresponsibility on the part of a marketing organization, they may urge their legislators to draft new legislation to regulate the behavior, or they may engage in litigation to force the organization to "play by the rules." Deceptive advertising in particular causes consumers to become defensive toward all promotional messages, and to become distrustful of all advertising; thus, it harms both consumers and marketers.[50]

3-8c Ethical Dimension

Economic and legal responsibilities are the most basic aspects of social responsibility, for good reason: failure to consider them may mean that a marketer does not operate long enough to engage in ethical or philanthropic activities. Beyond these dimensions lie marketing ethics—principles and standards that define acceptable conduct in marketing as determined by various stakeholders, including the public, government regulators, private-interest groups, consumers, industries, and the organization itself. The most basic of these principles have been codified as laws and regulations to encourage marketers to conform to society's expectations of conduct. Volkswagen suffered significant reputational and financial impact from its emissions scandal with attempting to cover up the actual emissions impact of its diesel vehicles. Specific brands included VW, Audi, and Porsche cars and SUVs with six-cylinder engines. The company initially agreed to a $15 billion settlement for its smaller vehicles and expanded it to include Audi and Porsche models. VW faced buybacks, repairs and financial settlements with defrauded customers. Consumers expect ethical conduct and truthful and transparent operations. This was not the case with VW.[51]

However, marketing ethics goes beyond legal issues. Ethical marketing decisions foster trust, which helps to build long-term marketing relationships. Trust is a key part of developing customer relationships. It has been found that transparency about how products are produced, as well as how a firm's philanthropic activities give back to the community, creates trust and intentions to purchase. This also creates positive word-of-mouth communication about the firm.[52] Marketers should be aware of ethical standards for acceptable conduct from several viewpoints—company, industry, government, customers, special-interest groups, and society at large. When marketing activities deviate from accepted standards, the exchange process can break down, resulting in customer dissatisfaction, lack of trust, and lawsuits. The 2016 Edelman Trust Barometer revealed that 62 percent of the informed public in America trust businesses to do what is right. Figure 3.3 compares American consumers' trust of business compared to citizens of other countries. The figure reveals that Americans' trust in business is lower than that of consumers in China, Brazil, and India.[53]

When managers engage in activities that deviate from accepted principles, continued marketing exchanges become difficult, if not impossible. The best time to deal with such problems is during the strategic planning process, not after major problems materialize. HCL Technologies, for instance, is an employee-centered company that encourages employees to make recommendations and convert their ideas into action. The company believes employees can take an active role in improving the company, stop problems before they occur, and better meet customer needs.[54]

ethical issue An identifiable problem, situation, or opportunity requiring a choice among several actions that must be evaluated as right or wrong, ethical or unethical

An **ethical issue** is an identifiable problem, situation, or opportunity requiring an individual or organization to choose from among several actions that must be evaluated as right or wrong, ethical or unethical. Any time an activity causes marketing managers or customers in their target market to feel manipulated or cheated, a marketing ethical issue exists, regardless of the legality of that activity. For example, the FDA has asked drug and meat companies to stop giving antibiotics to livestock in order to speed their growth. However, before the FDA got involved, Perdue Farms had already required its farmers to end the practice due

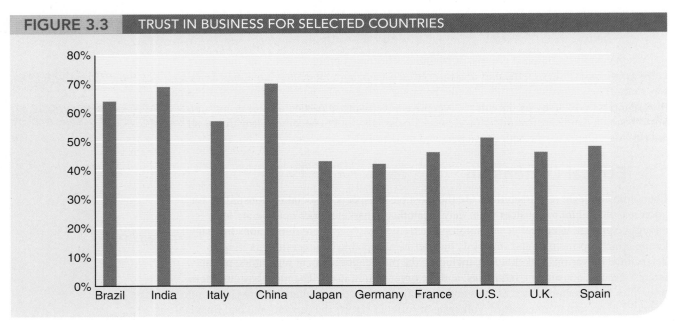

| FIGURE 3.3 | TRUST IN BUSINESS FOR SELECTED COUNTRIES |

Source: Edelman Insights, *2016 Edelman Trust Barometer*, www.edelman.com/insights/intellectual-property/2016-edelman-trust-barometer/global-results/ (accessed January 12, 2017).

to concerns from consumers. Market concerns over the safety of food turned this practice into an ethical issue. As a result of consumer pressure, companies such as Perdue, Tyson, and Walmart began selling meat products without antibiotics even before the issue caught regulators' attention.[55]

Regardless of the reasons behind specific ethical issues, marketers must be able to identify these issues and decide how to resolve them. To do so requires familiarity with the many kinds of ethical issues that may arise in marketing. Research suggests that the greater the consequences associated with an issue, the more likely it will be recognized as an ethics issue, and the more important it will be to making an ethical decision.[56] Examples of ethical issues related to product, price, distribution, and promotion (the marketing mix) appear in Table 3.3.

3-8d Philanthropic Dimension

At the top of the pyramid are philanthropic responsibilities. These responsibilities, which go beyond marketing ethics, are not required of a company, but they promote human welfare or goodwill, as do the economic, legal, and ethical dimensions of social responsibility. After natural disasters, for example, many corporations provide support to victims, waive certain fees, and/or aid in cleanup efforts.[57] The BMW Ultimate Drive program involves specially marked BMWs that drive across the USA to increase breast cancer awareness and raise funds for breast cancer research. BMW donates $1 to the Susan G. Komen Breast Cancer Foundation for every mile these cars are test driven by participants.[58]

More companies than ever are adopting a strategic approach to corporate philanthropy. Many firms link their products to a particular social cause on an ongoing or short-term basis, a practice known as **cause-related marketing**. Cincinnati-based Fifth Third Bancorp, for instance, partnered with Oregon-based NextJob to find employment opportunities for unemployed customers. The cause-related marketing campaign targeted bank customers who were behind on payments because they had lost their jobs. Together the companies launched a website that featured job seekers who needed employment. The campaign linked well with the bank's mortgage and home loans business.[59] A Cone study revealed that 93 percent of respondents have a more positive image of companies that support causes.[60] Some companies are beginning to extend the concept of corporate philanthropy beyond financial contributions by adopting a **strategic philanthropy approach**, the synergistic use of organizational core competencies and resources to address key stakeholders' interests and achieve both organizational and social benefits. Strategic

cause-related marketing The practice of linking products to a particular social cause on an ongoing or short-term basis

strategic philanthropy approach The synergistic use of organizational core competencies and resources to address key stakeholders' interests and achieve both organizational and social benefits

TABLE 3.3	ETHICAL ISSUES IN MARKETING
Issue Category	Examples
Product	• Failing to disclose risks associated with a product • Failing to disclose information about a product's function, value, or use • Failing to disclose information about changes in the nature, quality, or size of a product
Pricing	• Price fixing • Predatory pricing • Failing to disclose the full price of a purchase
Distribution	• Failing to live up to the rights and responsibilities associated with supply-chain member roles (e.g., manufacturers, wholesalers, distributors, retailers) • Manipulating product availability • Using coercion to force other intermediaries to behave in a certain way
Promotion	• False or misleading advertising • Using manipulative or deceptive sales promotions, tactics, and publicity • Offering or accepting bribes in personal selling situations

consumerism Organized efforts by individuals, groups, and organizations to protect consumers' rights

philanthropy involves employees; organizational resources and expertise; and the ability to link these assets to the concerns of key stakeholders, including employees, customers, suppliers, and society in general. Strategic philanthropy involves both financial and non-financial contributions to stakeholders (employee time, goods and services, and company technology and equipment, as well as facilities), but it also benefits the company. Salesforce.com, for example, believes in the benefits of strategic philanthropy so strongly that it incorporates community service into its corporate culture. Warby Parker, an American brand of prescription eyewear, donates one pair of eyeglasses to the nonprofit VisionSpring for each pair that is sold. This socially responsible initiative is a core part of Warby Parker's mission and business model.[61] The synergistic use of organizational core competencies and resources to address key stakeholders' interests achieve both organizational and social benefits.

Although social responsibility may seem to be an abstract ideal, managers make decisions related to social responsibility every day. To be successful, a business must determine what customers, government regulators, and competitors, as well as society in general, want or expect in terms of social responsibility. Two major categories of social responsibility issues are sustainability and consumerism.

Sustainability

One of the more common ways marketers demonstrate social responsibility is through programs designed to protect and preserve the natural environment. Most Fortune 500 companies now engage in recycling activities and make significant efforts to reduce waste and conserve energy. Many companies are making contributions to environmental protection organizations, sponsoring and participating in cleanup events, promoting recycling, retooling manufacturing processes to minimize waste and pollution, employing more environmentally friendly energy sources, and generally reevaluating the effects of their products on the natural environment. This approach to the environment is to reduce, reuse, and recycle.

As mentioned in Chapter 1, green marketing is a strategic process involving stakeholder assessment to create meaningful, long-term relationships with customers while maintaining, supporting, and enhancing the natural environment. The consumption of green products can be promoted by emphasizing the shared responsibility between the firm and consumers in protecting the environment.[62] For example, some retailers will assist consumers in recycling used electrical equipment. Many products certified as "green" by environmental organizations such as Green Seal carry a special logo identifying their organization as green marketers. Kimberly Clark became the first consumer-products company to become certified by the Forest Stewardship Council (FSC). Its tissues carry the FSC label to indicate that they were harvested from sustainable forests using environmentally friendly methods.[63] On the other hand, consumers are becoming very skeptical of greenwashing, which occurs when firms claim to protect the environment but fail to demonstrate their commitment.[64]

Consumerism

Consumerism consists of organized efforts by individuals, groups, and organizations seeking to protect consumers' rights. The movement's major forces are individual consumer advocates, consumer organizations and other interest groups, consumer education, and consumer laws.

To achieve their objectives, consumers and their advocates write letters or send e-mails to companies, lobby government agencies, broadcast public-service announcements, and boycott companies whose activities they deem irresponsible. Some consumers choose to boycott firms and products out of a desire

Method Daily

Green Product Offerings
Method produces biodegradable cleaning supplies. To reduce waste, it offers refills for its natural shower cleaner.

GOING GREEN

No Harm, No Foul: Harmless Harvest Connects with Stakeholders

In recent years, sociocultural preferences have changed to embrace healthier foods, leading to high demand for products such as coconut water. Today, the coconut water industry is a $1.3 billion market. However, with great demand comes high competition. Because they operate in a monopolistic competitive environment, players in the coconut water industry must differentiate their products. Coconut water company Harmless Harvest uses two characteristics to differentiate its products from competitors: taste and a socially responsible focus.

When Harmless Harvest founders Justin Guilbert and Douglas Riboud decided to start a company, they wanted the organization to create value not only for owners and customers, but also for every stakeholder in the supply chain—including the environment. After settling on a coconut variety from Thailand, the men used a proprietary multi-filter process to maintain the fresh, nutty richness of the coconut in its product.

The company also became Fair for Life certified. This certification has higher criteria than fair trade products. Harmless Harvest must adhere to higher standards to protect workers on coconut farms, pay fair wages, and use best farming practices to preserve the environment. Harmless Harvest's great taste and socially responsible practices have resonated with consumers. Not only did its product become one of Whole Foods' top sellers, it was also nominated by CircleUp25 as one of the most innovative brands of the year.[b]

to support a cause and make a difference.[65] For example, several organizations evaluate children's products for safety, often calling attention to dangerous products before Christmas so that parents can avoid them. Other actions by the consumer movement have resulted in seat belts and air bags in automobiles, dolphin-safe tuna, the banning of unsafe, three-wheel motorized vehicles, and numerous laws regulating product safety and information.

Also of great importance to the consumer movement are four basic rights spelled out in a "consumer bill of rights" drafted by President John F. Kennedy. These include the right to safety, the right to be informed, the right to choose, and the right to be heard. Ensuring consumers' *right to safety* means that marketers have an obligation not to market a product that they know could harm consumers. This right can be extended to imply that all products must be safe for their intended use, include thorough and explicit instructions for proper and safe use, and be tested to ensure reliability and quality. Consumers' *right to be informed* means that consumers should have access to and the opportunity to review all relevant information about a product before buying it. Many laws require specific labeling on product packaging to satisfy this right. In addition, labels on alcoholic and tobacco products inform consumers that these products may cause illness and other problems. The FTC provides a wealth of consumer information at its website (www.consumer.ftc.gov/) on a variety of topics ranging from automobiles and the Internet to diet, health, and fitness. The *right to choose* means that consumers should have access to a variety of products at competitive prices. They also should be assured of satisfactory quality and service at a fair price. Activities that reduce competition among businesses in an industry might jeopardize this right. The *right to be heard* ensures that consumers' interests will receive full and sympathetic consideration in the formulation of government policy. The right to be heard also promises consumers fair treatment when they complain to marketers about products. For example, the Consumer Financial Protection Bureau provides the opportunity to submit a complaint and get answers to questions. This right benefits marketers, too, because when consumers complain about a product the manufacturer can use this information to modify the product and make it more satisfying.

codes of conduct Formalized rules and standards that describe what a company expects of its employees

3-9 INCORPORATING SOCIAL RESPONSIBILITY AND ETHICS INTO STRATEGIC PLANNING

LO 3-9 Examine how social responsibility and ethics can be incorporated into strategic planning.

Although the concepts of marketing ethics and social responsibility are often used interchangeably, it is important to distinguish between them. *Ethics* relates to individual and group decisions—judgments about what is right or wrong in a particular decision-making situation—whereas *social responsibility* deals with the total effect of marketing decisions on society. The two concepts are interrelated because a company that supports socially responsible decisions and adheres to a code of conduct is likely to have a positive effect on society. Because ethics and social responsibility programs can be profitable as well, an increasing number of companies are incorporating them into their overall strategic market planning. Ben & Jerry's, for instance, built socially responsible principles into its original business model. When company strategies are implemented, they must align with the organization's core beliefs and values. As the advertisement indicates, Ben & Jerry's demonstrates its values and social responsibility in many different ways, including providing job-training programs, using non-genetically-modified ingredients, participating in the Caring Dairy initiative, and using fair trade ingredients in products.

Without ethics and compliance programs, and uniform standards and policies for conduct, it is hard for a company's employees to determine what conduct is acceptable within the company. In the absence of such programs and standards, employees generally will make decisions based on their observations of how their peers and superiors behave. While individuals may have good ethics, they often face new and complex decisions in the business environment. To improve ethics, many organizations have developed **codes of conduct** (also called *codes of ethics*) consisting of formalized rules and standards that describe what the company expects of its employees. The New York Stock Exchange now requires every member corporation to have a formal code of conduct. Codes of conduct promote ethical behavior by reducing opportunities for unethical behavior; employees know both what is expected of them and the punishment they face if they violate the rules. Such codes are important in preventing misconduct within the organization. Effective content, the frequency of communication regarding the code, the quality of communication, and the incorporation of the code into the organization by senior and local management can result in fewer instances of observed unethical behavior.[66] Codes help marketers deal with ethical issues or dilemmas that develop in daily operations by prescribing or limiting specific activities. Codes of conduct often include general ethical values such as honesty and integrity, general legal compliance, harmful acts, and obligations related to social values, as well as more marketing-specific issues such as confidentiality, responsibilities to employers and clients, obligations to the profession, and marketing-specific legal and technical compliance issues.[67]

It is important that companies consistently enforce standards and correct or impose negative consequences on those

Ben & Jerry's

Social Responsibility and Strategic Planning
Ben & Jerry's incorporates social responsibility into its strategies. Its advertisement explains that its ice cream is made with Fair Trade ingredients and does not contain GMOs. It also emphasizes its support for the humane treatment of cows and for job programs.

who violate codes of conduct. Barrett-Jackson, an auction company specializing in classic and collector cars, recognizes the importance of ethical conduct to its customers. Ethical standards are such a significant part of the company's culture that it hired a top auditing firm to conduct an independent examination of its practices. To create an effective ethics and compliance program and stave off the types of misconduct found in similar organizations, Barrett-Jackson constantly reviews and updates its policies.[68]

Table 3.4 lists some commonly observed types of misconduct as reported in the Global Business Ethics Survey. The key metrics of the survey are observed misconduct—such as abusive behavior, lying to stakeholders, and conflict of interest—pressure to compromise standards, reporting of observed misconduct, and retaliation against reporters. To succeed, a compliance program must be viewed as part of the overall marketing strategy implementation. If ethics officers and other executives are not committed to the principles and initiatives of marketing ethics and social responsibility, the program's effectiveness will be in question.

Firms have a responsibility to treat customers ethically. Service providers that ensure satisfactory, ethical service delivery create a perception of reasonableness that builds customer relationships. For example, trust is often developed after conflicts if the participants were able to reach agreement on their thoughts and beliefs.[69] Therefore, ethics in marketing can be effective in increasing firm performance. Increasing evidence indicates that being ethical and socially responsible pays off. Social responsibility has a synergistic effect on market orientation that leads to improved business performance.[70] More firms are moving beyond a market orientation that focuses on customers and competitors and are adopting a stakeholder orientation that focuses on all constituents. Such a relationship implies that being ethically and socially concerned is consistent with meeting the demands of customers and other stakeholders. By encouraging their employees to understand their markets, companies can help them respond to stakeholders' demands.[71]

There is a direct association between corporate social responsibility and customer satisfaction, profits, and market value.[72] In a survey of consumers, 89 percent indicated that when quality and price are similar among competitors, they would be more likely to buy from the company associated with a particular cause. Approximately 54 percent bought a product associated with a cause within a twelve-month period.[73]

Thus, recognition is growing that the long-term value of conducting business in a socially responsible manner far outweighs short-term costs.[74] Companies that fail to develop strategies and programs to incorporate ethics and social responsibility into their organizational culture may pay the price with poor marketing performance, the potential costs of legal violations, civil litigation, and damaging publicity when questionable activities are made public.

TABLE 3.4	OBSERVED MISCONDUCT IN THE U.S. WORKFORCE
Observed misconduct	30%
Abusive behavior	22%
Lying to stakeholders	22%
Conflict of interest	19%
Pressure to compromise standards	22%
Report observed misconduct	76%
Experience retaliation for reporting	53%

Source: Ethics and Compliance Initiative, *2016 Global Business Ethics Survey™: Measuring Risk and Promoting Workplace Integrity* (Arlington, VA: Ethics and Compliance Initiative 2016), p. 43.

Chapter Review

3-1 Summarize why it is important to examine and respond to the marketing environment.

The marketing environment consists of external forces that directly or indirectly influence an organization's acquisition of inputs and creation of outputs. To monitor changes in the marketing environment effectively, marketers engage in environmental scanning and analysis. Environmental scanning is the process of collecting information about the forces in the marketing environment; environmental analysis is the process of assessing and interpreting the information gathered through environmental scanning. This information helps marketing managers to minimize uncertainty and threats and capitalize on opportunities presented by environmental factors.

3-2 Explain how competitive factors affect an organization's ability to compete.

A marketer generally defines *competition* as other firms that market products which are similar to or can be substituted for its products in the same geographic area. These competitors can be classified into one of four types: brand competitors, product competitors, generic competitors, and total budget competitors. The number of firms controlling the supply of a product may affect the strength of competitors. The four general types of competitive structures are monopoly, oligopoly, monopolistic competition, and pure competition. Marketers monitor their competitors' activity and assess changes occurring in the competitive environment.

3-3 Articulate how economic factors influence a customer's ability and willingness to buy products.

General economic conditions, buying power, and willingness to spend can strongly influence marketing decisions and activities. The overall state of the economy fluctuates in a general pattern known as the business cycle, which consists of four stages: prosperity, recession, depression, and recovery. Consumers' goods, services, and financial holdings make up their buying power, or ability to purchase. Financial sources of buying power are income, credit, and wealth. After-tax income used for spending or saving is disposable income. Disposable income left after an individual has purchased the basic necessities of food, clothing, and shelter is discretionary income. Factors affecting buyers' willingness to spend include product price; level of satisfaction obtained from currently used products; family size; and expectations about future employment, income, prices, and general economic conditions.

3-4 Identify the types of political forces in the marketing environment.

The political, legal, and regulatory forces of the marketing environment are closely interrelated. Political forces influence the enactment of laws and regulations affecting specific marketers, and determine how much resources the government purchases and from which suppliers. They can also be important in helping organizations secure foreign markets. Companies engage with political forces in several ways, including maintaining good relationships with political officials, protesting the actions of legislative bodies, helping elect individuals who regard them positively to public office through campaign contributions, and employing lobbyists to communicate their concerns to elected officials.

3-5 Explain how laws, government regulations, and self-regulatory agencies affect marketing activities.

Federal legislation affecting marketing activities can be divided into procompetitive legislation—laws designed to preserve and encourage competition—and consumer protection laws, which generally relate to product safety and information disclosure. Actual effects of legislation are determined by how marketers and courts interpret the laws. Federal guidelines for sentencing concerning violations of these laws represent an attempt to force marketers to comply with the laws. Federal, state, and local regulatory agencies usually have power to enforce specific laws. They also have some discretion in establishing operating rules and drawing up regulations to guide certain types of industry practices. Industry self-regulation represents another regulatory force; marketers view this type of regulation more favorably than government action because they have more opportunity to take part in creating guidelines. Self-regulation may be less expensive than government regulation, and its guidelines are generally more realistic. However, such regulation generally cannot ensure compliance as effectively as government agencies.

3-6 Describe how new technology impacts marketing and society.

Technology is the application of knowledge and tools to solve problems and perform tasks more efficiently. Revolutionary changes in communication technology have allowed marketers to reach vast numbers of people; however, with this expansion of communication has come concern about privacy and intellectual property. Home, health, leisure, and work are all influenced to varying degrees by technology and technological advances. The *dynamics* of technology involves the constant change that challenges every aspect of our society. *Reach* refers to the broad nature of technology as it moves through and affects society. The ability to protect inventions from competitor imitation is also an important consideration when making marketing decisions.

3-7 Outline the sociocultural issues marketers must deal with as they make decisions.

Sociocultural forces are the influences in a society and its culture that result in changes in attitudes, beliefs, norms, customs, and lifestyles. Major sociocultural issues directly affecting marketers include demographic and diversity characteristics and cultural values. Changes in a population's demographic characteristics such as age, income, race, and ethnicity can lead to changes in that population's consumption of products. Changes in cultural values such as those relating to health, nutrition, family, and the natural environment have had striking effects on people's needs for products and therefore are closely monitored by marketers.

3-8 Define the four dimensions of social responsibility.

Social responsibility refers to an organization's obligation to maximize its positive impact and minimize its negative impact on society. Whereas social responsibility is achieved by balancing the interests of all stakeholders in an organization, ethics relates to acceptable standards of conduct in making individual and group decisions. At the most basic level, companies have an economic responsibility to be profitable so that they can provide a return on investment to their stockholders, create jobs for the community, and contribute goods and services to the economy. Marketers are also expected to obey laws and regulations. Marketing ethics refers to principles and standards that define acceptable conduct in marketing as determined by various stakeholders. Philanthropic responsibilities go beyond marketing ethics; they are not required of a company but promote human welfare and goodwill. Sustainability and consumerism are two important issues in social responsibility.

3-9 Examine how social responsibility and ethics can be incorporated into strategic planning.

An increasing number of companies are incorporating ethics and social responsibility programs into their overall strategic marketing planning. To promote socially responsible and ethical behavior while achieving organizational goals, marketers must monitor changes and trends in society's values. They must determine what society wants and attempt to predict the long-term effects of their decisions. To improve ethics, many organizations have developed codes of conduct consisting of formalized rules and standards that describe what the company expects of its employees. Increasing evidence indicates that being socially responsible and ethical results in valuable benefits: an enhanced public reputation (which can increase market share), costs savings, and profits.

 Go to www.cengagebrain.com for resources to help you master the content in this chapter as well as for materials that will expand your marketing knowledge!

Developing Your Marketing Plan

A marketing strategy is dynamic. Companies must continually monitor the marketing environment not only to create their marketing strategy, but also to revise it if necessary. Information about various forces in the marketplace is collected, analyzed, and used as a foundation for several marketing plan decisions. The following questions will help you understand how the information in this chapter contributes to the development of your marketing plan:

1. Describe the current competitive market for your product. Can you identify the number of brands or market share that they hold? Expand your analysis to include other products that are similar or could be substituted for yours.

2. Using the business-cycle pattern, in which of the four stages is the current state of the economy? Can you identify changes in consumer buying power that would affect the sale and use of your product?

3. Referring to Tables 3.2 and 3.3, do you recognize any laws or regulatory agencies that would have jurisdiction over your type of product?

4. Conduct a brief technology assessment, determining the impact that technology has on your product, its sale, or use.

5. Discuss how your product could be affected by changes in social attitudes, demographic characteristics, or lifestyles.

Key Concepts

environmental
   scanning   50
environmental
   analysis   50
competition   52
brand competitors   52
product competitors   52
generic competitors   52
total budget
   competitors   52

monopoly   52
oligopoly   53
monopolistic
   competition   53
pure competition   53
buying power   54
disposable income   54
discretionary income   54
willingness to spend
   55

business cycle   56
Federal Trade Commission
   (FTC)   59
Better Business
   Bureau   61
National Advertising
   Review Board
   (NARB)   61
technology   62
sociocultural forces   63

social responsibility   65
marketing
   citizenship   66
ethical issue   68
cause-related
   marketing   69
strategic philanthropy
   approach   69
consumerism   70
codes of conduct   72

Issues for Discussion and Review

1. Why are environmental scanning and analysis important to marketers?
2. What are four types of competition? Which is most
important to marketers?
3. Define *income, disposable income,* and *discretionary
income.* How does each type of income affect consumer buying power?
4. What factors influence a buyer's willingness to spend?
5. What are the goals of the Federal Trade Commission?
List the ways in which the FTC affects marketing
activities. Do you think that a single regulatory agency
should have such broad jurisdiction over so many marketing practices? Why or why not?
6. Name several nongovernmental regulatory forces.
Do you believe that self-regulation is more or less
effective than governmental regulatory agencies? Why?

7. Discuss the impact of technology on marketing
activities.
8. In what ways are cultural values changing? How are
marketers responding to these changes?
9. What is social responsibility, and why is it
important?
10. What are four dimensions of social responsibility?
What impact do they have on marketing
decisions?
11. What are some major social responsibility issues? Give
an example of each.
12. Describe consumerism. Analyze some active consumer
forces in your area.
13. What is the difference between ethics and social
responsibility?

VIDEO CASE 3
Apple vs. Samsung: Gloves Are Off

Both Apple and Samsung have been at the forefront of technology innovation. Technological forces are pushing for
newer and better products, and tech companies must constantly pursue product development to compete effectively
against each other. As a result, the tech environment has
become highly aggressive with firms going to great lengths
to protect their patents. A patent rewards an innovator for
a new invention or technology by providing the innovator
the sole rights to develop and sell that product for 20 years.
Patents offer the owner legal protection. If during that time
competitors try to sell the product, they can be sued for
damages.

In the United States, whoever files a patent first gets
legal protection. This can get complicated, however, when
it is hard to determine which company obtained a patent
first, or when a firm accuses another firm of violating
their patent by copying certain product features protected
under the patent. This was the case between Apple and
Samsung, leading to a legal battle that would take multiple
years to resolve. It started in 2011, when Apple accused
Samsung of violating its iPhone patent by copying certain
iPhone features for its Galaxy S. In its allegations, Apple
accused Samsung of copying the iPhone shape; color; tap-
to-zoom, flip-to-rotate, and slide-to-scroll features; and

more. It also claimed that Samsung violated the patent for its iPad.

Samsung claimed the opposite. It claimed that it had patented these components before Apple and that therefore Apple's iPhone violated Samsung's intellectual property rights. Samsung countersued. Soon the lawsuit had taken on global proportions as lawsuits were filed in the United States, South Korea, Germany, Japan, the United Kingdom, and other countries. Since the legal and regulatory environments differ in each country, the courts often came up with different verdicts. For instance, South Korea courts found that Apple had violated two of Samsung's patents, while Samsung violated one of Apple's. The United Kingdom ruled in favor of Samsung.

In the United States, Apple wanted more than $2 billion in damages from Samsung. In the original verdict, U.S. courts ruled that Samsung had violated Apple's patents and ordered Samsung to pay $1 billion in damages. Later appeals reduced this amount. In 2012, Apple filed a new lawsuit against Samsung claiming it had copied five features protected under Apple's patent. Samsung sued Apple, claiming it had violated two of the patents it owned.

This time the jury issued a mixed verdict. "Among the popular features, it found Samsung copied the slide-to-unlock button on some of its phones and autocorrect," said Betty Yu, a reporter from KPIX 5 CBS who covered the outcome. "Samsung accused Apple of infringing two of its patents and in the end was found guilty of just one. It involves photo and video organization in folders."

As a result of the verdict, Samsung was ordered to pay $120 million in damages to Apple, whereas Apple was told to pay Samsung $158,000. Analysts see the legal battle as being a fight over dominance rather than a concern over money. Both companies hold a large share of the smartphone market, and neither is willing to give up market share.

For consumers, the verdict is likely to have little impact. Sometimes legal battles over intellectual property can result in the losing company being ordered to stop selling the product within the country. However, this did not happen with the Apple vs. Samsung case.

"What does all this mean for you and me? Well, experts say that this really doesn't mean anything for us," Betty Yu says. "You can still use your phones involved in this case, and the newest devices aren't an issue."

As this case demonstrates, intellectual property is not always an easy path to navigate, especially for global companies who operate in countries with different laws. In China, for instance, intellectual property rights laws are more lax, and copying is more common. Although some might view Apple as being overly aggressive, maintaining control over intellectual property in the tech industry could mean the difference between company failure and success. Currently, Samsung overshadows Apple in the global smartphone market. However, newer competitors including Chinese firms Huawei, Lenovo, and Xiaomi are quickly gaining in market share.[75]

Questions for Discussion

1. In what type of competitive environment do you think Apple and Samsung operate?
2. How do technological forces impact how Apple and Samsung operate when it comes to protecting their intellectual property?
3. Why is it important for international tech firms to be familiar with the laws and regulations of the countries in which they operate?

Part 2

Rawpixel.com/Shutterstock.com

Marketing Research and Target Markets

PART 2 examines how marketers use information and technology to better understand and target customers. **CHAPTER 4** provides a foundation for analyzing buyers through a discussion of marketing information systems and the basic steps in the marketing research process. Understanding elements that affect buying decisions enables marketers to better analyze customers' needs and to evaluate how specific marketing strategies can satisfy those needs. **CHAPTER 5** deals with selecting and analyzing target markets, which is one of the major steps in marketing strategy development.

chapter 4

Marketing Research and Information Systems

Jacob Lund/Shutterstock.com

LEARNING OBJECTIVES

4-1 Define marketing research and its importance to decision makers.

4-2 Distinguish between exploratory and conclusive research.

4-3 Name the five basic steps in conducting marketing research, including the two types of data and four survey methods.

4-4 Describe the tools, such as databases, big data, and marketing analytics, useful to marketing decision making.

4-5 Identify ethical and international issues in marketing research.

MARKETING INSIGHTS

IKEA Keeps Its Eyes on the Consumer

IKEA goes to great lengths to collect consumer information to obtain its goal of becoming a "leader in life at home." For the third consecutive year, IKEA has published its Life at Home Report, this time focusing on a quantitative study of 12,000 respondents in 12 countries worldwide. This type of research is particularly important for IKEA to maintain a strong competitive edge in the United States.

Despite IKEA's widespread popularity, its growth in the United States has been lower than anticipated. With plans to open more stores, IKEA recognizes that it must further invest in marketing research to understand U.S. consumers' unique needs. It is therefore ramping up its relatively unorthodox marketing research strategy by increasing its personal home visits. IKEA usually visits approximately 500 to 600 homes per year, but in its bid to understand how it can make life easier for consumers, it increased this amount to 1,000. IKEA representatives visit the homes to observe behavior and ask questions about household needs. Although the personal interview is the most expensive form of marketing research, IKEA believes it is key to meeting the unique customer demands in the different geographic areas in which its stores are located.

IKEA also engages in online research. The company uses an online panel and combines this data with insights from surveys and observations to develop a digital data mining tool. All of this data allows IKEA to focus on areas of high growth, such as introducing new products for the kitchen. Ultimately, IKEA hopes that better understanding its customers will lead to the development of more successful products and greater sales volume.[1]

iStock.com/cbarnesphotography

marketing research The systematic design, collection, interpretation, and reporting of information to help marketers solve specific marketing problems or take advantage of marketing opportunities

Marketing research enables firms such as IKEA to implement the marketing concept by helping firms acquire information about whether and how their goods and services satisfy the desires of target-market customers. When used effectively, such information facilitates relationship marketing by helping marketers focus their efforts on trying to anticipate and meet the needs of their customers. Marketing research and information systems that provide practical and objective information to help firms develop and implement marketing strategies are therefore essential to effective marketing.

In this chapter, we focus on how marketers gather the information needed to make marketing decisions. First, we define marketing research and examine the individual steps of the marketing research process, including the various methods of collecting data. Next, we look at how technology aids in collecting, organizing, and interpreting marketing research data. In addition, we explore how big data and marketing analytics are used in marketing research today. Finally, we consider ethical and international issues in marketing research.

4-1 THE IMPORTANCE OF MARKETING RESEARCH

LO 4-1 Define marketing research and its importance to decision makers.

Marketing research is the systematic design, collection, interpretation, and reporting of information to help marketers solve specific marketing problems or take advantage of marketing opportunities. As the word *research* implies, it is a process for gathering the information needed that is not already available to decision makers. The purpose of marketing research is to inform an organization about customers' needs and desires, marketing opportunities for particular products, and changing attitudes and purchase patterns of customers. Market information increases the firm's ability to make informed decisions and respond to customer needs, which can lead to improved organizational performance. Detecting shifts in buyers' behaviors and attitudes helps companies react to the ever-changing marketplace. Strategic planning requires marketing research to facilitate the process of assessing such opportunities or threats.

Marketing research can help a firm better understand market opportunities, ascertain new products' potential for success, and determine the feasibility of a marketing strategy. It can also reveal surprising trends. For example, the average television viewership for NASCAR declined from 9 million in 2005 to 4.6 million in 2016. In addition, the audience is becoming older. This finding could indicate the need for additional research to determine approaches to increase viewership.[2] Failing to conduct research can prevent companies from maintaining a competitive advantage.

Changes in the economy have dramatically changed marketers' decision-making strategies. Increasingly, businesses need speed and agility to survive and to react quickly to changing consumer behaviors. Understanding the market is crucial for effective marketing strategies. Marketing research has shifted its focus toward smaller studies like test marketing, small-scale surveys, and short-range forecasting in order to learn about changing dynamics in the marketplace. However, large, high-value research projects remain necessary for long-term success. Though it is acceptable to conduct studies that take six months or more, many companies need real-time information to help them make good decisions. As we discuss in this chapter, the use of big data and marketing analytics are helping to integrate findings in order to help companies make tactical and strategic decisions. In the future, the marketing researcher will need to be able to identify the most efficient and effective ways of gathering information.[3]

The real value of marketing research is measured by improvements in a marketer's ability to make informed decisions. Many types of organizations

Source: SAP

Importance of Marketing Research
SAP HANA is used to analyze data that would be impossible for a single marketing researcher. The insights gleaned from this data can be used to predict future consumer trends, which would provide businesses using this platform with a competitive advantage.

use marketing research to help them develop marketing mixes that address the needs of customers. It is important in today's rapidly changing marketing environment that firms have the necessary organizational speed and agility to adapt to changes quickly. To improve research-gathering capacity and decision-making ability, some firms may choose to hire a consultant who can assist with gathering and assessing the data involved in marketing research. Take a look at the advertisement for SAP's HANA system, a computing platform and data management system that offers a range of services. The advertisement targeted toward businesses stresses the importance of knowing one's customers and anticipating their needs before anyone else does—including the customers themselves. SAP HANA uses big data to predict future trends. This type of marketing research can be crucial in developing and adapting marketing strategies to connect with customers.

> **exploratory research**
> Research conducted to gather more information about a problem or to make a tentative hypothesis more specific

Having a full understanding of issues can help a company increase performance and develop an advantage over competitors. Sony and Tinder are testing start-up Interana's data analytics program to organize online data more efficiently. Interana helps clients to store a file on each of their customers, making it easier to analyze customer data.[4] Marketers should treat information as one of its resources, just as finances and human capital are resources, and they must weigh the costs and benefits of obtaining information. Information should be considered worthwhile if it results in marketing activities that better satisfy the firm's target customers, lead to increased sales and profits, or help the firm achieve some other goal.

4-2 TYPES OF RESEARCH

LO 4-2 Distinguish between exploratory and conclusive research.

The nature and type of research a firm conducts will vary depending on the research design and the hypotheses under investigation. Marketing research can involve two forms of data. *Qualitative data* yields descriptive, non-numerical information. *Quantitative data* yields information that can be communicated through numbers or metrics. Marketers may choose to collect either or both, depending upon the information desired. To collect data, marketers conduct either exploratory research or conclusive research. Although each has a distinct purpose, they vary in levels of formalization and flexibility. Table 4.1 summarizes the differences.

4-2a Exploratory Research

When marketers need more information about a problem or want to make a tentative hypothesis more specific, they conduct **exploratory research**. The main purpose of exploratory research

TABLE 4.1	DIFFERENCES BETWEEN EXPLORATORY AND CONCLUSIVE RESEARCH	
Research Project Components	**Exploratory Research**	**Conclusive Research**
Research purpose	General: to generate insights about a situation	Specific: to verify insights and aid in selecting a course of action
Data needs	Vague	Clear
Data sources	Ill-defined	Well-defined
Data collection form	Open-ended, rough	Usually structured
Sample	Relatively small, subjectively selected to maximize generalization of insights	Relatively large, objectively selected to permit generalization of findings
Data collection	Flexible, no set procedure	Rigid, well-laid-out procedure
Data analysis	Informal, typically not quantitative	Formal, typically quantitative
Inferences/recommendations	More tentative than final	More final than tentative

customer advisory boards Small groups of actual customers who serve as sounding boards for new-product ideas and offer insights into their feelings and attitudes toward a firm's products and other elements of its marketing strategy

focus group An interview that is often conducted informally, without a structured questionnaire, in small groups of 8 to 12 people, to observe interaction when members are exposed to an idea or a concept

is to better understand a problem or situation and/or to help identify additional data needs or decision alternatives.[5] Exploratory research is usually associated with qualitative research techniques. The focus of qualitative research is not metrics and complex data analysis but rather stories, visual portrayals, interpretations, and expressive descriptions. Exploratory research does not usually provide quantitative data that assigns numeric values for statistical analysis.[6] For example, exploratory qualitative research could include online participant observation or even netnography, which is involvement in social networks, to understand brand perceptions. For instance, a researcher may get involved in an online PlayStation community to better understand the brand and consumer interests. This type of exploratory research can help marketers better understand how consumers view a topic or a product, which can assist a firm as it develops better products and more targeted marketing mixes.

Some organizations utilize **customer advisory boards**, which are small groups of actual customers who serve as sounding boards for new-product ideas and offer researchers insights into their feelings and attitudes toward a firm's marketing strategy, including products, pricing, distribution, and promotion. These advisory boards provide qualitative exploratory information. While these advisory boards can help companies maintain strong relationships with valuable customers, they can also generate a greater understanding of marketing research questions. Oracle maintains customer advisory boards for its subsidiary PeopleSoft to provide insights on how customers view the organization's business application products.[7]

One common method for conducting exploratory research is through a focus group. A **focus group** brings together multiple people to discuss a specific topic in a group setting facilitated by a moderator. For example, CVS maintains a mock-up store where it not only tests new products but also conducts focus groups with consumers.[8] Focus groups are often conducted informally, without a structured questionnaire. Therefore, they are a common technique associated with qualitative research. They allow customer attitudes, behaviors, lifestyles, needs, and desires to be explored in a flexible and creative manner. Questions are open-ended and stimulate respondents to answer in their own words. A traditional focus group session consists of 8 to 12 individuals and is led by a moderator, who is an independent individual hired by the research firm or the company. The moderator encourages all of the participants to engage in the conversation and directs the discussion by asking questions when needed. Blue Matrix Labs used a focus group of 20 kids separated into five groups of four to test a new type of water balloon product. The focus groups of children were allowed to play with the balloons and were then asked questions about how they liked the product (the moderators also used games to solicit feedback from the children). The company took the insights they gleaned and used them to develop the product's tagline and messaging.[9]

Focus groups can provide companies with ideas for new products or can be a forum to test marketing strategies for existing products. This format can yield detailed information, including on topics about which researchers might not have thought to ask participants, because new topics may arise when focus group members engage with one another.

In-person focus groups have some disadvantages, however. For instance, sometimes the focus group's discussion can be hindered by overly talkative, confrontational, or shy individuals. Some participants might be less than honest in an effort to be sociable or to receive money and/or food in exchange for their participation.[10] Furthermore, focus groups do not provide quantitative data, and are thus best used to uncover issues that can be explored using quantifiable marketing research techniques.

Because of their ease of use, online focus groups are a growing research trend. Participants either sign in to a website and insert their responses in the fields provided, or log into a video chat. Online focus groups can be a cost-effective way to gather data from large and geographically diverse groups. Technology exists to make conducting

Focus Groups
Companies bring consumers together to solicit feedback and gain a better understanding of their changing attitudes and desires.

online focus groups easy and cost-effective. Online focus groups are more convenient for the participants than traditional focus groups because they can participate in their own homes, no matter where they are located. However, this method is not well-adapted to asking participants about a product's smell or taste, so it is not suitable for all goods. When using a website login, researchers also cannot observe the participants' nonverbal cues and body language, which can often reveal gut reactions to questions or topics discussed. Marketers should keep these concerns in mind when designing a research project for a particular product.

Other forms of exploratory qualitative research include observation, conversation, and depth interviews that can last over an hour. Depth interviews provide more insight into an individual's perceptions than focus groups.[11] While these exploratory research techniques provide qualitative information, conclusive research provides quantitative in-depth analysis of problems and opportunities.

4-2b Conclusive Research

Conclusive research is designed to verify insights through an objective procedure to help marketers make decisions. It is helpful in reaching conclusions and provides quantitative information. It is used in the final stages of decision making, when the marketer has narrowed his or her decision down to a few alternatives. Conclusive research is helpful when a marketer requires a well-defined and structured research project to help decide which of a set of approaches is best for a specific product and target consumers. Conclusive research studies are typically formal, specific, and have verifiable methods. Two such types of conclusive research are descriptive research and experimental research.

If marketers need to understand the characteristics of certain phenomena to solve a particular problem, descriptive research can aid them. Descriptive research may range from general surveys of customers' educations, occupations, or ages to seeking out specific information on how often teenagers consume sports drinks or how often customers buy new shoes. For example, if Nike and Reebok wanted to target more young women, they might ask 15- to 35-year-old females how often they work out, how frequently they wear athletic shoes, and how many pairs of athletic shoes they buy in a year. Such descriptive research could be used to develop specific marketing strategies for the athletic shoe market. Descriptive studies generally demand significant prior knowledge and assume that the problem or issue is clearly defined. Some descriptive studies require statistical analysis and predictive tools. The marketer's primary task is to choose adequate methods for collecting and measuring data.

Descriptive research does not provide sufficient information to allow researchers to make causal inferences (i.e., that variable X causes a variable Y). Experimental research allows marketers to make these causal deductions about relationships between variables. The experiment controls one variable and randomizes one or more variables. Such experimentation requires that an independent variable (Variable X, one that is not influenced by or acted on by other variables) be manipulated and the resulting changes to a dependent variable (Variable Y, one that is influenced by the independent variable) be measured. Manipulation of the independent variable while controlling the other variables is what makes experimental research different from descriptive research. In this way, researchers can determine causality, which is highly important when developing marketing strategy.

| 4-3 THE MARKETING RESEARCH PROCESS

LO 4-3 Name the five basic steps in conducting marketing research, including the two types of data and four survey methods.

We will examine a generalized approach to the research process that should be adapted to the specific project. Marketing research should be customized to use methods that provide the best information for the marketing decision. Analytical approaches provide flexible and insightful information.[12]

conclusive research
Research designed to verify insights through objective procedures and to help marketers in making decisions

descriptive research
Research conducted to clarify the characteristics of certain phenomena to solve a particular problem

experimental research
Research that allows marketers to make causal inferences about relationships between variables

FIGURE 4.1   THE FIVE STEPS OF THE MARKETING RESEARCH PROCESS

1 Locating and defining issues or problems → **2** Designing the research project → **3** Collecting data → **4** Interpreting research findings → **5** Reporting research findings

To maintain the control needed to obtain accurate information, a firm should approach marketing research as a process with logical steps: (1) locating and defining problems or issues, (2) designing the research project, (3) collecting data, (4) interpreting research findings, and (5) reporting research findings (see Figure 4.1). These steps should be viewed as part of an overall approach to conducting research, rather than as a rigid set of rules. Marketers must consider each step and determine how they can be adapted to resolve the issues at hand.

4-3a Locating and Defining Problems or Issues

The first step in launching a research study is defining the problem or issue. This will encourage researchers to focus on the true nature and boundaries of a situation as it relates to marketing strategy or implementation. The first sign of a problem is typically a departure from normal functioning, such as the failure to meet an objective that was previously attainable. If a corporation's objective is a 12 percent sales increase and there was only a 6 percent increase under the current marketing strategy, marketers should analyze this discrepancy to adapt the marketing strategy to be more effective. A decrease in sales is a symptom of the problem, not the problem itself. Declining sales, increasing expenses, and decreasing profits all signal problems that could merit research for a firm. Conversely, a dramatic increase in sales or another positive event should prompt marketers to research the reasons for the change in order to leverage opportunities. Often, the discrepancy relates to marketing-related issues.

Marketing research often focuses on identifying and defining market opportunities or changes in the environment. When a firm discovers a market opportunity, it should conduct research to understand the situation and craft an appropriate marketing strategy. For example, UPS may want to know if it can deliver packages by a drone. This may require a survey of existing customers.

In order to identify and define an issue correctly, marketers must be careful not to be distracted by superficial symptoms. Addressing symptoms of the problem does not identify failures in marketing activities and leads to a continuation of the underlying issue. Researchers and decision makers should remain in the problem or issue definition stage as long as needed, until they are certain they have designed a research plan that addresses the issue. Taking the necessary steps to allow researchers to refine a broad, indefinite problem or issue into a precise and testable research statement is a prerequisite for the next step in the research process.

4-3b Designing the Research Project

Once the problem or issue has been defined, the next step is to create a **research design**, an overall plan for obtaining the information needed to address the issue. This step requires formulating a hypothesis and determining what type of research is most appropriate for testing the hypothesis to ensure the results are reliable and valid. The project should not be limited to a small set of research approaches or methods. Marketers should recognize that a large diversity of approaches is available and should be customized to address the most important research questions.[13]

Developing a Hypothesis

The objective statement of a marketing research project should include a hypothesis based on both previous research and expected research findings. A **hypothesis** is an informed

research design An overall plan for obtaining the information needed to address a research problem or issue

hypothesis An informed guess or assumption about a certain problem or set of circumstances

guess or assumption about a certain problem or set of circumstances. It is what a researcher seeks to prove or disprove and is based on all the insight and knowledge available about the problem or circumstances from previous research studies and other sources. As information is gathered, the researcher tests the hypothesis. For example, a marketer at a cosmetics company might propose the hypothesis that the fragrance of its scented beauty products will influence in-store purchase patterns. A marketing researcher would then gather data, perhaps through testing scents in the store and seeing whether sales change. The researcher would then analyze the data and draw conclusions as to whether the hypothesis is correct. Sometimes, several hypotheses are developed over the course of a research project. The hypotheses that are accepted or rejected become the study's conclusions.

Research Reliability and Validity

In designing research, marketing researchers must ensure that research techniques are both reliable and valid. A research technique has **reliability** if it produces almost identical results in repeated trials. To have **validity**, the research method must measure what it is supposed to measure, not something else. This means that not all reliable research findings are valid. For example, although a group of customers may express the same level of satisfaction based on a rating scale, as individuals they may not exhibit the same repurchase behavior because of different personal characteristics. If the purpose of rating satisfaction was to estimate potential repurchase behavior, this result may cause the researcher to question the validity of the satisfaction scale if satisfaction is not associated with repurchase behavior.[14] A study to measure the effect of advertising on sales is valid if advertising can be isolated from other factors and from variables that affect sales. Research projects should be replicable as well; otherwise, it is impossible to establish reliability.

4-3c **Collecting Data**

The next step in the marketing research process is collecting data to help prove (or disprove) the research hypothesis. The research design must specify what types of data to collect and how they will be collected.

Types of Data

Marketing researchers have two types of data at their disposal. **Primary data** are observed and recorded or collected directly from respondents. Primary data must be gathered by observing phenomena or surveying people of interest. **Secondary data** are compiled both inside and outside the organization for some purpose other than the current investigation. Secondary data include general reports compiled by other organizations and internal and online databases. Reports might address a variety of topics, including market share, retail inventory levels, and customers' buying behavior. They are useful for research if the information contained is pertinent to the hypothesis marketers are testing. Most marketing research comes from secondary sources, as they often provide the needed information at relatively low cost and effort. The Internet has increased the amount of secondary data available exponentially, making research both easier and more complicated. Now researchers are faced with the task of sorting through large volumes of secondary data, some of it of questionable quality, in order to find the information they need. There remain, however, large and reputable publications and databases that are useful.

Sources of Secondary Data

Marketers often begin the data-collection phase of the marketing research process by gathering secondary data. They may use available reports and other information from both internal and external sources to study a marketing problem.

reliability A condition that exists when a research technique produces almost identical results in repeated trials

validity A condition that exists when a research method measures what it is supposed to measure

primary data Data observed and recorded or collected directly from respondents

secondary data Data compiled both inside and outside the organization for some purpose other than the current investigation

Internal sources of secondary data, such as databases, sales records, and research reports, can be helpful because they provide information on the firm's own marketing activities. This information can be used to test hypotheses and pinpoint problems. From sales reports, for example, a firm can gather information such as the most popular times of the year for products, and which colors and sizes sell best. Marketers should look at any available tools for marketing, management, or financial purposes in their data search. Accounting records are often overlooked but can be a rich source of quantitative data. While they generally do not flow automatically to other departments, these records offer detailed information about costs, sales, customer accounts, and profits. Another source of internal secondary data is competitive information gathered by the sales force.

External sources of secondary data include trade associations, periodicals, government publications, unpublished sources, and online databases. Trade associations, such as the American Marketing Association, offer guides and directories that are full of information. Periodicals such as *Bloomberg Businessweek, The Wall Street Journal, Sales and Marketing Management, Advertising Age, Marketing Research,* and *Direct Selling News* publish general information that can help marketers define problems and develop hypotheses. Many marketers also consult federal government publications such as the *Statistical Abstract of the United States* and publications by the U.S. Census Bureau on Business, Agriculture, and the Population. Marketers can use searchable online databases, available through the Census website, to gather data on many different topics. Although the government only conducts its primary census every 10 years, it also conducts the American Community Survey (ACS), which is sent to population samples annually. The ACS is not as comprehensive as the decennial census, but it can provide marketers with an up-to-date picture of the nation's population. A company might use census data to determine, for example, whether the demographics, education, and income levels of a population in a specific area would make it a good place to construct a shopping mall.

The Internet is a very useful research tool. Search engines help marketers to quickly locate many types of secondary data or news and scholarly information research topics of interest. Many online retailers, for example, track customer purchases in order to gain a more complete understanding of their needs, desires, lifestyles, and income level. With this information, companies are able to cater recommendations to individuals based on the customer's previous purchases. Such a marketing system helps companies track the changing desires and buying habits of the most valuable customers. Furthermore, marketing researchers are increasingly monitoring blogs to discover what consumers are saying about their products—both positive and negative. Many retailers will send out products to popular bloggers with the hope that they will use them and feature the products and a review on their websites.

Methods of Collecting Primary Data

Collecting primary data is a lengthier, more expensive, and more complex process than collecting secondary data. To gather primary data, researchers use sampling procedures, survey methods, and observation. These efforts can be handled in-house by the firm's own research department or contracted to a private research firm such as ACNielsen or SymphonyIRI Group.

Sampling Because the time and resources available for research are limited, it is almost impossible to investigate all the members of a target market or other population. A **population**, or "universe," includes all the elements, units, or individuals of interest to researchers for a specific study. Consider a Gallup poll designed to predict the results of a presidential election. All registered voters in the United States constitute the population. By selecting a limited number of units—a **sample**—to represent the characteristics of a total population, researchers can predict the behaviors of the total population. **Sampling** in marketing research, therefore, is the process of selecting representative units from a population. Sampling techniques allow marketers to predict buying behavior fairly accurately without having to collect responses from a total population. Because it would be impossible in most situations to collect reactions from the entire market or market segment, most types of marketing research employ sampling techniques.

There are two basic types of sampling: probability sampling and nonprobability sampling. With **probability sampling**, every element in the population being studied has

population All the elements, units, or individuals of interest to researchers for a specific study

sample A limited number of units chosen to represent the characteristics of a total population

sampling The process of selecting representative units from a total population

probability sampling A type of sampling in which every element in the population being studied has a known chance of being selected for study

a known chance of being selected for study. Random sampling is a form of probability sampling. When marketers employ random sampling, all the units in a population have an equal chance of appearing in the sample. Likewise, the various events that can occur have an equal or known chance of taking place. For example, a specific card in a regulation playing deck has a 1 in 52 probability of being drawn. Sample units are ordinarily chosen by selecting from a table of random numbers statistically generated so that each digit, 0 through 9, will have an equal probability of occurring in each position in the sequence. The sequentially numbered elements of a population are sampled randomly by selecting the units whose numbers appear in the table of random numbers. There are random number generators, such as Random.org, available for free online, that will generate lists of random numbers for this purpose.

Another type of probability sampling is stratified sampling, in which the population of interest is divided into groups according to a common attribute, and a random sample is then chosen within each subgroup. A stratified sample may reduce some of the error that is a risk of a completely random sample, ensuring that a group is not accidentally over-represented. By segmenting a population into groups, the researcher makes sure that each segment receives its proportionate share of sample units and helps investigators avoid including too many or too few sample units from each subgroup. Samples are usually stratified when researchers believe there may be variations among different types of respondents. For instance, many political opinion surveys are stratified by gender, race, age, and/or geographic location.

The second type of sampling, nonprobability sampling, is more subjective than probability sampling because there is no way to calculate the probability that a specific element of the population being studied will be chosen. Quota sampling, for example, is highly judgmental because the final choice of participants is left to the researchers. In quota sampling, researchers divide the population into groups and then arbitrarily choose participants from each segment. In quota sampling, researchers impose some controls—usually limited to two or three variables, such as age, gender, or race—over the selection of participants to ensure that representative categories of respondents are included. A study of people who wear eyeglasses, for example, may be conducted by interviewing equal numbers of men and women. However, because quota samples are not probability samples, not everyone has an equal chance of being selected and sampling error therefore cannot be measured statistically. Quota samples are used most often in exploratory studies, when researchers have not yet generated hypotheses to test. In this case, the findings may provide valuable insights into a problem but cannot be extrapolated to the total population.

Survey Methods Marketing researchers often employ sampling to collect primary data through mail, telephone, personal interview, online, or social networking surveys. Table 4.2 summarizes and compares the advantages of the various survey methods. The results of such surveys are used to describe and analyze buying behavior. The survey method chosen depends on a variety of factors, including the nature of the problem or issue, the data needed to test the hypothesis, and the resources available to the researcher (e.g., funding and personnel). Marketers may employ more than one survey method depending on the goals of the research project. Surveys can be quite expensive, although online survey services have made the method much more affordable even for small firms. There are many companies that offer free or low-cost survey services, such as SurveyMonkey or Qualtrics.[15] Consider the advertisement for marketing research firm FocusVision. FocusVision uses an image of a multitool to describe its suite of products that can be used to collect both quantitative and qualitative data. For instance, FocusVision clients can use its Decipher platform to collect primary data through mobile and web surveys.

random sampling A form of probability sampling in which all units in a population have an equal chance of appearing in the sample, and the various events that can occur have an equal or known chance of taking place

stratified sampling A type of probability sampling in which the population is divided into groups with a common attribute and a random sample is chosen within each group

nonprobability sampling A sampling technique in which there is no way to calculate the likelihood that a specific element of the population being studied will be chosen

quota sampling A non-probability sampling technique in which researchers divide the population into groups and then arbitrarily choose participants from each group

All the tools you need are now in one place.

We've gathered worldwide leaders in qualitative and quantitative market research — so you can power all your research projects from one single source. Gain insight like never before through our full suite of market research products.

Source: FocusVision Worldwide, Inc

Collecting Primary Data
FocusVision offers a number of tools companies can use to collect both primary qualitative and quantitative market research.

TABLE 4.2	COMPARISON OF THE FOUR BASIC SURVEY METHODS			
	Mail Surveys	**Telephone Surveys**	**Online Surveys**	**Personal Interview Surveys**
Economy	Potentially lower in cost per interview than telephone or personal surveys. Low response rate a limitation.	Avoids interviewers' travel expenses. Limited by large part of population with cell phones.	The least expensive method. Non-response and privacy limits access to respondents.	The most expensive survey method. Shopping mall and focus-group interviews have lower costs than in-home interviews.
Flexibility	Inflexible. The questionnaire must be short and easy for respondents to complete.	Flexible because interviewers can ask probing questions, but observations are impossible.	Less flexible. Must be easy for online users to receive and return; short, concise questions work best.	The most flexible method. Respondents can react to visual materials. In-depth probes are possible.
Interviewer bias	Interviewer bias is eliminated. Questionnaires can be returned anonymously.	Some anonymity, but it may be hard to develop trust in respondents.	Interviewer bias is often eliminated, but privacy issues exist.	Interviewers' inability to maintain objectivity may result in bias.
Sampling and respondents' cooperation	Obtaining a complete mailing list is difficult. Nonresponse is a major disadvantage.	Sample limited to respondents with accessible telephones. Refusals are a problem.	The available e-mail address list may not be a representative sample for some purposes. Non-response an issue.	Not-at-homes are a problem, which may be overcome by focus-group and shopping mall interviewing.

Gathering information through surveys can be difficult because many people believe responding to surveys requires too much scarce personal time and may have concerns about invasions of privacy and how personal information will be used. The unethical use of selling techniques disguised as marketing surveys has also led to decreased cooperation. Hence, firms that choose to conduct surveys should anticipate a fairly high nonresponse rate. A danger in relying on survey responses when the nonresponse rate is high is that the results will not be representative of the sample as a whole.[16]

In a **mail survey**, questionnaires are sent to respondents who are encouraged to complete and return them. Mail surveys are used most often when the individuals in the sample are spread over a wide area and funds for the survey are limited. A mail survey is less expensive than a telephone or personal interview survey, as long as the response rate is high enough to produce reliable results.

Premiums, or incentives, that encourage respondents to return questionnaires can be effective in encouraging mail survey response rates and developing panels of respondents who are interviewed regularly. Such mail panels, selected to represent a target market or market segment, are especially useful in evaluating new products and providing general information about customers, as well as records of their purchases (in the form of purchase diaries). Mail panels and purchase diaries are much more widely used than custom mail surveys, but both panels and purchase diaries have shortcomings. People who take the time to fill out a diary may differ from the general population based on income, education, or behavior, such as the time available for shopping activities. Internet and social networking surveys have also greatly gained in popularity, although they are similarly limited—given that not all demographics utilize these media equally.

In a **telephone survey**, an interviewer records respondents' answers to a questionnaire over the phone. A telephone survey has some advantages over a mail survey. The rate of

mail survey A research method in which respondents answer a questionnaire sent through the mail

telephone survey A research method in which respondents' answers to a questionnaire are recorded by an interviewer on the phone

response is higher because it takes less effort to answer the telephone and talk than to fill out and return a questionnaire. If enough interviewers are available, a telephone survey can be completed very quickly. Political candidates or organizations that want an immediate reaction to an event may choose this method. In addition, a telephone survey permits interviewers to gain rapport with respondents and ask probing questions. Automated telephone surveys, also known as interactive voice response or "robosurveys," rely on a recorded voice to ask the questions while a computer program records respondents' answers. The primary benefit of automated surveys is the elimination of any bias that might be introduced by a live researcher. However, because of abuse of robosurveys during events such as political campaigns, many people have negative associations with them.

Another option is the **telephone depth interview**, which combines the traditional focus group's ability to probe with the confidentiality provided by a telephone survey. This type of interview is most appropriate for qualitative research projects among a small targeted group. This method can be appealing to busy respondents because they can choose the time and day for the interview. Although this method is difficult to implement, it can yield revealing information from respondents who otherwise would be unwilling to participate in marketing research.

A major shortcoming is that only a small proportion of the population likes to participate in telephone surveys or interviews. Many households are excluded from telephone directories by choice (unlisted numbers) or because the residents moved after the directory was published. Potential respondents often use telephone answering machines, voice mail, or caller ID to screen or block calls. Millions have also signed up for "Do Not Call Lists." Additionally, a shrinking proportion of the population has landlines, making conducting phone surveys more difficult. In fact, 49 percent of households have a cell phone but no landline telephones.[17] These factors can significantly limit participation and distort representation. Moreover, surveys and interviews conducted over the telephone are often limited to oral communication and do not include visual aids or observation. Many companies are using Skype so that interviewers can have personal interaction with respondents and show products. Although this method is difficult to implement, it can yield revealing information from respondents who otherwise would be unwilling to participate in marketing research.

In a **personal interview survey**, participants respond to questions face-to-face. Various audiovisual aids—pictures, products, diagrams, or prerecorded advertising copy—can be incorporated into a personal interview. Rapport gained through direct interaction usually permits more in-depth interviewing, including probes, follow-up questions, or psychological tests. In addition, because personal interviews can be longer than other survey types, they may yield more information. Respondents can be selected more carefully, and reasons for nonresponse can be explored. One such research technique is the **in-home (door-to-door) interview**. The in-home interview offers a clear advantage when thoroughness of self-disclosure and elimination of group influence are important. In an in-depth interview of 45 to 90 minutes, respondents can be probed to reveal their true motivations, feelings, behaviors, and aspirations. Door-to-door interviewing is increasingly difficult due to respondent and interviewer security and safety issues. This method is particularly limited in gated communities such as condos or apartments.

Over time, the nature of personal interviews has changed. In the past, most personal interviews, which were based on random sampling or prearranged appointments, were conducted in the respondent's home. Today, many personal interviews are conducted in shopping malls or other public areas. **Shopping mall intercept interviews** involve interviewing a percentage of individuals who pass by an "intercept" point in a mall. Like any face-to-face interviewing method, mall intercepts have advantages. The interviewer is in a position to recognize and react to respondents' nonverbal behavior. Respondents can view product prototypes, videotapes of commercials, and other materials, and provide their opinions. Also, the mall environment lets the researcher control for complex situational variables that may be present in individuals' homes.

telephone depth interview An interview that combines the traditional focus group's ability to probe with the confidentiality provided by telephone surveys

personal interview survey A research method in which participants respond to survey questions face-to-face

in-home (door-to-door) interview A personal interview that takes place in the respondent's home

shopping mall intercept interviews A research method that involves interviewing a percentage of individuals passing by "intercept" points in a mall

An **on-site computer interview** is a variation of the shopping mall intercept interview in which respondents complete a self-administered questionnaire displayed on a computer monitor. A computer software package can be used to conduct such interviews. After a brief lesson on how to operate the software, respondents proceed through the survey at their own pace. Questionnaires can be adapted so that respondents see only those items (usually a subset of an entire scale) that may provide useful information about their attitudes.

Online and Social Media Surveys As more and more consumers have Internet access and connect regularly, the Internet has become an increasingly important research and marketing resource. Internet surveys are quickly becoming the predominant tool for general population sampling, in part because of their relatively low cost and ability to target specific samples. In an **online survey**, questionnaires can be transmitted to respondents either through e-mail or via a website. Marketing researchers often send these surveys to online panel samples purchased from professional brokers or compiled by the company. E-mail is semi-interactive, meaning recipients can ask for question clarification or pose questions of their own. The potential advantages of online surveys are quick response time and lower cost than traditional mail, telephone, and personal interview surveys, if the response rate is adequate. Increasingly, firms use their websites to conduct surveys. They may include a premium, such as a chance to win a prize, to encourage participation. In addition, online surveys can be completed via mobile devices. For example, apps on smartphones can collect online information without active moment-to-moment participation by respondents.[18]

Online technology providers also offer software for conducting Internet surveys. One of the largest online survey providers is Qualtrics. Qualtrics provides software to firms who want to develop their own online surveys that they can circulate online.[19] The company also offers services such as concept testing, data collection, and employee feedback. It has 8,000 clients in 90 countries and runs approximately 2.1 million surveys each day.[20] Qualtrics's flexibility and research capabilities have caught the attention of many companies who want to learn more about their customers, including JetBlue. JetBlue used Qualtrics software to understand customer opinions on individual flights.[21]

Social networking sites are also used to conduct surveys. Marketers can also utilize digital media forums such as chat rooms, blogs, newsgroups, and research communities to identify trends in consumer interests and consumption patterns. However, using these forums for conducting surveys has limitations. Consumers must choose to visit a particular social media site or blog, which eliminates sample randomness, and it may be difficult to obtain a representative sample size if site traffic or participation rates are low. On the other hand, they can provide marketers with a general idea of consumer trends and preferences. Movies, consumer electronics, food, and computers are popular topics in many online communities. Indeed, by merely monitoring ongoing online conversations, marketers may be able to identify new-product opportunities and consumer needs. Free and low-cost services, such as Google Analytics, can help a firm monitor online traffic to a website and track whether users have linked from a social networking site. Klout is a company that measures the social influence of brands on social networking sites. The company collects search data as well as information from 13 social networks to determine the influence and reach of a brand.[22] Companies like Klout can help a firm better understand consumer needs and behaviors, as well as how to target them more effectively. A major advantage of online data is that it can be gathered at little incremental cost compared to alternative data sources.

Crowdsourcing combines the words *crowd* and *outsourcing* and calls for taking tasks usually performed by a marketer or researcher and outsourcing them to a crowd, or potential market, through an open call. In the case of digital marketing, crowdsourcing is often used to obtain the opinions or needs of the crowd (or potential markets). There are entire sites dedicated to crowdsourcing. Consider Lego's crowdsourcing platform Lego Ideas. Lego Ideas is a site that invites consumers to submit ideas for Lego sets.

on-site computer interview A variation of the shopping mall intercept interview in which respondents complete a self-administered questionnaire displayed on a computer monitor

online survey A research method in which respondents answer a questionnaire via e-mail or on a website

crowdsourcing Combines the words *crowd* and *outsourcing* and calls for taking tasks usually performed by a marketer or researcher and outsourcing them to a crowd, or potential market, through an open call

DIGITAL MARKETING

Digital Marketing Research Leads to Behavioral Advertising

It is no secret that online advertisers track consumer Internet activity and use the information to target ads toward each person's interests and preferences. These efforts used to be largely limited to individual websites tracking their own visitors. Now, however, technology enables the tracking of Internet users across sites. For example, every site with Facebook's "Like" button—as well as every smartphone app installed—sends Facebook information, which it then uses to target ads to its users.

Marketers claim this is a win–win for businesses and consumers. When ads are targeted to each user's behavior, users are more likely to see offerings in which they have an interest, improving their online experience. Targeted ads are also more efficient for businesses. Some privacy advocates, however, criticize the tracking of Internet users without their consent. Another concern is keeping information secure in a digital environment where hacking attempts are increasing. Privacy advocates therefore argue that behavioral advertising should be strictly regulated. Self-regulation is also an option. Facebook, for instance, now offers an online tool that allows users to opt out of having ads shown to them based on sites they have visited outside the social network.[a]

Those ideas that get 10,000 votes are reviewed by the firm for possible development. If the Lego set is chosen for development, the creator gets 1 percent of the product's total net sales.[23] Additionally, on threadless.com participants can submit and score T-shirt designs. Designs with the highest votes are printed and then sold. Crowdsourcing is a way for marketers to gather input straight from willing consumers and to actively listen to people's ideas and evaluations on products.

One Internet system that uses crowdsourcing to connect people from across the world is Amazon's Mechanical Turk (MTurk). MTurk is an online marketplace that connects requesters for tasks with workers willing to complete them. MTurk operates on the premise that there are still various tasks that only humans, and not computers, can complete. Based on this idea, MTurk allows companies and entrepreneurs to crowdsource human intelligence tasks (HITs) to workers worldwide. Workers who are equipped to complete these tasks have the flexibility to work their own hours from their homes. Money for the tasks is deposited into MTurk accounts.[24] The data generated from these crowdsourcing processes have been found to be just as reliable as data gathered through more traditional methods.[25] However, others have criticized MTurk because it is sometimes impossible to determine if respondents are representing themselves accurately. There has been a tendency for more respondents to be from countries outside of the United States. Freelancers who use MTurk have also complained that they are seen as little more than algorithms rather than skilled workers.[26]

Marketing research will likely rely heavily on online surveys in the future, particularly as negative attitudes toward other survey methods, such as telephone surveys, render them less representative and more expensive. Internet surveys have especially strong potential within organizations whose employees are networked and for associations that publish members' e-mail addresses. However, there are some ethical issues to consider when using e-mail for marketing research, such as unsolicited e-mail, which could be viewed as "spam," and privacy, as some survey respondents fear their personal information will be given or sold to third parties without their knowledge or permission. Additionally, as with direct mail, Internet surveys have a good chance of being discarded, particularly with users who receive dozens of e-mails every day.

A serious challenge for firms conducting online surveys is obtaining a sample that is representative of the population. While Internet surveys allow respondents to retain their anonymity and flexibility, they can also enable survey takers to abuse the system. For instance, some survey takers respond multiple times or pose as other people, particularly when the survey pays or offers a reward to respondents. To get around this problem, companies are developing screening mechanisms and instituting limits on how many surveys

Questionnaire Construction
Many more questionnaires are delivered online, often tied to an online shopping experience.

one person can take.[27] Survey programs, such as Qualtrics, automatically delete surveys that appear suspicious.

Questionnaire Construction A carefully constructed questionnaire is essential to the success of any survey. Questions must be clear, easy to understand, and directed toward a specific objective, meaning they must be designed to elicit information that meets the study's data requirements. Defining the objective of a questionnaire before construction will provide a guide to the substance of the questions and ensure that they yield useful information that contributes to the research project. The most important rule in composing questions is to maintain impartiality.

The questions are usually of three kinds: open-ended, dichotomous, and multiple-choice. Open-ended questions should be used carefully, as it is very difficult to code the responses in such a way as to easily analyze the data later. Problems may develop in the analysis of dichotomous or multiple-choice questions when responses for one outcome outnumber others. For example, a dichotomous question that asks respondents to choose between "buy" or "not buy" might require additional sampling from the disproportionately smaller group if there were not enough responses to analyze.[28] Researchers must also be very careful about questions that a respondent might consider too personal or that might require an admission of activities that other people are likely to condemn. Researchers must word questions carefully so as not to offend respondents.

Observation Methods When observing subjects of a research sample, researchers record individuals' overt behavior, taking note of physical conditions and events. They avoid direct contact with subjects and instead monitor their actions systematically. For instance, researchers might use observation methods to answer the question, "How long does the average McDonald's restaurant customer have to wait in line before being served?" Observation may include the use of ethnographic techniques, such as watching customers interact with a product in a real-world environment. Observation may also be combined with interviews. For instance, during a personal interview, the condition of a respondent's home or other possessions may be observed and recorded. The interviewer can also directly observe and confirm such demographic information as race, approximate age, and gender.

Data gathered through observation can sometimes be biased if the subject is aware of the observation process and adapts his or her behavior accordingly. However, a researcher can place an observer in a natural market environment, such as a grocery store, without influencing shoppers' actions. If the presence of a human observer is likely to bias the outcome or if human sensory abilities are inadequate, mechanical means may be used to record behavior. Mechanical observation devices include cameras, recorders, counting machines, scanners, and equipment that record physiological changes. A special camera can be used to record the eye movements of people as they look at an advertisement. Tracking the eye movements of online shoppers has revealed that function and non-functionality product characteristics result in greater eye movement and intensity,[29] suggesting that using these attributes in product descriptions could engage viewers more thoroughly. Cameras detect the sequence of reading and the parts of the advertisement that receive the greatest attention. The electronic scanners used in supermarkets are another mechanical means of gathering observational data. They provide accurate data on sales and customers' purchase patterns. In many cases, marketing researchers are able to buy the data from stores. Retailers have turned observation into a science, keeping vast databases of all individual shoppers' purchases and demographic information in order to assemble an aggregate overview of their shoppers, as well as a complete picture of each individual customer's lifestyle, habits, and product needs and how they change over time.[30]

Observation is straightforward and avoids a central problem of survey methods: motivating respondents to state their true feelings or opinions. However, observation tends to be descriptive and may not provide insights into causal relationships. Another drawback is that analyses based on observation are subject to the observer's biases or the limitations of the device being used.

Interpreting Research Findings
Marketing research teams spend considerable time overviewing data and interpreting the findings.

4-3d Interpreting Research Findings

After collecting data to test their hypotheses, marketers need to interpret the research findings. Interpretation of the data is easier if marketers carefully plan their data analysis methods early in the research process. They should allow for continual evaluation of the data during the entire collection period. In this way, marketers gain valuable insights into areas that should be probed during the formal analysis.

In most cases, the first step researchers will take is to assemble the data into a table format. Cross-tabulation may be useful, especially in tabulating joint occurrences, for data that will be used across categories of things or people studied. For example, using the two variables of gender and purchase rates of automobile tires, a cross-tabulation will show how men and women differ in purchasing automobile tires.

After the data are tabulated, they must be analyzed. **Statistical interpretation** focuses on what is typical and what deviates from the average. It indicates how widely responses vary and how they are distributed in relation to the variable being measured. When marketers interpret statistics, they must take into account estimates of expected error or deviation from the true values of the population. The analysis of data may lead researchers to accept or reject their hypothesis. Data require careful interpretation and a firm may choose to enlist an expert consultant or computer software to ensure accuracy. In a marketing environment increasingly filled with data, errors are possible and it is ever more important to interpret data correctly. If a researcher improperly analyzes data, he or she could reach the wrong conclusion, leading to a cascade of effects that might render a marketing strategy useless. Because so many firms engage in high-tech analysis, a firm must take steps to ensure that it has competitive tools at its disposal.

If the results of a study are valid, the decision maker should take action. If a question has been incorrectly or poorly worded, however, the results may produce poor decisions. Consider the research conducted for a food marketer that asked respondents to rate a product on criteria such as "hearty flavor," as well as how important each criterion was to the respondent. Although such results may have had utility for advertising purposes, they are less helpful in product development because it is not possible to objectively determine a meaning for the subjective term "hearty flavor." Managers must understand the research results and relate them to a context that permits effective decision making.

4-3e Reporting Research Findings

The final step in the marketing research process is to report the research findings. Before preparing the report, the marketer must objectively analyze the findings to determine whether the research is as complete as it can be and how well the data answer the research question and support or negate the hypothesis. Most research will not have answered the research question completely. Thus, the researcher must point out deficiencies and their causes in the report. While writing, researchers must keep the report's audience in mind and ensure that findings are relevant to the firm. They should also determine before writing how much detail and supporting data to include. Research is not useful unless it supports the organization's overall strategy and objectives.

If an outside research agency was contracted, it is important that it fully understand the client's business. Those responsible for preparing the report must facilitate adjusting the

statistical interpretation
Analysis of what is typical and what deviates from the average

findings to the environment, as it can change over time. The report must be helpful to marketers and managers on an ongoing basis.[31]

The report is usually a formal, written document. Researchers must allocate sufficient time when they plan and schedule the project for compiling and writing it, since this task can be time-consuming. Report writers should keep in mind that corporate executives prefer reports that are short, clear, and simply expressed. To address this desire, researchers often give their recommendations first, in an executive summary, followed by details on how the results were obtained. This way, executives can easily see the results of the report without spending time on the details. A technical report allows its users to analyze data and interpret recommendations because it describes the research methods and procedures and the most important data gathered. Thus, researchers must recognize the needs and expectations of the report user and adapt to them.

4-4 USING TECHNOLOGY TO IMPROVE MARKETING INFORMATION GATHERING AND ANALYSIS

LO 4-4 Describe the tools, such as databases, big data, and marketing analytics, useful to marketing decision making.

Technology and the Internet have made the information required for marketing decisions more accessible than ever. Marketers can easily track customer buying behavior, obtain detailed demographic profiles, and anticipate what buyers want—making it possible to fine-tune marketing mixes to satisfy customers. Big data enhances customer relationship management (CRM) by integrating data from all customer contacts and combining that information to improve customer retention. The use of big data is helping marketers discover customer insights that would have been hard to discover through traditional methods. Information technology permits for easy internal research and quick information gathering to help marketers better understand and satisfy customers. CRM has been enhanced by the ability to integrate and access data from all customer contacts.

Consumer feedback is an important aspect of marketing research, and new technology has enhanced this process. Most consumers read online product reviews on a myriad of sites, from Amazon to Yelp, when making purchase decisions. While this represents a tremendous opportunity for firms to generate new customers, they must also be aware of fake product reviews and the potentially negative effect they can have on consumer perception. Increasingly, too, while consumers utilize product reviews, they are also wary of them; companies have been found guilty of paying people claiming to be unbiased customers to write positive reviews of products.[32] Thus, as with any other resource, firms must manage digital resources with caution to maintain a high level of consumer trust and satisfaction.

Finally, companies of all sizes have unprecedented access to industry forecasts, business trends, and customer buying behavior—which improves communication, understanding of the marketing environment, and marketing research capabilities. Many firms use marketing information systems, CRM technologies, and cloud computing to network technologies and organize the marketing data available to them. In this section, we look at marketing information systems and specific technologies that are helping marketing researchers obtain and manage marketing research data.

4-4a Marketing Information Systems

marketing information system (MIS) A framework for managing and structuring information gathered regularly from sources inside and outside the organization

A **marketing information system (MIS)** is a framework for the day-to-day management and structuring of information gathered regularly from sources both inside and outside the organization. As such, an MIS provides a continuous flow of information about prices, advertising expenditures, sales, competition, and distribution expenses and can be an important asset for developing effective marketing strategies. The main focuses of an MIS are on data storage and retrieval, computer capabilities, and management's information requirements. MIS can help with producing regular sales reports by product or market categories, data on inventory levels, and records of salespeople's activities, which can all help in marketing decision making. Most firms develop a dashboard display where data can be integrated into useful management reports for strategic and tactical decisions.

database A collection of information arranged for easy access and retrieval

An effective MIS starts by determining the objective of the information—that is, by identifying decision needs that require certain information. The firm then specifies an information system for continuous monitoring to provide regular, pertinent information on both the external and internal environments. Shipping companies such as FedEx have interactive marketing information systems that provide instantaneous communication between the company and customers. Customers can track their packages via the Internet and receive immediate feedback concerning delivery. The company's website provides researchers with information about customer usage and allows customers to convey opinions on company services. The evolving telecommunications and computer technologies allow marketers to use information systems to cultivate one-to-one relationships with customers.

4-4b Databases

Most marketing information systems include internal databases. A **database** is a collection of information arranged for easy access and retrieval. It is a structured set of data that can be used in many ways. Databases allow marketers to tap into an abundance of information useful in making marketing decisions—internal sales reports, newspaper articles, company news releases, government economic reports, and bibliographies—often accessed through a computer system. Information technology has made it possible for firms to develop databases that are vastly enhanced in their speed and storage capacity to guide strategic planning and improve customer service.

Customer relationship management (CRM) employs database marketing techniques to identify different types of customers and develop specific strategies for interacting with each customer. CRM incorporates these three elements:

1. Identifying and building a database of current and potential consumers, including a wide range of demographic, lifestyle, and purchase information.

EMERGING TRENDS IN MARKETING

Making Meaning Out of Big Data: Marketing Analytics

The field of marketing research is changing. Where it was once dominated by focus groups and surveys, today's marketers are increasingly turning to marketing analytics to glean customer insights. A report found that large business-to-consumer firms are planning to increase their spending on marketing analytics by almost 100 percent in a three-year period. Eighty-three percent of business leaders pursue big data projects in the belief that it will provide their firms with a competitive advantage. The advantages of marketing analytics are not limited to business-to-consumer firms; approximately 79 percent of businesses that sell to other businesses believe analytics is important in identifying marketing channels that increase return on investment.

It is not enough simply to record big data. The hard part is determining which small bits of information among massive data files will reveal significant customer insights. However, interpreting big data correctly can help marketers recognize trends they never would have realized otherwise. For instance, one analytics firm helped a mobile phone manufacturer determine that the major reason consumers bought its phone was not because of the camera, which is what the firm thought, but because of a certain app built into the phone. There is no doubt that marketing analytics has begun to revolutionize marketers' understanding of customer trends and preferences.[b]

2. Delivering differential messages according to each consumer's preferences and characteristics through established and new media channels.
3. Tracking customer relationships to monitor the costs of retaining individual customers and the lifetime value of their purchases.[33]

Nearly all firms collect customer information in databases. For instance, many commercial websites require consumers to register and provide personal information before accessing the site or making a purchase. Frequent-flyer programs ask loyal customers to participate in surveys about their needs and desires and track their best customers' flight patterns by time of day, week, month, and year. Supermarkets frequently offer store discount cards, which allow them to gain consumer data on purchases through checkout scanners.

Marketing researchers can also use databases, such as LexisNexis or online commercial databases, for a fee, to obtain useful information for marketing decisions. To find research within a database, a user typically searches by keyword, topic, or company, and the database service generates abstracts, articles, or reports. Information provided by a single firm on household demographics, purchases, television viewing behavior, and responses to promotions such as coupons and free samples is called **single-source data**. For example, BehaviorScan Rx ad testing, offered by IRI, allows different TV advertisements to be played in the same market. It is also able to discover important links between TV viewing behaviors and consumer activities.[34] It is important that marketers gather longitudinal (long-term) information on customers to maximize the usefulness of single-source data.

4-4c **Big Data**

Big data has the potential to revolutionize the way businesses gather marketing research and develop tailored marketing campaigns. **Big data** involves massive data files that can be obtained from both structured and unstructured databases. Big data often consists of high-volume data that marketers can use to discover unique insights and make more knowledgeable marketing decisions.[35] Big data can include mountains of data collected from social networks, RFID, retailer scanning, purchases, logistics, and production.[36] The amount of data that can be gleaned from consumer activities and purchase patterns yields significant insights for marketers. The complexity of big data requires sophisticated software to store and analyze it.[37] It also requires marketers to identify and understand how to use this data to develop stronger customer relationships. Many firms such as Walmart, Whole Foods, and General Electric are adopting centralized systems to integrate disparate data and glean the most insights about consumers.[38]

Big data presents a new opportunity to use IT-enabled information to assist in marketing decision making. The amount of data is rapidly increasing through an array of generating sources, including mobile devices, Internet searches, behavioral observations, and tracking of purchase behavior. Marketers want to use this data to create competitive advantages that will help them discover new insights into customer behavior. Many companies are optimistic that increasingly advanced methodologies for analyzing and interpreting big data will lead to the development of new innovations with major impacts for society.[39]

The positive impact that big data has had upon marketing is undeniable. For instance, Samsung Mobile marketers used data on customers to prioritize key target markets and improve its marketing efforts. The result in the United States was an increase in brand preference from a relative score of -6 to $+2$.[40] According to research studies, 81 percent of companies that utilize big data effectively in marketing have seen sales increase as a result, as well as an increase of 73 percent in customer satisfaction.[41] Unlike other forms of marketing research, using big data can reveal specific details about consumers that would be hard to discover in other ways. The marketing vice president at DataSift—an organization that analyzes social data—has determined that his company's software can mine 400 pieces of data from a 140-character tweet.[42] For these reasons, Johnson & Johnson is partnering with IBM to use IBM's big-data service, Watson, to assess the probability of success for drugs before

single-source data Information provided by a single marketing research firm

big data Involves massive data files that can be obtained from both structured and unstructured databases

their release to the market. Johnson & Johnson hopes this partnership will help speed up its development of new drugs.[43]

Big data is important because marketers can look at patterns of consumption behavior and discover trends that predict future buying behaviors. Not all of these patterns would be as visible through traditional marketing research methods. It is obvious, for instance, that a woman buying baby supplies is likely pregnant or has a new baby. However, other consumption patterns are less obvious. Target has found that purchases of larger quantities of unscented lotions, cotton balls, scent-free soap, and supplements are also predictors of pregnancy. Target discovered these trends by analyzing its collection of data on consumer purchases. These discoveries have allowed the firm to accurately predict pregnancy. As a result, it has been able to send out marketing materials, such as coupons for diapers, to this demographic in the hopes that they will become future loyal customers.[44] Big data can therefore improve the relationship between company and consumer.

Despite the benefits of big data to marketing research, the challenge for marketers is to figure out how to use pieces of data to develop more targeted marketing strategies. Marketers must know what data to examine, which analytical tools to use, and how to translate this data into customer insights.[45] Big data is useless if an organization's marketers do not know how to use it. Mining big data for customer insights takes much time and energy. In one research study surveying marketers, a little more than half indicated that their organizations had a good understanding of big data. A major reason is that many marketers do not understand the definition of big data or its benefits.[46] Additionally, as with marketing research, big data can still be subject to bias, projection error, and sampling issues.[47]

Although big data yields tremendous insights into consumer preferences, lifestyles, and behaviors, it also creates serious privacy issues. Many consumers do not like to have their purchases or behaviors tracked, and sometimes using big data for marketing purposes creates conflict. On the other hand, social media networks such as Facebook and Twitter provide listening centers to monitor conversation about products and companies. Listening to different social media can reveal what consumers say about a specific brand, competitors, industry, and how consumers interact with all of these.[48] Pinpointing desires and needs of the target market creates big data files that require marketing analytics to aid in strategy development and to indicate how to adjust existing strategies. Although the benefits of big data for marketing are numerous, they may come at the expense of consumer privacy. While some consumers appreciate the added benefits of receiving marketing materials specifically targeted toward their needs, others feel uncomfortable with companies knowing so much about them. At the same time, companies that ignore big data miss out on the opportunity to develop stronger marketing strategies and customer relationships. Firms such as Zoomdata help to organize big data so that it can be visualized quickly in any data type. Zoomdata provides analytics that can provide marketing insights to make the right decision. Avoiding big data could cause a business to sacrifice a competitive advantage. Although there is no easy solution to this issue, consumers can do one thing if they do not want their store purchases tracked: pay in cash. However, some stores still track purchases by recording customer account numbers for frequent purchase rewards.

Big Data
Zoomdata is a company that assists organizations in analyzing big data.

4-4d Marketing Analytics

Big data is of little use without tools to measure and interpret the data to glean insights and develop better-targeted marketing campaigns. As digital marketing has become more popular, adding more complexity to the field of marketing, organizations have found the need to focus more extensively on how to measure the effectiveness of their marketing strategies. **Marketing analytics** uses tools and methods to measure and interpret the effectiveness of

marketing analytics Uses tools and methods to measure and interpret the effectiveness of a firm's marketing activities

a firm's marketing activities. The purpose of marketing analytics is to evaluate the company's return on investment (ROI) on their marketing strategies and make adjustments when necessary. This usually involves investing in software that can track, store, and analyze data. Big data linked to analytics software unlocks insights with decision-ready intelligence. For example, SAP provides advanced marketing analytics software with predictive features. Investing in marketing analytics involves the following four steps: (1) defining what to measure and which tools to use, (2) collecting data, (3) developing reporting capabilities, and (4) implementing the campaign and analyzing the results.[49] Having the right data and the right methods is necessary in our data-rich business environment.[50]

Marketing analytics is considered one of the most important marketing research tools to aid strategic decisions and implementation. Development in software can automate analysis of massive amounts of data available to marketers. Databases provide the opportunity to engage in data mining to better understand the attitudes and behaviors of consumers. Retailers create data from checkout scanners that can be used to determine purchasing patterns. For example, in a supermarket if consumers are buying Kashi cereal and Silk soy milk at the same time, maybe there could be a joint promotion.

Dashboards are a data management tool that visually communicate important information for decision making. Dashboards can convert data analytics to easy-to-use key performance indicators (KPIs). The dashboard is a way to provide a report of findings and make them available so a variety of marketers in different positions can use the data to make decisions. For example, Wave Analytics is an IT company that provides self-service analytics that the marketer can see instantly on any device. Therefore, decision makers can gain knowledge and take action. The ability to harness trillions of gigabytes of data and convert it to useable information provides marketing research findings on demand.

Marketing analytics is becoming an increasingly important part in companies' marketing activities, even among mid-sized and smaller organizations. More than 30 percent of companies have integrated marketing analytics into the daily activities of the marketing function, and marketing professionals believe that an increasing percentage of the marketing budget should go toward analytics. Web analytics have become highly important for measuring marketing effectiveness. More than 82 percent of marketers that use analytics tools measure their website traffic and performance.[51] Google Analytics is the most popular web analytics software and can be helpful for small businesses without a large marketing budget because its basic functions are free to use. Marketers use Google Analytics to measure website visitors, page views, the percentage of new visits, the average amount of time spent during a visit, and more.[52] Even more sophisticated marketing analytics software is available for marketers who want a more in-depth look at the effectiveness of their marketing activities that can be tied to ROI.

The highest goal marketers appear to have with marketing analytics is identifying how to develop better-targeted marketing strategies.[53] British Airways, for example, has successfully used marketing analytics to increase activities geared toward forming relationships with customers. It adopted a marketing analytics program that combined information on customer loyalty with information on the online behavior and buying patterns of the company's 20 million customers. The software has enabled the company to target thank-you messages to their most loyal customers and offer incentives.[54] The successful deployment of marketing analytics positively relates to favorable and sustainable marketing performance. Research shows that a one-unit increase in marketing analytics deployment results in an 8 percent increase in a company's return on assets.[55] It is therefore imperative that marketers investigate which marketing analytics metrics would best work for their companies to improve marketing performance and maintain competitive advantages.

Marketing Analytics
Google Analytics is the most popular web analytics software.

IB Photography/Shutterstock.com

4-5 ISSUES IN MARKETING RESEARCH

LO 4-5 Identify ethical and international issues in marketing research.

Marketers should identify and be aware of concerns that can influence the integrity of research, such as ethical issues and the international environment. Ethical issues are a constant risk in gathering and maintaining consistently high-quality information. International issues relate to environmental differences, such as culture, legal requirements, level of technology, and economic development.

4-5a The Importance of Ethical Marketing Research

Marketing managers and other professionals increasingly rely on marketing research, marketing information systems, and new technologies to make better decisions. Therefore, it is essential that professional standards be established by which to judge the reliability of marketing research. Such standards are necessary because of the ethical and legal issues that can develop in gathering marketing research data. For example, many consumers are wary of how their personal information collected by marketers will be used, especially whether it will be sold to third parties. Issues related to data privacy are discussed in Chapter 9.

Marketing research requires understanding of acceptable activities that ensure the integrity of gathering, analyzing, and reporting data. To provide standards and guidelines, organizations such as the Marketing Research Association have developed codes of conduct and guidelines that promote ethical marketing research. To be effective, such guidelines must instruct marketing researchers on how to avoid misconduct. Table 4.3 provides sample steps researchers should follow when introducing a questionnaire to a customer in order to ensure respondent cooperation and satisfaction.

Firms have the responsibility to refrain from misusing detailed data on customer demographics, interests, and behavior. This information has allowed companies to predict customer behavior and life changes more accurately, but many feel it infringes upon consumer privacy.[56] Amazon, Netflix, and eBay all use data to provide customized recommendations based on customers' interests, ratings, or past purchases. Companies use data collected by firms that specialize in tracking consumers' online behavior. While such data enable companies to offer more personalized services, policy makers fear that it could also allow them to

TABLE 4.3	GUIDELINES FOR QUESTIONNAIRE INTRODUCTION

- Allow interviewers to introduce themselves by name.
- State the name of the research company.
- Indicate that this questionnaire is a marketing research project.
- Explain that no sales will be involved.
- Note the general topic of discussion (if this is a problem in a blind study, a statement such as "consumer opinion" is acceptable).
- State the likely duration of the interview.
- Assure the anonymity of the respondent and the confidentiality of all answers.
- State the honorarium, if applicable (for many business-to-business and medical studies, this is done up-front for both qualitative and quantitative studies).
- Reassure the respondent with a statement such as, "There are no right or wrong answers, so please give thoughtful and honest answers to each question" (recommended by many clients).

Source: Reprinted with the permission of The Marketing Research Association.

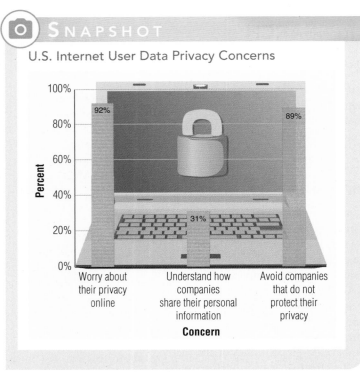

U.S. Internet User Data Privacy Concerns

Source: U.S. Consumer Privacy Index 2016, https://www.truste.com/resources/privacy-research/ncsa-consumer-privacy-index-us/ (accessed March 18, 2017).

discriminate against consumers who do not appear to be "valuable" customers.[57] Many consumers also believe that their online behavior could be used to identify them personally.[58]

4-5b International Issues in Marketing Research

As we shall see in Chapter 8, sociocultural, economic, political, legal, and technological forces vary in different regions of the world. These variations create challenges for the organizations that are attempting to understand foreign customers through marketing research. While the marketing research process is generally the same around the world, some regional differences exist. To make certain that firms are sufficiently aware of global and regional differences, many companies retain a research firm, or at least a researcher, with experience in the country of interest. Most of the largest marketing research firms derive a significant share of their revenues from research conducted outside the United States. For example, the Nielsen Company, the largest marketing research firm in the world, is a U.S. company but has a market presence in over 100 different countries. About 47.5 percent of Nielsen's revenue is generated from outside of the country.[59]

Experts recommend a two-pronged approach to conducting international marketing research. The first phase involves a detailed search for and analysis of secondary data to gain a greater understanding of a particular marketing environment and to pinpoint key regional issues that could affect primary research data. Secondary data can be particularly helpful in building a general understanding of the market, including economic, legal, cultural, and demographic issues, as well as in assessing the opportunities and risks of doing business in that market, and in forecasting demand. Marketing researchers often begin by gaining a general overview through country trade reports from the U.S. Department of Commerce, trade and general business publications such as *The Wall Street Journal,* and country-specific publications and websites. These sources can offer insights into a country's marketing environment and might indicate untapped market opportunities.

International Marketing Research
Marketing research firms strive to understand differences in global dietary norms; for instance, many Asian countries consider insects a delicacy.

The second phase involves field research using many of the methods described earlier, including focus groups and telephone surveys, to refine a firm's understanding of specific customer needs and preferences. Differences between countries can have a profound influence on data-gathering techniques. For instance, in-home (door-to-door) interviews are illegal in some places. In developing countries, many people have only cell phones, making telephone surveys less practical and less representative of the total population. Primary data gathering generally will have a greater chance of success if the firm employs local researchers who understand how to approach potential respondents and can do so in their own languages.[60] Regardless of the specific methods used to gather primary data, whether in the United States or abroad, the goal is to recognize the needs of specific target markets to craft the best possible marketing strategy to satisfy the needs of customers in each market, as we will see in the next chapter.

Chapter Review

4-1 Define marketing research and its importance to decision makers.

Marketing research is a critical step in developing a marketing strategy. It is the systematic design, collection, interpretation, and reporting of information to help marketers solve specific marketing problems or take advantage of marketing opportunities. It is a process for gathering information not currently available to decision makers. Marketing research can help a firm better understand market opportunities, ascertain the potential for success of new products, and determine the feasibility of a particular marketing strategy. The value of marketing research is measured by improvements in a marketer's ability to make decisions.

To maintain the control needed to obtain accurate information, marketers approach marketing research as a process with some basic logical steps: (1) locating and defining problems or issues, (2) designing the research project, (3) collecting data, (4) interpreting research findings, and (5) reporting research findings.

4-2 Distinguish between exploratory and conclusive research.

Marketers conduct exploratory research when they need more information about a problem or want to make a tentative hypothesis more specific. It can help marketers better understand how consumers view a topic or a product, which can help a firm develop better products and more targeted marketing mixes. The main purpose of exploratory research is to better understand a problem or situation and/or to help identify additional data needs or decision alternatives.

Conclusive research, on the other hand, is used to verify insights through an objective procedure. It is used in the final stages of decision making, when the marketer has narrowed his or her decision down to a few alternatives.

4-3 Name the five basic steps in conducting marketing research, including the two types of data and four survey methods.

The first step in launching a research study, problem or issue definition, focuses on uncovering the nature and boundaries of a situation or question related to marketing strategy or implementation. When a firm discovers a market opportunity, it may need to conduct research to understand the situation more precisely so it can craft an appropriate marketing strategy.

In the second step, marketing researchers design a research project to obtain the information needed to address the situation. This step requires formulating a hypothesis and determining what type of research to employ to test the hypothesis so the results are reliable and valid. A hypothesis is an informed guess or assumption about a problem or set of circumstances. Research is considered reliable if it produces almost identical results in repeated trials. It is valid if it measures what it is supposed to measure.

For the third step of the research process, collecting data, two types of data are available. Primary data are observed and recorded or collected directly from respondents. Secondary data are compiled inside or outside the organization for some purpose other than the current investigation. Sources of secondary data include an organization's own database and other internal sources, periodicals, government publications, unpublished sources, and online databases. Methods of collecting primary data include sampling, surveys, and observation. Sampling involves selecting representative units from a total population. In probability sampling, every element in the population being studied has a known chance of being selected for study. Nonprobability sampling is more subjective than probability sampling because there is no way to calculate the likelihood that a specific element of the population being studied will be chosen. Marketing researchers employ sampling to collect primary data through mail, telephone, online, or personal interview surveys. A carefully constructed questionnaire is essential to the success of any survey. In using observation methods, researchers record respondents' overt behavior and take note of physical conditions and events.

To apply research data to decision making, marketers must interpret and report their findings—the final two steps in the marketing research process. Statistical interpretation focuses on what is typical or what deviates from the average. After interpreting the research findings, the researchers must prepare a report on the findings that the decision makers can understand and use. Researchers must also take care to avoid bias and distortion.

4-4 Describe the tools, such as databases, big data, and marketing analytics, useful to marketing decision making.

Technology is essential to effective information gathering and analysis. Firms that do not utilize up-to-date technological tools are at a disadvantage. Many firms use technology to create a marketing information system (MIS), a framework for managing and structuring information gathered regularly from sources both inside and outside the organization. A database is a collection of information arranged for easy access and retrieval. Big data involves massive data files that can be obtained from both structured and unstructured databases. Marketing analytics uses tools and methods to measure and interpret the effectiveness of a firm's marketing activities.

4-5 Identify ethical and international issues in marketing research.

Eliminating unethical marketing research practices and establishing generally acceptable procedures for conducting research are important goals of marketing research. Both domestic and international marketing use the same marketing research process, but international marketing may require modifying data-gathering methods to address regional differences.

Go to www.cengagebrain.com for resources to help you master the content in this chapter as well as materials that will expand your marketing knowledge!

Developing Your Marketing Plan

Decisions about which market opportunities to pursue, what customer needs to satisfy, and how to reach potential customers are not made in a vacuum. The information provided by marketing research activities is essential in developing both the strategic plan and the specific marketing mix. Focus on the following issues as you relate the concepts in this chapter to the development of your marketing plan.

1. Define the nature and scope of the questions you must answer with regard to your market. Identify the types of information you will need about the market to answer those questions. For example, do you need to know about the buying habits, household income levels, or attitudes of potential customers?

2. Determine whether or not this information can be obtained from secondary sources.

3. Using Table 4.2, choose the appropriate survey method(s) you would use to collect primary data for one of your information needs. What sampling method would you use?

Key Concepts

marketing research 82
exploratory research 83
customer advisory
    boards 84
focus group 84
conclusive research 85
descriptive research 85
experimental research 85
research design 86
hypothesis 86
reliability 87

validity 87
primary data 87
secondary data 87
population 88
sample 88
sampling 88
probability sampling 88
random sampling 89
stratified sampling 89
nonprobability
    sampling 89

quota sampling 89
mail survey 90
telephone survey 90
telephone depth
    interview 91
personal interview
    survey 91
in-home (door-to-door)
    interview 91
shopping mall intercept
    interview 91

on-site computer
    interview 92
online survey 92
crowdsourcing 92
statistical interpretation 95
marketing information
    system (MIS) 96
database 97
single-source data 98
big data 98
marketing analytics 99

Issues for Discussion and Review

1. What is marketing research? Why is it important?
2. Describe the five steps in the marketing research process.
3. What is the difference between defining a research problem and developing a hypothesis?
4. Describe the different types of approaches to marketing research, and indicate when each should be used.
5. Where are data for marketing research obtained? Give examples of internal and external data.
6. What is the difference between probability sampling and nonprobability sampling? In what situation would random sampling be best? Stratified sampling? Quota sampling?
7. Suggest some ways to encourage respondents to cooperate in mail surveys.

8. If a survey of all homes with listed telephone numbers is to be conducted, what sampling design should be used?
9. Describe some marketing problems that could be solved through information gained from observation.
10. What is a marketing information system, and what should it provide?
11. Define a database. What is its purpose, and what does it include?
12. How can marketers use big data and marketing analytics to improve marketing strategies?
13. What role do ethics play in marketing research? Why is it important that marketing researchers be ethical?
14. How does marketing research in other countries differ from marketing research in the United States?

VIDEO CASE 4
Marketing Research Reveals Marketing Opportunities in the Baby Boomer Generation

For many years, marketers have focused on consumers between the ages of 18 and 34 to promote products. Marketers feel that wooing consumers early in life will ensure that they become lifetime loyal customers. While this seems logical, some research reveals that Baby Boomers might be a more profitable demographic. Statistics show that although spending for Millennials is actually shrinking, Baby Boomer spending has been increasing. Baby Boomers and older Americans are estimated to own 63 percent of all American financial assets.

The Baby Boomer generation is vastly different from the generations preceding it. Baby Boomers desire to have a variety of products available to them. Many of the products traditionally thought to belong to the younger generation, such as cars and technical products, are actually bought the most by older generations. With approximately 111 million Americans 50 years or older, marketers are beginning to research better ways for marketing to Baby Boomers.

In one study, researchers attempted to understand how older consumers shop and interact in stores. Because store marketers often target younger generations of consumers, little thought has been given to how accessible these stores are for older generations. The research design involved equipping participants with gloves, neck braces, helmets, blurry goggles, and other equipment to simulate what a person in his or her 70s with arthritis would experience. Researchers then observed how the participants took items off of shelves, got into their cars, and got up from chairs.

This research has been shared with many businesses that have interpreted the findings to create a retail environment better suited to this demographic. CVS, for instance, has lowered its shelves, made its store lighting softer, and installed magnifying glasses for hard-to-read labels. Other businesses are using this information to redesign their products. Diamond Foods Inc., for example, has designed the packaging of its Emerald snack nuts to be easier to open, a great help for older consumers whose hands become less mobile as they age. The company also studied consumers with arthritis, using that information to decrease the time it takes to rotate the caps to open its products. In-store customer service is also much more important to Baby Boomers than the Millennial generation.

Additionally, Baby Boomers have created an opportunity for businesses to market entirely new products. Baby Boomers tend to embrace fitness and exercise regimens as a way to stay fit and prolong their lives. Technology firms are seeing an opportunity to develop products to be installed in the homes of older consumers. These products monitor the movements of the inhabitants and alert family or experts if there are any changes in the inhabitants' movements. A decrease in mobility could signal a change in the person's physical and mental state, which may require medical attention. Although these devices might otherwise seem intrusive, Baby Boomers' desires to stay healthy and prolong life are increasing their demand. Many Baby Boomers are also concerned with preserving their more youthful appearance. Lingerie maker Maidenform has created shapewear, or clothes that help to "tone" the body, targeted toward people ages 35 to 54.

There is one description that marketers must avoid when marketing to Baby Boomers: any words or phrases that make them feel old. Marketing research has revealed that Baby Boomers do not like to be reminded that they are aging. Therefore, many marketing initiatives aimed at older consumers must be subtle. For this reason, Diamond Foods does not market the fact that its packages are easier to open because it does not want to make Baby Boomers feel aged. Even marketers of products that are for older people have overhauled their promotional campaigns to focus less on the concept of aging. Kimberly-Clark's Depend brand for incontinence was widely regarded as "adult diapers." This negative connotation led many to avoid them. To try to counteract this view, Kimberly-Clark released commercials that discussed the benefits of the product but also tried to "de-myth" the brand by discussing its similarity in look and feel to underwear. Many other businesses that sell similar products are following suit.

Although marketers have long focused on Millennials, the demand for products by Baby Boomers is changing the ways that businesses market to consumers. Marketing research is key to understanding the Baby Boomer demographic and creating the goods and services that best meet their needs.[61]

Questions for Discussion

1. Why are Baby Boomers such a lucrative market?
2. How has the marketing research process been used to understand how Baby Boomers shop and interact in stores?
3. How have stores used marketing research findings to tailor their stores and products to appeal to Baby Boomers?

chapter 5

Target Markets: Segmentation and Evaluation

ESB Professional/Shutterstock.com

LEARNING OBJECTIVES

5-1 Define what markets are and explain how they are generally classified.

5-2 List the five steps of the target market selection process.

5-3 Describe the differences among three targeting strategies.

5-4 Identify the major segmentation variables.

5-5 Describe what market segment profiles are and how they are used.

5-6 Explain how to evaluate market segments.

5-7 Identify the factors that influence the selection of specific market segments for use as target markets.

5-8 Discuss sales forecasting methods.

The Many Market Segments of Marriott

Marriott International already owned 19 hotel brands, including Ritz-Carlton, W, and Courtyard by Marriott, before it bought Starwood Hotels & Resorts in 2016. After the $13 billion deal, Marriott's marketers had 30 brands to consider—some of which had formerly been direct competitors. More than ever, these marketers are intensely interested in examining who stays at which hotels and why, and how elements like age, lifestyle, interest in technology, and price sensitivity affect such decisions.

For instance, the Ritz-Carlton hotel brand used to compete directly with the St. Regis brand in the market for luxury hotel accommodations. Once both were under Marriott, marketers dug deeper to better define the market for each brand beyond demographics like income and benefit expectations of upscale rooms, amenities, and services. They learned that travelers who choose Ritz-Carlton want a base from which to explore and enjoy new destinations. In contrast, travelers who choose St. Regis are status-conscious and seek unique on-site experiences like the hotel's famous midnight suppers.

Marriott's marketers also knew that some travelers are especially interested in technology and innovation. To attract these travelers, the company is implementing keyless entry and testing cutting-edge innovations like robot-based room service at some of its hotel brands, including Aloft and W. In addition, Marriott has launched a digital magazine site, *Travel Brilliantly*, to appeal to tech-savvy Millennials who want a fresh take on going places. The content features articles, images, and videos to entertain and inform Millennial travelers, so they keep Marriott in mind when they plan to travel.[1]

ValeStock/Shutterstock.com

Like Marriott, most organizations trying to compete effectively must identify specific customer groups toward whom they will direct marketing efforts. This includes developing and maintaining marketing mixes that satisfy the needs of those customers. In this chapter, we define and explore the concepts of markets and market segmentation. First we discuss the major requirements of a market. Then we examine the steps in the target market selection process, including identifying the appropriate targeting strategy, determining which variables to use for segmenting consumer and business markets, developing market segment profiles, evaluating relevant market segments, and selecting target markets. We conclude with a discussion of the various methods for developing sales forecasts.

5-1 WHAT ARE MARKETS?

LO 5-1 Define what markets are and explain how they are generally classified.

In Chapter 2, we defined a *market* as a group of individuals and/or organizations that have a desire or needs for products in a product class and have the ability, willingness, and authority to purchase those products. You, as a student, for example, are part of the market for textbooks. You are part of other markets as well, such as laptops, cell phones, clothes, food, and music. To truly be a market, a group must possess all four characteristics. For example, teenagers are not part of the market for alcohol. They may have the desire, willingness, and ability to buy liquor, but they do not have the authority to do so because teenagers are prohibited by law from buying alcoholic beverages.

Markets fall into one of two categories: consumer markets and business markets. These categories are based on the characteristics of the individuals and groups that make up a specific market and the purposes for which they buy products. A **consumer market** consists of purchasers and household members who intend to consume or benefit from the purchased products and do not buy products to make a profit or serve an organizational need. Consumer markets are sometimes also referred to as *business-to-consumer (B2C) markets.* Each of us belongs to numerous consumer markets for all the purchases we make in categories such as housing, food, clothing, vehicles, personal services, appliances, furniture, recreational equipment, and so on, as we shall see in Chapter 6.

A **business market** consists of individuals or groups that purchase a specific kind of product for one of three purposes: resale, direct use in producing other products, or use in general daily operations. For instance, a company that buys electrical wire to use in the production of lamps is part of a business market for electrical wire. Some products can be part of the business or consumer market, depending on their end use. For instance, if you purchase a chair for your home, that chair is part of the consumer market. However, if an office manager purchases the same chair for use in a business office, it is part of the business market. Business markets may be called *business-to-business (B2B), industrial,* or *organizational markets* and can be subclassified into producer, reseller, government, and institutional markets, as we shall see in Chapter 7.

Compare the two advertisements for Olay and Ryder. Olay Eyes is targeted at consumers and can be found in numerous retail stores. The ad appeals directly to the individual consumer by having a beautiful model showcase her anti-aging eye cream to promote how the product can "show strength, not your age." The Ryder ad, on the other hand, is targeted at businesses. The ad promotes Ryder's rental tractor rigs to businesses with a special offer of free miles and a free rental day for every five days of renting one of its trucks.

consumer market
Purchasers and household members who intend to consume or benefit from the purchased products and do not buy products to make profits or serve an organizational need

business market
Individuals or groups that purchase a specific kind of product for resale, direct use in producing other products, or use in general daily operations

Source: Olay Eyes

Ryder System, Inc

Types of Markets
Olay advertises to a consumer market, whereas Ryder advertises to a business market.

5-2 TARGET MARKET SELECTION PROCESS

LO 5-2 List the five steps of the target market selection process.

As indicated earlier, the first of two major components of developing a marketing strategy is selecting a target market. Although marketers may employ several methods for target market selection, they generally follow a five-step process. This process is shown in Figure 5.1, and we explore these steps in the following sections.

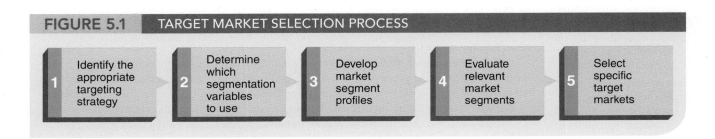

FIGURE 5.1 TARGET MARKET SELECTION PROCESS

1. Identify the appropriate targeting strategy
2. Determine which segmentation variables to use
3. Develop market segment profiles
4. Evaluate relevant market segments
5. Select specific target markets

5-3 STEP 1: IDENTIFY THE APPROPRIATE TARGETING STRATEGY

LO 5-3 Describe the differences among three targeting strategies.

A target market is a group of people or organizations for which a business creates and maintains a marketing mix specifically designed to satisfy the needs of group members. The strategy used to select a target market is affected by target market characteristics, product attributes, and the organization's objectives and resources. Failing to address the most effective segmentation variables can negatively impact financial results. Marketing research can help marketers discover and analyze customer behavior in order to select the best segmentation variables. Figure 5.2 illustrates the three basic targeting strategies: undifferentiated, concentrated, and differentiated.

5-3a Undifferentiated Targeting Strategy

An organization sometimes defines an entire market for a product as its target market. When a company designs a single marketing mix and directs it at the entire market for a particular product, it is using an **undifferentiated targeting strategy**. As Figure 5.2 shows, the strategy assumes that all customers in the target market have similar needs, and thus the organization can satisfy most customers with a single marketing mix with little or no variation. Products marketed successfully through the undifferentiated strategy include commodities and staple food items, such as sugar and salt and conventionally raised produce.

The undifferentiated targeting strategy is effective under two conditions. First, a large proportion of customers in a total market must have similar needs for the product, a situation termed a **homogeneous market**. A marketer using a single marketing mix for a total market of customers with a variety of needs would find that the marketing mix satisfies very few people. For example, marketers would have little success using an undifferentiated strategy to sell a "universal car" because different customers have varying needs. Second, the organization must have the resources to develop a single marketing mix that satisfies customers' needs in a large portion of a total market and the managerial skills to maintain it.

The reality is that, although customers may have similar needs for a few products, for most products their needs are different enough to warrant separate marketing mixes. In such instances, a company should use a concentrated or a differentiated strategy.

5-3b Concentrated Targeting Strategy through Market Segmentation

While most people will be satisfied with the same white sugar, not everyone wants the same car, furniture, or clothes. A market comprised of individuals or organizations with diverse product needs is called a **heterogeneous market**. For example, some individuals want a Ford truck because they have to haul heavy loads for their work, while others live in the city and enjoy the ease of parking and good gas mileage of a Smart car. The automobile market thus is heterogeneous.

For heterogeneous markets, market segmentation is the best approach. **Market segmentation** is the process of dividing a total market into groups, or segments, that consist of people or organizations with relatively similar product needs. The purpose is to enable a marketer to design a marketing mix that more precisely matches the needs of customers in the selected market segment. A **market segment** consists of individuals, groups, or organizations that share one or more similar characteristics that cause them to have relatively similar product needs. The total market for blue jeans is divided into multiple segments.

undifferentiated targeting strategy A strategy in which an organization designs a single marketing mix and directs it at the entire market for a particular product

homogeneous market A market in which a large proportion of customers have similar needs for a product

heterogeneous market A market made up of individuals or organizations with diverse needs for products in a specific product class

market segmentation The process of dividing a total market into groups with relatively similar product needs to design a marketing mix that matches those needs

market segment Individuals, groups, or organizations sharing one or more similar characteristics that cause them to have similar product needs

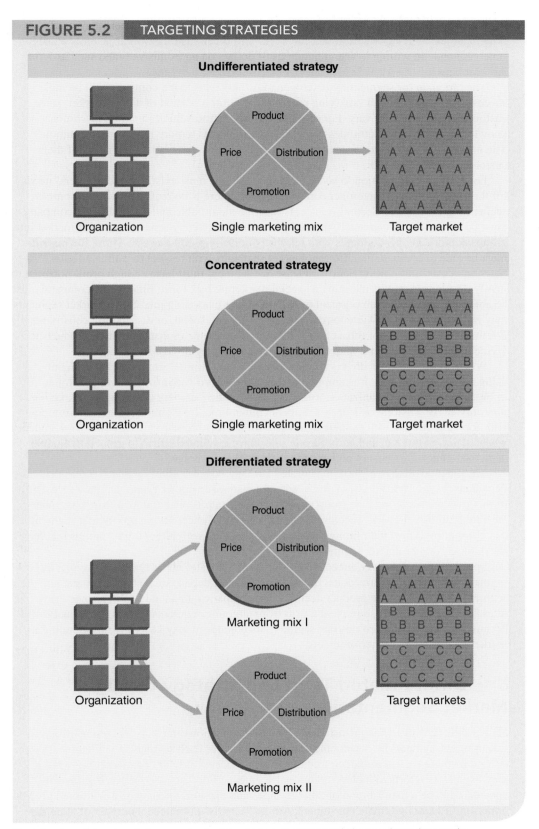

FIGURE 5.2   TARGETING STRATEGIES

Undifferentiated strategy

Product

Price · Distribution

Promotion

Organization · Single marketing mix · Target market

Concentrated strategy

Product

Price · Distribution

Promotion

Organization · Single marketing mix · Target market

Differentiated strategy

Product

Price · Distribution

Promotion

Marketing mix I

Product

Price · Distribution

Promotion

Organization

Marketing mix II · Target markets

The letters in each target market represent potential customers. Customers with the same letters have similar characteristics and similar product needs.

Price-sensitive customers can buy bargain jeans at Walmart or Ross. Others may need functional jeans, like Carhartt brand, for work. Still other customers wear jeans as a fashion statement and are willing to spend hundreds of dollars on an exclusive brand such as 7 for All Mankind.

The rationale for segmenting heterogeneous markets is that a company will be most successful in developing a satisfying marketing mix for a portion of a total market, since customers' needs tend to vary. For example, in the electric vehicles market, dissimilar knowledge and different attitudes toward electric vehicles require market segmentation.[2] The majority of organizations use market segmentation to best satisfy the needs of their customers.

For market segmentation to succeed, five conditions must exist. First, customers' needs for the product must be heterogeneous—otherwise, there is no reason to waste resources segmenting the market. Second, segments must be identifiable and divisible. The company must be able to find a characteristic, or variable, for effectively separating a total market into groups comprised of individuals with relatively uniform product needs. Third, the marketer must be able to compare the different market segments with respect to estimated sales potential, costs, and profits. Fourth, at least one segment must have enough profit potential to justify developing and maintaining a special marketing mix for it. Finally, the company must be able to reach the chosen segment with a particular marketing mix. Some market segments may be difficult or impossible to reach because of legal, social, or distribution constraints. For instance, producers of tobacco products cannot promote or distribute their products to U.S. children because those under the age of 18 cannot legally consume them.

When an organization directs its marketing efforts toward a single market segment using one marketing mix, it is employing a **concentrated targeting strategy**. Notice in Figure 5.2 that the organization using the concentrated strategy is aiming its marketing mix only at "B" customers. Happy Campers Gluten Free, for example, targets consumers with food allergies as well as their families, with healthy breads which are free from gluten, wheat, dairy, eggs, rice, and corn. Strong sales have enabled the firm to grow into a larger dedicated gluten-free bakery and expand their market coverage.[3]

The chief advantage of the concentrated strategy is that it allows a firm to specialize. The firm analyzes the characteristics and needs of a distinct customer group and then focuses all its energies on satisfying that group's needs. If the group is big enough, a firm may generate a large sales volume by reaching a single segment. Concentrating on a single segment can also permit a firm with limited resources to compete with larger organizations that have overlooked smaller market segments.

Specialization, however, means that a company allocates all its resources for one target segment, which can be hazardous. If a company's sales depend on a single segment and the segment's demand for the product declines, the company's financial health also deteriorates. The strategy can also prevent a firm from targeting segments that might be successful, because when a firm penetrates one segment, its popularity may keep it from extending its marketing efforts into other segments.

concentrated targeting strategy A market segmentation strategy in which an organization targets a single market segment using one marketing mix

differentiated targeting strategy A strategy in which an organization targets two or more segments by developing a marketing mix for each segment

5-3c **Differentiated Targeting Strategy through Market Segmentation**

With a **differentiated targeting strategy**, an organization directs its marketing efforts at two or more segments by developing a marketing mix for each segment (see Figure 5.2). After a firm uses a concentrated targeting strategy successfully in one market segment, it may expand its efforts to include additional segments. For instance, Adidas is primarily considered to be a man's brand of athletic shoes and apparel. Recognizing additional growth opportunities among female consumers, Adidas recently introduced a number of athleisure products that can outfit women from work to the gym. The company, which hired a former Lululemon executive as an advisor, is also airing prime-time commercials featuring more women.[4]

Take a look at the advertisement for Centrum vitamins, which is using a differentiated marketing strategy to reach two different market segments. Centrum MultiGummies for Women are targeted toward women, while the Centrum MultiGummies for Men are targeted at men. The advertisement promotes the vitamins' innovation and high quantity of vitamin D3, which many adults lack. The different vitamins are formulated specifically for the needs of the target market. To spur potential purchases, Centrum includes a $4.00 coupon within the advertisement.

A benefit of a differentiated approach is that a firm may increase sales in the total market because its marketing mixes are aimed at more customers. For this reason, a company with excess production capacity may find a differentiated strategy advantageous because the sale of products to additional segments may absorb excess capacity. On the other hand, a differentiated strategy often demands more production processes, materials, and people because the different ingredients in each marketing mix will vary. Thus, production costs may be higher than with a concentrated strategy.

Differentiated Targeting Strategy
The maker of Centrum MultiGummies targets adult women with MultiGummies for Women and adult males with MultiGummies for Men.

5-4 STEP 2: DETERMINE WHICH SEGMENTATION VARIABLES TO USE

LO 5-4 Identify the major segmentation variables.

Segmentation variables are the characteristics of individuals, groups, or organizations used to divide a market into segments. Location, age, gender, and rate of product usage can all be bases for segmenting markets. Marketers may use several variables in combination when segmenting a market. For example, Forever 21 stores became well-known for selling the latest fashion trends at affordable prices to Millennial women. Although it is expanding into fashion for older demographics, Forever 21's core market remains younger age groups.[5] Segmentation variables should be used to select the most attractive segments. The criteria for selection include areas where there is a sustainable competitive advantage that creates profitability. Therefore, a competitive analysis can be a strong predictor in finding the best segmentation variables.[6]

To select a segmentation variable, marketers consider several factors. The segmentation variable should relate to customers' needs for, uses of, or behavior toward the product. Consider that an automobile marketer is likely to segment the market for cars by income, age, and gender but not by religion, because people's car preferences do not vary much because of religion. Marketers must select measurable segmentation variables, such as age, location, or gender, if individuals or organizations in a total market are to be classified accurately.

There is no best way to segment markets, and the approach will vary depending on a number of factors. A company's resources and capabilities affect the number and size of segment variables used. The type of product and degree of variation in customers' needs also dictate the number and size of segments targeted. No matter what approach is used, choosing one or more segmentation variables is a critical step in effectively targeting a market. Selecting an inappropriate variable limits the chances of developing a successful marketing strategy. To help you better understand potential segmentation variables, we next examine the differences between the major variables used to segment consumer and business markets.

segmentation variables Characteristics of individuals, groups, or organizations used to divide a market into segments

| FIGURE 5.3 | SEGMENTATION VARIABLES FOR CONSUMER MARKETS |

Demographic variables
- Age
- Gender
- Race
- Ethnicity
- Income
- Education
- Occupation
- Family size
- Family life cycle
- Religion
- Social class

Geographic variables
- Region
- Urban, suburban, rural
- City size
- County size
- State size
- Market density
- Climate
- Terrain

Psychographic variables
- Personality attributes
- Motives
- Lifestyles

Behavioristic variables
- Volume usage
- End use
- Benefit expectations
- Brand loyalty
- Price sensitivity

5-4a Variables for Segmenting Consumer Markets

A marketer who is using segmentation to reach a consumer market can choose one or several variables. As Figure 5.3 shows, segmentation variables can be grouped into four major categories: demographic, geographic, psychographic, and behavioristic.

Demographic Variables

Demographers study aggregate population characteristics such as the distribution of age and gender, fertility rates, migration patterns, and mortality rates. Demographic characteristics that marketers commonly use include age, gender, race, ethnicity, income, education, occupation, family size, family life cycle, religion, and social class. Marketers segment markets by demographic characteristics because they are often closely linked to customers' needs and purchasing behaviors and can be readily measured.

Age is a common variable for segmentation purposes. A trip to the shopping mall highlights the fact that many retailers, including Zara, Forever 21, and American Eagle Outfitters, target teens and young adults. If considering segmenting by age, marketers need to be aware of age distribution, how that distribution is changing, and how it will affect the demand for different types of products. The proportion of consumers over the age of 55 is shrinking as Baby Boomers (born between 1946 and 1964) age. Meanwhile, Millennials (born between 1981 and 1997) now total 75.4 million, surpassing Baby Boomers.[7] In 1970, the median age of a U.S. citizen was 28.1. It is currently 37.8.[8] Because of the increasing average age of Americans, many marketers are searching for ways to market their products toward older adults. As Figure 5.4 shows, Americans in different age groups have different product needs because of their different lifestyles, family status, and health situations. Citizens 65 and older, for instance, spend the most on health care, while those between 35 and 64 spend the most on housing and food.

Gender is another demographic variable that is commonly used to segment markets for many products, including clothing, soft drinks, nonprescription medications, magazines, some food items, and personal-care products. Beer has traditionally been marketed to men, but High Heel Brewing, founded by a female brewmaster, targets women beer drinkers with unique flavors and stylish packaging.[9]

| FIGURE 5.4 | SPENDING LEVELS OF THREE AGE GROUPS FOR SELECTED PRODUCT CATEGORIES |

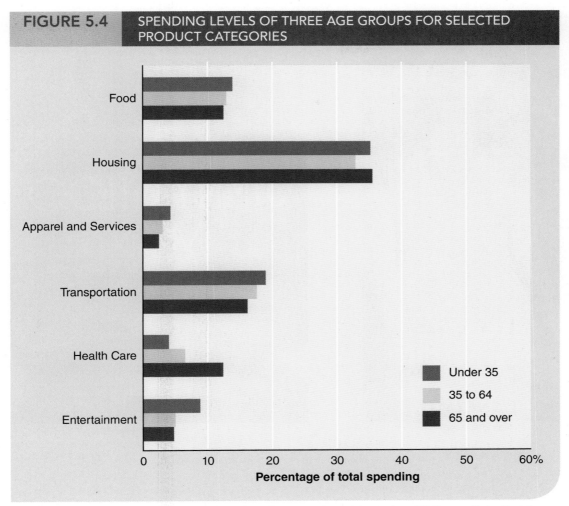

Source: Derived from Ann C. Foster, "Consumer Expenditures by Age," in *Beyond the Numbers*, U.S. Bureau of Labor Statistics, December 2015, https://www.bls.gov/opub/btn/volume-4/consumer-expenditures-vary-by-age.htm (accessed January 16, 2017).

The U.S. Census Bureau reports that females account for 50.8 percent and males for 49.2 percent of the total U.S. population.[10] Although they represent only slightly more than half of the population, women disproportionately influence buying decisions. It is estimated that women account for 85 percent of all consumer purchases, causing many marketers to consider female customers when making marketing decisions.[11] Take a look at the advertisements for Lancôme and Jimmy Choo fragrances. Lancôme is targeted at women. The Lancôme advertisement in a women's magazine features actress Julia Roberts and is tagged "La vie est belle," (Life is beautiful) to reinforce the brand's French identity. The Jimmy Choo Man advertisement in a men's magazine is targeted toward men and features a well-dressed model couple as well as a picture of the fragrance bottle and further identifies the product as "the fragrance for men." Although both these advertisements market fragrances, they clearly are segmented by gender due to their different areas of emphasis.

Marketers also use race and ethnicity as variables for segmenting markets for many products. Cosmetics, for example, is an industry where it is important to match the shade of the products with the skin color of customers. Iman Cosmetics is a line created by the Ethiopian supermodel Iman, with deeper colors designed to flatter the skin tones of women of color, be they Black, Hispanic, or Asian. These products are not made for, nor marketed to, light-skinned women.[12]

Lancôme

Jimmy Choo

Gender Segmentation
Fragrances are segmented based on gender. The Lancôme fragrance is aimed at women while the Jimmy Choo is targeted at men.

Because income strongly influences people's product purchases, it often provides a way to divide markets. Income affects customers' lifestyles and what they can afford to buy. Product markets segmented by income include sporting goods, housing, furniture, cosmetics, clothing, jewelry, home appliances, automobiles, and electronics. Although it may seem obvious to target higher-income consumers because of their larger purchasing power, many marketers choose to target lower-income segments because they represent a much larger population globally.

Among the factors that influence household income and product needs are marital status and the presence and age of children. These features, often combined and called the *family life cycle*, affect consumers' needs for housing, appliances, food and beverages, automobiles, and recreational equipment. Transitions between life-cycle stages—such as weddings— can also be lucrative for marketers. Consider that there are more than 2 million weddings performed in the United States each year, and the average cost of a wedding is $32,641. Marketers know that engaged couples will be highly receptive to wedding-related marketing messages, much like parents-to-be will be for baby-themed marketing, making them a very desirable market segment.[13] Family life cycles can be divided in various ways, as Figure 5.5 shows. This figure depicts the process broken down into nine categories.

The composition of the U.S. household in relation to the family life cycle has changed considerably over the last several decades. Single-parent families are on the rise, with one quarter of all children under age 18 living with a single parent. In fact, households with two married parents in their first marriage account for only 46 percent of all households in the United States, down from 73 percent in the 1960s.[14] Nearly 15 percent of Americans live alone, though that figure is skewed toward the elderly.[15] Previously small groups have recently risen in prominence, prompting an interest from marketers. For example, more than 8 million households

FIGURE 5.5   FAMILY LIFE-CYCLE STAGES AS A PERCENTAGE OF HOUSEHOLDS

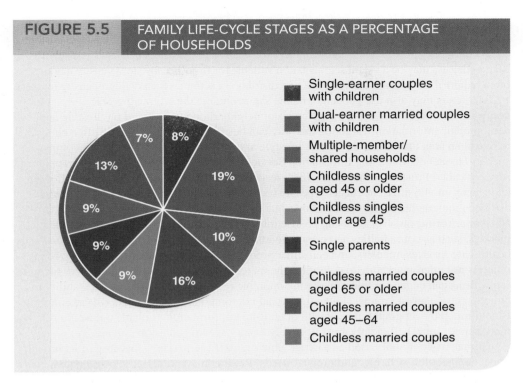

- Single-earner couples with children
- Dual-earner married couples with children
- Multiple-member/ shared households
- Childless singles aged 45 or older
- Childless singles under age 45
- Single parents
- Childless married couples aged 65 or older
- Childless married couples aged 45–64
- Childless married couples

market density The number of potential customers within a unit of land area

are comprised of unmarried couples living together, three times as many as in 1996.[16] Nearly 800,000 households include same-sex partners.[17] Thus, people live in many different situations, all of which have different requirements for goods and services. Tracking demographic shifts such as these helps marketers be informed and prepared to satisfy the needs of target markets through new marketing mixes that address consumers' changing lifestyles.

Geographic Variables

Geographic variables—climate, terrain, city size, population density, and urban/rural areas—also influence consumer product needs. Markets may be divided using geographic variables, because differences in location, climate, and terrain will influence consumers' needs. Consumers in the South, for instance, rarely have a need for snow tires. A company that sells products to a national market might divide the United States into Pacific, Southwest, Central, Midwest, South-east, Middle Atlantic, and New England regions. A firm that is operating in one or several states might regionalize its market by counties, cities, zip code areas, or other units.

City size can be an important segmentation variable. Many firms choose to limit marketing efforts to cities above a certain size because small populations have been calculated to generate inadequate profits. Other firms actively seek opportunities in smaller towns. A classic example is Walmart, which initially was located only in small towns and even today can be found in towns where other large retailers stay away. If a marketer chooses to divide by a geographic variable, such as city size, the U.S. Census Bureau provides reporting on population and demographics that can be of considerable assistance.

Market density refers to the number of potential customers within a unit of land area, such as a square mile. Although market density relates generally to population density, the correlation is not exact. For example, in two

iStock.com/AGrigorjeva

Geographic Segmentation
Climate affects numerous markets. Customers' needs for automotive accessories, such as tires, vary based on climate.

geodemographic segmentation A method of market segmentation that clusters people in zip code areas and smaller neighborhood units based on lifestyle and demographic information

micromarketing An approach to market segmentation in which organizations focus precise marketing efforts on very small geographic markets

different geographic markets of approximately equal size and population, market density for office supplies would be much higher in an area containing a large number of business customers, such as a city downtown, than in another area that is largely residential, such as a suburb. Market density may be a useful segmentation variable for firms because low-density markets often require different sales, advertising, and distribution activities than do high-density markets.

Marketers may also use geodemographic segmentation. **Geodemographic segmentation** clusters people by zip codes or neighborhood units based on lifestyle and demographic information. Targeting this way can be effective because people often choose to live in an area that shares their basic lifestyle and political beliefs. Information companies such as Donnelley Marketing Information Services and Nielsen provide geodemographic data services called Prospect Zone and PRIZM, respectively. PRIZM, for example, classifies zip code areas into 66 different cluster types, based on demographic information of residents.[18]

Geodemographic segmentation allows marketers to engage in micromarketing. **Micromarketing** involves focusing precise marketing efforts on very small geographic markets, such as communities and even individual neighborhoods. Providers of financial and health-care services, retailers, and consumer product companies use micromarketing. Many retailers use micromarketing to determine the merchandise mix for individual stores. Increasingly, firms can engage in micromarketing in online retailing, given the Internet's ability to target precise interest groups. Unlike traditional micromarketing, online micromarketing is not limited by geography. The wealth of consumer information available online allows marketers to appeal efficiently and effectively to very specific consumer niches.

Climate is commonly used as a geographic segmentation variable because of its broad impact on people's behavior and product needs. Product markets affected by climate include air-conditioning and heating equipment, fireplace accessories, clothing, gardening equipment, recreational products, and building materials.

Psychographic Variables

Marketers sometimes use psychographic variables, such as personality characteristics, motives, and lifestyles, to segment markets. A psychographic variable can be used by itself or in combination with other types of segmentation variables. For example, parents' attitudes and motives shape their purchases of software and technology for their children in ways that

EMERGING TRENDS IN MARKETING

Geofencing: Fenced In and Don't Know It?

Thanks to *geofencing*, a growing number of retailers can now target customers who are at or near a particular business location. Here's how it works: customers download a smartphone app so the marketer's network can track them crossing an electronic "fence." The fence's boundary may be two miles around a store or restaurant, or it may be the front door. Either way, once customers are inside the targeted area, the marketer can identify them, send promotional messages or discount coupons, or guide them directly to certain merchandise.

For example, all of Walmart's U.S. stores are geofenced, and the interiors are also mapped electronically. Once customers with the Walmart app go to a local store, they can activate the "Search

My Store" feature and follow the step-by-step route toward the products they want. The Walmart app also adds convenience when customers are picking up preordered merchandise. As soon as the network detects those customers at the store entrance, the app alerts staff to have all packages ready and waiting.

The Elephant Bar Restaurant chain uses geofencing for effective, on-the-spot targeting of repeat customers. When members of its rewards program are within two miles of its restaurants during operating hours, their phones receive a personalized text with a promotional offer. Geofencing works well for this restaurant group: About 40 percent of the recipients visit on the day they get a text.[a]

go beyond demographics. Using psychographic variables, marketing researchers can divide the family tech market into three segments. Enablers, who have confidence in their children's ability to make their own technology decisions, tend to seek out products based on their entertainment value. Limiters, who strive to minimize their children's screen time, generally focus on products that can further their children's academic skills. Finally, parents who prefer to actively spur and guide their children's technology use typically look for products that promote a balance of fun and educational value. Such segmentation suggests different strategies for reaching the different segments than would those based on basic demographics.[19]

Personality characteristics can be a useful means of segmentation when a product resembles many competing products and consumers' needs are not significantly related to other segmentation variables. However, segmenting a market according to personality traits can be risky. Although marketing practitioners have long believed consumer choice and product use vary with personality, marketing research has generally indicated only a weak relationship. It is difficult to measure personality traits accurately, especially because most personality tests were developed for clinical use, not for market segmentation purposes.

When appealing to a personality characteristic, a marketer almost always selects one that many people view positively. Individuals with this characteristic, as well as those who aspire to have it, may be influenced to buy the marketer's brand. Marketers taking this approach do not worry about measuring how many people have the positively valued characteristic. They assume a sizable proportion of people in the target market either have it or aspire to have it.

When motives are used to segment a market, the market is divided according to consumers' reasons for making a purchase. Personal appearance, affiliation, status, safety, and health are examples of motives affecting the types of products purchased and the choice of stores in which they are bought. Marketing efforts based on particular motives can be a point of competitive advantage for a firm.

Lifestyle segmentation groups individuals according to how they spend their time, the importance of things in their surroundings (homes or jobs, for example), beliefs about themselves and broad issues, and some demographic characteristics, such as income and education.[20] Take, for example, the advertisement for Yeti coolers. This advertisement shows a picture of a Yeti cooler superimposed over one of a man tending meat on a barbecue pit at night. However, it is not targeted to everyone who enjoys grilling and barbecuing. Rather, it appeals to the avid barbecuer who is willing to stay up all night to make sure the meat turns out just right. The ad also reminds interested consumers that Yeti coolers are indestructible and keep ice for days, so they are suitable for a rugged lifestyle. Lifestyle analysis provides a broad view of buyers because it encompasses numerous characteristics related to people's activities (e.g., work, hobbies, entertainment, sports), interests (e.g., family, home, fashion, food, technology), and opinions (e.g., politics, social issues, education, the future).

PRIZM, by Nielsen, is a service commonly used by marketers to segment by demographic variables. It can also be used to segment by psychographic variables and lifestyles. PRIZM combines demographics, consumer behavior, and geographic data to help marketers identify, understand, and reach their customers and prospects, resulting in a highly robust tool for marketers.[21] PRIZM divides U.S. households into demographically and behaviorally distinct segments that take into account such factors as likes, dislikes, lifestyles, and purchase behaviors. Used by thousands of marketers, including many Fortune 500 companies, PRIZM provides marketers with a common tool for understanding and reaching customers in a highly diverse and complex marketplace.

Segmentation Based on Lifestyles
This Yeti advertisement for large coolers is appealing to customers who engage in a certain lifestyle, which includes camping, hunting, and barbequing.

ReplyYes for Vinyl Collectors and Graphic Novel Fans

ReplyYes says "no" to demographic and geo-graphic segmentation variables and "yes" to psychographic and behavioristic variables. The company, based in Seattle, operates two e-commerce operations: The Edit markets vinyl records, and Origin Bound markets graphic novels. Every day, ReplyYes sends one text message about a single album or novel to consumers who have asked to receive these personalized offers. Customers simply text "yes" to initiate a purchase, complete the transaction with a couple of swipes or clicks, and watch for the item by mail within a week. For added context, customers are invited to "like" or "dislike" the featured product, which helps ReplyYes further refine its offers, individual by individual.

ReplyYes relies on segmentation according to lifestyle—such as people's interests in collecting albums or reading graphic novels—and behavior—such as heavy usage. CEO Dave Cotter explains that the company caters to "people who are totally passionate about a particular category" of product, whether it's vinyl records or graphic novels. The Edit has attracted tens of thousands of subscribers to its daily texts, and sold more than $1 million worth of records during its first eight months. On any given day, at least 300 buyers say yes to the album of the day. In fact, 68 percent of ReplyYes subscribers wind up making a purchase at some point, reflecting the power of segmentation to reach the right audience with the right offer at the right time.[b]

Behavioristic Variables

Firms can divide a market according to consumer behavior toward a product, which commonly involves an aspect of consumers' product use. For example, a market may be separated into users—classified as heavy, moderate, or light—and nonusers. To satisfy a specific group, such as heavy users, marketers may create a distinctive product and price, or initiate special distribution and promotion activities. Per capita consumption data can help determine different levels of usage by product category. To satisfy customers who use a product in a certain way, some feature—packaging, size, texture, or color—may be designed precisely to make the product easier to use, safer, or more convenient. Many web-based services have been modified to detect when the user is on a smartphone or other mobile device and to adjust the display for optimal appearance for mobile users.

Benefit segmentation is the division of a market according to benefits that consumers want from the product. Although most types of market segmentation assume a relationship between the variable and customers' needs, benefit segmentation differs in that the benefits customers seek *are* their product needs. Consider that a customer who purchases over-the-counter cold relief medication may be interested in two benefits: stopping a runny nose and relieving chest congestion. By determining desired benefits, marketers can divide people into groups by the benefits they seek. The effectiveness of such segmentation depends on three conditions: (1) the benefits sought must be identifiable, (2) using these benefits, marketers must be able to divide people into recognizable segments, and (3) one or more of the resulting segments must be accessible to the firm's marketing efforts.

Marketers can segment consumer markets using many characteristics. They do not, however, use the same variables to segment business characteristics. We will learn about business market segmentation in the next section.

benefit segmentation
The division of a market according to benefits that consumers want from the product

5-4b Variables for Segmenting Business Markets

Like consumer markets, business markets are frequently segmented for marketing purposes. Marketers segment business markets according to geographic location, type of organization, customer size, and product use.

Geographic Location

Earlier we noted that the demand for consumer products can vary considerably among geographic areas due to differences in climate, terrain, or regional customer preferences. Demand for business products also varies according to geographic location. For instance, producers of lumber may divide their markets geographically because customers' needs vary by region. Geographic segmentation may be especially appropriate for producers seeking to reach industries concentrated in certain locations, such as furniture and textile producers concentrated in the Southeast.

Type of Organization

A company sometimes segments a market by types of organization within that market because they often require different product features, price structures, distribution systems, and selling strategies. Given these variations, a firm may either concentrate on a single segment with one marketing mix (a concentrated targeting strategy) or focus on several groups with multiple mixes (a differentiated targeting strategy). A carpet producer, for example, could segment potential customers into several groups, such as automobile makers, home builders, commercial carpet contractors (firms that carpet large commercial buildings), carpet wholesalers, and retail carpet outlets. Consider the advertisement for Just Tanx. Just Tanx concentrates on businesses that use chemical containers and transportation services. As part of its marketing strategy, the advertisement promotes how Just Tanx can handle any intermodal chemical or bulk liquid challenge. The ad also highlights the firm's safety record, professionalism, insurance protection, and customer service, along with the fact that it is a woman-owned business.

Segmenting Business Markets
Just Tanx segments a business market based on product use.

Customer Size

An organization's size may affect its purchasing procedures and the types and quantities of products it needs. Size can thus be an effective variable for segmenting a business market. To reach a segment of a specific size, marketers may have to adjust one or more marketing-mix ingredients. For example, marketers may want to offer customers who buy in large quantities a discount as a purchase incentive. Personal selling is common and expected in business markets, where a higher level of customer service may be required—larger customers may require a higher level of customer service because of the size and complexity of their orders. Because the needs of large and small buyers tend to be distinct, marketers frequently use different marketing practices to reach target customer groups.

Product Use

Certain products, particularly basic raw materials such as steel, petroleum, plastics, and lumber, can be used numerous ways in the production of goods. These variations will affect the types and amounts of products purchased, as well as the purchasing method. Computers, for example, are used for engineering purposes, basic scientific research, and business operations such as word processing, accounting, and telecommunications. A computer maker, therefore, may segment the computer market by types of use because organizations' needs for computer hardware and software depend on the purpose for which products are purchased.

5-5 STEP 3: DEVELOP MARKET SEGMENT PROFILES

LO 5-5 Describe what market segment profiles are and how they are used.

A market segment profile describes the similarities among potential customers within a segment and explains the differences among people and organizations in different segments. A profile may cover such aspects as demographic characteristics, geographic factors, product benefits sought, lifestyles, brand preferences, and usage rates. Individuals and organizations within a market segment should be relatively similar with respect to several of their characteristics and product needs and differ considerably from those within other market segments. Marketers use market segment profiles to assess the degree to which their products fit potential customers' product needs. Market segment profiles support marketers in understanding how they can use their firms' capabilities to serve potential customer groups.

Market segment profiles help a marketer determine which segment or segments are most attractive relative to the firm's strengths, weaknesses, objectives, and resources. Although marketers may initially believe certain segments are attractive, a market segment profile may yield contrary information. Market segment profiles can be useful in helping a firm make marketing decisions relating to a specific market segment or segments.

5-6 STEP 4: EVALUATE RELEVANT MARKET SEGMENTS

LO 5-6 Explain how to evaluate market segments.

After analyzing the market segment profiles, a marketer should be able to narrow his or her focus to several promising segments that warrant further analysis. Marketers should examine sales estimates, competition, and estimated costs associated with each of these segments.

5-6a Sales Estimates

Potential sales for a market segment can be measured along several dimensions, including product level, geographic area, time, and level of competition.[22] With respect to product level, potential sales can be estimated for a specific product item (e.g., Diet Coke) or an entire product line (e.g., Coca-Cola Classic, Diet Coke, and Coca-Cola Zero Sugar comprise goods in a product line). A manager must also determine the geographic area to include in the estimate. In relation to time, sales estimates can be short range (one year or less), medium range (one to five years), or long range (longer than five years). The competitive level specifies whether sales are being estimated for a single firm or for an entire industry.

Market potential is the total amount of a product that customers will purchase within a specified period at a specific level of industry-wide marketing activity. Market potential can be stated in terms of dollars or units. A segment's market potential is affected by economic, sociocultural, and other environmental forces. The specific level of marketing effort will vary from one firm to another, but each firm's marketing activities together add up to the industry-wide marketing effort total. A marketing manager must also estimate whether and to what extent industry marketing efforts will change over time.

Company sales potential is the maximum percentage share of a market that an individual firm within an industry can expect to capture for a specific product. Several factors influence company sales potential for a market segment. First, the market potential places an absolute limit on the size of the company's sales potential—a firm cannot exceed the market potential. Second, the magnitude of industry-wide marketing activities has an indirect but definite impact on the company's sales potential. For instance, when Domino's Pizza advertises home-delivered pizza, it indirectly promotes pizza in general. Although the advertisement might spark a desire for pizza, you could decide to call the Pizza Hut down the street

market potential The total amount of a product that customers will purchase within a specified period at a specific level of industry-wide marketing activity

company sales potential The maximum percentage of a market that an individual firm within an industry can expect to obtain for a specific product

because it is more familiar to you. Third, the intensity and effectiveness of a company's marketing activities relative to competitors' activities affect the size of the company's sales potential. If a company spends twice as much as any of its competitors on marketing efforts, and if each dollar spent is more effective in generating sales, the firm's sales potential will be high relative to competitors'.

Two general approaches that measure company sales potential are breakdown and buildup. In the **breakdown approach**, the marketing manager first develops a general economic forecast for a specific time period. Next, the manager estimates market potential based on this forecast. The manager derives the company's sales potential from the forecast and an estimate of market potential. In the **buildup approach**, the marketing manager begins by estimating how much of a product a potential buyer in a specific geographic area, such as a sales territory, will purchase in a given period. The manager then multiplies that amount by the total number of potential buyers in that area. The manager performs the same calculation for each geographic area in which the firm sells products and then adds the totals to calculate market potential. To determine company sales potential, the manager must estimate, based on planned levels of company marketing activities, the proportion of the total market potential the company can reasonably attain.

breakdown approach
Measuring company sales potential based on a general economic forecast for a specific period and the market potential derived from it

buildup approach
Measuring company sales potential by estimating how much of a product a potential buyer in a specific geographic area will purchase in a given period, multiplying the estimate by the number of potential buyers, and adding the totals of all the geographic areas considered

5-6b Competitive Assessment

Besides obtaining sales estimates, it is crucial to assess competitors that are already operating in the segments being considered. A market segment that initially seems attractive based on sales estimates may turn out to be much less so after a competitive assessment. Such an assessment should ask several questions about competitors: How many exist? What are their strengths and weaknesses? Do several competitors already have major market shares and together dominate the segment? Can our company create a marketing mix to compete effectively against competitors' marketing mixes? Is it likely that new competitors will enter this segment? If so, how will they affect our firm's ability to compete successfully? Answers to such questions are important for proper assessment of the competition in potential market segments.

5-6c Cost Estimates

To fulfill the needs of a target segment, an organization must develop and maintain a marketing mix that precisely meets the wants and needs of that segment, which can be expensive. Distinctive product features, attractive package design, generous product warranties, extensive advertising, attractive promotional offers, competitive prices, and high-quality personal service use considerable organizational resources. In some cases, marketers may conclude that the costs to reach some segments are so high that they are basically inaccessible. Marketers also must consider whether the organization can reach a segment at costs equal to or below competitors' costs. If the firm's costs are likely to be higher, it will be unable to compete in that segment in the long run.

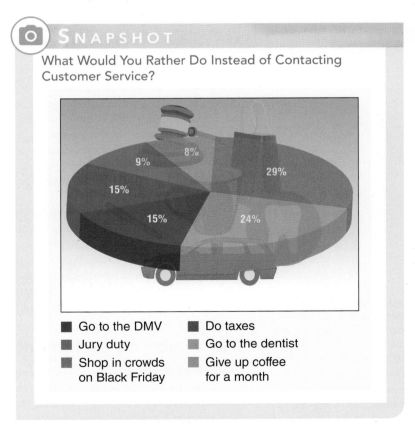

SNAPSHOT

What Would You Rather Do Instead of Contacting Customer Service?

- Go to the DMV
- Jury duty
- Shop in crowds on Black Friday
- Do taxes
- Go to the dentist
- Give up coffee for a month

29%, 24%, 15%, 15%, 9%, 8%

Source: CorvisaCloud survey of 1,214 adults

5-7 STEP 5: SELECT SPECIFIC TARGET MARKETS

LO 5-7 Identify the factors that influence the selection of specific market segments for use as target markets.

Assuming one or more segments offer significant opportunities to achieve organizational objectives, marketers must decide which offer the most potential at reasonable costs. Ordinarily, information gathered in the previous step—concerning sales estimates, competitors, and cost estimates—requires careful review in this final step to determining long-term marketing opportunities. At this time, the firm's management must investigate whether the organization has sufficient financial resources, managerial skills, employee expertise, and facilities to compete effectively in the selected segments. The firm must also consider the possibility that the requirements of some market segments are at odds with the firm's overall objectives, and that possible legal problems, conflicts with interest groups, and technological advancements will render certain segments unattractive. Finally, marketers must consider long-term versus short-term growth. If long-term prospects look poor, a marketer may ultimately choose not to target a segment because it would be difficult to recoup expenses.

Selecting appropriate target markets is important to an organization's effective adoption and use of the marketing concept philosophy. Identifying the right target market is the key to implementing a successful marketing strategy. Failure to do so can lead to low sales, high costs, and severe financial losses. A careful target market analysis places an organization in a strong position to serve customers' needs and achieve its objectives.

5-8 DEVELOPING SALES FORECASTS

LO 5-8 Discuss sales forecasting methods.

After a company selects a target market or markets, it must develop a **sales forecast**—the amount of a product the company expects to sell during a specific period at a specified level of marketing activity. The sales forecast differs from the company sales potential in that it concentrates on what actual sales will be at a certain level of company marketing effort. The company sales potential assesses what sales are possible at various levels of marketing activities, assuming certain environmental conditions exist. Businesses use the sales forecast for planning, organizing, implementing, and controlling activities. The success of numerous activities depends on the forecast's accuracy. Common problems in failing companies are improper planning and lack of realistic sales forecasts. For example, overly ambitious sales forecasts can lead to overbuying, overinvestment, and higher costs that can weaken a firm's strength and position.

To forecast sales, a marketer can choose from a number of forecasting methods, some arbitrary and quick and others more scientific, complex, and time consuming. A firm's choice of method, or methods, depends on the costs involved, type of product, market characteristics, time span and purpose of the forecast, stability of the historical sales data, availability of required information, managerial preferences, and forecasters' areas of expertise and experience.[23] Common forecasting techniques fall into five categories: executive judgment, surveys, time series analysis, regression analysis, and market tests.

5-8a Executive Judgment

Executive judgment is the intuition of one or more executives. This is an unscientific but expedient and inexpensive approach to sales forecasting. It is not a very accurate method, but executive judgment may work reasonably well when product demand is relatively stable and the forecaster has years of market-related experience. However, because intuition is heavily influenced by recent experience, the forecast may weight recent sales booms or slumps

sales forecast The amount of a product a company expects to sell during a specific period at a specified level of marketing activities

executive judgment A sales forecasting method based on the intuition of one or more executives

excessively. Another drawback to intuition is that the forecaster has only past experience as a guide for deciding where to go in the future.

5-8b Surveys

Another way to forecast sales is to question customers, sales personnel, or experts regarding their expectations about future purchases. In a **customer forecasting survey**, marketers ask customers what types and quantities of products they intend to buy during a specific period. This approach may be useful to a business with relatively few customers. Consider Lockheed Martin, the U.S. government's largest contractor. Because most of its contracts come from the same customer—the government—Lockheed Martin could conduct customer forecasting surveys effectively. PepsiCo, by contrast, has millions of customers and could not feasibly use a customer survey to forecast future sales.

In a **sales force forecasting survey**, the firm's salespeople estimate anticipated sales in their territories for a specified period. The forecaster combines these territorial estimates to arrive at a tentative forecast. A marketer may survey sales staff for several reasons, the most important being that the sales staff are the company personnel closest to customers on a daily basis. They therefore have first-hand knowledge about customers' product needs. Moreover, when sales representatives assist in developing the forecast, they are invested in the process and are more likely to work toward its achievement. In order for sales force forecasting to be effective, it is necessary to educate the sales force about the importance of forecasting, clearly define their responsibilities, and make it easy for them to participate.[24]

When a company wants an **expert forecasting survey**, it hires professionals to help prepare the sales forecast. These experts are usually economists, management consultants, advertising executives, college professors, or other individuals outside the firm with experience in a specific market. Drawing on this experience and their analyses of available information about the company and the market, experts prepare and present forecasts or answer questions. Using experts is a quick way to get information and is relatively inexpensive. However, because they work outside the firm, these forecasters may be less motivated than company personnel to do an effective job.

A more complex form of the expert forecasting survey incorporates the Delphi technique. In the **Delphi technique**, experts create initial forecasts, submit them to the company for averaging, and have the results returned to them so they can make individual refined forecasts. When making calculations using the Delphi technique, experts use the averaged results to eradicate outliers and to refine predictions. The procedure may be repeated several times until the experts, each working separately, reach a consensus. Because this technique gets rid of extreme data, the ultimate goal in using the Delphi technique is to develop a highly reliable sales forecast.

5-8c Time Series Analysis

With **time series analysis**, the forecaster uses the firm's historical sales data to discover a pattern, or patterns, in sales over time. If a pattern is found, it can be used to forecast sales. This forecasting method assumes that past sales patterns will continue into the future. The accuracy, and thus usefulness, of time series analysis hinges on the validity of this assumption.

In a time series analysis, a forecaster usually performs four types of analyses: trend, cycle, seasonal, and random factor. **Trend analysis** focuses on aggregate sales data, such as the company's annual sales figures, covering a period of many years to determine whether annual sales are generally rising, falling, or staying about the same. Through **cycle analysis**, a forecaster analyzes sales figures (often monthly sales data) for a three- to five-year period to ascertain whether sales fluctuate in a consistent, periodic manner. When performing a **seasonal analysis**, the analyst studies daily, weekly, or monthly sales figures to evaluate the degree to which seasonal factors, such as climate and holiday activities, influence sales. In a **random factor analysis**, the forecaster attempts to attribute erratic sales variations to random, nonrecurring events, such as a regional power failure, a natural disaster, or political unrest in a

customer forecasting survey A survey of customers regarding the types and quantities of products they intend to buy during a specific period

sales force forecasting survey A survey of a firm's sales force regarding anticipated sales in their territories for a specified period

expert forecasting survey Sales forecasts prepared by experts outside the firm, such as economists, management consultants, advertising executives, or college professors

Delphi technique A procedure in which experts create initial forecasts, submit them to the company for averaging, and then refine the forecasts

time series analysis A forecasting method that uses historical sales data to discover patterns in the firm's sales over time and generally involves trend, cycle, seasonal, and random factor analyses

trend analysis An analysis that focuses on aggregate sales data over a period of many years to determine general trends in annual sales

cycle analysis An analysis of sales figures for a three- to five-year period to ascertain whether sales fluctuate in a consistent, periodic manner

seasonal analysis An analysis of daily, weekly, or monthly sales figures to evaluate the degree to which seasonal factors influence sales

random factor analysis An analysis attempting to attribute erratic sales variations to random, nonrecurrent events

regression analysis A method of predicting sales based on finding a relationship between past sales and one or more independent variables, such as population or income

market test Making a product available to buyers in one or more test areas and measuring purchases and consumer responses to marketing efforts

foreign market. After performing each of these analyses, the forecaster combines the results to develop the sales forecast. Time series analysis is an effective forecasting method for products with reasonably stable demand, but not for products with erratic demand.

5-8d Regression Analysis

Like time series analysis, regression analysis requires the use of historical sales data. In **regression analysis**, the forecaster seeks to find a relationship between past sales (the dependent variable) and one or more independent variables, such as population, per capita income, or gross domestic product. Simple regression analysis uses one independent variable, whereas multiple regression analysis includes two or more independent variables. The objective of regression analysis is to develop a mathematical formula that accurately describes a relationship between the firm's sales and one or more variables. However, the formula indicates only an association, not a causal relationship. Once an accurate formula is established, the analyst plugs the necessary information into the formula to derive the sales forecast.

Regression analysis is useful when a precise association can be established. However, a forecaster seldom finds a perfect correlation. Furthermore, this method can be used only when available historical sales data are extensive. Thus, regression analysis is not useful for forecasting sales of new products.

5-8e Market Tests

A **market test** involves making a product available to buyers in one or more test areas and measuring purchases and consumer responses to the product, price, distribution, and promotion. Test areas are often mid-sized cities with populations of 200,000 to 500,000, but they can be towns or small cities with populations of 50,000 to 200,000. Test areas are chosen for their representativeness of a firm's target markets.

A market test provides information about consumers' actual, rather than intended, purchases. In addition, purchase volume can be evaluated in relation to the intensity of other marketing activities such as advertising, in-store promotions, pricing, packaging, and distribution. Forecasters base their sales estimates for larger geographic units on customer response in test areas. For example, PepsiCo's FritoLay unit test marketed Top N Go Walking Tacos—FritoLay snack chip brands served in a bag with street taco-inspired toppings—in a food truck that toured 30 states to measure product response. The food truck tour gave FritoLay insights into whether the marketing mix for Walking Tacos would be successful on a nationwide basis. After selling 23,000 Walking Tacos, the firm gauged demand to be sufficient to expand marketing nationwide in concession stands, convenience stores, and college campuses.[25]

Because it does not require historical sales data, a market test is effective for forecasting sales of new products or of existing products in new geographic areas. A market test also gives a marketer an opportunity to test the success of various elements of the marketing mix, including product ingredients and pricing. However, these tests are often time consuming and expensive. In addition, a marketer cannot be certain that consumer response during a market test represents the total market response, or that the same response will continue in the future.

5-8f Using Multiple Forecasting Methods

Although some businesses depend on a single sales forecasting method, most firms use several techniques. Sometimes a company is forced to use multiple methods when marketing diverse product lines, but even a single product line may require several forecasts, especially when the product is sold to different market segments. Thus, a producer of automobile tires may rely on one technique to forecast tire sales for new vehicles and on another to forecast sales of replacement tires. Variation in the length of forecasts may call for several forecasting methods as well. A firm that employs one method for a short-range forecast may find it inappropriate for long-range forecasting. Sometimes a marketer verifies results of one method by using one or more other methods and comparing outcomes.

Chapter Review

5-1 Define what markets are and explain how they are generally classified.

A market is a group of people who, as individuals or as organizations, have needs for products in a product class and have the ability, willingness, and authority to purchase such products. Markets can be categorized as consumer markets or business markets, based on the characteristics of the individuals and groups that make up a specific market and the purposes for which they buy products. A consumer market, also known as a *business-to-consumer (B2C) market*, consists of purchasers and household members who intend to consume or benefit from the purchased products and do not buy products for the main purpose of making a profit. A business market, also known as a *business-to-business (B2B)*, *industrial*, or *organizational market*, consists of individuals or groups that purchase a specific kind of product for one of three purposes: resale, direct use in producing other products, or use in general daily operations.

5-2 List the five steps of the target market selection process.

In general, marketers employ a five-step process when selecting a target market. Step one is to identify the appropriate targeting strategy. Step two is determining which segmentation variables to use. Step three is to develop a market segment profile. Step four is evaluating relevant market segments. Finally, step five is selecting specific target markets. Not all marketers will follow all of these five steps in this order, but this process provides a good general guide.

5-3 Describe the differences among three targeting strategies.

Step one of the target market selection process is to identify the appropriate targeting strategy. When a company designs a single marketing mix and directs it at the entire market for a particular product, it is using an undifferentiated targeting strategy. The undifferentiated strategy is effective in a homogeneous market, whereas a heterogeneous market needs to be segmented through a concentrated targeting strategy or a differentiated targeting strategy. Both of these strategies divide markets into segments consisting of individuals, groups, or organizations that have one or more similar characteristics and thus can be linked to similar product needs. When using a concentrated strategy, an organization directs marketing efforts toward a single market segment through one marketing mix. With a differentiated targeting strategy, an organization directs customized marketing efforts at two or more segments.

Certain conditions must exist for market segmentation to be effective. First, customers' needs for the product should be heterogeneous. Second, the segments of the market should be identifiable and divisible. Third, the total market should be divided so segments can be compared with respect to estimated sales, costs, and profits. Fourth, at least one segment must have enough profit potential to justify developing and maintaining a special marketing mix for that segment. Fifth, the firm must be able to reach the chosen segment with a particular marketing mix.

5-4 Identify the major segmentation variables.

The second step is determining which segmentation variables to use, which are the characteristics of individuals, groups, or organizations used to divide a total market into segments. The segmentation variable should relate to customers' needs for, uses of, or behavior toward the product. Segmentation variables for consumer markets can be grouped into four categories: demographic (e.g., age, gender, income, ethnicity, family life cycle), geographic (e.g., population, market density, climate), psychographic (e.g., personality traits, motives, lifestyles), and behavioristic (e.g., volume usage, end use, expected benefits, brand loyalty, price sensitivity). Variables for segmenting business markets include geographic location, type of organization, customer size, and product use.

5-5 Describe what market segment profiles are and how they are used.

Step three in the target market selection process is to develop market segment profiles. Such profiles describe the similarities among potential customers within a segment and explain the differences among people and organizations in different market segments. They are used to assess the degree to which the firm's products can match potential customers' product needs. Segments, which may seem attractive at first, may be shown to be quite the opposite after a market segment profile is completed.

5-6 Explain how to evaluate market segments.

Step four is evaluating relevant market segments. Marketers analyze several important factors, such as sales estimates, competition, and estimated costs associated with each segment. Potential sales for a market segment can be measured along several dimensions, including product level, geographic area, time, and level of competition. Besides obtaining sales estimates, it is crucial to assess competitors that are already operating in the segments being considered. Without competitive information, sales estimates may be misleading. The cost of developing a marketing mix that meets the wants and needs of individuals in that segment must also be considered. If the firm's costs to compete in that market are very high, it may be unable to compete in that segment in the long run.

5-7 Identify the factors that influence the selection of specific market segments for use as target markets.

The final step involves the actual selection of specific target markets. In this step, the company considers whether customers' needs differ enough to warrant segmentation and which segments to target. If customers' needs are heterogeneous, the decision of which segment to target must be made, or whether to enter the market at all. Considerations such as the firm's available resources, managerial skills, employee expertise, facilities, the firm's overall objectives, possible legal problems, conflicts with interest groups, and technological advancements must be considered when deciding which segments to target.

5-8 Discuss sales forecasting methods.

A sales forecast is the amount of a product the company actually expects to sell during a specific period at a specified level of marketing activities. To forecast sales, marketers can choose from a number of methods. The choice depends on various factors, including the costs involved, type of product, market characteristics, and time span and purposes of the forecast. There are five categories of forecasting techniques: executive judgment, surveys, time series analysis, regression analysis, and market tests. Executive judgment is based on the intuition of one or more executives. Surveys include customer, sales force, and expert forecasting. Time series analysis uses the firm's historical sales data to discover patterns in the firm's sales over time and employs four major types of analysis: trend, cycle, seasonal, and random factor. With regression analysis, forecasters attempt to find a relationship between past sales and one or more independent variables. Market testing involves making a product available to buyers in one or more test areas and measuring purchases and consumer responses to price, distribution, and promotion. Many companies employ multiple forecasting methods.

 Go to www.cengagebrain.com for resources to help you master the content in this chapter as well as materials that will expand your marketing knowledge!

Developing Your Marketing Plan

Identifying and analyzing a target market is a major component of formulating a marketing strategy. A clear understanding and explanation of a product's target market is crucial to developing a useful marketing plan. References to various dimensions of a target market are likely to appear in several locations in a marketing plan. To assist you in understanding how information in this chapter relates to the creation of your marketing plan, focus on the following considerations:

1. What type of targeting strategy is being used for your product? Should a different targeting strategy be employed?

2. Select and justify the segmentation variables that are most appropriate for segmenting the market for your product. If your product is a consumer product, use Figure 5.3 for ideas regarding the most appropriate segmentation variables. If your marketing plan focuses on a business product, review the information in the section entitled "Variables for Segmenting Business Markets."

3. Discuss how your product should be positioned in the minds of customers in the target market relative to the product positions of competitors.

Key Concepts

Issues for Discussion and Review

1. What is a market? What are the requirements for a market?
2. In your local area, identify a group of people with unsatisfied product needs who represent a market. Could this market be reached by a business organization? Why or why not?
3. Outline the five major steps in the target market selection process.
4. What is an undifferentiated strategy? Under what conditions is it most useful? Describe a present market situation in which a company is using an undifferentiated strategy. Is the business successful? Why or why not?
5. What is market segmentation? Describe the basic conditions required for effective segmentation. Identify several firms that use market segmentation.
6. List the differences between concentrated and differentiated strategies, and describe the advantages and disadvantages of each.
7. Identify and describe four major categories of variables that can be used to segment consumer markets. Give examples of product markets that are segmented by variables in each category.

8. What dimensions are used to segment business markets?
9. Define *geodemographic segmentation*. Identify several types of firms that might employ this type of market segmentation, and explain why.
10. What is a market segment profile? Why is it an important step in the target market selection process?
11. Describe the important factors that marketers should analyze to evaluate market segments.
12. Why is a marketer concerned about sales potential when trying to select a target market?
13. Why is selecting appropriate target markets important for an organization that wants to adopt the marketing concept philosophy?
14. What is a sales forecast? Why is it important?
15. What are the two primary types of surveys a company might use to forecast sales? Why would a company use an outside expert forecasting survey?
16. Under what conditions are market tests useful for sales forecasting? What are the advantages and disadvantages of market tests?
17. Under what conditions might a firm use multiple forecasting methods?

VIDEO CASE 5
Mike Boyle Wants Customers Who Want to Train

Everyone wants to be strong, healthy, and fit. But not everyone is the target market for Mike Boyle Strength and Conditioning (MBSC). With two Massachusetts locations, MBSC offers a variety of programs to help athletes at all levels build strength, improve endurance, and enhance performance. Co-founder Mike Boyle developed his approach to athletic training as a result of his experience working as a trainer for various sports teams and with Boston University. He's also trained professional athletes (such as soccer player Kristine Lilly) and celebrities (such as actress Jennifer Garner).

Over the years, Boyle noticed how many people join a gym with good intentions but then lose their motivation and rarely use the facilities. So when Boyle opened his first gym, he decided to go down a different marketing path. He wants to attract customers who expect to actively train, customers who will set personal goals and then come to the gym regularly to work with trainers, either one-on-one or in a small group. Boyle recognizes that his business doesn't just provide equipment and space for workouts—it also

offers social support and professional advice, encouraging customers to keep progressing toward their fitness and performance goals.

Some of MBSC's customers are school athletes in their teens or twenties. For these customers, MBSC offers age-appropriate programs such as middle-school athletic training, high-school performance training, and college break workout sessions. For adults, MBSC offers small-group strength and conditioning programs and private or semi-private personal training programs geared to customers' individual needs, including weight loss and better mobility. In addition, MBSC targets adults who are active in specific sports, such as golf, with programs to assess capabilities and provide training to improve performance.

As they age, professional athletes who want to continue their high-performance careers see MBSC's training regimen as a way to keep up their strength, speed, and endurance. Even men and women who aren't athletes see MBSC as a resource for taking their fitness to the next level, learning to prevent injuries, and getting in shape to look their best. MBSC also offers customers the option of adding massage therapy and physical therapy sessions when needed.

Boyle reaches out to a wider audience with "how to" videos designed to educate and encourage people who want to know about his training methods. His YouTube channel has 10,000 subscribers, his Twitter account has 33,800 followers, and his Facebook page has 1,000 likes. Boyle keeps up a dialogue with customers and prospects by posting notes on his blog about athletic performance, nutrition, school athletics, and other topics.

Today, MBSC serves customers as young as 11 years old, and at the other end of the spectrum, it has a number of members in their 80s. A small percentage of customers are professional athletes, with many more signing up for training to supplement their school sports activities. Because he was known for his work with the Boston Bruins hockey team and with Boston University's hockey team, Boyle

attracts many varsity hockey players from the Boston area. Boyle has little time these days for the kind of extended workouts he once enjoyed—but he does train every day in brief, intensive stints at his own gyms, serving as a role model for the ongoing benefits of maintaining strength and conditioning throughout life.[26]

Questions for Discussion

1. Which demographic variables does MBSC use in segmenting the market for its services? Be specific.
2. Which psychographic and behavioristic variables does MBSC use, and why?
3. Would you recommend that MBSC use an undifferentiated targeting strategy, a concentrated targeting strategy, or a differentiated targeting strategy to market its services? Explain your answer.

Part 3

ra2studio/Shutterstock.com

Customer Behavior and E-Marketing

PART 3 continues the focus on the customer. Understanding elements that affect buying decisions enables marketers to analyze customers' needs and evaluate how specific marketing strategies can satisfy those needs. **CHAPTER 6** examines consumer buying behavior, their decision processes, and the factors that influence buying decisions. **CHAPTER 7** stresses business markets, organizational buyers, the buying center, and the organizational buying decision process. **CHAPTER 8** looks at how marketers can reach global markets and the actions, involvement, and strategies that marketers employ internationally. **CHAPTER 9** examines how online social networking and digital media have affected marketing strategies with the creation of new communication channels, and the customer behavior related to these emerging technologies and trends.

chapter 6

Consumer Buying Behavior

iStock.com/gilaxia

LEARNING OBJECTIVES

6-1 Recognize the stages of the consumer buying decision process.

6-2 Classify the types of consumer decision making and the level of involvement.

6-3 Explain how situational influences may affect the consumer buying decision process.

6-4 Identify the psychological influences that may affect the consumer buying decision process.

6-5 Describe the social influences that may affect the consumer buying decision process.

6-6 Discuss consumer misbehavior.

Frito-Lay Measures Consumer Response to Its Traditional and New Snack Products

Frito-Lay, known for Lay's, Doritos, Tostitos, Smartfood, and other snack brands, is constantly cooking up new choices to keep customers coming back for more. The future growth of this $14 billion snack business owned by PepsiCo depends on its ability to cater to changing consumer tastes, preferences, and buying patterns. Competition is fierce, and Frito-Lay wants its brands to be on consumers' minds and in their shopping carts.

To attract attention and gauge interest in new flavors, Lay's regularly runs contests to crowdsource ideas for new potato-chip products. After judges screen the ideas for originality, fun, and taste potential, Lay's posts the finalists online so chip lovers can vote for their favorites. Lay's also wants to understand how brand fans feel about traditional chip varieties. Recently, it began selling several limited-time chip flavors and asked the public to vote on whether to replace one of the traditional flavors with a new flavor. Voters overwhelmingly preferred the traditional flavors.

Still, tastes can change quickly, which is why Frito-Lay's marketers monitor trends by checking out popular restaurant menu items and analyzing food comments on social media. "In our category, flavor and variety are really what drives people's interest," explains the chief marketing officer. Variety can mean different packaging and different sizes, offering choices even within the same brand and flavor. For example, Smartfood flavored popcorn now comes in single-serve bags and 35-calorie cups, not just big bags for families or parties. New choices keep Frito-Lay's brands in the public eye and allow snack lovers to try something new without leaving the company's product portfolio.[1]

buying behavior The decision processes and actions of people involved in buying and using products

consumer buying behavior The decision processes and purchasing activities of people who purchase products for personal or household use and not for business purposes

consumer buying decision process A five-stage purchase decision process that includes problem recognition, information search, evaluation of alternatives, purchase, and postpurchase evaluation

Frito-Lay and many other traditional and online marketers go to great lengths to understand their customers' needs and wants. This information provides insight into **buying behavior**, which is the decision processes and actions of people involved in buying and using products. **Consumer buying behavior** refers to the buying behavior of ultimate consumers—those who purchase products for personal or household use and not for business purposes. Marketers attempt to understand buying behavior for several reasons. First, customers' overall opinions and attitudes toward a firm's products have a great impact on the firm's success. Second, as we saw in Chapter 1, the marketing concept stresses that a firm should create a marketing mix that meets customers' needs. To find out what satisfies consumers, marketers must examine the main influences on what, where, when, and how they buy. Third, by gaining a deeper understanding of the factors that affect buying behavior, marketers are better positioned to predict how consumers will respond to marketing strategies.

In this chapter, we first examine the major stages of the consumer buying decision process, beginning with problem recognition, information search, and evaluation of alternatives, and proceeding through purchase and postpurchase evaluation. We follow this with an investigation into how the customer's level of involvement affects the type of decision making they use and a discussion of the types of consumer decision-making processes. Next, we explore situational influences—surroundings, time, purchase reason, and buyer's mood and condition—that affect purchasing decisions. We go on to consider psychological influences on purchasing decisions: perception, motives, learning, attitudes, personality and self-concept, and lifestyles. Next, we discuss social influences that affect buying behavior, including roles, family, reference groups, digital influences, opinion leaders, social classes, and culture and subcultures. We conclude with a discussion of consumer misbehavior.

6-1 CONSUMER BUYING DECISION PROCESS

LO 6-1 Recognize the stages of the consumer buying decision process.

The **consumer buying decision process**, shown in Figure 6.1, includes five stages: problem recognition, information search, evaluation of alternatives, purchase, and postpurchase evaluation. Before we examine each stage, consider these important points.

FIGURE 6.1 CONSUMER BUYING DECISION PROCESS AND POSSIBLE INFLUENCES ON THE PROCESS

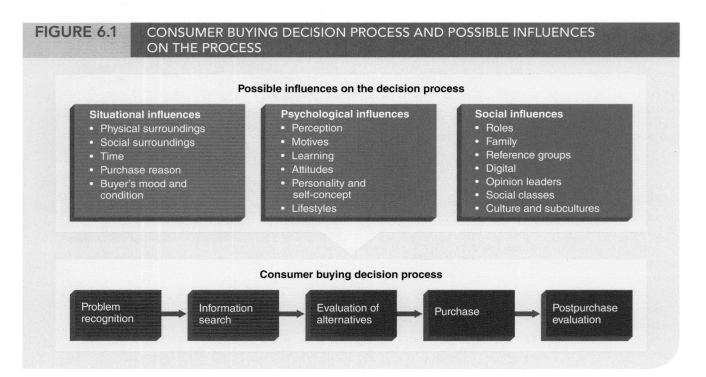

First, this process can be affected by numerous influences, which are categorized as situational, psychological, and social as shown in Figure 6.1. Second, the actual act of purchasing is usually not the first stage of the process. Third, not all decision processes result in a purchase. Individuals may end the process at any stage. Finally, not all consumer decisions include all five stages. The increasing use of mobile technology, especially smartphones, is speeding up the buying decision process for those who use them, in part by providing more opportunities to engage in the process whenever and wherever consumers happen to be.

6-1a Problem Recognition

Problem recognition occurs when a buyer becomes aware of a difference between a desired state and an actual condition. For example, a person may recognize a desire for clean floors, but lack a working vacuum cleaner to fulfill that need. The speed of consumer problem recognition can be rapid or slow. A person may not recognize a problem or need until marketers point it out. Marketers use sales personnel, advertising, and packaging to help trigger recognition of such needs or problems. For instance, marketers may use advertising to alert consumers of the need for pain medication. Consumers may not recognize the need for this product until they are suffering from aches or pains. Take a look at the advertisement for Tidy Cats, which pokes a little fun at the issue of unpleasant litter box odors. The advertisement presents before and after photos of a woman who has turned to Tidy Cats with Tidy Lock Protection to remedy her smelly cat litter problem. The ad first shows her "Stankface" in response to a stinky litter box as the problem that Tidy Cats cat litter solves, as shown in the after photo of the same woman smiling. The ad reinforces the product's ability to solve the problem.

Problem Recognition
This advertisement is attempting to stimulate problem recognition by comparing before-the-use of Tidy Cats with after-the-use of Tidy Cats.

6-1b Information Search

After recognizing the problem or need, the buyer will decide whether to pursue satisfying that need. If the consumer chooses to move forward, he or she will next search for product information to help resolve the problem or satisfy the need. For example, if a consumer realizes that he wants clean floors, he will conduct a search on different products that could fulfill this need.

An information search has two aspects. In an **internal search**, buyers search their memories for information about products that might solve their problem. If they cannot retrieve enough information from memory to make a decision, they seek additional information from outside sources in an **external search**. The external search may focus on communication with friends or relatives, comparison of available brands and prices, marketer-dominated sources, and/or public sources. An individual's personal contacts—friends, relatives, and coworkers—often are influential sources of information because the person trusts and respects them. However, consumers should take care not to overestimate the product knowledge of family and friends. Consumers may also use marketer-dominated sources of information, such as salespeople, advertising, websites, package labeling, and in-store demonstrations and displays because they typically require little effort.

The Internet has become a major resource during the consumer buying decision process, with its many sources for product descriptions and reviews and the ease of comparing prices. Buyers can also obtain information from independent sources—for instance, government

internal search An information search in which buyers search their memories for information about products that might solve their problem

external search An information search in which buyers seek information from sources other than their memories

consideration set A group of brands within a product category that a buyer views as alternatives for possible purchase

evaluative criteria Objective and subjective product characteristics that are important to a buyer

reports, news presentations, publications such as *Consumer Reports*, and reports from product-testing organizations. Consumers frequently view information from these sources as credible because of their factual and unbiased nature. For services that are hard to evaluate even after consumption (e.g., legal advice), consumers rely more on salespeople, friends and family, and independent consumer reports.[2] Buyers today routinely turn to user review sites and apps such as Yelp, Zagat, TripAdvisor, and Angie's List for insights into both goods and services.

Repetition, a technique often used by advertisers, increases consumers' information retention and recall. When they see or hear an advertising message for the first time, recipients may not grasp all of its important details, but they recall more details as the message is repeated. However, marketers should take care not to repeat a message too many times, as consumers can tire of it and begin to respond unfavorably. Information can be presented verbally, numerically, or visually. Marketers pay great attention to the visual components of their advertising materials.

6-1c Evaluation of Alternatives

A successful information search within a product category yields a group of brands that a buyer views as possible alternatives. This group of brands is sometimes called a **consideration set** (or an *evoked set*). Consumers assign a greater value to a brand they have heard of than to one they have not—even when they do not know anything else about the brand other than the name. For example, a consideration set of laptop computers might include devices from Apple, Samsung, Dell, or HP. A consumer will probably initially lean toward the one with which he or she is most familiar, or which his or her friends prefer, before conducting any additional searches.

To assess the products in a consideration set, the buyer uses **evaluative criteria**: objective characteristics (such as the size, speed, capacity) and subjective characteristics (such as style) that are important to him or her. Consider that one laptop buyer may prefer a large display, while another may want a computer with a lot of memory. The buyer assigns a certain level of importance to each criterion. However, some features and characteristics carry more weight than others, depending on consumer preferences. The buyer rates and eventually ranks brands in the consideration set using the selected evaluative criteria. It is possible that the evaluation stage may yield no brand the buyer is willing to purchase. In that case, a further information search may be necessary.

Marketers can influence consumers' evaluations by *framing* the alternatives—that is, describing the alternatives and their attributes in a certain manner. Framing can make a characteristic seem more important to a consumer and facilitate its recall from memory. For example, by stressing a car's superior comfort and safety features over those of a competitor's, a carmaker can direct consumers' attention toward these points. You have experienced the framing effect if you have ever walked into a gourmet grocery or high-end clothing store where the displays make the products seem so appealing you just have to buy them, only to return home and be less satisfied than you were in the store. Framing has a stronger influence on the decision processes of inexperienced buyers. If the evaluation of alternatives yields one or more brands that the consumer is willing to buy, he or she is ready to move on to the next stage of the decision process: the purchase.

6-1d Purchase

In the purchase stage, the consumer chooses to buy the product or brand yielded by the evaluation of alternatives. However, product availability may influence which brand is ultimately purchased. If the brand that ranked highest in evaluation is unavailable and the buyer is unwilling to wait until it is available again, the buyer may choose to purchase the brand that ranked second. For example, if a consumer is at the mall shopping for jeans and the preferred Levis are out of stock in her size but the Lucky brand jeans are not, the consumer may opt to purchase the Lucky brand to save another trip to the mall later.

During this stage, buyers also pick the seller from which they will buy the product—it could be a specific retail shop, chain, or online retailer. The choice of seller may affect final product selection and therefore the terms of sale, which, if negotiable, are determined at this stage. Consumers also settle other issues, such as price, delivery, warranties, maintenance agreements, installation, and credit arrangements, at this time. Finally, the actual purchase takes place (although the consumer can still decide to terminate the buying decision process even at this late stage).

6-1e Postpurchase Evaluation

After the purchase, the buyer evaluates the product to ascertain if its actual performance meets expected levels. Many criteria used in evaluating alternatives are applied again during postpurchase evaluation in order to make a comparison. The outcome of this stage is either satisfaction or dissatisfaction, which influences whether the consumer will repurchase the brand or product, complain to the seller, or communicate positively or negatively with other possible buyers. Postpurchase intent may differ between consumers. For example, the perceived value of the purchase has a weaker effect on the repurchase intent for women than for men. On the other hand, the costs and efforts of switching to a new store affect men's repurchase decisions much more than women.[3]

This stage is especially important for high-priced items. Shortly after the purchase of an expensive product, evaluation may result in **cognitive dissonance**, or doubts in the buyer's mind about whether purchasing the product was the right decision. Cognitive dissonance is most likely to arise when a person recently bought an expensive, high-involvement product that is found lacking compared to desirable features of competing brands. A buyer who is experiencing cognitive dissonance may attempt to return the product or may seek out positive information, such as reviews, to justify choosing it. For instance, a person would likely experience cognitive dissonance if he or she bought a pair of Nike shoes for full price and then found them on sale a week later. Marketers sometimes attempt to reduce cognitive dissonance by having salespeople call or e-mail recent customers to make sure they are satisfied with their new purchases.

As Figure 6.1 shows, three major categories of influences are believed to affect the consumer buying decision process: situational, psychological, and social. Although we discuss each major influence separately later in the chapter, their effects on the consumer decision process are interrelated.

6-2 TYPES OF CONSUMER DECISION MAKING AND LEVEL OF INVOLVEMENT

LO 6-2 Classify the types of consumer decision making and the level of involvement.

To acquire products that satisfy their current and future needs, consumers engage in different types of decision-making processes that vary depending on the nature of the product. The amount of effort, both mental and physical, that buyers expend in solving problems also varies considerably with the cost and type of product.

6-2a Types of Consumer Decision Making

There are three types of consumer decision making, which vary in involvement level and other factors: routinized response behavior, limited decision making, or extended decision making (see Table 6.1).

cognitive dissonance A buyer's doubts shortly after a purchase about whether the decision was the right one

TABLE 6.1	CONSUMER DECISION MAKING		
	Routinized Response	**Limited**	**Extended**
Product cost	Low	Low to moderate	High
Search effort	Little	Little to moderate	Extensive
Time spent	Short	Short to medium	Lengthy
Brand preference	More than one is acceptable, although one may be preferred	Several	Varies, usually many

A consumer uses **routinized response behavior** when buying frequently purchased, low-cost items that require very little search-and-decision effort. A consumer may have a brand preference, but will be satisfied with several brands in the product class or even a generic or store brand of the product. Typically, low-involvement products are bought through routinized response behavior—that is, almost automatically. For example, buyers spend little time or effort selecting most supermarket items such as bottled water, chips, or batteries.

Buyers engage in **limited decision making** when they purchase products occasionally or from unfamiliar brands in a familiar product category. This type of decision making requires slightly more time for information gathering and deliberation. For instance, if a more energy-efficient dry cleaner opens up closer to your home, you might seek additional information about it, perhaps by asking a friend who has used their services, watching a commercial about it, or visiting the company's website, before trying out their services.

The most complex type of decision making, **extended decision making**, occurs with high-involvement, unfamiliar, expensive, or infrequently purchased items—for instance, a car, a computer, or the services of a lawyer or doctor. The buyer uses many criteria to evaluate alternative brands or choices and spends much time seeking information and deciding before making the purchase.

Purchase of a specific product does not elicit the same type of decision-making process every time. We may engage in extended decision making the first time we buy a product, but find that limited decision making suffices when we buy it again. If a routinely purchased brand is discontinued or no longer satisfies us, we may use limited or extended decision making to switch to a new brand. Thus, if we notice that the brand of pain reliever we normally buy is no longer working well, we may seek out a different brand through limited decision making.

It is important to note that consumer decision making is not always rational. Most consumers occasionally make purchases solely on impulse and not on the basis of any of these three decision-making processes. **Impulse buying** involves no conscious planning and stems from a powerful urge to buy something immediately. Retailers set up gum, beef jerky, peanuts, and magazines close to the cash registers to encourage impulse buying.

6-2b Consumer Level of Involvement

A major factor in the type of decision-making process employed depends on the customer's **level of involvement**, which is the degree of interest in a product and the importance the individual places on that product. As an example, involvement with wine can be used to segment consumers who will visit a winery. Those consumers with high involvement with wine differ significantly in visitation motives and patterns than those identified as low involvement.[4] High-involvement products tend to be those that are visible to others

---

routinized response behavior A consumer problem-solving process used when buying frequently purchased, low-cost items that require very little search-and-decision effort

limited decision making A consumer problem-solving process used when purchasing products occasionally or needing information about an unfamiliar brand in a familiar product category

extended decision making A consumer problem-solving process employed when purchasing unfamiliar, expensive, or infrequently bought products

impulse buying An unplanned buying behavior resulting from a powerful urge to buy something immediately

level of involvement An individual's degree of interest in a product and the importance of the product for that person

(such as real estate, high-end electronics, or automobiles) and are more expensive. High-importance issues, such as health care, are also associated with high levels of involvement. Low-involvement products are much less expensive and have less associated social risk, such as grocery or drugstore items.

A person's interest in a product or product category that is ongoing and long-term is referred to as *enduring involvement.* Most consumers have an enduring involvement with only a very few activities or items—these are the product categories in which they have the most interest. Many consumers, for instance, have an enduring involvement with Apple products, a brand that inspires loyalty and trust. These consumers will expend a great deal of effort to purchase and learn about Apple products, waiting in line for the latest iPhone release and reading articles about the various features of the latest MacBook. In contrast, *situational involvement* is temporary and dynamic and results from a particular set of circumstances, such as the sudden need to buy a new laptop after the current one starts malfunctioning right before a research project is due. For a short time period, the consumer will research different computer brands, retailers, and prices, but will settle on a choice relatively quickly because the consumer needs a functional computer as soon as possible. Once the purchase is made, the consumer's interest and involvement taper off quickly. Consumer involvement may be attached to product categories (such as sports), loyalty to a specific brand, interest in a specific advertisement (e.g., a funny commercial) or a medium (such as a television show), or to certain decisions and behaviors (e.g., a love of shopping). Interest, such as finding an advertisement entertaining, does not necessarily mean the consumer will become involved with the brand. It may not satisfy a need the customer currently has, or he or she may be loyal to another brand.

Low-Involvement Products
Bottled water is a low-involvement product because it is inexpensive and purchased frequently. When buying bottled water, consumers usually employ routinized response behavior.

iStock.com/Danilin

There are several factors that influence a buyer's level of involvement. The most significant is the perceived risk of a purchase. In particular, high-priced items have greater risk of financial loss of future purchasing power. Buying a new car, for example, generally requires a monthly payment that will significantly reduce your purchasing power for other items in your monthly budget. Thus, high-priced products tend to be associated with a higher level of involvement. On the other hand, previous experience with a product is usually associated with lower levels of involvement because buyers do not need to engage in extensive decision making for a product they have purchased several times before. Finally, a buyer who is highly interested in something is likely to have a higher level of involvement than someone who is not. Consider an avid runner; he is more likely than most to be interested in running shoes and sports drinks, as well as magazines and blogs devoted to running and marathons. His level of involvement in a pair of running shoes is likely to be higher than for a college student who is just buying shoes to wear around campus.

6-3 SITUATIONAL INFLUENCES ON THE BUYING DECISION PROCESS

LO 6-3 Explain how situational influences may affect the consumer buying decision process.

Situational influences result from circumstances, time, and location that affect the consumer buying decision process. Imagine buying an automobile tire after noticing, while washing your car, that one of your current tires is badly worn. This is a different experience from buying a tire right after a blowout on the highway spoils your road trip. Situational

situational influences
Influences that result from circumstances, time, and location that affect the consumer buying decision process

factors can influence the buyer during any stage of the consumer buying decision process and may cause the individual to shorten, lengthen, or terminate the process. Situational factors can be classified into five categories: physical surroundings, social surroundings, time perspective, reason for purchase, and the buyer's momentary mood and condition.[5]

Physical surroundings include location, store atmosphere, scents, sounds, lighting, weather, and other factors in the physical environment in which the decision-making process occurs. A football stadium, for example, includes not only the field and bleachers but also concession stands, souvenir shops, entertainment, music, and the energy of the audience. Retail chains try to design their store environment and layout in a way that makes shopping as enjoyable and easy as possible, so consumers are more inclined to linger and make purchases. Marketers at banks, department stores, and specialty stores go to considerable effort and expense to create physical settings that are conducive to making purchase decisions. Abercrombie & Fitch, for example, sprays its men's fragrance, Fierce, in its stores and plays loud club music to attract young men and women—while repelling older shoppers. A&F may be exploiting the fact that overstimulating loud music has been found to weaken self-control, which could prompt impulse purchases.[6] Restaurant chains, such as Olive Garden and Chili's, invest heavily in facilities, often building from the ground up, to provide surroundings that are distinctive to the chain and that enhance customers' experiences. Even remodeling the physical surroundings of a store can directly affect sales. Remodeling tends to increase the sales to new customers, who will spend more per visit and return to the store more frequently than existing customers.[7]

However, in some settings, dimensions such as weather, traffic sounds, and odors are clearly beyond the marketers' control. General climatic conditions, for example, may influence a customer's decision to buy a specific type of vehicle (such as an SUV) with certain features (such as four-wheel drive). Current weather conditions, or other external factors, may be either encouraging or discouraging to consumers when they seek out specific products. Such factors may be favorable, as when forecasted bad weather causes customers to stock up and even hoard basic essentials.

Social surroundings include characteristics and interactions of others who are present during a purchase decision, such as friends, relatives, salespeople, and other customers. Buyers may feel pressured to behave in a certain way because they are in a public place such as a restaurant, store, or sports arena. Thoughts about who will be around when the product is used or consumed are another dimension of the social setting. Negative elements of physical surroundings, such as an overcrowded store or an argument between a customer and a salesperson, may cause consumers to leave the store before purchasing anything.

The time dimension influences the buying decision process in several ways. It takes varying amounts of time to progress through the steps of the buying decision process, including learning about, searching for, purchasing, and using a product. Time also plays a role when consumers consider the frequency of product use, the length of time required to use it, and the overall product life. Other time dimensions that can influence purchases include time of day, day of the week or month, seasons, and holidays. For example, a customer under time constraints is likely to either make a quick purchase decision or delay a decision. On the other hand, consumers may be willing to wait longer to purchase certain products depending upon their desire for them. An Apple enthusiast might spend a considerable time waiting for the newest iPhone to be released.

I WILL
REJECT 99.96% OF THE WORLD'S FINEST DIAMONDS BECAUSE THERE'S
A DIFFERENCE BETWEEN QUALITY AND TIFFANY-QUALITY.

THE TIFFANY® SETTING.
130 YEARS OF EXTRAORDINARY.

TIFFANY & CO.
NEW YORK SINCE 1837

Tiffany & Co.

Situational Influences
An engagement and a wedding are major events in people's lives. Purchases associated with major life events are very important. This reason for purchase results in customers taking considerable time and going to substantial efforts to ensure that the selection is just right.

The reason for purchase involves what the product purchase should accomplish and for whom. Generally, consumers purchase an item for their own use, for household use, or as a gift. Purchase choices are likely to vary depending on the reason. Consider the advertisement for the Tiffany engagement rings. The ad plays on the idea of the wedding vow by promising to reject most diamonds because they fail to live up to Tiffany's quality standards. The understated advertisement highlights the phrase "I will" and presents a beautiful ring backed by the iconic greenish blue color of the Tiffany brand to appeal to those thinking about marriage. Engagement rings are completely dependent upon the situation of getting engaged and likely are not purchased for anything else. As a result, buyers spend a great deal of time and money to find the perfect one.

The buyer's moods (e.g., anger, anxiety, or contentment) or conditions (e.g., fatigue, illness, or having cash on hand) may also affect the consumer buying decision process. Such moods or conditions are momentary and occur immediately before the situation where a buying decision will be made. They can affect a person's ability and desire to search for or receive information, or seek and evaluate alternatives. Moods can also significantly influence a consumer's postpurchase evaluation. If you are happy immediately after purchase, you may be more likely to attribute the mood to the product and will judge it favorably.

6-4 PSYCHOLOGICAL INFLUENCES ON THE BUYING DECISION PROCESS

LO 6-4 Identify the psychological influences that may affect the consumer buying decision process.

Psychological influences partly determine people's general behavior and thus influence their behavior as consumers. Primary psychological influences on consumer behavior are perception, motives, learning, attitudes, personality and self-concept, and lifestyles. Even though these psychological factors operate internally, they are strongly affected by external social forces.

6-4a **Perception**

People perceive the same event or thing at the same time in different ways. When you first look at the illustration, do you see two women or three columns? Similarly, the same individual may perceive an item in different ways at different times. **Perception** is the process of selecting, organizing, and interpreting information inputs to produce meaning. **Information inputs** are sensations received through sight, taste, hearing, smell, and touch. When we hear an advertisement on the radio, see a friend, smell food cooking at a restaurant, or touch a product, we receive information inputs. Perception is complicated and can be influenced and compounded by different factors. For instance, research has shown that advertisements for food items that appeal to multiple senses at once are more effective than ones that focus on taste alone.[8]

Perception can be interpreted in different ways because, although we constantly receive pieces of information, only a few reach our awareness. We would be completely overwhelmed if we paid equal attention to all sensory inputs, so we select some and ignore others. This process is called **selective exposure** because an individual selects (mostly unconsciously) which inputs will reach awareness.

psychological influences Factors that in part determine people's general behavior, thus influencing their behavior as consumers

perception The process of selecting, organizing, and interpreting information inputs to produce meaning

information inputs Sensations received through sight, taste, hearing, smell, and touch

selective exposure The process by which some inputs are selected to reach awareness and others are not

Perception
Do you see two women or three columns?

Juriah Mosin/Shutterstock.com

If you are concentrating on this paragraph, you probably are not aware that cars outside are making noise, that the room light is on, that a song is playing in the background, or even that you are touching the page. Even though you receive these inputs, they do not reach your awareness until they are brought to your attention. An individual's current set of needs affects selective exposure. Information inputs that relate to one's strongest needs are more likely to reach conscious awareness. It is not by chance that many fast-food commercials are aired near mealtimes. Customers are more likely to pay attention to these advertisements at these times.

The selective nature of perception may also result in two other conditions: selective distortion and selective retention. **Selective distortion** is changing or twisting received information. It occurs when a person receives information inconsistent with personal feelings or beliefs and he or she interprets the information, changing its meaning to align more closely with expectations. Selective distortion explains why people will reject logical information, even when presented with supporting evidence. Selective distortion can both help and hurt marketers. For example, a consumer may become loyal to a brand and remain loyal, even when confronted with evidence that another brand is superior. However, selective distortion can also lessen the impact of the message on the individual substantially. For instance, consumers are less likely to purchase a green product if they learn that the product was intentionally redesigned to benefit the environment. They prefer any environmental benefits to be an unintentional side effect. Consumers tend to believe that products intentionally designed to be more sustainable require product developers to take resources away from other areas, such as product quality.[9] In **selective retention**, a person remembers information inputs that support personal feelings and beliefs and forgets inputs that do not. After hearing a sales presentation and leaving a store, for example, a customer may quickly forget many selling points if they contradict personal beliefs or preconceived notions about a product.

The second step in the process of perception is perceptual organization. Information inputs that reach awareness are not received in an organized form. To produce meaning, an individual must organize and integrate new information with what is already stored in memory. People use several methods to achieve this. One method, called *closure*, occurs when a person fills in missing information in a way that conforms to a pattern or statement. In an attempt to draw attention to its brand, an advertiser may capitalize on closure by using incomplete images, sounds, or statements in its advertisements.

Interpretation, the third step in the perceptual process, involves assigning meaning to what has been organized. A person interprets information according to what he or she expects or what is familiar. For this reason, a manufacturer who changes a product or its package may face consumer backlash from customers looking for the old, familiar product or package and who do not recognize, or do not like, the new one. Unless a product or package change is accompanied by a promotional program that makes people aware of the change, an organization may suffer a sales decline.

Although marketers cannot control buyers' perceptions, they often try to influence them. Several problems may arise from such attempts, however. First, a consumer's perceptual process may operate such that a seller's information never reaches the target. For example, a buyer may entirely block out and not notice an advertisement in a magazine. Second, a buyer may receive information but perceive it differently than was intended, as occurs in selective distortion. For instance, when a toothpaste producer advertises that "35 percent of the people who use this toothpaste have fewer cavities," a customer could infer that 65 percent of users have more cavities. Third, a buyer who perceives information inputs to be inconsistent with prior beliefs is likely to forget the information quickly, as is the case with selective retention.

6-4b Motives

A **motive** is an internal energizing force that directs a person's activities toward satisfying needs or achieving goals. Buyers are affected by a set of motives rather than by just one.

selective distortion An individual's changing or twisting of information that is inconsistent with personal feelings or beliefs

selective retention Remembering information inputs that support personal feelings and beliefs and forgetting inputs that do not

motive An internal energizing force that directs a person's behavior toward satisfying needs or achieving goals

At any point in time, certain motives will have a stronger influence on a person than others. For example, the sensation of being cold is a strong motivator on the decision to purchase a new coat, making the feeling more urgent in the winter than it is in the summer. Motives can be physical feelings, states of mind, or emotions. Some motives may help an individual achieve his or her goals, whereas others create barriers to achievement. Motives also affect the direction and intensity of behavior.

Abraham Maslow, an American psychologist, conceived a theory of motivation based on a hierarchy of needs. According to Maslow, humans seek to satisfy five levels of needs, from most to least basic to survival, as shown in Figure 6.2.

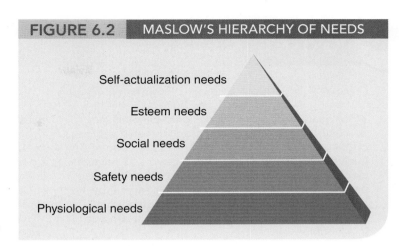

FIGURE 6.2   MASLOW'S HIERARCHY OF NEEDS

Self-actualization needs

Esteem needs

Social needs

Safety needs

Physiological needs

This pyramid is known as **Maslow's hierarchy of needs**. Maslow proposed that people are constantly striving to move up the hierarchy, fulfilling one level of needs, then aspiring to fulfill the next.

At the most basic level are *physiological needs*, requirements for survival such as food, water, sex, clothing, and shelter, which people try to satisfy first. Food and beverage marketers often appeal to physiological needs, such as sex appeal or hunger. Carl's Jr. is famous for its commercials of lingerie models eating burgers, appealing to two physiological needs at once—hunger and sex appeal.

At the next level are *safety needs*, which include security and freedom from physical and emotional pain and suffering. Life insurance, automobile air bags, carbon monoxide detectors, vitamins, and decay-fighting toothpastes are products that consumers purchase to ensure their safety needs are met.

Next are *social needs*: the human requirements for love and affection and a sense of belonging. Advertisements for cosmetics and other beauty products, jewelry, and even cars often suggest that purchasing these products will bring love and social acceptance, and are therefore appealing to social needs. Certain types of clothing, such as items emblazoned with logos or slogans, appeal to the customer's need to belong by displaying their affinity for popular brands.

At the level of *esteem needs*, people require respect and recognition from others as well as self-esteem, a sense of one's own worth. Owning a Mercedes, purchasing an expensive handbag, or flying first class can satisfy esteem needs. Purchasing products from firms such as Keurig Green Mountain Coffee, that have reputations for being socially responsible, can be motivated by a customer's desire to be perceived as a caring individual, thus contributing to satisfying esteem needs.

At the top of the hierarchy are *self-actualization needs*. These refer to people's needs to grow and develop and to become all they are capable of becoming. Many people never reach this level of the hierarchy, but it can be motivating to try. Some products that may send messages that they satisfy these needs include fitness center memberships, educational institutions, and self-improvement workshops. In its recruiting advertisements, the U.S. Army told its audience to "be all that you can be," a message that implied that people can reach their full potential by enlisting in the U.S. Army.

Maslow's hierarchy of needs The five levels of needs that humans seek to satisfy, from most to least important

iStock.com/NoDerog

Safety Needs
Crest brand toothpaste appeals to safety needs because it fights tooth decay, resulting in better health for the user.

Motives that influence which establishments a customer frequents are called **patronage motives**. A buyer may shop at a specific store because of such patronage motives as price, service, location, product variety, or friendliness of salespeople. To capitalize on patronage motives, marketers try to determine why regular customers shop at a particular store and to emphasize these characteristics in the marketing mix.

6-4c **Learning**

Learning refers to changes in a person's thought processes and behavior caused by information and experience. Consequences of behavior strongly influence the learning process. Behaviors that result in positive consequences tend to be repeated. For example, a consumer who is highly satisfied with a haircut at a salon is more likely to return to that salon and request the same hairdresser again. The individual will probably continue to purchase the good or service until it no longer provides satisfaction. When outcomes of the behavior are no longer satisfying or no longer contribute to achieving a desired goal, the person may switch to another product or organization. For instance, if the hairdresser leaves the salon, the consumer might stop going if there is no one else there that can do a comparable haircut.

Purchasing decisions require that customers process information, an ability that varies by individual. The type of information inexperienced buyers use may differ from the type used by experienced shoppers who are familiar with the product and purchase situation. Thus, two potential buyers of an antique desk may use different types of information in making their purchase decisions. The inexperienced buyer may judge the desk's value by price and appearance, whereas the more experienced buyer may look at the construction and condition of the desk as well as information about the manufacturer, period, and place of origin to assess the desk's quality and value. Consumers who lack experience may seek information from others when making a purchase and even take along an informed friend with experience. Experienced buyers have greater self-confidence and more knowledge about the product and can recognize which product features are reliable cues to quality.

Marketers help customers learn about their products by facilitating opportunities to gain experience with them, which makes customers feel more comfortable. They engage in

patronage motives Motives that influence where a person purchases products on a regular basis

learning Changes in an individual's thought processes and behavior caused by information and experience

shaping potential buyers' early experience through free samples, sometimes coupled with coupons, which can encourage trial and reduce purchase risk. For instance, because some consumers may be wary of trying new products outside of their routine, Costco, H-E-B's Central Market, and Whole Foods permit companies to sample their products in the stores' aisles. Personal-care products sometimes include a sample of another product in the package. In-store demonstrations foster knowledge of product uses. A software producer may use point-of-sale product demonstrations to introduce a new product. Adobe allows potential InDesign customers to download a free trial of the software for seven days to determine whether they like the software. Test drives give potential new-car purchasers some experience with the automobile's features.

Consumers also learn by experiencing products indirectly through information from salespeople, advertisements, websites, Internet videos, social media, friends, and relatives. Through sales personnel and advertisements, marketers offer information before (and sometimes after) purchases that can create favorable consumer attitudes toward the product. However, marketers may encounter problems in attracting and holding consumers' attention, providing them with information for making purchase decisions, and convincing them to try the product.

6-4d **Attitudes**

An **attitude** is an individual's enduring evaluation of feelings about and behavioral tendencies toward an object or idea. The things toward which we have attitudes may be tangible or intangible, living or nonliving. For example, we have attitudes about sex, religion, politics, and music, just as we do toward cars, football, and breakfast cereals. Although attitudes can change over time, they generally remain stable and do not vary, particularly in the short term. A person's attitudes toward different things do not have equal impact at any one time, and some are stronger than others. Individuals acquire attitudes through experience and interaction with other people.

An attitude consists of three major components: cognitive, affective, and behavioral. The cognitive component is the person's knowledge and information about the object or idea. For example, as consumers have become more knowledgeable about health, obesity, and quality ingredients, their attitudes toward soft drinks and fast food have become less favorable, and the sales of companies like McDonald's and Coca-Cola have declined. The affective component comprises the individual's feelings and emotions toward the object or idea. Emotions involve both psychological and biological elements. They relate to feelings and can create visceral responses that result in behaviors. Love, hate, anger, and fear are emotions that can influence behavior. For some people, certain brands, such as Apple, Starbucks, or REI, elicit a strong emotional response. Firms that successfully create an emotional experience or connection with customers establish a positive brand image that can result in customer loyalty. Southwest Airlines, for example, has forged an emotional connection with many of its customers through creative use of humor both during flights and on its website. The airline extends this playful focus and personal touches in every interaction to demonstrate its commitment to people—both customers and employees.[10] This means it is important for marketers to generate authentic, genuine messages that consumers can relate to on an emotional level. The behavioral component manifests itself in the person's actions regarding the object or idea. Changes in cognitive, affective, or behavioral components may possibly affect other components.

Consumer attitudes toward a company and its products greatly influence success or failure of the firm's marketing strategy. When consumers have strongly negative attitudes toward one or more aspects of a firm's marketing practices, they may not only stop using its products, but also urge relatives and friends to do likewise. Because attitudes play an important part in determining consumer behavior, marketers should regularly measure consumer attitudes toward prices, package designs, brand names, advertisements, salespeople, repair services, store locations, features of existing or proposed products, and social responsibility efforts.

attitude An individual's enduring evaluation of feelings about and behavioral tendencies toward an object or idea

attitude scale A means of measuring consumer attitudes by gauging the intensity of individuals' reactions to adjectives, phrases, or sentences about an object

Efforts to understand attitudes have resulted in two major academic models: the attitude toward the object model (the Fishbein model) and the behavioral intentions model (also known as the Theory of Reasoned Action). These models provide an understanding of the role of attitudes in decision making. The attitude toward the object model can be used to understand, and possibly predict, a consumer's attitude. It consists of three elements: beliefs about product attributes, the strength of beliefs, and the evaluation of beliefs. These elements combine to form what is called the overall attitude toward the object.[11]

The behavioral intentions model, rather than focusing on attributes, focuses on intentions to act or purchase. This model considers consumer perceptions of what other people, particularly peers, believe is the best choice among a set of alternatives. As its name indicates, this model focuses on attitudes toward the buying behavior, not toward the object. The subjective norm component is important in recognizing that individuals live in an inherently social environment and are influenced by what others think and believe. Consider attitudes toward personal appearance (such as clothing, hairstyles, piercings, and tattoos). Consumers will take into account what others will think of their decisions. Many people are motivated to comply with what others hold to be an acceptable norm and stay in close communication through traditional word-of-mouth communications, media, and online social networking.

Several methods help marketers gauge consumer attitudes. One of the simplest ways is to question people directly. The Internet and social networking sites are useful tools for marketers seeking to garner information on attitudes directly from consumers. Using sites such as Facebook, companies can ask consumers for feedback and product reviews.

SILKY SMOOTH TASTE WITHOUT THE SUGAR | Unlike the 12 grams of sugar in dairy milk,* Silk® Unsweetened Vanilla Almondmilk has 0 sugar and always tastes silky smooth.

Silk helps you bloom™

WhiteWave Services, Inc.

Communication to Influence Attitudes
The maker of Silk is seeking to change consumer attitudes about almond milk by highlighting a silky smooth taste and a lack of sugar.

Marketers also evaluate attitudes through attitude scales. An **attitude scale** usually consists of a series of adjectives, phrases, or sentences about an object. Respondents indicate the intensity of their feelings toward the object by reacting to the adjectives, phrases, or sentences. For example, a marketer who is measuring people's attitudes toward shopping might ask respondents to indicate the extent to which they agree or disagree with a number of statements, such as "shopping is more fun than watching television."

When marketers determine that a significant number of consumers have negative attitudes toward an aspect of a marketing mix, they may try to improve those attitudes. This task is generally lengthy, expensive, and difficult and can require extensive promotional efforts. To alter responses so that more consumers purchase a certain brand, a firm might launch an information-focused campaign to change the cognitive component of a consumer's attitude, or a persuasive (emotional) campaign to influence the affective component. Distributing free samples can help change the behavioral component by offering customers a no-cost means of trying out a product.

Both business and nonbusiness organizations try to change people's attitudes about many things using marketing messages, from health and safety to prices and product features. For example, look at the advertisement for Silk Almondmilk, a nondairy alternative to milk. With this ad, Silk is not just targeting those who do not drink regular milk. It is targeting health-conscious consumers by emphasizing the fact that Almondmilk has less sugar than conventional milk. To further influence consumers' perceptions of the product, the ad highlights the silky smooth texture of Almondmilk and depicts an almond holding up the product while standing on top of a carton of conventional milk, hinting that it might be a healthier alternative.

6-4e **Personality and Self-Concept**

Personality is a set of internal traits and distinct behavioral tendencies that result in consistent patterns of behavior in certain situations. An individual's personality is a unique combination of hereditary characteristics and personal experiences. Personalities typically are described as having one or more characteristics, such as compulsiveness, ambition, gregariousness, dogmatism, authoritarianism, introversion, extroversion, and competitiveness. Marketing researchers look for relationships between such characteristics and buying behavior. Even though a few links between several personality traits and buyer behavior have been identified, studies have not proven a definitive link. However, the weak association between personality and buying behavior may be the result of unreliable measures, rather than a true lack of a relationship.

Many marketers are convinced that personalities do influence types and brands of products purchased. Because of this believed relation, marketers aim advertising at specific personality types. For example, truck commercials often highlight rugged, all-American individualism. Marketers generally focus on positive personality characteristics, such as security consciousness, sociability, independence, or competitiveness, rather than on negatively valued ones, such as insensitivity or timidity.

A person's self-concept is closely linked to personality. **Self-concept** (sometimes called *self-image*) is one's perception or view of oneself. Individuals develop and alter their self-concepts based on an interaction between psychological and social dimensions. Research shows that buyers purchase products that reflect and enhance their self-concepts and that purchase decisions are important to the development and maintenance of a stable self-concept.[12] For example, consumers who feel insecure about their self-concept may purchase products that they believe will help bolster the qualities they would like to project. Consumers' self-concepts can influence whether they buy a product in a specific product category and may affect brand selection as well as the retailers they frequent.

personality A set of internal traits and distinct behavioral tendencies that result in consistent patterns of behavior in certain situations

self-concept A perception or view of oneself

lifestyle An individual's pattern of living expressed through activities, interests, and opinions

6-4f **Lifestyles**

As we saw in Chapter 4, many marketers attempt to segment markets by lifestyle. A **lifestyle** is an individual's pattern of living expressed through activities, interests, and opinions. Lifestyle patterns include the ways people spend time, the extent of their interaction with others, and their general outlook on life. People partially determine their own lifestyles, but lifestyle is also affected by personality and by demographic factors such as age, education, income, and social class. Lifestyles have a strong impact on many aspects of the consumer buying decision process, from problem recognition to postpurchase evaluation. Lifestyles influence consumers' product needs and brand preferences, types of media they use, and how and where they shop.

One of the most popular frameworks for understanding consumer lifestyles and their influences on purchasing behavior is a product called PRIZM (see Chapter 5). Originally developed by Claritas, PRIZM was acquired by Nielsen, one of the leading consumer behavior companies in the world.

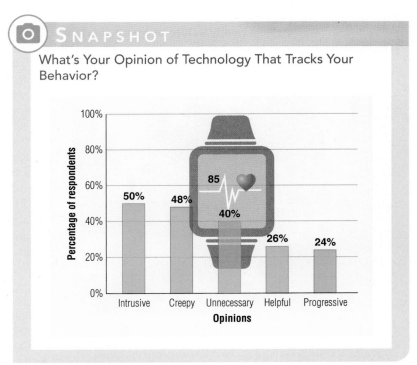

SNAPSHOT

What's Your Opinion of Technology That Tracks Your Behavior?

Percentage of respondents

- Intrusive: 50%
- Creepy: 48%
- Unnecessary: 40% (85)
- Helpful: 26%
- Progressive: 24%

Opinions

Source: Wearables.com/Center for Generational Kinetics survey of 1,007 consumers

social influences The forces other people exert on one's buying behavior

roles Actions and activities that a person in a particular position is supposed to perform based on expectations of the individual and surrounding persons

consumer socialization The process through which a person acquires the knowledge and skills to function as a consumer

It divides consumers in the United States into 66 distinct groups based on numerous variables such as education, income, technology use, employment, and social groups.[13] These groups can help marketers understand consumers and how factors like lifestyle and education will impact their purchasing habits.

6-5 SOCIAL INFLUENCES ON THE BUYING DECISION PROCESS

LO 6-5 Describe the social influences that may affect the consumer buying decision process.

Forces that other people exert on buying behavior are called social influences. As Figure 6.1 (located at the beginning of this chapter) shows, they are divided into seven major groups: roles, family, reference groups, digital, opinion leaders, social classes, and culture and subcultures.

6-5a Roles

All of us occupy positions within groups, organizations, and institutions. In these positions, we play one or more roles, which are sets of actions and activities a person in a particular position is supposed to perform based on the expectations of both the individual and surrounding persons. Because every person occupies numerous positions, they have many roles. For example, a man may perform the roles of son, husband, father, employee or employer, church member, civic organization member, and student in an evening college class. Thus, multiple sets of expectations are placed on each person's behavior.

An individual's roles influence both general behavior and buying behavior. The demands of a person's many roles may be diverse and even at times inconsistent or at odds. Consider the various types of clothes that you buy and wear depending on whether you are going to class, to work, to a party, or to the gym. You and others in these settings have expectations about what is acceptable attire for these events. Thus, the expectations of those around us affect our purchases of many different types of clothing and other products.

6-5b Family Influences

Family influences have a direct impact on the consumer buying decision process. Parents teach their children how to cope with a variety of problems, including those that help them deal with purchase decisions. Consumer socialization is the process through which a person acquires the knowledge and skills to function as a consumer. Often, children gain this knowledge and set of skills by observing parents and older siblings in purchase situations. Children observe brand preferences and buying practices in their families and, as adults, will retain some of these brand preferences and buying practices as they establish and raise their own families. Buying decisions made by a family are a combination of group and individual decisions.

The extent to which family members take part in family decision making varies among families and product categories. Traditionally, family decision-making processes have been grouped into four categories: autonomic, husband dominant, wife dominant, and syncratic by a study conducted in Belgium (and replicated in the United States), as shown in Table 6.2.[14] Although female roles have changed over time, women still make the majority of purchase decisions in households. Indeed, research indicates that women remain the primary decision makers for 85 percent of all consumer purchases.[15] When the family has a strong traditional sex-role orientation, certain tasks are stereotypically considered either

iStock.com/jhorrocks

Family Influences
The decision process related to purchasing a home is influenced by parents and children. In addition, children learn about buying housing, which they will apply when making similar decisions when they are adults.

TABLE 6.2	TYPES OF FAMILY DECISION MAKING	
Decision-Making Type	**Decision Maker**	**Types of Products**
Husband dominant	Male head of household	Lawn mowers, hardware and tools, stereos, automobile parts
Wife dominant	Female head of household	Children's clothing, women's clothing, groceries, household furnishings
Autonomic	Equally likely to be made by the husband or wife, but not by both	Men's clothing, luggage, toys and games, sporting equipment, cameras
Syncratic	Made jointly by husband and wife	Vacations, TVs, living room furniture, carpets, financial planning services, family cars

masculine or feminine, and more decisions tend to be husband-dominated than they are in less traditional families.[16]

The family life-cycle stage affects individual and joint needs of family members. Family life-cycle stage influences purchases ranging from housing, clothing, and personal-care items to entertainment and investment products. For example, consider how the car needs of recently married "twenty-somethings" compare to those of the same couple when they are "thirty-somethings" with a baby or "forty-somethings" with teenagers. Chrysler is developing an electric minivan, the Portal, which buyers can reconfigure as needed to match their changing life-cycle stages.[17] Family life-cycle changes can affect which family members are involved in purchase decisions and the types of products purchased. Children also have a strong influence on household purchase decisions.

When two or more family members participate in a purchase, their roles may dictate that each is responsible for performing certain purchase-related tasks, such as initiating the idea, gathering information, determining if the product is affordable, deciding whether to buy the product, or selecting the specific brand. The specific purchase tasks performed depend on the types of products being considered, the kind of family purchase decision process typically employed, and the presence and amount of influence children have in the decision process. Thus, different family members play different roles in the family buying process.

Within a household, an individual may perform one or more roles related to making buying decisions. The gatekeeper is the household member who collects and controls information, including price and quality comparisons, locations of sellers, and assessment of which brand best suits the household's needs. For example, if a family is planning a summer vacation, the gatekeeper will compare prices for hotels and airfare to determine the best deal. The influencer is a family member who tries to sway buying decisions by expressing his or her opinions. In the vacation example, an influencer might be a child who wants to go to Disney World or a teenager who wants to go snowboarding. The decider is a member who makes the buying choice. This role switches depending on the type and expense of the product being purchased. In the case of a vacation, the decider will more likely be the adults, who possess information, influence, and their own preferences. The buyer is the family member who actually makes the purchase. The user is a household member who consumes or uses the product. In the Disney World example, all members of the family are users.

6-5c **Reference Groups**

A **reference group** is a group, either large or small, with which a person identifies so strongly that he or she adopts the values, attitudes, and behavior of group members, regardless of group membership. Most people have several reference groups, such as families, work-related groups, fraternities or sororities, civic clubs, professional organizations, or church-related groups.

In general, there are three major types of reference groups: membership, aspirational, and disassociative. A membership reference group is one to which an individual actually belongs,

reference group A group that a person identifies with so strongly that he or she adopts the values, attitudes, and behavior of group members, regardless of group membership with which the individual identifies intensely enough to take on the values, attitudes, and behaviors of people in that group. An aspirational reference group is one to which a person aspires to belong. The aspiring member desires to be like group members. This is why companies may partner with celebrities to market their brands or products. A group that a person does not wish to be associated with is a disassociative or negative reference group. The individual does not want to take on the values, attitudes, and behavior of these group members.

A reference group may serve as an individual's point of comparison and source of information. A customer's behavior may change over time to be more in line with the actions and beliefs of group members. For instance, a person may switch to a different brand of shirt based on reference group members' advice and preferences. An individual may also seek information from the reference group about other factors regarding a prospective purchase, such as where to buy a certain product.

Reference groups can affect whether a person does or does not buy a product at all, buys a type of product within a product category, or buys a specific brand. The extent to which a reference group affects a purchase decision depends on the product's conspicuousness and on the individual's susceptibility to reference group influence. Generally, the more conspicuous a product, the more likely that reference groups will influence a consumer's purchase decision. A product's conspicuousness is determined by whether others can see it and whether it attracts attention. A marketer sometimes tries to use reference group influence in advertisements by suggesting that people in a specific group buy a product and are satisfied with it. Whether this kind of advertising succeeds depends on three factors: how effectively the advertisement communicates the message, the type of product, and the individual's susceptibility to reference group influence. In this type of appeal, the advertiser hopes that many people will accept the suggested group as a reference group and buy (or react more favorably to) the product.

6-5d Digital Influences

A generation ago, buyers were influenced by word-of-mouth referrals from a few neighbors, coworkers, or friends for each purchase. Today, however, buyers are strongly influenced by the opinions of hundreds or even thousands through digital sources such as social media networks, reviews on e-commerce sites, and review apps such as Yelp. A Pricewaterhouse-Coopers survey found that nearly half of online shoppers around the world reported that reading reviews, comments, and feedback on social media influenced their shopping decisions. Other activities that online shoppers say influence online buying behavior include receiving promotional offerings, staying on top of current fashion and product trends, and associating with particular brands or retailers.[18] Among women, 81 percent say they often purchase products they've seen shared on Facebook, Instagram, Pinterest, and other social networks. Nearly three-quarters of women surveyed say the ability to find recommendations on social media reduces the risk of buying a new product.[19]

Buyers are emotional, whether they realize it or not, and tapping into the experiences and opinions of others plays into that aspect of the buying decision process. By exploring the experiences of others as relayed on Amazon.com comments or Yelp reviews, shoppers can reduce their risk in trying an unknown product by gaining information from others. Online, consumers can not only find opinions but also obtain feedback as well as photos, videos, experiences, and how-to ideas that can lead them to particular brands or retailers.

Computers, smartphones, and wearables, as well as in-store kiosks and mobile payment devices affect both online and in-store shopping behaviors all around the world. These tools are profoundly altering in-store customer behavior but at different rates of impact, depending on the country.[20] Consumers today are increasingly online, no matter where they are. In the time it takes to stand in line at a coffee shop, a buyer in the information-search stage can read reviews on a product, find a store that sells it, and see a map showing the nearest store. When they log into Instagram, Facebook, or Twitter, they can see what their friends or favorite celebrities are wearing; they can also see whether their favorite brands might be introducing new products or having a sale. Thus, digital influences on the buying decision process have become increasingly important to marketers.

DIGITAL MARKETING

CoverGirl Signs Social Media Influencers

CoverGirl has been signing a new crop of brand ambassadors, reflecting the growing influence of those with huge followings on social media networks. Not long ago, the beauty brand teamed up with its first male cover model, teen makeup artist James Charles, to promote its So Lashy! mascara. Charles is featured in CoverGirl's social media ads as well as in its television commercials, print ads, and public relations efforts. With 1.4 million Instagram followers, nearly 200,000 Twitter followers, and 740,000 YouTube subscribers, this high school student from suburban New York brings social media star power to the brand.

Another recently-signed brand ambassador is Nura Afia, whose detailed YouTube makeup tutorials each attract hundreds of thousands of views.

Afia is the first CoverGirl to wear a hijab in the brand's commercials and print ads, also promoting So Lashy! mascara on social media. A Denver-based wife and mother, Afia maintains an Instagram account with more than 330,000 followers and frequently tweets beauty tips to thousands of Twitter followers. Her glamour and popularity help CoverGirl showcase its beauty products to wider and more diverse audiences.

Social media influencers like James Charles and Nura Afia join celebrity brand ambassadors like actress Zendaya, singer Katy Perry, and DJ Amy Pham in giving CoverGirl high visibility in traditional and digital media. Just as important, their trend-setting stature adds to their credibility as role models for how to achieve the newest looks with CoverGirl cosmetics.[b]

6-5e Opinion Leaders

An **opinion leader** is a member of an informal group who provides information about a specific topic, such as smartphones, to other group members seeking information. The opinion leader is in a position or has knowledge or expertise that makes him or her a credible source of information on a few topics. Opinion leaders are easily accessible—often through social media—and they are viewed by other group members as being well-informed about one or multiple topics. Opinion leaders are not the foremost authority on all topics, but because such individuals know they are opinion leaders, they feel a responsibility to remain informed about specific topics, and thus seek out advertisements, manufacturers' brochures, salespeople, and other sources of information. Opinion leaders have a strong influence on the behavior of others in their group, particularly relating to product adoption and purchases.

An opinion leader is likely to be most influential when consumers have high product involvement but low product knowledge, when they share the opinion leader's values and attitudes, and when the product details are numerous or complicated. Possible opinion leaders and topics are shown in Table 6.3.

TABLE 6.3	EXAMPLES OF OPINION LEADERS AND TOPICS
Opinion Leader	**Possible Topics**
Local religious leader	Charities to support, political ideas, lifestyle choices
"Movie buff" friend	Movies to buy, rent, stream, or see in theaters, television programs to watch
Family doctor	Prescription drugs, vitamins, health products
"Techie" acquaintance	Computer and other electronics purchases, software purchases, Internet service choices, video game purchases

opinion leader A member of an informal group who provides information about a specific topic to other group members

social class An open group of individuals with similar social rank

culture The accumulation of values, knowledge, beliefs, customs, objects, and concepts that a society uses to cope with its environment and passes on to future generations

6-5f Social Classes

In all societies, people rank others into higher or lower positions of respect. This ranking process, called social stratification, results in social classes. A **social class** is an open aggregate of people with similar social rank. A class is referred to as *open* because people can move into and out of it. Criteria for grouping people into classes vary from one society to another. In the United States, we take into account many factors, including occupation, education, income, wealth, race, ethnic group, and possessions. A person who is ranking someone into a class does not necessarily apply all of a society's criteria. Sometimes, too, the role of income tends to be overemphasized in social class determination. Although income does help determine social class, the other factors also play a role. Within social classes, both incomes and spending habits can differ significantly among members.

To some degree, individuals within social classes develop and assume common behavioral patterns. They may have similar attitudes, values, language patterns, and possessions. Social class influences many aspects of people's lives. Because people most frequently interact with others within their own social class, people are more likely to be influenced by others within their own class than by those in other classes. Social class can influence choice of religion, financial planning decisions, access to education, occupation, and leisure time activities.

Social class also influences people's spending, saving, and credit practices. It can determine the type, quality, and quantity of products a person buys and uses. For instance, it affects purchases of clothing, foods, financial and health-care services, travel, recreation, entertainment, and home furnishings. Behaviors within a social class can influence others as well. Most common is the "trickle-down" effect, in which members of lower classes attempt to emulate members of higher social classes, such as purchasing desirable automobiles, large homes, and even selecting certain names for their children. Couture fashions designed for the upper class influence the styles of the clothing sold in department stores frequented by the middle class, which eventually is sold to the working class who shop at discount clothing stores. Less often, status float will occur, when a product that is traditionally associated with a lower class gains status and popularity among upper classes. Social class also affects an individual's shopping patterns and types of stores patronized. In some instances, marketers attempt to focus on certain social classes through store location and interior design, product design and features, pricing strategies, personal sales efforts, and advertising. Many companies focus on the middle and working classes because they account for such a large portion of the population. Outside the United States, the middle class is growing rapidly in places such as India, China, and Brazil, making these consumers increasingly desirable targets for marketing messages.

Some firms target different classes with a range of products at different price points. Even designers who previously made clothing only for the wealthy have learned about the benefits of offering items at different price points. For instance, luxury fashion designers Victoria Beckham, Phillip Lim, and Missoni have created limited edition collections for sale exclusively at Target.[21]

6-5g Culture and Subcultures

Culture is the accumulation of values, knowledge, beliefs, customs, objects, and concepts that a society uses to cope with its environment and passes on to future generations. Culture permeates most things you do and objects you interact with, from the style of buildings in your town, to the education you receive, to the laws governing your country. Culture also includes society-specific core values and the degree of acceptability of a wide range of behaviors. For example, in U.S. culture, customers and businesses are expected to behave ethically.

Culture influences buying behavior because it saturates our daily lives. Our culture determines what we wear and eat and where we reside and travel. Society's interest in the healthfulness of food affects food companies' approaches to developing and promoting their products. Culture also influences how we buy and use products and the satisfaction we derive from them.

When U.S. marketers sell products in other countries, they must be aware of the tremendous impact specific cultures have on product purchases and use. Global marketers will find that people in other regions of the world have different attitudes, values, and needs, which call for different methods of doing business and different marketing mixes. Some international marketers fail because they do not or cannot adjust to cultural differences.

A culture consists of various subcultures. A **subculture** is a group of individuals whose characteristics, values, and behavioral patterns are similar within the group and different from those of people in the surrounding culture. U.S. culture is marked by many different subcultures, such as hipster, geek, biker, endurance sports enthusiast, and cowboy. Within subcultures, greater similarities exist in people's attitudes, values, and actions than within the broader culture. Relative to other subcultures, individuals in one subculture may have stronger preferences for specific types of clothing, furniture, food, or consumer electronics.

Subcultures can play a significant role in how people respond to advertisements, particularly when pressured to make a snap judgment. It is important for marketers to understand that a person can be a member of more than one subculture and that the behavioral patterns and values attributed to specific subcultures do not necessarily apply to all group members.

Subcultural boundaries may be based on geographic designations and demographic characteristics, such as age, religion, race, and ethnicity. The percentage of the U.S. population consisting of ethnic and racial subcultures has grown and is expected to continue to grow. By 2050, about one-half of the U.S. population will be members of racial and ethnic minorities. The three largest and fastest-growing ethnic U.S. subcultures are African Americans, Hispanics, and Asians.[22] The population growth of these ethnic and racial subcultures represents a tremendous opportunity for marketers because of cultural-specific tastes and desires. Businesses recognize that, to succeed, their marketing strategies have to take into account the values, needs, interests, shopping patterns, and buying habits of these various subcultures.

subculture A group of individuals whose characteristics, values, and behavioral patterns are similar within the group and different from those of people in the surrounding culture

African American Subculture

In the United States, the African American subculture represents 13.3 percent of the population.[23] That figure is expected to grow to 17.9 percent by 2060. African American consumers are more likely to shop online and interact with brands via social media, making this an effective route for marketers targeting this lucrative subculture. Younger African Americans have become trendsetters for all young American consumers regardless of race or ethnicity. The combined buying power of African American consumers is estimated to be approximately $1.4 trillion by 2020, up 338 percent since 1990.[24]

With so much buying power and growing influence of young African Americans, it's no surprise that companies are increasing their focus on the African American community. Allstate, for example, launched a national campaign on its YouTube, Instagram, and Facebook pages to highlight the contributions of ten prominent African Americans. The images and videos celebrate the positive impact these individuals have had on fields such as education, health, science, and entrepreneurship and strive to connect with black consumers with regard to insurance products.[25] Take a look at the advertisement for Clairol Beautiful Collection line of hair relaxers. Women of color

CLAIROL
PROFESSIONAL®

RELAX WITH A CLASSIC

With no ammonia and natural ingredients like Jojoba Oil, Vitamin E, and Aloe Vera, this color is gentle enough to use even after relaxing. Welcome to the next generation of classic style.

Available at Professional Beauty Supply Stores. Experience the collection at clairolpro.com
©2013 Clairol, A Division of P&G

Clairol Professional

Subcultures
Clairol is appealing to the subculture of African American women who like to straighten their hair with its line of Beautiful Collection hair products.

who like to wear their hair straight are the subculture targeted by this advertisement. Clairol underscores its long tradition of quality products for relaxing hair by showing a well-dressed woman from the 1950s facing a modern woman wearing contemporary clothing with the tagline, "Relax with a Classic."

Hispanic Subculture

Hispanics represent 17.6 percent of the U.S. population, but that figure is projected to grow to 24 percent by 2040. Hispanic buying power is estimated to be approximately $1.7 trillion by 2020.[26] When considering the buying behavior of Hispanics, marketers must keep in mind that this subculture is really composed of many diverse cultures coming from a huge geographic region that encompasses nearly two dozen nationalities, including Cuban, Mexican, Puerto Rican, Caribbean, Spanish, and Dominican. Each has its own history and unique culture that affect consumer preferences and buying behavior. Four clusters of the Hispanic market have been identified based upon language preferences, classified as retainers (those who speak Spanish as their main language), biculturals (alternate between Spanish and English), assimilators (speak English but acknowledge Hispanic background), and non-identifiers.[27] Marketers should also recognize that the terms *Hispanic* and *Latino* refer to an ethnic category rather than a racial distinction.

Hispanics represent a large and powerful subculture, and are an attractive consumer group for marketers. Target, for example, created its "Sin Traducción," ("Without Translation") campaign solely for its Hispanic customers to forge deeper connections. The retailer spends about 3 percent of its total advertising campaign funds on Hispanic media.[28] Macy's is reaching out to Latino customers in a variety of ways, but particularly through mobile media. The retailer has also introduced a collection of clothing, shoes, and jewelry from popular singer and telenovela star Ariadna Thalía Sodi Miranda (Thalía). The line features trendy items and includes colors and patterns designed to appeal to Latinas of different cultures.[29] Marketers should recognize that simply translating an English-speaking ad into Spanish may not resonate with Hispanic consumers—and may even backfire. Consider that when the California Milk Processing Board sought to translate its popular and long-running "Got Milk?" campaign into Spanish, it did not consult with actual Spanish speakers, and the resulting campaign, "Are You Lactating?" failed.[30]

Asian American Subculture

The term *Asian American* includes Filipinos, Chinese, Japanese, South Asian Indians, Koreans, and Vietnamese, encompassing people from more than 40 countries of origin. This group represents 5.6 percent of the U.S. population, and their combined buying power is expected to reach $1.1 trillion by 2020.[31] Asian Americans tend to identify strongly with their culture of origin; most prefer to refer to themselves by their country of origin (e.g., Japanese or Japanese American) rather than being referred to as Asian American.[32] The individual language, religion, and value system of each group influences its members' purchasing decisions.

Although Asian Americans are a smaller subculture than African Americans and Hispanics in the United States, they are growing faster. However, Asian Americans appear to be underserved relative to other subcultures.[33] For instance, advertisers spend less to reach this important segment.[34] However, ignoring such an important segment represents missed opportunities for marketers. Some companies are beginning to remedy this. Insurance company AIG, for example, opened a branch in California that targets Chinese Americans specifically but strives to appeal to all Asian American consumers. The opening ceremony for the branch featured an auspicious lion dance. The office has signs in both Chinese and English, and all employees speak English and at least one Asian language. To make its customers feel comfortable, it hosts meeting spaces that feel like tea rooms.[35]

consumer misbehavior
Behavior that violates generally accepted norms of a particular society

6-6 CONSUMER MISBEHAVIOR

LO 6-6 Discuss consumer misbehavior.

Approaching the topic of inappropriate consumer behavior requires some caution because of varying attitudes and cultural definitions of what comprises misbehavior. However, it is generally agreed that some conduct, such as shoplifting or purchasing illegal drugs, falls under the category of activities that are unacceptable by established norms. Therefore, we will define **consumer misbehavior** as behavior that violates generally accepted norms of a particular society. Shoplifting is one of the most obvious misconduct areas. U.S. retailers lose more than $32 billion annually due to individuals shoplifting grocery items, electronics, and more, as well as employee thefts, and the cost of these losses is passed on to consumers as higher prices.[36] Organized retail crime—where criminal groups engage in large-scale theft from retail and online stores—has become a major threat, not only to retailers, but to all organizations including governments. Experts estimate that organized retail crime alone costs businesses about $30 billion annually.[37] Aside from selling goods on the black market, consumer motivation for shoplifting includes the low risk of being caught, a desire to be accepted by a group of peers (particularly among young people), and the excitement associated with the activity.

Consumer fraud includes purposeful actions to take advantage of and/or damage others during a transaction. Using fraudulently obtained credit cards, debit cards, checks, or bank accounts falls into this category as does making false insurance claims. Although few realize it, purchasing a dress for a special event, wearing it once with the tags hidden, and then returning it is also fraud. Returning items for cash when those items were actually received as gifts or even stolen is another example of fraud. Retailers lose an estimated $9.1 to $15.9 billion annually to return fraud.[38] Some consumers engage in identity theft, which is a serious and growing legal problem—particularly as more shopping is conducted online, where regulations and security are more difficult to enforce.

Piracy is copying computer software, video games, movies, or music without paying the producer for them. It is estimated that global businesses spend approximately $500 billion to fix issues associated with pirated software. Global consumers spend approximately $25 billion and waste 1.2 billion hours to fix problems resulting from downloaded pirated software.[39] The recording industry broadcasts messages explaining why sharing music is not acceptable, but it remains a serious problem. Understanding motivations for piracy can be helpful in developing a plan to combat the issue (see Table 6.4).

Yet another area of concern with consumer misbehavior is abusive consumers. Rude customers engage in verbal or physical abuse, can be uncooperative, and may even break policies. Airlines remove abusive customers if they represent a threat to employees and other passengers. Belligerently drunk customers, especially in environments such as bars and airplanes, have to be removed in order to protect others. Understanding the psychological and social reasons for consumer misconduct can be helpful in preventing or responding to the problem.

TABLE 6.4	MOTIVATIONS FOR UNETHICAL OR ILLEGAL MISBEHAVIOR
• Justification/rationalization	• The thrill of getting away with it
• Economic reasons	• There is little risk of getting caught
• It is accepted by peers	• People think they are smarter than others

Source: Kevin J. Shanahan and Michael J. Hyman, "Motivators and Enablers of SCOURing: A Study of Online Piracy in the US and UK," *Journal of Business Research* 63, 9–10 (2010): 1095–1102.

Chapter Review

6-1 Recognize the stages of the consumer buying decision process.

The consumer buying decision process includes five stages: problem recognition, information search, evaluation of alternatives, purchase, and postpurchase evaluation. Not all decision processes culminate in a purchase, nor do all consumer decisions include all five stages. Problem recognition occurs when buyers become aware of a difference between a desired state and an actual condition. After recognizing the problem or need, buyers search for information about products to help resolve the problem or satisfy the need. In the internal search, buyers search their memories for information about products that might solve the problem. If they cannot retrieve from memory sufficient information to make a decision, they seek additional information through an external search. A successful search yields a group of brands, called a consideration set, which a buyer views as possible alternatives. To evaluate the products in the consideration set, the buyer establishes certain criteria by which to compare, rate, and rank different products. Marketers can influence consumers' evaluations by framing alternatives. In the purchase stage, consumers select products or brands on the basis of results from the evaluation stage and on other dimensions. Buyers also choose the seller from whom they will purchase the product. After the purchase, buyers evaluate the product to determine if actual performance meets expected levels.

6-2 Classify the types of consumer decision making and the level of involvement.

Buying behavior consists of the decision processes and acts of people involved in buying and using products. Consumer buying behavior is the buying behavior of ultimate consumers. An individual's level of involvement—the importance and intensity of interest in a product in a particular situation—affects the type of decision-making process used. Enduring involvement is an ongoing interest in a product class because of personal relevance, whereas situational involvement is a temporary interest that stems from the particular circumstance or environment in which buyers find themselves. There are three kinds of consumer decision making: routinized response behavior, limited decision making, and extended decision making. Consumers rely on routinized response behavior when buying frequently purchased, low-cost items requiring little search-and-decision effort. Limited decision making is used for products purchased occasionally or when buyers need to acquire information about an unfamiliar brand in a familiar product category. Consumers engage in extended decision making when purchasing an unfamiliar, expensive, or infrequently bought product. Purchase of a certain product does not always elicit the same type of decision making. Impulse buying is not a consciously planned buying behavior but involves a powerful urge to buy something immediately.

6-3 Explain how situational influences may affect the consumer buying decision process.

Three major categories of influences affect the consumer buying decision process: situational, psychological, and social. Situational influences are external circumstances or conditions existing when a consumer makes a purchase decision. Situational influences include surroundings, time, reason for purchase, and the buyer's mood and condition.

6-4 Identify the psychological influences that may affect the consumer buying decision process.

Psychological influences partly determine people's general behavior, thus influencing their behavior as consumers. The primary psychological influences on consumer behavior are perception, motives, learning, attitudes, personality and self-concept, and lifestyles. Perception is the process of selecting, organizing, and interpreting information inputs (sensations received through sight, taste, hearing, smell, and touch) to produce meaning. The three steps in the perceptual process are selection, organization, and interpretation. Individuals have numerous perceptions of packages, products, brands, and organizations that affect their buying decision processes. A motive is an internal energizing force that orients a person's activities toward satisfying needs or achieving goals. Learning refers to changes in a person's thought processes and behavior caused by information and experience. Marketers try to shape what consumers learn in order to influence what they buy. An attitude is an individual's enduring evaluation, feelings, and behavioral tendencies toward an object or idea and consists of three major components: cognitive, affective, and behavioral. Personality is the set of traits and behaviors that make a person unique. Self-concept, closely linked to personality, is one's perception or view of oneself. Researchers have found that buyers purchase products that reflect and enhance their self-concepts. Lifestyle is an individual's pattern of living expressed through activities, interests, and opinions. Lifestyles influence consumers' needs, brand preferences, and how and where they shop.

6-5 Describe the social influences that may affect the consumer buying decision process.

Social influences are forces that other people exert on buying behavior. They include roles, family, reference groups, social media, opinion leaders, social class, and culture and subcultures. Everyone occupies positions within groups, organizations, and institutions, and each position involves playing a role—a set of actions and activities that a person in a particular position is supposed to perform based on expectations of both the individual and surrounding persons. In a family, children learn from parents and older siblings how to make decisions, such as purchase decisions. Consumer socialization is the process through which a person acquires the knowledge and skills to function as a consumer. The consumer socialization process is partially accomplished through family influences.

A reference group is a group that a person identifies with so strongly that he or she adopts the values, attitudes, and behavior of group members, regardless of group membership. The three major types of reference groups are membership, aspirational, and disassociative. Buyers are increasingly influenced by the opinions of hundreds or even thousands through digital sources such as social media networks, reviews on ecommerce sites, and review apps. An opinion leader is a member of an informal group who provides information about a specific topic to other group members. A social class is an open group of individuals with similar social rank.

Social class influences people's spending, saving, and credit practices. Culture is the accumulation of values, knowledge, beliefs, customs, objects, and concepts that a society uses to cope with its environment and passes on to future generations. A culture is made up of subcultures, groups of individuals whose characteristic values and behavior patterns are similar to one another but different from those of the surrounding culture. U.S. marketers focus on three major ethnic subcultures: African American, Hispanic, and Asian American.

6-6 Discuss consumer misbehavior.

Consumer misbehavior is defined as behavior that violates generally accepted norms of a particular society. One form of consumer misbehavior involves shoplifting, or stealing goods from retail stores. Organized retail crime is on the rise and involves people paying others to shoplift certain goods from retail stores, which are then usually sold on the black market. Another form of consumer misbehavior is consumer fraud, which involves purposeful actions to take advantage of and/or damage others. Common examples of consumer fraud are false insurance claims, identity theft, returning an item of clothing after wearing it, and fraudulently obtaining credit cards, checks, and bank accounts. Another form of consumer misbehavior is piracy, the copying or sharing of music, movies, video games, and computer software. One final area of concern with regards to consumer misbehavior is abusive consumers, which include customers who are rude, verbally or physically abusive, and/or uncooperative, which may violate some companies' policies. In order to respond to or even prevent these growing problems, organizations need to understand the psychological and social reasons for consumer misbehavior.

 Go to www.cengagebrain.com for resources to help you master the content in this chapter as well as materials that will expand your marketing knowledge!

Developing Your Marketing Plan

Understanding the process that an individual consumer goes through when purchasing a product is essential for developing marketing strategy. Knowledge about the potential customer's buying behavior will become the basis for many of the decisions in the specific marketing plan. Using the information from this chapter, you should be able to determine the following:

1. See Table 6.1. What type of decision making are your customers likely to use when purchasing your product?
2. Determine the evaluative criteria that your target market(s) would use when choosing between alternative brands.
3. Using Table 6.2, what types of family decision making, if any, would your target market(s) use?
4. Identify the reference groups or subcultures that may influence your target market's product selection.

Key Concepts

buying behavior 134
consumer buying behavior 134
consumer buying decision process 134
internal search 135
external search 135

consideration set 136
evaluative criteria 136
cognitive dissonance 137
routinized response behavior 138
limited decision making 138

extended decision making 138
impulse buying 138
level of involvement 138
situational influences 139
psychological influences 141

perception 141
information inputs 141
selective exposure 141
selective distortion 142
selective retention 142
motive 142

Issues for Discussion and Review

1. What are the major stages in the consumer buying decision process? Are all these stages used in all consumer purchase decisions? Why or why not?
2. How does a consumer's level of involvement affect his or her choice of decision-making process?
3. Name the types of consumer decision-making processes. List some products you have bought using each type. Have you ever bought a product on impulse? If so, describe the circumstances.
4. What are the categories of situational factors that influence consumer buying behavior? Explain how each of these factors influences buyers' decisions.
5. What is selective exposure? Why do people engage in it?
6. How do marketers attempt to shape consumers' learning?
7. Why are marketers concerned about consumer attitudes?
8. In what ways do lifestyles affect the consumer buying decision process?
9. How do roles affect a person's buying behavior? Provide examples.
10. What are family influences, and how do they affect buying behavior?
11. What are reference groups? How do they influence buying behavior? Name some of your own reference groups.
12. How does an opinion leader influence the buying decision process of reference group members?
13. In what ways does social class affect a person's purchase decisions?
14. What is culture? How does it affect a person's buying behavior?
15. Describe the subcultures to which you belong. Identify buying behavior that is unique to one of your subcultures.
16. What is consumer misbehavior? Describe the various forms of consumer misbehavior.

VIDEO CASE 6
How Ford Drives Future Innovation

What do consumers care about today, what will they think about tomorrow, and what does it all mean for automotive manufacturers? Sheryl Connelly, Ford's manager of global consumer trends—the company's chief trend-watcher—has been studying consumer behavior worldwide, with an eye toward determining what consumers will want and need long before they know. By surveying consumers and analyzing emerging social trends, technological developments, political issues, environmental concerns, and economic changes, Connelly provides Ford's marketers with insights that shape and refine the company's future innovations.

For example, when Connelly looked at technological trends, she found that medical advances are allowing seniors to lead active lifestyles far longer than ever before. Yet as they age, drivers will need vehicles with features that help them adapt to changes in their physical and mental capabilities. Based on Connelly's conclusions, Ford has been adding features such as automated parking assistance

systems and ergonomic seats that enable drivers—old and young—to stay safe and comfortable behind the wheel.

Another trend Connelly recently identified is growing demand for products that are "more anticipatory and self-sufficient" in fulfilling consumers' needs. Self-driving cars will do this by steering themselves and maintaining a safe distance between other vehicles, freeing drivers from having to concentrate on the road as they travel. The company plans to have a self-driving car on the market within a few years, with a popular price tag. According to Connelly's research, buyers in the United States and the United Kingdom have less-positive attitudes about self-driving cars than buyers in China and India. Why? Because commuters in India and China battle more traffic congestion and face more challenging road conditions than drivers in the Western nations. Ford is also working on a voice-command system that will allow drivers to handle specific tasks such as opening a garage door simply by speaking instead of using their hands.

Increasingly, consumers want the benefits of mobility without the expense and responsibility of owning and maintaining vehicles individually. Especially in urban areas, consumers are flocking to alternatives such as hailing a ride to be driven somewhere or hiring a car to drive themselves for a few hours or a few days. In response, Ford has created a suite of mobility services branded "Ford Pass" to give customers and noncustomers alike more alternatives when they're deciding how to get where they want to go. For example, consumers who install the Ford Pass app can use it to locate a parking lot or spot, pay for parking, and arrange to share a ride with other people.

In addition, Connelly has noticed how many consumers are interested in environmental issues, such as conserving natural resources. Showcasing its sustainability initiatives, Ford looks carefully at its impact from raw materials to finished products and beyond. For example, the manufacturer is experimenting with ways to incorporate recycled materials as car parts.

Finally, Connelly's research has revealed a strong emphasis on self-reliance, which in turn means that buyers place a high value on product quality, versatility, and durability. Research shows that 76 percent of U.S. adults expect to keep and drive the same car for a decade or longer. As a result, Ford must be sure its cars, sport-utility vehicles, vans, and pickup trucks will deliver dependable transportation for years and years to first-time buyers, adults with families, seniors, and other consumer segments.[40]

Questions for Discussion

1. How does Ford take into account the diversity of consumer roles as it plans its future marketing? Explain Ford's approach in understanding two or more roles that can affect the buying decision process for vehicles.
2. In terms of psychological influences on buying, why would Ford make its "Ford Pass" app available to both customers and noncustomers?
3. Ford widely publicizes Sheryl Connelly's research findings about the broad trends affecting consumer behavior. During which stages of the consumer buying decision process is this publicity likely to prove influential, and why?

chapter 7 ●

Business Markets and Buying Behavior

iStock.com/Geber86

LEARNING OBJECTIVES

7-1 Distinguish among the four types of business markets.

7-2 Describe the North American Industry Classification System and how it can be used to identify and analyze business markets.

7-3 Identify the major characteristics of business customers and transactions.

7-4 Describe the buying center, stages of the business buying decision process, and the factors that affect this process.

7-5 Explore how the Internet facilitates business buying and marketing.

MARKETING INSIGHTS

Facebook Targets Businesses

Did you know Facebook has its own Facebook marketing page (www.facebook.com/marketing), with more than 11 million likes? The social media giant markets to businesses that seek to engage consumers or employees (or both) by using Facebook's communication tools. For example, businesses can buy targeted advertising based on the data Facebook collects about the two billion active users who log on each month. Whether the target audience is sports fans or pet lovers, Facebook can help a business get its ad in front of the right people. Already, 3 million businesses of all sizes are buying ads on Facebook pages, on Facebook Messenger, or within videos posted on Facebook, generating more than $17 billion in annual advertising revenue for Facebook.

Through the Facebook Audience Network, the firm monitors online browsing behavior as millions of consumers click and swipe their way around the Internet. By analyzing this information, Facebook can help businesses place ads to reach targeted audiences on other websites, not just Facebook. The company is also selling technology to give businesses more insight into who actually sees their ads.

For convenient internal communication, businesses like Starbucks and Danone (two early customers) can sign up for Workplace by Facebook and give employees access to a private, company-only Facebook page. The idea is to engage employees and facilitate work collaboration. Facebook charges a low monthly fee per user, which means a business pays only when employees actually use the page. What's next for Facebook as it targets businesses?[1]

Rawpixel.com/Shutterstock.com

Marketers are just as concerned with meeting the needs of business customers as they are consumers. Marketers at Facebook, for instance, go to considerable lengths to understand their customers so they can provide better, more satisfying products, and develop and maintain long-term customer relationships.

In this chapter, we look at business markets and business buying decision processes. We first discuss various kinds of business markets and the types of buyers that comprise those markets. Next, we explore several dimensions of business buying, such as characteristics of transactions, attributes and concerns of buyers, methods of buying, and distinctive features of demand for business products. We then examine how business buying decisions are made and who makes the purchases. Finally, we consider how businesses rely on technology and the Internet when marketing and building relationships with business customers.

7-1 BUSINESS MARKETS

LO 7-1 Distinguish among the four types of business markets.

As discussed in Chapter 5, a business market (also called a *business-to-business market* or *B2B market*) consists of individuals, organizations, or groups that purchase a specific kind of product for one of three purposes: resale, direct use in producing other products, or use in general daily operations. Marketing to businesses employs the same concepts—defining target markets, understanding buying behavior, and developing effective marketing mixes—as marketing to ultimate consumers. However, there are important structural and behavioral differences in business markets. A company that markets to another company must be aware of how its product will affect other firms in the marketing channel, such as resellers and other manufacturers. Business products can also be technically complex, and the market often consists of sophisticated buyers. For instance, the purchase of medical devices, robotics, and computer systems requires specialized expertise on the part of the buyer.

Because the business market consists of relatively smaller customer populations, a segment of a market could be as small as a few customers—or even just one. The market for railway equipment in the United States, for example, is limited to a few major carriers, including BNSF. Some products can be both business and consumer products. An Apple iPad might traditionally be thought of as a consumer product, but some restaurants are using them to list menu items or take orders. Salespeople at many car dealerships have also begun to use iPads for personal selling purposes. However, the quantity purchased and the buying methods differ significantly between the consumer and business markets, even for the same products. Business marketing is often based on long-term mutually profitable relationships across members of the marketing channel based on cooperation, trust, and collaboration. Manufacturers may even co-develop new products, with business customers sharing marketing research, production, scheduling, inventory management, and information systems. Business marketing can take a variety of forms, ranging from long-term buyer-seller relationships to quick exchanges of basic products at competitive market prices. For most business marketers, the goal is to understand customer needs and provide a value-added exchange that shifts the focus from attracting to retaining customers and developing relationships.

The four categories of business markets are producer, reseller, government, and institutional. In the remainder of this section, we discuss each of these types of markets.

Producer Markets
Chemical plants are part of a producer market because they produce products that organizations purchase to use as ingredients in the production of other products.

iStock.com/TomasSereda

7-1a Producer Markets

Individuals and business organizations that purchase products for the purpose of making a profit by using

TABLE 7.1	NUMBER OF ESTABLISHMENTS IN INDUSTRY GROUPS

Industry	Number of Establishments
Agriculture, forestry, fishing, and hunting	21,844
Mining, quarrying, and oil/gas extraction	29,754
Construction	667,099
Manufacturing	292,543
Transportation and warehousing	220,565
Utilities	17,962
Finance and insurance	470,951
Real estate	311,198

Source: "Statistics of U.S. Businesses (SUSB) Main," all industries, U.S. Bureau of the Census, www.census.gov/data/tables/2014/econ/susb/2014-susb-annual.html (accessed January 27, 2017).

them to produce other products or using them in their operations are classified as **producer markets**. Producer markets include buyers of raw materials, as well as purchasers of semifinished and finished items and services, used to make other products. Producer markets include a broad array of industries, including agriculture, oil and gas extraction, mining, construction, manufacturing transportation, services, and utilities. As Table 7.1 indicates, the number of business establishments in national producer markets is enormous. For instance, manufacturers buy raw materials and component parts for direct use in product creation. Grocery stores and supermarkets are part of producer markets for numerous support products, such as paper and plastic bags, shelves, counters, and scanners. Farmers are part of producer markets for farm machinery, fertilizer, seed, and livestock. Hospitals are part of producer markets for medical equipment. Service providers such as Federal Express, banks, and airlines are also an important part of producer markets. Hotels and restaurants, for example, are part of the producer market for the construction, agriculture, and utilities industries.

7-1b **Reseller Markets**

Reseller markets consist of intermediaries, such as wholesalers and retailers, which buy finished products and resell them for a profit. Aside from making minor alterations, resellers do not change the physical characteristics of the products they handle. Resellers also exist for services and intangible products. For instance, there are reseller markets for financial products such as stocks and bonds. Priceline, Orbitz, and Kayak act as resellers for hotel services. Except for items producers sell directly to consumers, all products sold to consumer markets are first sold to reseller markets.

Wholesalers purchase products for resale to retailers, other wholesalers, producers, governments, and institutions. Wholesalers can also be geographically concentrated. Of the 416,593 wholesale establishments in the United States, a large number are located in New York, California, Illinois, Texas, Ohio, Pennsylvania, New Jersey, and Florida.[2] Although some products are sold directly to end users, many manufacturers sell their products to wholesalers, which in turn sell the products to other firms—including retailers and other wholesalers—in the distribution system. Seafood, for example, goes through a number of intermediaries, including producer, processor, and wholesaler or distributor all the way down to the retailer and final customer. Thus, wholesalers are very important in helping producers get their products to customers.

Retailers purchase products and resell them to final consumers. There are more than 1 million retailers in the United States, employing nearly 16 million people and

producer markets Individuals and business organizations that purchase products to make profits by using them to produce other products or using them in their operations

reseller markets Intermediaries that buy finished products and resell them for a profit

generating approximately $4.5 trillion in annual sales.[3] The United States continues to be a powerful force in retailing. Half of the top 10 largest retail companies in the world are based in the United States. These retailers are Walmart, Costco, The Kroger Co., Walgreens Boots Alliance, The Home Depot Inc., and Amazon.com.[4] Some retailers—Safeway, PetSmart, and Staples, for example—carry a large number of items. Supermarkets may handle as many as 50,000 different products. In small, individually owned retail stores, owners or managers make purchasing decisions. In chain stores, a central office buyer or buying committee frequently decides whether store managers will stock a product on their shelves. For many products, however, local managers make the actual buying decisions for a particular store.

When making purchase decisions, resellers consider several factors. They evaluate the level of demand for a product to determine the quantity and the price at which the product can be resold. Retailers assess the amount of space required to handle a product relative to its potential profit, sometimes on the basis of sales per square foot of selling area. Because customers often depend on resellers to have products available when needed, resellers typically appraise a supplier's ability to provide adequate quantities when and where they are needed. Colgate Palmolive, for example, has an oral care division that helps retail customers such as Target assess their space and merchandise involving toothpaste, mouthwash, and other oral care products. Resellers also take into account the ease of placing orders and whether producers offer technical assistance or training programs. Before resellers buy a product for the first time, they will try to determine whether the product competes with or complements products they currently handle. These types of concerns distinguish reseller markets from other markets. Producers may even help resellers market the product to their end customers. Colgate-Palmolive has an office in Minnesota to assist Target in marketing oral care products.

government markets
Federal, state, county, or local governments that buy goods and services to support their internal operations and provide products to their constituencies

7-1c Government Markets

Federal, state, county, and local governments comprise government markets. These organizations spend billions of dollars annually for a wide range of goods and

ENTREPRENEURSHIP IN MARKETING

Picky Pyykkonen and the One Milk to Rule Them All

Travis Pyykkonen got the idea for his small business when shopping for milk for his young daughter in a suburban Chicago supermarket. Surprised to see little information on milk cartons about where the milk was from or how it was processed, he decided to dig deeper.

Pyykkonen met with dairy farmers who produce organic milk from grass-fed cows, learning about their methods and sampling their milk. He discovered that he liked the rich taste and texture of milk pasteurized in small batches at lower temperatures than typical in a large, commercial dairy. Pyykkonen was also aware of the growing trend for buying from local businesses, with consumers seeking out quality goods and services from local sources.

With all this in mind, Pyykkonen purchased 12 cows and named his new business 1871 Dairy, alluding to the legend that the 1871 Chicago fire was started by a cow kicking over a lantern. Just as some breweries market their beer as the product of a microbrewery, he marketed his milk as the product of a microdairy. Among his first major customers were high-end Chicago restaurants known for serving top-quality meals prepared from locally-sourced ingredients. He also began selling his branded milk to upscale grocery stores around Chicago. Now Pyykkonen plans to expand into another microdairy location. At a time when U.S. milk consumption is historically low, 1871 Dairy can price its milk higher than competing products from commercial dairies because business buyers value the product's quality, taste, and local character.[a]

services—from office supplies and health-care services to vehicles, heavy equipment, and weapons—to support their internal operations and provide citizens with products such as highways, education, energy, and national defense. Government spending accounts for about 36 percent of the United States' total gross domestic product (GDP).[5] The government also purchases services such as hotel rooms, food services, vehicle rentals, and legal and consulting services. The amount spent by federal, state, and local governments in recent decades has gone up because the total number of government units and the services they provide have both increased. Costs of providing these services have also risen.

Because government agencies spend public funds to buy the products needed to provide services, they are accountable to the public. This need for accountability explains their complex buying procedures. Some firms choose not to sell to government buyers because of the additional time and expense the red tape costs them. However, many marketers benefit enough from government contracts that they do not find these procedures to be a stumbling block. For certain products, such as defense-related items, the government may be the only customer.

Governments advertise their product needs through releasing bids or negotiated contracts. Although companies may be reluctant to approach government markets because of the complicated bidding process, once they understand the rules of this process, some firms routinely penetrate government markets. To make a sale under the bid system, firms must apply and be approved for placement on a list of qualified bidders. When a government unit wants to buy, it sends out a detailed description of the products to qualified bidders. Businesses whose products fit with the needs described will submit bids. The government unit is usually required to accept the lowest-priced bid.

When buying nonstandard or highly complex products, a government unit often uses a negotiated contract. Under this procedure, the government unit selects only a few firms and then negotiates specifications and terms. It eventually awards the contract to one of the negotiating firms.

institutional markets
Organizations with charitable, educational, community, or other nonbusiness goals

7-1d Institutional Markets

Organizations with charitable, educational, community, or other nonbusiness goals comprise **institutional markets**. Members of institutional markets include churches, some hospitals, fraternities and sororities, charitable organizations, and private colleges. Institutions purchase millions of dollars' worth of products annually to support their activities and provide goods, services, and ideas to various audiences. Because institutions often have different goals and fewer resources than other types of organizations, marketers may use special efforts to serve them. For example, Aramark provides a variety of products to institutional markets, including schools, hospitals, parks, and senior living centers. It frequently ranks as one of the most admired companies in its industry. For areas like university food service, Aramark aims its marketing efforts directly at students.[6]

Institutional Markets
This stained glass window producer supplies products mainly to churches, which are part of institutional markets.

North American Industry Classification System (NAICS) An industry classification system that generates comparable statistics among the United States, Canada, and Mexico

7-2 INDUSTRIAL CLASSIFICATION SYSTEMS

LO 7-2 Describe the North American Industry Classification System and how it can be used to identify and analyze business markets.

Marketers have access to a considerable amount of information about potential business customers through government and industry publications and websites. Marketers use this information to identify potential business customers and to estimate their purchase potential. The **North American Industry Classification System (NAICS)** is a single industry classification system used by the United States, Canada, and Mexico to generate comparable statistics among the three North American Free Trade Agreement (NAFTA) partners. The NAICS classification is based on production activities. NAICS is similar to the International Standard Industrial Classification (ISIC) system used in Europe and many other parts of the world.

NAICS divides industrial activity into 20 sectors with 1,170 industry classifications. NAICS is more comprehensive and up-to-date than the older Standard Industrial Classification (SIC), and it provides considerably more information about service industries and high-tech products.[7] Table 7.2 shows some NAICS codes for Apple Inc. and AT&T Wireless Inc. Industrial classification systems provide a consistent means of categorizing organizations into groups based on such factors as the types of goods and services provided. Although an industry classification system is a vehicle for segmentation, it is best used in conjunction with other types of data to determine exactly how many and which customers a marketer can reach.

A business marketer can identify and locate potential customers in specific groups by using state directories or commercial industrial directories, such as *Standard & Poor's Register* and Dun & Bradstreet's *Million Dollar Database*. These sources contain information about a firm, including its name, NAICS classification, address, phone number, and annual sales. By referring to one or more of these sources, marketers locate potential business customers by industry classification numbers, determine their locations, and develop lists of potential customers by desired geographic area.

TABLE 7.2	EXAMPLES OF NAICS CLASSIFICATION		
NAICS Hierarchy for AT&T Wireless Inc.		**NAICS Hierarchy for Apple Inc.**	
Sector 51	Information	Sector 31–33	Manufacturing
Subsector 517	Telecommunications	Subsector 334	Computer and Electronic Manufacturing
Industry Group 5171	Wired Telecommunication Carriers	Industry Group 3341	Computer and Peripheral Equipment Manufacturing
Industry Group 5172	Wireless Telecommunications Carriers		
Industry 51711	Wired Telecommunication Carriers	Industry 33411	Computer and Peripheral Equipment Manufacturing
Industry 51721	Wireless Telecommunications Carriers		
Industry 517110	Wired Telecommunication Carriers	U.S. Industry 334111	Electronic Computer Manufacturing
Industry 517210	Wireless Telecommunications Carriers		

Source: NAICS Association, www.census.gov/eos/www/naics/ (accessed January 30, 2017).

A more expedient, although more expensive, approach is to use a commercial data service. Dun & Bradstreet, for example, can provide a list of organizations that fall into a particular industrial classification group. For each company on the list, Dun & Bradstreet provides the name, location, sales volume, number of employees, type of products handled, names of chief executives, and other pertinent information. Either method can effectively identify and locate a group of potential customers by industry and location. Because some companies on the list will have greater potential than others, marketers must conduct further research to determine which customer or customer group to pursue.

To estimate the purchase potential of business customers or groups of customers, a marketer must find a relationship between the size of potential customers' purchases and a variable available in industrial classification data, such as the number of employees. For example, a paint manufacturer might attempt to determine the average number of gallons purchased by a type of potential customer relative to the number of employees. Once this relationship is established, it can be applied to customer groups to estimate the size and frequency of potential purchases. After deriving these estimates, the marketer is in a position to select the customer groups with the most sales and profit potential.

7-3 DIMENSIONS OF BUSINESS CUSTOMERS AND BUSINESS TRANSACTIONS

LO 7-3 Identify the major characteristics of business customers and transactions.

Now that we have considered different types of business customers and how to identify them, we look at several dimensions of marketing related to them, including transaction characteristics, attributes of business customers and some of their primary concerns, buying methods, major types of purchases, and the characteristics of demand for business products (see Figure 7.1).

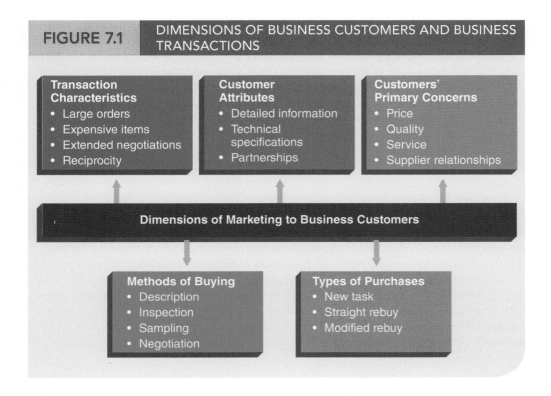

FIGURE 7.1   DIMENSIONS OF BUSINESS CUSTOMERS AND BUSINESS TRANSACTIONS

Transaction Characteristics
- Large orders
- Expensive items
- Extended negotiations
- Reciprocity

Customer Attributes
- Detailed information
- Technical specifications
- Partnerships

Customers' Primary Concerns
- Price
- Quality
- Service
- Supplier relationships

Dimensions of Marketing to Business Customers

Methods of Buying
- Description
- Inspection
- Sampling
- Negotiation

Types of Purchases
- New task
- Straight rebuy
- Modified rebuy

7-3a Characteristics of Transactions with Business Customers

Transactions between businesses differ from consumer sales in several ways. Orders by business customers tend to be much larger than individual consumer sales. Major government contractor Booz Allen Hamilton is sometimes awarded contracts worth up to half a billion dollars to supply medical and IT support assessments and services to various government agencies.[8] Suppliers of large, expensive, or complex goods often must sell products in large quantities to make profits. Consequently, they may prefer not to sell to customers who place small orders.

Some business purchases involve expensive items, such as complex military systems. For instance, Raytheon signed a $235 million contract with the U.S. Navy to provide SM-6 missiles for use on naval cruisers and destroyers beginning in 2018. The company has similar contracts to make the SM-6 for the Japanese, Korean, and Australian navies.[9] Other products, such as raw materials and component items, are used continuously in production, and their supply may need frequent replenishing. The contract regarding terms of sale of these items is likely to be a long-term agreement.

Discussions and negotiations associated with business purchases can require considerable marketing time and selling effort. Purchasing decisions are often made by committee, orders are frequently large and expensive, and products may need to be custom built to meet the specific needs of a customer. Several people or departments in the purchasing organization are often involved. For example, one department expresses a need for a product, a second department develops the specifications, a third stipulates maximum expenditures, and a fourth places the order.

Business customers look for solutions to reach their objectives. Therefore, suppliers need to identify their capabilities to position their products so they provide customer value. Staples recognized this need when it ran a television and radio advertising campaign illustrating how the office-supply retailer can help small businesses succeed in affordable ways.[10] To be successful, suppliers also have to differentiate their products from competitors. Building a brand reputation is an effective way to develop long-term relationships.[11] For instance, Federal Express develops long-term relationships with business customers by integrating customer solutions as a provider of many tracking, transportation, and delivery services.

One practice unique to business markets is **reciprocity**, an arrangement in which two organizations agree to buy from one another. Reciprocal agreements that threaten competition are illegal. The Federal Trade Commission and the Justice Department monitor and take actions to stop anticompetitive reciprocal practices, particularly among large firms. Nonetheless, a certain amount of reciprocal activity occurs among small businesses and, to a lesser extent, among larger companies. Because reciprocity influences purchasing agents to deal only with certain suppliers, it can lead to less than optimal purchases.

7-3b Attributes of Business Customers

Business customers also differ from consumers in their purchasing behavior because they are generally better informed about the products they purchase. They typically demand detailed information about a product's functional features and technical specifications to ensure that it meets their needs. Personal goals, however, may also influence business buying behavior. Most purchasing agents seek the psychological satisfaction that comes with organizational advancement and financial rewards. Buyers who consistently exhibit rational business buying behavior are likely to attain their personal goals because they help their firms achieve organizational objectives. Suppliers need to take into account

reciprocity An arrangement unique to business marketing in which two organizations agree to buy from each other

organizational behavior in the form of individual-level decisions. Often the reaction of an individual buyer triggers the purchase of products and affects the broader organizational acceptance of them.[12] Today, many suppliers and their customers build and maintain mutually beneficial relationships, sometimes called *partnerships*. Researchers find that even in a partnership between a small vendor and a large corporate buyer, a strong partnership can exist because high levels of interpersonal trust lead to higher levels of commitment to the partnership on the part of both organizations.[13] Consider JetBlue Airways' program to mentor small food businesses and prepare them for success, hopefully as future JetBlue suppliers of sustainable food items. The BlueBud program connects promising small firms with resources and opportunities to work with its leaders to develop business strategies aligned with JetBlue's.[14]

7-3c **Primary Concerns of Business Customers**

When making purchasing decisions, business customers take into account a variety of factors. Among their chief considerations are price, product quality, service, and supplier relationships. Price is an essential consideration for business customers because it influences operating costs and costs of goods sold, which in turn affect selling price, profit margin, and ultimately the ability to compete. A business customer is likely to compare the price of a product with the benefits the product will yield to the organization, often over a period of years. When purchasing major equipment, a business customer views price as the amount of investment necessary to obtain a certain level of return or savings on business operations. On the other hand, excellent service and product quality also enter into the decision. A product with a higher price could yield lower operating costs for the buyer in terms of service and quality. For instance, Caterpillar construction equipment may be sold at a higher price with superior service and parts availability.

Most business customers try to maintain a specific level of quality in the products they buy. To achieve this goal, most firms establish standards (usually stated as a percentage of defects allowed) for these products and buy them on the basis of a set of expressed characteristics. These standards, commonly called **product specifications**, are written statements describing a product's necessary characteristics, standards of quality, and other information essential to identifying the best supplier for the needed product. The auto industry, for instance, is turning toward aluminum to build vehicles because it is a lighter metal, which can help boost fuel efficiency. Metal companies like Alcoa wanting to sell aluminum to automakers must meet certain specifications in strength and lightness. A customer evaluates the quality of the products being considered to determine whether they meet specifications. In Alcoa's case, its success will depend on how automakers view the price and quality of its metal sheets. If a product fails to meet specifications or malfunctions for the ultimate consumer, the customer may switch to a different supplier. On the other hand, business customers are also likely to be cautious about buying products that exceed minimum required specifications because they often cost more than is necessary, which drives up the cost of goods and services. Business customers, therefore, must strike a balance between quality and price when making purchasing decisions. Specifications are designed to meet a customer's wants, and anything that does not contribute to meeting those wants may be considered wasteful.

Because their purchases tend to be large and may be complicated, business buyers value service. Services offered by suppliers directly and indirectly influence customers' costs, sales, and profits. Typical services business customers desire from suppliers are market information, inventory maintenance, on-time delivery, and repair services. Business buyers may need technical product information, data regarding demand, information about general economic conditions, or supply and delivery information. Purchasers of machinery are especially concerned about obtaining repair services and replacement parts quickly because inoperable equipment is costly, both in terms of repairs and lost productivity. Offering quality

product specifications
Written statements describing a product's necessary characteristics, standards of quality, and other information essential to identifying the best supplier for the needed product

customer service can be a means of gaining a competitive advantage over other firms, which leads some businesses to seek out ways to improve their customer service. Bain & Company targets these businesses with programs to improve their clients' service operations in retail establishments, call centers, and a variety of other service situations. For example, it has developed multiple frameworks of different steps their clients can take to become customer-centered service providers.[15]

Hello
my name is

...AND I'M
PAYING
TOO MUCH
FOR DIGITAL
ADVASTING.

FINALLY
ZERO MARGIN MEDIA BUYS

STEELHOUSE
ADVERTISING SUITE

STEELHOUSE.COM | 888-978-3354

SteelHouse

Concerns of Business Customers
Business customers are concerned about several major factors, including costs, acquiring the right product that works effectively, and customer service. Some of these concerns are expressed in this SteelHouse Advertising Suite ad.

Maintaining adequate inventory is critical to quality customer service, customer satisfaction, and managing inventory costs and distribution efficiency. Furthermore, on-time delivery is crucial to ensuring that products are available as needed. Reliable on-time delivery saves business customers money because it enables them to carry only the inventory needed at any given time.

Customer expectations about quality of service have increased and broadened over time. Using traditional service quality standards based only on manufacturing and accounting systems is not sufficient. Customers also expect to have access to communication channels that allow them to ask questions, voice complaints, submit orders, and track shipments. Increasingly, they expect to be able to do that on the fly through their cell phone or other mobile device. Marketers should develop customer service objectives and monitor customer service programs, striving for uniformity of service, simplicity, truthfulness, and accuracy. Firms can observe service by formally surveying customers or informally calling on customers and asking questions about the service they received. Spending the time and effort to ensure that customers are satisfied can greatly benefit marketers by increasing customer retention.

Businesses are also increasingly concerned about ethics and social responsibility. Sustainability in particular is rising as a consideration among customers making purchases. Managers are playing a key role in green marketing strategies through the integration of environmental values into the organizational culture.[16] This results in purchase decisions that favor sustainable and environmentally friendly products. In fact, improvement of environmental performance can indirectly improve financial performance.

Finally, business customers are concerned about the costs of developing and maintaining relationships with their suppliers. In the SteelHouse advertisement, note that the focus is on cost. SteelHouse recognizes that advertising costs are a major source of concern for most organizations. The ad plays on this worry by showing a nametag, like those worn at trade shows and other meetings, along with the admission, "I'm paying too much for digital advertising." SteelHouse promotes its advertising suite with zero margin media buys as a solution. By building trust with a particular supplier, buyers can reduce their search efforts and uncertainty about prices. Business customers have to keep in mind the overall fit of a supplier and its products with marketing objectives, including distribution and inventory-maintenance costs and efficiency.

GOING GREEN

Reduce, Reuse, Recycle, Repeat

Where some businesses see waste, other businesses see growth potential and a way to protect the planet. Momentum Recycling is building a new $11 million plant in Colorado to separate and process glass from recycled waste and deliver it to nearby factories that manufacture glass beer bottles. The factories need clean crushed glass as the raw material for making bottles, and that's one of Momentum Recycling's specialties. The company also profits from processing recycled glass to be made into insulation for buildings.

Leanne Bertram founded Clean Conscience Recycling to provide businesses in Alberta, Canada, with a convenient, cost-efficient alternative to sending waste to landfills. She works with construction companies to recycle and reuse discarded materials directly from building sites, making a difference to the local economy and the local ecology. Clean Conscience Recycling attracts business customers that want to get the job done without hassle or harm to the environment.

TerraCycle, based in New Jersey, has long been involved in transforming recycled plastic packaging and cigarette butts collected in local communities into saleable products such as purses, pencil cases, and gardening supplies. More recently, it has partnered with Procter & Gamble to turn plastic items that wash up on beaches into shampoo bottles for Head & Shoulders. TerraCycle is also working with the manufacturing giant Henkel to safely recycle adhesive-product packaging from industrial customers. Watch for more recycling initiatives as TerraCycle expands into new business markets to keep the planet green.[b]

7-3d **Methods of Business Buying**

Although no two business buyers do their jobs the same way, most use one or more of the following purchase methods: *description, inspection, sampling,* and *negotiation.* The most straightforward is description. When products are standardized and graded according to characteristics such as size, shape, weight, and color, a business buyer may be able to purchase simply by specifying quantity, grade, and other attributes. Commodities and raw materials may be purchased this way. Sometimes buyers specify a particular brand or its equivalent when describing the desired product. Purchases on the basis of description are especially common between a buyer and seller with an ongoing relationship built on trust.

Certain products, such as industrial equipment, used vehicles, and buildings, have unique characteristics and may vary with regard to condition. Depending on how they were used and for how long, two products may be in very different condition, even if they look identical on paper. Consequently, business buyers of such products must base purchase decisions on inspection.

Sampling entails evaluating a portion of the product on the assumption that its characteristics represent the entire lot. This method is appropriate when the product is homogeneous—for instance, grain—and examining the entire lot is not physically or economically feasible.

Some business purchases are based on negotiated contracts. In these instances, buyers describe exactly what they need and ask sellers to submit bids. They then negotiate with the suppliers that submit the most attractive bids. This approach is generally used for very large or expensive purchases, such as with commercial vehicles. This is frequently how the federal government conducts business. In other cases, the buyer may be unable to identify specifically what is to be purchased and can provide only a general description, as might be the case for a piece of custom-made equipment. A buyer and seller might negotiate a contract that specifies a base price and provides for the payment of additional costs and fees. These contracts are most commonly used for one-time projects such as buildings, capital equipment, and special projects.

new-task purchase An organization's initial purchase of an item to be used to perform a new job or solve a new problem

straight rebuy purchase A routine purchase of the same products under approximately the same terms of sale by a business buyer

modified rebuy purchase A new-task purchase that is changed on subsequent orders or when the requirements of a straight rebuy purchase are modified

derived demand Demand for business products that stems from demand for consumer products

7-3e Types of Business Purchases

Most business purchases are one of three types: new-task, straight rebuy, or modified rebuy. Each type is subject to different influences and thus requires business marketers to modify their selling approaches accordingly. For a **new-task purchase**, an organization makes an initial purchase of an item to be used to perform a new job or solve a new problem. A new-task purchase may require development of product and vendor specifications and procedures for future product purchases. To make the initial purchase, the business buyer usually needs to acquire a lot of information. New-task purchases are important to suppliers because they can result in a long-term buying relationship if customers are satisfied.

A **straight rebuy purchase** occurs when buyers purchase the same products routinely under approximately the same terms of sale. Buyers require little information for routine purchase decisions and tend to use familiar suppliers that have provided satisfactory service and products in the past. These marketers may set up automatic systems to make reordering easy and convenient for business buyers. A supplier may even monitor the business buyer's inventories and communicate to the buyer what should be ordered and when.

For a **modified rebuy purchase**, a new-task purchase is altered after two or three orders, or requirements associated with a straight rebuy purchase are modified. A business buyer might seek faster delivery, lower prices, or a different quality level of product specifications. Retaining existing customers should receive more attention than attracting new customers. If a long-term purchase contract does not exist, a firm should use all information available to develop retention strategies.[17] This means knowing what customers are likely to purchase and how their purchases might change over time. For example, the advertisement for Sprint Business highlights the firm's ability to supply flexible plans with dedicated support, extended warranties, and other "cool stuff, … no surprises, no really." As companies grow and change, their wireless service needs are likely to change as well, and the Sprint ad informs business buyers about how Sprint Business can flexibly accommodate their changing needs. Organizations that are satisfied with Sprint Business wireless services are likely to make similar orders over time, but demand for specific business products and supplies may fluctuate in cycles that mirror periods of high and low customer demand. A modified rebuy situation may cause regular suppliers to compete to keep the account. When a firm changes the terms of a service contract, such as modifying the speed or comprehensiveness of a telecommunication services package, it has made a modified rebuy purchase.

7-3f Demand for Business Products

Demand for business products (also called *industrial demand*) can be characterized in different ways, either as (1) derived, (2) inelastic, (3) joint, or (4) fluctuating.

Derived Demand

Because business customers, especially producers, buy products for direct or indirect use in the production of goods and services to satisfy consumers' needs, the demand for business products derives from the demand for consumer products; it is therefore called **derived demand**. In the long run, no demand for business products is totally unrelated to the demand for consumer products. The derived nature of demand is usually multilevel in that business marketers at different levels are affected by a change in consumer demand for a product. The component parts of computers are an example of something

Flexible data, Devices, Set-up, Dedicated support, Reports, Extended warranty, Refresh, Other stuff, Cool stuff, No CapEx, No surprises, No really.

A bold new way to get wireless

Mobility-as-a-Service
Per seat. Per month. All you need.

Find out more

sprint.com/maas

Sprint Business
For companies with people in them™

Types of Business Purchases
When purchasing wireless services, it is likely that a business will engage in a modified rebuy purchase.

that experiences derived demand. Demand for Intel processors, for instance, derives from the demand for computers. The "Intel inside" sticker featured on many computers is meant to stimulate derived demand by encouraging customers to choose a brand of computer with an Intel processor. Change in consumer demand for a product affects demand for all firms involved in the production of that product.

Inelastic Demand

With **inelastic demand**, a price increase or decrease does not significantly alter demand for a business product. A product has inelastic demand when the buyer is not sensitive to price or when there are no ready substitutes. Because many business products are more specialized than consumer products, buyers will continue to make purchases even as the price goes up. Because some business products contain many different parts, price increases that affect only one or two parts may yield only a slightly higher per-unit production cost.

Derived Demand
Intel attempts to generate derived demand by promoting that its products are inside many brands of computers. Thus, the sale of computers generates demand for Intel products.

Inelasticity of demand in the business market applies at the industry level, while demand for an individual firm's products may fluctuate. Suppose a spark plug producer increases the price of spark plugs sold to small-engine manufacturers, but its competitors continue to maintain lower prices. The spark plug company that raised its prices will experience reduced unit sales because most small-engine producers will switch to lower-priced brands. A specific firm, therefore, remains vulnerable to elastic demand, while demand across the industry as a whole will not fluctuate drastically.

Joint Demand

Certain business products, especially raw materials and components, are subject to joint demand. **Joint demand** occurs when two or more items are used in combination to produce a product. Consider a firm that manufactures computers. The firm will need the same number of CPUs as it does computer screens—these two products thus are demanded jointly by the firm. If a shortage of CPUs exists because of increased industry demand or reduced manufacturer productivity, the manufacturer buys fewer computer screens and produces fewer computers. Understanding the effects of joint demand is particularly important for a marketer that sells multiple jointly demanded items. Such a marketer realizes that when a customer purchases one of the jointly demanded items, an opportunity exists to sell related products.

Fluctuating Demand

Because the demand for business products is derived from consumer demand, it is subject to dramatic fluctuations. In general, when consumer products are in high demand, producers buy large quantities of raw materials and components to ensure that they can meet long-run production requirements. These producers may expand production capacity to meet demand as well, which entails acquiring new equipment and machinery, more workers, and more raw materials and component parts. Conversely, a decline in demand for certain consumer goods reduces demand for business products used to produce those goods.

Sometimes, price changes lead to surprising temporary changes in demand. A price increase for a business product initially may cause business customers to buy more of the item because they expect the price to continue to rise in the future. Similarly, demand for a business product may decrease significantly following a price cut because buyers are waiting for further price reductions. Fluctuations in demand can be substantial in industries in which prices change frequently.

inelastic demand Demand that is not significantly altered by a price increase or decrease

joint demand Demand involving the use of two or more items in combination to produce a product

business (organizational) buying behavior The purchase behavior of producers, government units, institutions, and resellers

buying center The people within an organization who make business purchase decisions

7-4 BUSINESS BUYING DECISIONS

LO 7-4 Describe the buying center, stages of the business buying decision process, and the factors that affect this process.

Business (organizational) buying behavior refers to the purchase behavior of producers, government units, institutions, and resellers. Although several factors that affect consumer buying behavior (discussed in Chapter 6) also influence business buying behavior, a number of factors are unique to businesses. In this section, we first analyze the buying center to learn who participates in business buying decisions. Then we focus on the stages of the buying decision process and the factors that affect it.

7-4a The Buying Center

Relatively few business purchase decisions are made by a single person. Often they are made through a buying center. The **buying center** is the group of people within the organization who make business purchase decisions. They include users, influencers, buyers, deciders, and gatekeepers.[18] One person may perform several roles within the buying center, and participants share goals and risks associated with their decisions.

Users are the organizational members who will actually use the product. They frequently initiate the purchase process and/or generate purchase specifications. After the purchase, they evaluate product performance relative to the specifications.

Influencers are often technical personnel, such as engineers, who help develop product specifications and evaluate alternatives. Technical personnel are especially important influencers when the products being considered involve new, advanced technology.

Buyers select suppliers and negotiate terms of purchase. They may also be involved in developing specifications. Buyers are sometimes called purchasing agents or purchasing managers. Their choices of vendors and products, especially for new-task purchases, are heavily influenced by others in the buying center. For straight rebuy purchases, the buyer plays a major role in vendor selection and negotiations.

Deciders actually choose the products. Although buyers may be deciders, it is not unusual for different people to occupy these roles. For routinely purchased items, buyers are commonly deciders. However, a buyer may not be authorized to make purchases that exceed a certain dollar limit, in which case higher-level management personnel are deciders.

Finally, *gatekeepers*, such as secretaries and technical personnel, control the flow of information to and among the different roles in the buying center. Buyers who deal directly with vendors also may be gatekeepers because they can control information flows. The flow of information from a supplier's sales representatives to users and influencers is often controlled by personnel in the purchasing department.

The number and structure of an organization's buying centers are affected by the organization's size and market position, the volume and types of products being purchased, and the firm's overall managerial philosophy on who should make purchase decisions. The size of a buying center is influenced by the stage of the buying decision process and by the type of purchase (new-task, straight rebuy, or modified rebuy). The size of the buying center is generally larger for a new-task purchase than for a straight rebuy. A marketer attempting to sell to a business customer should first determine who the people in the buying center are, the roles they play in the buying center, and which individuals are most influential in the decision process. Selling to a buying center requires using signals from the buying center to identify and adapt selling behaviors toward creating strong relationships.

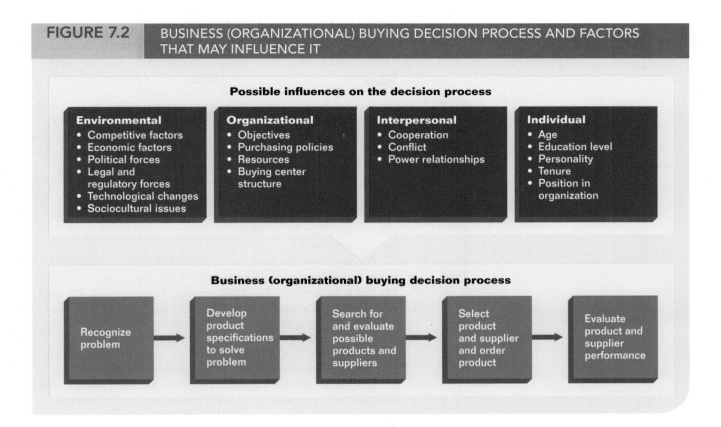

FIGURE 7.2 BUSINESS (ORGANIZATIONAL) BUYING DECISION PROCESS AND FACTORS THAT MAY INFLUENCE IT

Possible influences on the decision process

Environmental
- Competitive factors
- Economic factors
- Political forces
- Legal and regulatory forces
- Technological changes
- Sociocultural issues

Organizational
- Objectives
- Purchasing policies
- Resources
- Buying center structure

Interpersonal
- Cooperation
- Conflict
- Power relationships

Individual
- Age
- Education level
- Personality
- Tenure
- Position in organization

Business (organizational) buying decision process

Recognize problem → Develop product specifications to solve problem → Search for and evaluate possible products and suppliers → Select product and supplier and order product → Evaluate product and supplier performance

7-4b Stages of the Business Buying Decision Process

Like consumers, businesses follow a buying decision process. This process is summarized in the lower portion of Figure 7.2.

In the first stage, one or more individuals recognize that a problem or need exists. *Problem recognition* may arise under a variety of circumstances—for instance, when machines malfunction or a firm modifies an existing product or introduces a new one. It may be individuals in the buying center or other individuals in the firm who initially recognize that a problem exists.

The second stage of the process, *development of product specifications*, requires that buying center participants assess the problem or need and determine what is necessary to resolve or satisfy it. During this stage, users and influencers, such as engineers, provide information and advice for developing product specifications. By assessing and describing needs, the organization should be able to establish product specifications.

Searching for and evaluating potential products and suppliers is the third stage in the decision process. Search activities may involve looking in company files and trade directories, websites, contacting suppliers for information, soliciting proposals from known vendors, and examining various online and print publications. It is common for organizations, particularly those with a reputation for having open hiring policies, to specify a desire to work with diverse vendors, such as those owned by women or by minorities.

During this third stage, some organizations engage in value analysis, an evaluation of each component of a potential purchase. **Value analysis** examines quality, design, materials,

value analysis An evaluation of each component of a potential purchase

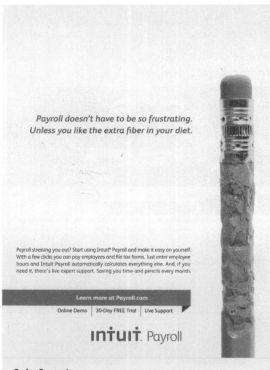

Source: Intuit, Inc.

Sole Sourcing
This advertisement for Intuit points to the problem some firms have with implementing and maintaining a smooth and efficient payroll process. Businesses that outsource payroll processing are likely to use just one vendor.

and possibly item reduction or deletion, in order to acquire the product in the most cost-effective way. Some vendors may be deemed unacceptable because they are not large enough to supply needed quantities.

Others may be excluded because of poor delivery and service records. Sometimes the product is not available from any vendor and the buyer will work with an innovative supplier to design and produce it. Buyers evaluate products to make sure they meet or exceed product specifications developed in the second stage of the business buying decision process. Usually suppliers are judged according to multiple criteria. A number of firms employ **vendor analysis**, a formal, systematic evaluation of current and potential vendors, focusing on such characteristics as price, product quality, delivery service, product availability, and overall reliability.

The results of deliberations and assessments in the third stage are used during the fourth stage of the process to *select the product to be purchased and the supplier*. In some cases, the buyer selects and uses several suppliers, a process known as **multiple sourcing**. Firms with federal government contracts are generally required to have several sources for an item to ensure a steady supply. At times, only one supplier is selected, a situation called **sole sourcing**. For organizations that outsource their payroll services, many of these companies will use just one provider. The Intuit advertisement focuses on a problem that many firms have with implementing and maintaining a smooth payroll process. The chewed pencil underscores what a headache payroll can be for

vendor analysis A formal, systematic evaluation of current and potential vendors

multiple sourcing An organization's decision to use several suppliers

sole sourcing An organization's decision to use only one supplier

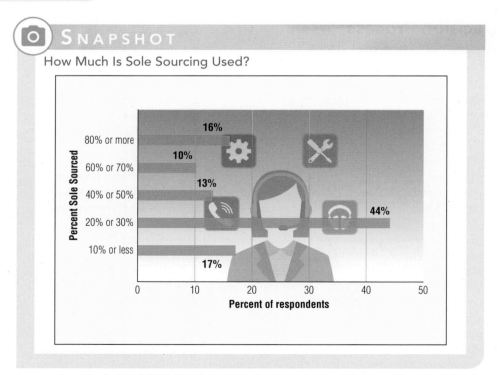

How Much Is Sole Sourcing Used?

Source: A Report by the Supply Chain Management Faculty at the University of Tennessee: Managing Risk in the Global Supply Chain (page 11), http://globalsupplychaininstitute.utk.edu/publications/documents/Risk.pdf.

many firms. The businesses that recognize that they have this problem are encouraged to purchase Intuit's payroll products to make the process easier and smoother because they cover all business payroll needs.

Sole sourcing has historically been discouraged except in the cases where a product is only available from one company. While still not common, more organizations now choose sole sourcing, partly because the arrangement means better communications between buyer and supplier, stability and higher profits for suppliers, and often lower prices for buyers. However, multiple sourcing remains preferable for most firms because it lessens the possibility of disruption caused by strikes, shortages, or bankruptcies. The actual product is ordered in this fourth stage, and specific details regarding terms, credit arrangements, delivery dates and methods, and technical assistance are finalized.

In the final stage, members of the buying center *evaluate the supplier's and product's performance by comparing it with specifications*. Sometimes the product meets the specifications but its performance fails to adequately solve the problem or satisfy the need recognized in the first stage. In that case, product specifications must be adjusted. The supplier's performance is also evaluated during this stage. If supplier performance is inadequate, the business purchaser seeks corrective action from the supplier or searches for a new one. Results of the evaluation become useful feedback in future business purchase decisions.

The business buying decision process is used in its entirety primarily for new-task purchases. Several stages, but not necessarily all, are used for modified rebuy and straight rebuy situations.

7-4c Influences on the Business Buying Decision Process

Figure 7.2 also lists the four major factors that influence business buying decisions: environmental, organizational, interpersonal, and individual. Environmental factors include competitive and economic factors, political forces, legal and regulatory forces, technological changes, and sociocultural issues. These factors can generate considerable uncertainty for an organization, including in buying decisions. Changes in one or more environmental forces, such as new government regulations or increased competition, can create opportunities and threats that affect purchasing decisions.

Organizational factors that influence the buying decision process include the company's objectives, purchasing policies, resources, and the size and composition of its buying center. An organization may also have certain buying policies to which buying center participants must conform that limit buying decisions. For instance, a firm's policies may mandate contract lengths that are undesirable to many sellers. An organization's financial resources might require special credit arrangements, also affecting purchase decisions.

Interpersonal factors are the relationships among people in the buying center. Trust is crucial in collaborative partnerships. This is especially true when customized products are involved—the buyer may not see the product until it is finished and must trust that the producer is creating it to specifications. Trust and clear communication ensure that all parties are satisfied with the outcome; however, interpersonal dynamics and varying communication abilities within the buying center may complicate processes.

Individual factors are the personal characteristics of participants in the buying center, such as age, education level, personality, and tenure and position in the organization. Personality and emotional reactions to suppliers and their products can be a key factor in a purchase. Consider a 55-year-old manager who has been in the organization for 25 years. This manager is likely to have a greater influence and power over buying center decisions than a 30-year-old employed at the firm only two years. The influence of various factors, such as relationships, age, and tenure, on the buying decision process depends on the buying situation, the type of product, and the type of purchase (new-task, modified rebuy, or straight rebuy). Employees' negotiating styles will vary as well. To be effective, marketers develop relationships with and understand both rational and emotional factors that can affect purchase decisions.

Promotion targeted to individuals in the buying center can influence individual decision making as well. Most trade publications carry advertising to influence buyers. Cintas, for example, launched its first-ever national advertising campaign using television, radio, print, and online ads to show how the commercial laundry and uniform provider can help a variety of businesses be "ready."[19] Trade shows are very popular when products can be demonstrated and samples provided. Personal selling is by far the most important influence of trust in maintaining strong relationships. Interestingly, business-to-business marketers seem to hesitate in embracing social media as a relationship marketing tool. When they use social media, they tend to focus on relationships rather than on functional or rational appeals for purchases.[20] When using Twitter or other social media sites, business-to-business marketers should try to post content to develop information and trust rather than close the sale.

7-5 RELIANCE ON THE INTERNET AND OTHER TECHNOLOGY

LO 7-5 Explore how the Internet facilitates business buying and marketing.

Whereas in the past, an organization seeking a type of product might contact product suppliers, speak with someone on the sales force, and request a catalog or brochure, business customers today first turn to the Internet to search for information and find sources. The Internet has become a major channel in organizational buying, accounting for $780 billion in sales.[21] Indeed, 62 percent of business buyers now purchase products online, and 30 percent of them researched at least 90 percent of products online before making a purchase. Moreover, 94 percent of B2B buyers engaged in online research prior to purchasing a product, and 55 percent report researching at least half their organizations' purchases online.[22] In many cases, business buyers' needs and wants have been shaped by their experiences as consumers shopping at sites such as Amazon.com, LandsEnd.com, and Walmart.com.

Organizational buyers often begin searching for a product after recognizing a need or problem. The Internet allows buyers to research potential solutions, read blogs, view webinars and YouTube videos, examine specifications, chat with peers about their experiences, and even find reviews of potential products long before beginning a formal buying process. Dealings with a sales representative now may take place much later in the process than in the past. B2B marketers should therefore take care that the content they post on their blogs, webinars, videos, eBooks, whitepapers, and even responses to forum queries include useful information about how their products might solve customers' problems or address their needs. John Deere, for example, uses its comprehensive website to showcase its products so that business buyers can research product details and find the right one to match their needs. The screenshot for John Deere's backhoe loaders offers general information about the features

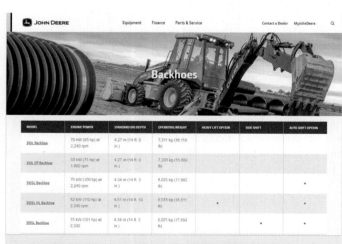

deere.com

Technology Facilitates the Buying Decision Process
Astute B2B marketers ensure that they provide detailed information about their products on their websites to streamline the research process for potential buyers.

of the product as well as detailed specifications for different models. It also highlights a quote from a user who appreciated being
asked for input when Deere designed new machines with improvements to boost productivity.

For most firms, online marketing efforts make the buying process far more efficient because it saves time and reduces costs. BOGA Paddle and Surf Company processes 80 percent of its dealer customers' orders online. The company, which relies on TradeGecko e-commerce software, has been able to capitalize on the growing trend of stand-up paddle-boarding to grow 55 percent per year since its inception. The software allows BOGA's sales representatives to access the firm's entire catalog on their smartphones in the field so that retailers know exactly what the firm has in stock and where their orders are.[23] As we shall see in Chapter 14, Internet technology has streamlined physical distribution and other supply-chain activities, resulting in significant cost savings.

Organizations can make purchases directly from a firm's website, such as computers from dell.com or hp.com. Like many larger companies, Dell and Hewlett Packard offer special access through a password-protected portal to B2B customers where they can track orders, see past orders, and access relevant information. Organizations can also purchase supplies from a retailer's website. Amazon Business, for example, offers 300,000 business buyers millions of products including office supplies, computers, food service supplies, and technology equipment using the successful and secure e-commerce platform of its parent, Amazon.com.[24]

Increasingly, businesses are turning to **B2B e-commerce sites**, which serve as online marketplaces where buyers and sellers from around the world can exchange information, goods, services, ideas, and payments. Variously known as trading exchanges, B2B exchanges, and ehubs, B2B e-commerce sites may be independent or private. Independent sites act as a neutral third party and charge a fee for providing a trading forum. Some sites may be focused on a specific industry, while others may offer products and attract businesses from many industries. AutoWurld.com, for example, is an independent e-commerce site for wholesale and retail buying and selling of motor vehicles. Dealers pay a flat fee of $395 per month to gain access to unlimited vehicle listings and sales transactions.[25] Alibaba, on the other hand, connects buyers in 190 countries with Chinese manufacturing firms offering millions of products in 40 categories for many industries and purposes.[26] Such exchanges are especially beneficial for small businesses because they allow them to expand their customer base while reducing the costs of marketing to and buying from other companies. Private B2B exchanges connect member firms, which typically share supply chains or complex customers, through a secure system that permits all the organizations to share significant information as well as facilitate exchanges. Exostar, for example, serves as a private exchange for companies in the aerospace, defense, health-care, pharmaceutical, and financial markets.

Businesses may also turn to online auctions, such as uBid and TradeOut, to find products. As with a traditional auction, a seller posts an item to an online auction, and potential buyers bid against each other on the item; the highest bidder wins the right to buy the item. Such auctions are especially popular for liquidating unsold, returned, and used merchandise. In a reverse auction, a buyer invites businesses to bid to supply the specified good or service in competition with each other; the lowest bidder wins the right to sell the product.

B2B e-commerce sites Online marketplaces where buyers and sellers from around the world can exchange information, goods, services, ideas, and payments

Chapter Review

7-1 Distinguish among the four types of business markets.

Business (B2B) markets consist of individuals, organizations, and groups that purchase a specific kind of product for resale, direct use in producing other products, or use in day-to-day operations. Producer markets include those individuals and business organizations that purchase products for the purpose of making a profit by using them to produce other products or as part of their operations. Intermediaries that buy finished products and resell them to make a profit are classified as reseller markets. Government markets consist of federal, state, county, and local governments, which spend billions of dollars annually for goods and services to support internal operations and to provide citizens with needed services. Organizations with charitable, educational, community, or other nonprofit goals constitute institutional markets.

7-2 Describe the North American Industry Classification System and how it can be used to identify and analyze business markets.

Business marketers have a considerable amount of information available for use in planning marketing strategies. The North American Industry Classification System (NAICS) is a single industry classification system used by the United States, Canada, and Mexico to generate comparable statistics. It provides marketers with information needed to identify business customer groups. Marketers can best utilize this data in conjunction with other information. After identifying target industries, a marketer can obtain the names and locations of potential customers by using government and commercial data sources. Marketers then must estimate potential purchases of business customers by finding a relationship between a potential customer's purchases and a variable available in industrial classification data.

7-3 Identify the major characteristics of business customers and transactions.

Transactions that involve business customers differ from consumer transactions in several ways. Business transactions tend to be larger and negotiations occur less frequently, though they are often lengthy. They may involve more than one person or department in the purchasing organization. They may also involve reciprocity, an arrangement in which two organizations agree to buy from each other. Business customers are usually better informed than ultimate consumers and are more likely to

seek information about a product's features and technical specifications.

Business customers are particularly concerned about quality, service, price, and supplier relationships. Quality is important because it directly affects the quality of products the buyer's firm produces. To achieve an exact level of quality, organizations often buy products on the basis of a set of expressed characteristics, called specifications. Because services have such a direct influence on a firm's costs, sales, and profits, factors such as market information, on-time delivery, and availability of parts are crucial to a business buyer. Although business customers do not depend solely on price to decide which products to buy, price is of primary concern because it directly influences a firm's profitability.

Business buyers use several purchasing methods, including description, inspection, sampling, and negotiation. Most organizational purchases are new-task, straight rebuy, or modified rebuy. In a new-task purchase, an organization makes an initial purchase of items to be used to perform new jobs or solve new problems. A straight rebuy purchase occurs when a buyer purchases the same products routinely under approximately the same terms of sale. In a modified rebuy purchase, a new-task purchase is changed the second or third time it is ordered or requirements associated with a straight rebuy purchase are modified.

Industrial demand differs from consumer demand along several dimensions. Industrial demand derives from demand for consumer products. At the industry level, industrial demand is inelastic. If an industrial item's price changes, product demand will not change as much proportionally. Some industrial products are subject to joint demand, which occurs when two or more items are used in combination to make a product. Finally, because organizational demand derives from consumer demand, the demand for business products can fluctuate significantly.

7-4 Describe the buying center, stages of the business buying decision process, and the factors that affect this process.

Business (or organizational) buying behavior refers to the purchase behavior of producers, resellers, government units, and institutions. Business purchase decisions are made through a buying center, the group of people involved in making such purchase decisions. Users are those in the organization who actually use the product. Influencers help develop specifications and evaluate alternative products for possible use. Buyers select suppliers and negotiate purchase terms. Deciders choose the products. Gatekeepers control the flow of information to and among individuals occupying other roles in the buying center.

The stages of the business buying decision process are problem recognition, development of product specifications to solve problems, search for and evaluation of products and suppliers, selection and ordering of the most appropriate product, and evaluation of the product's and supplier's performance.

Four categories of factors influence business buying decisions: environmental, organizational, interpersonal, and individual. Environmental factors include competitive forces, economic conditions, political forces, laws and regulations, technological changes, and sociocultural factors. Business factors include the company's objectives, purchasing policies, and resources, as well as the size and composition of its buying center. Interpersonal factors are the relationships among people in the buying center. Individual factors are personal characteristics of members of the buying center, such as age, education level, personality, and tenure and position in the organization.

7-5 Explore how the Internet facilitates business buying and marketing.

The Internet has become a major facilitator of business transactions with business buyers often beginning the buying process informally by searching online for information to solve a problem or address a need. They may find useful information in online catalogs, blogs, videos, webinars, white papers, and peer reviews to help them find the best products and suppliers. Online marketing efforts make the buying process more efficient by saving time and reducing costs. Organizational buyers can purchase directly from a company's website, from an online retailer, from a B2B e-commerce site, or through an online auction. A B2B e-commerce site is an online marketplace where buyers and sellers from around the world can exchange information, goods, services, ideas, and payments.

 Go to www.cengagebrain.com for resources to help you master the content in this chapter as well as materials that will expand your marketing knowledge!

Developing Your Marketing Plan

When developing a marketing strategy for business customers, it is essential to understand the process the business goes through when making a buying decision. Knowledge of business buying behavior is important when developing several aspects of the marketing plan. To assist you in relating the information in this chapter to the creation of a marketing plan for business customers, consider the following issues:

1. What are the primary concerns of business customers? Could any of these concerns be addressed with the strengths of your company?

2. Determine the type of business purchase your customer will likely be using when purchasing your product. How would this impact the level of information required by the business when moving through the buying decision process?

3. Discuss the different types of demand that the business customer will experience when purchasing your product.

Key Concepts

Issues for Discussion and Review

1. Identify, describe, and give examples of the four major types of business markets.
2. What function does an industrial classification system help marketers perform?
3. Why might business customers generally be considered more rational in their purchasing behavior than ultimate consumers?
4. What are the primary concerns of business customers?
5. List several characteristics that differentiate transactions involving business customers from consumer transactions.
6. What are the commonly used methods of business buying?
7. Why do buyers involved in straight rebuy purchases require less information than those making new-task purchases?
8. How does demand for business products differ from consumer demand?
9. What are the major components of a firm's buying center?
10. Identify the stages of the business buying decision process. How is this decision process used when making straight rebuys?
11. How do environmental, business, interpersonal, and individual factors affect business purchases?
12. How has the Internet facilitated the organizational buying process?

VIDEO CASE 7
Will Apple Pay Pay Off for Retailers?

When Apple introduced its mobile payment system in 2014, the company was looking to leverage the popularity of its iPhone by adding more functionality and convenience for millions of customers. With Apple Pay, iPhone owners (and Apple Watch wearers) first enter their credit or debit card information, which Apple confirms with the banks. Once this information is on file, Apple creates a digital "token" that will be electronically transmitted to the retailer when an iPhone owner pays for something. To complete a purchase, the customer simply waves the phone or taps it at the checkout, uses the iPhone's built-in fingerprint security to activate Apple Pay, and the phone instantly transfers the token as payment.

Even though Apple Pay offers consumers the benefits of convenience and security, Apple knew it wouldn't succeed without a large network of retailers, restaurants, and other businesses agreeing to accept its mobile payments. Among the earliest businesses to sign up with Apple was McDonald's, which agreed to honor Apple Pay in its 14,000 U.S. restaurants and drive-through locations. "We serve 27 million customers every day. This is a clear and compelling business opportunity for us," explained McDonald's chief information officer. Compared with cash transactions, Apple Pay transactions cost McDonald's a few pennies more to process because of bank fees. Yet the fast-food giant was willing to sign on because it saw competitive advantage and profit potential in wooing iPhone users interested in speedy checkout.

Another early business supporter was Walgreens, the nationwide drugstore chain with 85 million customers enrolled in its frequent buyer rewards program. Walgreens sells snacks, household products, and health and beauty items in addition to health-care products. Not only did Walgreens agree to accept Apple Pay at its checkout counters, but it was also the first U.S. retailer to add its rewards program to Apple Pay's easy sign-on system. As a result, Walgreens' customers tap twice at the checkout, once to activate the rewards account and display their savings, the second time to process the actual payment. By deciding to honor Apple Pay, Walgreens said it was "enabling a simple and convenient customer experience."

Several hundred thousand businesses had signed on to participate by the time Apple Pay launched in October 2014. Apple's ongoing efforts to increase business participation paid off: Eighteen months later, the network of participating businesses topped 2 million, and major companies such as Forever 21, Regal Cinemas, and Marriott Hotels were preparing to participate. Eyeing international expansion, Apple also initiated talks with banks in China to bring Apple Pay to millions of iPhone users there.

Even though more consumers are making more mobile payments year after year, not every U.S. retailer is willing or able to work with Apple Pay. Some aren't satisfied with the amount of consumer information that Apple Pay shares with participating merchants. Others would have to upgrade to new checkout technology for Apple Pay. Still others are locked into exclusive mobile payment deals with competing services.

Today, mobile payments represent a tiny fraction of all purchase transactions, dwarfed by cash as well as by credit and debit payments. And Apple Pay faces strong competition from Google, Samsung, and others operating in the mobile-payment market. To remain a leader, Apple will have to keep signing more participating businesses and showing consumers the benefits of paying by iPhone or Apple Watch whenever they make a purchase.[27]

Questions for Discussion

1. When a retailer is considering whether to participate in Apple Pay, is the decision process like a new-task purchase, a straight rebuy purchase, or a modified rebuy purchase? Explain your answer.
2. Which of the four categories of business markets is Apple Pay best suited for, and why?
3. Which environmental influences on the decision process seem to have been most important to McDonald's when it decided to honor Apple Pay?

ArtisticPhoto/Shutterstock.com

chapter 8

Reaching Global Markets

LEARNING OBJECTIVES

8-1 Define international marketing.

8-2 Differentiate between the six environmental forces that affect international marketing efforts.

8-3 List six important international trade agreements.

8-4 Identify methods of international market entry.

8-5 Describe the use of the marketing mix internationally.

184

Netflix Stream Becomes a Global River

Netflix is taking on the world as it becomes available in more countries. With a presence in about 130 countries, the streaming service wants to increase this number to 200. The company has entered into Italy, Spain, Portugal, and Japan. It became one of the first U.S. companies to expand into Cuba. Netflix has announced its intention to enter into every country in the world.

The key to Netflix's rapid international expansion is its globalized approach. Because Netflix is an Internet streaming service, it is easily obtained by any household with a strong enough Internet connection. Its products and distribution channels are therefore highly standardized. As more consumers become connected to the Internet worldwide, Netflix is taking advantage of the opportunity to reach them.

However, even companies with a globalization approach face certain challenges that vary by country. U.S. sanctions on Syria and North Korea currently prevent Netflix from entering those countries. It was also forced to abandon its plans to launch in China due to the country's government restrictions. Instead, Netflix has decided to license content to local firms rather than launching its own service. In Cuba, the price for its services is $7.99, which consists of half the monthly salary of the average Cuban worker. Payments must be made with credit or debit cards that are not accessible to the majority of Cubans. Netflix may therefore have to customize its payment options. Finally, Netflix's success depends upon how much of the population has sufficient Internet connections. Only about 26 percent of Cubans have Internet access. On the other hand, Japan has one of the fastest connections worldwide.[1]

sitthiphong/Shutterstock.com

Technological advances and rapidly changing political and economic conditions are making it easier than ever for companies to market their products overseas as well as at home. With most of the world's population and two-thirds of total purchasing power outside the United States, international markets represent tremendous opportunities for growth. For example, Procter & Gamble obtains only 44 percent of its net sales from North America.[2] Accessing these markets can promote innovation, while intensifying competition can spur companies to develop global strategies.

In deference to the increasingly global nature of marketing, we devote this chapter to the unique features of global markets and international marketing. We begin by considering the nature of global marketing strategy and the environmental forces that create opportunities and threats for international marketers. Next, we consider several regional trade alliances, markets, and agreements. Then we examine the modes of entry into international marketing and companies' degree of involvement in it, as well as some of the structures that can be used to organize multinational enterprises. Finally, we examine how firms may alter their marketing mixes when engaging in international marketing efforts. All of these factors must be considered in any marketing plan that includes an international component.

8-1 THE NATURE OF GLOBAL MARKETING STRATEGY

LO 8-1 Define international marketing.

International marketing involves developing and performing marketing activities across national boundaries. For instance, Walmart has approximately 2,300,000 employees and operates 11,500 stores in 28 countries; Starbucks serves tens of millions of customers a week at more than 24,000 shops in over 70 countries.[3] General Motors sells more cars in China than in the United States. Emirates airline, based in Dubai, has become the world's largest long-haul carrier. Dubai is building an airport that can handle four times as many passengers a year as New York's John F. Kennedy International Airport.[4]

Firms are finding that international markets provide tremendous opportunities for growth. To encourage international growth, many countries offer significant practical assistance and valuable benchmarking research that will help their domestic firms become more competitive globally. One example is Export.gov, a website managed by the U.S. Department of Commerce's International Trade Administration. Export.gov collects a variety of resources to help businesses that want to export to other countries.[5] A major element of the assistance that governmental organizations can provide for firms (especially small-and medium-sized firms) is knowledge of the internationalization process of firms.

Traditionally, most companies—such as McDonald's and KFC—have entered the global marketplace incrementally as they gained knowledge about various markets and opportunities. Beginning in the 1990s, however, some firms—such as eBay, Google, and Logitech—were founded with the knowledge and resources to expedite their commitment and investment in the global marketplace. These "born globals"—typically small, technology-based firms earning as much as 70 percent of their sales outside the domestic/home market—export their products almost immediately after being established in market niches in which they compete with larger, more established firms.[6] Whether a firm adopts the traditional approach, the born-global approach, or an approach that merges attributes of both approaches to market products, international marketing

international marketing
Developing and performing marketing activities across national boundaries

Emirates Airlines
Emirates airlines, based in Dubai, flies to more than 140 destinations.

Rebius/Shutterstock.com

strategy is a critical element of a firm's global operations. Today, global competition in most industries is intense and becoming increasingly fierce with the addition of newly emerging markets and firms.

8-2 ENVIRONMENTAL FORCES IN GLOBAL MARKETS

LO 8-2 Differentiate between the six environmental forces that affect international marketing efforts.

Firms that enter international markets often find that they must make significant adjustments in their marketing strategies. The environmental forces that affect foreign markets may differ dramatically from those that affect domestic markets. Alphabet Inc.'s Google search engine faces unique competition, regulatory issues, and consumer use patterns in the foreign markets it serves. Thus, a successful international marketing strategy requires a careful environmental analysis. Conducting research to understand the needs and desires of international customers is crucial to global marketing success. Many firms have demonstrated that such efforts can generate tremendous financial rewards, increase market share, and heighten customer awareness of their products around the world. In this section, we explore how differences in the sociocultural; economic; political, legal, and regulatory; social and ethical; competitive; and technological forces in other countries can profoundly affect marketing activities.

8-2a Sociocultural Forces

Cultural and social differences among nations can have significant effects on marketing activities. Because marketing activities are primarily social in purpose, they are influenced by beliefs and values regarding family, religion, education, health, and recreation. In terms of families, the world population is nearly 7.5 billion. By identifying such major sociocultural deviations among countries, marketers lay groundwork for an effective adaptation of marketing strategy. When Taco Bell originally expanded into South Korea, the menu was largely the same as in the United States, but more recently it has grown to include items like kimchi quesadillas, designed to appeal to local tastes. The kimchi quesadilla launch was a success, and the menu item now makes up 10 percent of sales in the country.[7] McDonald's was one of the first U.S. brands to be successful in China, but in 2017 it sold an 80 percent interest in its 2,400 Chinese stores to a state-owned enterprise. Chinese consumers became more concerned about their health and have less confidence in fast food.[8]

Local preferences, tastes, and idioms can all prove complicated for international marketers. Although football is a popular sport in the United States and a major opportunity for many television advertisers, soccer is the most popular televised sport in Europe and Latin America. And, of course, marketing communications often must be translated into other languages. Sometimes, the true meaning of translated messages can be misinterpreted or lost. Consider some translations that went awry in foreign markets: KFC's long-running slogan "Finger-lickin' good" was translated into Chinese as "Eat your fingers off," and Coors' "Turn it loose" campaign was translated into Spanish as "Drink Coors and get diarrhea."[9]

It can be difficult to transfer marketing symbols, trademarks, logos, and even products to international markets, especially if these are associated with objects that have profound religious or cultural significance in a particular culture. Clothing and language are both relative to culture. Cultural differences may also affect marketing negotiations and decision-making behavior. In many parts of Asia, a gift may be considered a necessary introduction before negotiation, whereas in the United States or Canada, a gift may be misconstrued as an illegal bribe.

Buyers' perceptions of other countries can influence product adoption and use. Consumers that have a global orientation tend to have a positive attitude toward purchasing global brands. On the other hand, when consumers think local and are ethnocentric, they are more negative toward global brands.[10] Multiple research studies have found that consumer preferences for products depend on both the country of origin and the product category of competing products.[11] When people are unfamiliar with products from another country, their perceptions of the country as a whole may affect their attitude toward the product and influence whether they will buy it. If a country has a reputation for producing quality products and therefore has a positive image in consumers' minds, marketers of products from that country will want to make the country of origin well known. BMW is a respected German brand that manufactures many of its vehicles in the United States, Mexico, and South Africa. In the case of BMW, the brand is more important than the country of origin to most consumers. BMW produces over 400,000 X models in South Carolina each year with 70 percent exported outside the United States. This makes BMW the largest exporter of cars in the United States.[12] On the other hand, marketers may want to dissociate themselves from a particular country in order to build a brand's reputation as truly global or because a country does not have a good reputation for quality. Traditionally, Chinese brands have been viewed as being of low quality. However, the global success of companies such as Lenovo, Xiaomi, and Alibaba are not only increasing China's brand reputation but are also challenging top competitors such as Hewlett-Packard, Apple, and Amazon. The extent to which a product's brand image and country of origin influence purchases is subject to considerable variation based on national culture characteristics.

When products are introduced from one nation into another, acceptance is far more likely if similarities exist between the two cultures. In fact, many similar cultural characteristics exist across countries. For international marketers, cultural differences have implications for product development, pricing, advertising, and packaging. For instance, the Middle East represents a lucrative market for personal-care firms, but they must formulate their products to adhere to Middle Eastern laws and customs. To be allowed under Islamic law, cosmetics cannot contain alcohol or pork by-products. Another challenge is trying to compete with local suppliers who create counterfeit products at lower costs. However, this has not deterred personal-care firms such as German consumer-goods maker Henkel. Henkel markets its Gliss shampoo as the first such product to address problems Middle Eastern women have due to lack of ventilation for their veiled hair.[13]

8-2b **Economic Forces**

Global marketers need to understand the international trade system, particularly the economic stability of individual nations, as well as trade barriers that may stifle marketing efforts. Economic differences among nations—differences in standards of living, credit, buying power, income distribution, national resources, exchange rates, and the like—dictate many of the adjustments firms must make in marketing internationally. Country-specific factors such as economic wealth and national culture have a direct influence on the success of a new product in specific countries.[14]

Instability is one of the guaranteed constants in the global business environment. The United States and the European Union are more stable economically than many other regions of the world. However, even these economies have downturns in regular cycles. A number of other countries, including Greece, Russia, Spain, and Thailand, have all experienced economic problems, such as recessions, high unemployment, corporate bankruptcies, instabilities in banking systems, and trade imbalances. For instance, the rising price of raw materials could increase inflation in developing countries where demand is growing.[15] On the other hand, a 40 percent decrease in oil prices that occurred between 2014 and 2017 before oil prices started to rise provided an economic benefit. The constantly fluctuating conditions in different economies require global marketers to carefully monitor the global environment and make changes quickly. Even more stable developing countries, such as Mexico and Brazil, tend to have greater fluctuations in their business cycles than the United States does. For example, instability in Russia due to economic sanctions, political conflicts, and a devaluing of the ruble damaged trade with Russia in the past few years. Economic instability can also disrupt the markets for U.S. products in places that otherwise might provide excellent marketing opportunities. On the other hand, competition from the sustained economic growth of countries like China and India can disrupt markets for U.S. products.

The value of the dollar, euro, and yen has a major impact on the prices of products in many countries. An important economic factor in the global business environment is currency valuation. Many countries have adopted a floating exchange rate, which allows the currencies of those countries to fluctuate, or float, according to the foreign exchange market. Table 8.1 compares the value of the dollar, euro, yen, and yuan. China has been criticized for undervaluing its currency, or valuing its currency below the market value. This gives it an advantage in selling exports, since the Chinese yuan has a lower value than other nations' currencies. However, China's central bank has begun to allow the value of the yuan to be driven by the market.[16] The value of the U.S. dollar is also important to the global economy. In the last few years, the value of the dollar has been strong relative to other currencies. This means that U.S. exports cost more if purchased with the euro or yen, and imports cost less. In 2017, the U.S. dollar reached a 14-year high against six of the world's major currencies. A strong dollar makes U.S. products less competitive in foreign markets.[17] On the other hand, because imports are cheaper, a 10 percent increase in the value of the U.S. dollar increases the trade deficit by 1 percent of the gross domestic product. The strong dollar damages companies like Boeing, 3M, and Caterpillar that have significant global sales.[18]

In terms of the value of all products produced by a nation, China has the largest gross domestic product in the world with more than $21 trillion, growing at a rate of 6.6 percent annually.[19] **Gross domestic product (GDP)** is an overall measure of a nation's economic standing; it is the market value of a nation's total output of goods and services for a given period. However, it does not take into account the concept of GDP in relation to population (GDP per capita). The United States has a GDP per capita of $57,300. Switzerland is roughly 230 times smaller than the United States—a little larger than the state of Maryland—but its population density is six times greater than that of the United States. Although Switzerland's GDP is much smaller than the United States' GDP, its GDP per capita is slightly higher. Even Canada, which is comparable in geographic size to the United States, has a lower GDP and GDP per capita.[20] Table 8.2 provides a comparative economic analysis of 15 countries, including the United States. Knowledge about per capita income, credit, and the distribution of income provides general insights into market potential.

Opportunities for international trade are not limited to countries with the highest incomes. Brazil, Russia, India, China, and South Africa (BRICS) have attracted attention as their economies are rapidly advancing. Relationship marketing has proven to be a highly effective tool in reaching these emerging markets. This is because businesses in these countries value long-term and close interactions with marketers that they can trust.[21] Other nations are progressing at a much faster rate than they were a few years ago, and these countries—especially in Latin America, Africa, eastern Europe, and the Middle East—have great market potential. In addition to infrastructure issues, another issue marketers encounter is how to price products high enough to earn a profit and yet make them affordable for lower-income consumers. Marketers must also understand the political and legal environments before they can convert buying power of customers in these countries into actual demand for specific products.

gross domestic product (GDP) The market value of a nation's total output of goods and services for a given period; an overall measure of economic standing

TABLE 8.1	EXCHANGE RATES OF GLOBAL CURRENCIES*			
	1 USD (U.S. Dollars)	**1 EUR** (Euro)	**1 JPY** (Japanese Yen)	**1 CNY** (China Yuan Renminbi)
1 USD	1.00	0.93	113.08	6.88
1 EUR	1.08	1.00	122.07	7.43
1 JPY	0.0088	0.0082	1.00	0.061
1 CNY	0.15	0.13	16.45	1.00

*As of January 31, 2017

TABLE 8.2	COMPARATIVE ANALYSIS OF SELECTED COUNTRIES				
Country	Population (in Millions)	GDP (U.S.$ in Billions)	Exports (U.S.$ in Billions)	Imports (U.S.$ in Billions)	Internet Users (in Millions)	Cell Phones (in Millions)
Brazil	205.8	3,135	189.7	143.8	139.1	280.7
Canada	35.4	1,674	402.4	419	32.1	29.5
China	1,373.5	21,270	2,011	1,437	721.4	1,300
Honduras	8.9	43.2	8.2	11.3	1.7	7.7
India	1,266.8	8,721	271.6	402.4	462.1	944
Japan	126.7	4,932	641.4	629.8	115.1	152.7
Jordan	8.1	86.2	7.1	17.9	3.5	11.1
Kenya	46.8	152.7	6.4	16.3	21.2	33.6
Mexico	123.2	2,307	359.3	372.8	58	102.2
Russia	142.4	3,745	259.3	165.1	102.3	221
South Africa	54.3	736.3	83.2	85	28.6	79.5
Switzerland	8.2	494.3	301.1	243.4	7.3	11.5
Turkey	80.3	1,670	150.1	197.8	46.2	71.9
Thailand	68.2	1,161	190	171.3	29	97.1
U.S.	323.9	18,560	1,471	2,244	286.9	317.4

Source: The CIA, *The World Fact Book,* www.cia.gov/library/publications/the-world-factbook/rankorder/rankorderguide.html (accessed January 31, 2017); "Internet Users by Country (2014)," Internet Live Stats, 2016, www.internetlivestats.com/internet-users-by-country/ (accessed January 31, 2017).

8-2c Political, Legal, and Regulatory Forces

The political, legal, and regulatory forces of the environment are closely intertwined in the United States. To a large degree, the same is true in many countries internationally. Typically, legislation is enacted, legal decisions are interpreted, and regulatory agencies are operated by elected or appointed officials. A country's legal and regulatory infrastructure is a direct reflection of the political climate in the country. In some countries, this political climate is determined by the people via elections, whereas in other countries leaders are appointed or have assumed leadership based on certain powers. Although laws and regulations have direct effects on a firm's operations in a country, political forces are indirect and often not clearly known in all countries. China is an example of state-directed or national capitalism. The government owns a majority of or has a partial stake in many businesses. State-backed firms accounted for one-third of the emerging world's foreign direct investment in the last decade. An issue with state-owned enterprises versus private ones is the nature of competition. State-backed companies do not have as many competitors because the government is supporting them. Unless state-owned firms work hard to remain competitive, costs for these companies will most likely increase.[22]

Rena Schild/Shutterstock.com

Political, Legal, & Regulatory
Political systems, laws, and regulatory bodies vary widely among nations and play a significant role in international marketing.

A nation's political system, laws, regulatory bodies, special-interest groups, and courts all have a great impact on international marketing. A government's policies toward public and private enterprise, consumers, and foreign firms influence marketing across national boundaries. Some countries have established import barriers, such as tariffs. An **import tariff** is any duty levied by a nation on goods bought outside its borders and brought into the country. Because they raise the prices of foreign goods, tariffs impede free trade between nations. Tariffs are usually designed either to raise revenue for a country or to protect domestic products. For example, China subsidizes its steelmakers, leading to an oversupply of steel on world markets. In 2016 the United States placed a tariff of 522 percent on cold-rolled Chinese steel, as has the European Union.[23]

Cuba
The U.S. embargo on Cuba restricts trade and travel.

Non-tariff trade restrictions include quotas and embargoes. A **quota** is a limit on the amount of goods an importing country will accept for certain product categories in a specific period of time. The United States maintains tariff-rate quotas on imported raw cane sugar, refined and specialty sugar, and sugar-containing products. The goal is to allow countries to export specific products to the United States at a relatively low tariff while acknowledging higher tariffs above predetermined quantities.[24] An **embargo** is a government's suspension of trade in a particular product or with a given country. The United States has had an embargo on Cuban imports and exports for over 50 years. Although diplomatic relations have been restored with Cuba, only Congress can lift the embargo. Embargoes are generally directed at specific goods or countries and are established for political, health, or religious reasons. An embargo may be used to suspend the purchase of a commodity like oil from a country that is involved in questionable conduct, such as human rights violations or terrorism. The United States and the European Union issued trade sanctions against Russia due to its involvement in the Ukraine conflict. The sanctions hurt European agricultural products, which resulted in much lower prices in Europe for these products due to over-supply. Laws regarding competition may also serve as trade barriers. The European Union has stronger antitrust laws than the United States. Being found guilty of anticompetitive behavior has cost companies like Intel billions of dollars. Because some companies do not have the resources to comply with more stringent laws, this can act as a barrier to trade.

Exchange controls, government restrictions on the amount of a particular currency that can be bought or sold, may also limit international trade. They can force businesspeople to buy and sell foreign products through a central agency, such as a central bank. Developing economies use exchange control to limit speculation against their currencies and or to limit foreign investment. For example, Greece placed restrictions on how much cash could be withdrawn from banks and restrictions on transfer of capital abroad during a financial crisis. On the other hand, to promote international trade, some countries have joined to form free trade zones, which are multinational economic communities that eliminate tariffs and other trade barriers. Such regional trade alliances are discussed later in the chapter. As mentioned earlier, foreign currency exchange rates also affect the prices marketers can charge in foreign markets. Fluctuations in the international monetary market can change the prices charged across national boundaries on a daily basis. Thus, these fluctuations must be considered in any international marketing strategy.

Countries may limit imports to maintain a favorable balance of trade. The **balance of trade** is the difference in value between a nation's exports and its imports. When a nation exports more products than it imports, a favorable balance of trade exists because money is flowing into the country. The United States has a negative balance of trade for goods and services of more than $453 billion.[25] A negative balance of trade is considered harmful, because it means U.S. dollars are supporting foreign economies at the expense of U.S.

import tariff A duty levied by a nation on goods bought outside its borders and brought into the country

quota A limit on the amount of goods an importing country will accept for certain product categories in a specific period of time

embargo A government's suspension of trade in a particular product or with a given country

exchange controls Government restrictions on the amount of a particular currency that can be bought or sold

balance of trade The difference in value between a nation's exports and its imports

companies and workers. At the same time, U.S. citizens benefit from the assortment of imported products and their typically lower prices.

Many non-tariff barriers, such as quotas and minimum price levels set on imports, port-of-entry taxes, and stringent health and safety requirements, still make it difficult for U.S. companies to export their products. For instance, the collectivistic nature of Japanese culture and the high-context nature of Japanese communication make some types of direct marketing messages used to sell products through television and print less effective and may predispose many Japanese to support greater regulation of direct marketing practices.[26] A government's attitude toward importers has a direct impact on the economic feasibility of exporting to that country.

8-2d Ethical and Social Responsibility Forces

Differences in national standards are illustrated by what the Mexicans call *la mordida*: "the bite." The use of payoffs and bribes is deeply entrenched in many governments. Because U.S. trade and corporate policy, as well as U.S. law, prohibits direct involvement in payoffs and bribes, U.S. companies may have a hard time competing with foreign firms that engage in these practices. Some U.S. businesses that refuse to make payoffs are forced to hire local consultants, public relations firms, or advertising agencies, which results in indirect payoffs that are also illegal under U.S. law. The ultimate decision about whether to give small tips or gifts where they are customary must be based on a company's code of ethics. However, under the Foreign Corrupt Practices Act (FCPA) of 1977, it is illegal for U.S. firms to attempt to make large payments or bribes to influence policy decisions of foreign governments. Walmart has been accused of using bribes to pave the way for the construction of new stores in Mexico, a major violation of the FCPA. Walmart spent $791 million on legal fees and on internal investigation and to revamp its compliance systems.[27] Nevertheless, facilitating payments, or small payments to support the performance of standard tasks, are often acceptable. The Foreign Corrupt Practices Act also subjects all publicly held U.S. corporations to rigorous internal controls and record-keeping requirements for their overseas operations.

Many other countries have also outlawed bribery. As we discussed in Chapter 3, the U.K. Bribery Act has redefined what many companies consider to be bribery versus gift-giving, causing multinational firms to update their codes of ethics. Companies with operations in the United Kingdom could still face penalties for bribery, even if the bribery occurred outside the country and managers were not aware of the misconduct.[28] Japan has its own anti-bribery law but has been lax in enforcing it. The Organisation for Economic Co-operation and Development is pressuring Japanese officials to toughen their stance against bribery.[29] It is thus essential for global marketers to understand the major laws in the countries in which their companies operate.

Differences in ethical standards can also affect marketing efforts. In China and Vietnam, for example, standards regarding intellectual property differ dramatically from those in the United States, creating potential conflicts for marketers of computer software, music, and books. Trade in counterfeit goods has been estimated at anywhere from $200 billion to more than $1.7 trillion worldwide, but the full scope is unknown according to the U.S. Chamber of Commerce.[30] Chinese-based Alibaba Group Holding Ltd., one of the biggest shopping sites in the world, has faced numerous problems with counterfeit products sold on its site. As the company expands, it has begun removing products that have been flagged as counterfeit.[31] The enormous amount of counterfeit products available worldwide, the time it takes to track them down, and legal barriers in certain countries make the pursuit of counterfeiters challenging for many companies.

When marketers do business abroad, they often perceive that other business cultures have different modes of operation. This uneasiness is especially pronounced for marketers who have not traveled extensively or interacted much with foreigners in business or social settings. For example, a perception exists among many in the United States that U.S. firms are different from those in other countries. This implied perspective of "us versus

GOING GREEN

Greenhouse Gas Emissions: China Takes its Foot Off the Pedal

China may have been slow on the environmental uptake, but it has made up for lost time. As the world's largest producer of greenhouse gases, the country had a tough job ahead of it. It responded by creating a Ministry of Environmental Protection with goals to clean up China's air and water and establish the country as an alternative energy powerhouse.

In a short amount of time, China launched a number of green initiatives. China has adopted stringent fuel economy standards and is encouraging manufacturers to develop electric vehicles. It also launched an extensive program investing in renewables. China has installed more wind and solar power farms than anywhere else in the world. It is also increasing fines for dumping waste. Six companies were fined $26 million for polluting rivers, the largest fine at the time.

However, after years of investment in renewables, China plans to scale back investments in wind and solar power because of slow economic growth and a slump in electricity demands. With China as such a large investor of renewable energy, the industry came to rely on the country's continued investment. The global renewable energy industry may struggle if China scales back too much. Yet despite these recent challenges, China has no plans to abandon its sustainability initiatives.[a]

them" is also common in other countries. In business, the idea that "we" differ from "them" is called the self-reference criterion (SRC). The SRC is the unconscious reference to one's own cultural values, experiences, and knowledge. When confronted with a situation, we react on the basis of knowledge we have accumulated over a lifetime, which is usually grounded in our culture of origin. Our reactions are based on meanings, values, and symbols that relate to our culture but may not have the same relevance to people of other cultures.

Many companies try to conduct global business based on the local culture. These businesspeople adapt to the cultural practices of the country they are in and use the host country's cultural practices as the rationalization for sometimes straying from their own ethical values when doing business internationally. For instance, by defending the payment of bribes or "greasing the wheels of business" and other questionable practices in this fashion, some businesspeople resort to cultural relativism—the concept that morality varies from one culture to another and that business practices are therefore differentially defined as right or wrong by particular cultures. Table 8.3 indicates the countries that businesspeople, risk analysts, and the general public perceive as the most and least corrupt. Most global companies are recognizing that they must establish values and standards that are consistent throughout the world. Because of differences in cultural and ethical standards, many work both individually and collectively to establish ethics programs and standards for international business conduct.

Levi Strauss' code of ethics, for example, bars the firm from manufacturing in countries where workers are known to be abused.

Many firms, including Texas Instruments, Coca-Cola, DuPont, HP, Levi Strauss & Company, and Walmart, endorse following international business practices responsibly. These companies support a globally based resource system called Business for Social Responsibility (BSR). BSR tracks emerging issues and trends, provides information on corporate leadership and best practices, conducts educational workshops and training, and assists organizations in developing practical business ethics tools. It addresses such issues as community investment, corporate social responsibility, the environment, governance, and accountability.[32] Other companies have developed their own unique initiatives to give back to global communities. For instance, Southwest Airlines upcycles old leather seat cushions for use in the creation of other products. Southwest has created a training program in Kenya

cultural relativism The concept that morality varies from one culture to another and that business practices are therefore differentially defined as right or wrong by particular cultures

TABLE 8.3		RANKING OF COUNTRIES BASED UPON CORRUPTION OF PUBLIC SECTOR			
Country Rank	CPI Score*	Least Corrupt	Country Rank	CPI Score*	Most Corrupt
1	90	Denmark	174	10	Somalia
2	90	New Zealand	174	11	South Sudan
3	89	Finland	173	12	North Korea
4	88	Sweden	172	13	Syria
5	86	Switzerland	171	14	Yemen
5	85	Norway	170	14	Sudan
7	84	Singapore	169	14	Libya
8	83	Netherlands	166	15	Afghanistan
9	82	Canada	166	16	Guinea-Bissau
10	81	Germany	166	17	Venezuela
11	81	Luxembourg	161	17	Iraq
12	81	United Kingdom	161	18	Eritrea
12	79	Australia	161	18	Angola

*CPI score relates to perceptions of the degree of public-sector corruption as seen by businesspeople and country analysts and ranges between 100 (highly clear) and 0 (highly corrupt). The United States is perceived as the 16th least-corrupt nation.
Source: Data from Transparency International, *Corruption Perceptions Index 2016* (Berlin, Germany, 2017).

where young adults learn how to turn this leather into goods such as backpacks and shoes. This program not only helps individuals in Kenya develop valuable skills, it also keeps the leather out of landfills.[33]

8-2e Competitive Forces

Competition is often viewed as a staple of the global marketplace. Customers thrive on the choices offered by competition, and firms constantly seek opportunities to outmaneuver their competition to gain customers' loyalty. Firms typically identify their competition when they establish target markets worldwide. Customers who are seeking alternative solutions to their product needs find the firms that can solve those needs. However, the increasingly interconnected international marketplace and advances in technology have resulted in competitive forces that are unique to the international marketplace.

Beyond the types of competition (i.e., brand, product, generic, and total budget competition) and types of competitive structures (i.e., monopoly, oligopoly, monopolistic competition, and pure competition), which are discussed in Chapter 3, firms that operate internationally must do the following:

- Be aware of the competitive forces in the countries they target.
- Identify the interdependence of countries and the global competitors in those markets.
- Be mindful of a new breed of customers: the global customer.

Each country has unique competitive aspects—often founded in the other environmental forces (i.e., sociocultural, technological, political, legal, regulatory, and economic forces)—that are often independent of the competitors in that market. The most globally competitive countries are listed in Table 8.4. Although competitors drive competition, nations establish the infrastructure and the rules for the types of competition that can take place. For example, the laws against antitrust in the European Union are often perceived as being stricter than those in the United States. Over the last seven years, Alphabet Inc.'s Google has been accused by the European Union's antitrust regulators of restricting competition. The claim

TABLE 8.4	RANKING OF THE MOST COMPETITIVE COUNTRIES IN THE WORLD		
Rank	**Country**	**Rank**	**Country**
1	Switzerland	11	Norway
2	Singapore	12	Denmark
3	United States	13	New Zealand
4	Netherlands	14	Taiwan, China
5	Germany	15	Canada
6	Sweden	16	United Arab Emirates
7	United Kingdom	17	Belgium
8	Japan	18	Qatar
9	Hong Kong SAR	19	Austria
10	Finland	20	Luxembourg

Source: Klaus Schwab (ed.), *The Global Competitiveness Report 2016–2017*, www3.weforum.org/docs/GCR2016 -2017/05FullReport/TheGlobalCompetitivenessReport2016-2017_FINAL.pdf (accessed January 31, 2017).

is that the search feature restricts advertisements sold by other companies. Also, there is a claim that Google pre-installs its search engine as a default on mobile devices.[34] Like the United States, other countries allow some monopoly structures to exist. Consider Sweden; their alcohol sales are made through the governmental store Systembolaget, which is legally supported by the Swedish Alcohol Retail Monopoly. According to Systembolaget, the Swedish Alcohol Retail Monopoly exists for one reason: "to minimize alcohol-related problems by selling alcohol in a responsible way."[35]

A new breed of customer—the global customer—has changed the landscape of international competition drastically. In the past, firms simply produced goods or services and provided local markets with information about the features and uses of their goods and services. Now, however, not only do customers who travel the globe expect to be able to buy the same product in most of the world's more than 200 countries, but they also expect that the product they buy in their local store in Miami will have the same features as similar products sold in London or even in Beijing. If either the quality of the product or the product's features are more advanced in an international market, customers will soon demand that their local markets offer the same product at the same or lower prices.

8-2f Technological Forces

Advances in technology have made international marketing much easier. The world is undergoing a digital revolution. Interactive Web systems, instant messaging, and podcast downloads (along with the traditional vehicles of voice mail, e-mail, and cell phones) make international marketing activities more affordable and convenient. Internet use and social networking activities have accelerated dramatically within the United States and abroad. In Japan, 115 million have Internet access, and more than 102 million Russians, 462 million Indians, and 720 million Chinese are logging on to the Internet (refer back to Table 8.2).[36] Today more than 3 billion people have access to the Internet. Facebook joined Ericsson, Qualcomm, Nokia, and Samsung into a coalition called Internet.org to reach the remaining two-thirds of the world population. One of the products they released was a free app, Free Basics, that was launched in the African countries of Zambia and Tanzania to give the population access to Facebook, Wikipedia, Google Search, and other popular sites.[37] Mark Zuckerberg reported that Internet.org has helped 40 million individuals get online.[38]

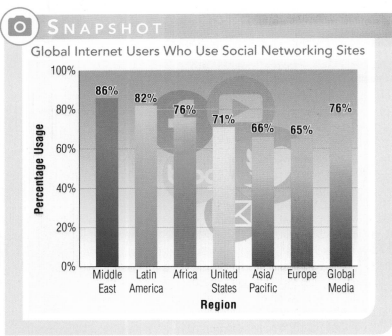

SNAPSHOT

Global Internet Users Who Use Social Networking Sites

Percentage Usage (y-axis: 0% to 100%)

- Middle East: 86%
- Latin America: 82%
- Africa: 76%
- United States: 71%
- Asia/Pacific: 66%
- Europe: 65%
- Global Media: 76%

Region (x-axis)

Source: Pew Research Center, Spring 2015 Global Attitudes Survey, Q74, percentage is based on median.

In many developing countries that lack the level of technological infrastructure found in the United States and Japan, marketers are beginning to capitalize on opportunities to leapfrog existing technology. For example, cellular and wireless phone technology is reaching many countries at a more affordable rate than traditional hard-wired telephone systems. Consequently, opportunities for growth in the cell phone market remain strong in Southeast Asia, Africa, and the Middle East. One opportunity created by the rapid growth in mobile devices in Kenya is mobile payment services. London-based Vodafone partnered with Kenyan telecom firm Safaricom to take advantage of this market opportunity with its M-PESA money transfer service, the most popular money transfer service in Kenya. It is estimated that twice as many Kenyans use their mobile phones for financial activities than have bank accounts.[39]

Despite the enormous benefits of digital technology, however, the digital economy may actually be increasing the divide between skilled wealthy workers and the rest of the labor force. Instead of increasing wages overall, wages have remained relatively flat. There is also the fear that technology will take over people's jobs. At a Foxconn factory in China, automation replaced many workers to reduce the risk of injury. However, technology also leads to the hire of skilled individuals to work on the automation. Despite the labor imbalance that some technologies are causing, they offer a great opportunity for entrepreneurs in developing countries to reach the rest of the world.[40]

8-3 REGIONAL TRADE ALLIANCES, MARKETS, AND AGREEMENTS

LO 8-3 List six important international trade agreements.

Although many more firms are beginning to view the world as one huge marketplace, various regional trade alliances and specific markets affect companies engaging in international marketing; some create opportunities, and others impose constraints. In fact, while trade agreements in various forms have been around for centuries, the last century can be classified as the trade agreement period in the world's international development. Today, there are nearly 200 trade agreements around the world compared with only a select handful in the early 1960s. In this section, we examine several of the more critical regional trade alliances, markets, and changing conditions affecting markets. These include the North American Free Trade Agreement, European Union, Southern Common Market, Asia-Pacific Economic Cooperation, Association of Southeast Asian Nations, and World Trade Organization.

8-3a The North American Free Trade Agreement (NAFTA)

North American Free Trade Agreement (NAFTA) An alliance that merges Canada, Mexico, and the United States into a single market

The **North American Free Trade Agreement (NAFTA)**, implemented in 1994, effectively merged Canada, Mexico, and the United States into one market of 450 million consumers. NAFTA eliminated virtually all tariffs on goods produced and traded among

Canada, Mexico, and the United States to create a free trade area. The estimated annual output for this trade alliance is more than $20.7 trillion.[41] NAFTA makes it easier for U.S. businesses to invest in Mexico and Canada, provides protection for intellectual property (of special interest to high-technology and entertainment industries), expands trade by requiring equal treatment of U.S. firms in both countries, and simplifies country-of-origin rules, hindering China and Japan's use of Mexico as a staging ground for further penetration into U.S. markets.

Canada's 36 million consumers are relatively affluent, with a per capita GDP of $50,000. Canada is the single largest trading partner of the United States, which in turn supports 1.7 million U.S. jobs.[42] NAFTA has also enabled additional trade between Canada and Mexico. Mexico is Canada's fifth largest export market and third largest import market.[43]

With a per capita GDP of $18,900, Mexico's more than 123 million consumers are less affluent than Canadian consumers.[44] However, the United States is Mexico's largest trading partner, and Mexico is the third largest trading partner of the United States. The United States gets imports totaling $295 billion from Mexico.[45] Many U.S. companies, including General Electric, HP, IBM, and General Motors, have taken advantage of Mexico's low labor costs and close proximity to the United States to set up production facilities, sometimes called *maquiladoras*. Production at the *maquiladoras*, especially in the automotive, electronics, and apparel industries, has grown rapidly as companies as diverse as Ford, John Deere, Kimberly-Clark, and VF Corporation set up facilities in north-central Mexican states. Moreover, increasing trade between the United States and Canada constitutes a strong base of support for the ultimate success of NAFTA.

Mexico is growing faster than Brazil and is estimated to soon become one of the top ten biggest global economies. Part of this might be due to Mexico's liberal free-trade policies. Mexico has free trade agreements with 45 countries. It could very likely become a hub for automakers as companies like Nissan, Audi, and Kia have built manufacturing sites in the country.[46] Loans to companies in Mexico have been increasing, and as one of the world's largest oil producers, Mexico has the opportunity to increase investment in this profitable commodity—although lower oil prices have the potential to slow down economic development. Additionally, while China has taken much outsourcing business away from Mexico, a turnaround may be approaching. With an increase in Chinese labor costs and the high transportation costs of transporting goods between China and the United States, many U.S. businesses that outsource are looking toward Mexico as a less costly alternative.[47]

Mexico's membership in NAFTA links the United States and Canada with other Latin American countries, providing additional opportunities to integrate trade among all the nations in the Western Hemisphere. Indeed, efforts to create a free trade agreement among the 34 nations of North and South America are under way. A related trade agreement—the Dominican Republic–Central American Free Trade Agreement (CAFTA-DR)—among Costa Rica, the Dominican Republic, El Salvador, Guatemala, Honduras, Nicaragua, and the United States has also been ratified in all those countries. The United States exports $29 billion to the CAFTA-DR countries annually.[48]

8-3b The European Union (EU)

The **European Union (EU)**, sometimes also referred to as the *European Community* or *Common Market*, was established in 1958 to promote trade among its members, which initially included Belgium, France, Italy, West Germany, Luxembourg, and the Netherlands. Today the Euro Zone (countries that have adopted the euro as their currency) consists of 340 million citizens in 19 separate countries with varying political landscapes.[49] In 1991, East and West Germany united, and by 2015, the EU included the United Kingdom, Spain, Denmark, Greece, Portugal, Ireland, Austria, Finland, Sweden, Cyprus, Poland, Hungary, the Czech Republic, Slovenia, Estonia, Latvia, Lithuania, Slovakia, Malta, Romania, Bulgaria, Belgium, France, Germany, Italy, Luxembourg, The Netherlands, and Croatia. The Former Yugoslav Republic of Macedonia, Montenegro, Serbia, and Turkey are candidate countries that hope to join the European Union in the near future.[50]

European Union (EU) An alliance that promotes trade among its member countries in Europe

EMERGING TRENDS IN MARKETING

IKEA: "African IKEA" Is Knocking on Your Door!

Nicknamed the "African IKEA," South African–based retailer Steinhoff International is entering the United States. Steinhoff manufactures and sells furniture and household goods globally. Much like IKEA, Steinhoff credits itself with targeting the value-conscious consumer. Steinhoff paid $3.8 billion to purchase U.S.-based Mattress Firm, the largest U.S. specialty mattress maker and owner of such brands as Tempur-Pedic.

Steinhoff International has its origins in West Germany where its founder started selling inexpensive furniture to neighboring East Germany in 1964. After East and West Germany were reunited, Steinhoff expanded into other areas of Europe. It came to South Africa in 1997 after acquiring a South African furniture store.

While Steinhoff has expanded its global reach with acquisitions in Europe and Australia, its purchase of Mattress Firm will be its first time entering the U.S. market. By acquiring an established firm, Steinhoff believes it will gain a quicker foothold into the U.S. market. South Africa's richest man even invested $1.8 billion to help with Steinhoff's global expansion strategy.

Interestingly, Steinhoff has not seen much success in the rest of Africa. Outside of South Africa, the company maintains a small market share on the continent. Some problems with expanding into Africa include supply chain challenges and high rent prices. Steinhoff is therefore finding it easier to expand farther away than in countries closer to home.[b]

Southern Common Market (MERCOSUR) An alliance that promotes the free circulation of goods, services, and production factors, and has a common external tariff and commercial policy among member nations in South America

In 2016, the United Kingdom voted to exit the European Union. This decision to exit, called "Brexit," resulted in the value of the pound falling sharply. There remain many questions about the impact of the proposed exit on trade relationships with other countries.[51]

Due to the massive industry collaboration between the United States and the EU, there have been discussions about the possibility of a trade agreement between the two entities. In many respects, the United States, the EU, and Asia have become largely interdependent in trade and investment. For instance, the United States and the EU have already adopted the "Open Skies" agreement to remove some of the restrictions on transatlantic flights, and the two often collaborate on ways to prevent terrorist attacks, cyber hacking, and crime. The United States and the EU hope that by working together, they can create mutually beneficial relationships that will provide benefits to millions of their citizens.[52]

8-3c The Southern Common Market (MERCOSUR)

The **Southern Common Market (MERCOSUR)** was established in 1991 under the Treaty of Asunción to unite Argentina, Brazil, Paraguay, and Uruguay as a free trade alliance. Venezuela joined in 2006. Currently, Bolivia, Chile, Colombia, Ecuador, and Peru are associate members. The alliance represents two-thirds of South America's population and has a combined GDP of more than $3.32 trillion, making it the fourth-largest trading bloc behind the EU, NAFTA, and the Association of Southeast Asian Nations.[53] Like NAFTA, MERCOSUR promotes "the free circulation of goods, services, and production factors among the countries" and establishes a common external tariff and commercial policy.[54]

South America and Latin America are catching the attention of many international businesses. The region

Regional Trade Alliance
Regional trade alliances connect economies, creating new opportunities and imposing constraints.

Ronnie Chua/Shutterstock.com

is advancing economically with an estimated growth rate of under 3 percent. Most of Latin America is dependent on the price of commodities. For example, lower oil prices in 2015 created some political instability.[55] Another trend is that several of the countries, including some of the MERCOSUR alliance, are starting to experience more stable democracies. Even Cuba, one of the traditionally harshest critics of capitalism in Latin America, is accepting more privatization. For example, while there is a growing flow of funds (remittances from the United States) and tourists from the United States, there is much uncertainty about future economic relations. About a third of Cubans are in the private sector, but the money for starting most of these businesses came from Cuban Americans' remittances that are greater than all of Cuba's exports.[56] Despite governmental restrictions, entrepreneurship is growing in Cuba.[57]

Asia-Pacific Economic Cooperation (APEC) An alliance that promotes open trade and economic and technical cooperation among member nations throughout the world

8-3d The Asia-Pacific Economic Cooperation (APEC)

The Asia-Pacific Economic Cooperation (APEC), established in 1989, promotes open trade and economic and technical cooperation among member nations, which initially included Australia, Brunei Darussalam, Canada, Indonesia, Japan, Korea, Malaysia, New Zealand, the Philippines, Singapore, Thailand, and the United States. Since then, the alliance has grown to include China, Hong Kong, Taiwan, Mexico, Papua New Guinea, Chile, Peru, Russia, and Vietnam. The 21-member alliance represents approximately 40 percent of the world's population, 54 percent of the world's GDP, and nearly 44 percent of global trade. APEC differs from other international trade alliances in its commitment to facilitating business and its practice of allowing the business/private sector to participate in a wide range of APEC activities.[58]

Companies of the APEC have become increasingly competitive and sophisticated in global business in the last few decades. Moreover, the markets of the APEC offer tremendous opportunities to marketers who understand them. In fact, the APEC region has consistently been one of the most economically dynamic parts of the world. In its first decade, the APEC countries generated almost 70 percent of worldwide economic growth, and the APEC region consistently outperformed the rest of the world.[59]

The most important emerging economic power is China, which has become one of the most productive manufacturing nations. Now the United States' largest trading partner, China has initiated economic reforms to stimulate its economy by privatizing many industries, restructuring its banking system, and increasing public spending on infrastructure. China is a manufacturing powerhouse; however, its high growth rate has decreased in recent years to below 6.8 percent.[60] Many foreign companies, including Nike, Samsung, and Adidas, have factories in China to take advantage of its low labor costs, and China has become a major global producer in virtually every product category. China has emerged as the world's largest economy in purchasing-power terms.[61] This means China is becoming a source of demand and investment to other countries in the Asia-Pacific region. For example, the most advanced Disney theme park—outside of Florida—opened in China.[62] The number of Internet users in China is 731 million according to the China Internet Network Information Centre, expanding by up to 6.2 percent in recent years.[63]

Pacific Rim regions like South Korea, Thailand, Singapore, Taiwan, and Hong Kong are also major manufacturing and financial centers. Even before Korean brand names, such as Samsung, Daewoo, and Hyundai, became household words, these products prospered under U.S. company labels, including GE, GTE, RCA, and JCPenney. Singapore boasts huge global markets for rubber goods and pharmaceuticals. Hong Kong is

Asia-Pacific Economic Cooperation
The Asia-Pacific Economic Cooperation (APEC) is made up of 21 members to promote regional economic growth.

hans engbers/Shutterstock.com

Association of Southeast Asian Nations (ASEAN) An alliance that promotes trade and economic integration among member nations in Southeast Asia

World Trade Organization (WTO) An entity that promotes free trade among member nations by eliminating trade barriers and educating individuals, companies, and governments about trade rules around the world

General Agreement on Tariffs and Trade (GATT) An agreement among nations to reduce worldwide tariffs and increase international trade

dumping Selling products at unfairly low prices

still a strong commercial center after being transferred to Chinese control. South Korea is becoming known for its pop culture.[64] Vietnam is one of Asia's fastest-growing markets for U.S. businesses, but Taiwan, given its stability and high educational attainment, has the most promising future of all the Pacific Rim nations as a strong local economy, and low import barriers draw increasing imports. The markets of APEC offer tremendous opportunities to marketers who understand them. Technology firms are experiencing their fastest growth overseas, much of it from APEC countries.[65]

8-3e Association of Southeast Asian Nations (ASEAN)

The **Association of Southeast Asian Nations (ASEAN)**, established in 1967, promotes trade and economic integration among 10 member nations in Southeast Asia. The trade pact includes Malaysia, the Philippines, Singapore, Thailand, Brunei Darussalam, Vietnam, Laos, Myanmar, Indonesia, and Cambodia.[66] The region is home to 600 million people and has a 5 percent growth rate in GDP. Currently, combined GDP is at $2.5 trillion, but analysts estimate the ASEAN region will have a combined GDP of $4.7 trillion by 2020.[67] With its motto, "One Vision, One Identity, One Community," member nations have expressed the goal of encouraging free trade, peace, and collaboration between member countries.[68] ASEAN's three pillars are sociocultural, political, and economic. The ASEAN Economic Community (AEC) attempts to unite the regional economy.[69] In 1993, the trade bloc passed the Common Effective Preferential Tariff to reduce or phase out tariffs between countries over a 10-year period as well as eliminate non-tariff trade barriers.[70] Nearly all categories of products are traded within the bloc tariff-free.

Yet, despite these positive growth rates, ASEAN is facing many obstacles in becoming a unified trade bloc. Thailand, for instance, has faced political uncertainties after the military ousted the government's prime minister.[71] There have also been conflicts between members themselves and concerns over issues such as human rights and disputed territories.[72] Therefore, there are great opportunities but also substantial risk.

On the other hand, while many choose to compare ASEAN with the European Union, ASEAN members are careful to point out their differences. Although members hope to increase economic integration, they expressed that there will be no common currency or fully free labor flows between members. In this way, ASEAN plans to avoid some of the pitfalls that occurred among nations in the EU during the latest worldwide recession.[73]

8-3f The World Trade Organization (WTO)

The **World Trade Organization (WTO)** is a global trade association that promotes free trade among 157 member nations. The WTO is the successor to the **General Agreement on Tariffs and Trade (GATT)**, which was originally signed by 23 nations in 1947 to provide a forum for tariff negotiations and a place where international trade problems could be discussed and resolved. Rounds of GATT negotiations reduced trade barriers for most products and established rules to guide international commerce, such as rules to prevent **dumping**, the selling of products at unfairly low prices.

The WTO came into being in 1995 as a result of the Uruguay Round (1988–1994) of GATT negotiations. Broadly, WTO is the main worldwide organization that deals with the rules of trade between nations; its main function is to ensure that trade flows as smoothly, predictably, and freely as possible between nations. About 160 nations are members of the WTO.[74]

Fulfilling the purpose of the WTO requires eliminating trade barriers; educating individuals, companies, and governments about trade rules around the world; and assuring global markets that no sudden changes of policy will occur. At the heart of the WTO are agreements that provide legal ground rules for international commerce and trade policy. Based in Geneva, Switzerland, the WTO also serves as a forum for dispute resolution.[75] For example, Indonesia and Argentina complained to the WTO about anti-dumping duties that the EU imposed on biodiesel imports from those two countries. These duties were decided upon after the EU determined that the two countries were dumping their biodiesel into the market. Both countries protested that the antidumping duties were against global trading rules.[76]

importing The purchase of products from a foreign source

exporting The sale of products to foreign markets

8-4 MODES OF ENTRY INTO INTERNATIONAL MARKETS

LO 8-4 Identify methods of international market entry.

Marketers enter international markets and continue to engage in marketing activities at several levels of international involvement. Traditionally, firms have adopted one of four different modes of entering an international market; each successive "stage" represents different degrees of international involvement. As Figure 8.1 shows, companies' international involvement today covers a wide spectrum, from purely domestic marketing to global marketing.

8-4a Importing and Exporting

Importing and exporting require the least amount of effort and commitment of resources. Importing is the purchase of products from a foreign source. Exporting, the sale of products to foreign markets, enables firms of all sizes to participate in global business. Trade is a major—and often challenging—activity between regions. A firm may find an exporting intermediary to take over most marketing functions associated with marketing to other

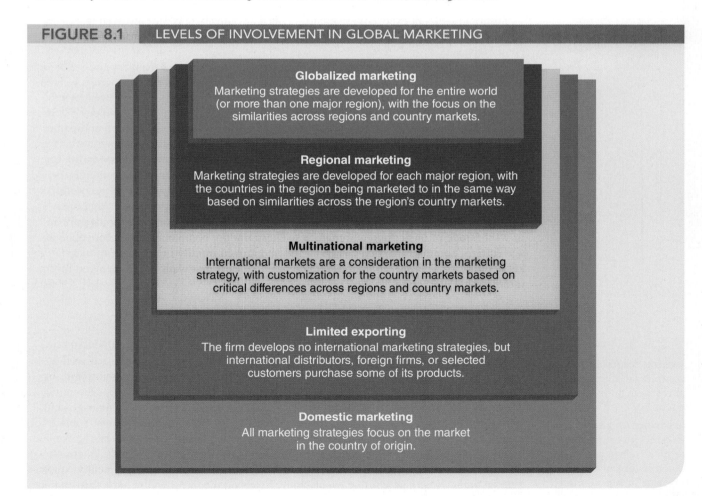

FIGURE 8.1   LEVELS OF INVOLVEMENT IN GLOBAL MARKETING

Globalized marketing
Marketing strategies are developed for the entire world (or more than one major region), with the focus on the similarities across regions and country markets.

Regional marketing
Marketing strategies are developed for each major region, with the countries in the region being marketed to in the same way based on similarities across the region's country markets.

Multinational marketing
International markets are a consideration in the marketing strategy, with customization for the country markets based on critical differences across regions and country markets.

Limited exporting
The firm develops no international marketing strategies, but international distributors, foreign firms, or selected customers purchase some of its products.

Domestic marketing
All marketing strategies focus on the market in the country of origin.

Importing and Exporting
Exchanging imports and exports can be challenging between regions.

countries. This approach entails minimal effort and cost. Modifications in packaging, labeling, style, or color may be the major expenses in adapting a product for the foreign market.

Export agents bring together buyers and sellers from different countries and collect a commission for arranging sales. Export houses and export merchants purchase products from different companies and then sell them abroad. They are specialists at understanding customers' needs in global markets. For example, China has an insatiable appetite for pork and pork imports, while Poland exports more apples than any other country. Using exporting intermediaries involves limited risk because no foreign direct investment is required.

Buyers from foreign companies and governments provide a direct method of exporting and eliminate the need for an intermediary. These buyers encourage international exchange by contacting overseas firms about their needs and the opportunities available in exporting to them. Indeed, research suggests that many small firms tend to rely heavily on such native contacts, especially in developed markets, and remain production oriented rather than market oriented in their approach to international marketing.[77] Domestic firms that want to export with minimal effort and investment should seek out export intermediaries. Once a company becomes involved in exporting, it usually develops more knowledge of the country and becomes more confident in its competitiveness.[78]

Marketers sometimes employ a **trading company**, which links buyers and sellers in different countries but is not involved in manufacturing and does not own assets related to manufacturing. Trading companies buy products in one country at the lowest price consistent with quality and sell them to buyers in another country. For instance, WTSC offers a 24-hour-per-day online world trade system that connects 20 million companies in 245 countries, offering more than 60 million products.[79] A trading company acts like a wholesaler, taking on much of the responsibility of finding markets while facilitating all marketing aspects of a transaction. An important function of trading companies is taking title to products and performing all the activities necessary to move the products to the targeted foreign country. For instance, large grain-trading companies that operate out-of-home offices in both the United States and overseas control a major portion of world trade of basic food commodities. These trading companies sell homogeneous agricultural commodities that can be stored and moved rapidly in response to market conditions. Trading companies reduce risk for firms that want to get involved in international marketing.

8-4b **Licensing and Franchising**

trading company A company that links buyers and sellers in different countries

licensing An alternative to direct investment that requires a licensee to pay commissions or royalties on sales or supplies used in manufacturing

When potential markets are found across national boundaries, and when production, technical assistance, or marketing know-how is required, **licensing** is an alternative to direct investment. The licensee (the owner of the foreign operation) pays commissions or royalties on sales or supplies used in manufacturing. The licensee may also pay an initial down payment or fee when the licensing agreement is signed. Exchanges of management techniques or technical assistance are primary reasons for licensing agreements. Yoplait, for example, is a French yogurt that is licensed for production in the United States; the Yoplait brand tries to maintain a French image. Similarly, sports organizations like the International Olympic Committee (IOC), which is responsible for the Olympic Games, typically concentrate on organizing their sporting events while licensing the merchandise and other products that are sold.

Licensing is an attractive alternative when resources are unavailable for direct investment or when the core competencies of the firm or organization are not related to the product being sold (such as in the case of Olympics merchandise). Licensing can also be a viable alternative when the political stability of a foreign country is in doubt. In addition, licensing is especially advantageous for small manufacturers wanting to launch a well-known brand internationally. For example, Questor Corporation owns the Spalding name but does not produce a single golf club or tennis ball itself; all Spalding sporting products are licensed worldwide.

Franchising is a form of licensing in which a company (the franchisor) grants a franchisee the right to market its product, using its name, logo, methods of operation, advertising, products, and other elements associated with the franchisor's business, in return for a financial commitment and an agreement to conduct business in accordance with the franchisor's standard of operations. This arrangement allows franchisors to minimize the risks of international marketing in four ways: (1) the franchisor does not have to put up a large capital investment, (2) the franchisor's revenue stream is fairly consistent because franchisees pay a fixed fee and royalties, (3) the franchisor retains control of its name and increases global penetration of its product, and (4) franchise agreements ensure a certain standard of behavior from franchisees, which protects the franchise name.[80]

8-4c Contract Manufacturing

Contract manufacturing occurs when a company hires a foreign firm to produce a designated volume of the firm's product (or a component of a product) to specification and the final product carries the domestic firm's name. The Gap, for example, relies on contract manufacturing for some of its apparel; Reebok uses Korean contract manufacturers to produce many of its athletic shoes. Marketing may be handled by the contract manufacturer or by the contracting company.

Three specific forms of contract manufacturing have become popular in the last decade: outsourcing, offshoring, and offshore outsourcing. **Outsourcing** is defined as the contracting of noncore operations or jobs from internal production within a business to an external entity that specializes in that operation. For example, outsourcing certain elements of a firm's operations to China and Mexico has become popular. The majority of all footwear is now produced in China, regardless of the brand name on the shoe you wear. Services can also be outsourced. Recent years, however, have seen an increase in domestic manufacturing within the United States. Firms with more than $1 billion in annual sales are estimated to make approximately 47 percent of their products in the United States within the next five years. On the other hand, higher costs make domestic manufacturing difficult for smaller organizations, and many are forced to outsource overseas to keep costs down.[81] Conflicts between globalism and protectionism associated with nationalism have emerged, but most economists believe all trade is beneficial.[82]

Offshoring is defined as moving a business process that was done domestically at the local factory to a foreign country, regardless of whether the production accomplished in the foreign country is performed by the local company (e.g., in a wholly-owned subsidiary) or a third party (e.g., subcontractor). Typically, the production is moved to reap the advantages

TonyV3112/Shutterstock.com

Global Franchising
KFC has franchises in a number of countries, including this one in Beijing, China.

contract manufacturing The practice of hiring a foreign firm to produce a designated volume of the domestic firm's product or a component of it to specification; the final product carries the domestic firm's name

outsourcing The practice of contracting noncore operations with an organization that specializes in that operation

offshoring The practice of moving a business process that was done domestically at the local factory to a foreign country, regardless of whether the production accomplished in the foreign country is performed by the local company (e.g., in a wholly-owned subsidiary) or a third party (e.g., subcontractor)

offshore outsourcing The practice of contracting with an organization to perform some or all business functions in a country other than the country in which the product will be sold

joint venture A partnership between a domestic firm and a foreign firm or government

strategic alliance A partnership that is formed to create a competitive advantage on a worldwide basis

direct ownership A situation in which a company owns subsidiaries or other facilities overseas

of lower cost of operations in the foreign location. **Offshore outsourcing** is the practice of contracting with an organization to perform some or all business functions in a country other than the country in which the product will be sold. Today, some clothing manufacturers that previously engaged in offshore outsourcing are moving production back to the United States to maintain quality and tighter inventory control.[83]

8-4d Joint Ventures

In international marketing, a **joint venture** is a partnership between a domestic firm and a foreign firm or government. Joint ventures are especially popular in industries that require large investments, such as natural resources extraction or automobile manufacturing. Control of the joint venture may be split equally, or one party may control decision making. Joint ventures are often a political necessity because of nationalism and government restrictions on foreign ownership.

Joint ventures also provide legitimacy in the eyes of the host country's citizens. Local partners have firsthand knowledge of the economic and sociopolitical environment and the workings of available distribution networks, and they may have privileged access to local resources (raw materials, labor management, and so on). However, joint venture relationships require trust throughout the relationship to provide a foreign partner with a ready means of implementing its own marketing strategy. Joint ventures are assuming greater global importance because of cost advantages and the number of inexperienced firms that are entering foreign markets. They may be the result of a trade-off between a firm's desire for completely unambiguous control of an enterprise and its quest for additional resources.

Strategic alliances are partnerships formed to create a competitive advantage on a worldwide basis. They are very similar to joint ventures, but while joint ventures are defined in scope, strategic alliances are typically represented by an agreement to work together (which can ultimately mean more involvement than a joint venture). In an international strategic alliance, the firms in the alliance may have been traditional rivals competing for the same market. They may also be competing in certain markets while working together in other markets where it is beneficial for both parties. Air France, for instance, has many competitors in the global airline market. However, Air France is also a part of the Sky Team Alliance, a collaboration involving 20 members including KLM, Aeromexico, Air France, Alitalia, Czech Airlines, Delta, Korean Air, Kenya Airways, Aeroflot, Air Europa, Vietnam Airlines, China Airlines, MEA, Saudia, Tarom Romanian Air Transport, China Eastern, Aerolineas Argentinas, XiamenAir, Garuda Indonesia, and China Southern. This alliance is designed to improve customer service among the firms.[84] Whereas joint ventures are formed to create a new identity, partners in strategic alliances often retain their distinct identities, with each partner bringing a core competency to the union.

Multinational Corporation
Microsoft operates in many countries outside of the United States.

Ken Wolter/Shutterstock.com

8-4e Direct Ownership

Once a company makes a long-term commitment to marketing in a foreign country that has a promising market as well as a suitable political and economic environment, **direct ownership** of a foreign subsidiary or division is a possibility. Most foreign investment covers only manufacturing equipment or personnel because the expenses of developing a separate foreign distribution system can be tremendous. The opening of retail stores in Europe, Canada, or Mexico can require a staggering financial investment in facilities, research, and management.

The term **multinational enterprise**, sometimes called *multinational corporation*, refers to a firm that has operations or subsidiaries in many countries. Often, the parent company is based in one country and carries on production, management, and marketing activities in other countries. The firm's subsidiaries may be autonomous so they can respond to the needs of individual international markets, or they may be part of a global network that is led by the headquarters' operations.

At the same time, a wholly-owned foreign subsidiary may be allowed to operate independently of the parent company to give its management more freedom to adjust to the local environment. Cooperative arrangements are developed to assist in marketing efforts, production, and management. A wholly-owned foreign subsidiary may export products to the home country, its market may serve as a test market for the firm's global products, or it may be a component of the firm's globalization efforts. Some U.S. automobile manufacturers, for example, import cars built by their foreign subsidiaries. A foreign subsidiary offers important tax, tariff, and other operating advantages. Table 8.5 lists some well-known global corporations, most of which have operations in several different countries.

multinational enterprise A firm that has operations or subsidiaries in many countries

8-5 CUSTOMIZATION VERSUS GLOBALIZATION OF INTERNATIONAL MARKETING MIXES

LO 8-5 Describe the use of the marketing mix internationally.

Like domestic marketers, international marketers develop marketing strategies to serve specific target markets. Traditionally, international marketing strategies have customized marketing mixes according to cultural, regional, and national differences. Table 8.6 provides a sample of international issues related to product, price, distribution, and promotion. For example, many developing countries lack the infrastructure needed for expansive distribution networks, which can make it harder to get the product to consumers. Realizing that both similarities and differences exist across countries is a critical first step to developing the appropriate marketing strategy effort targeted to particular international markets. Today, many firms strive to build their marketing strategies around similarities that exist instead of customizing around differences.

TABLE 8.5   MULTINATIONAL FIRMS FROM AROUND THE WORLD

Company	Country	Description
Royal Dutch Shell	Netherlands	Oil and gas
Toyota	Japan	Automobiles
Walmart	United States	Retail
Siemens	Germany	Engineering and electronics
Nestlé	Switzerland	Nutritional, snack-food, and health-related consumer goods
Samsung	South Korea	Subsidiaries specializing in electronics, electronic components, telecommunications equipment, medical equipment, and more
Unilever	United Kingdom	Consumer goods including cleaning and personal care, foods, beverages
Boeing	United States	Aerospace and defense
Lenovo	China	Computer technology
Subway	United States	Largest fast-food chain

TABLE 8.6	MARKETING-MIX ISSUES INTERNATIONALLY
Product Element	**Sample International Issues**
Core Product	Is there a commonality of the customer's needs across countries?
	What will the product be used for and in what context?
Product Adoption	How is awareness created for the product in the various country markets?
	How and where is the product typically bought?
Managing Products	How are truly new products managed in the country markets vis-à-vis existing products or products that have been modified slightly?
Branding	Is the brand accepted widely around the world?
	Does the home country help or hurt the brand perception of the consumer?
Distribution Element	
Marketing Channels	What is the role of the channel intermediaries internationally?
	Where is value created beyond the domestic borders of the firm?
Physical Distribution	Is the movement of products the most efficient from the home country to the foreign market or to a regional warehouse?
Retail Stores	What is the availability of different types of retail stores in the various country markets?
Retailing Strategy	Where do customers typically shop in the targeted countries: downtown, in suburbs, or in malls?
Promotion Element	
Advertising	Some countries' customers prefer firm-specific advertising instead of product-specific advertising.
	How does this affect advertising?
Public Relations	How is public relations used to manage the stakeholders' interests internationally?
	Are the stakeholders' interests different worldwide?
Personal Selling	What product types require personal selling internationally?
	Does it differ from how those products are sold domestically?
Sales Promotion	Is coupon usage a widespread activity in the targeted international markets?
	What other forms of sales promotion should be used?
Pricing Element	
Core Price	Is price a critical component of the value equation of the product in the targeted country markets?
Analysis of Demand	Is the demand curve similar internationally and domestically?
	Will a change in price drastically change demand?
Demand, Cost, and Profit Relationships	What are the fixed and variable costs when marketing the product internationally?
	Are they similar to the domestic setting?
Determination of Price	How do the pricing strategy, environmental forces, business practices, and cultural values affect price?

For many firms, **globalization** of marketing is the goal. It involves developing marketing strategies as though the entire world (or its major regions) were a single entity; a globalized firm markets standardized products in the same way everywhere. Global brands are emerging that are rapidly losing their associations with individual countries.[85] Nike and Adidas shoes, for example, are standardized worldwide. Other examples of globalized products include electronic communications equipment, Western-style clothing, movies, soft drinks, rock and alternative music, cosmetics, and toothpaste. Sony televisions, Starbucks coffee, and many products sold at Walmart all post year-to-year gains in the world market.

For many years, organizations have attempted to globalize their marketing mixes as much as possible by employing standardized products, prices, distribution channels, and promotion campaigns for all markets. The economic and competitive payoffs for globalized marketing strategies are certainly great. Brand name, product characteristics, packaging, and labeling are among the easiest marketing-mix variables to standardize; media allocation, retail outlets, and price may be more difficult. In the end, the degree of similarity among the various environmental and market conditions determines the feasibility and degree of globalization. A successful globalization strategy often depends on the extent to which a firm is able to implement the idea of "think globally, act locally."[86] Even take-out food lends itself to globalization: McDonald's, KFC, and Taco Bell restaurants satisfy hungry customers in both hemispheres, although menus may be altered slightly to satisfy local tastes. Dunkin' Donuts sells curry doughnuts in India and dulce de leche in South America. It plans to reopen stores in Brazil and has hired food specialists to help the company determine what types of foods appeal to the Brazilian market.[87]

International marketing demands some strategic planning if a firm is to incorporate foreign sales into its overall marketing strategy. International marketing activities often require customized marketing mixes to achieve the firm's goals. Globalization requires a total commitment to the world, regions, or multinational areas as an integral part of the firm's markets; world or regional markets become as important as domestic ones. Global brands exist in an increasingly local world where consumer behavior, economic conditions, and distribution systems differ. Therefore, global brands may shift to local responsibility for marketing strategy implementation.[88] Regardless of the extent to which a firm chooses to globalize its marketing strategy, extensive environmental analysis and marketing research are necessary to understand the needs and desires of the target market(s) and successfully implement the chosen marketing strategy.

A global presence does not automatically result in a global competitive advantage. However, a global presence generates five opportunities for creating value: (1) to adapt to local market differences, (2) to exploit economies of global scale, (3) to exploit economies of global scope, (4) to mine optimal locations for activities and resources, and (5) to maximize the transfer of knowledge across locations.[89] To exploit these opportunities, marketers need to conduct marketing research and work within the constraints of the international environment and regional trade alliances, markets, and agreements.

globalization The development of marketing strategies that treat the entire world (or its major regions) as a single entity

Chapter Review

8-1 Define international marketing.

International marketing involves developing and performing marketing activities across national boundaries. International markets can provide tremendous opportunities for growth and renewed opportunity for the firm.

8-2 Differentiate between the six environmental forces that affect international marketing efforts.

A detailed analysis of the environment is essential before a company enters an international market. Environmental aspects of special importance include sociocultural; economic; political, legal, and regulatory; social and ethical; competitive; and technological forces. Because marketing activities are primarily social in purpose, they are influenced by beliefs and values regarding family, religion, education, health, and recreation. Cultural differences may affect marketing negotiations, decision-making behavior, and product adoption and use. A nation's economic stability and trade barriers can affect marketing efforts. Significant trade barriers include import tariffs, quotas, embargoes, and exchange controls. Gross domestic product (GDP) and GDP per capita are common measures of a nation's economic standing. Political and legal forces include a nation's political system, laws, regulatory bodies, special-interest groups, and courts. In the area of ethics, cultural relativism is the concept that morality varies from one culture to another and that business practices are therefore differentially defined as right or wrong by particular cultures. In addition to considering the types of competition and the types of competitive structures that exist in other countries, marketers also need to consider the competitive forces at work and recognize the importance of the global customer who is well informed about product choices from around the world. Advances in technology have greatly facilitated international marketing.

8-3 List six important international trade agreements.

Various regional trade alliances and specific markets create both opportunities and constraints for companies engaged in international marketing. Important trade agreements include the North American Free Trade Agreement, European Union, Southern Common Market, Asia-Pacific Economic Cooperation, Association of Southeast Asian Nations, and World Trade Organization.

8-4 Identify methods of international market entry.

There are several ways to enter international marketing. Importing (the purchase of products from a foreign source) and exporting (the sale of products to foreign markets) are the easiest and most flexible methods. Marketers may employ a trading company, which links buyers and sellers in different countries but is not involved in manufacturing and does not own assets related to manufacturing. Licensing and franchising are arrangements whereby one firm pays fees to another for the use of its name, expertise, and supplies. Contract manufacturing occurs when a company hires a foreign firm to produce a designated volume of the domestic firm's product to specification, and the final product carries the domestic firm's name. Joint ventures are partnerships between a domestic firm and a foreign firm or government. Strategic alliances are partnerships formed to create competitive advantage on a worldwide basis. Finally, a firm can build its own marketing or production facilities overseas. When companies have direct ownership of facilities in many countries, they may be considered multinational enterprises.

8-5 Describe the use of the marketing mix internationally.

Although most firms adjust their marketing mixes for differences in target markets, some firms standardize their marketing efforts worldwide. Traditional full-scale international marketing involvement is based on products customized according to cultural, regional, and national differences. Globalization, however, involves developing marketing strategies as if the entire world (or regions of it) were a single entity; a globalized firm markets standardized products in the same way everywhere. International marketing demands some strategic planning if a firm is to incorporate foreign sales into its overall marketing strategy.

 Go to www.cengagebrain.com for resources to help you master the content in this chapter as well as for materials that will expand your marketing knowledge!

Developing Your Marketing Plan

When formulating marketing strategy, one of the issues a company must consider is whether or not to pursue international markets. Although international markets present increased marketing opportunities, they also require more complex decisions when formulating marketing plans. To assist you in relating the information in this chapter to the development of your marketing plan, focus on the following:

1. Review the environmental analysis that was completed in Chapter 3. Extend the analysis for each of the seven factors to include global markets.

2. Using Figure 8.1 as a guide, determine the degree of international involvement that is appropriate for your product and your company.

3. Discuss the concepts of customization and globalization for your product when moving to international markets. Refer to Table 8.6 for guidance in your discussion.

Key Concepts

Issues for Discussion and Review

1. How does international marketing differ from domestic marketing?
2. What factors must marketers consider as they decide whether to engage in international marketing?
3. Why are the largest industrial corporations in the United States so committed to international marketing?
4. Why do you think this chapter focuses on an analysis of the international marketing environment?
5. If you were asked to provide a small tip (or bribe) to have a document approved in a foreign nation where this practice is customary, what would you do?
6. How will NAFTA affect marketing opportunities for U.S. products in North America (the United States, Mexico, and Canada)?
7. What should marketers consider as they decide whether to license or enter into a joint venture in a foreign nation?
8. Discuss the impact of strategic alliances on international marketing strategies.
9. Contrast globalization with customization of marketing strategies. Is one practice better than the other?
10. What are some of the product issues that need to be considered when marketing luxury automobiles in Australia, Brazil, Singapore, South Africa, and Sweden?

VIDEO CASE 8
Alibaba and Global e-Commerce: Should Amazon Be Afraid?

From rural farmers to multimillionaires, millions of people in China are reaping economic opportunities from the growing e-commerce market. One entrepreneur earns $5 million in sales annually from his ladies' handbag e-commerce business—a far cry from his humble origins. Although his success might be the exception to the norm, many Chinese consumers with similar backgrounds have found jobs working in e-commerce.

"We grew up in a rural area which left us few choices. I never thought about my future or had any belief in it," the entrepreneur says.

At the center of this is Alibaba, an online marketplace founded by entrepreneur Jack Ma in 1999. Jack Ma conceived of an online portal that could connect Chinese manufacturers with buyers from other countries. He chose the name Alibaba because it was globally recognized based upon the famous character in the collection Arabian Nights. Today this multibillion-dollar firm has 500 million registered users. Its sales surpass those of eBay and Amazon combined. Alibaba runs a number of businesses that handle approximately 80 percent of all online shopping in China. Unlike Amazon, it does not own its own merchandise but acts as a portal to bring buyers and sellers together.

Alibaba has a number of trading platforms that sell to both business-to-business (B2B) and business-to-consumer (B2C) markets. Its B2C market portal, Taobao, has been termed the Chinese version of Amazon.com or eBay. Taobao has enabled rural farmers to start their own businesses and has created employment opportunities for locals. Because of its influence, entire "Taobao Villages" have sprung up across China. These villages consist of residents who operate in e-commerce. Today there are estimated to be 780 Taobao Villages in China.

This is just the beginning for Alibaba. In 2014 it was listed on the U.S. stock exchange with an initial public offering of $25 billion, the largest IPO to date. To emphasize its global intentions, Alibaba opened offices in France, Germany, and Italy. It is also focused on selling more international brands such as Macy's, Apple, and L'Oreal. In its quest to expand into media, Alibaba entered into a licensing agreement with Disney to sell a streaming device that will broadcast movies, television shows, e-books, games, and more.

Although it is listed on the U.S. stock exchange, investing in Alibaba differs from the traditional model due to regulatory and legal barriers. The Chinese government restricts foreign investment in certain areas, meaning that global investors outside of China cannot own shares of Alibaba outright. In reality, investors purchased shares of a shell corporation in the Cayman Islands. Alibaba itself owns all of its non-Chinese assets. Jack Ma has the most power in the company, and some investors are concerned about his tendency to make large decisions or transfer ownership without consulting many other people.

Another issue that Alibaba is coming across as it expands involves counterfeit products. In China counterfeit goods have traditionally been more accepted than in other countries. Its international e-commerce site AliExpress has gained widespread popularity in Russia, the United States, and Brazil, but its rise in popularity has been accompanied by a rise in counterfeit goods sold through the site. Regulators are worried that the site is allowing counterfeits to go straight from Chinese manufacturers to consumers on a global scale. In fact, Kering SA—a French luxury group—filed a lawsuit against Alibaba accusing the firm of knowingly allowing the sale of counterfeit products. Alibaba denies the charges and is working with government bodies to improve counterfeiting controls.

Despite the risks of investing in a firm that they cannot actually own, investors were eager to purchase shares during Alibaba's initial public offering. China is overtaking the United States as the largest e-commerce market, and the opportunities are too good for many investors to pass up. They believe Alibaba has the potential for massive global growth as it is less capital intensive and therefore more flexible than global rivals such as Amazon.com.[90]

Questions for Discussion

1. What are some of the barriers Alibaba is facing as it expands globally?
2. How has Taobao created economic opportunities for Chinese entrepreneurs that were inaccessible to them before?
3. Why would the sale of counterfeit products through its sites be damaging to Alibaba?

chapter 9

Digital Marketing and Social Networking

LEARNING OBJECTIVES

9-1 Define digital media, digital marketing, and electronic marketing.

9-2 Summarize the growth and importance of digital marketing.

9-3 Describe different types of digital media and how they can be used for marketing.

9-4 Describe how marketers can measure the success of a digital strategy.

9-5 Clarify how digital media affects the four variables of the marketing mix.

9-6 Identify legal and ethical considerations in digital marketing.

ipsy Has Beauty "Bagged"

Digital marketing has enabled the rise of the e-tailer, a retailer that operates solely online. Traditional brick-and-mortar businesses can take many years to become established in their industry. On the other hand, entrepreneurs and companies that have successfully capitalized on social media have seen demand for their products soar in a short amount of time. Such is the case with ipsy, a subscription-based beauty sampling service, founded by YouTube sensation Michelle Phan.

After Michelle Phan was rejected for a job at a Lancôme cosmetics counter, she turned to YouTube to display her passion for art and makeup. Phan's makeup tutorials gained a loyal following, with 690,000 followers three years after she started posting videos. She became such a sensation that Lancôme, which had previously rejected her for a job, signed Phan up as their first video makeup artist. One year later, Phan founded ipsy, an online subscription service.

The idea for ipsy came when Phan noticed how women prefer to purchase smaller samples of unfamiliar products. Because cosmetics are expensive, purchasing an unfamiliar cosmetic never tried before is a risky endeavor. Phan made small samples from well-known beauty brands available to subscribers for a monthly fee of $10.

The company has expanded to also serve as a community for beauty creators on YouTube with its offshoot, ipsy Open Studios. With influencer marketing at the center of ipsy's business model, the beauty subscription service has attracted more than 1.5 million subscribers.[1]

ipsy

LOG IN   GET STARTED

Zoeva 322 Tapered Highlighter

MR. WRITE (NOW)

Discover Your New Favorite Foundation.

5 Beauty Products | Only $10/month | Free Shipping*

GET STARTED

* Within the U.S.

ipsy.com

New Business Opportunities
Digital marketing creates many new business opportunities for marketers around the world.

Maxx-Studio/Shutterstock.com

Digital media creates exciting opportunities for companies to target specific markets, develop new marketing strategies, and gather information about customers. Using digital media channels, marketers are able to analyze and address consumer needs better. Fueled by changing technology, consumer behavior has changed with Internet-enabled consumer empowerment. This has resulted in a shift in the balance of power between consumer and marketer.[2]

One of the defining characteristics of information technology in the 21st century is accelerating change. New systems and applications advance so rapidly that unexpected new innovations appear that can change existing assumptions about digital marketing opportunities. For example, digital assistants that function as a personal information manager were not in wide use a few years ago. Now, Amazon and Google are connecting consumers to the Internet based on voice commands. You can order products, create a shopping list, and of course obtain music, news, and weather. How this will affect digital marketing will evolve.

E-mail, smartphones, social networking, drones and even driverless vehicles are shaping the marketing environment. All of these advances in technology relate to how consumers make decisions about products. In this chapter, we focus more on social media marketing, but digital marketing is a broad field that provides opportunity to develop relationships with consumers.

While digital marketing has many benefits and opportunities, there are also challenges. Today, consumers often have to sacrifice their privacy to engage in digital technology.[3] As firms gather information on consumers for marketing research, there are dangers of data breaches and online crime. Data analytics associated with big data to understand consumers opens the door to identity theft, online fraud, and cyber criminals. There are regulatory issues relating to what types of consumer data can be stored and what firms should do to protect consumer data. We address these issues later in the chapter. With more than 3.5 billion people accessing the Internet worldwide, marketers are seeing their digital marketing strategies reach consumers from different parts of the world like never before.[4]

In this chapter, we focus on digital marketing strategies, particularly new communication channels such as social networks, and discuss how consumers are changing their information searches and consumption behaviors to fit with these emerging technologies and trends. Most important, we analyze how marketers can use digital media to their advantage to connect with consumers more effectively, gather more information about their target markets, and convert this information into successful marketing strategies.

9-1 DEFINING DIGITAL MARKETING

LO 9-1 Define digital media, digital marketing, and electronic marketing.

Before we move on, we must first provide a definition of digital media. **Digital media** are electronic media that function using digital codes—when we refer to digital media, we are referring to media available via computers, mobile devices, and other digital devices that have been released in recent years. A number of terms have been coined to describe marketing activities on the Internet. **Digital marketing** uses all digital media, including the Internet and mobile and interactive channels, to develop communication and exchanges with customers. In this chapter, we focus on how the Internet relates to all aspects of marketing, including strategic planning. Thus, we use the term **electronic marketing**, (or **e-marketing**),

digital media Electronic media that function using digital codes; when we refer to digital media, we are referring to media available via computers, cellular phones, smartphones, and other digital devices that have been released in recent years

digital marketing Using all digital media, including the Internet and mobile and interactive channels, to develop communication and exchanges with customers

electronic marketing (e-marketing) The strategic process of pricing, distributing, and promoting products, and discovering the desires of customers using digital media and digital marketing

to refer to the strategic process of pricing, distributing, and promoting products, and discovering the desires of customers using digital media and digital marketing. Our definition of e-marketing goes beyond the Internet and includes mobile phones, banner ads, digital outdoor marketing, and social networks.

9-2 GROWTH AND BENEFITS OF DIGITAL MARKETING

LO 9-2 Summarize the growth and importance of digital marketing.

The phenomenal growth of the Internet has provided unprecedented opportunities for marketers to forge interactive relationships with consumers. As the Internet and digital communication technologies have advanced, they have made it possible to target markets more precisely and reach markets that were previously inaccessible. As the world of digital media continues to grow, e-marketing has developed strategies that include all digital media, including television advertising and other mobile and interactive media that do not use the Internet (advertising media are discussed in detail in Chapter 16). In fact, marketers are using the term *digital marketing* as a catch-all for capturing all digital channels for reaching customers. This area is progressing rapidly, and the digital world is evolving into effective marketing strategy integration.[5]

One of the most important benefits of e-marketing is the ability of marketers and customers to share information. Through websites, social networks, and other digital media, consumers can learn about everything they consume and use in life. As a result, the Internet is changing the way marketers communicate and develop relationships. Today's marketers can use the Internet to form relationships with a variety of stakeholders, including customers, employees, and suppliers. For example, IBM's digital assistant allows IBM customers to identify and digitally interact with key experts through a variety of platforms. IBM's Watson is an assistant in cognitive computing impacting fields as diverse as finance, medicine, and education. This results in the need to adjust marketing strategies to the digital world. Digital marketing and social media permit innovative forms of communication and co-created content in relationship-based interactions.[6]

For many businesses, engaging in digital and online marketing activities is essential to maintaining competitive advantages. Increasingly, small businesses can use digital media to develop strategies to reach new markets and access inexpensive communication channels. Large companies like Target use online catalogs and company websites to supplement their brick-and-mortar stores. At the other end of the spectrum, companies like Amazon.com and Alibaba are challenging traditional brick-and-mortar businesses. Amazon is taking on department stores and big box stores such as Walmart and Home Depot. Department stores such as Macy's and Sears have had to close hundreds of stores, and some shopping centers have gone out of business.[7] Social networking sites are advancing e-marketing by providing additional features, such as the ability to view daily deals or purchase items using Facebook. Finally, some corporate websites and social media sites provide feedback mechanisms through which customers can ask questions, voice complaints, indicate preferences, and otherwise communicate about their needs and desires.

One of the biggest mistakes a marketer can make when engaging in digital marketing is to treat it like a traditional marketing channel. Digital media offer a whole new dimension to marketing that marketers must

Benefits of Digital Marketing
Digital marketing provides access to products from any location at a time that is convenient for the consumer.

Andrey_Popov/Shutterstock.com

TABLE 9.1	CHARACTERISTICS OF ONLINE MEDIA	
Characteristic	**Definition**	**Example**
Addressability	The ability of the marketer to identify customers before they make a purchase	Amazon installs cookies on a user's computer that allow the company to identify the user when he or she returns to the website
Interactivity	The ability of customers to express their needs and wants directly to the firm in response to its marketing communications	Texas Instruments interacts with its customers on its Facebook page by answering concerns and posting updates
Accessibility	The ability for marketers to obtain digital information	Google can use web searches done through its search engine to learn about customer interests
Connectivity	The ability for consumers to be connected with marketers along with other consumers	Mary Kay offers users the opportunity to sign up for My MK, a system that connects customers with beauty consultants and allows them to develop their own personalized space
Control	The customer's ability to regulate the information they view as well as the rate and exposure to that information	Consumers use Kayak.com to discover the best travel deals

consider when concocting their companies' marketing strategies. The quality of a website will have a major impact on whether the customer exhibits loyalty to the site. Website aesthetics, navigational quality, information content, and information quality positively impact the level of a customer's relative loyalty to the e-retail website.[8] Some of the characteristics that distinguish online media from traditional marketing include addressability, interactivity, accessibility, connectivity, and control, as defined in Table 9.1.

9-3 TYPES OF CONSUMER-GENERATED MARKETING AND DIGITAL MEDIA

LO 9-3 Describe different types of digital media and how they can be used for marketing.

While digital media and e-marketing have generated exciting opportunities for organizations to interact with consumers, it is essential to recognize that social media are more consumer-driven than traditional media. Consumer-generated material is having a profound effect on marketing. As the Internet becomes more accessible worldwide, consumers are creating and reading consumer-generated content like never before. Social networks and advances in software technology provide an environment for marketers to use consumer-generated content.

Two major trends have caused consumer-generated information to gain importance:

1. The increased tendency of consumers to publish their own thoughts, opinions, reviews, and product discussions through blogs or other digital media.
2. Consumers' tendencies to trust other consumers over corporations. Consumers often rely on the recommendations of friends, family, and fellow consumers when making purchasing decisions.

By understanding where online users are likely to express their thoughts and opinions, marketers can use these forums to interact with consumers, address problems, and promote their companies. Types of digital media in which consumers are likely to participate include social networks, blogs, wikis, media-sharing sites, virtual reality gaming, mobile devices, digital assistants, applications and widgets, and more.

9-3a Social Media Marketing

Social media marketing involves obtaining communications with consumers through social media sites. Social media marketing enables firms to promote a message and create online conversations through multiple platforms. Large markets can be targeted and reached through paid media, owned media, and earned media.[9] Traditional paid media includes traditional print and broadcast but is now joined by paid advertising on social networks such as Facebook and Twitter. Marketers can place ads on Google just like they place an ad on television. On Facebook, which has more than 2.5 million advertisers, brands can pay to boost posts, create compelling photo carousel ads, promote their page, and more.[10] In addition to placing ads, marketers can own their own media outlets and create messages on social networks. Most firms have owned websites but can also develop websites through such social networking services as Facebook and LinkedIn. Finally, markets can have earned media when consumers are communicating on social media sites. These digital word-of-mouth posts or interactions can promote a product or firm. Although it is not controllable like advertising, if the communication is positive, it increases sales.[11]

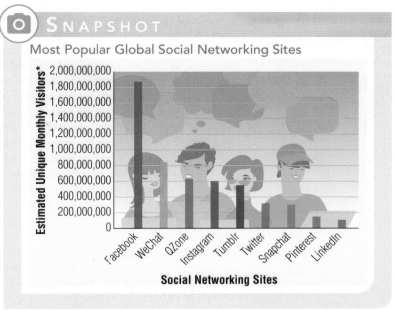

📷 SNAPSHOT

Most Popular Global Social Networking Sites

As of January 2017

Source: "Most Famous Social Network Sites Worldwide as of January 2017, Ranked by Number of Active Users (in Millions)," *Statista*, www.statista.com/statistics/272014/global-social-networks-ranked-by-number-of-users/ (accessed March 5, 2017).

User-generated content relates to consumers that create, converse, rate, collect, join, or simply read online materials. Marketers can't access the creative efforts of consumers that post or publish on publicly accessible websites, such as blogs like A Beautiful Mess and Modern Martha, or on social networking sites such as LinkedIn. These user-generated sites often involve self-disclosure where consumers share their knowledge, interests, and desire to join or associate with others. Participating in discussions to connect and network with others is a major motivating factor to influence others or to promote an interest or cause. There are many critics involved in user-generated content. These consumers comment, post evaluations on blogs, and post ratings and reviews. If you have ever posted a product review or rated a movie, you have engaged in this activity. Evaluating what critics post should be an important part in a company's digital marketing strategy. Of course, consumers read ratings to aid their shopping purchases. Yelp is one of the most comprehensive review sites on products and businesses. Yelp, with more than 77 million reviews, continues to expand their platform, adding Questions and Answers for users to ask venue-specific questions for other users to answer.[12] Therefore, these rating sites can be helpful to collect information used in marketing research and to monitor firm reputation.

Marketers need to analyze their target markets and determine the best social media approach to support marketing objectives. Social media should be included in both the corporate and marketing strategy. It should be a part of the firm's marketing plan and implementation efforts. Social media can be used to monitor target market competitors and understand the social and economic environment as a whole. Social media has the potential of building campaigns that produce advocates and enthusiasts of a firm's products. For example, Dodge uses social media to release product teasers and news to its engaged fans. The brand rewarded its most engaged social media fans by inviting a limited number to the unveiling of the 2018 Dodge Challenger SRT Demon.[13] Marketing should be focused on relationship building, and social media can influence consumer behavior and deliver value to the firm.

social network A website where users can create a profile and interact with other users, post information, and engage in other forms of web-based communication

Social networks have been integrated into marketing strategies. A **social network** is a website where users can create a profile and interact with other users, post information, and engage in other forms of web-based communication. Marketing is evolving from digital into strategic interactive marketing that facilitates two-way communication. Allowing consumers to opt-in or opt-out of programs facilitates communication without intruding on privacy.[14]

Another benefit of social networking is marketers' ability to reach out to new target markets. Snapchat is a mobile photo messaging application that allows users to send photos, messages, or videos to their friends for a certain amount of time. After that time, the post is deleted from both the recipient's phone and Snapchat servers. Snapchat has grown immensely popular with Millennials, a popular but difficult demographic for marketers to reach. When Snap Inc., Snapchat's parent company, debuted on the stock market, the stock value was up 44 percent by the end of its first day of trading, giving the company a $33 billion valuation.[15] Many countries also have their own, much smaller social networking sites that marketers should consider when trying to reach global populations. For instance, VK, based in Russia, is a popular social networking site in Europe, while QZone, which has 625 million users, is popular in China.[16] More information on how marketers use social networks is provided in later sections of this chapter.

Social networks are building business models for economic success. As Figure 9.1 demonstrates, social network usage is growing on every major platform, with the exception of Pinterest. Seventy-nine percent of online adults use Facebook, which continues to be the most popular social media platform by far. The second most popular platform, Instagram, attracts 32 percent of online adults.[17] As social networks evolve, both marketers and the owners of social networking sites are realizing the incredible opportunities such networks offer—an influx of advertising dollars for social networking owners and a large reach for the advertiser. The challenge to improve the brand is to expand the range of social media used and to target various stakeholders that should be a part of the dialogue. Therefore, social media is a part of corporate communication and brand building strategy.[18] The following social networks we examine are among the most important to marketers worldwide.

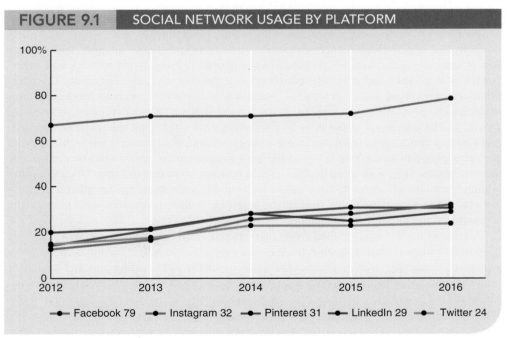

FIGURE 9.1   SOCIAL NETWORK USAGE BY PLATFORM

Legend: Facebook 79 — Instagram 32 — Pinterest 31 — LinkedIn 29 — Twitter 24

Note: *Percentage of online adults. Eighty-six percent of Americans currently Internet users. Survey conducted March 7–April 4, 2016.*
Source: Pew Research Center, "Social Media Update 2016," November 11, 2016, www.pewinternet.org/2016/11/11/social-media-update-2016/ (accessed March 5, 2017).

Facebook

Facebook is the number one social networking site in the world. When it was launched in 2004 by Harvard student Mark Zuckerberg and four of his classmates, it was initially limited to Harvard students. In 2006 the site was opened to anyone aged 13 or older. Internet users create Facebook profiles and then search the network for people with whom to connect. This social networking giant has nearly 2 billion users worldwide.[19]

Organizations also use Facebook and other digital media sites to give special incentives to customers. Doritos released 11,500 limited edition rainbow chip bags in support of the LGBT community, only the chips were never available for sale. To receive a bag, customers had to donate a sum of $10 or more to the It Gets Better Project and post a supportive quote on social media using #boldandbetter. This not only engaged customers, resulting in 30 times more Facebook shares than the brand's average, but also made the Doritos brand appear more authentic to the public.[20] Advertising on Facebook has also been increasing. The firm generates more than $8 billion in annual advertising revenues and allows advertisers to target ads to users based upon their web-browsing habits.[21]

Additionally, social networking sites are useful for relationship marketing, or the creation of relationships that mutually benefit the business and customer. Thanks to Facebook, companies that are focused upon building and enhancing customer relationships are able to understand who their customers are and how they can meet their needs.

Twitter

Twitter is a hybrid mix of a social networking site and a micro-blogging site that asks viewers one simple question: "What's happening?" Users can post answers of up to 140 characters, which are then available for their "followers" to read. A limitation of 140 characters may not seem like enough for companies to send an effective message, but some have become experts at using Twitter in their marketing strategies. For example, the National Football League features football highlights and clips on Twitter to engage sports enthusiasts.[22] Like other social networking sites, Twitter is being used to enhance customer service and create publicity about company products. Marketers are clearly taking notice of the various marketing opportunities Twitter has to offer.

Snapchat

While Snap Inc. admits it may never achieve profitability, posting a net loss of approximately $514 million in recent years, investors see value in Snapchat, which has more than 158 million daily active users.[23] The mobile app, launched in 2011, allows users to send messages and disappearing photos and videos to friends. The parent company prefers to think of itself as a camera company rather than a social media company, and plans to release more lifestyle products like Spectacles, camera glasses sold at Snapchat pop-up shops, outside of its social media platform.[24] Marketers are looking at Snapchat as an opportunity to reach their young, highly engaged audience. Brands like Taco Bell, Sour Patch Kids, and Birchbox have taken to Snapchat to engage with their audiences.

Snapchat, which features skippable, vertical video ads and custom photo filters, is used mostly by people under the age of 34. In fact, 85 percent of daily users are between 18 and 34.[25] Universal Pictures created a custom lens in the app, a special filter that alters a user's picture, to promote the movie *Fifty Shades Darker*, enabling users to add a masquerade mask to their photo. Other films promoted on Snapchat include *Office

Twitter
Twitter allows users to post messages and to follow individuals or organizations that are of interest.

Sattalat phukkum/Shutterstock.com

Christmas Party, Ghostbusters (2016), and *Sing*.[26] One of Snapchat's biggest challenges will be scaling its advertising dollars to achieve its revenue goals.

YouTube

Purchased by Google for $1.65 billion, YouTube allows users to upload and share videos worldwide. Users watch a billion hours of YouTube videos every day, making this popular video platform an important part of marketing strategy.[27] Though brands use the platform to release original video content, consumers far outnumber them on the platform. For example, in beauty searches, beauty brands on YouTube are outnumbered by beauty vloggers 14 to 1.[28] This makes it challenging for brands to control messaging about their products on the platform.

YouTube continues to diversify its video offering with YouTube Red and YouTube TV. YouTube Red expands upon the original platform allowing users to pay for uninterrupted music, ad-free and offline video, and original programming from top creators. As more homes cancel their cable packages, YouTube TV is an affordable alternative. For $35 per month, users can watch ABC, CBS, and NBC among other top networks, positioning the service as a competitor to Sling TV and DirecTV Now.[29]

LinkedIn

LinkedIn is the top networking site for businesses and business professionals. This networking tool allows users to post a public profile, similar to a resume, connect with colleagues, find job listings, and join private groups. Eighty percent of B2B marketers say LinkedIn is an effective business lead generator.[30] This platform can also be used to spread brand awareness and for corporate recruiting. HubSpot, an inbound marketing and sales platform with more than 175,000 followers, uses LinkedIn to spread their content, promote free webinars, and increase awareness around inbound marketing.[31]

blogs Web-based journals (short for "weblogs") in which writers editorialize and interact with other Internet users

9-3b **Blogs and Wikis**

Today's marketers must recognize the impact of consumer-generated material like blogs and wikis, as their significance to online consumers has increased a great deal. **Blogs** (short for "weblogs") are web-based journals in which writers can editorialize and interact with other Internet users. More than three-fourths of Internet users read blogs.[32] In fact, the blogging site Tumblr, which allows anyone to post text, hyperlinks, pictures, and other media for free, became one of the top ten online destinations. The site, which has been around for more than a decade, has approximately 336 million users that have created more than 146 billion posts.[33] Yahoo purchased Tumblr for $1.1 billion, demonstrating the belief that blogs are a growing segment of social media.[34]

Blogs give consumers control, sometimes more than companies would like. Whether or not the blog's content is factually accurate, bloggers can post whatever opinions they like about a company or its products. Although companies have filed lawsuits against bloggers for defamation, they usually cannot prevent the blog from going viral. Responding to a negative review is a delicate matter. For instance, although companies sometimes force bloggers to remove blogs, readers often create copies of the blog and spread it across the Internet after the original's removal. In other cases, a positive review of a product posted on a popular blog

Kaspars Grinvalds/Shutterstock.com

Blogs
Blogs such as this fashion blog allow consumers to stay current on clothing and accessory trends.

EMERGING TRENDS IN MARKETING

Social Media Challenges: Fraudsters and Fake News

Social networks have changed the marketing discipline, in many ways benefiting companies that use their services. However, there are always those who take advantage of social media to earn money through fraudulent means. A more recent concern is the propagation of fake news. During major events such as elections, fake news stories abound. The more popular the story shared on social media sites—whether factual or false—the higher up it is in users' news feeds. This has allowed fake news stories to spread virally across social media.

Although some of these perpetrators have their own personal agendas, many spread fake news on social media sites because it directs interested users to their own websites. Once users are on the fraudsters' websites, they are presented with a number of ads that earn the fraudsters money from advertisers if clicked on. Hence, fraudsters disseminating fake news want to convince users to visit their phony news websites because they hope users will click on ads posted there.

Due to the criticism Facebook and Google have faced, they started to take steps to identify fake news stories. Google announced that it would ban fake news from its advertising platform, while Facebook is coming up with tools members can use to flag suspicious news. Facebook is also looking into partnering with fact-checkers to check suspicious news and determine whether it is false.[a]

---

can result in large increases in sales. Thus, blogs can represent a potent threat to corporations as well as an opportunity.

Many businesses use blogs to their advantage. Rather than trying to eliminate blogs that cast their companies in a negative light, some marketers use blogs to answer consumer concerns or defend their corporate reputations. For instance, direct selling firm Tastefully Simple operates a blog of easy recipes. Users can look for recipes based on the main ingredient used, type of course, or cooking method.[35] As blogging changes the face of media, companies like Tastefully Simple are using this digital tool to build enthusiasm for their products and develop customer relationships.

A **wiki** is a type of software that creates an interface that enables users to add or edit the content of some types of websites. One of the best known is Wikipedia, an online encyclopedia with nearly 40 million article entries in 293 languages on nearly every subject imaginable.[36] Because Wikipedia can be edited and read by anyone, it is easy for online consumers to correct inaccuracies in content.[37] This site is expanded, updated, and edited by a large team of volunteer contributors. For the most part, only information that is verifiable through another source is considered appropriate. Because of its open format, Wikipedia has suffered from some high-profile instances of vandalism in which incorrect information was disseminated. Such problems have usually been detected and corrected quickly. Like all social media, wikis have advantages and disadvantages for companies. Wikis on controversial companies like Walmart and Nike often contain negative publicity about the companies, such as worker rights violations. However, some companies have begun to use wikis as internal tools for teams working on a project requiring lots of documentation.[38] Additionally, monitoring wikis provides companies with a better idea of how consumers feel about the company brand.

There is too much at stake financially for marketers to ignore blogs and wikis. Despite this fact, statistics show that less than a third of Fortune 500 companies have a corporate blog.[39] Marketers who want to form better customer relationships and promote their company's products must not underestimate the power of these two tools as new media outlets.

9-3c Media-Sharing Sites

Marketers share their corporate messages in more visual ways through media-sharing sites. Media-sharing sites allow marketers to share photos, videos, and podcasts but are more

wiki Type of software that creates an interface that enables users to add or edit the content of some types of websites

limited in scope in how companies interact with consumers. They tend to be more promotional-oriented. This means that while firms can promote their products through videos or photos, they usually do not interact with consumers through personal messages or responses. At the same time, the popularity of these sites has the potential to reach a global audience of consumers.

Photo-sharing sites allow users to upload and share their photos with the world. Well-known photo-sharing sites include Flickr, Shutterfly, Snapfish, and Instagram. Owned by Yahoo, Flickr is one of the most popular photo-sharing sites on the Internet. A Flickr user can upload images, edit them, classify the images, create photo albums, and share photos or videos with friends without having to e-mail bulky image files or send photos through the mail. Instagram is a mobile photo-sharing site that has surpassed Flickr in popularity. Instagram allows its 600 million users to manipulate their photos with different tints and share them with their friends.[40] To compete against Snapchat, Instagram introduced Instagram Stories, a way for its users to send their friends messages that disappear in 24 hours.[41] Facebook purchased Instagram for $1 billion with the intention to break into the mobile industry.[42] With more and more people using mobile apps or accessing the Internet through their smartphones, the use of photo sharing through mobile devices is increasing.

Other sites are emerging that take photo sharing to a new level. Pinterest is a photo-sharing bulletin board that combines photo sharing with elements of bookmarking and social networking. Users can share photos and images among other Internet users, communicating mostly through images that they "pin" to their boards. Other users can "repin" these images to their boards, follow each other, "like" images, and make comments. Marketers have found that an effective way of marketing through Pinterest is to post images conveying a certain emotion that represents their brand.[43] It has become so popular that it has surpassed Google+ in number of users. Because Pinterest users create boards that deal with their interests, marketers also have a chance to develop marketing messages encouraging users to purchase the product or brand that interests them. Pinterest hopes to learn how to influence a customer to proceed from showing interest in a product to having an intent to purchase. This knowledge will be helpful to advertisers marketing through Pinterest's website.[44] Pinterest added a feature called Lens that allows users to take a picture of an object and find a list of pins with similar looking objects, further establishing the platform as a discovery tool for shopping.[45]

Photo sharing represents an opportunity for companies to market themselves visually by displaying snapshots of company events, company staff, and/or company products. Nike, Audi, and MTV have all used Instagram in digital marketing campaigns.[46] Zales Jewelers has topic boards on Pinterest featuring rings as well as other themes of love, including songs, wedding cakes, and wedding dresses.[47] Digital marketing companies are also scanning photos and images on photo-sharing sites to gather insights about how brands are being displayed or used. These companies hope to offer these insights to big-name companies such as Kraft.[48] The opportunities for marketers to use photo-sharing sites to gather information and promote brands appear limitless.

Another popular form of media sharing is video-sharing sites. These sites allow virtually anybody to upload videos, from professional marketers at Fortune 500 corporations to the average Internet user. Some of the most popular video-sharing sites include YouTube, Vimeo, and Hulu. Video-sharing sites give companies the opportunity to upload ads and informational videos about their products. A few videos become viral at any given time, and although many of these gain popularity because they embarrass the subject in some way, others reach viral status because people find them entertaining

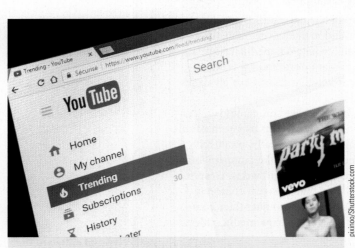

YouTube
YouTube allows users to post material and view or subscribe to channels of interest.

(viral marketing will be discussed in more detail in Chapter 15). Marketers are seizing upon opportunities to use this viral nature to promote awareness and use of their products.

A new trend in video marketing is the use of amateur filmmakers. Video-sharing websites give businesses the chance to capitalize on consumer-generated content. They also provide would-be video bloggers with the chance to create a name for themselves, which in turn could catch the attention of major companies. Consider the case of Bethany Mota, who started uploading videos to YouTube when she was 13. Since then she has started weekly videos featuring the makeup and clothing that she wears. As a charismatic presenter with 10.3 million subscribers, she has promoted different fashion brands, written a book, and even developed her own fashion, accessory, and fragrance collection at Aéropostale.[49] These types of videos are more authentic and create enthusiasm for products among consumer participants. They become an electronic word-of-mouth form of communication that supports brand image.

With the rise of bloggers and social media stars like Michelle Phan and Eva Gutowski, brands are turning to influencers to promote their products. Brands identify influencers who align with their brand image and often pay them for an endorsement or send complimentary product in exchange for a review. Roughly 22 percent of businesses are seeing higher customer acquisition rates through influencer marketing than through traditional channels like e-mail and search marketing.[50] Brands can contact influencers directly or use paid platforms like TapInfluence and BrandBacker to identify ideal partners and manage campaigns. Influenster is a product sampling program that puts products in the hands of influencers and micro-influencers in exchange for authentic, user-generated content on social media. With a community of more than 2 million, brands are able to identify users who fall into their target demographic through data collected on the platform along with pre-qualification surveys. Once a user receives a set of products, Influenster drives social posts, in-store actions, and product reviews by incentivizing the influencers with a "Brand Badge." To receive the digital badge and retain membership privileges, users must participate in activities dictated by the brand, such as writing a review on a blog, posting a photo on Instagram, or uploading video using the products on YouTube.[51]

Podcasting, traditionally used for music and radio broadcasts, is also an important digital marketing tool. **Podcasts** are audio or video files that can be downloaded from the Internet with a subscription that automatically delivers new content to listening devices or personal computers. Podcasts offer the benefit of convenience, giving users the ability to listen to or view content when and where they choose. They have also shown to be influential over consumer buying habits. For instance, listening to nutrition podcasts while in the grocery store increases the likelihood that shoppers will purchase healthier items.[52] Food marketers might use this information to improve how they market the health benefits of foods. Companies can use podcasts to demonstrate how to use their products or understand certain features. As podcasting continues to catch on, radio and television networks like CBC Radio, NPR, MSNBC, and PBS are creating podcasts of their shows to profit from this growing trend. Through podcasting, many companies hope to create brand awareness, promote their products, and encourage customer loyalty.

9-3d Mobile Devices

Mobile devices, such as smartphones, tablet computers, and other mobile computing devices, allow customers to leave their desktops and access digital networks from anywhere. More than 95 percent of Americans have a mobile device.[53] Many of these mobile devices are smartphones, which have the ability to access the Internet, download apps, listen to music, take photographs, and more. Figure 9.2 breaks down smartphone ownership by age. Mobile marketing is exploding—marketers spend over $22 billion on mobile advertising spending.[54]

Mobile marketing is effective in grabbing consumers' attention. In one study, 58 percent of consumers recalled a brand shown through a mobile video advertisement, compared to 10 percent who saw it on television. This rate is unusually high in a world where consumers

podcast Audio or video file that can be downloaded from the Internet with a subscription that automatically delivers new content to listening devices or personal computers

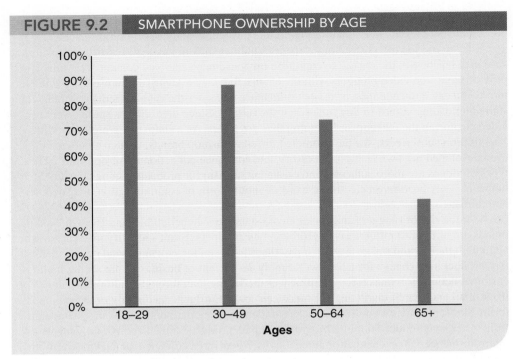

Among adults, the percentage who have a smartphone
Source: Pew Research Center, conducted September 29–November 6, 2016.

are often inundated with ads. Despite these promising trends, many brands have yet to take advantage of mobile marketing opportunities. Although most major businesses have websites, not all of these websites are easily viewable on mobile devices.[55]

To avoid being left behind, brands must recognize the importance of mobile marketing. Some of the more common mobile marketing tools include the following:

- SMS messages: SMS messages are text messages of 160 characters or less. SMS messages have been an effective way to send coupons to prospective customers.[56]
- Multimedia messages: Multimedia messaging takes SMS messaging a step further by allowing companies to send video, audio, photos, and other types of media over mobile devices. It is estimated that 98 percent of SMS and MMS messages are viewed, making this a valuable way of attracting consumers.[57]
- Mobile advertisements: Mobile advertisements are visual advertisements that appear on mobile devices. Companies might choose to advertise through search engines, websites, or even games accessed on mobile devices. Marketers spend approximately $22 billion on mobile advertising.[58]
- Mobile websites: Mobile websites are websites designed for mobile devices. Approximately 60 percent of all online traffic comes from mobile devices.[59]
- Mobile applications: Mobile applications are software programs that run on mobile devices and give users access to certain content.[60] Businesses release apps to help consumers access more information about their company or to provide incentives. These are discussed in further detail in the next section.

9-3e Applications and Widgets

mobile application A software program that runs on mobile devices and gives users access to certain content

Applications, or apps, are adding an entirely new layer to the marketing environment, as approximately 77 percent of all American adult smartphone users have applications on their mobile devices.[61] The most important feature of apps is the convenience and cost savings they offer to the consumer. Certain apps allow consumers to scan a product's barcode and then compare it with the prices of identical products in other stores or download store discounts.

To remain competitive, companies are beginning to use mobile marketing to offer additional incentives to consumers. Starbucks allows its app users to skip the lines by ordering ahead. App orders account for 21 percent of Starbuck's transactions.[62] Another application that marketers are finding useful is the QR scanning app. QR codes are black-and-white squares that sometimes appear in magazines, posters, and store-front displays. Smartphone users who have downloaded the QR scanning application can open their smartphones and scan the code, which contains a hidden message accessible with the app. The QR scanning app recognizes the code and opens the link, video, or image on the phone's screen. Marketers are using QR codes to promote companies and offer consumer discounts.[63]

Increasingly companies are taking advantage of beacon technology to target and communicate with app users based on their location. For example, retailers can place beacons throughout their stores, so when a shopper approaches one, it activates the retailer's app on the shopper's smartphone with custom messages and promotions. Macy's uses this technology in all of its U.S. stores to detect shoppers' locations and present personalized offers.[64] Similarly, Marriott's LocalPerks initiative locates the mobile devices of Marriott guests to determine their location and send them daily deals and other marketing messages.[65] One large barrier is that consumers need the company's app installed on their phone in order to receive beacon signals. Google aims to lower this barrier by sending Chrome browser-based notifications.[66] The applications for location-based technology will continue to expand as companies determine new ways to deliver value to their customers.

Mobile technology is also making inroads in transforming the shopping experience. Not only can shoppers use mobile applications to compare prices or download electronic discounts, they can also use them to tally up purchases and pay through their smartphones. As mobile payments gain traction, companies like Google, Apple, and Square are working to invest in this opportunity.[67] For instance, Google Wallet and Apple Pay are mobile apps that allow users to pay with their phones.[68] Square is a company launched by Twitter co-founder Jack Dorsey that provides organizations with smartphone and tablet swiping devices for credit cards. Another growing payment trend that has emerged with the rise of digital technology is digital currency. Bitcoin is a virtual peer-to-peer currency that can be used to make a payment via smartphone. The success of mobile payments in revolutionizing the shopping experience will depend upon retailers adopting digital payment systems, and companies like Starbucks are already jumping at the opportunity.

Widgets are small bits of software on a website, desktop, or mobile device that performs a simple purpose, such as providing stock quotes or blog updates. Marketers might use widgets to display news headlines, clocks, or games on their webpages.[69] For example, CNBC uses widgets to send alerts and financial news to subscribers. Widgets have been used by companies as a form of viral marketing—users can download the widget and send it to their friends with a click of a button.[70] Widgets downloaded to a user's desktop can update the user on the latest company or product information, enhancing relationship marketing between companies and their fans. For example, hotels, restaurants, and other tourist locations can download TripAdvisor widgets to their websites. These widgets display the latest company reviews, rewards, and other TripAdvisor content directly to their websites.[71] Widgets are an innovative digital marketing tool to personalize webpages, alert users to the latest company information, and spread awareness of the company's products.

Mobile Applications
Apps allow access to digital networks from a variety of mobile devices.

Scanrail/Shutterstock.com

widgets Small bits of software on a website, desktop, or mobile device that enable users to interface with the application and operating system

ENTREPRENEURSHIP IN MARKETING

The Virtual Grocery Cart: Instacart

Apoorva Mehta has learned from past mistakes that a successful business depends upon solving a problem the entrepreneur cares about. Mehta hated grocery shopping and wanted to make it more convenient for people. Instacart, an Internet-based grocery delivery service, was born.

Instacart is based on the sharing-economy concept popularized by Uber and Airbnb. Customers who want their groceries delivered use an app connecting them to a personal shopper. Instacart hires both part-time employees and independent contractors. Drivers are independent contractors who use their own cars for delivery.

Deliveries cost consumers $5.99. Instacart will often mark-up groceries, so groceries purchased through Instacart cost more than those purchased in-store.

Instacart has hit some obstacles as funding has tightened, forcing it to cut the pay of drivers and shoppers. However, Whole Foods has extended its partnership with Instacart and has purchased shares in the firm. Grocery stores such as Whole Foods like Instacart because it has helped them increase their numbers of customers. For many busy and on-the-go consumers, the extra cost is worth the convenience.[b]

9-4 MONITORING DIGITAL MEDIA BEHAVIORS OF CONSUMERS

LO 9-4 Describe how marketers can measure the success of a digital strategy.

Consumers now have a greater ability to regulate the information that they view as well as the rate and sequence of their exposure to that information. The Internet is sometimes referred to as a *pull* medium because users determine which websites they are going to view; the marketer has only limited ability to control the content to which users are exposed, and in what sequence. Today, blogs, wikis, podcasts, and ratings are used to publicize, praise, or challenge companies. Digital media require marketers to approach their jobs differently compared to traditional marketing. However, most companies in the United States do not routinely monitor consumers' postings to online social networking sites. In many cases, this represents a missed opportunity to gather information.

On the other hand, some companies are using the power of the consumer to their advantage. While negative ratings and reviews are damaging to a company, positive customer feedback is free publicity that often helps the company more than corporate messages do. Because consumer-generated content appears more authentic than corporate messages, it can go far in increasing a company's credibility. Additionally, while consumers can use digital media to access more information, marketers can also use the same sites to get information about the consumer—often more information than could be garnered through traditional marketing venues. They can examine how consumers are using the Internet to target marketing messages to their audience. Finally, marketers are also using the Internet to track the success of their online marketing campaigns, creating an entirely new way of gathering marketing research.

9-4a Online Monitoring and Analytics

Without digital media monitoring and evaluation, it will not be possible to maximize resources and minimize costs in social media marketing. The strength of measurement relates to the ability to have online analytics and metrics. Social media monitoring involves activities to track, measure, and evaluate a firm's digital marketing initiatives.[72] A strategic performance evaluation was discussed in Chapter 2, and monitoring and evaluating the digital marketing strategy is a part of this process. An advantage of digital marketing evaluations is that there are methods to capture the metrics that indicate the outcomes of strategies. Therefore, establishing an expected level of performance creates a benchmark against which performance can be compared. Metrics develop from listening and tracking. For example, a firm could set up a hashtag and promote it. Metrics can be quantitative or qualitative. For example, click-through rate (CTR) determines the percentage of consumers that clicked on a link on a site as a quantitative measure. In addition, a qualitative metric could reveal how consumers feel about a product.

Key performance indicators (KPIs) should be embedded at the onset of a social media strategy that can allow almost real-time measurement and evaluation. This provides a foundation for making iterative changes to implementation and tactical execution. As discussed in Chapter 4, marketing analytics uses tools and methods to measure and interpret the effectiveness of marketing activities. Applying analytics to social media performance can help develop better targeted social media campaigns. Selecting valid metrics requires specific objectives that the social media strategy is to obtain. Objectives that are quantitative could include the number of likes on an Instagram post or the CTR of a Facebook post. Table 9.2 provides a list of metrics based on exposure, engagement, influence, impact, and advocacy.

As pointed out in Chapter 2, a comprehensive performance evaluation requires gathering all valid metrics and understanding the way the strategy meets performance standards

TABLE 9.2   SOCIAL MEDIA METRICS

Exposure	Engagement	Influence	Impact	Advocacy
Quantitative	**Quantitative**	**Quantitative**	**Quantitative**	**Quantitative**
Page Visits	Repeat Visits	Links	New Subscribers	Online Ratings
Visitors, Unique Visitors	Time Spent on Site	Association with Brand Attributes	Number of Referrals to website	Ratio Mentions To Recommendations
Visits per Channel (Source)	Total Interactions on Post/Page	Purchase Consideration	Number of Content Downloads	Number of Brand Fans/Advocates
Reach Total Follower (Audience Count)	Likes, Shares Comments, +1s Click-Throughs	Likelihood to Recommend	Number of App Downloads Abandoned Shopping Carts (–)	
Opportunity-to-See	Number of Followers, Friends		Number of Sales Leads Conversion Rate	
CPM (cost per thousand exposures)	Total Audience of All Shares		Sales Repeat Sales	
	Interaction with Profile Use of Hashtags		Purchase Frequency Cost Savings	
	Qualitative	**Qualitative**	**Qualitative**	**Qualitative**
	Mentions People Talking About Brand	Sentiment (Positive, Neutral, Negative)	Satisfaction Loyalty	Content of Ratings/Reviews
		Net Promoter Score		Organic Posts by Advocates Employee
	Klout Score			Ambassadors

Credit Per Source: Barker/Barker/Bormann/Zahay/Roberts. Social Media Marketing, 2E. © 2017 South-Western, a part of Cengage, Inc. Reproduced by permission. www.cengage.com/permissions

TABLE 9.3	GOOGLE ANALYTICS
Real-Time	Data updates live so you can see pageviews, top social traffic, top referrals, top keywords, top active pages, and top locations in real time.
Audience	Audience reports provide insight into demographics, interest, geography, behavior, mobile use, and more.
Acquisition	In-bound traffic is monitored through acquisition reports, allowing you to compare traffic from search, referrals, e-mail, and social media.
Behavior	Evaluate your site's content by seeing how visitors interact with your content. Monitor landing pages, exit pages, site speed, bounce rate, and more.
Conversions	Google Analytics allows users to set goals and objectives to monitor web conversions, like signing up for an e-mail newsletter or completing a purchase.

or underperforms based on expectations. One way to approach this is to use Google Analytics, the largest analytics platform monitoring more than 30 million websites.[73] The Google Analytics dashboard is broken into five sections: Real-Time, Audience, Acquisition, Behavior, and Conversions. Table 9.3 explains the function of each section. Using this tool allows you to identify your website's strengths and weaknesses and uncover opportunities for growth. For example, you may find that organic search traffic is very high, but that your social media traffic is quite low, or you may see a spike in weekday traffic while weekends are slow. KPIs for your social media strategy can include likes, shares, reach, engagement rate, click-through rate (CTR), and conversions. In the conversions dashboard, marketers can set up custom conversion goals to see the impact social media has on their business.

By analyzing rich site traffic data, marketers can better understand their customer and measure the effectiveness of their marketing efforts. For example, PBS uses Google Analytics to monitor the web performance for multiple properties and track key events like user registrations and video views. After analyzing search engine trends, PBS experienced 30 percent more site traffic in the first year after implementation.[74] Google Analytics is arguably the most robust web analytics tool available, and it's free to anyone with a Google account. A premium version, Google Analytics 360 Suite, designed to help companies target potential customers is available for even more in-depth analytics. The tool identifies someone's habits from web and television to mobile, competing with companies like Salesforce and Oracle.[75]

Online Products
Amazon is redefining retailing as it continues to grow and become a bigger part of the online retail landscape.

Eric Broder Van Dyke/Shutterstock.com

9-5 E-MARKETING STRATEGY

LO 9-5 Clarify how digital media affects the four variables of the marketing mix.

More than one-third of the world's population uses the Internet, and this number is growing at a high rate.[76] These trends display a growing need for businesses to use the Internet to reach an increasingly web-savvy population. As more shoppers go online for purchases, the power of traditional brick-and-mortar businesses is lessening.

This makes it essential for businesses, small and large alike, to learn how to effectively use new social media. Most businesses are finding it necessary to use digital marketing to gain or maintain market share.

When Amazon.com first became popular as an online bookstore in the 1990s, the brick-and-mortar bookseller chain Barnes & Noble quickly made online shopping possible through its website, but did not abandon its physical stores. This "bricks-and-clicks" model is now standard for businesses from neighborhood family-owned restaurants to national chain retailers. The following sections will examine how businesses are using these social media forums to create effective marketing strategies on the web.

9-5a Product Considerations

In traditional marketing, marketers must anticipate consumer needs and preferences and then tailor their products to meet these needs. The same is true with marketing products using digital media. Digital media provide an opportunity to add a service dimension to traditional products and create new products only accessible on the Internet. For example, the digital platform Steam provides gamers access to thousands of video games for PC and Mac. These represent products that can only be found in the digital realm.

The ability to access information for any product can have a major impact on buyer decision making. However, with larger companies now launching their own extensive marketing campaigns, and with the constant sophistication of digital technology, many businesses are finding it necessary to upgrade their product offerings to meet consumer needs. In managing a product, it is important to pay attention to consumer-generated brand stories that address quality and performance and impact image.[77] As has been discussed throughout this chapter, the Internet represents a large resource to marketers for learning more about consumer wants and needs.

Some companies now use online advertising campaigns and contests to help develop better products. For example, Volition, a skin care and cosmetics company, crowdsources its new product ideas from its customers. If an idea makes it past the Volition team, tens of thousands of people in the Volition community will vote online whether the product should be produced and then receive a discount if the product is voted in. Using their fan base for new ideas has led to unique and innovative products, and as consumers share their product ideas to their social networks for support from friends and family, awareness increases for this beauty community.[78]

9-5b Pricing Considerations

Pricing relates to perceptions of value and is the most flexible element of the marketing mix. Digital media marketing facilitates both price and nonprice competition, because Internet marketing gives consumers access to more information about products and prices. As consumers become more informed about their options, the demand for low-priced products has grown, leading to the creation of daily deal sites. ShopStyle is an online destination that informs users about fashion trends and connects them with fashion brands and websites. Users can filter their searches by price as well as other criteria. ShopStyle competes on its wide product offering as well as price with its promise of exclusive offers provided to shoppers daily. Several marketers also use buying incentives like online coupons or free samples to generate consumer demand for their product offerings.

Digital connections can help the customer find the price of the product available from various competitors in an instant. Websites provide price information, and mobile applications can help the customer find the lowest price. Consumers can even bargain with retailers in the store by using a smartphone to show the lowest price available during a transaction. While this new access

Pricing Considerations
Online retailers can capture customers with strong value propositions through sales, reward programs, discount codes, and other promotional opportunities.

to price information benefits the consumer, it also places new pressures on the seller to be competitive and to differentiate products so that customers focus on attributes and benefits rather than price.

Retailers and other organizations are beginning to develop e-commerce stores on Facebook and social media sites so that customers can purchase the product they want directly. Facebook partnered with BigCommerce to create a "Shop" section on Facebook pages to allow merchants to share merchandise on the social platform and direct consumers to their website.[79] Brands like Smartwool, YETI and Polkadot Alley have taken advantage of the integration. For the business that wants to compete on price, digital marketing provides unlimited opportunities.

9-5c Distribution Considerations

The role of distribution is to make products available at the right time, at the right place, and in the right quantities. Digital marketing can be viewed as a new distribution channel that helps businesses increase efficiency. The ability to process orders electronically and increase the speed of communications via the Internet reduces inefficiencies, costs, and redundancies while increasing speed throughout the marketing channel. Shipping times and costs have become an important consideration in attracting consumers, prompting many companies to offer consumers low shipping costs or next-day delivery. Digital marketing is also creating new distribution methods for common products. For instance, Amazon.com has expanded into door-to-door deliveries of groceries. Green Amazon Fresh trucks can be found delivering groceries in Seattle, parts of California, New York, Boston, London, and more.[80] It has been estimated that Amazon needs only to capture 4 percent share in the markets in which it operates its grocery system within a ten-year period to be profitable.[81] In response, Whole Foods is also delivering groceries directly to consumers in some markets.

Many online retailers, such as Birchbox, Blue Nile, and Warby Parker, have established a presence in the traditional brick-and-mortar to create a physical presence and increase awareness. Unlike most, Blue Nile's shops, called a "Webroom," are showrooms only, meaning customers can touch and feel the products, but all orders are placed online, saving the company money in distribution costs and real estate costs associated with large storefronts. This trend is a result of increased online competition as well as a trend toward omni-channel retailing where retailers offer a seamless experience on mobile, desktop, or traditional retail spaces. For example, many retailers aim to offer consistent product assortments and pricing on all channels as well as streamline the return process. A customer may research a purchase online, shop in-store, browse an in-store digital catalog, and then use a coupon from the retailer's app at checkout. Seventy-three percent of shoppers use multiple channels while shopping, making a seamless shopping experience a way to differentiate a retailer from its competitors. The survey revealed customers researching online before in-store shopping led to 13 percent more in sales among omni-channel shoppers.[82]

9-5d Promotion Considerations

The majority of this chapter has discussed ways that marketers use digital media to promote products, from creating profiles on social networks to connecting with consumers to inserting brands into virtual social games. Social networking sites also allow marketers to approach promotion in entirely new, creative ways. ColourPop is an example of a digital marketing success story. The company is online only and does no traditional advertising. Instead, it relies on social buzz developed through digital marketing. The company, known for its low price point, became popular through Instagram and YouTube and has a number of Millennial fans, including 4.1 million followers on its Instagram account, 527,000 followers on Twitter, and 1.2 million likes on Facebook. As a result, ColourPop is thriving at a time when the beauty market is more crowded than ever.[83] Marketers who choose to engage in these opportunities have the chance to boost their firms' brand exposure. Califia Farms,

omni-channel Retailing where retailers offer a seamless experience on mobile, desktop, or traditional retail spaces

a natural beverage company, uses Instagram as a platform to showcase its iconic, award-winning packaging, teach consumers new ways to enjoy Califia Farms beverages, and educate consumers on the benefits of their ingredients.[84]

Online advertising includes many types of display advertising, including the use of text, logos, animation, video, photographs, or any other type of graphic display. Currently, Internet advertising revenues surpass $50 billion and continue to grow.[85] A major advantage of Internet advertising is being able to track advertising statistics. High-impact digital advertisements featuring large and interactive formats drive higher response ratios. Marketers are tracking and maximizing Internet advertising to improve the value of their products.[86] Google's AdWords is the dominant player in the online advertising market, and the company wants to take its success into the mobile realm as well. To achieve its goals, Google launched an initiative called Enhanced Campaigns and required users of its AdWords service to participate. Enhanced Campaigns requires advertisers to bid on advertisements across a number of devices, including mobile and tablets.[87] Despite the extensive use of online promotion from all types of industries, small businesses do not engage in paid Internet advertising as much due to smaller budgets. Facebook and other digital companies are studying ways to communicate to smaller businesses how paid advertising can create value for their companies.[88]

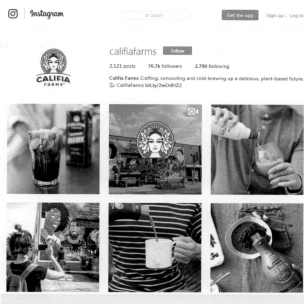

Promotion Considerations
Califia Farms uses social media to showcase their unique bottle design and teach consumers how to use their products.

Digital media has also opened opportunities for business-to-business promotions. As more companies adopt digital marketing strategies, the need for better platforms and digital solutions have grown. Digital promotions all attempt to increase brand awareness and market to consumers. As a result of online promotion, consumers are more informed, reading user-generated content before making purchasing decisions and increasingly shopping at Internet stores. Consumer consumption patterns are changing radically, and marketers must adapt their promotional efforts to meet these new patterns.

9-6 ETHICAL AND LEGAL ISSUES

LO 9-6 Identify legal and ethical considerations in digital marketing.

How marketers use technology to gather information—both online and offline—raises numerous legal and ethical issues. The popularity and widespread use of the Internet grew so quickly that global regulatory systems were unable to keep pace. The global regulatory environment is not uniform, with areas such as Europe more concerned about privacy than the United States. Even today, courts are debating over laws that would affect consumer Internet activities. For instance, are threats posted on Facebook protected speech according to the First Amendment? The U.S. Supreme Court ruled that a person could not be convicted based on threats unless there is evidence that a reasonable person would regard the communications as a threat, but protected speech is evaluated on a case by case basis. The Federal Trade Commission (FTC) regulates and makes rules for privacy, fraud, and misappropriation of copyrighted intellectual property, as well as other illicit Internet activities.

The FTC rules for online marketing are the same as for any other form of communication or advertising. These rules help maintain the credibility of the Internet as an advertising medium. To avoid deception, all online communication must tell the truth and cannot mislead consumers. In addition, all claims must be substantiated. If online communication is unfair and causes injury that is substantial and not reasonably avoidable and is not outweighed by other benefits, it is considered deceptive. The FTC identifies risk areas for online communication and issues warnings to consumers as misconduct is reported. Some of the areas include testimonials and endorsements, warranties and guarantees, free products, and mail and telephone orders. The FTC periodically joins with other law enforcement agencies to monitor the Internet for potentially false or deceptive online claims, including fraud, privacy, and intellectual property issues.

Influencer marketing is relatively new compared with other forms of digital marketing, so it should be no surprise there have been road bumps for early adopters. Due to concerns about dishonest advertising, the Federal Trade Commission (FTC) requires influencers to clearly disclose any connection they have with brands they promote. Neglecting to make a disclosure is viewed as deceptive advertising. Cases have been filed against Warner Bros. Home Entertainment, who paid PewDiePie, YouTube's number one most subscribed channel, for an endorsement of its video game *Middle-Earth: Shadow of Mordor*, and Lord & Taylor, who paid various influencers to promote their dresses, all without disclosures. According to the FTC, any level of compensation much be disclosed, whether a partnership is paid or an influencer strictly receives free product.[89]

9-6a **Privacy**

Unfortunately, consumers or firms that try to protect their privacy cannot control the Internet environment where cybercrime exists. The FTC attempts to regulate and prevent identity theft, online fraud, and provide information on privacy to consumers and marketers. The use of consumer data associated with marketing analytics sets the stage for hackers to steal or demand ransom for files. A data breach at Yahoo compromised at least 500 million users' data. Yahoo is still under investigation over the incident because it took the company two years to disclose the incident. There is a regulatory guideline that firms need to disclose material information about cybersecurity incidents once they determine it could affect investors.[90]

Determining what data is needed and how to protect it is the first step for protecting consumers. In our current environment, data breaches and piracy will continue to occur. All organizations involved in social media marketing have a responsibility to protect the consumer by understanding risks and the development of effective cybersecurity. All organizations need a contingency or crisis management plan to respond if a data breach occurs.[91]

One of the most significant privacy issues involves the use of personal information companies collect from website visitors in their efforts to foster long-term customer relationships. Some people fear that the collection of personal information from website users violates users' privacy, especially when it is done without their knowledge. Additionally, governments have issued subpoenas to companies like Google and Microsoft for user information when pursuing legal action. Smartphone companies like Apple Inc. resist sharing code that provides access to a person's phone records. On the other hand, the U.S. Justice Department gets some of its most effective evidence from e-mails in processing cases.

Due to consumer concerns over privacy, the FTC is considering developing regulations that would protect consumer privacy by limiting the amount of consumer information that businesses can gather online. Other countries are pursuing similar actions. The European Union passed a law requiring companies to get users' consent before using cookies to track their information. In the United States, some government officials have called for a "do not track" bill, similar to the "do not call" bill for telephones, to allow users to opt out of having their information tracked. Legislators reintroduced a Do Not Track Kids bill that would make it illegal for companies to track children between the ages of 13 and 15 over the Internet or mobile devices without parental permission (currently, marketers are prohibited from gathering information about consumers aged 13 or younger without parental permission). They also desire a system that would erase information that these teenagers found to be embarrassing.[92]

Certain laws pertaining to privacy have also taken on new meanings with the increase in digital marketing. For instance, the Federal Video Privacy Protection Act requires that any marketers who wish to disclose or share information about a consumer's video content consumption must obtain separate, independent consent from the consumer. This means that a company cannot share information about videos that users watched on their sites with other parties without permission.[93] Marketers are also seeing opportunities to capitalize on users' discontent with having their data collected. Social networking site Ello markets the fact that they do not collect customer data. Ello, created for artists, designers, musicians, illustrators, and architects, never sells ads or personal data to third parties. Wickr, a mobile messaging app, refuses to store information on its central server, preventing the organization from keeping a digital record of user activity, claiming no conversation can be tracked.[94]

While consumers may welcome such added protections, web advertisers, who use consumer information to target advertisements to online consumers, see it as a threat. In response to impending legislation, many web advertisers are attempting self-regulation in order to stay ahead of the game. For instance, the Digital Advertising Alliance (DAA) has adopted privacy guidelines for online advertisers. The DAA has created a "trusted mark" icon that websites adhering to their guidelines can display. However, because it is self-regulatory, not all digital advertisers may choose to participate in its programs.[95] Table 9.4 describes industry best practices for digital marketers to consider before launching digital marketing campaigns. It is important for digital marketers to craft campaigns that comply with FTC rules.

9-6b Online Fraud

Online fraud includes any attempt to purposely deceive online. Online fraud includes, among other things, attempts to deceive consumers into releasing personal information. Hacking has also become a major problem in the digital realm. Hackers break into websites and steal users' personal information. Home Depot, Target, and J.P. Morgan are some notable cases where cybercriminals hacked into these companies' systems and stole information. Sony experienced a devastating attack that shut down its entire computer network and resulted in the theft of 27-gigabytes of files.[96] The FTC considers ransomware as the most challenging cybersecurity issue at this time. Cybercriminals gain access to consumer and business computers, encrypt files, and then demand a ransom payment for providing a key to unlock the files.[97]

online fraud Any attempt to conduct fraudulent activities online, including deceiving consumers into releasing personal information

TABLE 9.4	BEST PRACTICES FOR DIGITAL MARKETING IMPLEMENTATION

1. Implement privacy during the conceptualization phase of the marketing campaign.

2. Disclose all passive tracking systems used to collect information.

3. Data collection involving third parties should involve clear guidelines regarding how the data will be used and who owns it. Provide ways for users to opt-out of tracking or e-mail marketing through visible notices.

4. Screen age of users if appropriate for the campaign. Collecting personal information of children under 13 requires parental consent. If marketing to children is allowed, ensure that the content and language is appropriate for the age range targeted.

5. Ensure that all tracking or data-collection activities that occur do not conflict with the company's online privacy policy.

6. Adopt security measures for any data collected from users. User information must be protected, particularly if it is identifiable.

7. Be aware of all legal requirements and industry codes of ethics on digital marketing.

Source: Adapted from Jesse Brody, "Terms and Conditions," *Marketing News*, November 2014, pp. 34-41; Direct Marketing Association, *Direct Marketing Association's Guidelines for Ethical Business Practice*, https://thedma.org/accountability/ethics-and-compliance/dma-ethical-guidelines/ (accessed March 25, 2017).

iStock.com/Paul Gregg

Online Fraud

Phishing is a type of fraud that occurs when cybercriminals trick users into providing their personal information by pretending to be a legitimate web entity. Cybercriminals then use this information to pose as the user online.

Organizations and social networking sites alike are developing ways to combat fraudulent activity on digital media sites. For instance, organizations known as brand-protection firms monitor social networks for fraudulent accounts.[98] Companies are purchasing more sophisticated security programs to protect clients' information. However, the best protection for consumers is to be careful when divulging information online. Privacy advocates advise that the best way to stay out of trouble is to avoid giving out personal information, such as Social Security numbers or credit card information, unless the site is definitely legitimate. Using a different password for each website users visit is another important way to avoid becoming the victim of online fraud. Passwords should be complex enough that a cybercriminal cannot easily guess it. However, many consumers do not do this because of the hassle it takes in remembering complex passwords for multiple sites.[99]

9-6c Intellectual Property and Illegal Activity

The Internet has also created issues associated with intellectual property and illicit e-commerce. Intellectual property is the copyrighted or trademarked ideas and creative materials developed to solve problems, carry out applications, and educate and entertain others. Each year, intellectual property losses in the United States total billions of dollars stemming from the illegal copying of computer programs, movies, compact discs, and books. Peer-to-peer file sharing sites such as Pirate Bay containing digital content—much of it copyrighted—makes it easier for copyright violations. Although authorities have tried to shut down Pirate Bay through raids and arrests, it continues to pop up again with servers in different countries.[100] The software industry is particularly hard-hit when it comes to the pirating of materials and illegal file sharing. The Business Software Alliance estimates the total losses of unlicensed software installations on personal computers is $52.2 billion.[101] Consumers view illegal downloading in different ways, depending on the motivation for the behavior. If the motivation is primarily utilitarian, or for personal gain, then the act is viewed as less ethically acceptable than if it is for a hedonistic reason, or just for fun.[102]

Consumers rationalize pirating software, video games, and music for a number of reasons. First, many consumers feel they just do not have the money to pay for what they want. Second, because their friends engage in piracy and swap digital content, they feel influenced to engage in this activity. Third, for some, the attraction is the thrill of getting away with it and the slim risk of consequences. Fourth, to some extent, there are people who think they are smarter than others; engaging in piracy allows them to show how tech savvy they are.[103]

Sales of counterfeit goods are another problem. Knockoffs of popular products seized by federal officials annually are valued at over $1 billion. Counterfeit products, particularly from overseas, are thriving on the Internet because they can be shipped directly to customers without having to be examined by customs officials when shipped through ports. Some firms, including UGG Boots, are creating online services allowing users to type in the address to verify whether the electronic retailer is a legitimate seller.[104]

As digital media continues to evolve, more legal and ethical issues will certainly arise. As a result, marketers and all other users of digital media should make an effort to learn and abide by ethical practices to ensure they get the most out of the resources available in this growing medium. Doing so will allow marketers to maximize the tremendous opportunities digital media has to offer.

Chapter Review

9-1 Define digital media, digital marketing, and electronic marketing.

Digital media are electronic media that function using digital codes—when we refer to digital media, we are referring to media available via computers, cellular phones, smartphones, and other digital devices that have been released in recent years. Digital marketing uses all digital media, including the Internet and mobile and interactive channels, to develop communication and exchanges with customers. Electronic marketing refers to the strategic process of pricing, distributing, and promoting products, and discovering the desires of customers using digital media and digital marketing. Our definition of e-marketing goes beyond the Internet and also includes mobile phones, banner ads, digital outdoor marketing, and social networks.

9-2 Summarize the growth and importance of digital marketing.

The phenomenal growth of the Internet has provided unprecedented opportunities for marketers to forge interactive relationships with consumers. As the Internet and digital communication technologies have advanced, they have made it possible to target markets more precisely and reach markets that were previously inaccessible. One of the most important benefits of e-marketing is the ability of marketers and customers to share information. Through websites, social networks, and other digital media, consumers can learn about everything they consume and use in life. As a result, the Internet is changing the way marketers communicate and develop relationships. For many businesses, engaging in digital marketing activities is essential to maintaining competitive advantages.

9-3 Describe different types of digital media and how they can be used for marketing.

Digital media in marketing is advancing at a rapid rate. The self-sustaining nature of digital technology means that current advances act as a catalyst to spur even faster development. As faster digital transmissions evolve, marketing applications are emerging that offer an opportunity for companies to reach consumers in new ways.

There are many types of digital media that can be used as marketing tools. A social network is a website where users can create a profile and interact with other users, post information, and engage in other forms of web-based communication. Blogs (short for "weblogs") are web-based journals in which writers can editorialize and interact with other Internet users. A wiki is a type of software that creates an interface that enables users to add or edit the content of some types of websites. Media-sharing sites allow marketers

to share photos, videos, and podcasts but are more limited in scope in how companies interact with consumers. One type of media sharing is podcasts, which are audio or video files that can be downloaded from the Internet with a subscription that automatically delivers new content to listening devices or personal computers. Virtual sites involve user-created, three-dimensional worlds that have their own economies and currencies, lands, and residents who come in every shape and size. Mobile devices are becoming an important mechanism for marketing. Mobile applications are software programs that run on mobile devices and give users access to certain content. Widgets are small bits of software on a website, desktop, or mobile device that performs a simple purpose, such as providing stock quotes or blog updates.

As a result of these new marketing channels, digital marketing is moving from a niche strategy to becoming a core consideration in the marketing mix. At the same time, digital technologies are largely changing the dynamic between marketer and consumer. Consumers use social networking sites and mobile applications to do a variety of activities. The menu of digital media alternatives continues to grow, requiring marketers to make informed decisions about strategic approaches.

9-4 Describe how marketers can measure the success of a digital strategy.

It is essential that marketers focus on the changing social behaviors of consumers and how they interact with digital media. Consumers now have a greater ability to regulate the information that they view as well as the rate and sequence of their exposure to that information. The Internet is sometimes referred to as a *pull* medium because users determine which websites they are going to view; the marketer has only limited ability to control the content to which users are exposed, and in what sequence. Marketers must modify their marketing strategies to adapt to the changing behaviors of online consumers.

Monitoring and evaluating digital media helps marketers maximize resources and minimize costs. Key performance indicators (KPIs) that relate to specific objectives are defined at the onset of a social media strategy for real-time measurement and evaluation. Tools like Google Analytics helps marketers to measure and interpret the effectiveness of marketing activities. Applying analytics to social media performance, from likes to clicks, can help develop better targeted social media campaigns.

9-5 Clarify how digital media affects the four variables of the marketing mix.

The reasons for a digital marketing strategy are many. The low costs of many digital media channels can provide major savings in promotional budgets. Digital marketing is allowing companies to connect with market segments that are harder to reach with traditional media. Despite the challenges involved in such a strategy, digital marketing is opening up new avenues in the relationship between businesses and consumers.

The marketing mix of product, price, distribution, and promotion continues to apply in digital marketing. From a product perspective, digital media provide an opportunity to add a service dimension to traditional products and create new products that could only be accessible on the Internet. Many businesses find it necessary to continually upgrade their product offerings to meet consumer needs. From a pricing dimension, digital media facilitates both price and nonprice competition, because Internet marketing gives consumers access to more information about products and prices. For distribution, the ability to process orders electronically and increase the speed of communications via the Internet reduces inefficiencies, costs, and redundancies while increasing speed throughout the marketing channel. Finally, marketers can promote their products to consumers in new and creative ways using digital media.

9-6 Identify legal and ethical considerations in digital marketing.

How marketers use technology to gather information—both online and offline—has raised numerous legal and ethical issues. Privacy is one of the most significant issues, involving the use of personal information that companies collect from website visitors in their efforts to foster long-term relationships with customers. Some people fear that the collection of personal information from website users may violate users' privacy, especially when it is done without their knowledge.

Online fraud includes any attempt to conduct dishonest activities online. Online fraud includes, among other things, attempts to deceive consumers into releasing personal information. Another concern is that hackers may break into websites and steal users' personal information, enabling them to commit identity theft. Organizations and social networking sites alike are developing ways to combat fraudulent activity on new digital media sites.

The Internet has also created issues associated with intellectual property as well as other illicit online activities. Intellectual property is the copyrighted or trademarked ideas and creative materials developed to solve problems, carry out applications, and educate and entertain others. Each year, intellectual property losses in the United States total billions of dollars stemming from the illegal copying of computer programs, movies, compact discs, and books. The software industry is particularly hard-hit when it comes to pirating materials and illegal file sharing. The selling of illegal drugs and counterfeit products is also becoming more common over the Internet.

 Go to www.cengagebrain.com for resources to help you master the content in this chapter as well as for materials that will expand your marketing knowledge!

Developing Your Marketing Plan

When developing a marketing strategy using new digital media, a marketer must be aware of the strengths and weaknesses of these new media. Digital media are relatively new to the field of marketing and have different pros and cons relative to traditional media sources. Different products and target markets may be more or less suited for different digital media outlets.

1. Review the key concepts of addressability, interactivity, accessibility, connectivity, and control in Table 9.1, and explain how they relate to social media. Think about how a marketing strategy focused on social media differs from a marketing campaign reliant on traditional media sources.

2. No matter what marketing media are used, determining the correct marketing mix for your company is always important. Think about how social media might affect the marketing mix.

3. Discuss different digital media and the pros and cons of using each as part of your marketing plan.

Key Concepts

digital media 214
digital marketing 214
electronic marketing
    (e-marketing) 214

social network
    218
blogs 220
wiki 221

podcast 223
mobile application 224
widgets 225

omni-channel 230
online fraud 233

Issues for Discussion and Review

1. How does e-marketing differ from traditional marketing?
2. How can marketers exploit characteristics of digital marketing to improve relations with customers?
3. Why are social networks becoming an increasingly important marketing tool? Find an example online in which a company has improved the effectiveness of its marketing strategy by using social networks.
4. How has new media changed consumer behavior? What are the opportunities and challenges that face marketers with this in mind?
5. Describe the ways marketers can measure digital strategy success.
6. How can marketers exploit the characteristics of the Internet to improve the product element of their marketing mixes?
7. Describe how social media affects the push-pull dynamic of distribution.
8. How do the characteristics of e-marketing affect the promotion element of the marketing mix?
9. How has digital media affected the pricing of products? Give examples of the opportunities and challenges presented to marketers in light of these changes.
10. Name and describe the major ethical and legal issues that have developed in response to the Internet. How should policymakers address these issues?

VIDEO CASE 9
Zappos Drives Sales through Relationship Building on Social Media

Zappos was one of the first companies to incorporate social media into their business, and they have established themselves as a leader in its use. Zappos focuses on building customer relationships through human interaction and emphasizes comments related to service and fun. For example, if a customer experienced a problem with an order or has a question about a product, the Zappos team ensures that these comments are responded to honestly, authentically, and in a timely manner. Sometimes customers will leave fun comments about their experience with the company. Zappos takes these comments just as seriously. The heart of their operation is to "deliver happiness." In return, up to 75 percent of sales are from repeat customers.

Zappos does not maintain a specific strategy for marketing on social media, nor do they have a policy for responding to customers. As with any Zappos's activity, marketing is guided by the company's core values, including creating "WOW" customer experiences and a culture characterized by fun and a little weirdness. Product Manager Robert Richman explains, "Social media is a communication tool … and we want to be available to people wherever they're at." If customers are congregating on Facebook, Zappos makes sure to have a presence there so they can engage them in conversation. In fact, Kenshoo, a digital marketing specialist, has recognized Zappos's Facebook activity for its effectiveness. Over a two-month period, the company initiated 85,000 visits to their webpage through status updates.

Forty-two percent of these updates led to purchases, while the other 58 percent left comments or likes on the webpage.

Rob Siefker, director of the customer loyalty team, emphasizes the importance of using Twitter. He states, "Most people went on Twitter as a way to interact with friends. Some companies went on there and solely focused on the business or service aspect. For us, part of service is being playful … it makes it much more human to the customer … it makes it much more personal." Most companies that use social media use it for promotion rather than for truly interacting with customers. This creates a distance between the company and the customer. Mr. Siefker points out that customers "feel when they are being marketed to, and they know there is a reason for it." However, Zappos strives to go beyond using digital media simply for promotion purposes. They want to forge a real connection with customers and describe themselves as a human company, requiring strong interactions between customers and the organization.

The company has been able to achieve rapid growth through their use of values in their marketing activities. They are a large company with a small business feel when it comes to how they treat their customers and how their customers feel about them. This is due in large part to their presence on social media and the way they cross-promote their activities across platforms. For example, if they receive or post a comment on Facebook, they will also share it on Twitter, YouTube, and Pinterest in order to reach other current or potential customers. While the company focuses mainly on current customers, this activity generates widespread effects such as word-of-mouth marketing that brings in more new customers. The current customers in this sense serve as brand advocates or brand enthusiasts.

Zappos also generates interest by encouraging customers to share promotions and purchases with friends. Another tactic they used on Facebook was to ask people to like their page. It read, "Let's be in a Like-Like relationship." Then they asked users to sign up for their e-mail list. The order in which they make these requests gives people the impression that Zappos is indeed concerned about building relationships. They also have exclusive content for people who opt to become fans. Once deemed a fan, people are able to see special offers, videos, and promotions and share comments about them. Finally, Zappos used an engagement strategy

called "Fan of the Week Contest," where people were encouraged to take and post photos of themselves with Zappos products. Then users voted on the best photo, and the one with the most votes won. Zappos would post the photo on their website for all to see. Overall, Zappos ensures that they are using social media to build relationships by bringing customers closer to the company. Marketing for Zappos is an authentic and human activity that is not about selling products but building relationships.[105]

Questions for Discussion

1. Describe some ways in which Zappos uses digital media tools.
2. How does Zappos encourage word-of-mouth marketing through digital media?
3. How does Zappos use digital media to create an authentic relationship with consumers?

Part 4

Kaspars Grinvalds/Shutterstock.com

Product and Price Decisions

We are now prepared to analyze the decisions and activities associated with developing and maintaining effective marketing mixes. **PART 4** explores the product and price ingredients of the marketing mix. **CHAPTER 10** focuses on basic product concepts and on branding and packaging decisions. **CHAPTER 11** analyzes various dimensions regarding product management, including line extensions and product modification, new-product development, product deletions, and the management of services as products. In **CHAPTER 12** we discuss a number of factors that affect how pricing decisions are made:

Product, Branding, and Packaging Concepts

chapter 10

Juanmonino/iStock Unreleased/Getty Images

LEARNING OBJECTIVES

10-1 Define the concept of a product.

10-2 Discuss how products are classified.

10-3 Explain the concepts of product line and product mix and how they are related.

10-4 Explore the product life cycle and its impact on marketing strategies.

10-5 Discuss the product adoption process.

10-6 Explain the major components of branding, including brand types, branding strategies, and brand protection.

10-7 Describe the major packaging functions and design considerations, and how packaging is used in marketing strategies.

10-8 Identify the functions of labeling and legal issues related to labeling.

What Are Technics and Shinola? Old and New Retro Brands

Decades ago, Panasonic put its Technics brand on state-of-the-art audio equipment such as turntables. But as vinyl records gave way to cassettes and CDs, followed by digital music, Panasonic shelved the Technics brand. In 2016, Panasonic revived it with a high-profile introduction of a new Technics turntable. The revival caused a stir among the new generation of vinyl fans who recognized the brand's long-time association with audio innovation. The Technics brand has an authentic 20th-century pedigree, but the audio technology it represents today is 21st century, all the way.

In contrast, Shinola is a retro brand reborn for a marketing purpose. Originally, Shinola was a brand of shoe polish. By the 1960s, Shinola was bankrupt and the brand was out of circulation, but the name lingered for years at the edges of American pop culture. Then entrepreneur Tom Kartsotis bought the Shinola brand in 2011 through his Texas-based company, Bedrock Brands, and added a 21st-century twist. Shinola would now brand hip, classically-styled products made in Detroit, bringing to mind the ingenuity of American manufacturing and contributing to the local economy.

Shinola wristwatches and bicycles proved so popular that the company soon introduced leather goods, a turntable, and a line of jewelry. It already operates 21 Shinola stores and is building a Shinola-branded boutique hotel in Detroit. "Everything we build has both form and function," says Shinola's chief marketing officer. "Though our mission is to create quality jobs, our products are design-led, offering great value with a great story that's built to last."[1]

Goran Bogicevic/Shutterstock.com

good A tangible physical entity

service An intangible result of the application of human and mechanical efforts to people or objects

idea A concept, philosophy, image, or issue

Technics and Shinola are brands that consumers use to identify specific products. In this chapter, we first define a product and discuss how products are classified. Next, we examine the concepts of product line and product mix. We then explore the stages of the product life cycle and the effect of each life-cycle stage on marketing strategies. Next, we outline the product adoption process. Then we discuss branding, its value to customers and marketers, brand loyalty, and brand equity. We examine the various types of brands and consider how companies choose and protect brands, the various branding policies employed, brand extensions, co-branding, and brand licensing. We also look at the role of packaging, the functions of packaging, issues to consider in packaging design, and how the package can be a major element in marketing strategy. We conclude with a discussion of labeling and some related legal issues.

10-1 WHAT IS A PRODUCT?

LO 10-1 Define the concept of a product.

WESTLAKE DERMATOLOGY®
SmartLipo

Westlake Dermatology

Services as Products
It can be difficult for service organizations such as Westlake Dermatology to illustrate services in their advertisements. Often, service organizations will use images to demonstrate the benefits of their service offerings.

As defined in Chapter 1, a *product* is a good, a service, or an idea received in an exchange. It can be either tangible or intangible and includes functional, social, and psychological utilities or benefits. It also includes supporting services, such as installation, guarantees, product information, and promises of repair or maintenance. A **good** is a tangible physical entity, such as a Nintendo Switch gaming system or a Starbucks latte. A **service**, in contrast, is intangible; it is the result of the application of human and mechanical efforts to people or objects. Examples of services include a concert performance by Beyoncé, online car insurance, a medical examination, and child day care. Many marketers of intangible products try to make them seem more tangible to consumers through advertisements that employ tangible images that provoke ideas. Skin treatments and cosmetic dermatology products are another example of services. In the advertisement for Westlake Dermatology, the business primarily displays a large image of a young woman in a swimsuit. The ad implies that users of its SmartLipo service will be able to dress similarly because they will have great skin to show off. An **idea** is a concept, philosophy, image, or issue. Ideas provide the psychological stimulation that aids in solving problems or adjusting to the environment. For example, Mothers Against Drunk Driving (MADD) promotes safe consumption of alcohol and stricter enforcement of laws against drunk driving. In the Frost Bank advertisement, marketers want to stimulate a concept in consumers' minds that Frost will satisfy consumers according to their banking needs.

It is useful to think of a total product offering as having three interdependent elements: the core product itself, its supplemental features, and its symbolic or experiential benefits (see Figure 10.1). The core product consists of a product's fundamental utility or main benefit and usually addresses a fundamental need of the consumer. Most consumers, however, appreciate additional features and services. For instance, a basic cell phone allows consumers to make calls, but increasingly consumers expect supplemental features such as unlimited texting, widely available high-speed Internet access, and apps. Consumers also may seek out symbolic benefits, such as a trendy brand name, when purchasing a phone.

Supplemental features provide added value or attributes that are in addition to the core product's utility or benefit. These features often include such perks as free installation, delivery, training, or financing. These supplemental attributes are not required to make the core product function effectively, but they help to differentiate one product brand from another and may increase customer loyalty. For example, Drury Hotels creates customer loyalty through strong customer service and supplemental benefits. In addition to its core product, the hotel's value package offers supplemental product features including free breakfast, free Wi-Fi, and free popcorn and soda in the hotel lobby, which reinforce its tagline, "the extras aren't extra."[2] These supplemental benefits differentiate the hotel chain in customers' minds, making them feel as if they are getting a better deal than they would receive at rival hotels.

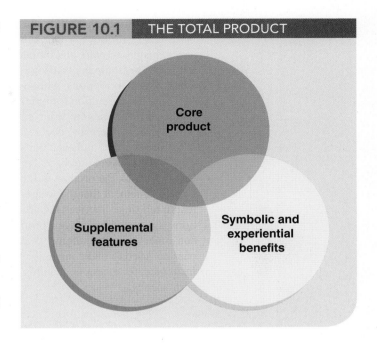

FIGURE 10.1   THE TOTAL PRODUCT

- Core product
- Supplemental features
- Symbolic and experiential benefits

Finally, customers also receive benefits based on their experiences with the product, which gives symbolic meaning to many products (and brands) for buyers. For some consumers, the simple act of shopping gives them pleasure, which lends symbolic value to the act and improves their attitudes about the products they are buying. Some retailers capitalize on this by striving to create a special, personalized experience for customers. Even well-established retail chains are recognizing the importance of an individualized customer experience for gaining a competitive advantage. McDonald's, known for its quick service, is testing a program in

EMERGING TRENDS IN MARKETING

Hello, Siri, Alexa, Cortana, and Google

Virtual assistants are adding fun and functionality to a wider variety of products, thanks to Apple's Siri, Amazon's Alexa, Microsoft's Cortana, and Google's Google (yes, that's the name). This technology, backed by artificial intelligence, enables a smartphone or another device to recognize and respond to voice commands, for hands-off convenience.

Apple built Siri into its iPhones as a virtual assistant starting in 2011. Siri's novelty helped propel the female-voiced feature into pop culture and set iPhones apart from competing phones. As virtual assistants move into the mainstream, Apple has adapted Siri to work with other digital devices.

Amazon's virtual assistant is Alexa, built into the online retailer's Echo speaker. Users can verbally ask the assistant to turn on the outside lights, check the time in Tokyo, play a favorite album, or place an order at Amazon. Now Amazon is allowing Alexa to appear in a wide range of products from other marketers, including cars and refrigerators.

Microsoft's Cortana virtual assistant became part of the Windows phone operating system in 2014. Cortana was originally a code name used during development, chosen because it's the name of an artificial intelligence charter in the *Halo* video game. Then Microsoft discovered that the name was more popular than alternatives like Naomi and Alyx, and kept it for the launch.

Google has its own virtual assistant for smart-home systems. Rather than choosing a separate name for this technology, Google wants customers to perceive it "as an extension and evolution of Google itself." Google is building this technology into its Home speaker, Pixel phones, and messaging app Allo, among other products.[a]

some of its stores that allows customers to customize their sandwiches by choosing bun, protein, and various topping bundles, such as buffalo bacon (blue cheese spread, buffalo sauce, bacon, tomato, and lettuce) and pico de gallo (guacamole, cheese, ranch sauce, and lettuce). The company is also offering larger and smaller sizes of its iconic Big Mac to give customers more options. Although customization takes more time and may conflict with McDonald's reputation for quick service, Millennials—McDonald's key target market for this venture—appear to value customization over time.[3]

The atmosphere and décor of a retail store, the variety and depth of product choices, the customer support, and even the sounds and smells all contribute to the experiential element. Thus, when buyers purchase a product, they are really buying the benefits and satisfaction they think the product will provide. A Rolex or Patek Philippe watch is purchased to make a statement that the wearer has high status or has achieved financial success—not just to tell time. Services in particular are purchased on the basis of expectations. Expectations, suggested by images, promises, and symbols, as well as processes and delivery, help consumers to make judgments about tangible and intangible products. Often symbols and cues are used to make intangible products more tangible, or real, to the consumer. Prudential Insurance, for example, features the Rock of Gibraltar on its logo to symbolize strength and permanency.

10-2 CLASSIFYING PRODUCTS

LO 10-2 Discuss how products are classified.

Products fall into one of two general categories. Products purchased to satisfy personal and family needs are **consumer products**. Those bought to use in a firm's operations, to resell, or to make other products are **business products**. Consumers buy products to satisfy their personal wants, whereas business buyers seek to satisfy the goals of their organizations. Product classifications are important because they may influence pricing, distribution, and promotion decisions. In this section, we examine the characteristics of consumer and business products and explore the marketing activities associated with some of these products.

10-2a **Consumer Products**

The most widely accepted approach to classifying consumer products is based on characteristics of consumer buying behavior. It divides products into four categories: convenience, shopping, specialty, and unsought products. However, not all buyers behave in the same way when purchasing a specific type of product. Thus, a single product might fit into several categories. To minimize complexity, marketers think in terms of how buyers *generally* behave when purchasing a specific item. Examining the four traditional categories of consumer products can provide further insight.

Convenience Products

Convenience products are relatively inexpensive, frequently purchased items for which buyers exert only minimal purchasing effort. They range from bread, soft drinks, and chewing gum to gasoline and newspapers. The buyer spends little time planning the purchase or comparing available brands or sellers. Even a buyer who prefers a specific brand will generally choose a substitute if the preferred brand is not conveniently available. A convenience product is normally marketed through many retail outlets, such as gas stations, drugstores, and supermarkets. Coca-Cola products, for instance, are available in grocery stores, convenience stores, gas stations, restaurants, and airports—among many other outlets. Because sellers experience high inventory turnover, per-unit gross margins can be relatively low. Producers of convenience products, such as Wrigley's chewing gum, expect little

consumer products Products purchased to satisfy personal and family needs

business products Products bought to use in an organization's operations, to resell, or to make other products

convenience products Relatively inexpensive, frequently purchased items for which buyers exert minimal purchasing effort

promotional effort at the retail level and thus must provide it themselves with advertising and sales promotion. Packaging and displays are also important because many convenience items are available only on a self-service basis at the retail level, and thus the package plays a major role in selling the product.

Shopping Products

Shopping products are items for which buyers are willing to expend considerable effort in planning and making the purchase. Buyers spend much time comparing stores and brands with respect to prices, product features, qualities, services, and perhaps warranties. Shoppers may compare products at a number of outlets such as Best Buy, Amazon.com, Lowe's, or Home Depot; they may begin their buying process at the websites of these stores. Appliances, bicycles, furniture, stereos, cameras, and shoes exemplify shopping products. These products are expected to last a fairly long time, are more expensive than convenience products but still within the budgets of most consumers, and are purchased less frequently than convenience items. Shopping products are distributed via fewer retail outlets than convenience products.

Because shopping products are purchased less frequently, inventory turnover is lower, and marketing channel members expect to receive higher gross margins to compensate for the lower turnover. In certain situations, both shopping products and convenience products may be marketed in the same location. For instance, retailers such as Target or Walmart carry shopping products such as televisions, furniture, and cameras as well as groceries and other convenience products. Pop Secret microwave popcorn is a convenience product that can be purchased in most stores that sell food items. On the other hand, Skechers GOrun athletic shoes are shopping products available in fewer outlets. People are willing to put forth considerable effort to find the right type and fit of athletic shoe to satisfy their performance footwear needs. Although Pop Secret is a convenience product, the company uses advertising to tout its flavor in comparison to a rival brand. In the Skechers advertisement, the ad displays the shoe and compares it to lightning while touting its advanced features.

shopping products Items for which buyers are willing to expend considerable effort in planning and making purchases

Convenience vs. Shopping Products
Convenience products such as Pop Secret do not require much shopping effort. However, customers might expend considerable shopping effort when purchasing Skechers GOruns.

specialty products Items, with unique characteristics, that buyers are willing to expend considerable effort to obtain

unsought products Products purchased to solve a sudden problem, products of which customers are unaware, and products that people do not necessarily think about buying

A marketer must consider several key issues to market a shopping product effectively, including how to allocate resources, whether personal selling is needed, and the level of cooperation in the supply chain. Although advertising shopping products often requires a large budget, an even larger percentage of the overall budget is needed if marketers determine that personal selling is required. The producer and the marketing channel members usually expect some cooperation from one another with respect to providing parts and repair services and performing promotional activities. Marketers should consider these issues carefully so that they can choose the best course for promoting these products.

Specialty Products

Specialty products possess one or more unique characteristics, and generally buyers are willing to expend considerable effort to obtain them. On average, this is the most expensive category of products. Buyers conduct research, plan the purchase of a specialty product, know exactly what they want, and will not accept a substitute. Examples of specialty products include fine jewelry or limited-edition collector's items. When searching for specialty products, buyers do not compare alternatives and are unlikely to base their decision on price. They are concerned primarily with finding an outlet that sells the preselected product. Vacheron Constantin watches are a specialty product with limited distribution. Vacheron Constantin strives to spark a desire for its prestige timepieces with an aesthetically pleasing advertisement featuring a close up of a watch to highlight its craftsmanship. The ad also calls attention to the watchmaker's long history and the fact that the watches are made in Geneva.

Marketers will approach their efforts for specialty products differently from convenience or shopping products in several ways. Specialty products are often distributed through a very limited number of retail outlets. Similar to shopping products, they are purchased infrequently, causing lower inventory turnover and thus requiring high gross margins to be profitable.

Unsought Products

Unsought products are those purchased when a sudden problem must be solved, products of which customers are unaware until they see them in a store or online, and products that people do not plan on purchasing. Emergency medical services and automobile repairs are examples of products needed quickly and suddenly to solve a problem. A consumer who is sick or injured has little time to plan to go to an emergency medical center or hospital and will find the closest location to receive service. Likewise, in the event of a broken fan belt in a car, a consumer likely will seek the nearest auto repair facility or call AAA to minimize the length of time before the car is operational again. In such cases, speed of problem resolution is more important than price or other features a buyer might normally consider if there were more time for making a decision. Companies such as ServiceMaster, which markets emergency services such as disaster recovery, carpet cleaning, and plumbing repair, are making the purchases of these unsought products more bearable by building trust with consumers through recognizable brands and superior functional performance.

OVERSEAS

Bearing the prestigious Hallmark of Geneva, this timepiece is the ideal companion for an extraordinary voyage that reveals a unique perspective on the world. It is the only watch of its kind.

CRAFTING ETERNITY SINCE 1755

OVERSEAS

VACHERON CONSTANTIN
GENÈVE

Vacheron Constantin Boutiques:
New York · Beverly Hills · South Coast Plaza · Las Vegas · Miami
Call 1(877) 701-1755, or contact concierge.us@vacheron-constantin.com
Discover more on overseas.vacheron-constantin.com

Vacheron Constantin

Specialty Products
High-end watches are a specialty product. Vacheron Constantin watches are priced from $4,000 to $50,000 and are available only in 36 U.S. locations.

10-2b **Business Products**

Business products are usually purchased on the basis of an organization's goals and objectives. Generally, the functional aspects of the product are more important than the psychological rewards sometimes associated with consumer products. Business products can be classified into seven categories according to their characteristics and intended uses: installations; accessory equipment; raw materials; component parts; process materials; maintenance, repair, and operating (MRO) supplies; and business services.

Installations

Unsought Products
A new windshield is an unsought product. Although the purchase of a windshield is necessary, this type of purchase is usually unplanned.

Installations include facilities, such as office buildings, factories, and warehouses, and major nonportable equipment, such as production lines and very large machines. Normally, installations are expensive and intended to be used for a considerable length of time. Because installations tend to be costly and involve a long-term investment of capital, these purchase decisions often are made by high-level management. Marketers of installations frequently must provide a variety of services, including training, repairs, maintenance assistance, and even aid in financing such purchases.

Accessory Equipment

Accessory equipment does not become part of the final physical product but is used in production or office activities. Examples include file cabinets, fractional-horsepower motors, calculators, and tools. Compared with major equipment, accessory items are usually less expensive, are purchased routinely with less negotiation, and are often treated as expense items rather than capital items because they are not expected to last as long. More outlets are required for distributing and selling accessory equipment than for installations, but sellers do not have to provide the multitude of services expected of installations marketers.

Raw Materials

Raw materials are the basic natural materials that actually become part of a physical product. They include minerals, chemicals, agricultural products, and materials from forests and oceans. Corn, for example, is a raw material that is found in many different products, including food, beverages (as corn syrup), and even fuel (as ethanol).

Component Parts

Component parts become part of the physical product and are either finished items ready for assembly or products that need little processing before assembly. Although they become part of a larger product, component parts often can be identified and distinguished easily even after the product is assembled. Spark plugs, tires, clocks, brakes, and headlights are all component parts of an automobile. Buyers purchase such items according to their own specifications or industry standards, and they expect the parts to be of a specified quality and delivered on time so that production is not slowed or stopped. Producers that are primarily assemblers, such as auto or computer manufacturers, depend heavily on suppliers of component parts. Apple, for example, procures component parts from companies in eight different Asian countries—including Foxconn, Pegatron, Sharp, Japan Display, Largan Precision, Alps Electric, and Cowell Electronics—in order to manufacture its iPhone 7 and 7 Plus.[4]

installations Facilities and nonportable major equipment

accessory equipment Equipment that does not become part of the final physical product but is used in production or office activities

raw materials Basic natural materials that become part of a physical product

component parts Items that become part of the physical product and are either finished items ready for assembly or products that need little processing before assembly

process materials Materials that are used directly in the production of other products but are not readily identifiable

MRO supplies Maintenance, repair, and operating items that facilitate production and operations but do not become part of the finished product

business services The intangible products that many organizations use in their operations

product item A specific version of a product that can be designated as a distinct offering among a firm's products

product line A group of closely related product items viewed as a unit because of marketing, technical, or end-use considerations

Process Materials

Process materials are used directly in the production of other products. Unlike component parts, however, process materials are not readily identifiable. For example, a salad dressing manufacturer includes vinegar as an ingredient in its dressing. The vinegar is a process material because it is not identifiable or extractable from other ingredients in the salad dressing. As with component parts, process materials are purchased according to industry standards or the purchaser's specifications.

MRO Supplies

MRO supplies are maintenance, repair, and operating items that facilitate production and operations but do not become part of the finished product. Many products that are purchased as consumer products could also be considered MRO supplies to businesses. These might include paper, pencils, cleaning supplies, and paints. MRO supplies are commonly sold through numerous outlets and are purchased routinely, much like convenience products in the consumer market. To ensure supplies are available when needed, buyers often deal with more than one seller.

Business Services

Business services are the intangible products that many organizations use in their operations. They include financial, legal, marketing research, information technology, and janitorial services. Firms must decide whether to provide these services internally or obtain them from outside the organization. This decision depends on the costs associated with each alternative and how frequently the services are needed. As an example, Accenture focuses on services that help companies with business processes and management systems and with integrating advanced technology into their operations.

| 10-3 PRODUCT LINE AND PRODUCT MIX

LO 10-3 Explain the concepts of product line and product mix and how they are related.

Marketers must understand the relationships among all the products of their organization to coordinate the marketing of the total group of products. The following concepts help to describe the relationships among an organization's products.

A **product item** is a specific version of a product that can be designated as a distinct offering among an organization's products. An American Eagle T-shirt represents a product item. A **product line** is a group of closely related product items that are considered to be a unit because of marketing, technical, or end-use considerations. Apple, for example, has product lines for smart devices (iPhones, iPads, and Apple Watches as well as their operating system); computers; software; iCloud and Apple Pay; and Apple Music, Apple TV, iPod, and iTunes.[5]

Specific product items in a product line, such as different lipstick shades or shampoos for oily and dry hair, usually reflect the desires of different target markets or the varying needs of consumers. Thus, to develop the optimal product line, marketers must understand buyers' goals. Firms with high market share are more likely to expand their product lines aggressively, as are marketers with relatively high prices or limited product lines.[6] This pattern can be seen in many industries—including the computer industry, where companies are likely to expand their product lines when industry barriers are low or perceived market opportunities exist.

iStock.com/eskaylim

Product Line
Pringles has a product line consisting of 17 different varieties of chips in the United States, as well as a number of healthy and limited-edition options.

FIGURE 10.2	THE CONCEPTS OF PRODUCT MIX WIDTH AND DEPTH APPLIED TO U.S. PROCTER & GAMBLE PRODUCTS

	Laundry	Oral care	Bar soaps	Deodorants	Shampoos	Tissue/Towel	Health
Depth	Dreft 1933 Tide 1946 Cheer 1950 Downy 1960 Bold 1965 Gain 1966 Era 1972 Febreze 2000	Crest 1955 Scope 1966 Oral-B 2006	Ivory 1879 Safeguard 1963 Olay 1993	Old Spice 1948 Secret 1956	Pantene 1947 Head & Shoulders 1961 Herbal Essence 2001 Aussie 2003	Charmin 1928 Puffs 1960 Bounty 1965	Pepto-Bismol 1901 Vicks 1905 Prilosec OTC 2003

Width

A product mix is the composite, or total, group of products that an organization makes available to customers. The width of product mix is measured by the number of product lines a company offers. Deere & Co. offers multiple product lines for the agricultural industry, including tractors, scrapers, grain harvesting equipment, agricultural management solutions, home and workshop products, and even crop insurance.[7] The depth of product mix is the average number of different product items offered in each product line. Procter & Gamble offers a broad product mix, comprised of all the health-care, beauty-care, laundry and cleaning, food and beverage, and paper products the firm manufactures, some of which are quite deep. Figure 10.2 shows the width and depth of part of Procter & Gamble's product mix. Procter & Gamble is known for using distinctive branding, packaging, segmentation, and consumer advertising to promote individual items in its product lines. Tide, Bold, Gain, Cheer, and Era, for example, are all Procter & Gamble detergents that share the same distribution channels and similar manufacturing facilities, but each is promoted as a distinctive product, adding depth to the product line.

10-4 PRODUCT LIFE CYCLES AND MARKETING STRATEGIES

LO 10-4 Explore the product life cycle and its impact on marketing strategies.

Product life cycles follow a similar trajectory to biological life cycles, progressing from birth to death. As Figure 10.3 shows, a product life cycle has four major stages: introduction, growth, maturity, and decline. As a product moves through each cycle, the strategies relating to competition, pricing, distribution, promotion, and market information must be evaluated and possibly adjusted. Astute marketing managers use the life-cycle concept to make sure that strategies related to the introduction, alteration, and deletion of products are timed and executed properly. By understanding the typical life-cycle pattern, marketers can maintain profitable product mixes.

10-4a Introduction

The introduction stage of the product life cycle begins at a product's first appearance in the marketplace. Sales start at zero and profits are negative because companies must invest in product development and launch prior to selling. Profits may remain low or below zero because initial revenues will be low while the company covers large expenses for promotion and distribution. Notice in Figure 10.3 how, as sales move upward from zero over time, profits also increase.

Sales may be slow at first because potential buyers must be made aware of a new product's features, uses, and advantages through marketing. Efforts to highlight a new product's

product mix The total group of products that an organization makes available to customers

width of product mix The number of product lines a company offers

depth of product mix The average number of different product items offered in each product line

product life cycle The progression of a product through four stages: introduction, growth, maturity, and decline

introduction stage The initial stage of a product's life cycle—its first appearance in the marketplace—when sales start at zero and profits are negative

growth stage The stage of a product's life cycle when sales rise rapidly and profits reach a peak and then start to decline

value can create a foundation for building brand loyalty and customer relationships.[8] Two difficulties may arise during the introduction stage. First, sellers may lack the resources, technological knowledge, and marketing expertise to launch the product successfully. Large companies often launch new products with advertising and social media campaigns to inform potential buyers about the value of their new offerings. When Apple introduced its Airpod headphones, it ran commercials featuring a gravity-defying dancer to showcase the versatility of the product.[9] However, a large marketing budget is not required to launch a successful product. Marketers can attract attention through such techniques as giving away free samples or through media appearances. Websites, such as Retailmenot.com, help firms with low cost promotion by listing coupons and samples for thousands of companies—exposing customers to great deals and new brands. Some firms also choose to host online brand communities to promote the new product and predict its success. Apple and eBay have become experts in hosting online brand communities to promote products.[10] Second, the initial product price may have to be high to recoup expensive marketing research or development costs, which can depress sales. Given these difficulties, it is not surprising that many products never last beyond the introduction stage.

Most new products start off slowly and seldom generate enough sales to bring immediate profits. Although new product success rates vary a great deal between companies and in different industries, it is estimated that only 15 to 25 percent of new products truly succeed in the marketplace.[11] Even among established and successful companies, new product success rates are rarely above 50 percent. As buyers learn about a new product and express interest, the firm should constantly monitor the product and marketing strategy for weaknesses and make corrections quickly to prevent the product's early demise. Marketing strategy should be designed to attract the segment that is most interested in, most able, and most willing to buy the product. At the end of the introduction stage, the growth stage begins as competitors enter the market.

10-4b Growth

During the **growth stage**, sales rise rapidly and profits reach a peak and then start to decline (see Figure 10.3). The growth stage is critical to a product's survival because competitive reactions to the product's success during this period will affect the product's life expectancy. An example of a product in the growth stage is 3D printers.

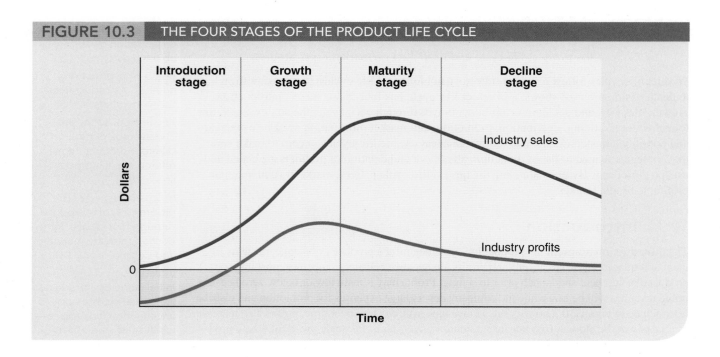

FIGURE 10.3   THE FOUR STAGES OF THE PRODUCT LIFE CYCLE

Profits begin to decline late in the growth stage as more competitors enter the market, driving prices down and creating the need for heavy promotional expenses. At this point, a typical marketing strategy seeks to strengthen market share and position the product favorably against aggressive competitors through emphasizing product benefits. Marketers should analyze competing brands' product positions relative to their own and adjust the marketing mix in response to their findings. Aggressive pricing, including price cuts, is also typical during this stage as a means of gaining market share—even if it means short-term loss of profits. The goal of the marketing strategy in the growth stage is to establish and fortify the product's market position by encouraging adoption and brand loyalty. To achieve greater market penetration, marketers may choose to use segmentation strategies more intensively, which requires developing product variations to satisfy the needs of consumers in several different market segments. For example, a packaged goods company might introduce new flavors of a successful cookie to appeal to different tastes or allergy-free versions to target those with food sensitivities.

Firms should seek to fill gaps in geographic market coverage during the growth period. As a product gains market acceptance, new distribution outlets usually become easier to secure. Marketers sometimes move from an exclusive or a selective exposure to a more intensive network of dealers to achieve greater market penetration. Marketers must also make sure the physical distribution system is running efficiently so that customers' orders are processed accurately and delivered on time.

Promotion expenditures in the growth stage may be slightly lower than during the introductory stage, but are still large. As sales continue to increase, promotion costs should drop as a percentage of total sales, which contributes significantly to increased profits. Advertising messages should stress brand benefits.

10-4c **Maturity**

During the maturity stage, sales curves peak and start to level off or decline, and profits continue to fall (see Figure 10.3). DVDs are an example of a product in the maturity phase as Internet streaming grows in popularity. This stage is characterized by intense competition because many brands are now in the market. Competitors emphasize improvements and differences in their versions of the product. As a result, during the maturity stage, weaker competitors are squeezed out of the market.

During the maturity phase, the producers who remain in the market are likely to change their promotional and distribution efforts. Advertising and dealer-oriented promotions are typical during this stage of the product life cycle. Marketers also must take into account that as the product reaches maturity, buyers' knowledge of it attains a high level. Consumers are no longer inexperienced generalists. They have become experienced specialists. Marketers of mature products sometimes expand distribution into global markets, in which case products may have to be adapted to fit differing needs of global customers more precisely. For instance, as Barbie doll sales decrease in the United States, Mattel has been trying to increase interest for Barbie in China. Because parents in China have a different view of toys from those of parents in the United States, Mattel has had to adapt Barbie to focus more on learning and intellectual pursuits.[12] If the iconic doll fails to take off there, Mattel may have to shift to a decline strategy for Barbie.

Because many products are in the maturity stage of their life cycles, marketers must know how to deal with them and be prepared to adjust their marketing strategies. There are many approaches to altering marketing strategies during the maturity stage. To increase the sales of mature products, marketers may suggest new uses for them.

As customers become more experienced and knowledgeable about products during the maturity stage (particularly about business products), the benefits they seek may change as well, necessitating product modifications. For instance, Stonyfield reformulated its yogurt products so that they would contain less sugar. Because many consumers are concerned about the amount of sugar in consumer packaged goods, Stonyfield recognized this as an opportunity to differentiate its mature brand from rivals.[13]

During the maturity stage, marketers actively encourage resellers to support the product. Resellers may be offered promotional assistance to lower their inventory costs. In general,

maturity stage The stage of a product's life cycle when the sales curve peaks and starts to decline as profits continue to fall

Unilever

Managing Products in the Maturity Stage
The Klondike Bar has reached the maturity stage of the product life cycle. To be competitive, the maker of Klondike Bars promotes a variety of flavors.

marketers go to great lengths to serve resellers and provide incentives for displaying and selling their brand.

Maintaining market share during the maturity stage requires promotion expenditures, which can be large if a firm seeks to increase a product's market share through new uses. Advertising messages in this stage may focus on differentiating a brand from the field of competitors, and sales promotion efforts may be aimed at both consumers and resellers. The advertisement for Klondike Bars, for example, promotes the brand's 13 different flavors. The ad includes an enticing image of a stack of different flavored Klondike Bars with their corners bitten off to show how delicious they look inside. Additionally, the ad reminds consumers that some flavors of Klondike Bars are old favorites like Oreo cookies and Reese's Pieces.

10-4d Decline

During the **decline stage**, sales fall rapidly (see Figure 10.3). When this happens, the marketer must consider eliminating items from the product line that no longer earn a profit. The marketer also may cut promotion efforts, eliminate marginal distributors, and finally, plan to phase out the product. This can be seen in the decline in demand for most sweetened carbonated beverages such as soda, which has been continuing for decades as consumers turn instead to bottled teas and flavored waters. Companies have responded to this shift in consumer preference by expanding their offerings of juices, waters, and healthier drink options.

In the decline stage, marketers must decide whether to reposition the product to extend its life, or whether it is better to

decline stage The stage of a product's life cycle when sales fall rapidly

eliminate it. Usually a declining product has lost its distinctiveness because similar competing or superior products have been introduced. Competition engenders increased substitution and brand switching among consumers as they become increasingly insensitive to minor product differences. For these reasons, marketers do little to change a product's style, design, or other attributes during its decline. New technology or social trends, product substitutes, or environmental considerations also may indicate that the time has come to delete the product.

During a product's decline, spending on promotion efforts is usually reduced considerably. Advertising of special offers and sales promotions, such as coupons and premiums, may slow the rate of decline temporarily. Firms will maintain outlets with strong sales volumes and eliminate unprofitable outlets. An entire marketing channel may be eliminated if it does not contribute adequately to profits. A channel not used previously, such as a factory outlet or Internet retailer, can help liquidate remaining inventory of a product that is being eliminated. As sales decline, the product becomes harder for consumers to find, but loyal buyers will seek out resellers who still carry it. As the product continues to decline, the sales staff at outlets where it is still sold will shift emphasis to more profitable products.

iStock.com/yanyong

Decline Stage
As more consumers choose to stream music, compact discs are on the decline. Many retail stores are offering CDs at lower prices to try and spur demand.

10-5 **PRODUCT ADOPTION PROCESS**

LO 10-5 Discuss the product adoption process.

product adoption process
The stages buyers go through in accepting a product

Acceptance of new products—especially new-to-the-world products—usually does not happen quickly. It can take a very long time for consumers to become aware of and overcome skepticism about a new product, particularly if it represents a dramatic innovation. Some cautious and critical remarks about products that went on to be successful are listed in Table 10.1. Many consumers prefer to wait until the "second generation," when kinks are more likely to have been worked out. Customers come to accept new products through an adoption process, detailed in Figure 10.4. The stages of the **product adoption process** are as follows:

Awareness. The buyer becomes aware of the product.
Interest. The buyer seeks information and is receptive to learning about the product.
Evaluation. The buyer considers the product's benefits and decides whether to try it, considering its value versus the competition.
Trial. The buyer examines, tests, or tries the product to determine if it meets his or her needs.
Adoption. The buyer purchases the product and can be expected to use it again whenever the need for this product arises.[14]

In the first stage, when consumers initially become aware that the product exists, they possess little information and are not yet concerned about obtaining more. Consumers enter the interest stage when they become motivated to learn about the product's features, uses, advantages, disadvantages, price, or location. During the evaluation stage, individuals consider whether the product will address the criteria that are crucial to meeting their specific needs. In the trial stage, consumers use or experience the product for the first time, possibly by purchasing a small quantity, taking advantage of free samples, or borrowing the product

TABLE 10.1	MOST NEW PRODUCTS HAVE THEIR SKEPTICS

"I think there is a world market for maybe five computers."
—Thomas Watson, chairman of IBM, 1943

"This 'telephone' has too many shortcomings to be seriously considered as a means of communication. The device is inherently of no value to us."
—Western Union internal memo, 1876

"The wireless music box has no imaginable commercial value. Who would pay for a message sent to nobody in particular?"
—David Sarnoff's associates in response to his urgings for investment in the radio in the 1920s

"The concept is interesting and well formed, but in order to earn better than a C, the idea must be feasible."
—A Yale University management professor in response to Fred Smith's paper proposing reliable overnight delivery service (Smith went on to found Federal Express Corp.)

"Who the hell wants to hear actors talk?"
—H. M. Warner, Warner Brothers, 1927

"A cookie store is a bad idea. Besides, the market research reports say America likes crispy cookies, not soft and chewy cookies like you make."
—Banker's response to Debbie Fields's idea of starting Mrs. Fields' Cookies

"We don't like their sound, and guitar music is on the way out."
—Decca Recording Company rejecting the Beatles, 1962

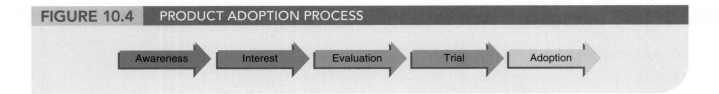

FIGURE 10.4   PRODUCT ADOPTION PROCESS

Awareness → Interest → Evaluation → Trial → Adoption

from someone else. Individuals move into the adoption stage when they need a product of that general type and choose to purchase the new product on a trial basis. However, entering the adoption stage does not mean that the person will eventually adopt the new product. Rejection may occur at any stage. Both product adoption and product rejection can be temporary or permanent.

When an organization introduces a new product, consumers in the target market enter into and move through the adoption process at different rates. For most products, there is also a group of nonadopters who never begin the process. For business marketers, success in managing production innovation, diffusion, and adoption requires great adaptability and significant effort in understanding customers.[15]

Depending on the length of time it takes them to adopt a new product, consumers tend to fall into one of five major adopter categories: innovators, early adopters, early majority, late majority, and laggards.[16] **Innovators** are the first to adopt a new product because they enjoy trying new products and do not mind taking a risk. **Early adopters** choose new products carefully and are viewed as people who are in-the-know by those in the remaining adopter categories. People in the **early majority** adopt just prior to the average person. They are deliberate and cautious in trying new products. Individuals in the **late majority** are skeptical of new products but eventually adopt them because of economic necessity or social pressure. **Laggards**, the last to adopt a new product, are oriented toward the past. They are suspicious of new products, and when they finally adopt one, it may already have been replaced by an even newer product.

10-6 BRANDING

innovators First adopters of new products

early adopters Careful choosers of new products

early majority Those adopting new products just before the average person

late majority Skeptics who adopt new products when they feel it is necessary

laggards The last adopters, who distrust new products

brand A name, term, design, symbol, or any other feature that identifies one marketer's product as distinct from those of other marketers

brand name The part of a brand that can be spoken

LO 10-6 Explain the major components of branding, including brand types, branding strategies, and brand protection.

Marketers must make many decisions about products, including choices about brands, brand names, brand marks, trademarks, and trade names. A **brand** is a name, term, design, symbol, or any other feature that identifies one marketer's product as distinct from those of other marketers.[17] A brand may identify a single item, a family of items, or all items of that seller. Some have defined a brand as not just the physical good, name, color, logo, or ad campaign, but everything associated with the product, including its symbolism and experiences.[18] Firms that try to shift the image of a brand risk losing market share. Coca-Cola learned this the hard way with its failed New Coke brand. However, simple brand changes have also led to major marketing successes. When MillerCoors temporarily repackaged its Miller Lite beer for a short-term promotion using its original white can design instead of the blue design it had used for the past decade, sales of the mature product increased dramatically. The result prompted MillerCoors to make the retro look permanent, and extended the white label to all Miller Lite cans, bottles, and coasters.[19]

A **brand name** is the part of a brand that can be spoken—including letters, words, and numbers—such as 7UP or V8. A brand name is essential, as it is often a product's only distinguishing characteristic without which a firm could not differentiate its products. To consumers, a brand name is as fundamental as the product itself. Indeed, many brand names have become synonymous with the product, such as Scotch Tape, Xerox copiers, and Kleenex tissues. Marketers must make efforts, through promotional activities, to ensure that such brand names do not become generic terms, which are not protected under the law.

The element of a brand that is not comprised of words—often a symbol or design—is a **brand mark**. Examples of brand marks include the McDonald's Golden Arches, Nike's "swoosh," and Mercedes Benz's three-pointed star. A **trademark** is a legal designation indicating that the owner has exclusive use of a brand or a part of a brand and that others are prohibited by law from its use. To protect a brand name or brand mark in the United States, an organization must register it as a trademark with the U.S. Patent and Trademark Office. Finally, a **trade name** is the full and legal name of an organization, such as Ford Motor Company, rather than the name of a specific product.

10-6a **Value of Branding**

Both buyers and sellers benefit from branding. Brands help buyers recognize specific products that meet their criteria for quality, which reduces the time needed to identify and purchase products by facilitating iden-

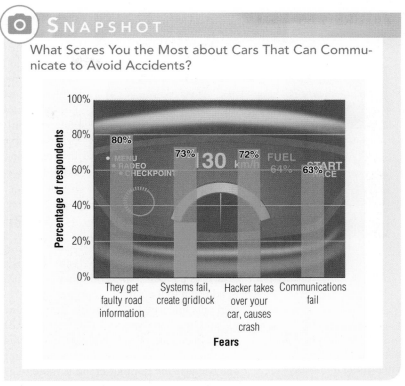

SNAPSHOT

What Scares You the Most about Cars That Can Communicate to Avoid Accidents?

Source: ORC International for the Chubb Group of Insurance Companies survey of 1,005 adults in the U.S.

tification of products that satisfy consumer needs. Without brands, product selection would be more difficult because buyers would have fewer guideposts indicating quality and product features. For many consumers, purchasing certain brands is a form of self-expression. For example, clothing brand names, such as Nike or Tommy Hilfiger, are important to many consumers because they convey signals about their lifestyle or self-image. Especially when a customer is unable to judge a product's quality, a brand indicates a quality level and image to the customer and reduces a buyer's perceived risk of purchase. Customers want to purchase brands whose quality they trust, such as Coca-Cola, Apple, and Panera. In addition, customers might receive a psychological reward from purchasing and owning a brand that symbolizes high status, such as Aston Martin or Chanel. On the other hand, conspicuous brand usage that is considered to be attention-getting can cause dilution in some cases. Some brand users with a low self-brand connection may have a harder time connecting with the brand. For example, showing-off behaviors such as wearing Gucci sunglasses indoors may be perceived negatively by brand users.[20]

Sellers also benefit from branding because brands are identifiers that make repeat purchasing easier for customers, thereby fostering brand loyalty. Furthermore, branding helps a firm introduce a new product by carrying the name and image of one or more existing products. Buyers are more likely to experiment with the new product because of familiarity with products carrying firms' existing brand names. It also facilitates promotional efforts because the promotion of each branded product indirectly promotes all other products bearing the same brand. As consumers become loyal to a specific brand, the company's market share will achieve a level of stability, allowing the firm to use its resources more efficiently.

Branding also involves a cultural dimension in that consumers bestow their own social meanings onto brands. A brand appeals to customers on an emotional level based on its symbolic image and key associations.[21] For some brands, such as Harley-Davidson and Apple, this can result in an almost cult-like following. These brands may develop communities of loyal customers that communicate through get-togethers, online forums, blogs,

brand mark The part of a brand not made up of words

trademark A legal designation of exclusive use of a brand

trade name Full legal name of an organization

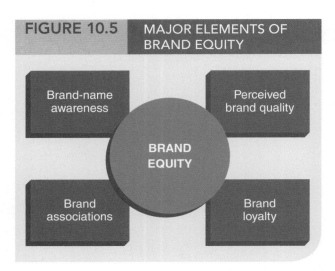

FIGURE 10.5 MAJOR ELEMENTS OF BRAND EQUITY

Brand-name awareness

Perceived brand quality

BRAND EQUITY

Brand associations

Brand loyalty

podcasts, and other means. They may even help consumers to develop their identity and self-concept and serve as a form of self-expression. In fact, the term *cultural branding* has been used to explain how a brand conveys a powerful myth that consumers find useful in cementing their identities.[22] It is also important for marketers to recognize that brands are not completely within their control because a brand exists independently in the consumer's mind. Every aspect of a brand is subject to a consumer's emotional involvement, interpretation, and memory. By understanding how branding influences purchases, marketers can foster customer loyalty.[23]

10-6b **Brand Equity**

A well-managed brand is an asset to an organization. The value of this asset is often referred to as brand equity. **Brand equity** is the marketing and financial value associated with a brand's strength in a market. In addition to the actual proprietary brand assets, such as patents and trademarks, four major elements underlie brand equity: brand-name awareness, brand loyalty, perceived brand quality, and brand associations (see Figure 10.5).[24]

brand equity The marketing and financial value associated with a brand's strength in a market

brand loyalty A customer's favorable attitude toward a specific brand

brand recognition A customer's awareness that the brand exists and is an alternative purchase

Being aware of a brand leads to brand familiarity, which in turn results in a level of comfort with the brand. A consumer is more likely to select a familiar brand than an unfamiliar one because the familiar brand is more likely to be viewed as reliable and of an acceptable level of quality. The familiar brand is also likely to be in a customer's consideration set, whereas the unfamiliar brand is not.

Brand loyalty is a customer's favorable attitude toward a specific brand. If brand loyalty is sufficiently strong, customers will purchase the brand consistently when they need a product in that specific product category. Customer satisfaction with a brand is the most common reason for loyalty to that brand.[25] Companies with the most brand loyalty include Lyft (rideshares), Red Bull (energy drinks), GEICO (car insurance), Dunkin' Donuts (coffee and baked goods), and Discover (credit cards).[26] Brand loyalty has advantages for the customer as well as the manufacturer and seller. It reduces a buyer's risks and shortens the time spent deciding which product to purchase. The degree of brand loyalty is highly variable between product categories, and it is challenging for a firm to foster brand loyalty for some products, such as fruits or vegetables, because customers can readily judge their quality by looking at them in the grocery store without referring to a brand. However, when consumers perceive products as being green or sustainable, their attitude toward the brand tends to improve.[27]

The rapid pace of technological transformation also presents challenges for marketers. With new computers, apps, and other digital devices entering the market at an ever more rapid pace, it can be difficult for marketers to sustain a high level of emotional engagement with consumers, and therefore retain their loyalty from year to year. Brand loyalty also varies by country, as different cultures may identify with a certain brand to a greater or lesser degree.

There are three degrees of brand loyalty: recognition, preference, and insistence. **Brand recognition** occurs when a customer is aware that the brand exists and views

Product with Brand Loyalty
Many consumers are extremely brand loyal to Starbucks and are unwilling to accept a substitute.

it as an alternative purchase if the preferred brand is unavailable or if the other available brands are unfamiliar. This is the weakest form of brand loyalty. **Brand preference** is a stronger degree of brand loyalty. A customer has a definite preference for one brand over competitive offerings, and will purchase this brand if it is available. However, if the brand is not available, the customer will accept a substitute rather than expending the additional effort required to find and purchase the preferred brand. **Brand insistence** is the strongest and least common level of brand loyalty. A customer will accept no substitute, and is willing to spend a great deal of time and effort to acquire that brand. If a brand-insistent customer goes to a store and finds the brand unavailable, he or she will seek the brand elsewhere rather than purchase a substitute. Brand insistence also can apply to service products, such as Hilton Hotels, or sports teams, such as the Dallas Cowboys. Although it occurs rarely, marketers aspire to achieve brand insistence.

Brand loyalty is an important component of brand equity because it reduces a brand's vulnerability to competitors' actions. It allows an organization to keep its existing customers and avoid spending significant resources to gain new ones. Loyal customers provide brand visibility and reassurance to potential new customers. And because customers expect their brands to be available when and where they shop, retailers strive to carry the brands known for their strong customer following.

Customers associate a particular brand with a certain level of overall quality. As mentioned previously, customers frequently use a brand name as a proxy for an actual assessment of a product's quality. In many cases, customers cannot actually judge the quality of the product for themselves and instead must rely on the brand as a quality indicator. A consumer looking to purchase a new car might have never purchased a Subaru or an Audi vehicle. However, because the brands rank among the highest in quality, a potential car buyer might give preference to them over other brands.[28] Perceived high brand quality helps to support a premium price, allowing a marketer to avoid severe price competition. Also, favorable perceived brand quality can ease the introduction of brand extensions because consumers' high regard for the brand is likely to translate into high regard for the related products.

The set of associations linked to a brand is another key component of brand equity. At times, a marketer works to connect a particular lifestyle or—in some instances—a certain personality type with a specific brand. These types of brand associations contribute significantly to the brand's equity. Brand associations sometimes are facilitated by using trade characters, such as the GEICO Gecko, the Pillsbury Dough Boy, and the Keebler Elves. Placing these trade characters in advertisements and on packaging helps consumers to link the ads and packages with the brands. This practice is particularly effective with younger consumers, which is why many cereals and candies feature licensed characters such as Dora the Explorer.[29] For instance, GEICO's advertising usually portrays its gecko trade character describing how consumers can save money with GEICO car insurance.

Although difficult to measure, brand equity represents the value of a brand to an organization—it includes both tangible assets and intangibles such as public perception and consumer loyalty. Table 10.2 lists the top 10 brands with the highest economic value. Any company that owns a brand listed in Table 10.2 would agree that equity is likely to be the greatest single asset in the organization's possession.

10-6c **Types of Brands**

There are three categories of brands: manufacturer, private distributor, and generic. **Manufacturer brands** are initiated by producers and ensure that producers

brand preference The degree of brand loyalty in which a customer prefers one brand over competitive offerings

brand insistence The degree of brand loyalty in which a customer strongly prefers a specific brand and will accept no substitute

manufacturer brands Brands initiated by producers

Lanier/Getty Images

Stimulating Brand Associations
GEICO Insurance uses the Gecko as a trade character to stimulate favorable brand associations.

TABLE 10.2	THE 10 MOST VALUABLE BRANDS IN THE WORLD	
Rank	**Brand**	**Brand Value ($ Millions)**
1	Google	$ 229,198
2	Apple	228,460
3	Microsoft	121,824
4	AT&T	107,387
5	Facebook	102,551
6	Visa	100,800
7	Amazon.com	98,988
8	Verizon	93,220
9	McDonald's	88,654
10	IBM	86,206

Source: "2016 BrandZ Top 100 Global Brands," Kantar Millward Brown, http://wppbaz.com/charting/19 (accessed February 24, 2017).

are identified with their products at the point of purchase—for example, Green Giant, Dell Computer, and Levi's jeans. A manufacturer brand usually requires a producer to become involved in distribution, promotion, and, to some extent, pricing decisions.

Private distributor brands (also called *private brands*, *store brands*, or *dealer brands*) are initiated and owned by resellers—wholesalers or retailers. The major characteristic of private brands is that the manufacturers are not identified on the products. Retailers and wholesalers use private distributor brands to develop more efficient promotion, generate higher gross margins, and change store image. Private distributor brands give retailers or wholesalers freedom to purchase products of a specified quality at the lowest cost without disclosing the identities of the manufacturers. Wholesaler brands include IGA (Independent Grocers' Alliance) and Topmost (General Grocer). Successful private brands are distributed nationally, and many rival the quality of manufacturer brands. Familiar retailer brand names include Target's Archer Farms and Up and Up, Walmart's Great Value, and Whole Foods' 365 Everyday Value. Sometimes retailers with successful private distributor brands start manufacturing their own products to gain more control over product costs, quality, and design in the hope of increasing profits. Sales of private labels have grown considerably as the quality of store brands has increased. Sales of store brands account for $115 billion in revenue. It is estimated that one in four products sold at supermarkets are store brands.[30]

Some products, on the other hand, are not branded at all, often called *generic branding*. **Generic brands** indicate only the product category and do not include the company name or other identifying terms. These items are typically staples that would be marketed using an undifferentiated strategy because they lack special features, such as sugar, salt, or aluminum foil. Generic brands usually are sold at lower prices than comparable branded items and compete on the basis of price and value. The prevalence of generic brands has decreased over time, particularly as the quality and value of private brands has increased.

private distributor brands Brands initiated and owned by resellers

generic brands Brands indicating only the product category

10-6d **Selecting a Brand Name**

Marketers consider several factors in selecting a brand name. First, the name should be easy for customers (including foreign buyers if the firm intends to market its products in other countries) to say, spell, and recall. Short, one-syllable names, such as Cheer, often satisfy this requirement. Second, the brand name should indicate in some way the product's major benefits and, if possible, should suggest the product's uses and special characteristics. Marketers should always avoid negative or offensive references. For example, the brand names of household cleaning products such as Ajax dishwashing liquid, Vanish toilet bowl cleaner, Formula 409 multipurpose cleaner, Cascade dishwasher detergent, and Wisk laundry detergent connote strength and effectiveness. Consumers are more likely to recall and to evaluate favorably names that convey positive attributes or benefits.[31] Third, to set it apart from competitors, the brand name should be distinctive. Research has shown that creating a brand personality that aligns with the products sold and the target market's self-image is important to brand success—if the target market feels aligned with the brand, they are more likely to develop brand loyalty.[32] If a marketer intends to use a brand for a product line, that brand must be compatible with all products in the line. Finally, a brand should be designed so that it can be used and recognized in all types of media. Finding the right brand name has become a challenging task because many obvious names have already been used.

Marketers can devise brand names from single or multiple words—for example, Dodge Charger. Letters and numbers, alone or in combination, are used to create such brands as BMW's i8 sports car or WD-40 lubricant. Words, numbers, and letters are combined to yield brand names, such as Samsung Galaxy S7 Edge. To avoid terms that have negative connotations, marketers sometimes use fabricated words that have absolutely no meaning when created—for example, Häagen-Dazs. For marketing in China, U.S. brands strive to use names that translate well and have significant meaning in Chinese, but stay true to their U.S. identities. Thus Starbucks goes by Starry Hope, which is consistent with its U.S. logo. Nike calls itself "Nai ke," which translates to "endurance and perseverance" but sounds like its U.S. name; rival Reebok is called "Rui bu," which means "fast steps."[33]

Who actually creates brand names? Brand names are generally created by individuals or a team within the organization. Sometimes a name is suggested by individuals who are close to the development of the product. Some organizations have committees that participate in brand-name creation and approval. Large companies that introduce numerous new products annually are likely to have a department that develops brand names. At times, outside consultants and companies that specialize in brand-name development are used.

10-6e **Protecting a Brand**

A marketer also should design a brand so that it can be protected easily through registration. A series of court decisions has created a broad hierarchy of protection based on brand type. From most protectable to least protectable, these brand types are fanciful (Exxon), arbitrary (Dr Pepper), suggestive (Spray 'n Wash), and descriptive (Minute Rice). Generic terms, such as aluminum foil, are not protectable. Surnames and descriptive, geographic, or functional names are difficult to protect.[34] However, research shows that consumers prefer these descriptive and suggestive brand names and find them easier to recall compared with fanciful and arbitrary brand names.[35] Although registration protects trademarks domestically for 10 years, and trademarks can be renewed indefinitely, a firm should develop a system for ensuring that brands are protected and its trademarks are renewed as needed.

To guard its exclusive rights to a brand, a company must ensure that the brand is not likely to be considered an infringement on any brand already registered with the U.S. Patent and Trademark Office. Patent infringement cases are at a record high, in part because the Internet allows for easier searching of possible infringement cases. However, proving that patent infringement has occurred may be complex because infringement is determined by the courts, which base their decisions on whether a brand causes consumers to be confused, mistaken, or deceived about the source of the product. McDonald's is the company

iStock.com/fmdesign

Brand Protection
Companies try to protect their brands by using certain phrases and symbols in their advertisements and on their packaging. Note the use of the ® symbol after Lysol.

probably most famous for aggressively protecting its trademarks against infringement by launching charges against a number of companies with *Mc* names because it fears that use of the prefix will give consumers the impression that these companies are associated with or owned by McDonald's.

A marketer should guard against allowing a brand name to become a generic term because these terms cannot be protected as exclusive brand names. For example, *aspirin*, *escalator*, and *shredded wheat*—all brand names at one time—eventually were declared generic terms that refer to product classes. Thus, they could no longer be protected. To keep a brand name from becoming a generic term, the firm should spell the name with a capital letter and use it as an adjective to modify the name of the general product class and include the word *brand* after the brand name, as in Kleenex Brand tissues.[36] An organization can deal with this problem directly by advertising that its brand is a trademark and should not be used generically. The firm also can indicate that the brand is a registered trademark by using the symbol ®.

A U.S. firm that tries to protect a brand in a foreign country is likely to encounter additional problems. In many countries, brand registration is not possible. In such places, the first firm to use a brand in such a country automatically has the rights to it. In some instances, U.S. companies actually have had to buy their own brand rights from a firm in a foreign country because the foreign firm was the first user in that country.

Marketers trying to protect their brands also must contend with brand counterfeiting. In the United States, for instance, one can purchase fake General Motors parts, Cartier and Rolex watches, Louis Vuitton handbags, Walt Disney character dolls, Microsoft software, Warner Brothers clothing, Mont Blanc pens, and a host of other products illegally marketed by manufacturers that do not own the brands. Annual losses caused by counterfeit products are estimated at $461 billion. Counterfeit products not only harm manufacturers, but can also harm consumers when their manufacture is subpar or they are made of harmful ingredients.[37]

10-6f Branding Policies

Before establishing branding policies, a firm must decide whether to brand its products at all. If a company's product is homogeneous and is similar to competitors' products, it may be difficult to brand in a way that will result in consumer loyalty. Raw materials and commodities such as coal, carrots, or gravel are hard to brand because of their homogeneity and their physical characteristics.

If a firm chooses to brand its products, it may use individual or family branding, or a combination. **Individual branding** is a policy of naming each product differently. Nestlé S.A., the world's largest food and nutrition company, uses individual branding for many of its 6,000 different brands, such as Nescafé coffee, PowerBar nutritional food, Maggi soups, and Häagen-Dazs ice cream. A major advantage of individual branding is that if

individual branding A policy of naming each product differently

an organization introduces a product that fails in the marketplace, the negative images associated with it do not influence consumers' decisions to purchase the company's other products. An individual branding policy also may facilitate market segmentation when a firm wishes to enter many segments of the same market. Separate, unrelated names can be used, and each brand can be aimed at a specific segment. However, with individual branding a firm cannot capitalize on the positive image associated with successful products.

When using **family branding**, all of a firm's products are branded with the same name, or part of the name, such as the cereals Kellogg's Frosted Flakes, Kellogg's Rice Krispies, and Kellogg's Corn Flakes. In some cases, a company's name is combined with other words, such as with Arm & Hammer Heavy Duty Detergent, Arm & Hammer Pure Baking Soda, and Arm & Hammer Carpet Deodorizer. Unlike individual branding, family branding means that the promotion of one item with the family brand promotes the firm's other products. Examples of other companies that use family branding include Apple, Fisher-Price, and Heinz.

Family Branding
The maker of Heinz products employs family branding on its condiments. Note that the name "Heinz" appears on each bottle.

An organization is not limited to a single branding policy. A company that uses primarily individual branding for many of its products also may use family branding for a specific product line. Branding policy is influenced by the number of products and product lines the company produces, the number and types of competing products available, and the size of the firm.

10-6g Brand Extensions

A **brand extension** occurs when an organization uses one of its existing brands to brand a new product in a different product category. For example, furniture retailer West Elm planned to open a chain of boutique hotels under the West Elm brand name with DDK, a hospitality firm. The hotels will be furnished with West Elm furniture, which guests will be able to buy online.[38] A brand extension should not be confused with a line extension. The major difference between the two is that a line extension uses an existing brand on a new product in the same product category, such as new flavors or sizes. Line extensions will be discussed in more detail in Chapter 11.

If a brand is extended too many times or extended too far outside its original product category, it can be weakened through dilution of its image and symbolic impact. Table 10.3 describes brand extensions that failed because they were too dissimilar to their core product. Research has found that a line extension into premium categories can be an effective strategy to revitalize a brand, but the extension needs to be closely linked to the core brand.[39] Successful branding strategies for new product categories depend largely on how they fit with the product categories of the parent brand, as well as how the positioning of the new product is similar to how the parent brand is positioned.[40] Other research supports this by suggesting that diluting a brand by extending it into dissimilar product categories can suppress consumer consideration and choice for the original products carrying the brand.[41]

10-6h Co-Branding

Co-branding is the use of two or more brands on one product. Marketers employ co-branding to capitalize on the brand equity of multiple brands. For instance, Benjamin Moore partnered

family branding Branding all of a firm's products with the same name

brand extension Using an existing brand to brand a new product in a different product category

co-branding Using two or more brands on one product

TABLE 10.3	WORST BRAND EXTENSIONS	
Brand Name	**Core Product**	**Failed Brand Extension**
Smith & Wesson	Firearms	Mountain Bikes
Bic	Pens	Bic Underwear
Cosmopolitan	Magazine	Yogurt
Wrigley	Candy	Life Savers Soda
Coors	Beer	Rocky Mountain Spring Water
Colgate	Consumer products	Colgate Kitchen Entrees
Frito-Lay	Snack foods	Lemonade
Harley-Davidson	Motorcycles	Perfume

Source: "Top 25 Biggest Product Flops of All Time," *DailyFinance*, www.aol.com/photos/top-25-biggest-product-flops-of-all-time/ (accessed February 24, 2017).

with the retailer, Target, to release a co-branded line of paint colors that coordinate with Target's kids' furniture and accessories collection.[42] Co-branding is popular in several processed-food categories and in the credit card industry. The brands used for co-branding can be owned by the same company. For example, Kraft's Lunchables product teams the Kraft cheese brand with Oscar Mayer lunchmeats, another Kraft-owned brand. Many food items are co-branded as well. Cinnabon, for instance, has released co-branded items with Kellogg's (cereal) and Pillsbury (Toaster Strudel).

Effective co-branding capitalizes on the trust and confidence customers have in the brands involved. For instance, Harley Davidson successfully teamed up with Best Western to develop a rewards program for motorcycle enthusiasts. At more than 1,200 hotels throughout the United States, motorcycle enthusiasts can receive a free wipe-down motorcycle towel and other benefits. The partnership was so successful that it was extended for three years and expanded to areas outside of the United States.[43] The brands should not lose their identities, and it should be clear to customers which brand is the main brand. It is important for marketers to understand before entering a co-branding relationship that when a co-branded product is unsuccessful, both brands are implicated in the failure. To gain customer acceptance, the brands involved must represent a complementary fit in the minds of buyers. Trying to link a brand such as Harley-Davidson with a brand such as Healthy Choice would not achieve co-branding objectives because customers are not likely to perceive these brands as compatible.

10-6i Brand Licensing

A popular branding strategy involves **brand licensing**, an agreement in which a company permits another organization to use its brand on other products for a licensing fee. Royalties may be as low as 2 percent of wholesale revenues or higher than 10 percent. The licensee is responsible for all manufacturing, selling, and advertising functions and bears the costs if the licensed product fails. The top U.S. licensing company is Walt Disney Company. The NFL, the NCAA, NASCAR, and MLB are all leaders in the retail sales of licensed sports-related products. The advantages of licensing range from extra revenues and the low cost of brand expansion to generating free publicity, developing a new image, or protecting a trademark. The major disadvantages are a lack of manufacturing control and the risks of making consumers feel bombarded with too many unrelated products bearing the same name.

brand licensing An agreement whereby a company permits another organization to use its brand on other products for a licensing fee

|10-7 PACKAGING

LO 10-7 Describe the major packaging functions and design considerations, and how packaging is used in marketing strategies.

Packaging involves the development of a container to hold a product. A package can be a vital part of a product, making it more versatile, safer, and easier to use. It also conveys vital information about the product and is an opportunity to display interesting graphic design elements. Like a brand name, a package can influence customers' attitudes toward a product and their decisions to purchase. For example, packaging convenience can be a major factor in purchase. Producers of jellies, sauces, and ketchups package their products in squeezable plastic containers that can be stored upside down to make dispensing and storing the product more convenient. Package characteristics help to shape buyers' impressions of a product at the time of purchase and during use. In this section, we examine the main functions of packaging and consider several major packaging decisions. We also analyze the role of the package in a marketing strategy.

10-7a **Packaging Functions**

At the most basic level, packaging materials serve the purpose of protecting the product and maintaining its functional form. For instance, fluids such as milk and orange juice require packages that are waterproof and durable to preserve and protect their contents. Packaging should prevent damage that could affect the product's usefulness and value and thus lead to higher costs. Packaging techniques have also been developed to prevent product tampering. Some packages are designed to deter shoplifting through the inclusion of antitheft devices.

Another function of packaging is to offer convenience to users. For example, single-serving containers for food and drinks that do not require refrigeration appeal to children, parents, and those with active lifestyles because they are easily portable. Packaging can prevent product waste, make storage easier for retailers and for consumers, and even promote greater consumption. Additionally, packaging can promote a product by communicating its features, uses, benefits, and image. Sometimes a reusable package is developed to make the product more desirable.

DIGITAL MARKETING

Inside Unboxing Videos

What's inside the box? Millions of consumers are watching unboxing videos on YouTube and, increasingly, on Snapchat, to check out new products. Unboxing videos help marketers connect with consumers as a new product is about to be introduced, heightening anticipation and fueling word of mouth.

For example, Benefit Cosmetics provides new products to selected brand influencers with large social media followings. The company thinks about how to market to influencers so they will be excited about unboxing the new product on video. "You need to let influencers fall in love with your packages and keep them going through the layers," explains Benefit's social media manager. Often, the influencers post their first impressions of a new product and its packaging on Snapchat, later posting on Instagram and Facebook.

When Radiohead released the deluxe vinyl version of its album *A Moon-Shaped Pool*, the band posted an unboxing video on Twitter. Shot with a vintage look, the video showed off features like the detailed book of lyrics included with the album package. Band fans quickly retweeted the video thousands of times, spreading the word about the new release.

Adidas encourages YouTube posts of unboxing videos to reach many thousands of sneaker fans interested in seeing the sole of a new sneaker, not to mention the latest color and style. The company's media agency says this allows Adidas to target brand fans by appealing to their passion for the product rather than targeting only by age and gender. Who will be the first to see a new sneaker, a new eye-shadow, or a new LP unboxed on YouTube?[b]

Reusable Packaging
Reusable packaging is attractive to many consumers because they can extend the use of the packaging long after they have consumed the original product.

dcwcreations/Shutterstock.com

SC Johnson encourages consumers to reuse their Windex bottles by selling smaller recyclable refill packages. These refills help reduce the waste that comes with purchasing an entirely new bottle of Windex each time the old one runs out.[44]

10-7b Major Packaging Considerations

Marketers must take many factors into account when designing and producing packages. Obviously, a major consideration is cost. Although a number of different packaging materials, processes, and designs are available, costs can vary greatly. In recent years, buyers have shown a willingness to pay more for improved packaging.

Marketers should consider how much consistency is desirable between the package designs of different products produced by an organization. In many cases, consistency may be the best policy, especially if a firm's products are unrelated or aimed at vastly different target markets. However, to promote an overall company image, a firm may decide that all packages should be similar or should all feature one major design element. This approach is called **family packaging**. It is generally used only for lines of products, as with Campbell's soups, Weight Watchers' foods, or Planters Nuts.

family packaging Using similar packaging for all of a firm's products or packaging that has one common design element

A package's promotional role is an important consideration. Through verbal and nonverbal symbols, the package can inform potential buyers about the product's content, features, uses, advantages, and hazards. A firm can create desirable images and associations by its choice of color, design, shape, and texture. Many cosmetics manufacturers, for example, design their packages to create impressions of luxury and exclusivity. A package designer must consider size, shape, texture, color, and graphics as well as functionality. A package must obviously be the right size to hold the product, but clever design can make a package appear taller or shorter or larger or smaller, depending on the desire of the marketer and expectations of consumers.

Packaging also must meet the needs of resellers. Wholesalers and retailers consider whether a package facilitates transportation, storage, and handling. Resellers may refuse to carry certain products if their packages are cumbersome or require too much shelf space. Concentrated versions of laundry detergents and fabric softeners aid retailers and shoppers alike by offering products in smaller containers that are easier to transport, store, and display.

10-7c Packaging and Marketing Strategy

Packaging can be a major component of a marketing strategy. A new cap or closure, a better box or wrapper, or a more convenient container may give a product a competitive advantage. The right type of package for a product can help it to gain market recognition very quickly. Frito-Lay gained attention when it introduced a limited-time promotional packaging for Tostitos that had a unique sensor that can detect alcohol on a consumer's breath. Timed for sale just before the Super Bowl, the bags flashed a red light if the sensor detected a trace of alcohol and displayed a "Don't Drink and Drive" message along with a $10 code for an Uber ride.[45] Marketers should view packaging as a major strategic tool, especially for consumer convenience products. When considering the strategic uses of packaging, marketers also must analyze the cost of packaging and package changes.

10-7d Altering the Package

At times, a marketer changes a package or labeling because the existing design is no longer in style, especially when compared with the packaging of competitive products. Wild Planet

Foods, for example, redesigned the packaging for its shelf-stable sustainable seafood products using a cleaner, more modern look to symbolize the freshness and quality of its tuna, salmon, and sardine products.[46] A package may be redesigned because new product features need to be highlighted or because new packaging materials have become available. Cleaning supply company Seventh Generation sells its 4x concentrated laundry detergent in a paper bottle, which encloses a plastic shell. The design is innovative, completely recyclable, and requires fewer materials to make.[47]

An organization may also decide to change a product's packaging to make the product safer or more convenient to use. When Procter & Gamble released its popular Tide Pods product, it did not anticipate that many children would mistake the colorful packaging and pods for candy. Procter & Gamble developed a double safety latch for the packaging and redesigned the transparent container to make it opaque. These moves were meant to make the pods look less like candy and harder for children to open. However, continued ingestions led Procter & Gamble and other laundry pod manufacturers to make additional modifications to make the packaging safer.[48]

A product's packaging can also be altered to make it easier to handle in the distribution channel—for example, by changing the outer carton or using special bundling, shrink-wrapping, or pallets. In some cases, the shape of the package may be altered to allow it to fit in smaller shipping containers or easier to load onto trucks. Outer containers for products are sometimes changed so that they will proceed more easily through automated warehousing systems.

Marketers also use innovative or unique packages that are inconsistent with traditional packaging practices to make the brand stand out from its competitors. Basing their packaging on research that wine drinkers tend to decide which product to purchase in the store, not in advance, Stack Wine offers its products in unique single-serve cups. The cups are filled with wine, sealed, and come stacked together in four packs. The unique packaging is eye-catching and practical, designed for parties, camping, or other situations where wine glasses are not readily available. It is also a convenient product for the occasional wine drinker, who does not want to open an entire bottle just to have one glass.[49] Unusual packaging sometimes requires expending considerable resources, not only when designing the package but also for making customers aware of the unique package and why it is an improvement. Research suggests that uniquely shaped packages that attract attention are likely to be perceived as containing a higher volume of product than comparable products that generate less attention.[50]

Finally, a firm's packaging strategy can accommodate multiple packaging. Rather than packaging a single unit of a product, marketers sometimes use twin-packs, tri-packs, six-PACKS, or other forms of multiple packaging. For certain types of products, multiple packaging may increase demand because it increases the amount of the product available at the point of consumption (e.g., in one's house). It also may increase consumer acceptance of the product by encouraging the buyer to try the product several times.

10-8 LABELING

LO 10-8 Identify the functions of labeling and legal issues related to labeling.

Labeling is closely related with packaging and is used for identification, promotional, informational, and legal purposes. Labels can be small or large relative to the size of the product and they carry varying amounts of information. The stickers on a banana or apple, for example, are small and display only the brand name of the fruit, the type, and perhaps a stock-keeping unit number. A label can be part of the package itself or a separate feature attached to the package. The label on a can of Coke is actually part of the can, whereas the label on a two-liter bottle of Coke is separate and can be removed. Information presented on a label may include the brand name and mark, the registered trademark symbol, package size and content, product features, nutritional information, presence of allergens, type and style of the product, number of servings, care instructions, directions for use and safety precautions, the name and address of the manufacturer, expiration dates, seals of approval, and other facts.

labeling Providing identifying, promotional, or other information on package labels

iStock.com/Gwengoat

Labeling as Marketing Strategy
Labeling can be an important part of the marketing strategy. This label can be attached to the packaging to communicate that the product was made in the USA. Labeling can include claims about where the product was made as well as other information that is potentially valuable to the buyer.

Labels can facilitate the identification of a product by displaying the brand name in combination with a unique graphic design. For example, Heinz Ketchup and Coca-Cola are both easy to identify on a supermarket shelf because of their iconic labels, which feature the name and recognizable brand marks. By drawing attention to products and their benefits, labels can strengthen an organization's promotional efforts. Labels may contain promotional messages such as "30 percent more free," or provide information about a new or improved product feature, such as "new, improved scent."

Several federal laws and regulations specify information that must be included on the labels of certain products. Garments must be labeled with the name of the manufacturer, country of manufacture, fabric content, and cleaning instructions. Labels on nonedible items such as shampoos and detergents must include both safety precautions and directions for use. The Nutrition Labeling Act of 1990 requires the FDA to review food labeling and packaging, focusing on nutrition content, label format, ingredient labeling, food descriptions, and health messages. Any food product making a nutritional claim must follow standardized nutrition labeling. Food product labels must state the number of servings per container, serving size, number of calories per serving, number of calories derived from fat, number of carbohydrates, and amounts of specific nutrients such as vitamins. The Food and Drug Administration also instituted a law requiring chain restaurants and vending machines to place the calorie information of their products on menus and menu boards.[51]

Also of concern to many manufacturers are the Federal Trade Commission's (FTC) guidelines regarding "Made in USA" labels, a problem owing to the increasingly global nature of manufacturing. Additionally, consumers in many countries attach high brand value to American-made brands, giving U.S. companies an even greater incentive to employ a "Made in USA" label. The FTC requires that "all or virtually all" of a product's components be made in the United States if the label says "Made in USA."[52] The "Made in USA" labeling issue remains complicated, as so many products involve parts sourced, produced, or assembled in places around the globe. As business shows little sign of becoming less international, the FTC criteria for "Made in USA" are likely to be challenged and may be changed or adapted over time.

Chapter Review

10-1 Define the concept of a product.

A product is a good, a service, an idea, or any combination of the three received in an exchange. It can be either tangible or intangible and includes functional, social, and psychological utilities or benefits. When consumers purchase a product, they are buying the benefits and satisfaction they think the product will provide.

10-2 Discuss how products are classified.

Products can be classified on the basis of the buyer's intentions. Consumer products are those purchased to satisfy personal and family needs. Business products are purchased for use in a firm's operations, to resell, or to make other products. Consumer products can be subdivided into convenience, shopping, specialty, and unsought products.

Business products can be classified as installations, accessory equipment, raw materials, component parts, process materials, MRO supplies, and business services.

10-3 Explain the concepts of product line and product mix and how they are related.

A product item is a specific version of a product that can be designated as a distinct offering among an organization's products. A product line is a group of closely related product items that are considered a unit because of marketing, technical, or end-use considerations. The composite, or total, group of products that an organization makes available to customers is called the product mix. The width of the product mix is measured by the number of product lines the company offers. The depth of the product mix is the average number of different products offered in each product line.

10-4 Explore the product life cycle and its impact on marketing strategies.

The product life cycle describes how product items in an industry move through four stages: introduction, growth, maturity, and decline. The sales curve is at zero at introduction, rises at an increasing rate during growth, peaks during the maturity stage, and then declines. Profits peak toward the end of the growth stage of the product life cycle.

10-5 Discuss the product adoption process.

When customers accept a new product, they usually do so through a five-stage adoption process. The first stage is awareness, when buyers become aware that a product exists. Interest, the second stage, occurs when buyers seek information and are receptive to learning about the product. The third stage is evaluation; buyers consider the product's benefits and decide whether to try it. The fourth stage is trial; during this stage, buyers examine, test, or try the product to determine if it meets their needs. The last stage is adoption, when buyers actually purchase the product and use it whenever a need for this general type of product arises.

10-6 Explain the major components of branding, including brand types, branding strategies, and brand protection.

A brand is a name, term, design, symbol, or any other feature that identifies one seller's good or service and distinguishes it from those of other sellers. Branding helps buyers to identify and evaluate products, helps sellers to facilitate product introduction and repeat purchasing, and fosters brand loyalty. Brand equity is the marketing and financial value associated with a brand's strength. It represents the value of a brand to an organization. The four major elements

underlying brand equity include brand-name awareness, brand loyalty, perceived brand quality, and brand associations.

There are three degrees of brand loyalty. Brand recognition occurs when a customer is aware that the brand exists and views it as an alternative purchase if the preferred brand is unavailable or if the other available brands are unfamiliar. Brand preference is a stronger degree of brand loyalty. Brand insistence is the strongest and least common level of brand loyalty.

A manufacturer brand is initiated by a producer. A private distributor brand is initiated and owned by a reseller, sometimes taking on the name of the store or distributor. A generic brand indicates only the product category and does not include the company name or other identifying terms. When selecting a brand name, a marketer should choose one that is easy to say, spell, and recall and that alludes to the product's uses, benefits, or special characteristics. Brand names can be devised from words, letters, numbers, nonsense words, or a combination of these. Companies protect ownership of their brands through registration with the U.S. Patent and Trademark Office.

Individual branding designates a unique name for each of a company's products. Family branding identifies all of a firm's products with a single name. A brand extension is the use of an existing name on a new or improved product in a different product category. Co-branding is the use of two or more brands on one product. Through a licensing agreement and for a licensing fee, a firm may permit another organization to use its brand on other products. Brand licensing enables producers to earn extra revenue, receive low-cost or free publicity, and protect their trademarks.

10-7 Describe the major packaging functions and design considerations, and how packaging is used in marketing strategies.

Packaging involves the development of a container and a graphic design for a product. Effective packaging offers protection, economy, safety, and convenience. It can influence a customer's purchase decision by promoting features, uses, benefits, and image. When developing a package, marketers must consider the value to the customer of efficient and effective packaging, offset by the price the customer is willing to pay. Other considerations include how to make the package tamper resistant, whether to use multiple packaging and family packaging, how to design the package as an effective promotional tool, and how best to accommodate resellers. Packaging can be an important part of an overall marketing strategy and can be used to target certain market segments. Modifications in packaging can revive a mature product and extend its product life cycle. Producers alter packages to convey new features or to make them safer or more convenient. If a package has a secondary use, the product's value to the consumer may increase. Innovative packaging enhances a product's distinctiveness.

10-8 Identify the functions of labeling and legal issues related to labeling.

Labeling is closely related to packaging and is used for identification, promotional, and informational and legal purposes. Various federal laws and regulations require that certain products be labeled or marked with warnings, instructions, nutritional information, manufacturer's identification, and perhaps other information.

 Go to www.cengagebrain.com for resources to help you master the content in this chapter as well as for materials that will expand your marketing knowledge.

Developing Your Marketing Plan

Identifying the needs of consumer groups and developing products that satisfy those needs is essential when creating a marketing strategy. Successful product development begins with a clear understanding of fundamental product concepts. The product concept is the basis on which many of the marketing plan decisions are made. When relating the information in this chapter to the development of your marketing plan, consider the following:

1. Using Figure 10.2 as a guide, create a matrix of the current product mix for your company.

2. Discuss how the profitability of your product will change as it moves through each of the phases of the product life cycle.

3. Create a brief profile of the type of consumer who is likely to represent each of the product adopter categories for your product.

4. Discuss the factors that could contribute to the failure of your product. How will you define product failure?

Key Concepts

good 242
service 242
idea 242
consumer products 244
business products 244
convenience products 244
shopping products 245
specialty products 246
unsought products 246
installations 247
accessory equipment 247
raw materials 247
component parts 247

process materials 248
MRO supplies 248
business services 248
product item 248
product line 248
product mix 249
width of product mix 249
depth of product mix 249
product life cycle 249
introduction stage 249
growth stage 250
maturity stage 251
decline stage 252

product adoption process 253
innovators 254
early adopters 254
early majority 254
late majority 254
laggards 254
brand 254
brand name 254
brand mark 255
trademark 255
trade name 255
brand equity 256
brand loyalty 256

brand recognition 256
brand preference 257
brand insistence 257
manufacturer brands 257
private distributor brands 258
generic brands 258
individual branding 260
family branding 261
brand extension 261
co-branding 261
brand licensing 262
family packaging 264
labeling 265

Issues for Discussion and Review

1. Is a personal computer sold at a retail store a consumer product or a business product? Defend your answer.
2. How do convenience products and shopping products differ? What are the distinguishing characteristics of each type of product?
3. How does an organization's product mix relate to its development of a product line? When should an enterprise add depth to its product line rather than width to its product mix?

4. How do industry profits change as a product moves through the four stages of its life cycle?
5. What are the stages in the product adoption process, and how do they affect the commercialization phase?
6. How does branding benefit consumers and marketers?
7. What is brand equity? Identify and explain the major elements of brand equity.
8. What are the three major degrees of brand loyalty?

9. Compare and contrast manufacturer brands, private distributor brands, and generic brands.
10. Identify the factors a marketer should consider in selecting a brand name.
11. What is co-branding? What major issues should be considered when using co-branding?

12. Describe the functions a package can perform. Which function is most important? Why?
13. What are the main factors a marketer should consider when developing a package?
14. In what ways can packaging be used as a strategic tool?
15. What are the major functions of labeling?

VIDEO CASE 10
GaGa: Not Just a Lady

Several years before Lady Gaga made her musical debut, Jim King started a company he named GaGa after his beloved grandmother. King, a Rhode Island television news anchor turned entrepreneur, planned to use his grandmother's recipe for frozen dessert as the basis of his first product. Because the lemony dessert contains more butterfat than sherbet and less butterfat than ice cream, he couldn't legally label it as either. So King came up with the idea of calling the product "SherBetter," using the word play to suggest that it's similar to sherbet, but better.

King wasn't intending to compete with major ice cream firms like Hood, Breyers, and Ben & Jerry's. First, as a tiny start-up business, GaGa couldn't begin to match the marketing resources of the national brands. Second, GaGa's focus would be much narrower than the big brands, because sherbets and sorbets make up only a tiny fraction of the overall market for ice cream products. King determined that GaGa would compete on the basis of high quality, all-natural ingredients, and a fresh, creamy taste. He coined the slogan "Smooth as ice cream, fresh like sherbet" to describe SherBetter's appeal.

After he cooked up batches of SherBetter in his home kitchen, King drove from grocery store to grocery store until he made a sale to his first retail customer, Munroe Dairy. This initial order for 500 pints of lemon SherBetter was enough to get GaGa off to a solid start. During the first four years of business, the company marketed just one product—the original lemon SherBetter in pint containers. In that time, Stefani Germanotta shot to fame under the stage name of Lady Gaga, giving GaGa's frozen desserts an unexpected but welcome boost in brand awareness and sales.

Four years after founding GaGa, King realized that he could increase sales and enlarge his brand's visibility in supermarket frozen-food cases by expanding with sufficient products to fill a shelf. Over the next four years, he introduced raspberry, orange, and several other new flavors of SherBetter packed in pint containers. He also launched a line of frozen dessert novelty bars, called "SherBetter on a stick" because they're shaped like ice-cream bars. In addition, he decided to develop a tropical flavor to enhance his product offerings. That led to the introduction of toasted coconut SherBetter, a flavor that tested very well during GaGa's research. As he gained experience, King learned to account for cannibalization of existing products when he launched new products, knowing that overall sales would gain over time.

However, King didn't anticipate that supermarkets would display SherBetter pints and bars in separate freezer sections several doors away from each other. This complicated GaGa's marketing effort, because customers might not know they could buy SherBetter in both bars and pints unless they looked in both frozen-food sections. GaGa simply couldn't afford advertising to promote bars and pints. Instead, King and his wife Michelle, who serves as marketing director, began setting up a table outside the frozen-foods case in different supermarkets and distributing free samples on weekends. They found that when they offered samples, customers responded positively and the store sold a lot of GaGa products that day. This opened the door to repeat purchasing and brand loyalty.

One lesson King learned is that the GaGa brand is more memorable than the SherBetter product name. As a result, he changed the product packaging to emphasize the GaGa brand and its playful implications. After hiring professionals to analyze the company's marketing activities, he also learned that he should focus on what makes GaGa's products unique rather than trying to fit into the broader ice cream product category. The basics of high quality, a unique recipe, and a fun brand have helped King acquire distribution in 1,500 supermarkets and grocery stores throughout the Eastern United States.[53]

Questions for Discussion

1. When GaGa began adding novelty bars in new flavors, what was the effect on the width and depth of its product mix?
2. Why is packaging particularly important for a company like GaGa, which can't afford advertising?
3. Do you think GaGa's SherBetter pints and bars are likely to follow the product life cycle of traditional ice cream products? Explain your answer.

chapter 11 ●

Developing and Managing Goods and Services

iStock.com/StockRocket

iStock.com/StockRocket

LEARNING OBJECTIVES

11-1 Explain how companies manage existing products through line extensions and product modifications.

11-2 Explore how businesses develop a product idea into a commercial product.

11-3 Discuss the importance of product differentiation and the elements that differentiate one product from another.

11-4 Explain how businesses position their products.

11-5 Discuss how product deletion is used to improve product mixes.

11-6 Summarize how the characteristics of services influence the development of marketing mixes for services.

11-7 Describe organizational structures used for managing products.

MARKETING INSIGHTS

Different Cars, Different Product Positioning at Hyundai

From the subcompact Accent, compact Elantra, and sporty Veloster to the Santa Fe SUV, luxury Genesis, and earth-friendly Ioniq, Hyundai has vehicles for nearly every wallet, lifestyle, and garage. Hyundai originally broke into the U.S. market through budget pricing. Over time, the South Korean automaker prepared for future growth and profitability by reshaping perceptions of its cars and trucks. Key to that effort was the introduction of a 10-year, 100,000-mile warranty to reassure customers about vehicle quality and reliability.

One of Hyundai's newer product lines is its Ioniq cars, geared for "green" customers who want fuel efficiency without harming the planet. Knowing that these customers do not share all the same preferences or priorities, the company developed three Ioniq models: a hybrid gas-electric, an all-electric, and a plug-in electric. This allows Ioniq to compete more effectively, feature for feature, against high-profile, eco-friendly vehicles like the Toyota Prius, the Nissan Leaf, and the Chevy Bolt.

In addition, Hyundai is moving up the luxury ladder with its Genesis vehicles. Just like Toyota with the Lexus marque, Hyundai has made Genesis a stand-alone premium brand to compete with high-end vehicles from Lexus, BMW, Mercedes, and Cadillac, among others. Genesis has its own engineering team and its own design team, headed by a former designer of Bugatti high-performance cars. They're driving development of upscale vehicles that will make Genesis a standout for aesthetic appeal, comfort, and performance, as well as for value. Genesis cars have already won design awards, helping Hyundai draw more buyers into showrooms from coast to coast.[1]

Darren Brode/Shutterstock.com

To provide products that satisfy target markets and achieve the firm's objectives, marketers like Hyundai must develop, adjust, and maintain effective product mixes. An organization's product mix may require adjustment for a variety of reasons. Because customers' attitudes and product preferences change over time, their desire for certain products may wane. For instance, Americans' breakfast preferences are shifting from cold cereals, such as Frosted Flakes and Lucky Charms, toward healthier, more natural, and more portable fare like yogurt and snack bars as well as fast-food breakfast items. Cereal makers have responded to the decline in sales of traditional cereals by introducing new products such as cereal-based snack bars as well as reformulating cereals to make them more appealing to more consumers.[2] In other cases, a company needs to alter its product mix for competitive reasons. A marketer may have to delete a product from the mix because a competitor dominates the market for that product. Similarly, a firm may have to introduce a new product or modify an existing one to compete more effectively. A marketer may expand the firm's product mix to take advantage of excess marketing and production capacity.

In this chapter we examine several ways to improve an organization's product mix. First, we discuss managing existing products through effective line extension and product modification. Next, we examine the stages of new-product development. Then we go on to discuss the ways companies differentiate their products in the marketplace and follow with a discussion of product positioning and repositioning. Next, we examine the importance of deleting weak products and the methods companies use to eliminate them. Then we explore the characteristics of services as products and how their characteristics affect the development of marketing mixes for services. Finally, we look at the organizational structures used to manage products.

| 11-1 MANAGING EXISTING PRODUCTS

LO 11-1 Explain how companies manage existing products through line extensions and product modifications.

An organization can benefit by capitalizing on its existing products. By assessing the composition of the current product mix, a marketer can identify weaknesses and gaps. This analysis can then lead to improvements of the product mix through line extensions and product modifications.

11-1a **Line Extensions**

line extension Development of a product closely related to one or more products in the existing product line but designed specifically to meet somewhat different customer needs

A **line extension** is the development of a product closely related to one or more products in the existing product line but designed specifically to meet somewhat different customer needs. For example, McDonald's introduced two new sizes of its perennial Big Mac burger to appeal to customers who desire a larger burger or a more portable version. The $5.00 Grand Mac has two patties totaling a third of a pound, while the $3.00 Mac Jr. has one patty and less than 500 calories even with the usual Big Mac fixings.[3]

Many of the so-called new products introduced each year are, in fact, line extensions. Line extensions are more common than new products because they are a less expensive, lower-risk alternative for increasing sales. A line extension may focus on a different market segment or may be an attempt to increase sales within the same market segment by more precisely satisfying the needs of people in that segment. For example, Henry's Hard Soda (owned by MillerCoors) introduced a new flavor—grape—to its line of alcoholic sodas as well as sparkling, reduced-calorie adult beverages to target consumers looking for alternatives

Line Extensions
These products are line extensions of the original Oreo cookie. In the United States, there are more than 50 Oreo line extensions.

to beer and wine.[4] The success of a line extension is enhanced if the parent brand has a high-quality brand image and if there is a good fit between the line extension and its parent.[5]

11-1b Product Modifications

Product modification means changing one or more characteristics of a product. A product modification differs from a line extension because the original product does not remain in the line. For example, automakers use product modifications annually when they create new models of the same brand. Once the new models are introduced, the manufacturers stop producing last year's model. Like line extensions, product modifications entail less risk than developing new products.

Product modification can indeed improve a firm's product mix, but only under certain conditions. First, the product must be modifiable. Second, customers must be able to perceive that a modification has been made. Third, the modification should make the product more consistent with customers' desires so that it provides greater satisfaction. One drawback to modifying a successful product is that the consumer who had experience with the original version of the product may view a modified version as a riskier purchase. There are three major ways to modify products: quality, functional, and aesthetic modifications.

Quality Modifications

Quality modifications are changes relating to a product's dependability and durability. The changes usually are executed by altering the materials or the production process. For instance, for a service such as air travel, quality modifications may involve increasing leg room in the seating area.

Reducing a product's quality may allow an organization to lower its price and direct the item at a different target market. In contrast, increasing the quality of a product may give a firm an advantage over competing brands. Higher quality may enable a company to charge a higher price by creating customer loyalty and lowering customer sensitivity to price. Case in point, many firms, including Nestlé USA, Kellogg, and Kraft Heinz, are modifying their products to eliminate artificial colors and flavors in response to growing consumer preference for natural and simple ingredients. Kellogg's removed artificial colors and flavors from its Eggo products, while Kraft substituted natural colors and flavors for its classic Mac & Cheese.[6] However, higher quality may require the use of more expensive ingredients, components, and processes, thus forcing the organization to cut costs in other areas. Some firms, such as Caterpillar, are finding ways to increase quality while reducing costs.

Functional Modifications

Changes that affect a product's versatility, effectiveness, convenience, or safety are called **functional modifications**; they usually require that the product be redesigned. Product categories that have undergone considerable functional modification include agricultural equipment, appliances, cleaning products, automobiles, and telecommunications services. Consider Ford, which, despite having the best-selling pickup truck in the United States, continues to use functional modifications to stand out above the competition. For the 2018 model year, Ford modified the F-150 with new information technology including Apple Car Play and Android Auto, as well the option to have a diesel engine for the first time. The new model also includes more wheel and seat-color

product modification
Change in one or more characteristics of a product

quality modifications
Changes relating to a product's dependability and durability

functional modifications
Changes affecting a product's versatility, effectiveness, convenience, or safety

Functional Modifications in the Automobile Industry
One of the ways in which automobile companies are engaging in functional modification is by developing vehicles that can run on electric energy.

aesthetic modifications
Changes to the sensory appeal of a product

options.[7] Functional modifications can make a product useful to more people and thus enlarge its market. Companies can also place a product in a favorable competitive position by providing benefits that competing brands do not offer. Additionally, they can help an organization achieve and maintain a progressive image. Finally, functional modifications are sometimes made to reduce the possibility of product liability lawsuits, such as adding a kill switch on a machine.

Aesthetic Modifications

Aesthetic modifications change the sensory appeal of a product by altering its taste, texture, sound, smell, or appearance. A buyer making a purchase decision is swayed by how a product looks, smells, tastes, feels, or sounds. Thus, an aesthetic modification may strongly affect purchases. The fashion industry relies heavily on aesthetic modifications from season to season. For example, Armani clothing, shoes, watches, and leather goods are leaders in the haute couture industry. In order to maintain its reputation for the utmost level of quality and style, the company performs aesthetic modifications on its products regularly. This ensures that Armani maintains its reputation for cutting-edge design and quality. In addition, aesthetic modifications attempt to minimize the amount of illegal product counterfeiting that occurs through constant change in design.

Aesthetic modifications can help a firm differentiate its product from competing brands and thus gain a sizable market share. The major drawback in using aesthetic modifications is that their value is determined subjectively. Although a firm may strive to improve the product's sensory appeal, customers actually may find the modified product less attractive.

| 11-2 DEVELOPING NEW PRODUCTS

LO 11-2 Explore how businesses develop a product idea into a commercial product.

A firm develops new products as a means of enhancing its product mix and adding depth to a product line. Developing and introducing new products is frequently expensive and risky. However, failure to introduce new products is also risky. Consider the case of Kodak, once one of the world's best known brands, which marketed film and other products for cameras and imaging products. Although Kodak invested significant resources into developing a line of digital cameras, it persisted in trying to make them function like the conventional cameras it knew so well. Even after it became clear that consumers were shifting rapidly to digital cameras and later to smartphones, Kodak continued to define itself as a film company and failed to adapt to the disruption of digital technology and consumers' changing preferences. Although Kodak survives as an imaging company, consumers seldom describe the digital images they share on social media as "Kodak moments."[8]

The term *new product* can have more than one meaning. A genuinely new product offers innovative benefits. For example, Dyson's new Supersonic hairdryer uses proprietary technology and design that makes it quieter, less prone to burning users or damaging hair, and less likely to tire users' arms.[9]

Zapp2Photo/Shutterstock.com

New Product
Google Home allows you to play music, obtain information, and adjust lighting and temperatures in your home. Although smart speakers with voice assistants are not new, Google Home is a new product offering for Google.

However, products that are different and distinctly better are often viewed as new. For instance, the Colgate Optic White Toothbrush and Whitening Pen features special bristles that help remove tooth stains and comes with a whitening pen for applying a special gel directly on the teeth to make them even whiter. The pen is stored inside the toothbrush.[10] Toothbrushes already exist, as do teeth whitening products. However, consumers who want whiter teeth without expensive dental treatments or hard-to-use strips are likely to view this is a useful new product. A new product can also be a product that a given firm has not marketed previously, although similar products have been available from other companies. Google Home, for example, is not the first smart speaker with digital assistant available, but it is a new product offering for Google. Finally, a product can be viewed as new when it is brought to one or more markets from another market.

In recent years, a growing number of companies have found success by identifying ways to change how things are done in an industry and then developing products to lead the way. **Disruptive innovation**, first described by Professor Clayton Christensen of Harvard Business School, identifies old technologies that can be exploited in new ways or develops new business models to give customers more than they've come to expect from current products in a specific market. Companies like Google, Netflix, iTunes, Uber and Lyft, and Warby Parker have become successful by recognizing unmet or poorly satisfied needs and developing products to satisfy them. Michael Dubin, for example, founded Dollar Shave Club after recognizing that buying refill cartridges for men's razors was boring, expensive, and often frustrating when retailers keep them locked up. He also realized that most men don't change their cartridges often enough. Dollar Shave Club is a subscription service that sends four or five cartridges every month for as little as $1/month. Its more than 3 million subscribers can also get other skin care products shipped as well. The company's great success has spawned imitators and spurred shaving giant Gillette to launch its own subscription service.[11]

Before a product is introduced, it goes through the seven phases of the **new-product development process** shown in Figure 11.1: (1) idea generation, (2) screening, (3) concept testing, (4) business analysis, (5) product development, (6) test marketing, and (7) commercialization. A product may be dropped—and many are—at any stage of development. In this section, we look at the process through which products are developed from idea inception to fully commercialized product.

11-2a **Idea Generation**

Businesses and other organizations seek product ideas that will help them to achieve their objectives. This activity is **idea generation**. The fact that only a few ideas are good enough to be successful commercially underscores the challenge of the task.

At the heart of innovation is a purposeful, focused effort to identify new ways to serve a market.[12] New-product ideas can come from several sources. They may come from internal sources—marketing managers, researchers, sales personnel, engineers, franchisees, or other organizational personnel. Brainstorming and incentives or rewards for good ideas are typical intra-firm devices for stimulating development of ideas. For example, the idea for 3M Post-it Notes came from an employee. As a church choir member, he used slips of paper to mark songs in his hymnal. Because the pieces of paper fell out, he suggested developing an adhesive-backed note. Over time, employees have become more empowered to express their own product ideas to their supervisors. This collaborative process can be particularly useful to help marketers iron out the details of a new product concept.[13]

disruptive innovation Identifies old technologies that can be exploited in new ways or develops new business models to give customers more than they've come to expect from current products in a specific market

new-product development process A seven-phase process for introducing products

idea generation Seeking product ideas that will help organizations to achieve objectives

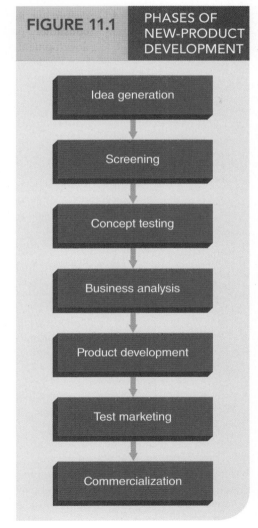

FIGURE 11.1 PHASES OF NEW-PRODUCT DEVELOPMENT

Idea generation

Screening

Concept testing

Business analysis

Product development

Test marketing

Commercialization

New-product ideas also may arise from sources outside the firm, such as customers, competitors, advertising agencies, management consultants, and research organizations. Increasingly, firms are bringing consumers into the product idea development process through online campaigns. The Internet gives marketers the chance to tap into consumer ideas by building online communities and listening to their product needs and wants. These communities provide consumers with a sense of empowerment and allow them to give insight for new product ideas that can prove invaluable to the firm.[14] The Internet and social media have become very important tools for gathering information from stakeholders, particularly when a firm is targeting younger consumers. Frito-Lay, for example, holds an annual contest inviting consumers to submit photos, videos, or written descriptions of their ideas for a new Lay's potato chip flavor idea to a special Lay's website. The winner receives $1 million, and Frito-Lay gets a fresh new flavor.[15] The interactivity of the Internet allows other stakeholders not only to suggest and analyze new product ideas but also to interact with one another on evaluating and filtering these ideas. Asking customers what they want from products has helped many firms become successful and remain competitive.

Many of today's most successful companies solicit ideas from inventors and outside consultants. Procter & Gamble is one such firm. The company's Connect + Develop website uses crowdsourcing to encourage creative individuals to submit innovative ideas for new products.[16] Many firms offer product development consulting and can be good sources for stimulating new product ideas. For example, Kaleidoscope offers product design, engineering, and development services to companies in the health-care, medical, consumer goods, electronics, and high-tech industries.[17] When outsourcing new-product development activities to outside organizations, the best results are achieved from spelling out the specific tasks with detailed contractual specifications. Asking customers what they want from products has helped many firms become successful and remain competitive. As more global consumers become interconnected through the Internet, marketers have the chance to tap into consumer ideas by building online communities with them.

11-2b Screening

In the process of **screening**, the ideas with the greatest potential are selected for further review. During screening, product ideas are analyzed to determine whether they match the organization's mission, objectives, and resources. Cannibalization is another issue that should be examined during the screening process. If a product idea results in a product similar to the firm's existing products, marketers must assess the degree to which the new product could eat into the sales of current products. Additionally, the company should analyze its overall abilities to produce and market the product. Other aspects of an idea to be weighed are the nature and wants of buyers and possible environmental changes. At times, a checklist of new-product requirements is used when making screening decisions. This practice encourages evaluators to be systematic and thus reduces the chances of overlooking some pertinent fact. Most new product ideas are rejected during the screening phase.

11-2c Concept Testing

To evaluate ideas properly, it may be necessary to test product concepts. In **concept testing**, a small sample of potential buyers is presented with a product idea through a written or oral description (and perhaps a few drawings) to determine their attitudes and initial buying intentions regarding the product. Asian fast-casual restaurant chain Pei Wei, for example, maintains a test kitchen in a working Scottsdale, AZ, restaurant to try out potential new products and get authentic feedback from actual Pei Wei customers.[18] For a single product idea, an organization can test one or several concepts of the same product. Concept testing is a low-cost procedure that allows a company to determine customers'

screening Choosing the most promising ideas for further review

concept testing Seeking potential buyers' responses to a product idea

initial reactions to a product idea before it invests considerable resources in research and development.

During concept testing, the concept is described briefly, and then a series of questions is presented to a test panel. For a potential food product, a sample may be offered. The questions vary considerably depending on the type of product being tested. Typical questions include the following: In general, do you find this proposed product attractive? Which benefits are especially attractive to you? Which features are of little or no interest to you? Do you feel that this proposed product would work better for you than the product you currently use? Compared with your current product, what are the primary advantages of the proposed product? If this product were available at an appropriate price, would you buy it? How often would you buy this product? How could this proposed product be improved?

11-2d Business Analysis

During the **business analysis** stage, the product idea is evaluated to determine its potential contribution to the firm's sales, costs, and profits. In the course of a business analysis, evaluators ask various questions: Does the product fit with the organization's existing product mix? Is demand strong enough to justify entering the market, and will the demand endure? What types of environmental and competitive changes can be expected, and how will these changes affect the product's future sales, costs, and profits?

It is crucial that a firm determine whether its research, development, engineering, and production capabilities are adequate to develop the product; whether new facilities must be constructed, how quickly they can be built, and how much they will cost; and whether the necessary financing for development and commercialization is on hand or is obtainable based upon terms consistent with a favorable return on investment.

In the business analysis stage, firms seek market information. The results of consumer polls, along with secondary data, supply the specifics needed to estimate potential sales, costs, and profits. For many products in this stage (when they are still just product ideas), forecasting sales accurately is difficult. This is especially true for innovative and completely new products. Organizations sometimes employ break-even analysis to determine how many units they would have to sell to begin making a profit. At times, an organization also uses payback analysis, in which marketers compute the time period required to recover the funds that would be invested in developing the new product. Because break-even and payback analyses are based on estimates, they are usually viewed as useful but not particularly precise tools.

11-2e Product Development

Product development is the phase in which the organization determines if it is technically feasible to produce the product and if it can be produced at costs low enough to make the final price reasonable. To test its acceptability, the idea or concept is converted into a prototype, or working model. When Dyson was working to develop its Supersonic hair dryer, it went through 600 prototypes before it found the right one.[19] The prototype should reveal tangible and intangible attributes associated with the product in consumers' minds. The product's design, mechanical features, and intangible aspects must be linked to wants in the marketplace. Through marketing research and concept testing, product attributes that are important to buyers are identified. These characteristics must be communicated to customers through the design of the product.

After a prototype is developed, its overall functioning must be tested. Its performance, safety, convenience, and other functional qualities are tested both in a laboratory and in the field. Functional testing should be rigorous and lengthy enough to test the product thoroughly. The form or design of a product can actually influence how consumers view the product's functional performance.[20] Manufacturing issues that come to light at this stage may require adjustments.

business analysis Evaluating the potential contribution of a product idea to the firm's sales, costs, and profits

product development Determining if producing a product is technically feasible and cost effective

test marketing Introducing a product on a limited basis to measure the extent to which potential customers will actually buy it

A crucial question that arises during product development is how much quality to build into the product. For example, a major dimension of quality is durability. Higher quality often calls for better materials and more expensive processing, which increase production costs and, ultimately, the product's price. In determining the specific level of quality, a marketer must ascertain approximately what price the target market views as acceptable. In addition, a marketer usually tries to set a quality level consistent with that of the firm's other products. Obviously, the quality of competing brands is also a consideration.

The development phase of a new product is frequently lengthy and expensive; thus a relatively small number of product ideas are put into development. If the product appears sufficiently successful during this stage to merit test marketing, then, during the latter part of the development stage, marketers begin to make decisions regarding branding, packaging, labeling, pricing, and promotion for use in the test marketing stage.

11-2f Test Marketing

A limited introduction of a product in geographic areas chosen to represent the intended market is called **test marketing**. The aim of test marketing is to determine the extent to which potential customers will buy the product. Wendy's, for example, test marketed a truffle bacon cheeseburger and bacon truffle fries at some Massachusetts and Tennessee locations.[21] Test marketing is not an extension of the development stage; it is a sample launching of the entire marketing mix. Test marketing should be conducted only after the product has gone through development and initial plans regarding the other marketing-mix variables. Companies use test marketing to lessen the risk of product failure. The dangers of introducing an untested product include undercutting already profitable products and, should the new product fail, loss of credibility with distributors and customers.

Test marketing provides several benefits. It lets marketers expose a product in a natural marketing environment to measure its sales performance. The company can strive to identify weaknesses in the product or in other parts of the marketing mix. A product weakness discovered after a nationwide introduction can be expensive to correct. Moreover, if consumers' early reactions are negative, marketers may be unable to persuade consumers to try the product again. Thus, making adjustments after test marketing can be crucial to the success of a new product. On the other hand, test marketing results may be positive enough to warrant accelerating the product's introduction. Test marketing also allows marketers to experiment with variations in advertising, pricing, and packaging in different test areas and to measure the extent of brand awareness, brand switching, and repeat purchases resulting from these alterations in the marketing mix.

Selection of appropriate test areas is very important because the validity of test market results depends heavily on selecting test sites that provide accurate representations of the intended target market. U.S. cities commonly used for test marketing appear in Table 11.1. The criteria used for choosing test cities depend upon the product's attributes, the target market's characteristics, and the firm's objectives and resources.

Test marketing is not without risks. It is expensive, and competitors may try to interfere. A competitor may attempt to "jam" the test program by increasing its own advertising or promotions, lowering prices, and offering special incentives, all to combat the recognition and purchase of the new brand. Any such tactics can invalidate test results. Sometimes, too, competitors copy the product in the testing stage and rush to introduce a

TABLE 11.1	COMMON TEST MARKET CITIES
Rank	**City**
1	Columbus, Ohio
2	Peoria, Illinois
3	Albany, New York
4	Jacksonville, Florida
5	Lexington, Kentucky
6	Des Moines, Iowa
7	Battle Creek, Michigan
8	Greensboro, North Carolina
9	Cleveland, Ohio
10	Phoenix, Arizona

similar product. It is desirable to move to the commercialization phase as soon as possible after successful testing.

Because of these risks, many companies use alternative methods to measure customer preferences. One such method is simulated test marketing. Typically, consumers at shopping centers are asked to view an advertisement for a new product and are given a free sample to take home. These consumers are interviewed subsequently over the phone and asked to rate the product. The major advantages of simulated test marketing are greater speed, lower costs, and tighter security, which reduce the flow of information to competitors and reduce jamming. Several marketing research firms, such as ACNielsen Company, offer test marketing services to provide independent assessments of proposed products. Not all test-marketed products are launched. At times, problems discovered during test marketing cannot be resolved.

11-2g Commercialization

During the commercialization phase, plans for full-scale manufacturing and marketing must be refined and settled and budgets for the project prepared. Early in the commercialization phase, marketing management analyzes the results of test marketing to find out what changes in the marketing mix are needed before the product is introduced. The results of test marketing may suggest the need to change one or more of the product's physical attributes, modify the distribution plans to include more retail outlets, alter promotional efforts, or change the product's price. However, as more and more changes are made based on test marketing findings, the test marketing projections may become less valid.

During the early part of this stage, marketers not only must gear up for larger-scale production but also must make decisions about warranties, repairs, and replacement parts. The type of warranty a firm provides can be a critical issue for buyers, especially for expensive, technically complex goods such as appliances or frequently used items such as mattresses. Tempur-Pedic, for example, offers a 90-day, no-risk, in-home trial of its innovative mattresses. If, after 90 days, the customer is not satisfied, the retailer will pick up the mattress for a modest return fee. Establishing an effective system for providing repair services and replacement parts is necessary to maintain favorable customer relationships. Although the producer may furnish these services directly to buyers, it is more common for the producer to provide such services through regional service centers. Regardless of how services are provided, it is important to customers that they be performed quickly and correctly.

The product enters the market during the commercialization phase. When introducing a product, a firm may spend enormous sums for advertising, personal selling, and other types of promotion, as well as for plant and equipment. Such expenditures may not be recovered for several years. Smaller firms may find this process difficult, but even so, they may use press releases, blogs, podcasts, social media, and other tools to capture quick feedback as well as promote the new product. Another low-cost promotional tool is product reviews in newspapers and magazines, which can be especially helpful when they are positive and target the same customers.

Products are not usually launched nationwide overnight but are introduced through a process called a *rollout*. Through a rollout, a product is introduced in stages, starting in one geographic area and gradually expanding into adjacent areas. It may take several years to market the product nationally. Sometimes, the test cities are used as initial marketing areas, and introduction of the product becomes a natural extension of test marketing. A product test marketed in Sacramento, California, and Fort Collins, Colorado, could be introduced first in those cities. After the stage 1 introduction is complete, stage 2 could include market coverage of the states where the test cities are located. In stage 3, marketing efforts might be extended into adjacent states. All remaining states then would be covered in stage 4. Figure 11.2 demonstrates these four stages of commercialization.

Gradual product introductions do not always occur state by state; other geographic combinations, such as groups of counties that cross state borders, are sometimes used. Products destined for multinational markets also may be rolled out one country or region

commercialization Deciding on full-scale manufacturing and marketing plans and preparing budgets

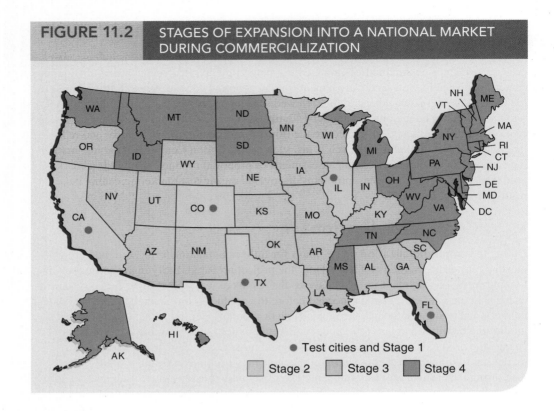

FIGURE 11.2   STAGES OF EXPANSION INTO A NATIONAL MARKET DURING COMMERCIALIZATION

● Test cities and Stage 1
Stage 2   Stage 3   Stage 4

at a time. Gradual product introduction is desirable for several reasons. It reduces the risks of introducing a new product. If the product fails, the firm will experience smaller losses if it introduced the item in only a few geographic areas than if it marketed the product nationally. Furthermore, a company cannot introduce a product nationwide overnight because a system of wholesalers and retailers necessary to distribute the product cannot be

ENTREPRENEURSHIP IN MARKETING

How Safe Is Your Phone? Maybe Leather, Linen, and Wood Can Help

Entrepreneurs Brian and Kari Holmes were thinking about old-fashioned American craftsmanship when the couple founded their Minneapolis-based business, Pad & Quill, in 2010. They started with $1,200 and the idea that iPhone users would appreciate an artistic, high-quality case made with care, "a beautiful product that is functional," as Brian Holmes explains.

Although he knew he could cut costs by having his cell phone cases manufactured overseas, Holmes also believed that well-crafted, higher-end "made in America" products would appeal to a sizable niche market. It took time to locate a production partner capable of manufacturing wood and leather cases to Pad & Quill's exacting standards, but he eventually found a suitable company close

by in St. Paul, Minnesota. Another benefit of local production was fast turnaround, allowing Pad & Quill to speed its new products to market.

After a challenging first year spent testing products and gauging demand, Pad & Quill became profitable during its second year, selling products online only. Now annual revenues are approaching $3 million as the company expands its product line to include leather and wooden cases for other Apple products as well as leather wallets and bags. Every time Apple announces a new phone or some other device, Pad & Quill rushes to check the specifications so it can develop a functional and visually-pleasing case for customers willing to pay a little more for "made in America" craftsmanship and quality.[a]

established so quickly. The development of a distribution network may take considerable time. Also, the number of units needed to satisfy national demand for a successful product can be enormous, and a firm usually cannot produce the required quantities in a short time. Finally, gradual introduction allows for fine-tuning of the marketing mix to satisfy target customers.

Despite the good reasons for introducing a product gradually, marketers realize that this approach creates some competitive problems. A gradual introduction allows competitors to observe what the firm is doing and to monitor results, just as the firm's own marketers are doing. If competitors see that the newly introduced product is successful, they may quickly enter the same target market with similar products. In addition, as a product is introduced region by region, competitors may expand their marketing efforts to offset promotion of the new product. Marketers should realize that too much delay in launching a product can cause the firm to miss out on seizing market opportunities, creating competitive offerings, and forming cooperative relationships with channel members.[22]

11-3 PRODUCT DIFFERENTIATION THROUGH QUALITY, DESIGN, AND SUPPORT SERVICES

LO 11-3 Discuss the importance of product differentiation and the elements that differentiate one product from another.

Some of the most important characteristics of products are the elements that distinguish them from one another. **Product differentiation** is the process of creating and designing products so that customers perceive them as different from competing products. Customer perception is critical in differentiating products. Perceived differences might include quality, features, styling, price, and image. A crucial element used to differentiate one product from another is the brand. In this section, we examine three aspects of product differentiation that companies must consider when creating and offering products for sale: product quality, product design and features, and product support services. These aspects involve the company's attempt to create real differences among products. Later in this chapter, we discuss how companies position their products in the marketplace based on these three aspects.

11-3a Product Quality

Quality refers to the overall characteristics of a product that allow it to perform *as expected* in satisfying customer needs. The words *as expected* are very important to this definition because quality usually means different things to different customers. For some, durability signifies quality. The Craftsman line of tools at Sears is an example of a product with a reputation for durability; indeed, Sears provides a lifetime guarantee on the durability of its tools. For other consumers, a product's ease of use may indicate quality.

The concept of quality also varies between consumer and business markets. For business markets, technical suitability, ease of repair, and company reputation are important characteristics. Unlike consumers, most businesses place far less emphasis on price than on product quality. A business is likely to be more concerned with a desk chair's functionality and comfort, for instance, than price or aesthetics.

One important dimension of quality is **level of quality**, the amount of quality a product possesses. The concept is a relative one because the quality level of one product is difficult to describe unless it is compared with that of other products. The American Customer Satisfaction Index, compiled by the National Quality Research Center at the University of Michigan, ranks customer satisfaction among a wide variety of businesses. According to its survey, Dial had the highest rating of customer satisfaction in the personal care and cleaning products industry.[23] Consider how the advertisement for Blue Apron emphasizes level of

product differentiation Creating and designing products so that customers perceive them as different from competing products

quality Characteristics of a product that allow it to perform as expected in satisfying customer needs

level of quality The amount of quality a product possesses

Level of Quality
Blue Apron focuses on a high level of quality by promoting fresh ingredients, easy-to-follow recipes, and simple weekly delivery.

quality. The image of the inside of a Blue Apron meal box showcases the beautiful fruits, vegetables, and well labeled ingredients customers can expect from the meal-making kits. The ad reinforces the image with the tagline, "incredible ingredients make incredible meals" to tempt consumers to try out the service. The ad even offers $30 off the first delivery as a further inducement to give Blue Apron a try. On the other hand, products that fail to obtain a certain level of quality may cause dissatisfied customers to curtail their overall spending, which could stifle economic growth.

A second important dimension is consistency. **Consistency of quality** refers to the degree to which a product has the same level of quality over time. Consistency means giving customers the quality they expect every time they purchase the product. As with level of quality, consistency is a relative concept. It implies a quality comparison within the same brand over time.

The consistency of product quality can also be compared across competing products. It is at this stage that consistency becomes critical to a company's success. Companies that can provide quality on a consistent basis have a major competitive advantage over rivals. FedEx, for example, offers reliable delivery schedules and a variety of options. It is considered among the best consumer shipping companies in terms of quality.[24] No company has ever succeeded by creating and marketing low-quality products that do not satisfy consumers. Many companies have taken major steps, such as implementing total quality management (TQM), to improve the quality of their products and become more competitive.

11-3b Product Design and Features

Product design refers to how a product is conceived, planned, and produced. Design is a very complex topic because it involves the total sum of all the product's physical characteristics. Many companies are known for the outstanding designs of their products: Apple for electronics and computers, Cuisinart for kitchen appliances, and Merrell for hiking boots. Good design is one of the best competitive advantages any brand can possess.

One component of design is **styling**, or the physical appearance of the product. The style of a product is one design feature that can allow certain products to sell very rapidly. Good design means more than just appearance; it also involves a product's functionality and usefulness. A pair of jeans may look great, but if they fall apart after three washes, clearly the design was poor. Most consumers seek products that both look good and function well.

Product features are specific design characteristics that allow a product to perform certain tasks. By adding or subtracting features, a company can differentiate its products from those of the competition. Product features also can be used to differentiate products within the same company. For instance, Nike offers a range of shoes designed for purposes from walking, to running, to weightlifting, to cross-training in a gym. In general, the more features a product has, the higher is its price, and often, the higher is the perceived quality.

For a brand to have a sustainable competitive advantage, marketers must determine the product designs and features that customers desire. Information from marketing research efforts and from databases can help in assessing customers' product design and feature

consistency of quality The degree to which a product has the same level of quality over time

product design How a product is conceived, planned, and produced

styling The physical appearance of a product

product features Specific design characteristics that allow a product to perform certain tasks

preferences. Being able to meet customers' desires for product design and features at prices they can afford is crucial to a product's long-term success. Marketers must be careful not to misrepresent or overpromise regarding product features or performance.

customer services Human or mechanical efforts or activities that add value to a product

11-3c Product Support Services

Many companies differentiate their product offerings by providing support services. Usually referred to as **customer services**, these services include any human or mechanical efforts or activities a company provides that add value to a product. Examples of customer services include delivery and installation, financing arrangements, customer training, warranties and guarantees, repairs, layaway plans, convenient hours of operation, adequate parking, and information through toll-free numbers and websites. Trader Joe's stands out among supermarkets for its stellar customer service. Marketers at Trader Joe's strive to ensure that nothing interrupts the positive experience and to create opportunities for employees to connect with customers. The approach ensures that shoppers find and purchase exactly what they want. To create a more personal environment, the stores do not even have loudspeakers. As a result, Trader Joe's customers are highly loyal and sales per square foot frequently are triple that of competitors.[25]

Whether as a major or minor part of the total product offering, all marketers of goods sell customer services. Providing good customer service may be the only way that a company can differentiate its products when all products in a market have essentially the same quality, design, and features. This is especially true in the computer industry. When buying a laptop computer, for example, consumers shop more for fast delivery, technical support, warranties, and price than for product quality and design, as witnessed by the high volume of "off-the-shelf," non-customized, sometimes lagging in technology, discount laptops sold at Best Buy, Costco, Walmart, Target, and the like. Through research, a company can discover the types of services customers want and need. Add-on features can also enhance a product in the eyes of the consumer. Consumers often infer a higher level of quality from the mere availability of add-on services.[26]

DIGITAL MARKETING

Starbucks Brews Up Mobile Order-and-Pay

Competition is heating up for Starbucks, the Seattle-based company that popularized "coffee culture" and operates 25,000 cafés worldwide. Now Starbucks is further sharpening its competitive edge by applying technology to make customer service even more convenient. The company already offers mobile payment options, allowing customers to pay for their orders with a smartphone app. More than 8 million Starbucks customers take advantage of this way to speed up purchases.

Now Starbucks is taking the next step by introducing apps for mobile ordering and payment with a tap or a voice command, so customers can avoid waiting in line at the café. Customers set up the iPhone or Android app with instructions for their usual orders, and include payment details. Then they simply tap to have an order ready for pickup

at the designated café. The app can even respond to voice commands, using artificial intelligence to understand what customers say, asking about any changes or additions to the order, and sending the order to the café. Soon customers will be able to ask Alexa, the Amazon virtual assistant, to handle the transaction by saying, "Alexa, order my Starbucks."

Mobile order-and-pay has been highly successful—so much so that the highest-traffic U.S. cafés initially struggled to keep up with the barrage of mobile orders. CEO Howard Schultz acknowledged the challenge of "too much demand" and instituted changes such as refining behind-the-scenes work routines to better manage peak volume. As Starbucks adds mobile ordering and payment to its services in other nations, the company is planning carefully to maintain quality service.[b]

product positioning Creating and maintaining a certain concept of a product in customers' minds

11-4 PRODUCT POSITIONING AND REPOSITIONING

LO 11-4 Explain how businesses position their products.

Product positioning refers to the decisions and activities intended to create and maintain a certain concept of the firm's product (relative to competitive brands) in customers' minds. When marketers introduce a product, they try to position it so that it appears to have the characteristics that the target market most desires. This projected image is crucial. Crest, for example, is positioned as a fluoride toothpaste that fights cavities, whereas Rembrandt is positioned as a whitening toothpaste to fight stains.

11-4a Perceptual Mapping

A product's position is the result of customers' perceptions of the product's attributes relative to those of competitive brands. Buyers make numerous purchase decisions on a regular basis. To avoid a continuous reevaluation of numerous products, buyers tend to group, or "position," products in their minds to simplify buying decisions. Rather than allowing customers to position products independently, marketers often try to influence and shape consumers' concepts or perceptions of products through advertising. Marketers sometimes analyze product positions by developing perceptual maps, as shown in Figure 11.3. Perceptual maps are created by questioning a sample of consumers about their perceptions of products, brands, and organizations with respect to two or more dimensions. To develop a perceptual map like the one in Figure 11.3, respondents would be asked how they perceive selected pain relievers in regard to price and type of pain for which the products are used. Also, respondents would be asked about their preferences for product features to establish "ideal points" or "ideal clusters," which represent a consensus about a specific group of customers' desires in terms of product features. Then marketers can see how their brand is perceived compared with the ideal points.

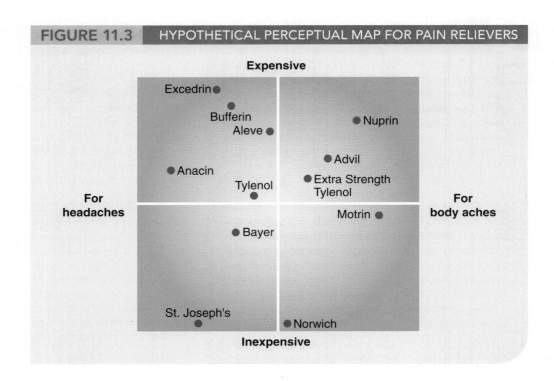

FIGURE 11.3   HYPOTHETICAL PERCEPTUAL MAP FOR PAIN RELIEVERS

11-4b Bases for Positioning

Marketers can use several bases for product positioning. A common basis for positioning products is to use competitors. A firm can position a product to compete head-on with another brand, as PepsiCo has done against Coca-Cola, or to avoid competition, as 7UP has done relative to other soft-drink producers. Head-to-head competition may be a marketer's positioning objective if the product's performance characteristics are at least equal to those of competitive brands and if the product is priced lower. Head-to-head positioning may be appropriate even when the price is higher if the product's performance characteristics are superior. Interestingly, smaller or less well-known brands in industries that have dominant competitors can actually increase visibility and sales by emphasizing the size and proximity of their competitor's brand compared to their own.[27] SodaStream, which manufactures a consumer home carbonation product, uses a head-to-head positioning strategy against the dominant players in the soda market, Pepsi and Coca-Cola. SodaStream positions itself as a healthier, more eco-friendly brand, and portrays its top competitors as environmentally harmful due to the large amounts of plastic bottle waste that ends up in landfills.

Conversely, positioning to avoid competition may be best when the product's performance characteristics do not differ significantly from those of competing brands. Moreover, positioning a brand to avoid competition may be appropriate when that brand has unique characteristics that are important to some buyers. Volvo, for example, has for years positioned itself away from competitors by focusing on the safety characteristics of its cars. Whereas some auto companies mention safety issues in their advertisements, many are more likely to focus on style, fuel efficiency, performance, or terms of sale. Avoiding competition is critical when a firm introduces a brand into a market in which the company already has one or more brands. Marketers usually want to avoid cannibalizing sales of their existing brands unless the new brand generates substantially larger profits.

A product's position can be based on specific product attributes or features. Apple's iPhone, for instance, is positioned based on product attributes such as its sleek design and compatibility with other Apple products and accessories, such as apps and music through the iTunes store. Style, shape, construction, and color help to create the image and the appeal. If buyers can easily identify the benefits, they are, of course, more likely to purchase the product. When the new product does not offer certain preferred attributes, there is room for another new product.

Other bases for product positioning include price, quality level, and benefits provided by the product. GEICO, for instance, is positioned on the basis of its low insurance prices, customer satisfaction, and 24/7 licensed agents. The GEICO advertisement uses colorful macaroons to show consumers that it offers more than its competitors. The ad also reminds consumers that GEICO is the second largest auto insurer and has been around for 80 years, telling consumers, "The choice is yours, and it's simple." The target market can also be a positioning basis caused by marketing. This type of positioning relies heavily on promoting to the types of people who use the product.

11-4c Repositioning

Positioning decisions are not just for new products. Evaluating the positions of existing products is important because a brand's market share and profitability may be strengthened by product repositioning. When introducing a new product into a

Product Positioning
GEICO positions itself as a marketer of inexpensive car insurance that provides a high level of customer satisfaction through 24/7 licensed agents.

product deletion Eliminating a product from the product mix

product line, one or more existing brands may have to be repositioned to minimize cannibalization of established brands and thus ensure a favorable position for the new brand.

Repositioning can be accomplished by physically changing the product, its price, or its distribution. Rather than making any of these changes, marketers sometimes reposition a product by changing its image through promotional efforts. Wyndham Hotel Group repositioned each of its 16 lodging brands to broaden their appeal and distinguish them in an increasingly crowded hospitality market. In addition to updating and refreshing individual hotels, the company also gave the brands new slogans backed by promotional efforts. Travelodge, for example, now has the slogan, "Your Basecamp for Adventure," and has partnered with the National Parks Conservation Association to highlight nearby national parks.[28] Finally, a marketer may reposition a product by aiming it at a different target market.

11-5 PRODUCT DELETION

LO 11-5 Discuss how product deletion is used to improve product mixes.

Generally, a product cannot satisfy target market customers and contribute to the achievement of an organization's overall goals indefinitely. **Product deletion** is the process of eliminating a product from the product mix, usually because it no longer satisfies a sufficient number of customers. Chick-fil-A, for instance, discontinued its Spicy Chicken Biscuit due to flagging sales. Although some customers took to social media to protest the deletion, the product accounted for just one half of 1 percent of the chain's breakfast sales.[29] A declining product reduces an organization's profitability and drains resources that could be used to modify other products or develop new ones. A marginal product may require shorter production runs, which can increase per-unit production costs. Finally, when a dying product completely loses favor with customers, the negative feelings may transfer to some of the company's other products.

Most organizations find it difficult to delete a product. A decision to drop a product may be opposed by managers and other employees who believe that the product is necessary to the product mix. Salespeople who still have some loyal customers are especially upset when a product is dropped. Companies may spend considerable resources and effort to revive a slipping product's marketing mix to improve its sales and thus avoid having to eliminate it.

Some organizations delete products only after the products have become heavy financial burdens. A better approach is some form of systematic review in which each product is

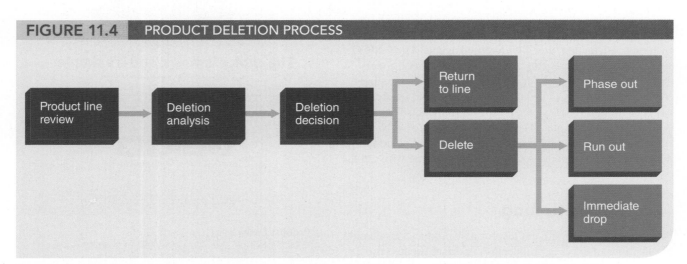

FIGURE 11.4   PRODUCT DELETION PROCESS

Product line review → Deletion analysis → Deletion decision → Return to line → Phase out

Delete → Run out

Immediate drop

Source: Martin L. Bell, *Marketing Concepts and Strategy*, 3rd ed., p. 267; Copyright 1979. Houghton Mifflin Company. Reprinted by permission of Mrs. Martin L. Bell.

evaluated periodically to determine its impact on the overall effectiveness of the firm's product mix. Such a review should analyze the product's contribution to the firm's sales for a given period, as well as estimate future sales, costs, and profits associated with the product. It also should gauge the value of making changes in the marketing strategy to improve the product's performance. A systematic review allows an organization to improve product performance and ascertain when to delete products. For instance, analysis by Procter & Gamble led the company to slash its portfolio by 100 brands, including CoverGirl, Nice 'n Easy, and Duracell, divesting less profitable products over a two year period to focus more resources on its more successful brands.[30]

There are three basic ways to delete a product: phase it out, run it out, or drop it immediately (see Figure 11.4). A *phase-out* allows the product to decline without a change in the marketing strategy; no attempt is made to give the product new life. A *run-out* exploits any strengths left in the product. Intensifying marketing efforts in core markets or eliminating some marketing expenditures, such as advertising, may cause a sudden jump in profits. This approach is commonly taken for technologically obsolete products, such as older models of computers and CD players. Often, the price is reduced to get a sales spurt. The third alternative, an *immediate drop* of an unprofitable product, is the best strategy when losses are too great to prolong the product's life.

11-6 MANAGING SERVICES

LO 11-6 Summarize how the characteristics of services influence the development of marketing mixes for services.

Many products are services rather than tangible goods. The organizations that market service products include for-profit firms, such as those offering financial, personal, and professional services, and nonprofit organizations, such as educational institutions, churches, charities, and governments. In this section, we focus initially on the growing importance of service industries in our economy. Then we address the unique characteristics of services. Finally, we deal with the challenges these characteristics pose in developing and managing marketing mixes for services.

11-6a Nature and Importance of Services

All products—whether goods, services, or ideas—are to some extent intangible. Services are usually provided through the application of human and/or mechanical efforts directed at people or objects. For example, a service such as education involves the efforts of service providers (teachers) directed at people (students), whereas janitorial and interior decorating services direct their efforts at objects. Services also can involve the use of mechanical efforts directed at people (air or public transportation) or objects (freight transportation). A wide variety of services, such as health care and landscaping, involve both human and mechanical efforts. Although many services entail the use of tangibles such as tools and machinery, the primary difference

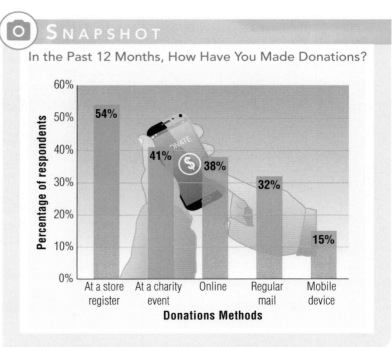

SNAPSHOT

In the Past 12 Months, How Have You Made Donations?

Source: Cone Communications Digital Activism Study of 873 adults

between a service and a good is that a service is dominated by the intangible portion of the total product. Services, as products, should not be confused with the related topic of customer services. While customer service is part of the marketing of goods, service marketers also provide customer services.

The importance of services in the U.S. economy led the United States to be known as the world's first service economy. In most developed countries, including Germany, Japan, Australia, and Canada, services account for about 70 percent of the gross domestic product (GDP). More than one-half of new businesses are service businesses, and service employment is expected to continue to grow. A practice that has gained popularity among a number of U.S. businesses is **homesourcing**, in which customer-contact jobs, such as at call centers, are outsourced to the homes of workers. Home-based customer service agents are growing twice as fast as more traditional customer contact centers.[31]

11-6b Characteristics of Services

The issues associated with marketing service products are not exactly the same as those associated with marketing goods. To understand these differences, it is first necessary to understand the distinguishing characteristics of services. Services have six basic characteristics: intangibility, inseparability of production and consumption, perishability, heterogeneity, client-based relationships, and customer contact.[32]

Intangibility

As already noted, the major characteristic that distinguishes a service from a good is intangibility. **Intangibility** means a service is not physical and therefore cannot be touched. For example, it is impossible to touch the education that students derive from attending classes—the intangible benefit is becoming more knowledgeable. In addition, services cannot be physically possessed. Figure 11.5 depicts a tangibility continuum from pure goods (tangible)

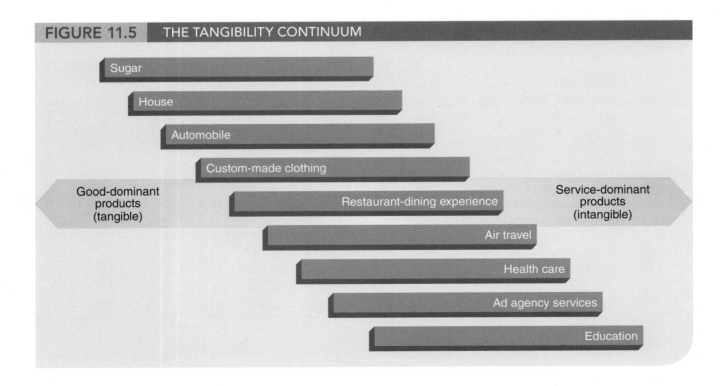

FIGURE 11.5   THE TANGIBILITY CONTINUUM

Sugar
House
Automobile
Custom-made clothing
Restaurant-dining experience
Air travel
Health care
Ad agency services
Education

Good-dominant products (tangible)　　　Service-dominant products (intangible)

to pure services (intangible). Pure goods, if they exist at all, are rare because practically all marketers of goods also provide customer services. Intangible, service-dominant products such as education and health care are clearly service products. Most products fall somewhere in the middle of this continuum. Products such as a restaurant meal or a hotel stay have both tangible and intangible dimensions.

Inseparability of Production and Consumption

Another important characteristic of services that creates challenges for marketers is **inseparability**, which refers to the fact that the production of a service cannot be separated from its consumption by customers. For instance, an airline flight is produced and consumed simultaneously—that is, services are produced, sold, and consumed at the same time. In goods marketing, a customer can purchase a good, take it home, and store it until ready for use. The manufacturer of the good may never see an actual customer. Customers, however, often must be present at the production of a service (such as investment consulting or surgery) and cannot take the service home. Indeed, both the service provider and the customer must work together to provide and receive the service's full value. Because of inseparability, customers not only want a specific type of service but also expect it to be provided in a specific way by a specific individual. For example, the production and consumption of a medical exam occur simultaneously, and the patient knows in advance who the physician is and generally understands how the exam will be conducted. Inseparability implies a shared responsibility between the customer and service provider. When delays or service failures occur, customers experience dissatisfaction with the service experience. Training programs for employees in the service sector should stress the importance of the customer in the service experience so that employees understand that the shared responsibility exists. For uncontrollable or unforeseen situations that damage the service experience, service providers should find the most optimal method of communicating problems to customers. Speedy communication often has the effect of decreasing customer dissatisfaction when a service failure occurs.[33]

Perishability

Services are characterized by **perishability** because the unused service capacity of one time period cannot be stored for future use. For example, empty seats on an air flight today cannot be stored and sold to passengers at a later date. Other examples of service perishability include unsold basketball tickets, unscheduled dental appointment times, and empty hotel rooms. Although some goods (e.g., meat, milk, or produce) are perishable, goods generally are less perishable than services. If a pair of jeans has been sitting on a department store shelf for a month, the quality is not affected. Goods marketers can handle the supply-demand problem through production scheduling and inventory techniques. Service marketers do not have the same advantage, and they face several hurdles in trying to balance supply and demand. They can, however, plan for demand that fluctuates according to day of the week, time of day, or season.

Heterogeneity

Services delivered by people are susceptible to **heterogeneity**, or variation in quality. Quality of manufactured goods is easier to control with standardized procedures, and mistakes are easier to isolate and

inseparability Being produced and consumed at the same time

perishability The inability of unused service capacity to be stored for future use

heterogeneity Variation in quality

Perishability of Services
For airlines, empty seats represent lost revenue that cannot be recovered. Obviously, yesterday's empty airline seats cannot be sold today. For this reason, airlines often offer incentives to fill empty seats even if it means lowering the price.

Heterogeneity of Services
Do you like to go to the same hair care professional most of the time? If so, it is probably because you want the same quality of hair care, such as a haircut that you have received from this individual in the past.

correct. Because of the nature of human behavior, however, it is very difficult for service providers to maintain a consistent quality of service delivery. This variation in quality can occur from one organization to another, from one service person to another within the same service facility, and from one service facility to another within the same organization. For example, the staff people at one bookstore location may be more knowledgeable and therefore more helpful than those in another bookstore owned by the same chain. Heterogeneity usually increases as the degree of labor intensiveness increases. Many services, such as auto repair, education, and hairstyling, rely heavily on human labor. Other services, such as telecommunications, health clubs, and public transportation, are more equipment intensive. People-based services are often prone to fluctuations in quality from one time period to the next. For example, the fact that a hairstylist gives a customer a good haircut today does not guarantee that customer a haircut of equal quality from the same hairstylist at a later date. Equipment-based services, in contrast, suffer from this problem to a lesser degree than people-based services. For instance, automated teller machines have reduced inconsistency in the quality of teller services at banks, and barcode scanning has improved the accuracy of service at the checkout counters in grocery stores.

Client-Based Relationships

The success of many services depends on creating and maintaining **client-based relationships**, which are interactions with customers that result in satisfied customers who use a service repeatedly over time.[34] In fact, some service providers, such as lawyers, accountants, and financial advisors, call their customers *clients* and often develop and maintain close long-term relationships with them. For such service providers, it is not enough to attract customers. They are successful only to the degree to which they can maintain a group of clients who use their services on an ongoing basis. For example, an accountant may serve a family in his or her area for decades. If the members of this family like the quality of the accountant's services, they are likely to recommend the accountant to other families. If several families repeat this positive word-of-mouth communication, the accountant likely will acquire a long list of satisfied clients.

Social media have made it easier for customers to share information about service companies. On Pinterest, users create separate pinboards for different categories, such as a wedding or party they are planning, and other users can use these boards for ideas and inspiration. Companies who engage users on Pinterest through pin-its, re-pins, and rich pins increase brand awareness and marketing to interested consumers. Sixty-nine percent of consumers who visit Pinterest claim to have found an item on the site that they eventually purchased, compared to 40 percent for Facebook.[35] Word-of-mouth (or going viral, which is the online equivalent) is a key factor in creating and maintaining client-based relationships. To ensure that it actually occurs, the service provider must take steps to build trust, demonstrate customer commitment, and satisfy customers so well that they become very loyal to the provider and unlikely to switch to competitors.

client-based relationships Interactions that result in satisfied customers who use a service repeatedly over time

customer contact The level of interaction between provider and customer needed to deliver the service

Customer Contact

Not all services require a high degree of customer contact, but many do. **Customer contact** refers to the level of interaction between the service provider and the customer that is necessary to deliver the service. High-contact services include health care, real estate, and legal. Examples of low-contact services are tax preparation, auto repair, and dry cleaning. Technology has enabled many service-oriented businesses to reduce their level of customer contact. Most airlines, for example, have apps through which fliers can book flights, choose seats, check in, and more on their phone or tablet. The use of technology appears to be most effective in situations where employees do not engage in many relationship-building interactions with customers. In the case of high-contact encounters, the use of technology results in customer psychological discomfort and, ultimately, lower service-encounter evaluations than if the technology were not present.[36]

Service with High Customer Contact
Health-care services require high customer contact.

Note that high-contact services generally involve actions directed toward people, who must be present during production. A hairstylist's customer, for example, must be present during the styling process. When the customer must be present, the process of production may be just as important as its final outcome. Although it is sometimes possible for the service provider to go to the customer, high-contact services typically require that the customer go to the production facility. Thus, the physical appearance of the facility may be a major component of the customer's overall evaluation of the service. Even in low-contact service situations, the appearance of the facility is important because the customer likely will need to be present to initiate and finalize the service transaction. Consider customers of auto-repair services. They bring in the vehicle and describe its symptoms, but often do not remain during the repair process.

Employees of high-contact service providers represent a very important ingredient in creating satisfied customers. A fundamental precept of customer contact is that satisfied employees lead to satisfied customers. In fact, research indicates that employee satisfaction is the single most important factor in providing high service quality. Thus, to minimize the problems that customer contact can create, service organizations must take steps to understand and meet the needs of employees by training them adequately, empowering them to make decisions, and rewarding them for customer-oriented behavior.[37] Southwest Airlines encourages customer loyalty and employee retention through training their staff and broadcasting instances of customer satisfaction and standout customer service through social media channels. Social media can be an inexpensive and effective means of training and engaging employees, as well as spreading awareness of stellar service to customers.[38]

11-6c Developing and Managing Marketing Mixes for Services

The characteristics of services create a number of challenges for service marketers (see Table 11.2). These challenges are especially evident in the development and management of marketing mixes for services. Although such mixes contain the four major marketing-mix variables—product, price, distribution, and promotion—the characteristics of services require that marketers consider additional issues.

TABLE 11.2	SERVICE CHARACTERISTICS AND MARKETING CHALLENGES
Service Characteristics	**Resulting Marketing Challenges**
Intangibility	Difficult for customer to evaluate. Customer does not take physical possession. Difficult to advertise and display. Difficult to set and justify prices. Service process usually not protectable by patents.
Inseparability of production and consumption	Service provider cannot mass-produce services. Customer must participate in production. Other consumers affect service outcomes. Services are difficult to distribute.
Perishability	Services cannot be stored. Balancing supply and demand is very difficult. Unused capacity is lost forever. Demand may be very time-sensitive.
Heterogeneity	Service quality is difficult to control. Service delivery is difficult to standardize.
Client-based relationships	Success depends on satisfying and keeping customers over the long term. Generating repeat business is challenging. Relationship marketing becomes critical.
Customer contact	Service providers are critical to delivery. Requires high levels of service employee training and motivation. Changes a high-contact service into a low-contact service to achieve lower costs without reducing customer satisfaction.

Sources: K. Douglas Hoffman and John E. G. Bateson, *Services Marketing: Concepts, Strategies, and Cases* (Mason, OH: Cengage Learning, 2011); Valarie A. Zeithaml, A. Parasuraman, and Leonard L. Berry, *Delivering Quality Service: Balancing Customer Perceptions and Expectations* (New York: Free Press, 1990); Leonard L. Berry and A. Parasuraman, *Marketing Services: Competing through Quality* (New York: Free Press, 1991), 5.

11-6d Development of Services

A service offered by an organization generally is a package, or bundle, of services consisting of a core service and one or more supplementary services. A *core service* is the basic service experience or commodity that a customer expects to receive. A *supplementary service* is a supportive one related to the core service that is used to differentiate the service bundle from that of competitors. For example, when a student attends a tutoring session for a class, the core service is the tutoring. Bundled with the core service might be access to outlines with additional information, handouts with practice questions, or online services like a chat room or wiki to address questions that arise outside the designated tutoring time.

As discussed earlier, heterogeneity results in variability in service quality and makes it difficult to standardize services. However, heterogeneity provides one advantage to service marketers: it allows them to customize their services to match the specific needs of individual customers. Customization plays a key role in providing competitive advantage for the service provider. Being able to personalize the service to fit the exact needs of the customer accommodates individual needs, wants, or desires.[39] Chipotle, Subway, and Freebirds, for example, allow each customer to participate in developing his or her own customized taco, sandwich, or burrito. Health care is an example of an extremely customized service. The services provided differ from one patient to the next.

Such customized services can be expensive for both provider and customer, and some service marketers therefore face a dilemma: how to provide service at an acceptable level of quality in an efficient and economic manner and still satisfy individual customer needs. To cope with this problem, some service marketers offer standardized packages. For example, a lawyer may offer a divorce package at a specified price for an uncontested divorce. When service bundles are standardized, the specific actions and activities of the service provider usually are highly specified. Automobile quick-lube providers frequently offer a service bundle for a single price; the specific actions to be taken are quite detailed about what will be done to a customer's car. Various other equipment-based services are also often standardized into packages. For instance, cable television providers offer several packages, such as "Basic," "Standard," "Premier," and "Hollywood."

The characteristic of intangibility makes it difficult for customers to evaluate a service prior to purchase. Intangibility requires service marketers, such as hairstylists or attorneys, to market promises to customers. The customer must place some degree of trust in the service provider to perform the service in a manner that meets or exceeds those promises. Service marketers should take steps to avoid sending messages that consumers might construe as promises that raise customer expectations beyond what the firm can provide. To cope with the problem of intangibility, marketers employ tangible cues, such as well-groomed, professional-appearing contact personnel and clean, attractive physical facilities, to assure customers about the quality and professionalism of the service.

The inseparability of production and consumption and the level of customer contact also influence the development and management of services. The fact that customers are present and may take part in the production of a service means that other customers can affect the outcome of the service. For instance, a restaurant might give a small discount if children are well-behaved. Service marketers can reduce problems by encouraging customers to share the responsibility of maintaining an environment that allows all participants to receive the intended benefits of the service environment.

11-6e **Pricing of Services**

Services should be priced with consumer price sensitivity, the nature of the transaction, and its costs in mind.[40] Prices for services can be established on several different bases. The prices of such services as pest-control, dry cleaning, sports events, and a physician's consultation usually are based on the performance of specific tasks. Other service prices are based on time spent on the task. For example, attorneys, consultants, counselors, piano teachers, and plumbers usually charge by the hour or day.

Some services use demand-based pricing. When demand for a service is high, the price is also high. Conversely, when demand for a service is low, so is the price. The perishability of services means that when demand is low, the unused capacity cannot be stored and is lost—resulting in foregone profits for the firm. Every empty seat on an airline flight or in a movie theater represents lost revenue. Some services are time-sensitive, meaning that a significant number of customers desire the service around the same time. This point in time is called *peak demand*. A provider of time-sensitive services brings in most of its revenue during peak demand. For an airline, peak demand is usually early and late in the day. Marketers may also want to consider that some consumers find demand-based pricing to be a more interesting way to shop for goods and services because it requires them to search for the best deals.[41]

Providers of time-sensitive services can use demand-based pricing to manage the problem of balancing supply and demand. They charge top prices during peak demand and lower prices during off-peak demand to encourage more customers to use the service. This is why the price of a matinee movie is generally lower than the price of the same movie shown at a later time. **Off-peak pricing** is the practice of reducing prices of services used during slow periods in order to boost demand. The New York Jets engage in demand-based pricing. The cost of individual seats can rise or fall depending on the opposing team and the expected weather for the football game.[42]

off-peak pricing The practice of reducing prices of services used during slow periods in order to boost demand

In cases where customers tend to purchase services in a bundle, marketers must decide whether to offer the services at one price, price them separately, or use a combination of the two methods. Some service providers offer a one-price option for a specific bundle of services and make add-on services available at additional charges. Most cable television providers offer a standard package, and customers can add services according to their needs for additional fees. However, the trend of á la carte television services is growing. More consumers are choosing to forgo cable or satellite and paying for only those channels they want to stream. As a result, some networks like HBO and CBS are offering standalone streaming services for customers who do not want the full package.[43]

Because of the intangible nature of services, customers rely heavily at times on price as an indicator of quality. If customers perceive the available services in a service category as being similar in quality, and if the quality of such services is difficult to judge even after these services are purchased, customers may seek out the lowest-priced provider. For example, many customers search for auto insurance providers with the lowest rates because insurance companies tend to offer packages that are easily comparable between firms. If the quality of different service providers is likely to vary, customers may rely heavily on the price-quality association. For example, if you have to have an appendectomy, will you choose the surgeon who charges $1,500 or the surgeon who only charges $399?

11-6f Distribution of Services

Marketers deliver services in various ways. In some instances customers go to a service provider's facility. For instance, most health-care, dry-cleaning, and spa services are delivered at the service providers' facilities. Some services are provided at the customer's home or business. Lawn care, computer systems installation, and carpet cleaning are examples. Some services are delivered primarily at "arm's length," meaning that no face-to-face contact occurs between the customer and the service provider. A number of equipment-based services can be delivered at arm's length, including electric, Internet, cable television, and telephone services. It can be costly for a firm to install the systems required to deliver high-quality customer service at arm's length, but this can be essential in keeping customers satisfied and maintaining market share. Focusing too much effort on making sales or retaining customers, on the other hand, can result in a failure to listen to customer needs. Comcast, which often delivers its services at arm's length, has gained a reputation for poor customer service. This is partially due to the fact that customer service representatives have been perceived as too pushy or reluctant to cancel subscriptions with the company.[44]

Distribution of Services
A number of services are distributed digitally.

easy camera/Shutterstock.com

Marketing channels for services are usually short and direct, meaning that the producer delivers the service directly to the end user. Some services, however, use intermediaries. For example, travel agents facilitate the delivery of airline services, independent insurance agents participate in the marketing of various insurance policies, and financial planners market investment services. Restaurants are increasingly using third-party intermediaries to deliver hot meals to customers who prefer not (or are unable) to leave their homes or workplaces. A growing number of services, such as DeliverMeFood, GrubHub, and Eat24, connect restaurants and customers with website or smartphone ordering and swift delivery. These services are especially popular with corporate and hotel customers.[45]

Service marketers are less concerned with warehousing and transportation than are goods marketers.

They are very concerned, however, about inventory management, especially balancing supply and demand for services. The service characteristics of inseparability and level of customer contact contribute to the challenges of demand management. In some instances, service marketers use appointments and reservations as approaches for scheduling the delivery of services. Health-care providers, attorneys, accountants, and restaurants often use reservations or appointments to plan and pace the delivery of their services. To increase the supply of a service, marketers use multiple service sites and also increase the number of contact service providers at each site.

To make delivery more accessible to customers and to increase the supply of a service, as well as reduce labor costs, some service providers have decreased the use of contact personnel and replaced them with equipment. In other words, they have changed a high-contact service into a low-contact one. By installing ATMs, banks have increased production capacity and reduced customer contact. The transition to more automated services is not always seamless, however. Some customers do not like that automated services are less personal and would prefer to talk to a staff person. When designing service delivery, marketers must pay attention to the degree of personalization that customers in their target market desire.

11-6g **Promotion of Services**

The intangibility of services results in several promotion-related challenges to service marketers. Because it may not be possible to depict the actual performance of a service in an advertisement or to display it in a store, explaining a service to customers can be a difficult task. Promotion of services typically includes tangible cues that symbolize the service. Consider Liberty Mutual Insurance, which features the Statue of Liberty on its logo. This image symbolizes strength and reliability to consumers. Although such symbols have nothing to do with the actual services, they make it much easier for customers to understand the intangible attributes associated with services.

To make a service more tangible, promotions for services may show pictures of facilities, equipment, and service personnel. For example, advertisements for fitness centers may depict the equipment available. Marketers may also promote their services as a tangible expression of consumers' lifestyles. Additionally, branded marketing can help service firms hone their messages for maximum impact. JPMorgan Chase kept this in mind when it revamped its banking website in part to create a consistent message across all available channels, including its smartphone app. The new website employs a simple, responsive, and personal design to echo the bank's highly used Chase Mobile App. Many of the website's buttons and menus are identical to those used in the app. The website also includes discussions and advice about financial health and stories about neighborhoods. The changes have already resulted in longer stays on the website, allowing Chase to build stronger relationships with its customers.[46]

Compared with marketers of goods, service providers are more likely to promote price, guarantees, performance documentation, availability, and training and certification of contact personnel. For example, it is common for gyms and yoga or aerobics studios to highlight their trainers' degrees and certifications as a way to assure customers that their trainers are well-qualified to help them reach their fitness goals. When preparing advertisements, service marketers are careful to use concrete, specific language to help make services more tangible in the minds of customers. Service companies are also careful not to promise too much regarding their services so that customer expectations do not rise to unattainable levels.

Through their actions, service contact personnel can be directly or indirectly involved in the personal selling of services. Personal selling may be important because personal influence can help the customer visualize the benefits of a given service. Because service contact personnel may engage in personal selling, some companies invest heavily in training.

Because of the heterogeneity and intangibility of services, word-of-mouth communication is important in service promotion. What other people say about a service provider

product manager The person within an organization responsible for a product, a product line, or several distinct products that make up a group

brand manager The person responsible for a single brand

venture team A cross-functional group that creates entirely new products that may be aimed at new markets

can have a tremendous impact on whether an individual decides to use that provider. Some service marketers attempt to stimulate positive word-of-mouth communication by asking satisfied customers to tell their friends and associates about the service and give a high rating on Yelp. Groupon and Living Social, which offer discounted deals at local businesses in participating cities, offer a free deal to customers who refer friends who then become new customers.

11-7 ORGANIZING TO DEVELOP AND MANAGE PRODUCTS

LO 11-7 Describe organizational structures used for managing products.

It should be obvious by now that managing products is a complex task. Often, the traditional functional form of organization does not fit a company's product management needs. In this case, management must find an organizational approach that accomplishes the tasks necessary to develop and manage products. Alternatives to functional organization include the product or brand manager approach and the venture team approach.

A **product manager** is responsible for a product, a product line, or several distinct products that make up an interrelated group within a multiproduct organization. A **brand manager** is responsible for a single brand. Mondelēz International, Inc., for example, has one brand manager for Oreos and one for Chips Ahoy! Both product and brand managers operate cross-functionally to coordinate the activities, information, and strategies involved in marketing an assigned product. Product managers and brand managers plan marketing activities to achieve objectives by coordinating a mix of price, distribution, and promotion (especially sales promotion and advertising). The product or brand manager approach to organization is used by many large, multiple-product companies.

Product management is used for intangible products or services as well as goods. For instance, the software industry has adopted Procter & Gamble's concept of a brand manager to be responsible for a software application that is a branded product rather than just managing functions. Microsoft employs a product manager approach for software brands such as Excel.[47]

A **venture team** creates entirely new products that may be aimed at new markets. Unlike a product manager, a venture team is responsible for all aspects of developing a product: research and development, production and engineering, finance and accounting, and marketing. Venture team members are brought together from different functional areas of the organization. In working outside established divisions, venture teams have greater flexibility to apply inventive approaches to develop new products that can take advantage of opportunities in highly segmented markets. Companies are increasingly using such cross-functional teams for product development in an effort to boost product quality. Quality may be positively related to information integration within the team, customers' influence on the product development process, and a quality orientation within the firm. When a new product has demonstrated commercial potential, team members may return to their functional areas, or they may join a new or existing division to manage the product.

iStock.com/mindscanner

Product Manager Responsibilities
Product managers operate cross-functionally to coordinate marketing activities associated with products, including advertising, branding, design, and distribution.

Chapter Review

11-1 Explain how companies manage existing products through line extensions and product modifications.

Organizations must be able to adjust their product mixes to compete effectively and achieve their goals. Using existing products, a product mix can be improved through line extension and through product modification. A line extension is the development of a product closely related to one or more products in the existing line but designed specifically to meet different customer needs. Product modification is the changing of one or more characteristics of a product. This approach can be achieved through quality modifications, functional modifications, and aesthetic modifications.

11-2 Explore how businesses develop a product idea into a commercial product.

Before a product is introduced, it goes through a seven-phase new-product development process. In the idea-generation phase, new-product ideas may come from internal or external sources. In the process of screening, ideas are evaluated to determine whether they are consistent with the firm's overall objectives and resources. Concept testing, the third phase, involves having a small sample of potential customers review a brief description of the product idea to determine their initial perceptions of the proposed product and their early buying intentions. During the business analysis stage, the product idea is evaluated to determine its potential contribution to the firm's sales, costs, and profits. In the product development stage, the organization determines if it is technically feasible to produce the product and if it can be produced at a cost low enough to make the final price reasonable. Test marketing is a limited introduction of a product in areas chosen to represent the intended market. Finally, in the commercialization phase, full-scale production of the product begins, and a complete marketing strategy is developed.

11-3 Discuss the importance of product differentiation and the elements that differentiate one product from another.

Product differentiation is the process of creating and designing products so that customers perceive them as different from competing products. Product quality, product design and features, and product support services are three dimensions of product differentiation that companies consider when creating and marketing products.

11-4 Explain how businesses position their products.

Product positioning refers to the decisions and activities that create and maintain a certain concept of the firm's product in the customer's mind. Organizations can position a product to compete head to head with another brand if the product's performance is at least equal to the competitive brand's performance and if the product is priced lower. When a brand possesses unique characteristics that are important to some buyers, positioning it to avoid competition is appropriate. Companies also increase an existing brand's market share and profitability through product repositioning.

11-5 Discuss how product deletion is used to improve product mixes.

Product deletion is the process of eliminating a product that no longer satisfies a sufficient number of customers. Although a firm's personnel may oppose product deletion, weak products are unprofitable, consume too much time and effort, may require shorter production runs, and can create an unfavorable impression of the firm's other products. A product mix should be systematically reviewed to determine when to delete products. Products to be deleted can be phased out, run out, or dropped immediately.

11-6 Summarize how the characteristics of services influence the development of marketing mixes for services.

Services are intangible products involving deeds, performances, or efforts that cannot be physically possessed. They have six fundamental characteristics: intangibility, inseparability of production and consumption, perishability, heterogeneity, client-based relationships, and customer contact. Intangibility means that a service cannot be seen, touched, tasted, or smelled. Inseparability refers to the fact that the production of a service cannot be separated from its consumption. Perishability means that unused service capacity of one time period cannot be stored for future use. Heterogeneity is variation in service quality. Client-based relationships are interactions with customers that lead to the repeated use of a service over time. Customer contact is the interaction needed to deliver a service between providers and customers.

11-7 Describe organizational structures used for managing products.

Often, the traditional functional form or organization does not lend itself to the complex task of developing and managing products. Alternative organizational forms include the product or brand manager approach, and the venture team approach. A product manager is responsible for a product, a product line, or several distinct products that make up an interrelated group within a multiproduct organization. A brand manager is a product manager who is responsible for a single brand. A venture team is sometimes used to create entirely new products that may be aimed at new markets.

 Go to www.cengagebrain.com for resources to help you master the content in this chapter as well as for materials that will expand your marketing knowledge!

Developing Your Marketing Plan

A company's marketing strategy may be revised to include new products as it considers its SWOT analysis and the impact of environmental factors on its product mix. When developing a marketing plan, the company must decide whether new products are to be added to the product mix, or if existing ones should be modified. The information in this chapter will assist you in the creation of your marketing plan as you consider the following:

1. Identify whether your product will be the modification of an existing one in your product mix, or the development of a new product.

2. If the product is an extension of one in your current product mix, determine the type(s) of modifications that will be performed.
3. Using Figure 11.1 as a guide, discuss how your product idea would move through the stages of new-product development. Examine the idea using the tests and analyses included in the new-product development process.
4. Discuss how the management of this product will fit into your current organizational structure.

Key Concepts

line extension 272
product modification 273
quality modifications 273
functional modifications 273
aesthetic modifications 274
disruptive innovation 275
new-product development process 275

idea generation 275
screening 276
concept testing 276
business analysis 277
product development 277
test marketing 278
commercialization 279
product differentiation 281
quality 281
level of quality 281

consistency of quality 282
product design 282
styling 282
product features 282
customer services 283
product positioning 284
product deletion 286
homesourcing 288
intangibility 288

inseparability 289
perishability 289
heterogeneity 289
client-based relationships 290
customer contact 290
off-peak pricing 293
product manager 296
brand manager 296
venture team 296

Issues for Discussion and Review

1. What is a line extension, and how does it differ from a product modification?
2. Compare and contrast the three major approaches to modifying a product.
3. Identify and briefly explain the seven major phases of the new-product development process.
4. Do small companies that manufacture just a few products need to be concerned about developing and managing products? Why or why not?
5. Why is product development a cross-functional activity within an organization? That is, why must finance,

engineering, manufacturing, and other functional areas be involved?
6. What is the major purpose of concept testing, and how is it accomplished?
7. What are the benefits and disadvantages of test marketing?
8. Why can the process of commercialization take a considerable amount of time?
9. What is product differentiation, and how can it be achieved?
10. Explain how the term *quality* has been used to differentiate products in the automobile industry in recent

years. What are some makes and models of automobiles that come to mind when you hear the terms *high quality* and *poor quality*?

11. What is product positioning? Under what conditions would head-to-head product positioning be appropriate? When should head-to-head positioning be avoided?

12. What types of problems does a weak product cause in a product mix? Describe the most effective approach for avoiding such problems.

13. How important are services in the U.S. economy?
14. Identify and discuss the major service characteristics.
15. For each marketing-mix element, which service characteristics are most likely to have an impact?
16. What type of organization might use a venture team to develop new products? What are the advantages and disadvantages of such a team?

VIDEO CASE 11
How Sriracha Became a Hot Product

Entrepreneur David Tran cooked up his first batch of hot-pepper sauce in 1975, when he was still living in his native Vietnam. He packaged the sauce in recycled baby-food jars, and family members made customer deliveries by bicycle. When Tran came to America in 1980, he made a living by cooking up batches of his distinctively hot sauce and selling it by the bucketful to Asian restaurants around Chinatown in Los Angeles.

Tran named his company Huy Fong after the freighter that brought him to America. To convey the authenticity of the bright-red sauce made from freshly-crushed jalapeno chili peppers, Tran called it sriracha, which is an actual town in Thailand. He packaged the fiery sauce in a clear squeeze bottle to showcase its "hot" color and quality, added white lettering in English and Chinese, and topped the bottle with a green squirt cap, features that differentiate his product from other sauces. The red rooster sketched on every bottle represents Tran's Chinese zodiac sign.

Although Tabasco and other hot sauces had been popular condiments for years, the fresh quality and unique tang of Tran's sriracha sauce quickly made it a mainstay in restaurants and consumer kitchens through word-of-mouth only—without advertising or even a sales force. The firm soon needed a larger production facility and, as demand multiplied year after year, it enlarged its production facility a second time.

Now Huy Fong cooks up hundreds of thousands of bottles of its signature sauce every day, using locally-grown jalapeno peppers that can be harvested, transported, washed, ground, and stirred into sriracha within only six hours. Because no two crops of peppers are exactly the same, some individual batches may be hotter than others, as Huy Fong warns customers on its website. Annual sales exceed $80 million as Huy Fong's sauces are shipped throughout North America and beyond. Long lines of Sriracha fans wait to tour Huy Fong's production plant in Irwindale, California, where they can watch Tran's sauce being made and buy chili-red T-shirts in the Rooster Room gift shop (or online).

When Tran began selling his made-in-America sauce back in 1980, he did not trademark the sriracha name. As a result, his company cannot sue any time another marketer uses the word in a brand name or to describe a particular item. It has also opened the door to competition from sriracha food products made by well-established, deep-pocketed corporations like Tabasco, Heinz, and Kikkoman. When Tran heard that Tabasco was about to launch its own sriracha sauce, his comment was: "My 'rooster killer' jumped into the market."

Despite the sriracha rivalry, Tran believes that widespread use of the word *sriracha* serves as a form of advertising for his product, which is positioned as the pioneer of the category. The entrepreneur also uses the fame of being sriracha's originator to forge partnerships with food marketers that want to add his sauce's flavor to their products.

Pop Gourmet, for example, has a deal to use Huy Fong's sriracha in its popcorn. Neither licensing fees nor royalties are involved, only prominent display of Tran's trademarked rooster on the popcorn's vivid-red packaging. Sriracha popcorn has become Pop Gourmet's best-selling product, and the firm is introducing additional snacks featuring sriracha. Now other marketers have received Tran's permission to use his sauce in their products, reinforcing the product's positioning as the original, most authentic, and best-known of all sriracha sauces.[48]

Questions for Discussion

1. Because chili peppers are agricultural products, their level of spiciness can fluctuate from crop to crop. What does this mean for consumers' perceptions of the quality of Huy Fong sriracha sauce?
2. If you were to create a perceptual map for sriracha sauces, which four dimensions would you choose? Where would you put Huy Fong's sriracha on this perceptual map, and why?
3. What are the possible benefits and risks of Huy Fong allowing other marketers to use his sauce, and include his brand, when they introduce line extensions?

chapter 12

Pricing Concepts and Management

iStock.com/niarchos

LEARNING OBJECTIVES

12-1 Identify issues related to developing pricing objectives.

12-2 Discuss the importance of identifying the target market's evaluation of price.

12-3 Explore the role of demand and the price elasticity of demand.

12-4 Describe the relationships among demand, costs, and profits.

12-5 Explain how marketers analyze competitors' prices.

12-6 Analyze the bases used for setting prices.

12-7 Compare the different types of pricing strategies.

12-8 Describe the selection of a specific price.

12-9 Identify seven methods companies can use to price products for business markets.

At Disney, Prices are in Tiers, Guests are Not

Every year, Disneyland in California welcomes 18 million visitors and Disney World Magic Kingdom in Florida welcomes nearly 20 million visitors. In fact, famous rides like Pirates of the Caribbean and fun features like fireworks are bringing millions of families and children of all ages into all of Disney's U.S. theme parks. But high demand means theme-park crowding and long waits for popular rides during school vacations and other peak periods.

Now Disney is seeking to reduce crowding and encourage visits during less-popular periods by offering three price tiers for admission tickets. The lowest price tier, "value," applies to off-peak midweek periods, such as Mondays through Thursdays when schools are in session and demand is lowest. The middle price tier, "regular," applies to most weekends and summer weeks. Nearly half of the days on Disney's theme-park calendars fall into this "regular" tier. The top tier, "peak," applies to July weekends, many December days, and spring break from school, when demand is highest. In addition, Disney offers annual passes, priced to save money for local customers who visit often.

One year after instituting tiered pricing, Disney increased its one-day admission price in all three tiers by a few dollars. The one-day ticket for Disneyland that used to cost $66 in 2007 now costs as much as $124 per day. Meanwhile, the company continues to debut exciting new rides and expand its parks to bring visitors back again and again, because crowding is less of a problem. How will Disney's tiered pricing affect customer loyalty and theme-park attendance in the future?[1]

iStock.com/Jorge Villalba

Price and Nonprice Competition
Generally, providers of wireless phone services compete on the basis of price competition. Providers of medical services engage in nonprice competition.

Price is an integral part of any marketing mix. Before setting a product's price, an organization must determine whether it will compete on price alone or some combination of factors. Many firms, including luxury perfume makers, use pricing as a tool to make their products stand out from those of other firms. However, rival firms may likewise employ pricing as a major competitive tool. **Price competition** occurs when a seller emphasizes a product's low price and sets a price that equals or beats that of competitors. To use this approach most effectively, a seller must have the flexibility to change prices rapidly and aggressively in response to competitors' actions. Consider Walmart's perennial everyday low prices strategy. The company even vows to match lower prices from other retailers including Amazon.com.[2] While price competition allows a marketer to set prices based on demand for the product or in response to changes in the firm's finances, so can competitors. It is a major drawback of price competition that competitors can meet or outdo an organization's price cuts. If unforeseen circumstances that force a seller to raise prices do not also affect other firms, competitors will likely maintain their lower prices.

Nonprice competition is competition based on factors other than price. It is used most effectively when a marketer like Disney can distinguish its product through distinctive product quality, customer service, promotion, packaging, or other features. However, buyers must be able to perceive these distinguishing characteristics and consider them desirable for nonprice competition to be effective. An advantage is that, once customers have chosen a brand for nonprice reasons such as unique features, they may not be attracted as easily to competing firms and brands.

In this chapter, we examine the eight stages of a process that marketers can use when setting prices. Figure 12.1 illustrates these stages. Stage 1 is developing a pricing objective that is compatible with the organization's overall marketing objectives. Stage 2 entails assessing the target market's evaluation of price. In Stage 3, marketers should examine a product's demand and the price elasticity of demand. Stage 4 consists of analyzing demand, cost, and profit relationships—it is a necessary step in estimating the economic feasibility of various price alternatives. Stage 5 involves evaluating competitors' prices, which helps determine the role of price in the marketing strategy. Stage 6 requires choosing a basis for setting prices. Stage 7 is selecting a pricing strategy, or determining the role of price in the marketing mix. Stage 8 involves determining the final price. This final step depends on environmental forces and marketers' understanding and use of a systematic approach to establishing prices. These stages are not rigid, and not all marketers will follow all the steps. They are merely guidelines that provide a logical sequence for establishing prices.

12-1 DEVELOPMENT OF PRICING OBJECTIVES

LO 12-1 Identify issues related to developing pricing objectives.

The first step in setting prices is developing **pricing objectives**—goals that describe what a firm wants to achieve through pricing. Specifying pricing objectives is an important task because they form the basis for decisions for other stages of the pricing process. Thus, pricing

price competition Emphasizes price as an issue and matching or beating competitors' prices

nonprice competition Emphasizes factors other than price to distinguish a product from competing brands

pricing objectives Goals that describe what a firm wants to achieve through pricing

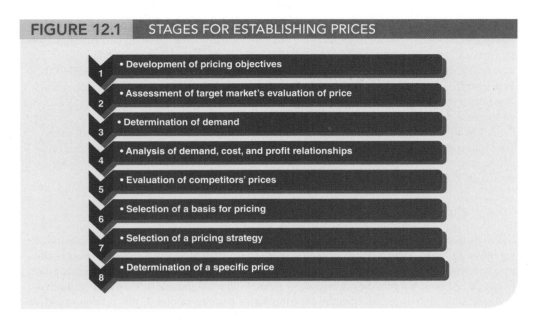

FIGURE 12.1   STAGES FOR ESTABLISHING PRICES

1 • Development of pricing objectives

2 • Assessment of target market's evaluation of price

3 • Determination of demand

4 • Analysis of demand, cost, and profit relationships

5 • Evaluation of competitors' prices

6 • Selection of a basis for pricing

7 • Selection of a pricing strategy

8 • Determination of a specific price

objectives must be stated explicitly and in measurable terms, and should include a time frame for accomplishing them.

Marketers need to ensure that pricing objectives are consistent with the firm's marketing and overall objectives because pricing objectives influence decisions in many functional areas of a business, including finance, accounting, and production. A marketer can use both short- and long-term objectives and can employ one or multiple pricing objectives. For instance, a firm may wish to increase market share by 18 percent over the next three years, achieve a 15 percent return on investment, and promote an image of quality in the marketplace. In this section, we identify some of the pricing objectives that companies might set.

12-1a Survival

Survival is one of the most fundamental pricing objectives. Achieving this objective generally means temporarily setting prices low, even at times below costs, in order to attract more sales. Because price is a flexible ingredient in the marketing mix, it can be useful in keeping a company afloat by increasing sales volume. Most organizations will tolerate setbacks, such as short-run losses and internal upheaval, if necessary for survival.

12-1b Profit

Although a business may claim that its objective is to maximize profits for its owners, the objective of profit maximization is rarely operational because its achievement is difficult to measure. Therefore, profit objectives tend to be set at levels that the owners and top-level decision makers view as satisfactory and attainable. Specific profit objectives may be stated in terms of either actual dollar amounts or a percentage of sales revenues.

12-1c Return on Investment

Pricing to attain a specified rate of return on the company's investment is a profit-related pricing objective. A return on investment (ROI) pricing objective generally requires some trial and error, as it is unusual for all required data and inputs to be available when setting prices. Many pharmaceutical companies also use ROI pricing objectives because of their great investment in research and development.

12-1d Market Share

Many firms establish pricing objectives to maintain or increase market share, which is a product's sales in relation to total industry sales. Gillette, for instance, reduced the prices of its mid-level razors in a bid to regain some market share lost to start-up razor clubs like Harry's and Dollar Shave Club. Gillette's market share fell from 71 to 59 percent after Dollar Shave Club entered the market with its subscription razor refill service.[3] Many firms recognize that high relative market shares often translate into high profits for firms. The Profit Impact of Market Strategies (PIMS) studies, conducted over the past 50 years, have shown that both market share and product quality influence profitability.[4] Thus, marketers often use an increase in market share as a primary pricing objective.

Maintaining or increasing market share need not depend on growth in industry sales. An organization can increase its market share even if sales for the total industry are flat or decreasing. On the other hand, a firm's sales volume can increase while its market share decreases if the overall market grows.

12-1e Cash Flow

Some companies set prices so they can recover cash as quickly as possible. Financial managers understandably want to recover capital spent to develop products. Choosing this pricing objective may have the support of a marketing manager if he or she anticipates a short product life cycle. Although it may be acceptable in some situations, the use of cash flow and recovery as an objective oversimplifies the contribution of price to profits. If this pricing objective results in high prices, competitors with lower prices may gain a large share of the market.

12-1f Status Quo

In some cases, an organization is in a favorable position and desires nothing more than to maintain the status quo. Status quo objectives can focus on several dimensions, such as maintaining a certain market share, meeting (but not beating) competitors' prices, achieving price stability, and maintaining a favorable public image. A status quo pricing objective can reduce a firm's risks by helping to stabilize demand for products. A firm that chooses status quo pricing objectives risks minimizing pricing as a competitive tool, which could lead to a climate of nonprice competition. Professionals such as accountants and attorneys often operate in such an environment.

Product Quality
Cartier offers high-quality jewelry and prices its products accordingly.

12-1g Product Quality

A company may have the objective of leading its industry in product quality. A high price on a product may signal to customers that the product is of a high quality. Attaining a high level of product quality is also more expensive for the firm, as the costs of materials, research, and development may be greater. This is the case with Cartier, a French company that designs and manufactures high-end jewelry and watches. The advertisement shows a close-up of the Calibre de Cartier Diver watch. Because Cartier watches cost thousands of dollars and will not be purchased for everyday events, the text of the advertisement details the quality standards of the watch and reminds potential buyers that Cartier has been around since 1847. As previously mentioned, the PIMS studies have shown that both product quality and market share are good indicators of profitability. The products and brands that customers perceive to be of high quality are more likely to survive in a competitive marketplace because customers trust these products more, even if the prices are higher.

12-2 ASSESSMENT OF THE TARGET MARKET'S EVALUATION OF PRICE

LO 12-2 Discuss the importance of identifying the target market's evaluation of price.

After developing pricing objectives, marketers next must assess the target market's evaluation of price. Despite the general assumption that price is a major issue for buyers, the importance of price varies depending on the type of product and target market, and the purchase situation. For instance, buyers are more sensitive to gasoline prices than luggage prices. We purchase gasoline regularly and we notice fluctuations in price, but luggage is an investment and we expect to pay more for it. With respect to the type of target market, adults frequently must pay more than children for goods and services, including clothing, meals, and movie tickets.

The purchase situation also affects the buyer's view of price. Most moviegoers would never pay in other situations the prices charged for soft drinks, popcorn, and candy at concession stands. The markup for popcorn in movie theaters can be up to 1,275 percent.[5] Nevertheless, consumers are willing to pay the markup to enhance their movie experience by enjoying buttery popcorn at the theater. By assessing the target market's evaluation of price, a marketer is in a better position to know how much emphasis to put on price in the overall marketing strategy. Information about the target market's price evaluation may also help a marketer determine how far above the competition the firm can set its prices.

Today, because some consumers are seeking less-expensive products and the Internet allows consumers to shop more selectively than ever before, some manufacturers and retailers are focusing on the value of their products in communications with customers. Value is more than just a product's price. It combines price with quality attributes, which customers use to differentiate between competing brands. Generally, consumers want to maximize the value they receive for their money. Consumers may even perceive products to have great value that are not the least expensive, such as organic produce, if they have desirable features or characteristics. Consumers are also generally willing to pay a higher price for products that offer convenience and time savings. Companies that offer both affordable prices and high quality, like Target, have altered consumers' expectations about how much quality they must sacrifice for low prices. Understanding the importance of a product to customers, as well as their expectations about quality and value, helps marketers assess correctly the target market's evaluation of price.

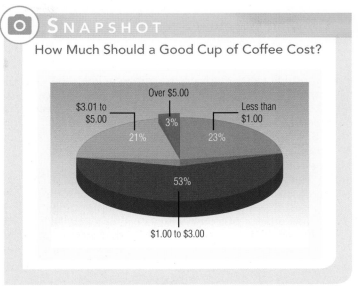

SNAPSHOT

How Much Should a Good Cup of Coffee Cost?

- Over $5.00: 3%
- $3.01 to $5.00: 21%
- Less than $1.00: 23%
- $1.00 to $3.00: 53%

Source: PayPal survey of 610 coffee drinkers

12-3 ANALYSIS OF DEMAND

LO 12-3 Explore the role of demand and the price elasticity of demand.

Another significant factor in pricing decisions is demand. Marketers use marketing research and forecasting techniques to estimate sales potential and determine the relationship between a product's price and the quantity demanded.

12-3a Demand Curves

For most products, demand and price are inversely related: The quantity demanded goes up as the price goes down and vice versa. Consider how prices have fallen precipitously

ENTREPRENEURSHIP IN MARKETING

Growing Gwynnie Bee

Christine Hunsicker realized that renting plus-size clothing to women would be a great business opportunity after studying the research. First, she learned that 75 percent of adult women wear a size 10 or larger. In fact, two-thirds of these women wear at least a size 14. According to estimates, overall U.S. spending on clothing by plus-size women added up to $17 billion. Yet relatively few fashion designers were producing plus-size clothing.

Hunsicker also recognized that many clothing purchases would hang in closets, unworn, for long periods. She reasoned that if a customer is going to wear a piece of clothing only once or twice, "it makes absolutely zero sense to own that item." That's what convinced her to rent rather than sell fashion clothing for plus-size women.

Hunsicker founded Gwynnie Bee in 2011, offering monthly rentals of clothing in sizes 10 to 32. Customers log onto Gwynnie Bee, browse the thousands of fashions for rent, and select up to 10 items to rent by mail each month, with the company paying postage both ways. Customers can keep items as long as they wish and they have the option to buy any item they choose.

Now Hunsicker is partnering with fashion brands to extend their clothing lines into larger size ranges exclusively for Gwynnie Bee's customers. Customers are flocking to try Gwynnie Bee because, the founder says, "The plus-size market is dramatically underserved. Anyone coming in with an offering that speaks to that consumer has a lot of room to grow."[a]

for flat-screen television sets. This change in price is largely due to strong competition and newer technologies such as 3D and curved screens. In order to compensate, most makers of flat-screen TVs responded by continuing to lower prices. Thus, an inverse relationship exists between price and quantity demanded. As long as the marketing environment and buyers' needs, ability (purchasing power), willingness, and authority to buy remain stable, this fundamental inverse relationship holds.

Figure 12.2 illustrates the effect on the quantity demanded of a product at different prices. The normal **demand curve** (*D*) is a graphic representation of the quantity of products a firm expects to sell at different prices, in this case P1 and P2, holding other factors constant. As you can see, as price falls, quantity demanded (Q) rises for products that adhere to a normal demand curve. Demand depends on other factors in the marketing mix, including product quality, promotion, and distribution. An improvement in any of these factors may cause an increase in demand that shifts the demand curve outward, allowing a firm to sell more products at the same price.

Several types of demand exist, and not all conform to the normal demand curve shown in Figure 12.2. Prestige products, for example some cosmetics, tend to sell better at higher prices than at lower ones. Prestige products are desirable partly because their expense makes buyers feel elite. If the price fell drastically, making the products affordable for a large number of people, they would lose some of their appeal. The demand curve on the right side of Figure 12.2 shows the relationship between price and quantity demanded for prestige products. As you can see, the curve has a very different shape that shows that quantity demanded is greater, not less, at higher prices—to a point. For a certain price range—from *P*1 to *P*2—the quantity demanded (*Q*1) increases to *Q*2. After that point, however, continuing to raise the price backfires and demand decreases again. The figure shows that if price increases from *P*2 to *P*3, quantity demanded returns to the *Q*1 level.

12-3b Demand Fluctuations

demand curve A graph of the quantity of products a firm expects to sell at various prices if other factors remain constant

Consumer demand is influenced by many more factors than just price. Changes in buyers' needs, variations in the effectiveness of other marketing-mix variables, the presence of substitutes, and dynamic environmental factors can all influence demand. Restaurants and utility companies experience large fluctuations in demand at different periods throughout

| **FIGURE 12.2** | DEMAND CURVE ILLUSTRATING THE TYPICAL PRICE/QUANTITY RELATIONSHIP |

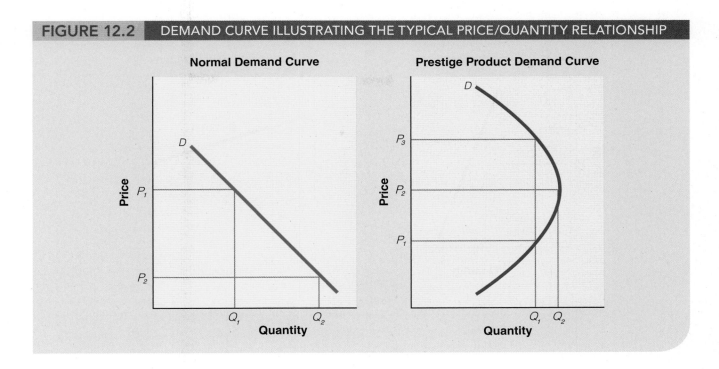

the day. Toy manufacturers, fireworks suppliers, and air-conditioning and heating contractors face demand fluctuations because of the seasonal nature of their products. Consider that
flowers are in higher demand in the United States around Valentine's Day and Mother's Day.
In some cases, demand fluctuations are predictable. It is no surprise to restaurants and utility
company managers that demand fluctuates. However, changes in demand for other products may be less predictable, leading to problems for some companies. Other organizations
anticipate demand fluctuations and develop new products and prices to meet consumers'
changing needs.

12-3c **Assessing Price Elasticity of Demand**

We have seen how marketers analyze the target market's conception of price for different products and how that affects the quantity of product sold under normal and prestige
demand curves. The next step is to assess price elasticity of demand. **Price elasticity of
demand** provides a measure of the sensitivity of consumer demand for a product or product category to changes in price. Elasticity is formally defined as the percentage change in
quantity demanded relative to a given percentage change in price (see Figure 12.3).[6] For a
product with inelastic demand, an increase in price (from $P1$ to $P2$) does not affect quantity
demanded (from $Q1$ to $Q2$) very much. Utilities and gasoline are examples of products that
are fairly inelastic because we still require them to go about our normal routines, even if
the price increases. For a product with highly elastic demand, you can see that a relatively
small increase in price, such as from $P1$ to $P2$, results in a huge change in quantity sold,
from $Q1$ to $Q2$. Non-essential items or those with ready substitutes tend to have more
elastic demand.

   If marketers can determine a product's price elasticity of demand, setting a price is easier.
By analyzing total revenues as prices change, marketers can determine whether a product is
price elastic. Total revenue is price multiplied by quantity. Thus, 10,000 cans of paint sold in
one year at a price of $10 per can is equal to $100,000 of total revenue. If demand is *elastic*,
a shift in price causes an opposite change in total revenue: an increase in price will decrease
total revenue, and a decrease in price will increase total revenue. *Inelastic* demand results
in a change in the same direction as total revenue: an increase in price will increase total

**price elasticity of
demand** A measure of
the sensitivity of demand
to changes in price

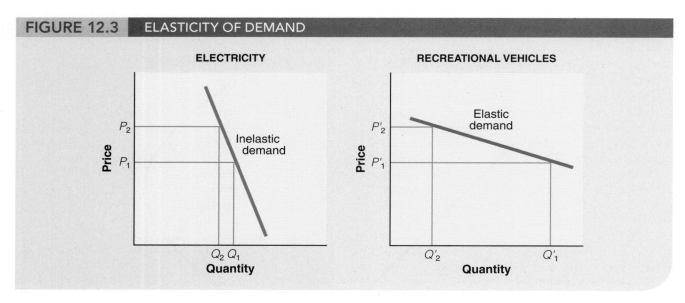

FIGURE 12.3   ELASTICITY OF DEMAND

revenue, and a decrease in price will decrease total revenue. The following formula determines the price elasticity of demand:

$$\text{price elasticity of demand} = \frac{\%\text{ change in quantity demanded}}{\%\text{ change in price}}$$

For instance, if demand falls by 8 percent when a seller raises the price by 2 percent, the price elasticity of demand is –4 (the negative sign indicating the inverse relationship between price and demand). If demand falls by 2 percent when price is increased by 4 percent, elasticity is –1/2. The less elastic the demand, the more beneficial it is for the seller to raise the price. Most products are inelastic in the long run—for example, you can hold out on buying a new car for a certain amount of time, but if the price remains high you will eventually have to replace your car at the higher price. Marketers cannot base prices solely on elasticity considerations. They must also examine the costs associated with different sales volumes and evaluate what happens to profits.

Price Elasticity of Demand
Gasoline is an example of a product that has inelastic demand. When the price of gasoline goes up, consumers do not significantly reduce consumption. When the price goes down, consumers do not significantly increase their consumption.

12-4 DEMAND, COST, AND PROFIT RELATIONSHIPS

LO 12-4 Describe the relationships among demand, costs, and profits.

In a marketing environment where consumers can comparison shop for items from retailers across the globe, marketers must be more aware than ever of effects on demand, costs, and profit potential. Customers have become less tolerant of price increases, putting manufacturers in the position of having to find ways to maintain high quality and low costs. To stay in business, a company must set prices that not only cover costs but also meet customers' expectations for quality, features, and price. In this section, we explore two approaches marketers take to analyze demand, cost, and profit relationships: marginal analysis and break-even analysis.

12-4a Marginal Analysis

Marginal analysis examines what happens to a firm's costs and revenues when production (or sales volume) changes by a single unit. Both production costs and revenues must be evaluated. To determine the costs of production, it is necessary to identify several types of potential costs. **Fixed costs** do not vary with changes in the number of units produced or sold. For example, a manufacturer's rent for a factory does not change because production increases, more employees are hired, or sales go up. Rent may increase, but it is not in relation to production or revenue. **Average fixed cost** is the fixed cost per unit produced and is calculated by dividing fixed costs by the number of units produced.

Variable costs are directly related to changes in the number of units produced or sold. The wages for adding a second shift of workers and the cost of inputs to produce twice as much product are variable costs because they increase as production increases. Variable costs are usually held constant per unit. That is, as long as there are no increases in efficiency, twice as many workers and twice as many raw materials result in double the production. **Average variable cost**, the variable cost per unit produced, is calculated by dividing the variable costs by the number of units produced.

Total cost is the sum of the average fixed costs and the average variable costs, multiplied by the quantity produced. The **average total cost** is the sum of the average fixed cost and the average variable cost. **Marginal cost (MC)** is the extra cost a firm incurs when it produces one additional unit of a product.

Table 12.1 illustrates an example of the relationships between various costs. Notice that average fixed cost declines as output increases. This is because a manufacturer generally gains cost and production savings from larger outputs, as the fixed cost becomes a smaller proportion of the average total cost and the producer can take advantage of efficiencies. Average variable cost and average total cost both follow a U-shaped curve. In this example, average total cost is lowest at five units of production, which is an average total cost of $22.00, whereas average variable cost is lowest at three units at a cost of $10.67. This means

fixed costs Costs that do not vary with changes in the number of units produced or sold

average fixed cost The fixed cost per unit produced

variable costs Costs that vary directly with changes in the number of units produced or sold

average variable cost The variable cost per unit produced

total cost The sum of average fixed and average variable costs, times the quantity produced

average total cost The sum of the average fixed cost and the average variable cost

marginal cost (MC) The extra cost incurred by producing one more unit of a product

TABLE 12.1	COSTS AND THEIR RELATIONSHIPS					
1 Quantity	2 Fixed Cost	3 Average Fixed Cost (2) ÷ (1)	4 Average Variable Cost	5 Average Total Cost (3) + (4)	6 Total Cost (5) × (1)	7 Marginal Cost
1	$40	$40.00	$20.00	$60.00	$50	
						$10
2	40	20.00	15.00	35.00	70	
						2
3	40	13.33	10.67	24.00	72	
						18
4	40	10.00	12.50	22.50	90	
						20
5	40	8.00	14.00	22.00	110	
						30
6	40	6.67	16.67	23.33	140	
						40
7	40	5.71	20.00	25.71	180	

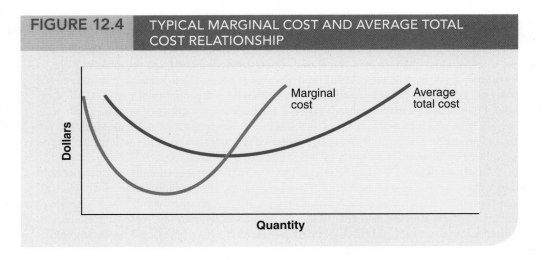

FIGURE 12.4   TYPICAL MARGINAL COST AND AVERAGE TOTAL COST RELATIONSHIP

that average total costs continue to fall after the costs of producing additional products start to increase.

Figure 12.4 shows this phenomenon. Remember that marginal cost is what it takes to produce one additional unit of product. The marginal cost curve crosses the average total cost curve at its lowest point, which is the point where production is the most efficient in terms of costs. This is the point at which manufacturers should maintain their production. In the example laid out in Table 12.1, this occurs between five and six units of production. Average total cost decreases as long as marginal cost is less than average total cost and increases when marginal cost rises above average total cost.

Marginal revenue (MR) is the change in total revenue that arises from the sale of an additional unit of a product. Figure 12.5 depicts marginal revenue and a demand curve. Most firms face downward-sloping demand curves for their products. In other words, they must lower their prices to sell additional units. This situation means that each additional unit of product sold provides the firm with less revenue than the previous unit sold, which you can see illustrated in Figure 12.5. Marginal revenue decreases as price decreases and quantity sold increases. Eventually, marginal revenue will reach zero, and the sale of additional units actually causes the firm to lose money.

marginal revenue (MR)
The change in total revenue resulting from the sale of an additional unit of a product

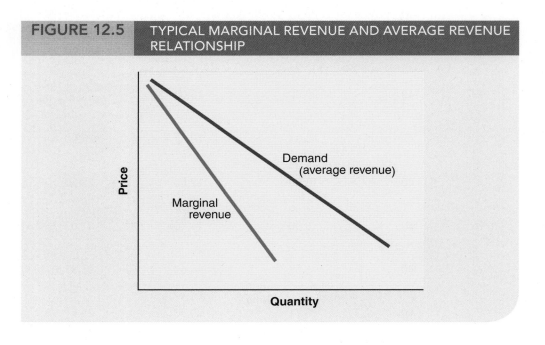

FIGURE 12.5   TYPICAL MARGINAL REVENUE AND AVERAGE REVENUE RELATIONSHIP

TABLE 12.2		MARGINAL ANALYSIS METHOD FOR DETERMINING THE MOST PROFITABLE PRICE				
1 Price	2 Quantity Sold	3 Total Revenue (1) × (2)	4 Marginal Revenue	5 Marginal Cost	6 Total Cost	7 Profit (3) − (6)
$57	1	$57	$57	$60	$60	$−3
50	2	100	43	10	70	30
38	3	114	14	2	72	42
33*	**4**	**132**	**18**	**18**	**90**	**42**
30	5	150	18	20	110	40
27	6	162	12	30	140	22
25	7	175	13	40	180	−5

*Boldface indicates the best price–profit combination.

Before the firm can determine whether a unit will be profitable, it must calculate costs and revenue, because profit equals revenue minus cost. If MR is the increase in revenue generated by the sale of a single additional unit of a product, and MC is the additional cost a single unit adds to a firm, subtracting MR from MC will tell us whether the unit is profitable. Table 12.2 provides an example of the relationships between price, quantity sold, total revenue, marginal revenue, marginal cost, and total cost. It indicates to a marketer the various combinations of price and cost where maximum profits are possible. Notice that the total cost and the marginal cost in Table 12.2 also appear in Table 12.1.

Profit (which is Total Revenue minus Total Cost) is the highest at the point where MC = MR. In Table 12.2, note that this point occurs at four units and a price of $33. Beyond this point, the additional cost of producing another unit exceeds the additional revenue generated, and profits decrease. If the price were based on minimum average total cost—$22 in Table 12.1—it would result in a lower profit—$40 in Table 12.2—for five units priced at $30, versus a profit of $42 for four units priced at $33.

Graphically, Figure 12.6 combines the information given in Figures 12.4 and 12.5. It shows that any unit for which MR exceeds MC adds to a firm's profits, and any unit for

FIGURE 12.6	COMBINING THE MARGINAL COST AND MARGINAL REVENUE CONCEPTS FOR OPTIMAL PROFIT

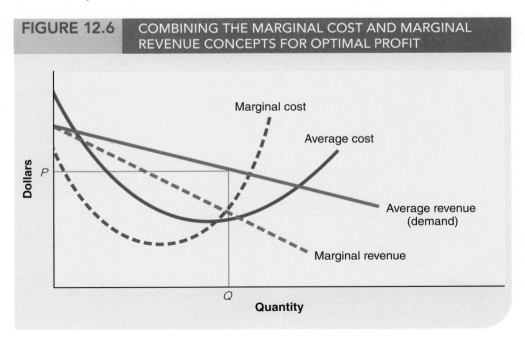

breakeven point The point at which the costs of producing a product equal the revenue made from selling the product

which MC exceeds MR subtracts from profits. The level at which it is best for a firm to produce is where MR equals MC, because this is the most profitable level of production.

This discussion of marginal analysis may give the false impression that pricing can be highly precise and mathematical. If revenue (demand) and cost (supply) remained constant, marketers could set prices for maximum profits. In practice, however, costs and revenues change frequently. The competitive tactics of other firms or government actions can quickly change the marketing environment and undermine a company's expectations for revenue, as can changing economic conditions. Thus, marginal analysis is only a model from which to work. Moreover, it offers little help in pricing new products before costs and revenues are established. On the other hand, most marketers can benefit by understanding the relationship between marginal cost and marginal revenue in setting prices of existing products.

12-4b Break-Even Analysis

The point at which the costs of producing a product equal the revenue made from selling the product is the **breakeven point**. If a paint manufacturer has total costs of $100,000 and sells $100,000 worth of paint in the same year, the company has broken even.

Figure 12.7 illustrates the relationships between costs, revenue, profits, and losses involved in determining the breakeven point. Knowing the number of units necessary to break even is important in setting the price because it helps a firm to calculate how long it will take to recoup expenses at different price points. For example, if a product priced at $100 per unit has an average variable cost of $60 per unit, the contribution to fixed costs is $40. If total fixed costs are $120,000, the breakeven point in units is determined as follows:

$$\text{break-even point} = \frac{\text{fixed costs}}{\text{per-unit contribution to fixed costs}}$$

$$= \frac{\text{fixed costs}}{\text{price-variable costs}}$$

$$= \frac{\$120,000}{\$40}$$

$$= 3,000 \text{ units}$$

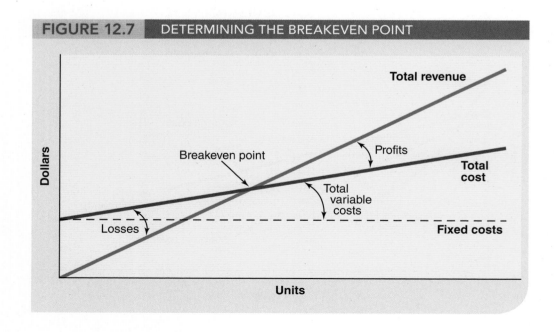

FIGURE 12.7   DETERMINING THE BREAKEVEN POINT

To calculate the breakeven point in terms of dollar sales volume, the seller multiplies the breakeven point in units by the price per unit. In the preceding example, the breakeven point in terms of dollar sales volume is 3,000 (units) times $100, or $300,000.

To use breakeven analysis effectively, a marketer should determine the breakeven point for several alternative prices in order to compare the relative effects on total revenue, total costs, and the breakeven point. Although this comparative analysis may not tell the marketer exactly what price to charge, it will identify highly undesirable prices that should definitely be avoided.

Break-even analysis is simple and straightforward. It does assume, however, that the quantity demanded is basically fixed (inelastic) and that the major task in setting prices is to recover costs. It focuses more on how to break even than on how to achieve a pricing objective, such as percentage of market share or return on investment. Nonetheless, marketing managers can use this concept to determine whether and when a product will achieve a break-even volume.

12-5 EVALUATION OF COMPETITORS' PRICES

LO 12-5 Explain how marketers analyze competitors' prices.

In most cases, marketers are in a better position to establish prices when they know the prices charged for competing brands, which is the next step in establishing prices. Identifying competitors' prices should be a regular part of marketing research. Some grocery and department stores even employ comparative shoppers who systematically collect data on prices. Companies may also purchase price lists from syndicated marketing research services. Even if a marketer has access to competitors' price lists, they may not reflect the actual prices at which competitive products sell because negotiation is involved.

Knowing the prices of competing brands is essential for a marketer. Regardless of a firm's actual costs, it does not want to sell its product at a price a great deal above competitors' because products may not sell well, or a great deal below because customers may believe the product is of a low quality. Firms tend to overprice products in market environments that have less competition or that maintain a strong technological orientation. Overpricing might help an organization in the short run, but it can have negative repercussions in the long term.[7] Particularly in an industry in which price competition prevails, a marketer needs competitive price information to ensure that a firm's prices are the same as, or slightly lower than, competitors'. In some instances, an organization's prices are designed to be slightly above competitors' prices, such as with Apple brand products, to lend an exclusive image.

12-6 SELECTION OF A BASIS FOR PRICING

LO 12-6 Analyze the bases used for setting prices.

The sixth step in establishing prices involves selecting a basis for pricing: cost, demand, and/or competition. The appropriate pricing basis is affected by the type of product, the market structure of the industry, the brand's market share position relative to competing brands, and customer characteristics. Although we discuss each basis separately in this section, an organization generally considers at least two, or perhaps all three, dimensions. For example, if a company uses cost as a primary basis for setting prices, its marketers are still aware of and concerned about competitors' prices. If a company uses demand as a basis for pricing, marketers still must consider costs and competitors' prices. Indeed, cost is a factor in every pricing decision because it establishes a price minimum below which the firm will not be able to recoup its production and other costs. Demand, likewise, sets an effective price maximum above which customers are unlikely to buy the product. Setting appropriate prices can be a difficult balance for firms. A high price may reduce demand for the product, but a low price will hurt profit margins and may instill in customers a perception that the product is of low quality. Firms must weigh many different factors when setting prices, including costs, competition, customer buying behavior and price sensitivity, manufacturing capacity, and product life cycles.

12-6a Cost-Based Pricing

With **cost-based pricing**, a flat dollar amount or percentage is added to the cost of the product, which means marketers apply a desired level of profit to the cost of the product. Cost-based pricing does not necessarily take into account the economic aspects of supply and demand, nor must it relate to just one pricing strategy or pricing objective. It is a straightforward and easy-to-implement method. Two common forms of cost-based pricing are cost-plus and markup pricing.

Cost-Plus Pricing

With **cost-plus pricing**, the seller's costs are determined (usually during a project or after a project is completed), and then a specified dollar amount or percentage of the cost is added to the seller's cost to establish the price. When production costs are difficult to predict, cost-plus pricing is appropriate. Projects involving custom-made equipment and commercial construction are often priced using this technique. The government also frequently uses cost-based pricing in granting defense contracts. One pitfall for the buyer is that the seller may increase stated costs in order to gain a larger profit base. Furthermore, some costs, such as overhead, may be difficult to determine. In periods of rapid inflation, cost-plus pricing is popular, especially when the producer must use raw materials that frequently fluctuate in price.

Markup Pricing

With **markup pricing**, commonly used by retailers, a product's price is derived by adding a predetermined percentage of the cost, called *markup,* to the cost of the product. For instance, most retailers mark up prices by 25 to 50 percent, whereas warehouse clubs, like Costco and Sam's Club, have a lower average markup of around 14 percent.[8] Markups can range a great deal, depending on the product and the situation. Although the percentage markup in a retail store varies from one category of goods to another—35 percent of cost for hardware items and 100 percent of cost for greeting cards, for example—the same percentage is often used to determine the prices on items within a single product category, and the percentage markup may be largely standardized across an industry at the retail level. Using a rigid percentage markup for a specific product category reduces pricing to a routine task that can be performed quickly.

The following example illustrates how percentage markups are determined and distinguishes between two methods of stating a markup. Assume a retailer purchases a can of tuna at 45 cents and adds a 15-cent markup to the cost, making the price 60 cents. There are two ways to look at the markup, as a percentage of cost or a percentage of selling price, as follows:

$$\text{Markup as percentage of cost} = \frac{\text{markup}}{\text{cost}}$$

$$= \frac{15}{45}$$

$$= 33.3\%$$

$$\text{Markup as percentage of selling price} = \frac{\text{markup}}{\text{selling price}}$$

$$= \frac{15}{60}$$

$$= 25.0\%$$

The markup as a percentage of cost is 33.3 percent, while the markup as a percentage of price is only 25 percent. Obviously, when discussing a percentage markup, it is important to know whether the markup is based on cost or selling price.

12-6b Demand-Based Pricing

Marketers sometimes base prices on the level of demand for the product. When **demand-based pricing** is used, customers pay a higher price at times when demand for the product is strong and a lower price when demand is weak. Many entertainment venues have implemented demand-based pricing for ticket sales. The Minnesota Twins baseball team, for example, uses demand-based pricing for single-game tickets, with final prices being influenced by factors such as opponent, time of year, and date.[9] Offering cheaper tickets or extra perks on traditionally slow

Demand-Based Pricing
Airline companies engage in demand-based pricing. When demand for a specific flight is higher, the fares are higher, and when the demand is lower, the fares will be lower.

iStock.com/uvendemir

days and more expensive tickets or greater restrictions on traditionally crowded days, such as summer weekends, can boost sales on slow days while spreading out venue attendance to relieve crowded conditions. The belief behind this pricing basis is that it is better to take a lower profit margin on a sale than no revenue at all.

Many service industries, including the airline, hotel, bus, car rental, ride sharing, and entertainment venues, use *dynamic pricing* to balance supply and demand. For instance, ride-sharing services Uber and Lyft charge higher rates on Saturday nights and other local peak demand times. Likewise, in some industries, *yield management* is a strategy of maximizing revenues by making numerous price changes in response to demand, competitors' prices, or environmental conditions. For example, Uber, like many firms in the transportation and travel industries, explains that it continually adjusts fares based on factors such as estimated traffic, estimated time and distance of the expected route, and the number of drivers available in order to ensure that the supply of drivers matches rider demand in real time.[10]

To use demand-based pricing, a marketer must be able to estimate the quantity of product consumers will demand at different times and how demand will be affected by changes in the price. The marketer then chooses the price that generates the highest total revenue. Demand-based pricing is appropriate for industries in which companies have a fixed amount of available resources that are perishable, such as airline seats, hotel rooms, concert seats, and so on. The effectiveness of demand-based pricing depends on the marketer's ability to estimate demand accurately. Compared with cost-based pricing, demand-based pricing places a firm in a better position to attain high profit levels, assuming demand is strong at times and buyers value the product at levels sufficiently above the product's cost.

12-6c Competition-Based Pricing

With **competition-based pricing**, an organization considers costs to be secondary to competitors' prices. This is a common method among producers of relatively homogeneous products, particularly when the target market considers price to be an important purchase consideration. A firm that uses competition-based pricing may choose to price below competitors' prices or at the same level. Competitors believe that Amazon's competition-based pricing model has been an attempt to gain monopoly control of many retail markets. Amazon uses highly sophisticated analytics to gauge consumer demand and compare its prices to competitors in order to gain an edge. To stay ahead of the competition, Amazon adjusts its prices millions of times each day to ensure that it undercuts competitors on the most popular items.[11]

demand-based pricing Pricing based on the level of demand for the product

competition-based pricing Pricing influenced primarily by competitor's prices

price skimming Charging the highest possible price that buyers who most desire the product will pay

penetration pricing Setting prices below those of competing brands to penetrate a market and gain a significant market share quickly

12-7 SELECTION OF A PRICING STRATEGY

LO 12-7 Compare the different types of pricing strategies.

A *pricing strategy* is a course of action designed to achieve pricing objectives, which are set to help marketers solve the practical problems of setting prices. The extent to which a business uses any of the following strategies depends on its pricing and marketing objectives, the markets for its products, the degree of product differentiation, the product's life-cycle stage, and other factors. Figure 12.8 contains a list of the major types of pricing strategies. We will discuss the various pricing strategies in the remainder of this section.

12-7a New-Product Pricing

The two primary types of new-product pricing strategies are price skimming and penetration pricing. An organization can use one or both over a period of time.

Price Skimming

Some consumers are willing to pay a high price for an innovative product, either because of its novelty or because of the prestige or status that ownership confers. **Price skimming** is the strategy of charging the highest possible price for a product during the introduction stage of its life cycle. The seller essentially "skims the cream" off the market, which helps a firm to recover the high costs of R&D more quickly. In addition, a skimming policy may hold down demand for the product in instances where the firm's production capacity is limited during the introduction stage. A danger is that a price skimming strategy may make the product appear more lucrative than it actually is to potential competitors. A firm also risks misjudging demand and facing insufficient sales at the high price.

Penetration Pricing

At the opposite extreme, **penetration pricing** is the strategy of setting a low price for a new product. The main purpose of setting a low price is to build market share quickly in order to encourage product trial by the target market and discourage competitors from entering the market. If the low price stimulates sales, the firm may be able to order longer production runs, increasing economies of scale and resulting in decreased production costs per unit. A disadvantage of penetration pricing is that it places a firm in a less-flexible pricing position. It is more difficult to raise prices significantly than it is to lower them.

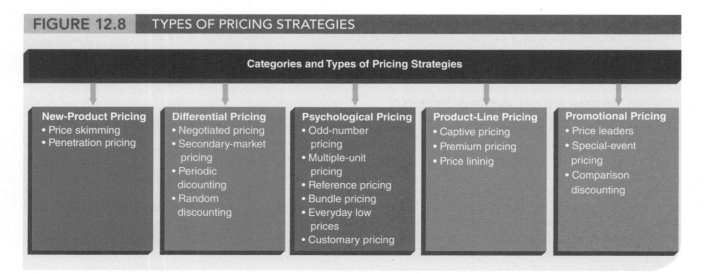

| FIGURE 12.8 | TYPES OF PRICING STRATEGIES |

Categories and Types of Pricing Strategies

New-Product Pricing	Differential Pricing	Psychological Pricing	Product-Line Pricing	Promotional Pricing
• Price skimming	• Negotiated pricing	• Odd-number pricing	• Captive pricing	• Price leaders
• Penetration pricing	• Secondary-market pricing	• Multiple-unit pricing	• Premium pricing	• Special-event pricing
	• Periodic dicounting	• Reference pricing	• Price lininig	• Comparison discounting
	• Random discounting	• Bundle pricing		
		• Everyday low prices		
		• Customary pricing		

12-7b **Differential Pricing**

An important issue in pricing decisions is whether to use a single price or different prices for the same product. A single price is easily understood by both employees and customers. Since many salespeople and customers dislike negotiating prices, having a single price reduces the risk of a marketer developing an adversarial relationship with customers.

    Differential pricing means charging different prices to different buyers for the same quality and quantity of product. For example, many theaters offer discounted tickets for daytime matinee performances, and airlines have different pricing tiers for airline seats depending on whether customers paid extra to board early or other perks. For differential pricing to be effective, the market must consist of multiple segments with different price sensitivities. When this method is employed, caution should be used to avoid confusing or antagonizing customers. Differential pricing can occur in several ways, including negotiated pricing, secondary-market pricing, periodic discounting, and random discounting.

Negotiated Pricing
Car buyers, such as the couple shown in this image, engage in negotiated pricing. It is understood that a buyer is not expected to pay the sticker price for a car.

iStock.com/LuckyBusiness

Negotiated Pricing

Negotiated pricing occurs when the final price is established through bargaining between the seller and the customer. Negotiated pricing occurs in a number of industries and at all levels of distribution. Even when there is a predetermined stated price or a price list, manufacturers, wholesalers, and retailers still may negotiate to establish the final sales price. Customers rarely pay the list price on a car, for instance, because they go to a car dealership expecting to negotiate with the seller until they arrive at a price that is satisfactory to both the customer and the seller. Loyal customers engaging in negotiations with salespeople often receive bigger discounts because of their relationship with the company and because they expect certain rewards for their loyalty.[12] Managing personal chemistry between the negotiators is just as important as settling on prices. The negotiation process can help build relationships and increase understanding between different parties in a supply-chain relationship.

Secondary-Market Pricing

Secondary-market pricing means setting one price for the primary target market and a different price for another market. Often the price charged in the secondary market is lower. However, when the costs of serving a secondary market are higher than normal, secondary-market customers may have to pay a higher price. Examples of secondary markets include a geographically isolated domestic market, a market in a foreign country, or a segment willing to purchase a product during off-peak times (such as "early bird" dinners at restaurants and off-season vacation rentals). Secondary markets give an organization an opportunity to use excess capacity and stabilize the allocation of resources.

Periodic Discounting

Periodic discounting is the temporary reduction of prices on a patterned or systematic basis. For example, many retailers have annual holiday sales, and some apparel stores have regular seasonal sales. From the marketer's point of view, a major problem with periodic discounting is that customers can predict when the reductions will occur and may delay their purchases until they can take advantage of the lower prices. Periodic discounting is less effective in an environment where many consumers shop online because they can more easily compare shops for a better deal even during non-sale times.

differential pricing
Charging different prices to different buyers for the same quality and quantity of product

negotiated pricing
Establishing a final price through bargaining between seller and customer

secondary-market pricing Setting one price for the primary target market and a different price for another market

periodic discounting
Temporary reduction of prices on a patterned or systematic basis

random discounting Temporary reduction of prices on an unsystematic basis

psychological pricing Strategies that encourage purchases based on consumers' emotional responses, rather than on economically rational ones

odd-number pricing The strategy of setting prices using odd numbers that are slightly below whole-dollar amounts

multiple-unit pricing The strategy of setting a single price for two or more units

reference pricing Pricing a product at a moderate level and positioning it next to a more expensive model or brand

Random Discounting

To alleviate the problem of customers knowing when discounting will occur, some organizations employ **random discounting**. That is, they reduce their prices temporarily on a nonsystematic basis. When price reductions occur randomly, current users of that brand are not able to predict when the reductions will occur. Therefore, they are less likely to delay their purchases in anticipation of buying the product at a lower price. Marketers also use random discounting to attract new customers. Marketers must be careful not to use random discounting too often, however, because customers will learn to wait for the discounts.

12-7c **Psychological Pricing**

Psychological pricing strategies encourage purchases based on consumers' emotional responses, rather than on economically rational ones. These strategies are used primarily for consumer products, rather than business products, because most business purchases follow a systematic and rational approach. In retail environments, how customers interpret price fairness, value, and feelings toward prices at a particular store affect their perceptions of the store's price image as well as their repurchase intentions.[13]

Odd-Number Pricing

Many retailers believe that consumers respond more positively to odd-number prices, such as $4.99, than to whole-dollar prices, such as $5.00. **Odd-number pricing** is the strategy of setting prices using odd numbers that are slightly below whole-dollar amounts. Nine and five are the most popular ending figures for odd-number prices.

Sellers who use this strategy believe that odd-number prices increase sales because consumers register the dollar amount, not the cents. The strategy is not limited to low-priced items. Auto manufacturers may set the price of a car at $11,999 rather than $12,000. Odd-number pricing has been the subject of various psychological studies, but the results have been inconclusive.

Bundle Pricing
Most providers of travel services engage in bundle pricing.

iStock.com/YinYang

Multiple-Unit Pricing

Many retailers (and especially supermarkets) practice **multiple-unit pricing**, setting a single price for two or more units of a product, such as two cans for 99 cents rather than 50 cents per can. Especially for frequently purchased products, this strategy can increase sales through encouraging consumers to purchase multiple units when they might otherwise have only purchased one at a time. Customers who see the single price and who expect eventually to use more than one unit of the product will purchase multiple units.

Reference Pricing

Reference pricing means pricing a product at a moderate level and physically positioning it next to a more expensive model or brand in the hope that the customer will use the higher price as a reference point (i.e., a comparison price).

Because of the comparison, the customer is expected to view the moderate price more favorably than he or she would if the product were considered in isolation.

Bundle Pricing

Bundle pricing is the packaging together of two or more products, usually of a complementary nature, to be sold for a single price. To be attractive to customers, the single price usually is considerably less than the sum of the prices of the individual products. Being able to buy the bundled combination in a single transaction may be of value to the customer, increasing convenience and a sense of value. Bundle pricing is used commonly for banking and travel services, computers, and automobiles with option packages. Bundle pricing can help to increase customer satisfaction. It can also help firms to sell slow-moving inventory and increase revenues by bundling the inventory with products with a higher turnover.

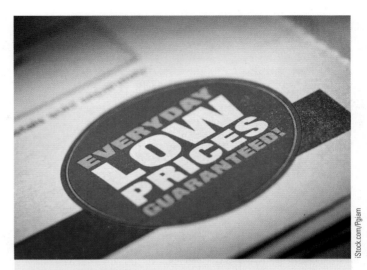

Every Day Low Prices
Walmart is a major user of the Everyday Low Price strategy.

Everyday Low Prices (EDLPs)

To reduce or eliminate the use of frequent short-term price reductions, some organizations use an approach referred to as **everyday low prices (EDLPs)**. When EDLPs are used, a marketer sets a low price for its products on a consistent basis, rather than setting higher prices and frequently discounting them. EDLPs, though not deeply discounted, are set low enough to make customers feel confident that they are receiving a good deal. EDLPs are employed by retailers, such as Walmart, and by manufacturers, such as Procter & Gamble. A company that uses EDLPs benefits from reduced promotional costs, reduced losses from frequent markdowns, and more stable sales. Studies show that when customers are uncertain about store prices, they are more likely to choose a retail establishment with an EDLP strategy over a retailer that offers large discounts infrequently.[14] A major problem with this approach is that customers can have mixed responses to it. In some instances, customers believe that EDLPs are a marketing gimmick, and not truly the good deal that they proclaim.

Customary Pricing

In **customary pricing**, certain goods are priced on the basis of tradition. Examples of customary, or traditional, prices would be those set for candy bars and chewing gum. This is a less common pricing strategy now than it was in the past. An example would be the 25-cent gumballs sold in gumball machines—the price has remained at that level for probably as long as you can remember.

12-7d **Product-Line Pricing**

Rather than considering products on an item-by-item basis when determining pricing strategies, some marketers employ product-line pricing. *Product-line pricing* means establishing and adjusting the prices of multiple products within a product line. Product-line pricing can provide marketers with flexibility in setting prices. For example, marketers can set prices so that one product is profitable, whereas another is less profitable but increases market share by virtue of having a low price. When marketers employ product-line pricing, they have several strategies from which to choose. These include captive pricing, premium pricing, and price lining.

bundle pricing Packaging together two or more complementary products and selling them for a single price

everyday low prices (EDLPs) Setting a low price for products on a consistent basis

customary pricing Pricing on the basis of tradition

iStock.com/adventtr

Captive Pricing

Companies that produce and market razors engage in captive pricing by charging high prices for replacement razor blade cartridges. To continue using a specific razor, the customer must purchase additional blade cartridges.

Captive Pricing

When marketers use **captive pricing**, the basic product in a product line is priced low, but the price on the items required to operate or enhance it are higher. A common example of captive pricing is printer ink. The printer is generally priced quite low, but the printer ink replacement cartridges are usually very expensive. This pricing strategy is effective because consumers must purchase far more replacement cartridges than printers over their lifetimes. Razorblades and single-serving coffee pods are additional well-known examples.

Premium Pricing

Premium pricing occurs when the highest-quality product or the most versatile and most desirable version of a product in a product line is assigned the highest price. Other products in the line are priced to appeal to price-sensitive shoppers or to those who seek product-specific features. Marketers that use premium pricing often realize a significant portion of their profits from premium-priced products. Examples of product categories in which premium pricing is common are small kitchen appliances, beer, ice cream, and television cable service. Pet food is another example. Pet owners are becoming more willing to pay premium prices for grain-free dog food in the belief that it is healthier for their pets.

Price Lining

Price lining is the strategy of selling goods only at certain predetermined prices that reflect explicit price breaks. For example, a shop may sell men's ties only at $22 and $37. This strategy is used widely in clothing and accessory stores. It eliminates minor price differences from the buying decision—both for customers and for managers who buy merchandise to sell in these stores.

12-7e **Promotional Pricing**

Price, as an ingredient in the marketing mix, often is coordinated with promotion. The two variables sometimes are so interrelated that the pricing policy is promotion-oriented. Examples of promotional pricing include price leaders, special-event pricing, and comparison discounting.

Price Leaders

Sometimes a firm prices a few products below the usual markup, near cost, or even below cost, which results in what are known as **price leaders**. This type of pricing is used most often in supermarkets and restaurants to attract customers by offering especially low prices on a few items, with the expectation that they will purchase other items as well. Management expects that sales of regularly priced products will more than offset the reduced revenues from the price leaders.

Special-Event Pricing

To increase sales volume, many organizations coordinate price with advertising or sales promotions for seasonal or special situations. **Special-event pricing** involves advertised sales or price cutting linked to a holiday, season, or event. If the pricing objective is survival, then special sales events may be designed to generate necessary operating capital.

captive pricing Pricing the basic product in a product line low, but pricing related items at a higher level

premium pricing Pricing the highest-quality or most versatile products higher than other models in the product line

price lining The strategy of selling goods only at certain predetermined prices that reflect definite price breaks

price leaders Products priced below the usual markup, near cost, or below cost

special-event pricing Advertised sales or price cutting linked to a holiday, season, or event

Comparison Discounting

comparison discounting
Setting a price at a specific level and comparing it with a higher price

Comparison discounting sets the price of a product at a specific level and simultaneously compares it with a higher price. The higher price may be the product's previous price, the price of a competing brand, the product's price at another retail outlet, or a manufacturer's suggested retail price. Customers may find comparison discounting informative, and it can have a significant impact on them.

However, because this pricing strategy on occasion has led to deceptive pricing practices, the Federal Trade Commission has established guidelines for comparison discounting. If the higher price against which the comparison is made is the price formerly charged for the product, sellers must have made the previous price available to customers for a reasonable period of time. If sellers present the higher price as the one charged by other retailers in the same trade area, they must be able to demonstrate that this claim is true. When they present the higher price as the manufacturer's suggested retail price, then the higher price must be close to the price at which a reasonable proportion of the product was sold. Some manufacturers' suggested retail prices are so high that very few products actually are sold at those prices. In such cases, it would be deceptive to use comparison discounting. The Internet has allowed consumers to be more wary of comparison discounting and less susceptible to deception, as they can easily compare the listed price for a product with comparable products online.

12-8 DETERMINATION OF A SPECIFIC PRICE

LO 12-8 Describe the selection of a specific price.

A pricing strategy will yield a certain price or range of prices, which is the final step in the pricing process. However, marketers may need to refine this price in order to make it

EMERGING TRENDS

How Much Should a Life-Saving Product Cost?

How should marketers price life-saving products? That's the controversy swirling around ready-to-inject epinephrine treatments for life-threatening allergic reactions. In 2007, Mylan bought the rights to EpiPen, a long-established pharmaceutical product that many consumers and schools keep handy in case of emergency. Mylan hiked the EpiPen price again and again, until a two-pack of injector pens carried a list price of $609, dramatically higher than the sub-$100 price in 2007.

Because buyers must purchase fresh injectors every year, the steep price for a must-have product sparked consumer outrage and triggered a government investigation. Under pressure, Mylan announced a generic version of EpiPen two-packs priced at $300 and offered a savings card to help insured consumers cover the co-payment. The company also paid $465 million to settle charges that U.S. government programs had overpaid for EpiPen products.

Although EpiPen has high brand awareness and high market share, thanks to branded and generic EpiPen products, its market share has dropped from about 95 percent to about 71 percent as competitors enter the market. CVS began selling a generic two-pack version of Adrenaclick for $110. When the retailer offers a $100 coupon, the effective price is only $10. Kaléo recently relaunched its Auvi-Q twin-pack of epinephrine injectors with a list price of $4,500, after retooling manufacturing to upgrade quality. Kaléo also limits the consumer's out-of-pocket costs to $360 per purchase, with some insured consumers paying nothing for the injectors.

How do you think life-saving products should be priced?[b]

consistent with circumstances, such as a sluggish economy, and with pricing practices in a particular market or industry. Johnson & Johnson, for example, has pledged to be transparent with its pricing strategies for pharmaceutical products at a time when many firms have come under fire for rapidly escalating prices on life-saving drugs. The company even releases a transparency report demonstrating that it has held average list price increases below 10 percent for five years.[15] Pricing strategies should help a firm in setting a final price. If they are to do so, marketers must establish pricing objectives, have considerable knowledge about target market customers, and determine demand, price elasticity, costs, and competitive factors. Additionally, the way marketers use pricing in the marketing mix will affect the final price.

12-9 PRICING FOR BUSINESS MARKETS

LO 12-9 Identify seven methods companies can use to price products for business markets.

Many of the pricing issues discussed thus far in this chapter deal with pricing in general. However, setting prices for business products can be quite different from setting prices for consumer products, owing to several factors such as size of purchases, transportation considerations, and geographic issues. In this section, we examine three types of pricing associated with business products: geographic pricing, transfer pricing, and discounting.

12-9a Geographic Pricing

Geographic pricing strategies deal with delivery costs. *F.O.B. origin pricing* stands for "free on board at the point of origin," which means that the price does not include freight charges. It requires the buyer to pay the delivery costs, which include transportation from the seller's warehouse to the buyer's place of business. *F.O.B. destination* indicates that the product price does include freight charges, and therefore the seller is responsible for these charges.

12-9b Transfer Pricing

When one unit in an organization sells a product to another unit, **transfer pricing** occurs. A transfer price is determined by calculating the cost of the product, which can vary depending on the types of costs included in the calculations. The choice of the costs to include when calculating the transfer price depends on the company's management strategy and the nature of the units' interaction. An organization also must ensure that transfer pricing is fair to all units involved in the purchase.

12-9c Discounting

geographic pricing Reductions for transportation and other costs related to the physical distance between buyer and seller

transfer pricing Prices charged in sales between an organization's units

discount A deduction from the price of an item

A **discount** is a deduction off the price of an item. Producers and sellers offer a wide variety of discounts to their customers, including trade, quantity, cash, and seasonal discounts as well as allowances. *Trade discounts* are taken off the list prices and are offered to marketing intermediaries, or middlemen. *Quantity discounts* are given to customers who buy in large quantities. Quantity discounts are offered because the seller's per-unit selling cost is usually lower for larger purchases. *Cash discounts* are incentives offered for prompt payment. A seller may offer a discount of "2/10, net 30," meaning that the buyer may take a 2 percent discount if the bill is paid within ten days and that the bill must be paid in full within 30 days. A *seasonal discount* is a price reduction to buyers who purchase out of season. It helps the seller to maintain steadier production during the year. An *allowance* is a reduction in price to achieve a desired goal. Trade-in allowances, for example, are price reductions granted for turning in used equipment, like aircraft, when purchasing new equipment. Table 12.3 describes some of the reasons for using these discounting techniques, as well as some examples.

TABLE 12.3	DISCOUNTS USED FOR BUSINESS MARKETS	
Type	**Reasons for Use**	**Examples**
Trade (functional)	To attract and keep effective resellers by compensating them for performing certain functions, such as transportation, warehousing, selling, and providing credit.	A college bookstore pays about one-third less for a new textbook than the retail price a student pays.
Quantity	To encourage customers to buy large quantities when making purchases and, in the case of cumulative discounts, to encourage customer loyalty.	Numerous companies serving business markets allow a 2 percent discount if an account is paid within 10 days.
Seasonal	To allow a marketer to use resources more efficiently by stimulating sales during off-peak periods.	Florida hotels provide companies holding national and regional sales meetings with deeply discounted accommodations during the summer months.
Allowance	In the case of a trade-in allowance, to assist the buyer in making the purchase and potentially earn a profit on the resale of used equipment. In the case of a promotional allowance, to ensure that dealers participate in advertising and sales support programs.	A farm equipment dealer takes a farmer's used tractor as a trade-in on a new one. Nabisco pays a promotional allowance to a supermarket for setting up and maintaining a large end-of-aisle display for a two-week period.

Chapter Review

12-1 Identify issues related to developing pricing objectives.

The stages in the process of setting prices are (1) developing pricing objectives, (2) assessing the target market's evaluation of price, (3) determining demand, (4) analyzing demand, cost, and profit relationships, (5) evaluating competitors' prices, (6) selecting a basis for pricing, (7) selecting a pricing strategy, and (8) determining a specific price.

Setting pricing objectives is critical because pricing objectives form the foundation upon which the decisions of all subsequent stages are based. Organizations may use numerous pricing objectives, including short-term and long-term ones, and objectives will vary for different products and market segments. Pricing objectives are overall goals that describe the role of price in a firm's long-range plans. There are several major types of pricing objectives. The most fundamental pricing objective is the organization's survival. Price usually can be easily adjusted to increase sales volume or combat competition to help the organization stay alive. Profit objectives, which are usually stated in terms of sales dollar volume or percentage change, are normally set at a satisfactory level rather than at a level designed to maximize profits. A sales growth objective focuses on increasing the profit base by raising sales volume. Pricing for return on investment (ROI) has a specified profit as its objective. A pricing objective to maintain or increase market share links market position to success. Other types of pricing objectives include cash flow, status quo, and product quality.

12-2 Discuss the importance of identifying the target market's evaluation of price.

Assessing the target market's evaluation of price tells the marketer how much emphasis to place on price and may help determine how far above the competition the firm can set its prices. Understanding how important a product is to customers relative to other products, as well as customers' expectations of quality, helps marketers assess the target market's evaluation of price.

12-3 Explore the role of demand and the price elasticity of demand.

An organization must identify the demand for its product. The classic demand curve is the quantity of products expected to be sold at various prices if other factors hold constant. It illustrates that as price falls, the quantity demanded usually increases. However, for prestige products there is a direct positive relationship between price and quantity demanded: demand increases as price increases. Price elasticity of demand, the percentage change in quantity demanded relative to a given percentage change in price, must also be determined. If demand is elastic, a change in price causes an opposite change in total revenue. Inelastic demand results in a parallel change in total revenue when a product's price is changed.

12-4 Describe the relationships among demand, costs, and profits.

Analysis of demand, cost, and profit relationships can be accomplished through marginal analysis or break-even analysis. Marginal analysis examines what happens to a firm's costs and revenues when production (or sales volume) is changed by one unit. Marginal analysis combines the demand curve with the firm's costs to determine the price that will yield a maximum profit. Fixed costs are those that do not vary with changes in the number of units produced or sold. Average fixed cost is the fixed cost per unit produced. Variable costs vary directly with changes in the number of units produced or sold. Average variable cost is the variable cost per unit produced. Total cost is the sum of average fixed cost and average variable cost, times the quantity produced. The optimal price is the point at which marginal cost (the cost associated with producing one more unit of the product) equals marginal revenue (the change in total revenue that occurs when one additional unit of the product is sold). Marginal analysis is only a model—which means it can provide guidance but offers little help in pricing new products before costs and revenues are established.

Break-even analysis, determining the number of units that must be sold to break even, is important in setting price. The point at which the costs of production equal the revenue from selling the product is the breakeven point. To use break-even analysis effectively, a marketer should determine the breakeven point for each of several alternative prices. This makes it possible to compare the effects on total revenue, total costs, and the breakeven point for each price under consideration. However, this approach assumes the quantity demanded is basically fixed and the major task is to set prices to recover costs.

12-5 Explain how marketers analyze competitors' prices.

A marketer needs to be aware of the prices charged for competing brands. This allows the firm to keep its prices in line with competitors' when nonprice competition is used. If a company uses price as a competitive tool, it can price its brand below competing brands.

12-6 Analyze the bases used for setting prices.

The three major dimensions on which prices can be based are cost, demand, and competition. When using cost-based pricing, the firm determines price by adding a dollar amount or percentage to the cost of the product. Two common cost-based pricing methods are cost-plus and markup pricing. Demand-based pricing is based on the level of demand for the product. To use this method, a marketer must be able to estimate the amounts of a product buyers will demand at different prices. Demand-based pricing results in a high price when demand for a product is strong and a low price when demand is weak. In the case of competition-based pricing, costs and revenues are secondary to competitors' prices.

12-7 Compare the different types of pricing strategies.

A pricing strategy is an approach or a course of action designed to achieve pricing and marketing objectives. Pricing strategies help marketers solve the practical problems of establishing prices. The most common pricing strategies are differential pricing, new-product pricing, product-line pricing, psychological pricing, and promotional pricing.

When marketers employ differential pricing, they charge different buyers different prices for the same quality and quantity of products. For example, with negotiated pricing, the final price is established through bargaining between seller and customer. Secondary-market pricing involves setting one price for the primary target market and a different price for another market. Often the price charged in the secondary market is lower than in the primary market. Marketers employ periodic discounting when they temporarily lower their prices on a patterned or systematic basis. The reason for the reduction may be a seasonal change, a model-year change, or a holiday. Random discounting occurs on an unsystematic basis.

Two strategies used in new-product pricing are price skimming and penetration pricing. With price skimming, the organization charges the highest price that buyers who most desire the product will pay. A penetration price is a low price designed to penetrate a market and gain a significant market share quickly.

Product-line pricing establishes and adjusts the prices of multiple products within a product line. This strategy includes captive pricing, in which the marketer prices the basic product in a product line low and prices related items higher. With premium pricing, prices on higher-quality or more versatile products are set higher than those on other models in the product line. Price lining is when the organization sets a limited number of prices for selected groups or lines of merchandise.

Psychological pricing attempts to influence customers' perceptions of price to make a product's price more attractive. With reference pricing, marketers price a product at a moderate level and position it next to a more expensive model or brand. Bundle pricing is packaging together two or more complementary products and selling them at a single price. With multiple-unit pricing, two or more identical products are packaged together and sold at a single price. To reduce or eliminate use of frequent short-term price reductions, some organizations employ everyday low prices (EDLP), setting a low price for products on a consistent basis. When employing odd-number pricing, marketers try to influence buyers' perceptions of the price or the product by ending the price with certain numbers. Customary pricing is based on traditional prices. With prestige pricing, prices are set at an artificially high level to convey prestige or a quality image.

Price leaders are products priced below the usual markup, near cost, or below cost. Special-event pricing involves advertised sales or price cutting linked to a holiday, season, or event. Marketers that use a comparison discounting strategy price a product at a specific level and compare it with a higher price.

12-8 Describe the selection of a specific price.

A pricing strategy will yield a certain price or range of prices, which is the final step in the pricing process. However, marketers may need to refine this price in order to make it consistent with circumstances, such as a sluggish economy, and with pricing practices in a particular market or industry. Pricing strategies should help a firm in setting a final price.

12-9 Identify seven methods companies can use to price products for business markets.

Setting prices for business products can be different from setting prices for consumer products, owing to several factors such as size of purchases, transportation considerations, and geographic issues. The three main types of pricing associated with business products are geographic pricing, transfer pricing, and discounting.

Geographic pricing involves reductions for transportation costs or other costs associated with the physical distance between buyer and seller. With an F.O.B. factory price, the buyer pays for shipping from the factory. An F.O.B. destination price means the producer pays for shipping.

Transfer pricing occurs when a unit in an organization sells products to another unit in the organization. The choice of the costs to include when calculating the transfer price depends on the company's management strategy and the nature of the units' interaction.

Discounts include trade, quantity, cash, seasonal, and allowance. A trade discount is a price reduction for performing such functions as storing, transporting, final processing, or providing credit services. If an intermediary purchases in large enough quantities, the producer gives a quantity discount, which can be either cumulative or noncumulative. A cash discount is a price reduction for prompt payment or payment in cash. Buyers who purchase goods or services out of season may be granted a seasonal discount. An allowance, such as a trade-in allowance, is a concession in price to achieve a desired goal.

 Go to www.cengagebrain.com for resources to help you master the content in this chapter as well as for materials that will expand your marketing knowledge!

Developing Your Marketing Plan

Setting the right price for a product is a crucial part of a marketing strategy. Price helps to establish a product's position in the mind of the consumer and can differentiate a product from its competition. Several decisions in the marketing plan will be affected by the pricing strategy that is selected. To assist you in relating the information in this chapter to the development of your marketing plan, focus on the following:

1. Using Table 12.1 as a guide, discuss each of the seven pricing objectives. Which pricing objectives will you use for your product? Consider the product life cycle, competition, and product positioning for your target market during your discussion.
2. Review the various types of pricing strategies. Which of these is the most appropriate for your product?
3. Select a basis for pricing your product (cost, demand, and/or competition). How will you know when it is time to revise your pricing strategy?

Key Concepts

Issues for Discussion and Review

1. Identify the eight stages in the process of establishing prices.
2. How does a return on investment pricing objective differ from an objective of increasing market share?
3. Why must marketing objectives and pricing objectives be considered when making pricing decisions?
4. Why should a marketer be aware of competitors' prices?
5. Why do most demand curves demonstrate an inverse relationship between price and quantity?
6. List the characteristics of products that have inelastic demand, and give several examples of such products.
7. Explain why optimal profits should occur when marginal cost equals marginal revenue.
8. Chambers Company has just gathered estimates for conducting a break-even analysis for a new product. Variable costs are $7 a unit. The additional plant will cost $48,000. The new product will be charged $18,000 a year for its share of general overhead. Advertising expenditures will be $80,000, and $55,000 will be spent on distribution. If the product sells for $12, what is the breakeven point in units? What is the breakeven point in dollar sales volume?
9. What are the benefits of cost-based pricing?
10. Under what conditions is cost-plus pricing most appropriate?
11. A retailer purchases a can of soup for 24 cents and sells it for 36 cents. Calculate the markup as a percentage of cost and as a percentage of selling price.
12. What is differential pricing? In what ways can it be achieved?
13. For what types of products would price skimming be most appropriate? For what types of products would penetration pricing be more effective?
14. Describe bundle pricing, and give three examples using different industries.
15. Why do customers associate price with quality? When should prestige pricing be used?
16. Compare and contrast a trade discount and a quantity discount.
17. What is the reason for using the term *F.O.B.* (free on board at the point of origin)?

VIDEO CASE 12
Warby Parker Puts Affordable Eyewear in Focus

Bringing down the high price of fashion eyeglasses was the goal that four friends set out to achieve when they founded Warby Parker in 2010. The business idea grew out of cofounder Dave Gilboa's personal experience. When he was a graduate student, he lost his glasses while hiking and was so outraged by the high price of replacing them that he squinted for months rather than buy new glasses. Eyeglasses are made from wire, plastic, screws, and glass, yet the retail price is often many times the actual cost of the materials, yielding a hefty profit margin. Adding a designer logo to a pair of frames pushes the final price even higher. Talking with friends, Gilboa learned he wasn't the only person unhappy about having to spend a lot for eyeglasses. So Gilboa teamed up with Neil Blumenthal, Andy Hunt, and Jeff Raider to create a business plan for a new kind of eyewear company, selling quality eyeglasses directly to customers with a price tag below $100 per pair.

Direct marketing keeps Warby Parker's distribution costs low and avoids the kind of intermediary markups that typically increase the final price. In-house designers develop all frame styles, which means no licensing fees for the right to use famous fashion logos. Customers benefit because Warby Parker passes the savings along in the form of affordable price tags for quality eyewear. The company also has a social conscience: It donates a pair of glasses to someone in need for every pair it sells.

Customers in Warby Parker's target market recognize the value of paying less for glasses by changing their buying behavior. The customer can select up to five eyeglass frames from online inventory and have these choices delivered for a five-day free at-home trial before purchasing a pair. Warby Parker pays the postage both ways, so the customer risks nothing. Frame prices begin at $95 per pair, although optional extras such as progressive lenses will increase the final price. After deciding on a frame, the customer submits a prescription, clicks to finalize the order, and receives new glasses by mail within one to two weeks.

Originally, Warby Parker marketed its eyeglasses only online. Initial sales were so brisk that the startup surpassed its first-year sales objectives by the end of the first three weeks. Six months after its online debut, Warby Parker had already sold 85,000 pairs—and donated an equal number to people in need. But not everything is online. Customers have always been able to visit the company's New York City headquarters, see frames in person, and try them on before ordering. This proved so popular that Warby Parker decided to expand its in-person retail operations.

Today, Warby Parker is opening new stores year after year, targeting cities where the company's database shows high concentrations of customers. It already operates 47 stores in 22 states, with some stores equipped for optical examinations. Some stores include photo kiosks so customers can snap fun photos of themselves wearing different frames and post to social media for advice from friends. The photos don't just help customers make buying decisions—they keep the Warby Parker brand in the public eye and help the firm stay in touch with customers who opt to receive communications. What's next for Warby Parker as it shakes up the eyewear industry with direct marketing, retail stores, low prices, fun styles, and social responsibility?[16]

Questions for Discussion

1. Based on your knowledge of pricing concepts, why does Warby Parker stress that the price tag for frames starts at $95?
2. Given Warby Parker's original idea of selling online to minimize distribution costs and keep prices low, do you agree with its more recent decision to open dozens of stores? Explain your answer.
3. Should Warby Parker charge more for frames purchased in stores than for frames purchased online, to offset the higher cost of rent and store employees? Why or why not?

Part 5

Monkey Business Images/Shutterstock.com

Distribution Decisions

Developing products that satisfy customers is important, but it is not sufficient to guarantee a successful marketing strategy. Products must also be available in adequate quantities in accessible locations at the times when customers desire them. **PART 5** deals with the distribution of products and the marketing channels and institutions that help to make products available. **CHAPTER 13** discusses supply-chain management, marketing channels, and the decisions and activities associated with the physical distribution of products, such as order processing, materials handling, warehousing, inventory management, and transportation. **CHAPTER 14** explores retailing and wholesaling, including types of retailers and wholesalers, direct marketing and selling, and strategic retailing issues.

chapter 13

Marketing Channels and Supply-Chain Management

iStock.com/narvikk

LEARNING OBJECTIVES

13-1 Describe the foundations of supply-chain management.

13-2 Explain the role and significance of marketing channels and supply chains.

13-3 Identify the intensity of market coverage.

13-4 Explore strategic issues in marketing channels, including leadership, cooperation, and conflict.

13-5 Explain physical distribution as being a part of supply-chain management.

13-6 Examine legal issues in channel management.

Seizing the Moment: Marketing Channels for Championship Gear

Fifteen minutes. That's all the time Fanatics needs to post official championship-logo caps and clothing for sale after a major league sports or college team wins a big game. The company aims to have clothing available "at Internet speed," an executive explains. Actually, 15 minutes isn't the company's record time. When Northwestern University's basketball team got into the NCAA Final Four, Fanatics had commemorative T-shirts for sale online four minutes after the buzzer sounded. The company prepares by creating designs in advance when possible. Right after the game, Fanatics sends the design to the winning team or league for approval. Minutes later, with responses in hand, Fanatics finalizes and posts the product online, ready to manufacture on demand when customers order.

For traditional retailers, stocking the right team merchandise can be more challenging. Before the

AFC and NFC championship football games, Dick's Sporting Goods orders T-shirts showing all four teams as winners, knowing it will sell only the winning team shirts and donate losing shirts to charity. "Providing excited fans with championship gear immediately following big games outweighs the costs of being prepared for both outcomes," explains a Dick's manager.

When the Chicago Cubs played in the World Series, major retailers and small stores alike ordered merchandise in anticipation of the final game. That night, immediately after the Cubs won, Dick's and others with Chicago-area stores opened their doors and sold until stock was depleted. Many retailers had trucks on the road overnight, picking up additional Cubs merchandise to sell the next morning, while fans continued to celebrate the victory.[1]

iStock.com/meyes

The **distribution** component of the marketing mix focuses on the decisions and activities involved in making products available to customers when and where they want to purchase them. Fanatics has become an expert at making trendy products available when they are wanted—as soon as a team wins big—through a variety of marketing channels. Choosing which channels of distribution to use to reach customers in a timely manner is a major decision in the development of marketing strategies.

In this chapter, we focus on marketing channels and supply-chain management. First, we explore the concept of the supply chain and its various activities. Second, we elaborate on marketing channels and the need for intermediaries and analyze the primary functions they perform. Next, we outline the types and characteristics of marketing channels, discuss how they are selected, and explore how marketers determine the appropriate intensity of market coverage for a product. We then examine the strategic channel issues of leadership, cooperation, and conflict. We also look at the role of physical distribution within the supply chain, including its objectives and basic functions. Finally, we review several legal issues that affect channel management.

13-1 FOUNDATIONS OF THE SUPPLY CHAIN

LO 13-1 Describe the foundations of supply-chain management.

An important function of distribution is to create an effective **supply chain**, which includes all the organizations and activities involved with the flow and transformation of products from raw materials through to the end customer. It may help to think of the firms involved in a total distribution system as existing along a conceptual line, the combined impact of which result in an effective supply chain. Firms that are "upstream" in the supply chain (e.g., suppliers) and "downstream" (e.g., wholesalers and retailers) work together to serve customers and generate competitive advantage. Historically, marketing focused solely on certain downstream supply-chain activities, but today marketing professionals recognize that they can reduce costs, boost profits, and better serve customers by effectively integrating activities along the entire length of the supply chain. Doing so requires marketing managers to work with other managers in operations, logistics, and supply. **Operations management** is the total set of managerial activities used by an organization to transform resource inputs into goods, services, or both.[2] **Logistics management** involves planning, implementing, and controlling the efficient and effective flow and storage of products and information from the point of origin to consumption in order to meet customers' needs and wants. The annual cost of business logistics in the United States is huge, at $1.41 trillion. To put this in perspective, the percentage of logistics costs comprising GDP is valued at 7.9 percent.[3] **Supply management** (e.g., purchasing, procurement, sourcing) in its broadest form refers to the processes that enable the progress of value from raw material to final customer and back to redesign and final disposition.

Supply-chain management (SCM) refers to the coordination of all the activities involved with the flow and transformation of supplies, products, and information throughout the supply chain to the ultimate consumer. It integrates the functions of operations management, logistics management, supply management, and marketing channel management so that products are produced and distributed in the right quantities, to the right locations, and at the right times. It includes activities like manufacturing, research, sales, advertising, and shipping. SCM involves all entities that facilitate product distribution and benefit from cooperative efforts, including suppliers of raw materials and other components to make goods and services, logistics and transportation firms, communication firms, and other firms that indirectly take part in marketing exchanges. Supply-chain managers must encourage cooperation between organizations in the supply chain and understand the trade-offs required to achieve optimal levels of efficiency and service.

In an efficient supply chain, upstream firms provide direct or indirect input to make the product, and downstream firms are responsible for delivery of the product and after-market

---

distribution The decisions and activities that make products available to customers when and where they want to purchase them

supply chain All the organizations and activities involved with the flow and transformation of products from raw materials through to the end customer

operations management The total set of managerial activities used by an organization to transform resource inputs into goods, services, or both

logistics management Planning, implementing, and controlling the efficient and effective flow and storage of products and information from the point of origin to consumption in order to meet customers' needs and wants

supply management The processes that enable the progress of value from raw material to final customer and back to redesign and final disposition

supply-chain management (SCM) The coordination of all the activities involved with the flow and transformation of supplies, products, and information throughout the supply chain to the ultimate consumer

services to the ultimate customers. To ensure quality and customer satisfaction, firms must be involved in the management of every aspect of their supply chain, in close partnership with all involved upstream and downstream organizations. This has led more businesses to seek out companies like Truckstop, shown in the advertisement. The ad explains how Truckstop Pro software provides tools and analysis to help companies maximize their transportation activities within the supply chain. The ad, which includes a picture of a businesswoman looking out the window, encourages potential clients to visit the firm's website for more detail about its expertise and capabilities.

Supply-chain management should begin with a focus on the customer, who is the ultimate consumer and whose satisfaction should be the goal of all the efforts of channel members. Cooperation among channel members should improve customer satisfaction while also increasing coordination, reducing costs, and increasing profits. When the buyer, the seller, marketing intermediaries, and facilitating agencies work together, the cooperative relationship results in compromise and adjustments that meet customers' needs regarding delivery, scheduling, packaging, or other requirements.

Demand for innovative goods and services has increased and changed over time. Marketers need to be flexible in order to respond to the changing needs of customers through developing and distributing new products and modifying existing ones. Supply-chain managers can use data available through improved information technology to learn about a firm's customers, which helps to improve products in the downstream portion of the supply chain. Marketers now understand that managing the entire supply chain is critically important in ensuring that customers get the products when, where, and how they want them. Amazon has set the gold standard for supply-chain management—offering

Technology Facilitates Supply-Chain Management
Truckstop Pro provides services and technology to facilitate supply-chain management for business customers.

customers nearly anything they can imagine through a user-friendly website that features product reviews and ratings, a variety of shipping options, and an easy return policy. The company has teamed up with suppliers all over the country to create a seamless distribution system that can even provide same-day delivery in some areas. Many companies have struggled to compete with and adapt to such a large and flexible competitor.

Technology has improved supply-chain management capabilities globally. Advances in information technology, in particular, have created an almost seamless distribution process for matching inventory needs to manufacturer requirements in the upstream portion of the supply chain and to customers' requirements in the downstream portion of the chain. With integrated information sharing among chain members, firms can reduce costs, improve service, and provide increased value to the end customer. Information is a crucial component in operating supply chains efficiently and effectively.

13-2 THE ROLE OF MARKETING CHANNELS IN SUPPLY CHAINS

LO 13-2 Explain the role and significance of marketing channels and supply chains.

A **marketing channel** (also called a *channel of distribution* or *distribution channel*) is a group of individuals and organizations that direct the flow of products from producers to customers within the supply chain. The major role of marketing channels is to make products available at the right time at the right place in the right quantities. This is accomplished

marketing channel A group of individuals and organizations that direct the flow of products from producers to customers within the supply chain

marketing intermediaries Middlemen that link producers to other intermediaries or ultimate consumers through contractual arrangements or through the purchase and resale of products

through achieving synergy among operations management, logistics management, and supply management. Providing customer satisfaction should be the driving force behind marketing channel decisions. Buyers' needs and behaviors are therefore important concerns of channel members.

Some marketing channels are direct, meaning that the product goes straight from the producer to the customer. For instance, when you buy fruit from a farm stand, the product goes straight from the manufacturer to the customer. Most channels, however, have one or more **marketing intermediaries** that link producers to other intermediaries or to ultimate consumers through contractual arrangements or through the purchase and resale of products. Marketing intermediaries perform the activities described in Table 13.1. They also play key roles in customer relationship management, not only through their distribution activities but also by maintaining databases and information systems to help all members of the marketing channel maintain effective customer relationships. For example, UltraShip TMS provides transportation management software to streamline logistics and create efficiencies throughout the supply chain.[4]

Wholesalers and retailers are examples of intermediaries. Wholesalers buy and resell products to other wholesalers, retailers, and industrial customers. Retailers purchase products and resell them to the end consumers. Consider your local supermarket, which probably purchased the Advil on its shelves from a wholesaler. The wholesaler purchased that pain medicine, along with other over-the-counter and prescription drugs, from manufacturers like McNeil Consumer Healthcare.

13-2a The Significance of Marketing Channels

Although it is not necessary to make marketing channel decisions before other marketing decisions, they can have a strong influence on the other elements of the marketing mix (i.e., product, pricing, and promotion). Channel decisions are critical because they determine a product's market presence and accessibility. Without marketing channel operations that reach the right customers at the right time, even the best goods and services will not be successful. Consider that small businesses are likely to purchase computers from chain specialty stores, such as Best Buy and Staples, putting computer companies without distribution through these outlets at a disadvantage. In fact, even Dell—which pioneered the direct-sales model in the computer industry—also sells its computers at Best Buy. The option of buying Dell systems directly from Dell or in retail stores like Best Buy means that customers can purchase what they need when and where they want. The in-store option gives customers a chance to test out computers in person before making a purchase.

Marketing channel decisions have strategic significance because they generally entail long-term commitments among a variety of firms (e.g., suppliers, logistics providers, and

TABLE 13.1	MARKETING ACTIVITIES PERFORMED BY INTERMEDIARIES
Marketing Activities	**Sample Activities**
Marketing information	Analyze sales data and other information in databases and information systems. Perform or commission marketing research.
Marketing management	Establish strategic and tactical plans for developing customer relationships and organizational productivity.
Facilitating exchanges	Choose product assortments that match the needs of customers. Cooperate with channel members to develop partnerships.
Promotion	Set promotional objectives. Coordinate advertising, personal selling, sales promotion, publicity, and packaging.
Price	Establish pricing policies and terms of sales.
Physical distribution	Manage transportation, warehousing, materials handling, inventory control, and communication.

operations firms). Once a firm commits to a distribution channel, it is difficult to change. Marketing channels also serve multiple functions, including creating utility and facilitating exchange efficiencies. Although some of these functions may be performed by a single channel member, most functions are accomplished through the joint efforts of channel members.

Marketing Channels Create Utility

Marketing channels create four types of utility: time, place, possession, and form. *Time utility* means making products available when the customer wants them. Services like Movies On Demand or streaming on Netflix allow customers to watch a movie or TV show whenever they want. *Place utility* is making products available in locations where customers wish to purchase them. For example, Zappos allows customers to shop for shoes and accessories anywhere they have access to a mobile device and an Internet connection. *Possession utility* means that the customer has access to the product to use or to store for future use. Possession utility can occur through ownership or through arrangements that give the customer the right to use the product, such as a lease or rental agreement. Channel members sometimes create *form utility* by assembling, preparing, or otherwise refining the product to suit individual customer needs.

Marketing Channels Facilitate Exchange Efficiencies

Even if producers and buyers are located in the same city, there are costs associated with exchanges of goods and services. Marketing intermediaries can reduce these expenses by performing services and functions efficiently. As Figure 13.1 shows, when four buyers seek

FIGURE 13.1   EFFICIENCY IN EXCHANGES PROVIDED BY AN INTERMEDIARY

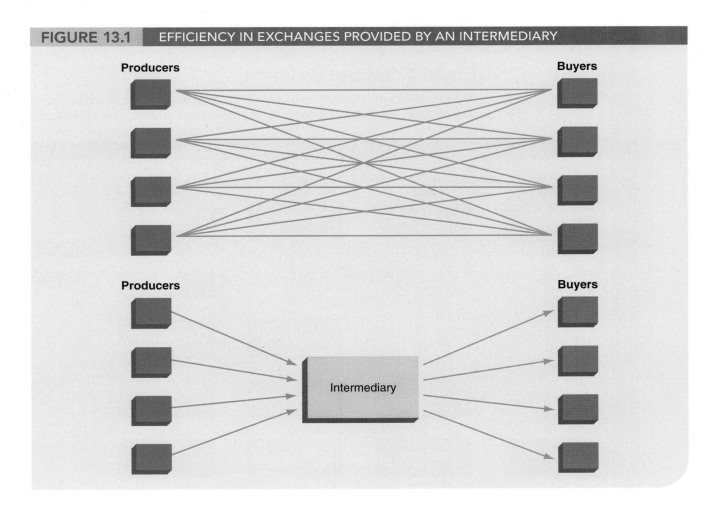

products from four producers, 16 separate transactions are possible. If one intermediary serves both producers and buyers, the number of possible transactions is cut in half. Intermediaries are specialists in facilitating exchanges. They provide valuable assistance because of their access to and control over important resources used in the proper functioning of marketing channels.

Nevertheless, the media, consumers, public officials, and even other marketers freely criticize intermediaries, especially wholesalers. Detractors accuse wholesalers of being inefficient and adding to costs. Buyers often think that making the distribution channel as short as possible will decrease the price for products, but this is not the case.

Critics who suggest that eliminating wholesalers will lower prices for customers fail to recognize that this would not eliminate the need for the services the wholesalers provide. Although wholesalers can be eliminated, their functions cannot. Other channel members would have to perform those functions, perhaps not as efficiently, and customers still would have to pay for them. In addition, all producers would deal directly with retailers or customers, meaning that every producer would have to keep voluminous records and hire adequate personnel to deal with a multitude of customers. In the end, customers could end up paying a great deal more for products because prices would reflect the costs of an inefficient distribution channel. To mitigate criticisms, wholesalers should perform only the marketing activities that are desired and must strive to be as efficient and customer-focused as possible.

13-2b Types of Marketing Channels

Because marketing channels that are appropriate for one product may be less suitable for others, firms can select many different distribution paths. The various marketing channels can be classified generally as channels for consumer products and channels for business products.

Channels for Consumer Products

Figure 13.2 illustrates several channels used in the distribution of consumer products. Channel A depicts the direct movement of products from producer to consumers. For instance, a

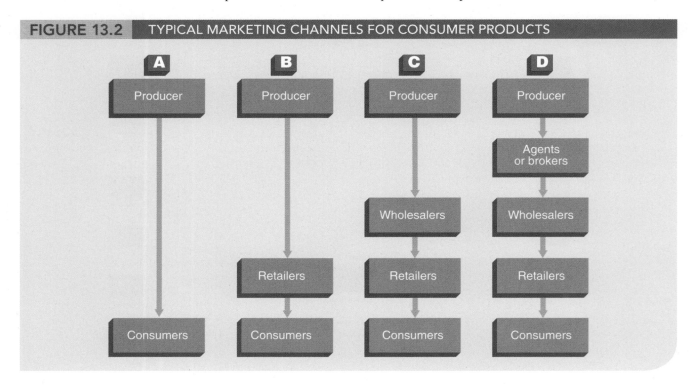

FIGURE 13.2   TYPICAL MARKETING CHANNELS FOR CONSUMER PRODUCTS

haircut received at a barber shop moves through channel A because there is no intermediary between the person performing the service and the one receiving it. Direct marketing via the Internet has become a critically important part of many companies' distribution strategies, often as a complement to selling products in retail stores. A firm must evaluate the costs and benefits of going direct versus those involved in using intermediaries.

Channel B, which moves goods from the producer to a retailer and then to customers, is a frequent choice of large retailers because it allows them to buy in quantity from manufacturers. Retailers like Target and Walmart sell many items to consumers that were purchased directly from producers. New automobiles and new college textbooks are also sold through this type of marketing channel.

Channel C is a common distribution channel for consumer products. It takes goods from the producer to a wholesaler, then to a retailer, and finally to consumers. It is a practical option for producers that sell to hundreds of thousands of customers through thousands of retailers. Some home appliances, hardware, and many convenience goods are marketed through this type of channel. Consider the number of retailers marketing KitchenAid mixers. It would be rather difficult, if not impossible, for KitchenAid to deal directly with each of the many retailers that sell its brand.

Channel D, wherein goods pass from producer, to agents, to wholesalers, to retailers, and finally to consumers, is used frequently for products intended for mass distribution, such as processed foods. For example, to place its Wheat Thins crackers in specific retail outlets, supply-chain managers at Nabisco may hire an agent (or a food broker) to sell the crackers to wholesalers. Wholesalers then sell the Wheat Thins to supermarkets, vending-machine operators, and convenience stores.

Contrary to what you might think, a long channel may actually be the most efficient distribution channel for some goods. When several channel intermediaries perform specialized functions at which they are experts, costs may be lower than when one channel member tries to perform them all. Efficiencies arise when firms that specialize in certain elements of producing a product or moving it through the channel are more effective at performing specialized tasks than the manufacturer. This results in added value to customers.

DIGITAL MARKETING

REI Urges Customers to #OptOutside

The day after Thanksgiving is Black Friday, traditionally the biggest shopping day of the year. In recent years, some brick-and-mortar stores have been getting a jump on Black Friday by opening on Thanksgiving, to compete with online retailers that never close. However, when stores open on Thanksgiving, employees and consumers can't enjoy a family day or experience the outdoors together.

REI, a retailer of outdoor clothing and equipment, is urging employees and customers to go outdoors on Black Friday and Thanksgiving instead of shopping. In 2015 and again in 2016, CEO Jerry Stritzke closed all stores on Thursday and Friday, stopped processing online orders, and gave all 12,287 employees paid time off. Despite the risk of revenue loss, Stritzke wanted customers to have a greener, outdoor experience rather than staying inside or heading to the mall.

REI's campaign used the hashtag #OptOutside to spread the message in ads and on social media. The campaign went viral, with millions of people choosing nature instead of shopping. Not only did REI's revenues not suffer, sales were up as customers rushed to buy from a retailer with strong green values. Will REI close on Thanksgiving and Black Friday every year? This is likely to be a year-by-year decision. Meanwhile, "I like the idea that there is a conversation about being open on Thanksgiving," Stritzke says. "A part of me is hoping that the vast majority of retailers pulls back from invading that holiday day."[a]

industrial distributor An independent business organization that takes title to industrial products and carries inventories

Channels for Business Products

Figure 13.3 shows four of the most common channels for business products. As with consumer products, manufacturers of business products sometimes work with more than one level of wholesaler.

Channel E illustrates the direct channel for business products. In contrast to consumer goods, business products, especially expensive equipment, are most likely to be sold through direct channels. Business customers prefer to communicate directly with producers, especially when expensive or technically complex products are involved. For instance, business buyers of Boeing jets receive not only planes and accessories that cost tens of millions of dollars, but also ongoing maintenance and technical support. This makes communication and customer support even more significant and would be impossible to obtain through an intermediary.

In channel F, an industrial distributor facilitates exchanges between the producer and the customer. An **industrial distributor** is an independent business that takes title to products and carries inventories. Industrial distributors usually sell standardized items, such as maintenance supplies, production tools, and small operating equipment. Some industrial distributors carry a wide variety of product lines. Applied Industrial Technologies Inc., for instance, carries 5 million industrial parts from 4,000 manufacturers and works with a wide variety of companies from small janitorial services companies to giant manufacturers.[5] Other industrial distributors specialize in one or a small number of lines. Industrial distributors carry an increasing percentage of business products. Overall, these distributors can be most effective when a product has broad market appeal, is easily stocked and serviced, is sold in small quantities, and is needed on demand to avoid high losses.

Industrial distributors offer sellers several advantages. They can perform the required selling activities in local markets at a relatively low cost to a manufacturer and reduce a producer's financial burden by providing customers with credit services. Also, because industrial distributors often maintain close relationships with their customers, they are aware of local needs and can pass on market information to producers. By holding adequate inventories in local markets, industrial distributors reduce producers' capital requirements. Using industrial distributors also has disadvantages. They may be difficult to manage because they are independent firms. They often stock competing brands, so a producer cannot depend on them to promote its brand aggressively. Furthermore, industrial distributors

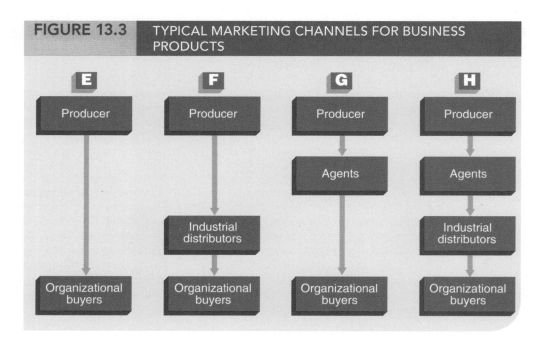

FIGURE 13.3   TYPICAL MARKETING CHANNELS FOR BUSINESS PRODUCTS

incur expenses from maintaining inventories and are less likely to handle bulky or slow-selling items, or items that need specialized facilities or extra selling efforts. In some cases, industrial distributors lack the specialized knowledge necessary to sell and service technical products.

The third channel for business products, channel G, employs a *manufacturers' agent*, an independent businessperson who sells complementary products from several producers in assigned territories and is compensated through commissions. Unlike an industrial distributor, a manufacturers' agent does not acquire title to the products and usually does not take possession. Acting as a salesperson on behalf of the producers, a manufacturers' agent has little or no latitude in negotiating prices or sales terms.

Using manufacturers' agents can benefit an organizational marketer. They usually possess considerable technical and market information and have an established set of customers. A manufacturers' agent can be an asset for an organization with seasonal demand because the seller does not have to support a year-round sales force. The fact that manufacturers' agents are typically paid on commission may also be an economical alternative for a firm that has limited resources and cannot afford a full-time sales force. The use of manufacturers' agents also has drawbacks. The seller has little control over the actions of manufacturers' agents. Because they work on commission, manufacturers' agents prefer to concentrate on larger accounts. They are often reluctant to spend time following up with customers after the sale, put forth special selling efforts, or provide sellers with market information because they are not compensated for these activities and they reduce the amount of productive selling time. Because they rarely maintain inventories, manufacturers' agents have a limited ability to provide customers with parts or repair services quickly.

Finally, channel H includes both a manufacturers' agent and an industrial distributor. This channel may be appropriate when the producer wishes to cover a large geographic area, but maintains no sales force due to highly seasonal demand or because it cannot afford one. This channel can also be useful for a business marketer that wants to enter a new geographic market without expanding its sales force.

Multiple Marketing Channels and Channel Alliances

To reach diverse target markets, manufacturers may use more than one marketing channel simultaneously, with each channel involving a different group of intermediaries. A manufacturer often uses multiple channels when the same product is directed to both consumers and business customers. For example, when Heinz markets ketchup for household use, the product is sold to supermarkets through grocery wholesalers or directly to retailers, whereas ketchup sold to restaurants or institutions follows a different distribution channel.

A **strategic channel alliance** exists when the products of one organization are distributed through the marketing channels of another. The products of the two firms are often similar with respect to target markets or uses, but they are not direct competitors. A brand of bottled water might be distributed through a marketing channel for soft drinks, or a cereal producer in the United States might form a strategic channel alliance with a European food processor to facilitate international distribution. Such alliances can provide benefits for both the organization that owns the marketing channel and the company whose brand is being distributed through the channel.

Quite often, companies today use multiple channels to reach the same target market. For example, L.L. Bean markets products through its longstanding catalog, its website, and through its own retail stores. In such cases, the firm is using **multichannel distribution**—the use of a variety of marketing channels to ensure maximum distribution. The primary reason for using a multichannel strategy is to reach target customers wherever and whenever they may choose to interact with a company or its products. Some consumers may prefer to shop in a brick-and-mortar store where they can personally compare and sample products, while others prefer shopping for an item on their smartphone as soon as they recognize a need for the product. The advertisement for Clinique's Dramatically Different Moisturizing

strategic channel alliance An agreement whereby the products of one organization are distributed through the marketing channels of another

multichannel distribution The use of a variety of marketing channels to ensure maximum distribution

Clinique Laboratories, LLC

Using Multiple Marketing Channels
Clinique uses multiple marketing channels. This product can be purchased directly from Clinique online, in brick-and-mortar stores, and also from Amazon.com.

products, which pictures the versions of the product available, touts that it is loved by customers and dermatologists alike. The ad also highlights the fact that the products can be bought at Clinique's website as well as in stores.

Some products can forgo physical distribution altogether. **Digital distribution** involves delivering content through the Internet to a computer or other device. For example, when you watch a TV show on Netflix or Hulu, those networks stream the content to your device so that you can consume them at the same time that they are streamed. In today's high-tech world, it is also possible to rent digital content, such as a textbook, or subscribe to software, such as Office 365, for a specific period of time after downloading them to a computer, tablet, or smartphone. Some services can also be distributed through digital channels such as booking travel services through Expedia.com or Hotels.com.

It is important to recognize that the line between different marketing channels is becoming increasingly blurred. Consider that today's consumer expects to be able to order a product online from, say Home Depot or Target, and pick up the order at their nearest retail store to avoid paying a shipping charge. Many companies have distribution channels that include physical retail stores as well as Amazon.com or eBay. Younger consumers today have learned to shop online wherever they may be through their smartphone, though they may visit a retail store to assess a product for themselves, and then order it directly from the manufacturer's website or Amazon. Marketers are having to adjust their strategies to respond to the blurred lines between multiple marketing channels by ensuring they are using every channel their target market prefers to use and sending a consistent message across all distribution channels. Amazon.com, for example, is opening kiosks on some college campuses where students can pick up their Amazon orders. The move lets Amazon reach half a million future customers.[6]

13-2c **Selecting Marketing Channels**

Selecting appropriate marketing channels is important because they are difficult to change once chosen. Although the process varies across organizations, channel selection decisions are usually affected by one or more of the following factors: customer characteristics, product attributes, type of organization, competition, marketing environmental forces, and characteristics of intermediaries (see Figure 13.4).

Customer Characteristics

Marketing managers must consider the characteristics of target market members in channel selection. As we have already seen, the channels that are appropriate for consumers are different from those for business customers. Because of variations in product use, product complexity, consumption levels, and need for services, firms develop different marketing strategies for each group. Business customers often prefer to deal directly with producers (or very knowledgeable channel intermediaries such as industrial distributors), especially for highly technical or expensive products, such as mainframe computers, jet airplanes, or heavy machinery, that require strict specifications and technical assistance. Businesses also frequently buy in considerable quantities.

digital distribution
Delivering content through the Internet to a computer or other device

FIGURE 13.4   SELECTING MARKETING CHANNELS

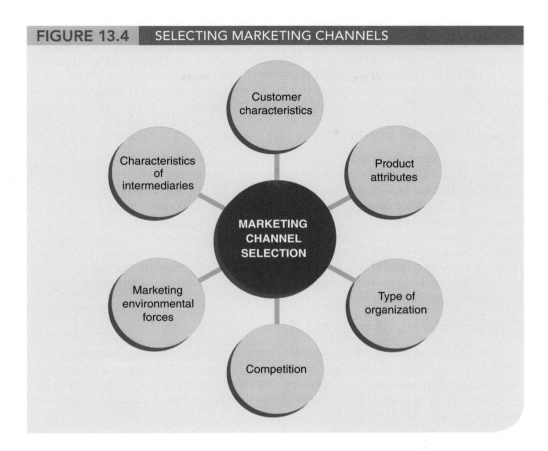

Consumers, on the other hand, generally buy limited quantities of a product, purchase from retailers, and often do not mind limited customer service. When customers are concentrated in a small geographic area, a direct channel may be best, but when many customers are spread across a state or nation, distribution through multiple intermediaries is likely to be more efficient.

Product Attributes

The attributes of a product can have a strong influence on the choice of marketing channels. Marketers of complex and expensive products, such as automobiles, will likely employ short channels, as will marketers of perishable products, such as dairy, fruits, and vegetables. Less-expensive, standardized products with long shelf lives, like soft drinks and canned goods, can go through longer channels with many intermediaries. Fragile products that require special handling are more likely to be distributed through short channels to minimize the amount of handling and risk of damage.

Type of Organization

The characteristics of the organization will have a great impact on the distribution channels chosen. Owing to their size, larger firms are in a better position to deal with vendors or other channel members. They are also likely to have more distribution centers, which reduce delivery times to customers. Large companies can also use an extensive product mix as a competitive tool. A smaller company that uses regional or local channel members might be in a strong position to cater its marketing mix to serve customers in that particular area, compared with a larger, less-flexible organization. However, smaller firms may not have the resources to develop their own sales force, ship their products long distances, maintain a large inventory, or extend credit. In such cases, they may have to include other channel members that have the resources to provide these services to customers.

Competition

Competition is another important factor for supply-chain managers to consider. The success or failure of a competitor's marketing channel may encourage or dissuade an organization from taking a similar approach. In a highly competitive market, it is important for a company to keep its costs low so it can offer lower prices than its competitors if necessary.

Environmental Forces

Environmental forces can play a role in channel selection. Adverse economic conditions might force an organization to use a low-cost channel, even though it reduces customer satisfaction. In contrast, a growing economy may allow a company to choose a channel that previously had been too costly. New technology might allow an organization to add to or modify its channel strategy, such as adding online retailing. Government regulations can also affect channel selection. As labor and environmental regulations change, an organization may be forced to modify its existing distribution channel structure to comply with new laws. Firms might choose to enact such changes before they are mandated in order to appear proactive. International governmental regulations can complicate the supply chain a great deal, as laws vary from country to country.

Characteristics of Intermediaries

When an organization believes that a current intermediary is not promoting its products adequately or offering the correct mix of services, it may reconsider its channel choices. In these instances, the company may choose another channel member to handle its products; it may select a new intermediary; or it might choose to eliminate intermediaries altogether and perform the functions itself.

13-3 INTENSITY OF MARKET COVERAGE

LO 13-3 Identify the intensity of market coverage.

In addition to deciding which marketing channels to use to distribute a product, marketers must determine the appropriate intensity of coverage—that is, the number and kinds of outlets in which a product will be sold. This decision depends on the characteristics of the product and the target market. To achieve the desired intensity of market coverage, distribution must correspond to behavior patterns of buyers. In Chapter 10, we divided consumer products into four categories—convenience, shopping, specialty, and unsought—according to how consumers make purchases. In considering products for purchase, consumers take into account such factors as replacement rate, product adjustment (services), duration of consumption, and time required to locate the product.[7] These variables directly affect the intensity of market coverage. The three major levels of market coverage are intensive, selective, and exclusive distribution.

13-3a Intensive Distribution

Intensive distribution uses all available outlets for distributing a product. Intensive distribution is appropriate for products that have a high replacement rate, require almost no service, and are often bought based on price cues. Most convenience products like bread, chewing gum, soft drinks, and newspapers are marketed through intensive distribution. Multiple channels may be used to sell through all possible outlets. For example, goods such as soft drinks, snacks, laundry detergent, and pain relievers are available at convenience stores, service stations, supermarkets, discount stores, and other types of retailers. To satisfy consumers seeking to buy these products, they must be available at a store nearby and be obtained with minimal search time. For these products, consumers want speed in obtaining them while receiving a reliable level of quality and flexibility to buy the product wherever it is most convenient for them at the lowest price possible. Sales of low-cost convenience products may be directly related to product availability.

intensive distribution
Using all available outlets
to distribute a product

Intensive and Selective Distribution
Grocery products, like Yoplait, Chobani, and Dannon yogurt, are usually sold through intensive distribution. Consumers can find such products in a variety of different outlets. Clothing, such as ties, is marketed through selective distribution and is not available in as many retail stores.

13-3b Selective Distribution

Selective distribution uses only some available outlets in an area to distribute a product. Selective distribution is appropriate for shopping products, which includes durable goods like televisions or stereos. Shopping products are more expensive than convenience goods, and consumers are willing to spend more time and possibly visit several retail outlets and websites to compare prices, designs, styles, and other features.

Selective distribution is desirable when a special effort, such as customer service from a channel member, is important to customers. Shopping products require differentiation at the point of purchase. Selective distribution is often used to motivate retailers to provide adequate service. Dealers can offer higher-quality customer service when products are distributed selectively, such as Apple products, which are distributed only through authorized Apple dealers and Apple stores, and some cosmetics, which are available only in certain department stores.

13-3c Exclusive Distribution

Exclusive distribution uses only one outlet in a relatively large geographic area. This method is suitable for products purchased infrequently, consumed over a long period of time, or requiring a high level of customer service or information. It is used for expensive, high-quality products with high profit margins, such as Porsche, BMW, and other luxury automobiles. It is not appropriate for convenience products and most shopping products because an insufficient number of units would be sold to generate an acceptable level of profits on account of those products' lower profit margins.

Exclusive distribution is often used as an incentive to sellers when only a limited market is available for products. Consider Patek Philippe watches that may sell for $10,000 or more. These watches, like luxury automobiles, are available in only a few select locations. A producer using exclusive distribution expects dealers to carry a complete inventory, train personnel to ensure a high level of product knowledge and quality customer service, and participate in promotional programs.

Some products are appropriate for exclusive distribution when first introduced, but as competitors enter the market and the product moves through its life cycle, prices decrease and other types of market coverage and distribution channels become necessary. A problem that can arise with exclusive (and selective) distribution is that unauthorized resellers acquire and sell products or counterfeits, violating the agreement between a manufacturer and its exclusive authorized dealers.

selective distribution Using only some available outlets in an area to distribute a product

exclusive distribution Using a single outlet in a fairly large geographic area to distribute a product

ENTREPRENEURSHIP IN MARKETING

Meet Kemar Newell, Founder of Flip

Kemar Newell is a "sneakerhead," interested in rare and limited-edition sneakers. He knows that avid collectors like to scour eBay and other auction websites for new and interesting pairs of sneakers—and they are willing to bid much more than the original retail price for special sneakers. Meanwhile, sellers want to be able to connect with interested buyers and complete a profitable auction transaction as efficiently as possible. In all, thousands of buyers and sellers are active in this $1 billion market.

So Newell, a former engineer with Apple and Google, applied his entrepreneurial skills to found Flip, a sneaker auction marketplace that's accessible via smartphone app. The Flip app streamlines the process of listing a pair of collectible sneakers for sale, with photo and description, in a matter of moments. Flip's employees review every listing, checking that the starting price is at least 30 percent lower than the estimated resale value, which gives buyers some room to bid. Flip takes a 10 percent commission on every sale. And the site guarantees a sale: if a pair of sneakers doesn't sell within 90 minutes, Flip will buy it from the seller.

When Newell launched Flip, he had 15,000 pairs of sneakers listed and ready for auction, with more pairs listed every day. Collectors who register their preferences are notified when a pair they might like comes up for auction, so they can bid. "Flip is that fair chance you get at that shoe you missed out on originally," Newell says.[b]

13-4 STRATEGIC ISSUES IN MARKETING CHANNELS

LO 13-4 Explore strategic issues in marketing channels, including leadership, cooperation, and conflict.

In order to maintain customer satisfaction and an effective supply chain, managers must retain a strategic focus on certain competitive priorities, including developing channel leadership, fostering cooperation between channel members, managing channel conflict, and possibly consolidating marketing channels through channel integration.

13-4a Competitive Priorities in Marketing Channels

Increasingly, firms are recognizing that supply chains can be a source of competitive advantage and a means of maintaining a strong market orientation because supply-chain decisions cut across all functional areas of business. Building the most effective and efficient supply chain can sustain a business and help it to use resources effectively and be more efficient. Many well-known firms, including Amazon, Dell, FedEx, Toyota, and Walmart, owe much of their success to outmaneuvering rivals with unique supply-chain capabilities.

Many countries now offer firms opportunities to create an effective and efficient supply chain. Although developed nations like the United States and Germany remain highly competitive manufacturing countries, China ranks number one on Deloitte's survey of global manufacturing competitiveness, indicating the country's superior capabilities to produce goods at a low price and efficiently distribute them where they need to go.[8] India, Mexico, and Taiwan have risen to prominence as well.

To unlock the potential of a supply chain, firms must integrate activities so that all functions are coordinated into an effective system. Supply chains driven by firm-established goals focus on the "competitive priorities" of speed, quality, cost, or flexibility as the performance objective. Managers must remember, however, to keep a holistic view of the supply chain so that goals such as "speed" or "cost" do not result in dissatisfied or underpaid workers or other such abuses in factories. This is particularly a concern among firms that use international manufacturers because it can be more difficult to monitor working conditions internationally.

13-4b Channel Leadership, Cooperation, and Conflict

Each channel member performs a specific role in the distribution system and agrees (implicitly or explicitly) to accept rights, responsibilities, rewards, and sanctions for non-conformity. Moreover, each channel member holds certain expectations of other channel members. Retailers, for instance, expect wholesalers to maintain adequate inventories and deliver goods on time. Wholesalers expect retailers to honor payment agreements and keep them informed of inventory needs. Manufacturers, wholesalers, and retailers expect shipping companies to deliver products on schedule and at a reasonable cost. Any one organization's failure to meet expectations can disrupt the entire supply chain. After South Korea's Hanjin Shipping Company declared bankruptcy, ports around the world refused entry to Hanjin ships until the firm could secure funding to pay the port fees. As a result, Hanjin ships loaded with millions of dollars of merchandise from around the world were left anchored offshore unable to be offloaded for months, disrupting supply chains for a large variety of products.[9]

Channel partnerships can facilitate effective supply-chain management when partners agree on objectives, policies, and procedures for physical distribution efforts associated with the supplier's products. Such partnerships eliminate redundancies and reassign tasks for maximum system-wide efficiency. Channel cooperation reduces wasted resources, such as time, energy, or materials. A coordinated supply chain can also be more environmentally friendly, a consideration that is increasingly important to many organizations and their stakeholders. For example, in order to reduce the carbon footprint of the U.S. auto industry's production processes, equipment manufacturers and suppliers partnered with the Environmental Protection Agency to form the Suppliers Partnership for the Environment. It is a forum for companies and their supply-chain partners to share environmental best practices and optimize supply-chain productivity. The result is a more efficient and less polluting supply chain.[10] In this section, we discuss channel member behavior—including leadership, cooperation, and conflict—that marketers must understand to make effective channel decisions.

Channel Leadership

Many marketing channel decisions are determined through channel member compromise, with a better marketing channel as the end goal. Some marketing channels, however, are organized and controlled by a single leader, or **channel captain** (also called *channel leader*). The channel captain may be a producer, wholesaler, or retailer. Channel captains may establish channel policies and coordinate development of the marketing mix. To attain desired objectives, the captain must possess **channel power**, the ability to influence another channel member's goal achievement.

When a manufacturing channel captain determines that it must increase sales volume to achieve production efficiency, it may encourage growth through offering channel members financing, business advice, ordering assistance, advertising services, sales and service training, and support materials. These benefits usually come with requirements related to sales volume, service quality, training, and customer satisfaction.

Retailers may also be channel captains. Walmart, for example, dominates the supply chain by virtue of its sheer size, the magnitude of its resources, and a strong,

channel captain The dominant leader of a marketing channel or a supply channel

channel power The ability of one channel member to influence another member's goal achievement

Channel Leadership
Nike provides channel leadership in the distribution of its products.

nationwide customer base. To be part of Walmart's supply chain, other channel members must agree to Walmart's rules. Small retailers too may assume leadership roles when they gain strong customer loyalty in local or regional markets. Retailers that are channel captains control many brands and sometimes replace uncooperative producers. Increasingly, leading retailers are concentrating their buying power among fewer suppliers, which makes it easier to coordinate and maintain a high level of quality and transparency along the entire supply chain. These more selective relationships often involve long-term commitments, which enable retailers to place smaller and more frequent orders as needed, rather than waiting for large-volume discounts, or placing large orders and assuming the risks associated with carrying more inventory than needed.

Wholesalers can assume channel leadership roles as well. Wholesaler leaders may form voluntary chains with several retailers, which they supply with bulk buying or management services, and which may also market their own brands. In return, the retailers shift most of their purchasing to the wholesaler leader. The Independent Grocers' Alliance (IGA) is one of the best-known wholesaler leaders in the United States with nearly 5,000 outlets in more than 30 countries.[11] IGA's power is based on its expertise in advertising, pricing, and purchasing knowledge that it makes available to independent business owners. Wholesaler channel leaders may help retailers with store layouts, accounting, and inventory control.

Channel Cooperation

Because the supply chain is an interrelated system, the success of one firm in the channel depends in part on other member firms. Cooperation enables retailers, wholesalers, suppliers, and logistics providers to speed up inventory replenishment, improve customer service, and cut the costs of bringing products to the consumer.[12] Without cooperation, neither overall channel goals nor individual member goals will be realized. Thus, marketing channel members should make a coordinated effort to satisfy market requirements. Channel cooperation leads to greater trust among channel members and improves the overall functioning of the channel. Cooperation also leads to more satisfying relationships among channel members.

There are several ways to improve channel cooperation. If a marketing channel is viewed as a unified supply chain competing with other systems, individual members will be less likely to take actions that put other members at a disadvantage. Channel members should agree on common objectives and their tasks should be precisely defined so that roles are structured for maximum effectiveness in working toward achieving objectives. Starting from a common basis allows channel members to set benchmarks for reviewing intermediaries' performance and helps to reduce conflicts as each channel member knows what is expected of it.

Channel Conflict
Textbook publishers, which traditionally have marketed college textbooks through campus bookstores and now sell textbooks through their own websites, may be experiencing channel conflict.

Channel Conflict

Although all channel members work toward the same general goal—distributing products profitably and efficiently—members sometimes may disagree about the best methods for attaining this goal. The Internet has increased the potential for conflict and resentment between manufacturers and intermediaries. When a manufacturer such as Apple or Dell makes its products available through the Internet, it is employing a direct channel that competes with the retailers that also sell its products. If self-interest creates misunderstanding about role expectations, the end result is frustration and conflict for the whole channel.

For individual organizations to function together, each channel member must clearly communicate and understand the role expectations. For example, using social media to communicate helps supplier-retailer partners achieve common goals, develop relationships, increase customer interaction, and promote the supplier, brand, and competitive environment across the different levels.[13] On the other hand, communication difficulties are a potential form of channel conflict because ineffective communication leads to frustration, misunderstandings, and ill-coordinated strategies, jeopardizing further coordination.

Although there is no single method for resolving conflict, partners can improve relations if two conditions are met. First, the role of each channel member must be clearly defined and followed. Channel members must have a clear understanding of goals and expectations as well as the metrics that different members will use to measure progress and determine incentive rates.[14] To minimize misunderstanding, all members must be able to expect unambiguous performance levels from one another. Second, members of channel partnerships must agree on means of coordinating channels, which requires strong, but not polarizing, leadership. To prevent channel conflict, producers or other channel members may provide competing resellers with different brands, allocate markets among resellers, define policies for direct sales to avoid
potential conflict over large accounts, negotiate territorial issues among regional distributors, and provide recognition to certain resellers for their importance in distributing to others.

13-4c Channel Integration

Channel members can either combine and control activities or pass them to another channel member. Channel functions may be transferred between intermediaries and producers, even to customers. As mentioned earlier in the chapter, supply-chain functions cannot be eliminated. Unless buyers themselves perform the functions, they must pay for the labor and resources needed to perform them.

Various channel stages may be combined, either horizontally or vertically, under the management of a channel captain. Such integration can help to stabilize product supply, reduce costs, and increase channel member coordination.

Vertical Channel Integration

Vertical channel integration combines two or more stages of the channel under one management. This may occur when one member of a marketing channel purchases the operations of another member, or simply performs the functions of another member, eliminating the need for that intermediary. Tesla, for example, manufactures 80 percent of its electric vehicles, which it sells directly to the consumer rather than through dealerships. The company is also building and operating its own Supercharger stations across the nation where Tesla owners can recharge their electric cars in just a few minutes.[15]

Vertical channel integration represents a more progressive approach to distribution, in which channel members become extensions of one another as they are combined under a single management. Vertically integrated channels can be more effective against competition because of increased bargaining power and the ease of sharing information and responsibilities. At one end of a vertically integrated channel, a manufacturer might provide advertising and training assistance, and at the other end the retailer might buy the manufacturer's products in large quantities and actively promote them.

Integration has been successfully institutionalized in a marketing channel called the **vertical marketing system (VMS)**, in which a single channel member coordinates or manages all activities to maximize efficiencies, resulting in an effective and low-cost distribution system that does not duplicate services. Vertical integration brings most or all stages of the marketing channel under common control or ownership. It can help speed the rate at which goods move through a marketing channel. VMSs account for a large share of retail sales in consumer goods.

vertical channel integration Combining two or more stages of the marketing channel under one management

vertical marketing system (VMS) A marketing channel managed by a single channel member to achieve efficient, low-cost distribution aimed at satisfying target market customers

Most vertical marketing systems take one of three forms: corporate, administered, or contractual. A *corporate VMS* combines all stages of the marketing channel, from producers to consumers, under a single owner. For example, the Inditex Group, which owns popular clothing retailer Zara, utilizes a corporate VMS to achieve channel efficiencies and maintain a maximum amount of control over the supply chain. Zara's clothing is trendy, requiring the shortest time possible from product development to offering the clothing in stores. Inventory is characterized by very high turnover and frequent changes. Because it has control over all stages of the supply chain, Inditex can maintain an advantage through speed and keeping prices low.[16] Supermarket chains that own food-processing plants and large retailers that purchase wholesaling and production facilities are other examples of corporate VMSs.

In an *administered VMS*, channel members are independent, but informal coordination achieves a high level of interorganizational management. Members of an administered VMS may adopt uniform accounting and ordering procedures and cooperate in promotional activities for the benefit of all partners. Although individual channel members maintain autonomy, as in conventional marketing channels, one channel member (such as a producer or large retailer) dominates the administered VMS so that distribution decisions take the whole system into account.

A *contractual VMS* is the most popular type of vertical marketing system. Channel members are linked by legal agreements spelling out each member's rights and obligations. Franchise organizations, such as McDonald's and KFC, are contractual VMSs. Other contractual VMSs include wholesaler-sponsored groups in which independent retailers band together under the contractual leadership of a wholesaler. Retailer-sponsored cooperatives, which own and operate their own wholesalers, are a third type of contractual VMS. Ace Hardware is a retail cooperative of 4,794 stores with revenues of $4.7 billion and strong growth despite competition from big box stores like Home Depot and Lowe's. Each Ace Hardware store contributes to advertising and marketing for the whole group and can capitalize on the well-known brand to build their neighborhood stores.[17]

Horizontal Channel Integration

Combining organizations at the same level of operation under one management constitutes **horizontal channel integration**. An organization may integrate horizontally by merging with other organizations at the same level in the marketing channel. The owner of a dry-cleaning firm, for example, might buy and combine several other existing dry-cleaning establishments. Likewise, Sherwin-Williams acquired rival paint firm Valspar for $11.3 billion in part to fast-track its move into international markets.[18]

Although horizontal integration permits efficiencies and economies of scale in purchasing, marketing research, advertising, and specialized personnel, it is not always the most effective method of improving distribution. Problems that come with increased size often follow, resulting in decreased flexibility, difficulties coordinating between members, and the need for additional marketing research and large-scale planning. Unless distribution functions for the various units can be performed more efficiently under unified management than under the previously separate managements, horizontal integration will neither reduce costs nor improve the competitive position of the integrating firm.

horizontal channel integration Combining organizations at the same level of operation under one management

physical distribution Activities used to move products from producers to consumers and other end users

13-5 PHYSICAL DISTRIBUTION IN SUPPLY-CHAIN MANAGEMENT

LO 13-5 Explain physical distribution as being a part of supply-chain management.

Physical distribution, also known as *logistics,* refers to the activities used to move products from producers to consumers and other end users. These activities include order processing, inventory management, materials handling, warehousing, and transportation. Physical distribution systems must meet the needs of both the supply chain and ultimate consumers.

Distribution activities are thus an important part of supply-chain management and can require a high level of cooperation.

Within the marketing channel, physical distribution activities may be performed by a producer, wholesaler, or retailer, or they may be outsourced. In the context of distribution, *outsourcing* is contracting physical distribution tasks to third parties. **Third-party logistics (3PL) firms** have special expertise in core physical distribution activities such as warehousing, transportation, inventory management, and information technology and can often perform these activities more efficiently. In recent years, 3PL firms have become increasingly sophisticated in their offerings. Today, outsourcing logistics to third-party organizations, such as trucking companies, warehouses, and data-service providers, can reduce marketing channel costs, improve information flow and analysis, and boost service and customer satisfaction for all supply-chain partners.[19]

The Internet and technological advancements have revolutionized logistics, allowing many manufacturers to carry out actions and services entirely online, bypassing shipping and warehousing considerations, and transforming physical distribution by facilitating just-in-time delivery, precise inventory visibility, and instant shipment-tracking capabilities. For example, video game and computer software manufacturers such as Microsoft and Sony have increasingly made their products available for download. Emerging technologies such as autonomous vehicles—forklifts, robots, drones, and even self-driving trucks—will further advance physical distribution.[20] Technological advances create new and different challenges for manufacturers, such as how to maintain a high level of customer service when customers never enter a store or meet with a salesperson and how to deal with returns of a product that does not exist in a physical form. However, technology enables companies to avoid expensive mistakes, reduce costs, and generate increased revenues. Moreover, information technology enhances the transparency of the supply chain by allowing all marketing channel members to track the movement of goods throughout the supply chain and improve their customer service.

Planning an efficient physical distribution system is crucial to developing an effective marketing strategy because it can decrease costs and increase customer satisfaction. When making distribution decisions, speed of delivery, flexibility, and quality of service are often as important to customers as costs. Companies that offer the right goods, in the right place, at the right time, in the right quantity, and with the right support services are able to sell more than competitors that do not. Even when the demand for products is unpredictable, suppliers must be able to respond quickly to inventory needs. In such cases, physical

third-party logistics (3PL) firms Firms that have special expertise in core physical distribution activities such as warehousing, transportation, inventory management, and information technology and can often perform these activities more efficiently

FIGURE 13.5 PROPORTIONAL COST OF EACH PHYSICAL DISTRIBUTION FUNCTION AS A PERCENTAGE OF TOTAL DISTRIBUTION COSTS

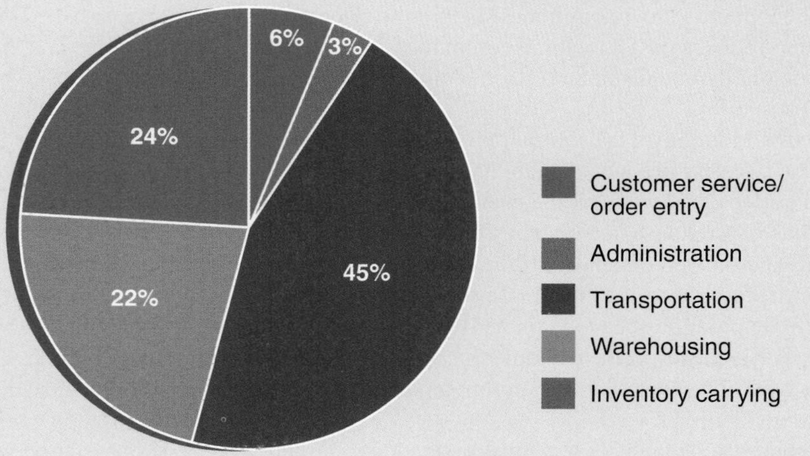

distribution costs may be a minor consideration when compared with service, dependability, and timeliness.

Although physical distribution managers try to minimize the costs associated with order processing, inventory management, materials handling, warehousing, and transportation, decreasing the costs in one area often raises them in another. Figure 13.5 shows the percentage of total costs that physical distribution functions represent. A total-cost approach to physical distribution that takes into account all these different functions enables managers to view physical distribution as a system and shifts the emphasis from lowering the costs of individual activities to minimizing overall costs.

Physical distribution managers must therefore be sensitive to the issue of cost trade-offs. Trade-offs are strategic decisions to combine (and recombine) resources for greatest cost-effectiveness. The goal is not always to find the lowest cost. Higher costs in one functional area of a distribution system may be necessary to achieve lower costs in another. When distribution managers regard the system as a network of integrated functions, trade-offs become useful tools in implementing a unified, cost-effective distribution strategy.

Another important goal of physical distribution involves **cycle time**, the time needed to complete a process. For instance, reducing cycle time while maintaining or reducing costs and/or maintaining or increasing customer service is a winning combination in supply chains and ultimately results in greater customer satisfaction. Firms should look for ways to reduce cycle time while maintaining or reducing costs and maintaining or improving customer service. Consider Dollar Shave Club, which grew from a tiny business with an irreverent viral video to a large business that ships razor blades to subscribers across the country. To reduce cycle time while maintaining high customer satisfaction and quality, the company turned to a third-party logistics specialist, which allowed it to focus on providing excellent customer service while ensuring on-time deliveries to subscribers.[21] In the rest of this section, we take a closer look at a variety of physical distribution activities, including order processing, inventory management, materials handling, warehousing, and transportation.

13-5a **Order Processing**

Order processing is the receipt and transmission of sales order information. Although management sometimes overlooks the importance of these activities, efficient order processing facilitates product flow. Computerized order processing provides a platform for information management, allowing all supply-chain members to increase their productivity. When carried out quickly and accurately, order processing contributes to customer satisfaction, decreased costs and cycle time, and increased profits.

Order processing entails three main tasks: order entry, order handling, and order delivery. Order entry begins when customers or salespeople place purchase orders via customer-service counter, telephone, regular mail, e-mail, or a website. Electronic ordering has become the most common. It is less time consuming than a paper-based ordering system and reduces costs. In some companies, sales representatives receive and enter orders personally and also handle complaints, prepare progress reports, and forward sales order information.

Order handling involves several tasks. Once an order is entered, it is transmitted to a warehouse to verify product availability and, if necessary, to the credit department to set terms and prices, and to check the customer's credit rating. If the credit department approves the purchase, warehouse personnel assemble the order. In many warehouses this step is carried out by automated machines. If the requested product is not in stock, a production order is sent to the factory, or the customer is offered a substitute.

When the order has been assembled and packed for shipment, the warehouse schedules delivery with a carrier. If the customer pays for rush service, overnight delivery by a mail carrier is used. The customer is then sent an invoice, inventory records are adjusted, and the order is delivered.

Whether a company uses a manual or an electronic order-processing system depends on which method provides the greater speed and accuracy within cost limits. Manual processing

cycle time The time needed to complete a process

order processing The receipt and transmission of sales order information suffices for small-volume orders and can be more flexible in certain situations. Most companies, however, use **electronic data interchange (EDI)**, which uses computer technology to integrate order processing with production, inventory, accounting, and transportation. Within the supply chain, EDI functions as an information system that links marketing channel members and outsourcing firms together. It boosts accuracy, reduces paperwork for all members of the supply chain, and allows them to share information on invoices, orders, payments, inquiries, and scheduling. Many companies encourage suppliers to adopt EDI to reduce distribution costs and cycle times.

13-5b **Inventory Management**

Inventory management involves developing and maintaining adequate assortments of products to meet customers' needs. It is a key component of any effective physical distribution system. Inventory decisions have a major impact on physical distribution costs and the level of customer service provided. When too few products are carried in inventory, the result is *stockouts*, or shortages of products. Stockouts can result in customer dissatisfaction that leads to lower sales, even loss of customers and brand switching. When a firm maintains too many products (especially too many low-turnover products) in inventory, costs increase, as do risks of product obsolescence, pilferage, and damage. The objective of inventory management is to minimize inventory costs while maintaining an adequate supply of goods to satisfy customers. To achieve this objective, marketers focus on two major issues: when to order and how much to order.

To determine when to order, a marketer calculates the *reorder point*: the inventory level that signals the need to place a new order. To calculate the reorder point, the marketer must know the order lead time, the usage rate, and the amount of safety stock required. The *order lead time* refers to the average time lapse between placing the order and receiving it. The *usage rate* is the rate at which a product's inventory is used or sold during a specific time period. *Safety stock* is the amount of extra inventory a firm keeps to guard against stockouts resulting from above-average usage rates and/or longer-than-expected lead times. The reorder point can be calculated using the following formula:

$$\text{Reorder Point} = (\text{Order Lead Time} \times \text{Usage Rate}) + \text{Safety Stock}$$

Thus, if order lead time is 10 days, usage rate is 3 units per day, and safety stock is 20 units, the reorder point is 50 units.

Efficient inventory management with accurate reorder points is crucial for firms that use a **just-in-time (JIT)** approach, in which supplies arrive just as they are needed for use in production or for resale. Companies that use JIT (sometimes referred to as *lean distribution*) can maintain low inventory levels and purchase products and materials in small quantities only when needed. Usually there is no safety stock in a JIT system. Suppliers are expected to provide consistently high-quality products. JIT inventory management requires a high level of coordination between producers and suppliers, but it eliminates waste and reduces inventory costs. This approach is popular among many well-known firms, including Toyota, Dell Computer, and Harley-Davidson. More recently, Trinity Health, which operates 90 U.S. hospitals, began to apply JIT distribution methods to save an estimated $20 million in inventory carrying costs and improvements in supply chain efficiency with the help of 3PL partner XPO

Warehousing and Inventory Management
Warehousing and inventory management efforts are expensive but are important elements in providing customer satisfaction.

iStock.com/oh4nn

electronic data interchange (EDI) A computerized means of integrating order processing with production, inventory, accounting, and transportation

inventory management Developing and maintaining adequate assortments of products to meet customers' needs

just-in-time (JIT) An inventory-management approach in which supplies arrive just when needed for production or resale

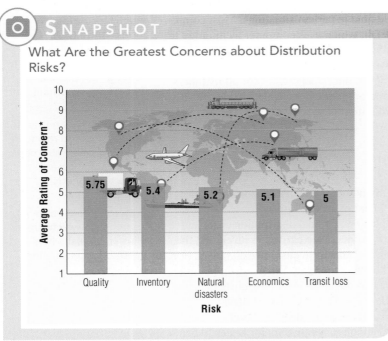

SNAPSHOT

What Are the Greatest Concerns about Distribution Risks?

Bar values: Quality **5.75**, Inventory **5.4**, Natural disasters **5.2**, Economics **5.1**, Transit loss **5**

Y-axis: Average Rating of Concern* (1–10)
X-axis: Risk

*Rating of Concern on a Scale of 1–10 (10 indicating greatest concern)
Source: "Managing Risk in the Global Supply Chain," Supply Chain Management Faculty at the University of Tennessee, p. 13, http://globalsupplychaininstitute.utk.edu/publications/documents/Risk.pdf (accessed March 6, 2017).

Logistics.[22] When a JIT approach is used in a supply chain, suppliers may move operations close to their major customers in order to provide goods as quickly as possible.

13-5c Materials Handling

Materials handling, the physical handling of tangible goods, supplies, and resources, is an important factor in warehouse operations, as well as in transportation from points of production to points of consumption. Efficient procedures and techniques for materials handling minimize inventory management costs, reduce the number of times a good is handled, improve customer service, and increase customer satisfaction. Systems for packaging, labeling, loading, and movement must be coordinated to maximize cost reduction and customer satisfaction.

Increasingly, companies are using **radio frequency identification (RFID)**—which uses radio waves to identify and track materials tagged with special microchips—through every phase of handling. RFID has greatly improved shipment tracking and reduced cycle times. Hundreds of RFID tags can be read at a time, which represents an advantage over barcodes. Firms are discovering that RFID technology has very broad applications, from tracking inventory to paying for goods and services. It is also useful for asset management and data collection. Inditex, for example, uses RFID chips inside the larger security tags of its clothes in 2,000 Zara stores in 48 countries. When an item is sold, the RFID tag records the time and orders an identical product from the company's stockroom. This has streamlined the inventory process and made inventory management easier. The use of RFID allows Zara stores to stock the right products at the right time, boosting customer service.[23]

Product characteristics often determine handling. For example, the characteristics of bulk liquids and gases dictate how they can be moved and stored. Internal packaging is also an important consideration in materials handling—goods must be packaged correctly to prevent damage or breakage during handling and transportation. Many companies employ packaging consultants during the product design process to help them decide which packaging materials and methods will result in the most efficient handling.

Unit loading and containerization are two common methods used in materials handling. With *unit loading,* one or more boxes are placed on a pallet or skid. These units can then be loaded efficiently by mechanical means, such as forklifts, trucks, or conveyer systems. *Containerization* involves consolidating many items into a single, large container that is sealed at its point of origin and opened at its destination. Containers are usually 8 feet wide, 8 feet high, and 10 to 40 feet long. Their uniform size means they can be stacked and shipped via train, barge, or ship. Once containers reach their destinations, wheel assemblies can be added to make them suitable for ground transportation by truck. Because individual items are not handled in transit, containerization greatly increases efficiency and security in shipping.

13-5d Warehousing

Warehousing, the design and operation of facilities for storing and moving goods, is another important physical distribution function. Warehousing creates time utility by

materials handling Physical handling of tangible goods, supplies, and resources

radio frequency identification (RFID) Using radio waves to identify and track materials tagged with special microchips

warehousing The design and operation of facilities for storing and moving goods enabling firms to compensate for dissimilar production and consumption rates. When mass production creates a greater stock of goods than can be sold immediately, companies warehouse the surplus until customers are ready to buy it. Warehousing also helps to stabilize prices and to facilitate the availability of seasonal items.

Choosing appropriate warehouse facilities is an important strategic consideration because these facilities allow a company to reduce transportation and inventory costs and improve service to customers. The wrong type of warehouse can lead to inefficient physical distribution and added costs. Warehouses fall into two general categories: private and public. In many cases, a combination of private and public facilities provides the most flexible warehousing approach.

Companies operate **private warehouses** for shipping and storing their own products. A firm usually leases or purchases a private warehouse when its warehousing needs in a given geographic market are substantial and stable enough to warrant a long-term commitment to a fixed facility. Private warehouses are also appropriate for firms that require special handling and storage and that want control of warehouse design and operation. Retailers like Sears find it economical to integrate private warehousing with purchasing and distribution for their retail outlets. When sales volumes are fairly stable, ownership and control of a private warehouse may be most convenient and offer cost benefits. Private warehouses, however, face fixed costs, such as insurance, taxes, maintenance, and debt expense. They limit a firm's flexibility if they wish to move inventories to different locations. Many private warehouses are being eliminated by direct links between producers and customers, reduced cycle times, and outsourcing to third-party logistics firms with warehousing services.

Public warehouses lease storage space and related physical distribution facilities to other companies. They sometimes provide distribution services, such as receiving, unloading, inspecting, filling orders, providing financing, displaying products, and coordinating shipments. Distribution Unlimited Inc., for example, offers a wide range of such services through its facilities in New York, which contain more than 8 million total square feet of warehouse space.[24]

Public warehouses are especially useful to firms that have highly seasonal production or demand, low-volume storage needs, and inventories that must be maintained in many locations. They are also useful for firms that are testing or entering new markets, or require additional storage space. Additionally, public warehouses also serve as collection points during product-recall programs. Whereas private warehouses have fixed costs, public warehouses offer variable (and possibly lower) costs because users rent space and purchase warehousing services only as needed.

Many public warehouses furnish security for products that are used as collateral for loans, a service provided at either the warehouse or the site of the owner's inventory. *Field public warehouses* are established by public warehouses at the owner's inventory location. The warehouser becomes custodian of the products and issues a receipt that can be used as collateral for a loan. Public warehouses also provide *bonded storage*, a warehousing arrangement in which imported or taxable products are not released until the products' owners pay U.S. customs duties, taxes, or other fees. Bonded warehouses enable firms to defer tax payments on such items until they are delivered to customers.

Distribution centers are large facilities used for receiving, warehousing, and redistributing products to stores or customers. They are specially designed for rapid flow of products. They are usually one-story buildings with access to transportation networks, such as major highways and/or railway lines. Many distribution centers are automated, with computer-directed robots, forklifts, and hoists that collect and move products to loading docks. Amazon, for example, relies on "fulfillment centers" around the world, each using robots, computer systems, and hundreds of employees to process and fulfill customer orders.[25] Distribution over large geographic areas can be complicated, and having strategically located distribution centers can help a company meet consumer demand. Although some public warehouses offer such specialized services, most distribution centers are privately owned. They serve customers in regional markets and, in some cases, function as consolidation points for a company's branch warehouses.

private warehouses
Company-operated facilities for storing and shipping products

public warehouses
Storage space and related physical distribution facilities that can be leased by companies

distribution centers
Large, centralized warehouses that focus on moving rather than storing goods

transportation The movement of products from where they are made to intermediaries and end users

13-5e **Transportation**

Transportation, the movement of products from where they are made to intermediaries and end users, is the most expensive physical distribution function. Transportation in the United States costs $890 billion, 63.2 percent of total logistics activities' costs.[26] Because product availability and timely deliveries depend on transportation functions, transportation decisions directly affect customer service. In some cases, a firm may choose to build its distribution and marketing strategy around a unique transportation system, if that system can ensure on-time deliveries and give the firm a competitive edge. Companies may build their own transportation fleets (private carriers) or outsource the transportation function to a common or contract carrier.

Transportation Modes

The basic transportation modes for moving physical goods are railroads, trucks, waterways, airways, and pipelines. Each has distinct advantages. Many companies adopt physical handling procedures that facilitate the use of two or more modes in combination. Table 13.2 gives more detail on the characteristics of each transportation mode.

Railroads like Union Pacific and Canadian National carry heavy, bulky freight that must be shipped long distances over land. Railroads commonly haul minerals, sand, lumber, chemicals, and farm products, as well as automobiles and low-value manufactured goods. Many companies locate factories or warehouses near rail lines for convenient loading and unloading.

Trucks provide the most flexible schedules and routes of all major transportation modes in the United States because they can go almost anywhere. Because trucks do not have to conform to a set schedule and can move goods from factory or warehouse to customer, wherever there are roads, they are often used in conjunction with other forms of transport that cannot provide door-to-door deliveries, such as waterways and railroads. Trucks are more expensive and somewhat more vulnerable to bad weather than trains. They are also subject to size and weight restrictions on the loads they carry. Trucks are sometimes criticized for higher levels of freight loss and damage and for delays caused by the re-handling of small shipments.

Waterways are the cheapest method of shipping heavy or low-value, nonperishable goods. Water carriers offer considerable capacity. Powered by tugboats and towboats, barges

TABLE 13.2	CHARACTERISTICS AND RATINGS OF TRANSPORTATION MODES BY SELECTION CRITERIA				
Selection Criteria	**Railroads**	**Trucks**	**Pipelines**	**Waterways**	**Airplanes**
Cost	Moderate	High	Low	Very low	Very high
Speed	Average	Fast	Slow	Very slow	Very fast
Dependability	Average	High	High	Average	High
Load flexibility	High	Average	Very low	Very high	Low
Accessibility	High	Very high	Very limited	Limited	Average
Frequency	Low	High	Very high	Very low	Average
Products carried	Coal, grain, lumber, paper and pulp products, chemicals	Clothing, computers, books, groceries and produce, livestock	Oil, processed coal, natural gas	Chemicals, bauxite, grain, motor vehicles, agricultural implements	Flowers, food (highly perishable), technical instruments, emergency parts and equipment, overnight mail

that travel along intra-coastal canals, inland rivers, and navigation systems can haul at least 10 times the weight of a rail car, and oceangoing vessels can haul thousands of containers. The vast majority of international cargo is transported by water at least part of the way. However, many markets are inaccessible by water transportation and must be supplemented by rail or truck. Droughts and floods also may create difficulties for users of inland waterway transportation. Nevertheless, the growing need to transport goods long distances across the globe will likely increase its use in the future.

Air transportation is the fastest but most expensive form of shipping. It is used most often for perishable goods, for high-value and low-bulk items, and for products that require quick delivery over long distances. Some air carriers transport combinations of passengers, freight, and mail. Despite its expense, air transit can reduce warehousing and packaging costs and losses from theft and damage, thus helping to lower the aggregate cost of the mode. Although air transport accounts for a small minority of total cargo carried, it is an important form of transportation in an increasingly time-sensitive business environment.[27] In fact, the success of many businesses is now based on the availability of overnight air delivery service provided by organizations such as UPS, FedEx, DHL, RPS Air, and the U.S. Postal Service. Many firms offer overnight or same-day shipping to customers.

Pipelines, the most automated transportation mode, usually belong to the shipper and carry the shipper's products. Most pipelines carry petroleum products or chemicals. Slurry pipelines carry pulverized coal, grain, or wood chips suspended in water. Pipelines move products slowly but continuously and at relatively low cost. They are dependable and minimize the problems associated with product damage and theft. However, contents are subject to as much as 1 percent shrinkage, usually from evaporation. Pipelines also have been a concern to environmentalists, who fear that pipelines disrupt animals' migratory routes and that leaks can harm plants and animals and threaten water quality.

Choosing Transportation Modes

Logistics managers select a transportation mode based on the combination of cost, speed, dependability, load flexibility, accessibility, and frequency that is most appropriate for their products and generates the desired level of customer service. Table 13.2 shows relative rankings of each transportation mode by these selection criteria.

Marketers compare alternative transportation modes to determine whether the benefits from a more expensive mode are worth the higher costs. A firm wishing to establish international distribution may consider a large logistics firm for its vast network of global partners. Expeditors International, for instance, has 16,000 associates in 331 locations throughout the world. The company provides tailored solutions and integrated information systems to perform supply-chain management functions around the globe.[28]

intermodal transportation
Two or more transportation modes used in combination

Coordinating Transportation

To take advantage of the benefits offered by various transportation modes and compensate for shortcomings, marketers often combine and coordinate two or more modes. **Intermodal transportation** is easier than ever because of developments within the transportation industry. Intermodal shipping combines the flexibility of trucking with the low cost or speed of other forms of transport. Containerization facilitates intermodal transportation by consolidating shipments into sealed containers of uniform size for transport by *piggyback* (using truck trailers and railway flatcars), *fishyback* (using truck trailers and water carriers), and *birdyback* (using truck trailers and air carriers). As transportation costs have increased

Intermodal Transportation
Containers facilitate intermodal transportation because they can be transported by ships, trains, and trucks.

iStock.com/rtem_Egorov

and firms seek to find the most efficient methods possible, intermodal shipping has gained popularity.

Specialized outsourcing agencies provide other forms of transport coordination. Known as **freight forwarders**, these firms combine shipments from several organizations into efficient lot sizes. Small loads (less than 500 pounds) are much more expensive to ship than full carloads or truckloads and may make shipping cost-prohibitive for smaller firms. Freight forwarders help such firms by consolidating small loads from various organizations to allow them to collectively qualify for lower rates. Freight forwarders' profits come from the margin between the higher rates firms would have to pay and the lower carload rates the freight forwarder pays for full loads. Because large shipments also require less handling, freight forwarders can reduce delivery time and the likelihood of shipment damage. Freight forwarders also have the insight to determine the most efficient carriers and routes and are useful for shipping goods to foreign markets. Some companies prefer to outsource their shipping to freight forwarders because the forwarders provide door-to-door service.

Another transportation innovation is the development of **megacarriers**, freight transportation companies that offer several shipment methods, including rail, truck, and air service. Prior to the development of megacarriers, transportation companies generally only specialized in one mode. To compete with megacarriers, air carriers have increased their ground-transportation services. As the range of transportation alternatives expands, carriers also put greater emphasis on customer service in order to gain a competitive advantage.

13-6 LEGAL ISSUES IN CHANNEL MANAGEMENT

LO 13-6 Examine legal issues in channel management.

The numerous federal, state, and local laws governing distribution channel management in the United States are based on the principle that the public is best served by protecting competition and free trade. Under the authority of such federal legislation as the Sherman Antitrust Act and the Federal Trade Commission Act, courts and regulatory agencies determine under what circumstances channel management practices violate this underlying principle and must be restricted. Although channel managers are not expected to be legal experts, they should be aware that attempts to control distribution functions may have legal repercussions. When shipping internationally, managers must also be aware of international laws and regulations that might affect their distribution activities. The following practices are among those frequently subject to legal restraint.

13-6a Restricted Sales Territories

To tighten control over product distribution, a manufacturer may try to prohibit intermediaries from selling outside of designated sales territories. Intermediaries themselves often favor this practice because it provides them with exclusive territories where they can minimize competition. Over the years, courts have adopted conflicting positions in regard to restricted sales territories. Although the courts have deemed restricted sales territories a restraint of trade among intermediaries handling the same brands (except for small or newly established companies), they have also held that exclusive territories can actually promote competition among dealers handling different brands. At present, the producer's intent in establishing restricted territories and the overall effect of doing so on the market is evaluated on a case-by-case basis.

13-6b Tying Agreements

When a supplier (usually a manufacturer or franchiser) furnishes a product to a channel member with the stipulation that the channel member must purchase other products as well, it has negotiated a **tying agreement**. Suppliers may implement tying agreements as

freight forwarders Organizations that consolidate shipments from several firms into efficient lot sizes

megacarriers Freight transportation firms that provide several modes of shipment

tying agreement An agreement in which a supplier furnishes a product to a channel member with the stipulation that the channel member must purchase other products as well

a means of getting rid of slow-moving inventory, or a franchiser may tie the purchase of equipment and supplies to the sale of franchises, justifying the policy as necessary for quality control and protection of the franchiser's reputation.

A related practice is *full-line forcing*, in which a supplier requires that channel members purchase the supplier's entire line to obtain any of the supplier's products. Manufacturers sometimes use full-line forcing to ensure that intermediaries accept new products and that a suitable range of products is available to customers.

The courts accept tying agreements when the supplier is the only firm able to provide products of a certain quality, as long as the intermediary is free to carry competing products, and when a company has just entered the market. Most other tying agreements are considered illegal.

exclusive dealing A situation in which a manufacturer forbids an intermediary from carrying products of competing manufacturers

13-6c **Exclusive Dealing**

When a manufacturer forbids an intermediary to carry products of competing manufacturers, the arrangement is called **exclusive dealing**. Manufacturers receive considerable market protection in an exclusive-dealing arrangement and may cut off shipments to intermediaries that violate the agreement.

The legality of an exclusive-dealing contract is generally determined by applying three tests. If the exclusive dealing blocks competitors from 15 percent of the market or more, the sales volume is large, and the producer is considerably larger than the retailer, then the arrangement is considered anticompetitive. If dealers and customers in a given market have access to similar products or if the exclusive-dealing contract strengthens an otherwise weak competitor, the arrangement is allowed.

13-6d **Refusal to Deal**

For nearly a century, courts have held that producers have the right to choose or reject the channel members with which they will do business. Within existing distribution channels, however, suppliers may not legally refuse to deal with wholesalers or dealers merely because they resist policies that are anticompetitive or in restraint of trade. Suppliers are further prohibited from organizing channel members in refusal-to-deal actions against other members that choose not to comply with illegal policies.

Chapter Review

13-1 Describe the foundations of supply-chain management.

The distribution component of the marketing mix focuses on the decisions and activities involved in making products available to customers when and where they want to purchase them. An important function of distribution is the joint effort of all involved organizations to be part of creating an effective supply chain, which includes all the organizations and activities involved with the flow and transformation of products from raw materials through to the end customer. Operations management is the total set of managerial activities used by an organization to transform resource inputs into goods, services, or both. Logistics management involves planning, implementing, and controlling the efficient and effective flow and storage of goods, services, and information from the point of origin to consumption in order to meet customers' needs and wants. Supply management in its broadest form refers to the processes that enable the progress of value from raw material to final customer and back to redesign and final disposition. Supply-chain management (SCM) refers to the coordination of all the activities involved with the flow and transformation of supplies, products, and information throughout the supply chain to the ultimate consumer. It integrates the functions of operations management, logistics management, supply management, and marketing channel management so that goods and services are produced and distributed in the right quantities, to the right locations, and at the right time.

The supply chain includes all entities—shippers and other firms that facilitate distribution, producers, wholesalers, and retailers—that distribute products and benefit from cooperative efforts.

13-2 Explain the role and significance of marketing channels and supply chains.

A marketing channel, or channel of distribution, is a group of individuals and organizations that direct the flow of products from producers to customers. The major role of marketing channels is to make products available at the right time, at the right price, in the right place, and in the right amounts. In most channels of distribution, producers and consumers are linked by marketing intermediaries. The two major types of intermediaries are retailers, which purchase products and resell them to ultimate consumers, and wholesalers, which buy and resell products to other wholesalers, retailers, and business customers.

Marketing channels serve many functions. They create time, place, and possession utilities by making products available when, where, and at the price customers want and providing customers with access to product use through sale or rental. Marketing intermediaries facilitate exchange efficiencies, often reducing the costs of exchanges by performing certain services and functions. Although some critics suggest eliminating wholesalers, the functions of the intermediaries in the marketing channel must be performed. As such, eliminating intermediaries results in other organizations in the channel having to perform those functions. Because intermediaries serve both producers and buyers, they reduce the total number of transactions that otherwise would be needed to move products from producer to the end customer.

Channels of distribution are broadly classified as channels for consumer products and for business products. Within these two broad categories, different products require different channels. Although consumer goods can move directly from producer to consumers, consumer channels that include wholesalers and retailers are more economical for many goods. Distribution of business products differs from that of consumer products in the types of channels used. A direct distribution channel is most common in business marketing. Also used are channels containing industrial distributors, manufacturers' agents, and a combination of agents and distributors. Most producers have multiple or dual channels so the distribution system can be adjusted for various target markets.

A strategic channel alliance exists when the products of one firm are distributed through the marketing channels of another. Multichannel distribution—the use of a variety of marketing channels to ensure maximum distribution—is increasingly used to reach target customers wherever and whenever they may choose to interact with a company or its products. Some products use digital distribution to deliver content through the Internet to a computer or other device. It is important to recognize that the line between different marketing channels is becoming increasingly blurred.

Selecting an appropriate marketing channel is a crucial decision for supply-chain managers. To determine which channel is most appropriate, managers must think about customer characteristics, the type of organization, product attributes, competition, environmental forces, and the availability and characteristics of intermediaries. Careful consideration of these factors will assist a supply-chain manager in selecting the correct channel.

13-3 Identify the intensity of market coverage.

An effective marketing channel is managed such that products receive appropriate market coverage. There are three levels of market coverage: intensive, selective, and exclusive. Different types of products are best handled using different intensities of market coverage. In choosing intensive distribution, producers strive to make a product available to all possible dealers. In selective distribution, only some outlets in an area are chosen to distribute a product that requires more consideration and effort on the part of the consumer before purchase. Exclusive distribution is used for more expensive items and usually gives a single dealer rights to sell a product in a large geographic area.

13-4 Explore strategic issues in marketing channels, including leadership, cooperation, and conflict.

Each channel member performs a different role in the system and agrees to accept certain rights, responsibilities, rewards, and sanctions for nonconformity. Although many marketing channels are determined by consensus, some are organized and controlled by a single leader, or channel captain. A channel captain may be a producer, wholesaler, or retailer. A marketing channel functions most effectively when members cooperate. When members deviate from or ignore their roles, channel conflict can arise.

Channel members can transfer, but not eliminate, supply-chain functions. When various channel stages are combined under a single channel captain this is called channel integration. Vertical integration combines two or more stages of the distribution channel under one management. A vertical marketing system (VMS) is managed centrally for the mutual benefit of all channel members. Vertical marketing systems may take corporate, administered, or contractual forms. Horizontal integration combines institutions at the same level of channel operation under a single management. Horizontal integration can be problematic in that it may not reduce costs, nor improve the competitiveness, of a firm.

13-5 Explain physical distribution as being a part of supply-chain management.

Physical distribution, or logistics, refers to the activities used to move products from producers to customers and other end users. These activities include order processing, inventory management, materials handling, warehousing, and transportation. An efficient physical distribution system is an important component of an overall marketing strategy, because it can decrease costs and increase customer satisfaction. Within the marketing channel, physical distribution activities are often performed by a wholesaler, but they may also be performed by a producer or retailer, or outsourced to a third party. Third-party logistics (3PL) firms have special expertise in core physical distribution activities such as warehousing, transportation, inventory management, and information technology and can often perform these activities more efficiently. Efficient physical distribution systems can decrease costs and transit time while increasing customer service.

Order processing is the receipt and transmission of sales order information. It consists of three main tasks—order entry, order handling, and order delivery—that may be done manually but are more often handled through electronic data interchange (EDI) systems. Inventory management involves developing and maintaining adequate assortments of products to meet customers' needs. Logistics managers must strive to find the optimal level of inventory to satisfy customer needs while keeping costs down. Materials handling, the physical handling of products, is a crucial element in warehousing and transporting products. Radio frequency identification (RFID) uses radio waves to identify and track materials tagged with special microchips through every phase of handling. Warehousing involves the design and operation of facilities for storing and moving goods and may be privately owned or public. Transportation, the movement of products from where they are made to where they are purchased and used, is the most expensive physical distribution function. The basic modes of transporting goods include railroads, trucks, waterways, airways, and pipelines. These modes can be combined—called intermodal transportation—in order to take advantage of the benefits of each different mode.

13-6 Examine legal issues in channel management.

Federal, state, local, and international laws regulate channel management to protect competition and free trade. Courts may prohibit or permit a practice depending on whether it violates this underlying principle. Channel management practices are subject to legal restraint, including restricted sales territories, tying agreements, exclusive dealing, and refusal to deal. When these practices strengthen weak competitors or increase competition among dealers, they may be permitted. In most other cases, when competition may be weakened, they are considered illegal.

 Go to www.cengagebrain.com for resources to help you master the content in this chapter as well as materials that will expand your marketing knowledge!

Developing Your Marketing Plan

One of the key components in a successful marketing strategy is the plan for getting the products to your customer. To make the best decisions about where, when, and how your products will be made available to the customer, you need to know more about how these distribution decisions relate to other marketing mix elements in your marketing plan. To assist you in relating the information in this chapter to your marketing plan, consider the following issues:

1. Marketing intermediaries perform many activities. Using Table 13.1 as a guide, discuss the types of activities where a channel member could provide needed assistance.

2. Using Figure 13.2 (or 13.3 if your product is a business product), determine which of the channel distribution paths is most appropriate for your product. Given the nature of your product, could it be distributed through more than one of these paths?

3. Determine the level of distribution intensity that is appropriate for your product. Consider the characteristics of your target market(s), the product attributes, and environmental factors in your deliberation.

4. Discuss the physical functions that will be required for distributing your product, focusing on materials handling, warehousing, and transportation.

Key Concepts

distribution 332
supply chain 332
operations management 332
logistics management 332
supply management 332
supply-chain management (SCM) 332
marketing channel 333
marketing intermediaries 334
industrial distributor 338
strategic channel alliance 339

multichannel distribution 339
digital distribution 340
intensive distribution 342
selective distribution 343
exclusive distribution 343
channel captain 345
channel power 345
vertical channel integration 347
vertical marketing system (VMS) 347

horizontal channel integration 348
physical distribution 348
third-party logistics (3PL) firm 349
cycle time 350
order processing 350
electronic data interchange (EDI) 351
inventory management 351
just-in-time (JIT) 351
materials handling 352

radio-frequency identification (RFID) 352
warehousing 352
private warehouses 353
public warehouses 353
distribution centers 353
transportation 354
intermodal transportation 355
freight forwarders 356
megacarriers 356
tying agreement 356
exclusive dealing 357

Issues for Discussion and Review

1. Define supply-chain management. Why is it important?
2. Describe the major functions of marketing channels. Why are these functions better accomplished through the combined efforts of channel members?
3. List several reasons consumers often blame intermediaries for distribution inefficiencies.
4. Compare and contrast the four major types of marketing channels for consumer products. Through which type of channel is each of the following products most likely to be distributed?
   a. New automobiles
   b. Saltine crackers
   c. Cut-your-own Christmas trees
   d. New textbooks
   e. Sofas
   f. Soft drinks
5. Outline the four most common channels for business products. Describe the products or situations that lead marketers to choose each channel.
6. Describe an industrial distributor. What types of products are marketed through an industrial distributor?
7. Under what conditions is a producer most likely to use more than one marketing channel?

8. Identify and describe the factors that may influence marketing channel selection decisions.
9. Explain the differences among intensive, selective, and exclusive methods of distribution.
10. "Channel cooperation requires that members support the overall channel goals to achieve individual goals." Comment on this statement.
11. Explain the major characteristics of each of the three types of vertical marketing systems (VMSs): corporate, administered, and contractual.
12. Discuss the cost and service trade-offs involved in developing a physical distribution system.
13. What are the main tasks involved in order processing?
14. Explain the trade-offs that inventory managers face when they reorder products or supplies. How is the reorder point computed?
15. Explain the major differences between private and public warehouses. How do they differ from a distribution center?
16. Compare and contrast the five major transportation modes in terms of cost, speed, and dependability.
17. Under what conditions are tying agreements, exclusive dealing, and dual distribution judged illegal?

VIDEO CASE 13
Taza Cultivates Channel Relationships with Chocolate

Taza Chocolate is a small Massachusetts-based manufacturer of stone-ground organic chocolate made in the classic Mexican tradition. Founded in 2006, Taza markets most of its products through U.S. retailers, wholesalers, and distributors. Individual customers around the world can also buy Taza chocolate bars, baking squares, chocolate-covered nuts, and other specialty items directly from the Taza website. If they live in Somerville, Massachusetts, they might even find a Taza employee riding a "chococycle," selling products and distributing samples at an upscale food truck festival or a weekend market festival.

Taza seeks to make personal connections with all the certified organic growers who supply its ingredients. "Because our process here at the factory is so minimal," says the company's director of sales, "it's really important that we get a very high-quality ingredient. To make sure that we're getting the absolute cream of the [cocoa] crop, we have a direct face-to-face human relationship between us and the actual farmer who's producing those beans."

Dealing directly with suppliers allows Taza to meet its social responsibility goals while ensuring the kind of quality that commands a premium price. "We're a premium brand," explains the director of sales, "and because of the way we do what we do, we have to charge more than your average chocolate bar." A Taza chocolate bar that sells at a retail price of $4.50 carries a wholesale price of about $2.70. The distributor's price, however, is even lower, closer to $2.00.

Distributors buy in the largest quantities, which for Taza means a pallet load rather than a case that a wholesaler would buy. "But wholesale will always be our bread and butter, where we really move the volume and we have good margins," says Taza's director of sales. In the company's experience, distributors are very price-conscious and more interested than wholesalers in promotions and extras.

Taza offers factory tours at its Somerville site, charging a small entrance fee that includes a donation to Sustainable Harvest International. There, visitors can watch the bean-to-bar process from beginning to end, learning about the beans and the stone-ground tradition that differentiates Taza from European chocolates. Visitors enjoy product samples along the way and, at the end of the tour, they can browse through the factory store and buy freshly made specialties like chipotle chili chocolate and ginger chocolate. On holidays like Halloween and Valentine's Day, Taza hosts special tastings and limited-edition treats to attract customers to its factory store. Its annual beer-and-chocolate pairing event, hosted with the Drink Craft Beer website, is another way to introduce Taza to consumers who appreciate quality foods and drinks.

Taza's marketing communications focus mainly on Facebook, Twitter, blogs, e-mail, and specialty food shows. Also, the company frequently offers samples in upscale and organic food stores in major metropolitan areas. As it does with its growers, Taza seeks to forge personal relationships with its channel partners. "When we send a shipment of chocolate," says the sales director, "sometimes we'll put in a little extra for the people who work there. That always helps because [it's] building that kind of human relationship."

Privately owned Taza has begun shipping to Canada and a handful of European countries. Its channel arrangements must allow for delivering perishable products that stay fresh and firm, no matter what the weather. As a result, distributors often hold some Taza inventory in refrigerated warehouses to have ready for next-day delivery when retailers place orders.[29]

Questions for Discussion

1. Which distribution channels does Taza use, and why are they appropriate for this company?
2. In what ways does Taza benefit from selling directly to some consumers? What are some potential problems of selling directly to consumers?
3. In what ways are Taza's distribution efforts influenced by the fact that its products are organic?

iStock.com/gmutlu

chapter 14

Retailing, Direct Marketing, and Wholesaling

LEARNING OBJECTIVES

14-1 Describe the purpose and function of retailers in the marketing channel.

14-2 Classify the major types of retailers.

14-3 Explore strategic issues in retailing.

14-4 Identify the various forms of direct marketing, direct selling, and vending.

14-5 Describe franchising and its benefits and weaknesses.

14-6 Explain the nature and functions of wholesalers.

Target Puts Its Bulls-Eye on College Campuses and on Urban Areas

Minneapolis-based Target is bringing its "cheap chic" retailing to college campus areas and to urban locations as it battles intense competition and changes in consumer behavior. The red-and-white bulls-eye already appears on more than 1,800 U.S. stores. The typical Target store covers 140,000 square feet, large enough to hold a wide variety of products for convenient one-stop shopping. In the digital age, however, with price comparisons and purchases as close as a click, Target must go beyond everyday low prices to bring shoppers into its stores.

Targeting college students, Target has been opening smaller stores close to campuses like Penn State and University of Florida. It has also been opening smaller stores in hip downtown areas like New York City's TriBeCa neighborhood, targeting the people who live and work nearby. Target calls these "flexible-format stores" because the configurations and merchandise selection are carefully tailored to local needs. Stores near campuses carry a larger selection of dorm décor products and electronics, while stores in cities carry more children's merchandise. Some stores are as small as 21,000 square feet, others are as large as 45,000 square feet—considerably smaller than the usual Target store and therefore easier for shoppers to navigate.

Over time, Target is using what it learns from customer response to these stores as input to refine its strategy and compete more effectively with stores down the street and online retailers like Amazon. Target expects the smaller stores to do double-duty as pickup locations for customers who have ordered online but want to collect their purchases locally. Will the flexible-format stores attract customers and boost profitability?[1]

iStock.com/YvanDube

Retailers like Target are the most visible and accessible marketing channel members to consumers. They represent an important link in the marketing channel because they are both marketers for and customers of producers and wholesalers. They perform many supply-chain functions, such as buying, selling, grading, risk taking, and developing and maintaining information databases about customers. Retailers are in a strategic position to develop relationships with consumers and partnerships with producers and intermediaries in the marketing channel.

In this chapter, we examine the nature of retailing, direct marketing, and wholesaling and their roles in supplying consumers with goods and services. First, we identify the major types of retail stores and explore strategic issues in retailing: location, retail technology, retail positioning, store image, and category management. Next, we discuss direct marketing, including online retailing, catalog marketing, direct-response marketing, telemarketing, and television home shopping. We also explore direct selling and vending. Then we look at the strengths and weaknesses of franchising, a popular form of retailing. Finally, we examine the importance of wholesalers in marketing channels, including their functions and classifications.

|14-1 RETAILING

LO 14-1 Describe the purpose and function of retailers in the marketing channel.

Retailing includes all transactions in which the buyer is the ultimate consumer and intends to consume the product for personal, family, or household use. A **retailer** is an organization that purchases products for the purpose of reselling them to ultimate consumers. Although most retailers' sales are made directly to the consumer, nonretail transactions occur occasionally, when retailers sell products to other businesses.

Retailing is vital to the U.S. economy. Every time you buy a meal, a smartphone, a movie ticket, or some other product from a retailer, the money you spend flows through the economy to the store's employees, to the government, and to other businesses and consumers. There are 3.8 million retail establishments in the United States, and they employ nearly 29 million people. Retailers contribute $1.2 trillion, or 7.7 percent, directly to the U.S. gross domestic product.[2]

Retailers add value for customers by providing services and assisting in making product selections. They can also enhance consumers' perception of the value of products by making buyers' shopping experiences easier or more convenient, such as providing free delivery or offering a mobile shopping option. Retailers can facilitate comparison shopping to allow customers to evaluate different options. For example, car dealerships often cluster in the same general vicinity, as do furniture stores. Product value is also enhanced when retailers offer services, such as technical advice, delivery, credit, and repair. Finally, retail sales personnel are trained to be able to demonstrate to customers how products can satisfy their needs or solve problems.

Retailers can add significant value to the supply chain, representing a critical link between producers and ultimate consumers by providing the environment in which exchanges occur. Retailers play a major role in creating time, place, and possession utility, and, in some cases, form utility. Retailers perform marketing functions that benefit ultimate consumers by making available broad arrays of products that can satisfy their needs.

Historically, retail stores have offered consumers a physical place to browse and compare merchandise in order to find what they need. However, traditional retailing is evolving to address changing consumer demographics and buying behavior and adopt new technologies to improve the shopping experience. Many retailers now engage in **multichannel retailing** by employing multiple distribution channels that complement their brick-and-mortar stores with websites, catalogs, and apps where consumers can research products, read other buyers' reviews, and make actual purchases. The most effective multichannel retail strategies integrate the firm's goals, products, systems, and technologies seamlessly across all platforms

retailing All transactions in which the buyer intends to consume the product through personal, family, or household use

retailer An organization that purchases products for the purpose of reselling them to ultimate consumers

multichannel retailing Employing multiple distribution channels that complement brick-and-mortar stores with websites, catalogs, and apps where consumers can research products, read other buyers' reviews, and make actual purchases

so that a customer can research a product through the firm's website at home, find specific information about the product and locate the nearest one through an app on their smartphone while in the car, and checkout in a store or online.

The key to success in retailing is to have a strong customer focus with a retail strategy that provides the level of service, product quality, and innovation that targeted consumers desire. New store formats, service innovations, and advances in information technology have helped retailers to serve customers better. Consider that investments in technology and infrastructure are letting major online retailers compete with traditional retailers on distribution through offering next-day or even same-day in-store pickup or home delivery in major markets, providing even greater satisfaction to customers. This strategy can be expensive for the retailer and is aimed at attracting customers who need items right away. Amazon's one-day shipping option has enabled it to gain an edge with this type of customer.

Retailing is increasingly international. In particular, many retailers see significant growth potential in some international markets. The market for a product category such as cell phones is maturing in areas such as North America and Europe, but producers forecast strong future demand in places like India, China, and Brazil. These countries all have large, relatively new middle classes with consumers hungry for goods and services. In India, for example, the fast-growing middle class with rising disposable income has led companies like Amazon, Tesla, Procter & Gamble, and McDonald's to enter the market or expand operations there.[3] Many major U.S. retailers have international outlets in order to capitalize on international growth. On the other hand, international retailers, such as Aldi, IKEA, and Zara, have also found receptive markets in the United States.

general-merchandise retailer A retail establishment that offers a variety of product lines that are stocked in considerable depth

department stores Large retail organizations characterized by a wide product mix and organized into separate departments to facilitate marketing efforts and internal management

14-2 MAJOR TYPES OF RETAIL STORES

LO 14-2 Classify the major types of retailers.

Many types of retail stores exist. One way to classify them is by the breadth of products they offer. Two general categories include general-merchandise retailers and specialty retailers.

14-2a General-Merchandise Retailers

A retail establishment that offers a variety of product lines that are stocked in considerable depth is referred to as a **general-merchandise retailer**. The types of product offerings, mixes of customer services, and operating styles of retailers in this category vary considerably. The primary types of general-merchandise retailers are department stores, discount stores, convenience stores, supermarkets, superstores, hypermarkets, warehouse clubs, and warehouse showrooms (see Table 14.1).

Department Stores

Department stores are large retail organizations characterized by wide product mixes with at least 25 employees. To facilitate marketing efforts and internal management, department stores like Macy's, Sears, and Nordstrom's organize related product lines into separate departments such as cosmetics, housewares, apparel, home furnishings, and appliances. This arrangement facilitates marketing and internal management. Often, each department functions as a self-contained business, with buyers for individual departments acting fairly autonomously. At typical

Department Stores
Department stores like Macy's offer a wide variety of product lines.

iStock.com/ozgurdonmaz

TABLE 14.1	GENERAL-MERCHANDISE RETAILERS	
Type of Retailer	**Description**	**Examples**
Department store	Large organization offering a wide product mix and organized into separate departments	Macy's, Sears, JCPenney
Discount store	Self-service, general-merchandise store offering brand-name and private-brand products at low prices	Walmart, Target, Dollar General
Convenience store	Small, self-service store offering narrow product assortment in convenient locations	7-Eleven, Allsup's
Supermarket	Self-service store offering complete line of food products and some non-food products	Kroger, Safeway, Publix, HEB
Superstore	Giant outlet offering all food and non-food products found in supermarkets, as well as most routinely purchased products	Walmart Supercenters, SuperTarget
Hypermarket	Combination supermarket and discount store, larger than a superstore	Carrefour, Lulu
Warehouse club	Large-scale, members-only establishments combining cash-and-carry wholesaling with discount retailing	Sam's Club, Costco
Warehouse showroom	Facility in a large, low-cost building with large on-premises inventories and minimal service	IKEA

department stores, a large proportion of sales comes from apparel, accessories, and cosmetics. Most carry a broad assortment of other products as well, including gift items, luggage, electronics, home accessories, and sports equipment. Some department stores offer services, such as automobile insurance, hair care, income tax preparation, and travel and optical services. In some cases, space for these specialized services is leased to other businesses, with proprietors managing their own operations and paying rent to the store. Most department stores also sell products through websites, which can service customers who live in smaller markets where they have no access to a store or who prefer to shop online or through apps.

Department stores are distinctly service-oriented. Their total product may include credit, delivery, personal assistance, merchandise returns, and a pleasant atmosphere. Although some so-called department stores are actually large, departmentalized specialty stores, most department stores are shopping stores. Consumers can compare price, quality, and service at one store with competing stores. Along with large discount stores, department stores are often considered retailing leaders in a community and are generally found in areas with populations of more than 50,000. However, in recent years, department stores have faced intense competition from discount stores and online retailing, and many chains have closed stores to reduce costs.

Discount Stores

Discount stores are self-service, general-merchandise outlets that regularly offer brand-name and private-brand products at low prices. Discounters accept lower profit margins than conventional retailers in exchange for high sales volume. To keep inventory turnover high, they carry a wide, but carefully selected, assortment of products, from appliances to housewares to clothing. Major discount establishments also offer food products, toys, automotive services, garden supplies, and sports equipment.

Walmart and Target have grown to become not only the largest discount stores in the country, but some of the largest retailers in the world. Walmart is the world's largest retailer,

discount stores Self-service, general-merchandise stores that offer brand-name and private-brand products at low prices

EMERGING TRENDS

Stores Inside Stores

Retailers are teaming up for greater impact and higher traffic, opening stores within stores to increase customer appeal with complementary product offerings. One of the most successful pairings is department store JCPenney and beauty specialty retailer Sephora. More than 600 JCPenney stores currently have Sephora stores prominently placed on the main floor. Sephora stocks a wide range of cosmetics products not available at JCPenney and offers personalized assistance plus try-before-you-buy convenience. Even as JCPenney closes some stores to cut costs and boost profitability, the retailer is opening additional Sephora stores and Salons by InStyle. "These offer clear differentiators for us, while driving traffic and frequency of business to our locations," according to JCPenney's CEO.

Macy's has an Apple store inside the department store's flagship location in New York City.

That flagship also hosts an Etsy shop with items made by artisans who sell online through Etsy. A new deal will be bringing LensCrafters' stores into Macy's branches across the country.

Other department stores are inviting smaller specialty retailers to open inside their branches. Bloomingdale's, for example, hosts the Combatant Gentlemen menswear stores in four cities. Combatant Gentlemen was online-only until it found space inside Bloomingdale's, an arrangement that saves time and money compared with opening independent stores. For its part, the department store is happy to host the Combatant Gentlemen. "The shop-in-shop concept gives us the opportunity to appeal to new customers while giving our existing customers new products and experiences," explains a Bloomingdale's executive.[a]

---

with revenues more than four times higher than its next competitor Costco, and Target is ranked eleventh.[4] Not all discounters are large and international. Some, such as Meijer Inc., which has stores in the Midwest United States, are regional discounters. Most discount stores operate in large (50,000 to 80,000 square feet), no-frills facilities. They usually offer everyday low prices, rather than relying on sales events.

Discount retailing developed on a large scale in the early 1950s, when postwar production caught up with strong consumer demand for goods. At first, they were often cash-only operations with minimal services located in warehouse districts, offering goods at savings of 20 to 30 percent over conventional retailers. Facing increased competition from department stores and other discount stores, some discounters have improved store services, atmosphere, and location, raising prices and sometimes blurring the distinction between discount store and department store.

As conventional discount stores have grown larger and pricier in recent years, low-income and thrifty consumers have turned to extreme-value stores (also known as dollar stores and single-price stores). **Extreme-value stores** are a fraction of the size of conventional discount stores and typically offer very low prices—generally $1 to $10—on smaller size name-brand nonperishable household items. Dollar General, Dollar Tree, and 99¢ Only Stores offer lower per-unit prices than discount stores but often charge considerably more when priced per ounce than stores whose customers can afford to stock up on supersized items.

Convenience Stores

A **convenience store** is a small, self-service store that is open long hours and carries a narrow assortment of products, usually items such as soft drinks and other beverages, snacks, newspapers, tobacco, and gasoline, as well as services such as ATMs. The primary product offered by the "corner store" is convenience. According to the National Association of Convenience Stores, there are more than 154,000 convenience stores in the United States alone, which together boast nearly $548 billion in annual sales.[5] They are typically less

extreme-value stores
Retailers that are a fraction of the size of conventional discount stores and typically offer very low prices on smaller size name-brand nonperishable household items

convenience store A small, self-service store that is open long hours and carries a narrow assortment of products, usually convenience items

than 5,000 square feet, open 24 hours a day and 7 days a week, and stock about 500 items. The convenience store concept was developed in 1927 when Southland Ice in Dallas began stocking basics such as milk and eggs in addition to ice for customers who wanted to replenish their supplies. In addition to national chains, there are many family-owned independent convenience stores.

Supermarkets

Supermarkets are large, self-service stores that carry a complete line of food products and some non-food products such as cosmetics and nonprescription drugs. Supermarkets are arranged by department for maximum efficiency in stocking and handling products, but have central checkout facilities. They offer lower prices than smaller neighborhood grocery stores, usually provide free parking, and may also provide services such as check cashing.

Consumers make the majority of their grocery purchases in supermarkets. However, increased availability of grocery items at discount stores and other competitors have eroded supermarkets' market share of the grocery segment. In larger cities, online grocers have reduced the need to go to grocery stores and put pressure on supermarkets to increase marketing efforts and make shopping more convenient. Retailers like Kroger, Whole Foods, and Costco have partnered with Instacart to provide personal shopping and pick-up or delivery services in many metropolitan areas. Safeway and Publix supermarket chains offer their own delivery services.

Another type of supermarket that may take back market share from discount stores is the *hard discounter*. Hard discounters maintain a no-frills environment and have a minimal assortment of goods they can sell at very low prices. These supermarkets first emerged in Europe. Now German grocery chains Aldi and Lidl have expanded outside of Europe and into the United States.

Superstores

Superstores, which originated in Europe, are giant retail outlets that carry not only the food and non-food products ordinarily found in supermarkets, but also routinely purchased consumer products such as housewares, hardware, small appliances, clothing, and personal-care products. Superstores combine features of discount stores and supermarkets and generally carry about four times as many items as supermarkets. Superstores also offer additional services, including dry cleaning, automotive repair, check cashing, and bill paying. Examples include Walmart Supercenters, some Kroger stores, and SuperTarget stores.

To cut handling and inventory costs, superstores use sophisticated operating techniques and often have tall shelving that displays entire assortments of products. Superstores can occupy an area of as much as 200,000 square feet (compared with 45,000 square feet in traditional supermarkets). Sales volume is typically two to three times that of supermarkets, partly because locations near good transportation networks help generate the in-store traffic needed for profitability.

supermarkets Large, self-service stores that carry a complete line of food products, along with some non-food products

superstores Giant retail outlets that carry food and non-food products found in supermarkets, as well as most routinely purchased consumer products

hypermarkets Stores that combine supermarket and discount store shopping in one location

Hypermarkets

Hypermarkets combine supermarket and discount store shopping in one location. Larger than superstores, they range from 225,000 to 325,000 square feet and offer 45,000 to 60,000 different types of low-priced products. They commonly allocate 40 to 50 percent of their space to grocery products and the remainder to general merchandise, including apparel, appliances, housewares, jewelry, hardware, and automotive supplies. Many also lease space to noncompeting businesses such as banks, optical shops, and fast-food restaurants. All hypermarkets focus on low prices and vast selections.

Retailers have struggled with introducing the hypermarket concept in the United States. Although Kmart, Walmart, and Carrefour all opened hypermarkets in the United States, most of these stores ultimately closed. Such stores may be too large for time-constrained

U.S. shoppers. Hypermarkets have been more successful in Europe, South America, Mexico, the Middle East, and India.

Warehouse Clubs

Warehouse clubs, a rapidly growing form of mass merchandising, are large-scale, members-only operations that combine cash-and-carry wholesaling with discount retailing. Sometimes called *buying clubs*, warehouse clubs offer the same types of products as discount stores, but in a limited range of sizes and styles. Whereas most discount stores carry around 40,000 items, a warehouse club handles only 3,500 to 5,000 products, usually brand leaders. Sam's Club stores, for example, stock about 4,000 items. Costco currently leads the warehouse club industry with sales of more than $116 billion. Sam's Club is second with $57 billion in store sales.[6] All these establishments offer a broad product mix, including food, beverages, books, appliances, housewares, automotive parts, hardware, and furniture.

Warehouse Clubs
Sam's Club is a warehouse club that has a wide product mix and limited depth.

To keep prices lower than those of supermarkets and discount stores, warehouse clubs offer few services. They also keep advertising to a minimum. Their facilities, often located in industrial areas, have concrete floors and aisles wide enough for forklifts. Merchandise is stacked on pallets or displayed on pipe racks. Customers must perform some marketing functions, like transportation of purchases, themselves. Warehouse clubs appeal to price-conscious consumers and small retailers unable to obtain wholesaling services from large distributors.

Warehouse Showrooms

Warehouse showrooms are retail facilities with five basic characteristics: large, low-cost buildings, warehouse materials-handling technology, vertical merchandise displays, large on-premises inventories, and minimal services. IKEA, a Swedish company, sells furniture, household goods, and kitchen accessories in warehouse showrooms and through catalogs. These high-volume, low-overhead operations offer few services and few personnel. Lower costs are possible because some marketing functions have been shifted to consumers, who must transport, finance, and perhaps assemble products. Most consumers carry away purchases in the manufacturer's carton, although stores will deliver for a fee.

14-2b **Specialty Retailers**

In contrast to general-merchandise retailers with their broad product mixes, specialty retailers emphasize narrow and deep assortments. Despite their name, specialty retailers do not sell specialty items (except when specialty goods complement the overall product mix). Instead, they offer substantial assortments in a few product lines. We examine three types of specialty retailers: traditional specialty retailers, category killers, and off-price retailers.

Traditional Specialty Retailers

Traditional specialty retailers are stores that carry a narrow product mix with deep product lines. Sometimes called *limited-line retailers*, they may be referred to as *single-line retailers* if they carry unusual depth in one product category. Specialty retailers commonly sell such shopping products as apparel, jewelry, sporting goods, fabrics, computers, and pet supplies. The Limited, James Avery, and Foot Locker are examples of retailers offering limited product lines but great depth within those lines.

warehouse clubs Large-scale, members-only establishments that combine features of cash-and-carry wholesaling with discount retailing

warehouse showrooms Retail facilities in large, low-cost buildings with large, on-premises inventories and minimal services

traditional specialty retailers Stores that carry a narrow product mix with deep product lines

category killer A very large specialty store that concentrates on a major product category and competes on the basis of low prices and product availability

off-price retailers Stores that buy manufacturers' seconds, overruns, returns, and off-season merchandise for resale to consumers at deep discounts

Because they are usually small, specialty stores may have high costs in proportion to sales, and satisfying customers may require carrying some products with low-turnover rates. However, these stores sometimes obtain lower prices from suppliers by purchasing limited lines of merchandise in large quantities. Successful specialty stores understand their customers and know what products to carry, which reduces the risk of unsold merchandise. Specialty stores usually offer better selections and more sales expertise than department stores, their main competitors. By capitalizing on fashion, service, personnel, atmosphere, and location, specialty retailers position themselves strategically to attract customers in specific market segments. However, traditional specialty stores have struggled to adapt to increased competition from online retailing. California-based Sports Chalet, for example, strained for years to keep up with changing consumer preferences while strong competition from online retailers and larger rivals eroded the firm's market share. After a decade of financial struggles, the firm's parent company declared bankruptcy and closed all 47 Sports Chalet stores.[7]

Category Killers

A more recent kind of specialty retailer is called the **category killer**, which is a very large specialty store that concentrates on a major product category and competes on the basis of low prices and broad product availability. These stores are referred to as category killers because they expand rapidly and gain sizable market shares, taking business away from smaller, higher-cost retail outlets. Examples of category killers include Home Depot and Lowe's (home improvement chains), Staples (office supplies), Barnes & Noble (bookseller), Petco and PetSmart (pet-supply chains), and Best Buy (consumer electronics). Online retailing has also placed pressure on category killers and taken away market share in recent years. Some retailers such as Best Buy and Toys "R" Us have built competitive websites and adopted price-matching policies in the hopes of better competing against their online rivals.

Off-Price Retailers

Off-price retailers are stores that buy manufacturers' seconds, overruns, returns, and off-season production runs at below-wholesale prices for resale to consumers at deep discounts. Unlike true discount stores, which pay regular wholesale prices for goods and usually carry second-line brand names, off-price retailers offer limited lines of national-brand and designer merchandise, usually clothing, shoes, or housewares. Consumers appreciate the ability to purchase name-brand goods at discounted prices, and sales at off-price retailers, such as T.J. Maxx, Marshalls, Stein Mart, and Burlington Coat Factory, have grown. Off-price retailers typically perform well in recessionary times, as consumers who want to own name-brand items search for good values. The success of off-price retailers has caught the attention of department stores like Macy's, which have had to close stores in the face of declining sales. To compete, Macy's is adding off-price retailers called Macy's Backstage inside select Macy's department stores. These stores-within-the store will sell merchandise at sharp discounts and have separate buyers.[8]

Off-price stores charge 20 to 50 percent less than department stores for comparable merchandise, but offer few customer services. They often feature community dressing rooms and central checkout counters. Some of these stores do not take returns or allow exchanges. Off-price stores may or may not sell goods with the original labels intact. They

iStock.com/SweetBabeeJay

iStock.com/1MoreCreative

Traditional Specialty Stores and Off-Price Specialty Stores
Banana Republic is a traditional specialty store, while Marshall's is an example of an off-price specialty retailer.

turn over their inventory 9 to 12 times a year, three times as often as traditional specialty stores. They compete with department stores for many of the same customers: price-conscious customers who are knowledgeable about brand names.

To ensure a regular flow of merchandise into their stores, off-price retailers establish long-term relationships with suppliers that can provide large quantities of goods at reduced prices. Manufacturers may approach retailers with samples, discontinued products, or items that have not sold well. Also, off-price retailers may seek out manufacturers, offering to pay cash for goods produced during the manufacturers' off-season. Although manufacturers benefit from such arrangements, they also risk alienating their specialty and department store customers. Department stores tolerate off-price stores as long as they do not advertise brand names, limit merchandise to last season's or

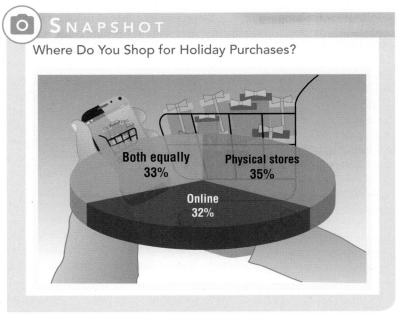

SNAPSHOT

Where Do You Shop for Holiday Purchases?

Both equally
33%

Physical stores
35%

Online
32%

Source: SDL Holiday Shopper Study of 500 shoppers

lower-quality items, and are located away from the department stores. When off-price retailers sell stocks of in-season, top-quality merchandise, tension builds between department stores and manufacturers.

14-3 STRATEGIC ISSUES IN RETAILING

LO 14-3 Explore strategic issues in retailing.

Whereas most business purchases are based on economic planning and necessity, consumer purchases are likely to be influenced by social and psychological factors. Because consumers shop for various reasons—to search for specific items, alleviate boredom, or learn about something new—retailers must do more than simply fill space with merchandise. They must make desired products available, create stimulating shopping environments, and develop marketing strategies that increase store patronage. In this section, we discuss how location, retail positioning, store image, and category management are used strategically by retailers.

14-3a Location of Retail Stores

You have likely heard the phrase "Location, location, location," commonly used in the real estate business. Location is certainly critical to business success. Making good location decisions is even more important because, once decided, it is the least flexible variable of the marketing mix. It is such an important strategic decision because location dictates the limited geographic trading area from which a store draws its customers. Retailers consider various factors when evaluating potential locations, including location of the firm's target market within the trading area, kinds of products being sold, availability of public transportation, customer characteristics, and competitors' locations. Increasingly, companies use marketing analytics of big data collected from their marketing information systems to identify optimal locations for new stores.

In choosing a location, a retailer must obviously consider the rental, leasing, or ownership terms of a potential property as well as the characteristics of the site itself. They research the types of stores in the area and the size, shape, and visibility of the lot or building under consideration. They usually evaluate the relative ease of movement to and from the site, including factors such as pedestrian and vehicular traffic, parking, and transportation. Retailers should look for compatibility with nearby retailers, because stores that complement one another draw more customers with similar product needs for everyone.

neighborhood shopping centers A type of shopping center usually consisting of several small convenience and specialty stores

community shopping centers A type of shopping center with one or two department stores, some specialty stores, and convenience stores

regional shopping centers A type of shopping center with the largest department stores, widest product mixes, and deepest product lines of all shopping centers

Some retailers choose to locate in downtown central business districts, whereas others prefer sites within shopping centers. Some retailers, including Toys "R" Us, Walmart, Home Depot, and many fast-food restaurants, opt for freestanding structures that are not connected to other buildings, but may be located within planned shopping centers. Sometimes, retailers choose to locate in less orthodox settings where competition will be lower and where consumers have fewer other options. Pop-ups—which are located inside another retailer, stand alone, or at special events for just a few days or weeks—can generate consumer buzz and help restauranteurs and specialty retailers determine if there is sufficient interest in their concept before investing significant resources in a conventional space. Another cost-saving strategy is sharing a single store with a compatible retailer, which may enable multiple small retailers to afford a storefront in a more desirable location. In some parts of the United States, food trailers, sometimes organized into outdoor food courts, have become popular and may provide a less expensive opportunity to grow a small business.

There are several different types of shopping centers, including neighborhood, community, regional, superregional, lifestyle, power, and outlet centers. **Neighborhood shopping centers,** also called *strip malls,* usually consist of several small convenience and specialty stores, such as small grocery stores, gas stations, and fast-food restaurants. These retailers consider their target markets to be consumers who live within two to three miles of their stores, or within a few minutes' walking or driving time. Because most purchases are based on convenience or personal contact, stores within a neighborhood shopping center generally do not coordinate selling efforts. Generally, product mixes consist of essential items, and the depth of product lines is limited.

Community shopping centers include one or two department stores and some specialty stores, as well as convenience stores. They draw consumers looking for shopping and specialty products not available in neighborhood shopping centers. Because these centers offer a wider variety of stores, they serve larger geographic areas and consumers are willing to drive longer distances to community shopping centers to shop. Community shopping centers are planned, and retailer efforts are coordinated to attract shoppers. Special events, such as art exhibits, automobile shows, and sidewalk sales, stimulate traffic. Managers of community shopping centers look for tenants that complement the centers' total assortment of products. Such centers have wide product mixes and deep product lines.

Regional shopping centers usually have the largest department stores, widest product mixes, and deepest product lines of all shopping centers. Many shopping malls are regional shopping centers, although some are community shopping centers. With 150,000 or more consumers in their target market, regional shopping centers must have well-coordinated management and marketing activities. Target markets may include consumers traveling

Location of Retail Stores
Victoria's Secret stores are usually located in regional malls whereas Lowe's stores are often located in freestanding buildings in high-traffic areas.

from a distance to find products and prices not available in their hometowns. Because of the expense of leasing space in regional shopping centers, tenants are likely to be national chains. Large centers usually advertise, have special events, furnish transportation for some consumer groups (such as seniors), maintain their own security forces, and carefully select the mix of stores. The largest of these centers, sometimes called **superregional shopping centers**, have the widest and deepest product mixes and attract customers from many miles away. Superregional centers often have special attractions beyond stores, such as skating rinks, amusement centers, or upscale restaurants. Mall of America, in the Minneapolis area, is the largest shopping mall in the United States with 520 stores, including major department stores like Nordstrom and Bloomingdale's, and 50 restaurants. The shopping center also includes a walk-through aquarium, a miniature golf course, a seven-acre Nickelodeon theme park, sports and virtual reality entertainment center, and a hotel, and the complex holds hundreds of special events each year.[9]

With traditional mall sales declining, some shopping center developers are looking to new formats that differ significantly from traditional shopping centers. A **lifestyle shopping center** is typically an open-air shopping center that features upscale specialty stores, dining, and entertainment, most usually owned by national chains.[10] Like San Jose's Santana Row, they are typically located near affluent neighborhoods and may have fountains, benches, and other amenities that encourage "casual browsing." Often resembling traditional "Main Street" shopping districts, lifestyle centers feature appealing architectural design and are designed to foster consumer loyalty by creating a sense of place. Some lifestyle shopping centers, like the Domain in Austin, Texas, include residences above the stores. To attract a wide variety of people, this type of center is designed to facilitate numerous types of activities and cultural events.

Some shopping center developers are bypassing the traditional department store anchor and combining off-price stores and small stores with category killers in **power shopping center** formats. These centers may be anchored by stores such as Gap, PetSmart, and Home Depot. The number of power shopping centers is growing, resulting in a variety of formats vying for the same retail dollar.

Factory outlet malls feature discount and factory outlet stores carrying traditional manufacturer brands, such as Polo Ralph Lauren, Nike, Guess, and Sunglass Hut. Some outlet centers feature upscale products from last season, discounted for quick sale. Manufacturers own these stores and make a special effort to avoid conflict with traditional retailers of their products. Manufacturers place these stores in noncompetitive locations, often outside of metropolitan areas. Factory outlet centers attract value-conscious customers seeking quality and major brand names. They operate in much the same way as regional shopping centers, but usually draw customers, some of whom may be tourists, from a larger shopping radius. Promotional activity is at the heart of these shopping centers. Craft and antique shows, contests, and special events attract consumer traffic.

14-3b **Retail Technology**

Today's consumers expect to be able to research and shop for a product wherever and whenever they want—in a mall, subway train, classroom, living room, or anywhere else. Younger shoppers in particular expect retailers to offer convenience, information, and a seamless experience across multiple platforms. Consider Nordstrom, which is famously guided by its mission to "provide a fabulous customer experience by empowering customers and the employees who serve them." The retailer has made strategic investments into point-of-sale systems that allow salespeople to view a customer's requests and needs online, an innovation lab, apps, mobile checkout, support for salespeople texting, a cloud-based men's personalized clothing service, and use of social media to build relationships with consumers and generate buzz. Integration of the firm's websites and apps with its inventory management control system lets customers find an item in a store or online and have it delivered to their home or office. Mobile checkout lets a salesperson who has been helping a customer in the store check them out on the spot rather than having to look for a register. These efforts contribute to Nordstrom's mission and ensure that customers have a great experience across all of the firm's platforms.[11]

superregional shopping centers A type of shopping center with the widest and deepest product mixes that attracts customers from many miles away

lifestyle shopping center A type of shopping center that is typically open air and features upscale specialty stores, dining, and entertainment

power shopping center A type of shopping center that combines off-price stores with category killers

Most retailers today have websites that, at a minimum, tell shoppers where they are, what their hours are, who they are, and what they sell. Many small retailers' websites highlight products in current inventory even if they are unable to offer online transactions. For most retailers, though, a website where customers can research products, purchase them, and otherwise interact with the firm is vital. Larger retailers such as Starbucks, Bank of America, and Amazon now have their own apps for customers to carry out those activities on their tablet or smartphone wherever they may be. Starbucks' app, for example, allows customers to order and pay right from their phone and accumulate loyalty reward points.

Retailers of all sizes can take advantage of technology to improve the store experience for a variety of customers. One way is through the use of *beacons* that can send real-time messages and offers to customers with Bluetooth-enabled smartphones. They are increasingly being used in airports, sports stadiums, hotels, fast-food restaurants, and bank branches. Citibank, for example, is using beacons in some branches to enable some customers after-hours entry using their iPhone or Apple Watch.[12]

There are a number of exciting new technologies designed to improve consumers' shopping experience whether they are in the store or at home shopping online. At some Ralph Lauren and Rebecca Minkoff stores, for example, smart mirrors can improve the dressing room experience by letting customers view clothing in different light and request a clerk bring the item in different colors or sizes without having to leave the dressing room. Soon, they'll be able to purchase the item via their smartphone before leaving the dressing room as well.[13] Virtual fit lets shoppers see how a product, such as eyeglasses, might look on them, using the cameras built into today's computers and smart devices. Self-checkout lets shoppers scan the items in their own shopping cart with their smartphone and pay for the merchandise out of a digital wallet, such as Apple Pay, so they don't have to wait in line. The technology even allows shoppers who subscribe to loyalty programs to get their rewards as they scan their own items.[14]

The reality is that evolving consumer demographics and preferences is spurring retailers to adapt in a variety of ways that are blurring the line between the various types of retailers more than ever before. Consider that most shoppers now research products online and then head to the nearest store to make the actual purchase—a practice sometimes called *webrooming*. For most consumers, there is no clear line between the brick-and-mortar store, the

DIGITAL MARKETING

Domino's AnyWare for Ordering Anywhere

Whenever and wherever customers want to order a pizza or another menu item, Domino's is ready with AnyWare, its anywhere-technology initiative. The idea is to give customers choices and make ordering quick and convenient, whether by calling, texting, tweeting, clicking, tapping, or saying a phrase.

Customers can always dial up Domino's. But if they're on the go and want to order via smartphone app, Domino's can make it happen. In fact, Domino's now has zero-click ordering, accessible by smartphone or Apple Watch. Customers enter their favorite orders in advance and provide payment and delivery details. Then they're ready to order by simply opening the app. After a 10-second delay to allow for changes (such as adding a beverage or requesting a new topping), the order goes to the nearest Domino's for delivery. Similarly, Twitter users can set up a favorite order in advance, including payment and delivery details, then place an order by tweeting a pizza emoji. Facebook users can use Facebook Messenger to order. Customers who own a voice-activated speaker made by Amazon or Google can order by talking to Alexa or Google Home.

Domino's has built a $9 billion business by making ordering easy. Already, 60 percent of Domino's orders are placed without a traditional phone call, and two-thirds of those orders involve a mobile device. Soon, Domino's AnyWare experts will introduce new options supported by artificial intelligence—the same technology that powers Amazon's Alexa and Google's voice-activated devices.[b]

store's website, and its app, and they move back and forth depending on their circumstances and desires. Online retailer Amazon.com has blurred the line even further by opening its own brick-and-mortar grocery store in Seattle, where a sophisticated system using cameras, microphones, and the Amazon Go app lets shoppers enter, pick up their items, and leave without actually passing through a checkout stand.[15]

14-3c **Retail Positioning**

The large variety of shopping centers and the expansion of product offerings by traditional stores, along with the increased use of retail technology, have all contributed to intense retailing competition. Retail positioning is therefore an important consideration. **Retail positioning** involves identifying an unserved or underserved market segment and reaching it through a strategy that distinguishes the retailer from others in the minds of customers in the market segment. In recent years, a number of discount and specialty store chains have positioned themselves to appeal to time and cash-strapped consumers with convenient locations and layouts as well as low prices. This strategy has helped them gain market share at the expense of large department stores.

14-3d **Store Image**

To attract customers, a retail store must project an image—a functional and psychological picture in the consumer's mind—that appeals to its target market. Store environment, merchandise quality, and service quality are key determinants of store image. **Atmospherics**, the physical elements in a store's design that appeal to consumers' emotions and encourage buying, help to create an image and position a retailer. Retailers can use different elements— music, color, and complexity of layout and merchandise presentation—to influence customer attention, mood, and shopping behavior.

Exterior atmospheric elements include the appearance of the storefront, display windows, store entrances, and degree of traffic congestion. Exterior atmospherics are particularly important to new customers, who tend to judge an unfamiliar store by its outside appearance and may not enter if they feel intimidated by the building or inconvenienced by the parking lot.

Interior atmospheric elements include aesthetic considerations, such as lighting, wall and floor coverings, dressing facilities, and store fixtures. Interior sensory elements contribute significantly to atmosphere. Bars, for example, consider several factors when it comes to atmospherics, including music tempo and volume, lighting, cleanliness, and physical layout. Most bars tend to sell a similar range of products, so they use atmospherics extensively to differentiate themselves and create a unique environment. In order for a bar to be successful and retain customers, it must monitor atmospheric variables and focus on maintaining customer comfort levels, which may vary depending on target audience. Bar patrons tend to be recreationally and socially motivated, rather than task motivated, so the layout must create a sense of flow and spread the crowd to the right places so customers do not feel claustrophobic.[16]

Color can attract shoppers to a retail display. Many fast-food restaurants use bright colors, such as red and yellow, because these have been shown to make customers feel hungrier and eat faster, which increases turnover. Sound is another important sensory component of atmosphere. A low-end, family dining restaurant might play fast pop music to encourage customers to eat quickly and leave, increasing turnover and sales. A high-end restaurant, on the other hand, will opt to play classical music to enhance the dining experience

retail positioning Identifying an unserved or underserved market segment and serving it through a strategy that distinguishes the retailer from others in the minds of consumers in that segment

atmospherics The physical elements in a store's design that appeal to consumers' emotions and encourage buying

iStock.com/SolStock

Atmospherics
Atmospherics in restaurants can greatly influence customers' experiences. The owner of this restaurant spent considerable resources on atmospherics such as fixtures, lighting, music, and furniture to favorably influence the customer experience and increase customer satisfaction.

and encourage patrons to indulge in multiple courses. Many retailers employ scent, especially food aromas, to attract customers. Most consumers expect the scent of a store to be congruent with the products that are sold there. For example, Starbucks should smell like its coffee, Panera like its freshly baked bread, and Yankee Candle like its scented candles. Studies show that scents which consumers can process easily tend to increase spending, whereas more complex scents do not.[17] Online retailers are not exempt from concern over atmospherics either. Such elements as the layout of a site and the content of digital ads that appear on that site can affect consumer mood and shopping behavior.[18]

14-3e Category Management

Category management is a retail strategy of managing groups of similar, often substitutable products produced by different manufacturers. It developed in the food industry because supermarkets were concerned about competitive behavior among manufacturers. Supermarkets use category management to allocate space for their many product categories, such as cosmetics, cereals, and soups. The assortment of merchandise a store chooses is strategic and meant to improve sales and enhance customer satisfaction.

Category management is part of developing a collaborative supply chain, which enhances value for customers. Successful category management involves collecting and analyzing data on sales and consumers and sharing the information between the retailer and manufacturer. Walmart, for example, has developed strong supplier relationships with major manufacturers like Procter & Gamble. Collaborative supply chains should designate one source to develop a system for collecting information on demand, consumer behavior, and optimal product allocations. The key is cooperative interaction between the manufacturers of category products and the retailer to create maximum success for all parties in the supply chain. Because category management can be such an important consideration for retailers, many global firms belong to the Category Management Association, which provides networking opportunities and information for member firms.[19]

| 14-4 DIRECT MARKETING, DIRECT SELLING, AND VENDING

LO 14-4 Identify the various forms of direct marketing, direct selling, and vending.

Although retailers are the most visible members of the supply chain, many products are sold outside the confines of a retail store. Direct selling and direct marketing account for an increasing proportion of product sales globally. Products also may be sold in automatic vending machines, but these account for a very small minority of all retail sales.

14-4a Direct Marketing

Direct marketing is the use of the telephone, Internet, and nonpersonal media to communicate product and organizational information to customers, who can then purchase products via mail, telephone, or the Internet. Direct marketing is one type of nonstore retailing. Sales through direct marketing activities are significant, accounting for about 8.5 percent of the United States' entire GDP.[20]

Nonstore retailing is the selling of products outside the confines of a retail facility. It is a form of direct marketing that accounts for an increasing percentage of total retail sales, particularly as online retailing becomes more prevalent. Direct marketing can occur through online retailing, catalog marketing, direct-response marketing, telemarketing, and television home shopping.

Online Retailing

Online retailing makes products available to buyers through Internet connections. Online retailing is a rapidly-growing segment that most retailers view as vital to business. Online retail

category management A retail strategy of managing groups of similar, often substitutable products produced by different manufacturers

direct marketing The use of the telephone, Internet, and nonpersonal media to introduce products to customers, who can then purchase them via mail, telephone, or the Internet

nonstore retailing The selling of products outside the confines of a retail facility

online retailing Retailing that makes products available to buyers through Internet connections

sales in the United States have grown to $395 billion, almost 42 percent of all retail sales.[21] One company that sells only online is Wayfair, which is striving to become the Amazon of furniture sales. The company offers 7 million products to furnish every room in the house, which it distributes through a network of 7,000 suppliers. For each item on its website, Wayfair specifies up to 100 pieces of information to help overcome consumer reluctance to buy furniture without trying it out first.[22]

Online retailing satisfies an increasing expectation among consumers to have multiple channels available to obtain the goods and services they desire at their convenience. Consumers can perform a wide variety of shopping-related tasks online, including purchasing virtually anything they desire. They can track down rare collectibles, refill their eyeglass prescriptions, and even purchase high-end jewelry or gourmet products. Banks and brokerages offer consumers online access to their accounts, where they can perform a wide variety of activities, such as money transfers and stock trading. With advances in computer technology continuing and consumers ever more pressed for time, online retailing will continue to escalate.

Online Retailing
Amazon sells millions of products online, which can be grouped into more than 40 different categories.

Catalog Marketing

In **catalog marketing**, an organization provides a catalog from which customers make selections and place orders by mail, telephone, or the Internet. Catalog marketing began in 1872, when Montgomery Ward issued its first catalog to rural families. There are thousands of catalog marketing companies in the United States, many of which also publish online. Some catalog marketers sell products spread over multiple product lines, while others are more specialized. Many companies, including Lands' End, Pottery Barn, and Crate & Barrel, employ a multichannel strategy and sell via catalogs, online, and through retail stores in major metropolitan areas. These retailers generally offer considerable product depth for just a few lines of products. Still other catalog companies specialize in products from a single product line such as JC Whitney's century-old auto-parts catalogs.

The advantages of catalog retailing include efficiency and convenience for customers because they do not have to visit a store. The retailer benefits by being able to locate in remote, low-cost areas, save on expensive store fixtures, and reduce both personal selling and store operating expenses. On the other hand, catalog retailing is inflexible, provides limited service, and is most effective for a select set of products.

catalog marketing A type of marketing in which an organization provides a catalog from which customers make selections and place orders by mail, telephone, or the Internet

direct-response marketing A type of marketing in which a retailer advertises a product and makes it available through mail or telephone orders

Direct-Response Marketing

Direct-response marketing occurs when a retailer advertises a product and makes it available through mail or telephone orders. Generally, customers use a credit card, but other forms of payment may be permitted. Direct-response marketing through television remains a multi-billion-dollar industry, although it now competes with the Internet for customers' attention. This marketing method has resulted in some products

Catalog Marketing
IKEA uses catalog marketing to sell its products. IKEA also employs online marketing and has brick-and-mortar stores.

gaining widespread popularity. You may have heard of the Shake Weight, Snuggie, and Magic Bullet—all of which became popular through direct-response television marketing campaigns. Direct-response marketing is also conducted by sending letters, samples, brochures, or booklets to prospects on a mailing list and asking that they order the advertised products by mail or telephone. In general, products must be priced above $20 to justify the advertising and distribution costs associated with direct-response marketing.

Telemarketing

A number of organizations use the telephone to strengthen the effectiveness of traditional marketing methods. **Telemarketing** is the performance of marketing-related activities by telephone. Some organizations use a prescreened list of prospective clients. Telemarketing can help to generate sales leads, improve customer service, speed up payments on past-due accounts, raise funds for nonprofit organizations, and gather marketing data.

However, increasingly restrictive telemarketing laws have made it a less appealing marketing method. In 2003, the U.S. Congress implemented a national do-not-call registry, which has more than 223 million numbers on it. The Federal Trade Commission (FTC) enforces violations, and companies are subject to fines of up to $16,000 for each call made to numbers on the list. The Federal Communications Commission (FCC) ruled that companies are no longer allowed to call customers using prerecorded marketing calls—"robocalls"—and require an "opt-out" mechanism for consumers who do not wish to receive calls. Companies that are still allowed to make telemarketing phone calls must pay for access to the do-not-call registry and must obtain updated numbers from the registry at least every three days. Certain exceptions do apply to no-call lists. For example, charitable, political, and telephone survey organizations are not restricted by the national registry. However, new technologies and less expensive calling rates mean that some unscrupulous firms are ignoring the do-not-call registry and using robocalls for telemarketing purposes. The FTC fined Consumer Education Group $2.3 million for repeatedly making telemarketing calls to registered phone numbers.[23]

Television Home Shopping

Television home shopping presents products to television viewers, encouraging them to order through toll-free numbers and pay with credit cards. The Home Shopping Network originated and popularized this format. The most popular products sold through television home shopping are jewelry (40 percent of total sales), clothing, housewares, and electronics. Most homes in the United States have access to at least one home shopping channel, with the Home Shopping Network and QVC being the largest.

The television home shopping format offers several benefits. Products can be demonstrated easily, and an adequate amount of time can be spent showing the product so viewers are well-informed. The length of time a product is shown depends not only on the time required for performing demonstrations, but also on whether the product is selling. Once the calls peak and begin to decline, hosts switch to a new product. Other benefits are that customers can shop at their convenience and from the comfort of their homes.

14-4b **Direct Selling**

Direct selling is the marketing of products to ultimate consumers through face-to-face sales presentations at home or in the workplace. The top five global direct selling companies are Amway, Avon, Herbalife, Vorwerk & Co., and Infinitus. Three of these companies—Avon, Amway, and Herbalife—are based in the United States. Direct selling is a highly valuable industry. Amway alone has nearly $9.5 billion in annual sales.[24] Direct selling was once associated with door-to-door sales, but it has evolved into a professional industry where most contacts with buyers are prearranged through electronic communication

telemarketing The performance of marketing-related activities by telephone

television home shopping A form of selling in which products are presented to television viewers, who can buy them by calling a toll-free number and paying with a credit card

direct selling Marketing products to ultimate consumers through face-to-face sales presentations at home or in the workplace or personal contacts. Today, companies identify customers through the mail, telephone, Internet, social networks, or shopping-mall intercepts and then set up appointments with salespeople. Direct selling is most successful in other countries, particularly collective societies like China, where Amway has higher sales than its domestic market, the United States.

Although the majority of direct selling takes place on an individual, or person-to-person, basis, it sometimes also includes the use of a group, or "party," plan. With a party plan, a consumer acts as a host and invites friends and associates to view merchandise in a group setting, where a salesperson demonstrates products. The informal atmosphere helps salespeople to overcome customers' reluctance and encourages them to buy. Tupperware and Mary Kay were the pioneers of this selling technique and remain global leaders.

Direct Selling
Mary Kay engages in direct selling through its consultants. The company also markets products online.

Direct selling has benefits and limitations. It gives the marketer an opportunity to demonstrate the product in an environment—usually customers' homes—where it most likely would be used. The seller can give the customer personal attention, and the product can be presented to the customer at a convenient time and location. Product categories that have been highly successful for direct selling include cosmetics and personal-care products, health products, jewelry, accessories, and household products. Personal attention to the customer is the foundation on which direct sellers have built their businesses. However, because commissions for salespeople are high, ranging from 30 to 50 percent of the sales price, and great effort is required to identify promising prospects, overall costs of direct selling make it the most expensive form of retailing. Furthermore, some customers view direct selling negatively, owing to unscrupulous and fraudulent practices used by some direct sellers. Some communities even have local ordinances that control or, in some cases, prohibit direct selling. Despite these negative views held by some individuals, direct selling is still alive and well, bringing in annual revenues of over $32.1 billion in the United States and $183.7 billion worldwide.[25]

14-4c **Automatic Vending**

Automatic vending is the use of machines to dispense products. Automatic vending is one of the most impersonal forms of retailing, and it accounts for a very small minority of all retail sales. Small, standardized, routinely purchased products, such as snacks and drinks, are best suited for sale in vending machines because consumers buy them out of convenience. Machines in areas of heavy foot traffic provide efficient and continuous service to consumers. High-volume areas, such as in commercial centers of large cities or in airports, may offer a wider range of automatic vending product options. Vending machines have even taken on cult popularity among some urban-dwelling consumers. In some cities, customers can find a wide variety of products dispensed via vending machines, even high-end items such as gold bars, cars, and iPods as well as cosmetics and food. Snap, the social media site, developed a unique smiling yellow vending machine to distribute its $130 Spectacles video sunglasses.[26]

Because vending machines need only a small amount of space and no sales personnel, this retailing method has some advantages over stores. The advantages are partly offset, however, by the high costs of equipment and the need for servicing and repairs. Many machines can now convey status reports via the Internet, helping marketers identify which items are selling and need to be restocked and which may have become stale and need to be replaced with items with a greater likelihood of selling.

automatic vending The use of machines to dispense products

franchising An arrangement in which a supplier (franchisor) grants a dealer (franchisee) the right to sell products in exchange for some type of consideration

| 14-5 FRANCHISING

LO 14-5 Describe franchising and its benefits and weaknesses.

Franchising is an arrangement in which a supplier, or franchisor, grants a dealer, or franchisee, the right to sell products in exchange for some type of consideration. The franchisor may receive a percentage of total sales in exchange for furnishing equipment, buildings, management know-how, and marketing assistance to the franchisee. The franchisee supplies labor and capital, operates the franchised business, and agrees to abide by the provisions of the franchise agreement. Table 14.2 lists the leading U.S. franchises, as well as the types of products they sell, number of franchise outlets, and start-up costs.

Because of changes in the international marketplace, shifting employment options in the United States, the large U.S. service economy, and corporate interest in more joint-venture activity, franchising is a very popular retail option. There are 732,842 franchise establishments in the United States, which provide 7.6 million jobs across a variety of industries, and generate $674 billion in sales.[27]

Franchising offers several advantages to both the franchisee and the franchisor. It enables a franchisee to start a business with limited capital and benefit from the business experience of others. Franchised outlets are generally more successful than independently owned businesses. Generally speaking, franchises have lower failure rates than independent retail establishments. However, franchise failure rates vary greatly depending on the particular franchise. Nationally advertised franchises, such as Subway and Burger King, are often

TABLE 14.2   TOP U.S. FRANCHISORS AND THEIR START-UP COSTS

Rank	Franchise and Description	Start-up Costs
1	**7-Eleven Inc.** Convenience store	$37,000–$1,600,000
2	**McDonald's** Fast food	$1,000,000–$2,200,000
3	**Dunkin' Donuts** Bakeries	$229,000–$1,700,000
4	**The UPS Store** Business support centers	$159,000–$435,000
5	**Jimmy John's Gourmet Sandwiches** Sandwiches	$326,000–$555,000
6	**Dairy Queen** Fast food	$361,000–$1,800,000
7	**Ace Hardware** Hardware	$273,000–$1,600,000
8	**Wingstop Restaurants** Chicken	$303,000–$923,000
9	**Sport Clips** Haircare	$183,000–$352,000
10	**RE/MAX LLC** Real estate services	$38,000–$224,000

Source: "2017 Top Franchises from Entrepreneur's Franchise 500 List," *Entrepreneur*, www.entrepreneur.com /franchise500 (accessed March 10, 2017).

assured of sales as soon as they open because customers already know what to expect. If business problems arise, the franchisee can obtain guidance and advice from the franchisor at little or no cost. Also, the franchisee receives materials to use in local advertising and can benefit from national promotional campaigns sponsored by the franchisor.

Through franchise arrangements, the franchisor gains fast and selective product distribution without incurring the high cost of constructing and operating its own outlets. The franchisor, therefore, has more available capital for expanding production and advertising. It can also ensure, through the franchise agreement, that outlets are maintained and operated according to its own standards. Some franchisors do permit their franchisees to modify their menus, hours, or other operating elements to better match their target market's needs. The franchisor benefits from the fact that the franchisee, being a sole proprietor in most cases, is likely to be very highly motivated to succeed. Success of the franchise means more sales, which translates into higher income for the franchisor.

Franchising
Chick-Fil-A is a franchise, so individual stores are owned and managed by the franchisee.

Franchise arrangements also have several drawbacks. The franchisor dictates many aspects of the business: decor, menu, design of employees' uniforms, types of signs, hours of operation, and numerous details of business operations. In addition, franchisees must pay to use the franchisor's name, products, and assistance. Usually, there is a one-time franchise fee and continuing royalty and advertising fees, often collected as a percentage of sales. Franchisees often must work very hard, putting in 10 to 12 hours a day six or seven days a week. In some cases, franchise agreements are not uniform, meaning one franchisee may pay more than another for the same services. Finally, the franchisor gives up a certain amount of control when entering into a franchise agreement. Consequently, individual establishments may not be operated exactly according to the franchisor's standards.

14-6 WHOLESALING

LO 14-6 Explain the nature and functions of wholesalers.

Wholesaling refers to all transactions in which products are bought for resale, for making other products, or for general business operations. It does not include exchanges with ultimate consumers. A **wholesaler** is an individual or organization that sells products that are bought for resale, making other products, or general business operations. In other words, wholesalers buy products and resell them to reseller, government, and institutional users. For instance, Sysco, the nation's number-one food-service distributor, supplies restaurants, hotels, schools, industrial caterers, and hospitals with everything from frozen and fresh food and paper products to medical and cleaning supplies. Wholesaling activities are not limited to goods. Service companies, such as financial institutions, also use active wholesale networks. There are 416,593 wholesaling establishments in the United States, and more than half of all products sold in this country pass through these firms.[28]

Wholesalers may engage in many supply-chain management activities, which we will discuss below. In addition to bearing the primary responsibility for the physical distribution of products from manufacturers to retailers, wholesalers may also establish information systems that help producers and retailers better manage the supply chain from producer to customer. Many wholesalers use information technology and the Internet to share information among intermediaries, employees, customers, and suppliers and facilitating agencies, such as trucking companies and warehouse firms. Some firms make their databases and marketing

wholesaling Transactions in which products are bought for resale, for making other products, or for general business operations

wholesaler An individual or organization that sells products that are bought for resale, for making other products, or for general business operations

information systems available to their supply-chain partners to facilitate order processing, shipping, and product development and to share information about changing market conditions and customer desires. As a result, some wholesalers play a key role in supply-chain management decisions.

14-6a Services Provided by Wholesalers

Wholesalers provide essential services to both producers and retailers. By initiating sales contacts with a producer and selling diverse products to retailers, wholesalers serve as an extension of the producer's sales force. Wholesalers also provide financial assistance. They often pay for transporting goods, reduce a producer's warehousing expenses and inventory investment by holding goods in inventory, extend credit and assume losses from buyers who turn out to be poor credit risks, and can be a source of working capital when they buy a producer's output in cash. Wholesalers also serve as conduits for information within the marketing channel, keeping producers up-to-date on market developments and passing along the manufacturers' promotional plans to other intermediaries. Using wholesalers, therefore, gives producers a distinct advantage because the specialized services that wholesalers perform allow producers to concentrate on developing and manufacturing products that match customers' needs and wants.

Wholesalers support retailers by assisting with marketing strategy, especially the distribution component. Wholesalers also help retailers select inventory. They are often specialists on market conditions and experts at negotiating final purchases. In industries in which obtaining supplies is important, skilled buying is indispensable. Effective wholesalers make an effort to understand the businesses of their customers. They can reduce a retailer's burden of looking for and coordinating supply sources. If the wholesaler purchases for several different buyers, expenses can be shared by all customers. Furthermore, whereas a manufacturer's salesperson offers retailers only a few products at a time, independent wholesalers always have a wide range of products available. Thus, through partnerships, wholesalers and retailers can forge successful relationships for the benefit of customers. Organizations like the National Association of Wholesaler-Distributors can provide firms with solutions to their wholesaler issues, including finding firms that carry out various services.[29]

The distinction between services performed by wholesalers and those provided by other businesses has blurred in recent years. Changes in the competitive nature of business, especially the growth of strong retail chains like Walmart, Home Depot, and Best Buy, are altering supply-chain relationships. In many product categories, such as electronics, furniture, and even food products, retailers have discovered that they can deal directly with producers, performing wholesaling activities themselves at a lower cost. However, when a wholesaler is eliminated from a marketing channel, wholesaling activities still have to be performed by a member of the supply chain, whether a producer, retailer, or facilitating agency. Most retailers can rely on computer technology to expedite ordering, track deliveries, and monitor handling of goods. Thus, technology has allowed retailers to take over some wholesaling functions.

14-6b Types of Wholesalers

A wholesaler is classified according to several criteria, including whether it is independently owned or owned by a producer, whether it takes title to (owns) the products it handles, the range of services provided, and the breadth and depth of its product lines. Using these criteria, we discuss three general types of wholesaling establishments: merchant wholesalers, agents and brokers, and manufacturers' sales branches and offices.

Merchant Wholesalers

merchant wholesalers Independently owned businesses that take title to goods, assume ownership risks, and buy and resell products to other wholesalers, business customers, or retailers

Merchant wholesalers are independently owned businesses that take title to goods, assume risks associated with ownership, and generally buy and resell products to other wholesalers,

ZUMA Press Inc/Alamy Stock Photo

Merchant Wholesaler
Grainger is a full service, limited-line wholesaler of electrical equipment and supplies.

business customers, or retailers. A producer is likely to rely on merchant wholesalers when selling directly to customers would be economically unfeasible. Merchant wholesalers are also useful for providing market coverage, making sales contacts, storing inventory, handling orders, collecting market information, and furnishing customer support. Some merchant wholesalers are even involved in packaging and developing private brands. Merchant wholesalers go by various names, including *wholesaler, jobber, distributor, assembler, exporter,* and *importer.* They fall into two broad categories: full service and limited service.

Full Service Wholesalers

Full service wholesalers perform the widest possible range of wholesaling functions. Customers rely on them for product availability, suitable product assortments, breaking large shipments into smaller ones, financial assistance, and technical advice and service. Full service wholesalers handle either consumer or business products and provide numerous marketing services to their customers. Many large grocery wholesalers help retailers with store design, site selection, personnel training, financing, merchandising, advertising, coupon redemption, and scanning. Macdonalds Consolidated is a Canadian full service wholesaler of meat, dairy, and produce goods for grocery retailers in North America. Macdonalds offers such services as communications management, document management, retailer flyers, and merchandising, and it offers rebates for valued customers.[30] Although full service wholesalers often earn higher gross margins than other wholesalers, their operating expenses are also higher because they perform a wider range of functions.

Full service wholesalers are categorized as general-merchandise, limited-line, and specialty-line wholesalers. **General-merchandise wholesalers** carry a wide product mix, but offer limited depth within product lines. They deal in products such as drugs, nonperishable foods, cosmetics, detergents, and tobacco. **Limited-line wholesalers** carry only a few product lines, such as groceries, lighting fixtures, or oil-well drilling equipment, but offer an extensive assortment of products within those lines. AmerisourceBergen Corporation, for example, is a limited-line wholesaler of pharmaceuticals and health products.[31]

General-line wholesalers provide a range of services similar to those of general-merchandise wholesalers. **Specialty-line wholesalers** offer the narrowest range of products,

full service wholesalers Merchant wholesalers that perform the widest range of wholesaling functions

general-merchandise wholesalers Full service wholesalers with a wide product mix but limited depth within product lines

limited-line wholesalers Full service wholesalers that carry only a few product lines but many products within those lines

specialty-line wholesalers Full service wholesalers that carry only a single product line or a few items within a product line

rack jobbers Full service, specialty-line wholesalers that own and maintain display racks in stores

limited-service wholesalers Merchant wholesalers that provide some services and specialize in a few functions

cash-and-carry wholesalers Limited-service wholesalers whose customers pay cash and furnish transportation

truck wholesalers Limited-service wholesalers that transport products directly to customers for inspection and selection

drop shippers Limited-service wholesalers that take title to goods and negotiate sales but never actually take possession of products

mail-order wholesalers Limited-service wholesalers that sell products through catalogs

usually a single product line or a few items within a product line. **Rack jobbers** are full service, specialty-line wholesalers that own and maintain display racks in supermarkets, drugstores, and discount and variety stores. They set up displays, mark merchandise, stock shelves, and maintain billing and inventory records. Rack jobbers specialize in non-food items with high profit margins, such as health and beauty aids, books, magazines, hosiery, and greeting cards.

Limited-Service Wholesalers

Limited-service wholesalers provide fewer marketing services than do full service wholesalers and specialize in just a few functions. Producers perform the remaining functions or pass them on to customers or other intermediaries. Limited-service wholesalers take title to merchandise, but often do not deliver the merchandise, grant credit, provide marketing information, store inventory, or plan ahead for customers' future needs. Because they offer restricted services, limited-service wholesalers charge lower rates and have smaller profit margins than do full service wholesalers. The decision about whether to use a limited-service or a full service wholesaler depends on the structure of the marketing channel and the need to manage the supply chain to create a competitive advantage. Although limited-service wholesalers are less common than other types, they are important in the distribution of products like specialty foods, perishable items, construction materials, and coal.

Table 14.3 summarizes the services provided by four typical limited-service wholesalers: cash-and-carry wholesalers, truck wholesalers, drop shippers, and mail-order wholesalers. **Cash-and-carry wholesalers** are intermediaries whose customers—usually small businesses—pay cash and furnish transportation. Cash-and-carry wholesalers usually handle a limited line of products with a high turnover rate, such as groceries, building materials, and electrical or office supplies. Many small retailers that other types of wholesalers will not take on because of their small size survive because of cash-and-carry wholesalers. **Truck wholesalers**, sometimes called *truck jobbers*, transport a limited line of products directly to customers for on-the-spot inspection and selection. They are often small operators who drive their own trucks. They usually have regular routes, calling on retailers and other institutions to determine their needs. **Drop shippers**, also known as *desk jobbers*, take title to products and negotiate sales but never take actual possession of the products. They forward orders from retailers, business buyers, or other wholesalers to manufacturers and arrange for carload shipments of items to be delivered directly from producers to these customers. They assume responsibility for products during the entire transaction, including the costs of any unsold goods. **Mail-order wholesalers** use catalogs instead of a sales force to sell products to retail and business buyers. Wholesale mail-order houses generally feature

TABLE 14.3	SERVICES THAT LIMITED-SERVICE WHOLESALERS PROVIDE			
	Cash-and-Carry	Truck	Drop Shipper	Mail Order
Physical possession of merchandise	Yes	Yes	No	Yes
Personal sales calls on customers	No	Yes	No	No
Information about market conditions	No	Some	Yes	Yes
Advice to customers	No	Some	Yes	No
Stocking and maintenance of merchandise in customers' stores	No	No	No	No
Credit to customers	No	No	Yes	Some
Delivery of merchandise to customers	No	Yes	No	No

cosmetics, specialty foods, sporting goods, office supplies, and automotive parts. Mail-order wholesaling enables buyers to choose and order particular catalog items for delivery through various mail carriers. This is a convenient and effective method of selling items to customers in remote areas that other wholesalers might find unprofitable to serve. The Internet has provided an opportunity for mail-order wholesalers to serve a larger number of buyers, selling products over their websites and having the products shipped by the manufacturers.

Agents and Brokers

Agents and brokers negotiate purchases and expedite sales but do not take title to products. Sometimes called *functional middlemen*, they perform a limited number of services in exchange for a commission, which generally is based on the product's selling price. **Agents** represent either buyers or sellers on a permanent basis, whereas **brokers** are intermediaries that buyers or sellers employ temporarily.

Although agents and brokers perform even fewer functions than limited-service wholesalers, they are usually specialists in particular products or types of customers and can provide valuable sales expertise. They know their markets well and often form long-lasting associations with customers. Agents and brokers enable manufacturers to expand sales when resources are limited, benefit from the services of a trained sales force, and hold down personal selling costs. Table 14.4 summarizes the services provided by agents and brokers.

Manufacturers' agents, which account for more than half of all agent wholesalers, are independent intermediaries that represent two or more sellers and usually offer complete product lines to customers. They sell and take orders year-round, much as a manufacturer's sales force does. Restricted to a particular territory, a manufacturer's agent handles noncompeting and complementary products. The relationship between the agent and the manufacturer is governed by written contracts that outline territories, selling price, order handling, and terms of sale relating to delivery, service, and warranties. Manufacturers' agents have little or no control over producers' pricing and marketing policies. They do not extend credit and may be unable to provide technical advice. Manufacturers' agents are commonly used in sales of apparel, machinery and equipment, steel, furniture, automotive products, electrical goods, and some food items.

Selling agents market either all of a specified product line or a manufacturer's entire output. They perform every wholesaling activity except taking title to products. Selling agents usually assume the sales function for several producers simultaneously, and some firms may use them in place of a marketing department. In fact, selling agents are used most often by small producers or by manufacturers that have difficulty maintaining a marketing department because of such factors as seasonal production. In contrast to manufacturers' agents, selling agents generally have no territorial limits and have complete authority over prices, promotion, and distribution. To avoid conflicts of interest, selling agents represent

agents Intermediaries that represent either buyers or sellers on a permanent basis

brokers Intermediaries that bring buyers and sellers together temporarily

manufacturers' agents Independent intermediaries that represent two or more sellers and usually offer customers complete product lines

selling agents Intermediaries that market a whole product line or a manufacturer's entire output

TABLE 14.4	SERVICES THAT AGENTS AND BROKERS PROVIDE			
	Manufacturers' Agents	Selling Agents	Commission Merchants	Brokers
Physical possession of merchandise	Some	Some	Yes	No
Long-term relationship with buyers or sellers	Yes	Yes	Yes	No
Representation of competing product lines	No	No	Yes	Yes
Limited geographic territory	Yes	No	No	No
Credit to customers	No	Yes	Some	No
Delivery of merchandise to customers	Some	Yes	Yes	No

commission merchants
Agents that receive goods on consignment from local sellers and negotiate sales in large, central markets

sales branches
Manufacturer-owned intermediaries that sell products and provide support services to the manufacturer's sales force

sales offices Manufacturer-owned operations that provide services normally associated with agents

noncompeting product lines. They play a key role in advertising, marketing research, and credit policies of the sellers they represent, at times even advising on product development and packaging.

Commission merchants receive goods on consignment from local sellers and negotiate sales in large, central markets. Sometimes called *factor merchants*, these agents have broad powers regarding prices and terms of sale. They specialize in obtaining the best price possible under market conditions. Most often found in agricultural marketing, commission merchants take possession of truckloads of commodities, arrange for necessary grading or storage, and transport the commodities to auction or markets where they are sold. When sales are completed, the agents deduct a commission and the expense of making the sale and turn over remaining profits to the producer. Commission merchants also offer planning assistance and sometimes extend credit, but usually do not provide promotional support.

A broker's primary purpose is to bring buyers and sellers together. Thus, brokers perform fewer functions than other intermediaries. They are not involved in financing or physical possession, have no authority to set prices, and assume almost no risks. Instead, they offer customers specialized knowledge of a particular commodity and a network of established contacts. Brokers are especially useful to sellers of products such as supermarket goods and real estate. Food brokers, for example, connect food and general merchandise firms to retailer-owned and merchant wholesalers, grocery chains, food processors, and business buyers.

Manufacturers' Sales Branches and Offices

Sometimes called *manufacturers' wholesalers*, manufacturers' sales branches and offices resemble merchant wholesalers' operations. **Sales branches** are manufacturer-owned intermediaries that sell products and provide support services to the manufacturer's sales force. Situated away from the manufacturing plant, they are usually located where large customers are concentrated and demand is high. They offer credit, deliver goods, give promotional assistance, and furnish other services. Customers include retailers, business buyers, and other wholesalers. Manufacturers of electrical supplies, plumbing supplies, lumber, and automotive parts often have branch operations.

Sales offices are manufacturer-owned operations that provide services normally associated with agents. Like sales branches, they are located away from manufacturing plants, but unlike sales branches, they carry no inventory. A manufacturer's sales office (or branch) may sell products that enhance the manufacturer's own product line.

Manufacturers may set up these branches or offices to reach their customers more effectively by performing wholesaling functions themselves. A manufacturer also might set up such a facility when specialized wholesaling services are not available through existing intermediaries. Performing wholesaling and physical distribution activities through a manufacturer's sales branch or office can strengthen supply-chain efficiency. In some situations, though, a manufacturer may bypass its sales office or branches entirely—for example, if the producer decides to serve large retailer customers directly.

Chapter Review

14-1 Describe the purpose and function of retailers in the marketing channel.

Retailing includes all transactions in which buyers are ultimate consumers who intend to consume products for personal, family, or household use. Retailers, organizations that sell products primarily to ultimate consumers,

are important links in the marketing channel because they are both marketers for and customers of wholesalers and producers. Retailers add value, provide services, and assist in making product selections. Many retailers now engage in multichannel retailing by employing multiple distribution channels that complement their brick-and-mortar stores with websites, catalogs, and apps.

14-2 Classify the major types of retailers.

Retail stores can be classified according to the breadth of products offered. Two broad categories are general merchandise retailers and specialty retailers. There are eight primary types of general merchandise retailers. Department stores are large retail organizations organized by departments and characterized by wide product mixes in considerable depth. Discount stores are self-service, low-price, general merchandise outlets. Extreme-value stores are much smaller than conventional discount stores and offer even lower prices on smaller size name-brand nonperishable household items. Convenience stores are small, self-service stores that are open long hours and carry a narrow assortment of products, usually convenience items. Supermarkets are large, self-service food stores that carry some non-food products. Superstores are giant retail outlets that carry all the products found in supermarkets and most consumer products purchased on a routine basis. Hypermarkets combine aspects of supermarket and discount store shopping in one location. Warehouse clubs are large-scale, members-only discount operations. Finally, warehouse and catalog showrooms are low-cost operations characterized by industrial methods of materials handling and display, large inventories, and minimal services.

Specialty retailers offer substantial assortments in a few product lines. They carry narrow product mixes with deep product lines. Category killers are large specialty stores that concentrate on a major product category and compete on the basis of low prices and enormous product availability. Off-price retailers sell brand-name manufacturers' seconds and product overruns at deep discounts.

14-3 Explore strategic issues in retailing.

To increase sales and store patronage, retailers must consider a number of key strategic issues. Location determines the area from which a store draws its customers. It is the least flexible ingredient in the marketing mix and should be considered carefully. When evaluating potential sites, retailers take into account a variety of factors, including the location of the firm's target market within the trading area, kinds of products sold, availability of public transportation, customer characteristics, and competitors' locations. Retailers can choose among several types of locations, including freestanding structures, traditional business districts, traditional planned shopping centers (neighborhood, community, regional, and superregional), or nontraditional shopping centers (lifestyle, power, and outlet). As consumer demographics and shopping trends change, retailers are adjusting by exploiting new technologies to improve the store experience and give consumers more shopping platforms.

Retail positioning involves identifying an unserved or underserved market segment and reaching it through a strategy that distinguishes the retailer from the competition. Store image, which is a subjective element, derives from atmospherics, location, products offered, customer services, prices, promotion, and the store's overall reputation. Atmospherics refers to the physical and sensory elements of a store's design that can be adjusted to appeal to consumers' emotions and thus induce them to buy. Category management is a retail strategy of managing groups of similar, often substitutable, products produced by different manufacturers.

14-4 Identify the various forms of direct marketing, direct selling, and vending.

Direct marketing is the use of the telephone, Internet, and nonpersonal media to communicate product and organizational information to customers, who can then purchase products via mail, telephone, or online. Direct marketing is a type of nonstore retailing, the selling of goods or services outside the confines of a retail facility. Direct marketing may occur online (online retailing), through a catalog (catalog marketing), advertising (direct-response marketing), telephone (telemarketing), or television (television home shopping). Two other types of nonstore retailing are direct selling and automatic vending. Direct selling is the marketing of products to ultimate consumers through face-to-face sales presentations at home or in the workplace. Automatic vending is the use of machines to dispense products.

14-5 Describe franchising and its benefits and weaknesses.

Franchising is an arrangement in which a supplier grants a dealer the right to sell products in exchange for some type of consideration. Franchise enables a franchisee to start a business with limited capital and benefit from the business experience of others. Franchised outlets are generally more successful and have lower failure rates than independently owned businesses. The franchisee can obtain guidance and advice from the franchisor at little or no cost. Also, the franchisee receives materials to use in local advertising and can benefit from national promotional campaigns. However, the franchisor can dictate many aspects of the business. Franchisees must pay to use the franchisor's name, products, and assistance. Franchisees often must work very hard, putting in long days without breaks. In some cases, franchise agreements are not uniform, meaning one franchisee may pay more than another for the same services. Finally, the franchisor gives up control when entering into a franchise agreement.

14-6 Explain the nature and functions of wholesalers.

Wholesaling consists of all transactions in which products are bought for resale, making other products, or general business operations. Wholesalers are individuals or organizations that facilitate and expedite wholesale exchanges. For producers, wholesalers are a source of financial assistance and information. By performing specialized accumulation and allocation functions, they allow producers to concentrate on manufacturing products. Wholesalers provide retailers with buying expertise, wide product lines, efficient distribution, and warehousing and storage.

There are different types of wholesalers. Merchant wholesalers are independently owned businesses that take title to goods and assume ownership risks. They are either full service wholesalers, offering the widest possible range of wholesaling functions, or limited-service wholesalers, providing only some marketing services and specializing in a few functions. Full service merchant wholesalers include a variety of types. General-merchandise wholesalers offer a wide, but relatively shallow product mix. Limited-line wholesalers offer extensive assortments within a few product lines. Specialty-line wholesalers carry only a single product line or a few items within a line. Finally, rack jobbers own and service display racks in supermarkets and other stores. Limited-service merchant wholesalers include various types as well. Cash-and-carry wholesalers sell to small businesses, require payment in cash, and do not deliver. Truck wholesalers sell a limited line of products from their own trucks directly to customers. Drop shippers own

goods and negotiate sales, but never take possession of products. And mail-order wholesalers sell to retail and business buyers through direct-mail catalogs.

Agents and brokers negotiate purchases and expedite sales in exchange for a commission, but they do not take title to products. Usually specializing in certain products, they can provide valuable sales expertise. Agents represent buyers or sellers on a permanent basis, and brokers are intermediaries that buyers and sellers employ temporarily to negotiate exchanges. Manufacturers' agents offer customers the complete product lines of two or more sellers. Selling agents market a complete product line or a producer's entire output and perform every wholesaling function except taking title to products. Commission merchants are agents that receive goods on consignment from local sellers and negotiate sales in large, central markets.

Manufacturers' sales branches and offices are owned by manufacturers. Sales branches sell products and provide support services for the manufacturer's sales force in a given location. Sales offices carry no inventory and function much as agents do.

 Go to www.cengagebrain.com for resources to help you master the content in this chapter as well as for materials that will expand your marketing knowledge!

Developing Your Marketing Plan

Distribution decisions in the marketing plan entail the movement of your product from the producer to the final consumer. An understanding of how and where your customer prefers to purchase products is critical to the development of the marketing plan. As you apply the information in this chapter to your plan, focus on the following issues:

1. Considering your product's attributes and your target market's (or markets') buying behavior, will your product likely be sold to the ultimate customer or to another member of the marketing channel?
2. If your product will be sold to the ultimate customer, what type of retailing establishment is most suitable to

your product? Consider the product's characteristics and your target market's buying behavior. Refer to Table 14.1 for types of general merchandise retailers.
3. Discuss how the characteristics of the retail establishment, such as location and store image, have an impact on the consumer's perception of your product.
4. Are direct marketing or direct selling methods appropriate for your product and target market?
5. If your product will be sold to another member in the marketing channel, discuss whether a merchant wholesaler, agent, or broker is most suitable as your channel customer.

Key Concepts

retailing 364
retailer 364
multichannel retailing 364
general-merchandise retailer 365
department stores 365
discount stores 366

extreme-value stores 367
convenience store 367
supermarkets 368
superstores 368
hypermarkets 368
warehouse clubs 369
warehouse showrooms 369

traditional specialty retailers 369
category killer 370
off-price retailers 370
neighborhood shopping center 372
community shopping center 372

regional shopping center 372
superregional shopping center 373
lifestyle shopping center 373
power shopping center 373

Issues for Discussion and Review

1. What value is added to a product by retailers? What value is added by retailers for producers and ultimate consumers?
2. What are the major differences between discount stores and department stores?
3. In what ways are traditional specialty stores and off-price retailers similar? How do they differ?
4. What major issues should be considered when determining a retail site location?
5. Describe the three major types of traditional shopping centers. Give an example of each type in your area.
6. Discuss the major factors that help to determine a retail store's image. How does atmosphere add value to products sold in a store?
7. How is door-to-door selling a form of retailing? Some consumers believe that direct-response orders bypass the retailer. Is this true?

8. If you were opening a retail business, would you prefer to open an independent store or own a store under a franchise arrangement? Explain your preference.
9. What services do wholesalers provide to producers and retailers?
10. What is the difference between a full service merchant wholesaler and a limited-service merchant wholesaler?
11. Drop shippers take title to products but do not accept physical possession of them, whereas commission merchants take physical possession of products but do not accept title. Defend the logic of classifying drop shippers as merchant wholesalers and commission merchants as agents.
12. Why are manufacturers' sales offices and branches classified as wholesalers? Which independent wholesalers are replaced by manufacturers' sales branches? By sales offices?

VIDEO CASE 14
Sephora: Brick or Click or App

In less than 50 years, Sephora has grown from a single store in France selling beauty products to an international retail presence of 2,000 stores selling 15,000 products in 33 countries. The company was founded in 1969, and from the start, in-store customers were encouraged to browse, examine, and test fragrances and cosmetics from a wide range of manufacturers. LVMH, a French company that owns upscale beauty brands like Guerlain and luxury fashion brands like Christian Dior, purchased Sephora in 1997. After successful expansion in Europe, Sephora entered the U.S. market in 1998 and launched an online store in 1999.

Where to open stores is a key decision for Sephora, as it is for every retailer. Because Sephora is in the beauty business, location is as much a decision about showcasing the brand and creating excitement as it is about attracting shoppers. The company has especially large, high-profile stores in prestigious neighborhoods like New York City's Fifth Avenue and Chicago's Magnificent Mile. Not only do these appeal to tourists and people who work nearby, they also make a public statement about the brand identity, the depth of merchandise available, and the personalized service.

When considering expansion possibilities, Sephora analyzes its database of online customers to identify geographic regions in which it has a sizable customer base. For example, Sephora decided to open its first store in Colorado after determining that many customers in the area were frequent buyers of merchandise on Sephora.com. The company also operates stores in shopping centers from coast to coast and hundreds of smaller stores inside JCPenney department stores (see this chapter's Emerging Trends box).

Unlike some retailers, Sephora does not pay its employees (known as "cast members") a commission for selling products, nor does it set sales quotas. As a result, employees can take the time to learn about each individual customer's needs, suggest various product options tailored to each customer, give away free samples, and demonstrate product use and technique during a complimentary makeover. Between Sephora's training and product-knowledge workshops conducted by manufacturers of every brand carried by the store, employees are ready and able to offer guidance about the full range of skin care products, cosmetics, and fragrances.

The Sephora Innovation Lab is busy developing new configurations and fixtures to enhance the in-store experience as well as providing digital options for customers. For the revamp of a Sephora store in San Francisco, the Lab created a separate area for group beauty lessons and a huge digital screen rotating user-generated content and merchandise images. For customer convenience, the Lab came up with a mobile app called Pocket Contour, which helps customers determine face shape and learn to apply the latest in contour makeup.

To encourage and reward customer loyalty, Sephora offers three frequent-buyer programs. The basic program includes a free birthday gift and free beauty classes. One level up, for customers who spend at least $350 in a year, the benefits include exclusive seasonal savings and gifts. The top level, for customers who spend at least $1,000 in a year, the benefits include free two-day shipping for online orders and invitations to special beauty events. All program members can view and manage their product preferences and purchases online or with an app. By opening "My Beauty Bag," customers can see what color or brand they purchased on a previous trip, and either reorder or buy something new in the store or via the app. No matter how customers like to browse and shop, Sephora wants to make the experience fun, convenient, and consistent with brand image.[32]

Questions for Discussion

1. What is Sephora's retail positioning and how does it differentiate the company?
2. Why would Sephora invest so heavily in apps and other technology that can substitute for the in-store customer experience?
3. Sephora is already using direct marketing to sell via online retailing. Would you suggest that the company participate in other direct marketing techniques? Explain your answer.

Part 6

Anton_Ivanov/Shutterstock.com

Promotion Decisions

PART 6 focuses on communication with target market members and other relevant groups. A specific marketing mix cannot satisfy people in a particular target market unless they are aware of the product and know where to find it. Some promotion decisions relate to a specific marketing mix; others are geared toward promoting the entire organization. **CHAPTER 15** discusses integrated marketing communications. It describes the communication process and the major promotional methods that can be included in promotion mixes. **CHAPTER 16** analyzes the major steps in developing an advertising campaign. It also explains what public relations is and how it can be used. **CHAPTER 17** deals with personal selling and the role it can play in a firm's promotional efforts. This chapter also explores the general characteristics of sales promotion and describes sales promotion techniques.

chapter 15

Integrated Marketing Communications

LEARNING OBJECTIVES

15-1 Define integrated marketing communications.

15-2 Describe the steps of the communication process.

15-3 Recognize the definition and objectives of promotion.

15-4 Summarize the four variables of the promotion mix.

15-5 Explain the factors that are used to determine a product's promotion mix.

15-6 Describe how word-of-mouth communication affects promotion.

15-7 Discuss how product placement impacts promotion.

15-8 List major criticisms and defenses of promotion.

Toyota Camry Finds the Key to Integrated Marketing

When Toyota was about to introduce its newest Camry model, it knew it needed to invest heavily in promotion. The company partnered with advertising agency Saatchi & Saatchi to develop an effective integrated marketing campaign. The team centered its campaign on the theme of love. It wanted to portray its newer model as sexy and edgy—a theme that would resonate with younger buyers.

The first step was to sell off the previous year's inventory. Using data collected from interested consumers, the team sent e-mails encouraging consumers to purchase the previous Camry model before it was gone. Interested consumers were directed to a sell-down landing page where they were encouraged to schedule test drives of the Camry.

The second step was to build buzz around its newest Camry model. In addition to traditional media, the team used Internet and mobile channels to portray the special bond between owners and the Toyota Camry. For instance, it released "teasers" on social media sites prompting consumers to consider their relationships with their vehicles. A microsite was created that used the idea of courtship to interact with users and take them though the improved features of the new Camry model.

Customer engagement soared. About 150,000 consumers interacted with the campaign, more than 11,000 consumers scheduled test drives, and the amount of sales generated as a result of the campaign was estimated at more than $27 million for dealers involved in the project. The campaign was so effective that it earned nine international marketing awards, including an Internet Advertising Competition (IAC) Award for Outstanding Achievement in Internet Advertising from the Web Marketing Association.[1]

integrated marketing communications Coordination of promotion and other marketing efforts for maximum informational and persuasive impact

Organizations like Toyota employ a variety of promotional methods to communicate with their target markets. Sometimes the messages are planned in advance, or they may be a response to a dramatic change in the marketing environment. Providing information to customers and other stakeholders is vital to initiating and developing long-term relationships with them.

This chapter looks at the general dimensions of promotion. First, we discuss the nature of integrated marketing communications. Next, we analyze the meaning and process of communication. We then define and examine the role of promotion and explore some of the reasons promotion is used. We consider major promotional methods and the factors that influence marketers' decisions to use particular methods. We explain the positive and negative effects of personal and electronic word-of-mouth communication. Finally, we examine benefits and criticisms of promotion.

15-1 THE NATURE OF INTEGRATED MARKETING COMMUNICATIONS

LO 15-1 Define integrated marketing communications.

Integrated marketing communications refers to the coordination of promotion and other marketing efforts to ensure maximum informational and persuasive impact on customers. Coordinating multiple marketing tools to produce this synergistic effect requires a marketer to employ a broad perspective. A major goal of integrated marketing communications is to send a consistent message to customers. Snickers developed an integrated marketing campaign called "You're not you when you're hungry" to demonstrate the satisfaction of a Snickers bar. Snickers, as an official sponsor of the NFL, debuts many of its most successful ads in the Super Bowl. Their recent "You're not you when you're hungry" ad features Adam Driver (Kylo Ren from *Star Wars: The Force Awakens* and Adam Sackler from HBO's *Girls*). This global platform has redefined success for Snickers with sales growth over three times the previous period, and the Betty White commercial generated media coverage for 91 days following the Super Bowl.[2]

Because various units both inside and outside most companies have traditionally planned and implemented promotional efforts, customers have not always received consistent messages. Integrated marketing communications allow an organization to coordinate and manage its promotional efforts to transmit consistent messages. Integrated marketing communications also enable synchronization of promotion elements and can improve the efficiency and effectiveness of promotion budgets. Thus, this approach creates not only long-term customer relationships but also the efficient use of promotional resources.

The concept of integrated marketing communications is increasingly effective for several reasons. Mass media advertising, a very popular promotional method in the past, is used less frequently today because of its high cost and lower effectiveness in reaching some target markets. Marketers take advantage of more precisely targeted promotional tools, such as direct mail, the Internet, special-interest magazines, DVDs, smartphones, mobile applications, social media, and outdoor advertising. Database marketing and marketing analytics are also allowing marketers to more precisely target individual

Featureflash Photo Agency/Shutterstock.com

Integrated Marketing Communications
Adam Driver from *Star Wars: The Force Awakens* appears in the Snickers "You're not you when you're hungry" campaign.

customers. Until recently, suppliers of marketing communications were specialists. Advertising agencies provided advertising campaigns, sales promotion companies provided sales promotion activities and materials, and public relations organizations engaged in publicity efforts. Today, a number of promotion-related companies provide one-stop shopping for the client seeking advertising, sales promotion, and public relations, thus reducing coordination problems for the sponsoring company. Because the overall cost of marketing communications has risen significantly, marketers demand systematic evaluations of communication efforts and a reasonable return on investment.

The types of communication used and the way in which they are used are changing as both information technology and customer interests become increasingly dynamic. For example, companies and politicians can hold press conferences where viewers can tweet their questions and have them answered on-screen. Some companies are creating their own branded content to exploit the many vehicles through which consumers obtain information. Under Armour teamed with famed Olympic athlete Michael Phelps to create a day in his life called "The Water Diviner." The writing, visuals, and lighting make this a compelling piece and won it recognition by Advertising Age as one of the top ten best branded content partnerships. As the most decorated Olympian in history, there remains significant fascination with Michael Phelps, and Under Armour has found an innovative way to create a partnership that enhances their branding.[3] Companies are turning toward branded content and other innovative communication media to engage users in ways that they can feel entertained without feeling the pressure of being inundated with traditional marketing messages.

Marketers and customers have almost unlimited access to data about each other. Integrating and customizing marketing communications while protecting customer privacy has become a major challenge. Through digital media, companies can provide product information and services that are coordinated with traditional promotional activities. In fact, gathering information about goods and services is one of the main reasons people go online. This has made digital marketing a growing business. Marketers spend nearly 30 percent of their marketing budget on digital marketing.[4] The biggest concern of marketers is from fake news, questionable metrics, ethics issues which social media platforms have created, creator-perceived risk, and scrutiny. Almost 50 percent of advertisers will not spend money on risky platforms.[5] College students in particular say they are influenced by Internet ads when buying online or researching product purchases. The sharing of information and use of technology to facilitate communication between buyers and sellers are essential for successful customer relationship management.

15-2 THE COMMUNICATION PROCESS

LO 15-2 Describe the steps of the communication process.

Communication is essentially the transmission of information. For communication to take place, both the sender and receiver of information must share some common ground. They must have a common understanding of the symbols, words, and pictures used to transmit information. Thus, we define **communication** as a sharing of meaning. Implicit in this definition is the notion of transmission of information because sharing necessitates transmission.

As Figure 15.1 shows, communication begins with a source. A **source** is a person, group, or organization with a meaning it attempts to share with an audience. A source could be an electronics salesperson wishing to communicate the attributes of OLED and 4K television to a buyer in the store or a TV manufacturer using television ads to inform thousands of consumers about its products. Developing a strategy can enhance the effectiveness of the source's communication. For example, a strategy in which a salesperson attempts to influence a customer's decision by eliminating competitive products from consideration has been found to be effective. A **receiver** is the individual, group, or organization that decodes a coded message, and an *audience* is two or more receivers.

communication A sharing of meaning through the transmission of information

source A person, group, or organization with a meaning it tries to share with a receiver or an audience

receiver The individual, group, or organization that decodes a coded message

coding process Converting meaning into a series of signs or symbols

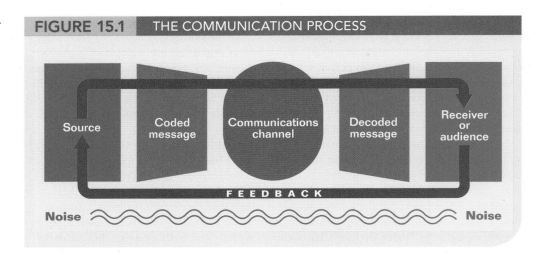

FIGURE 15.1   THE COMMUNICATION PROCESS

Source → Coded message → Communications channel → Decoded message → Receiver or audience

FEEDBACK

Noise ～～～～～ Noise

To transmit meaning, a source must convert the meaning into a series of signs or symbols representing ideas or concepts. This is called the **coding process**, or *encoding*. When coding meaning into a message, the source must consider certain characteristics of the receiver or audience. This is especially true for advertising. It is important to encode messages so as to prevent consumers from avoiding a conscious reception. Costs to the consumer in attention, time, and emotional response can diminish the impact of the message.[6] General Motors uses the tagline, "We are professional grade" and, in this ad, "Precision matters." Using a hummingbird, GM creates an analogy that the precision with which this bird can pollinate a flower is parallel to the commitment that GM workers have to producing high-quality, well engineered and manufactured cars and trucks. Precision is emphasized in all that GM does and produces. Such signs or symbols help the consumer to better understand and remember the ad message.

To share meaning, the source should use signs or symbols familiar to the receiver or audience. As marketers attempt to persuade consumers, they need to understand the specific lifestyles and attitudes that are acceptable to each target market to improve the effectiveness of their messaging. Marketers that understand this realize the importance of knowing their target market and ensuring that an advertisement or promotion uses language the target market understands and that shows behaviors acceptable within the culture. With the growth of the Hispanic market, marketers are increasingly using Spanish-language media in their advertisements and messaging.

When coding a meaning, a source needs to use signs or symbols that the receiver or audience uses to refer to the concepts the source intends to convey. Instead of technical jargon, thoughtful language that helps consumers understand the message is more likely to result in positive attitudes and purchase intentions. Marketers try to avoid signs or symbols that may have several meanings for an audience. For example, *soda* as a general term for soft drinks may not work well in national advertisements. Although in some parts of the United States the word means "soft drink," in other regions it may connote bicarbonate of soda, an ice cream drink, or something one mixes with alcoholic beverages.

2015 General Motors

Creating Meaning Through Visualization
General Motors emphasizes their commitment to quality by emphasizing that "precision matters" with this graphic of a hummingbird pollinating a flower.

TABLE 15.1	HOW AMERICANS GET THEIR NEWS
Type of Medium	**% Using Each Medium**
Television (cable, local, network nightly)	57%
Online (social media, websites, apps)	38%
Radio	25%
Paper newspapers	20%

Note: One percent said they never got news on any platform (not shown). Survey Conducted January 12–February 8, 2016. Source: Amy Mitchell, Jeffrey Gottfried, Michael Barthel, Elisa Shearer, "The Modern News Consumer," *Pew Research Center*, July 7, 2016, www.journalism.org/2016/07/07/pathways-to-news/ (accessed February 4, 2017).

communications channel The medium of transmission that carries the coded message from the source to the receiver

decoding process Converting signs or symbols into concepts and ideas

noise Anything that reduces a communication's clarity and accuracy

feedback The receiver's response to a decoded message

To share a coded meaning with the receiver or audience, a source selects and uses a **communications channel**, the medium of transmission that carries the coded message from the source to the receiver or audience. Transmission media include printed words (newspapers and magazines), broadcast media (television and radio), and digital communication (social media platforms such as Facebook and YouTube). Table 15.1 summarizes the leading communications channels from which people obtain information and news. Most Americans use multiple devices to access news, as the table demonstrates. The majority use four different devices or technologies during the day. Although television is still the most common source for obtaining news, more than half of Americans access the news through their mobile devices during the day.[7] Print news sources continue to decline as digital and television give the latest news stories.

In the **decoding process**, signs or symbols are converted into concepts and ideas. Seldom does a receiver decode exactly the same meaning the source intended. When the result of decoding differs from what was coded, noise exists. **Noise** is anything that reduces the clarity and accuracy of the communication; it has many sources and may affect any or all parts of the communication process. Noise sometimes arises within the communications channel itself. Radio or television transmission difficulties (satellite or cable) and poor or slow Internet connections are sources of noise. Noise also occurs when a source uses signs or symbols that are unfamiliar to the receiver or have a meaning different from the one intended. Noise may also originate in the receiver; a receiver may be unaware of a coded message when perceptual processes block it out through a lack of understanding.

The receiver's response to a decoded message is **feedback** to the source. The source usually expects and normally receives feedback, although perhaps not immediately. During feedback, the receiver or audience provides the original source with a response to the message. The feedback provided to Procter & Gamble on the success of this Tide ad would be the number of coupons redeemed. Calls to action, such as coupons, visits to websites, and digital marketing response rates are some of the best ways to measure the impact and collect feedback from consumers on the receptiveness to the offer. Feedback is coded, sent through a communications channel, and decoded by the receiver, the source of the original communication. Thus, communication is a circular process, as indicated in Figure 15.1.

Collecting Feedback
Tide uses coupon ads to stimulate sales and collect feedback from its customers as to how interested they are in this type of promotion.

channel capacity The limit on the volume of information a communication channel can handle effectively

promotion Communication to build and maintain relationships by informing and persuading one or more audiences

As marketers interact directly through personal selling sales promotions, feedback is provided immediately. Instant feedback lets marketers adjust messages quickly to improve the effectiveness of their communications. For example, when a salesperson realizes through feedback that a customer does not understand a sales presentation, the salesperson adapts the presentation to make it more meaningful to the customer. This is why face-to-face communication is the most adaptive and flexible, especially compared to digital, web-based, or other non-personal communications. In interpersonal communication, feedback occurs through talking, touching, smiling, nodding, eye movements, and other body movements and postures.

When mass communication like advertising is used, feedback is often slow and difficult to recognize. Also, it may be several months or even years before the effects of this promotion will be known. Some relevant and timely feedback can occur in the form of sales increases, inquiries about products, or online registrations for promotions or reward programs.

Each communication channel has a limit on the volume of information it can handle effectively. This limit, called **channel capacity**, is determined by the least efficient component of the communication process. Consider communications that depend on speech. An individual source can speak only so fast, and there is a limit to how much an individual receiver can take in through listening. Beyond that point, additional messages cannot be decoded; thus, meaning cannot be shared. To be effective, a 30-second advertising message should not exceed 75 words because most announcers cannot articulate words into understandable messages at a rate beyond 150 words per minute.

15-3 THE ROLE AND OBJECTIVES OF PROMOTION

LO 15-3 Recognize the definition and objectives of promotion.

Promotion is communication that builds and maintains favorable relationships by informing and persuading one or more audiences to view an organization positively and accept its products. Many organizations spend considerable resources on promotion to build and enhance relationships with current and potential customers as well as other stakeholders. Thoughtful promotion reinforces market positioning versus the competition and creates a reason for purchase. Chipotle Mexican Grill introduced a promotion designed to reinforce consumers' understanding of the quality and freshness of their guacamole and to create a reason for customers to visit or return to Chipotle. "Cado Crusher" is a game that can be played online that allows you to make your own guacamole and appreciate Chipotle's fresh ingredients, and after playing you receive a coupon for free chips and guacamole with a purchase. Their promotional partner is Avocados from Mexico. Joint promotions support the goals of each partner, and Chipotle is a good customer with each store using five cases of

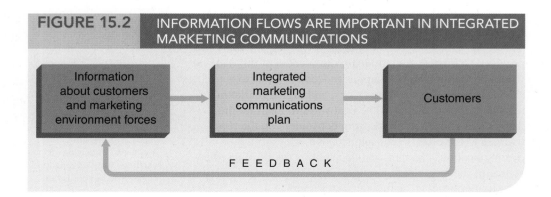

FIGURE 15.2   INFORMATION FLOWS ARE IMPORTANT IN INTEGRATED MARKETING COMMUNICATIONS

avocados a day.[8] Marketers also indirectly facilitate favorable relationships by focusing information about company activities and products on interest groups (such as environmental and consumer groups), current and potential investors, regulatory agencies, and society in general. For instance, some organizations promote responsible use of products criticized by society, such as tobacco, alcohol, and violent movies or video games.

TABLE 15.2	POSSIBLE OBJECTIVES OF PROMOTION`
Create awareness	Retain loyal customers and reach new ones
Stimulate demand	Facilitate retail and wholesale support
Encourage product trial	Challenge competitors' promotions
Identify prospects	Reduce sales fluctuations
Stimulate word of mouth	Generate positive social media posts

Companies sometimes promote programs that help selected groups. Such cause-related marketing links the purchase of products to philanthropic efforts for one or more causes. By contributing to causes that its target markets support, cause-related marketing can help marketers boost sales, increase loyalty, and generate goodwill.

To maximize promotional effectiveness, marketers strive for proper planning, implementation, coordination, and control of communications. Effective management of integrated marketing communications is based on information about and feedback from customers and the marketing environment, often obtained from an organization's marketing information system (see Figure 15.2). How successfully marketers use promotion to maintain positive relationships depends to some extent on the quantity and quality of information the organization receives and listens to from customers. Social media, blogging, and customer feedback through websites has been a very effective way to listen to customers. Because customers share information and opinions through many different sources, integrated marketing communications planning also takes into account these informal methods of communication. Because promotion is communication that can be managed, we now analyze what this communication is and how it works.

Promotional objectives vary considerably from one organization to another and within organizations over time. Large firms with multiple promotional programs operating simultaneously may have quite varied promotional objectives. For the purpose of analysis, we focus on the ten promotional objectives shown in Table 15.2. Although the list is not exhaustive, one or more of these objectives underlie many promotional programs.

15-3a **Create Awareness**

A considerable amount of promotion efforts focus on creating awareness. For an organization that is introducing a new product or a line extension, making customers aware of the product is crucial to initiating the product adoption process. A marketer that has invested heavily in product development strives to create product awareness quickly to generate revenues to offset the high costs of product development and introduction. Apple frequently begins to build awareness about new products months before it releases them. It holds an annual conference, where CEO Tim Cook creates interest and excitement about its new products.

Creating awareness is important for existing products, too. Orville Redenbacher has been making microwavable popcorn for decades. However, this ad creates the awareness that they are the only market leader who uses real butter in their popcorn. Many other competitors use butter flavoring as opposed to the real thing. Promotional efforts may aim to increase awareness of brands, product features, image-related

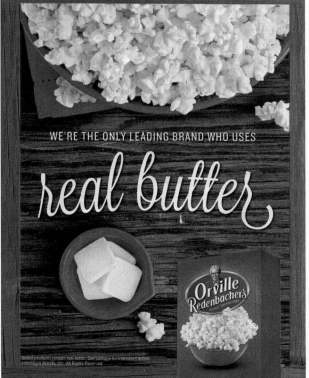

Generating Brand Awareness
Orville Redenbacher's use of real butter in its microwave popcorn helps to differentiate the product, and this ad stimulates that awareness.

issues (such as ethical or socially responsive behavior), or operational characteristics (such as store hours, locations, and credit availability). Some promotional programs are unsuccessful because marketers fail to generate awareness of critical issues among a significant portion of target market members. Other times, the campaign itself is at fault. For example, when the state of Rhode Island launched a $5 million campaign to promote tourism, they were not aware the footage in the 110 second video was of not only Rhode Island, but also Iceland. The company that cut the video was instructed to only use Rhode Island videos. Needless to say, those familiar with Rhode Island were confused when viewing the promotional materials, and the campaign's effectiveness was impacted.[9]

15-3b Stimulate Demand

When an organization is the first to introduce an innovative product, it tries to stimulate **primary demand**—demand for a product category rather than for a specific brand of product—through **new introductory promotion**. New introductory promotion informs potential customers about the product: what it is, what it does, how it can be used, and where it can be purchased. Because this promotion is used in the introductory stage of the product life cycle, meaning there are no competing brands, it neither emphasizes brand names nor compares brands. This tactic was taken when introducing chia seeds to the food market. Advertisers therefore had to engage in new introductory advertising to spread awareness of the product category before focusing on specific brands. IAMS attracts cat owners who are concerned about their pet's health and well-being with a line of products that assists in managing digestion, energy, and weight. The goal of the ad is to increase brand awareness of IAMS among cat owners who are willing to invest in their cat's health.

To build **selective demand**, demand for a specific brand, a marketer employs promotional efforts that point out the strengths and benefits of a specific brand. Building selective demand also requires singling out attributes important to potential buyers. Selective demand can be stimulated by differentiating the product from competing brands in the minds of potential buyers. Arnold focuses on two markets in these advertisements. The whole grain breads represent a broader, health-conscious market. The Sandwich Thins represent Arnold's goal of reaching a smaller segment of that market with a thin, whole wheat sandwich with lower calories than traditional whole wheat bread, focusing on weight-conscious consumers.

Selective demand can also be stimulated by increasing the number of product uses and promoting them through advertising campaigns, as well as through price discounts, free samples, coupons, consumer contests and games, and sweepstakes. For example, Macy's department store uses One Day Sales to create demand for Macy's products, increase exposure to the brand, and build selective demand. In a time when traditional retailers are struggling to compete against online competitors, discounting can be a tactic that generates selective demand. In addition, selective demand can be stimulated by encouraging existing customers to use more of the product.

15-3c Encourage Product Trial

When attempting to move customers through the product adoption cycle, marketers may successfully create awareness and interest, but customers may stall during the evaluation stage. In this case, certain types of promotion—such as free

IAMS Cat Food
IAMS uses this advertisement to generate awareness for its line of healthy cat food products.

Stimulating Product Demand
Arnold focuses on two markets with these ads, the health-conscious whole-grain segment and the smaller segment who are also weight-conscious.

samples, coupons, test drives, or limited free-use offers, contests, and games—are employed to encourage product trial. Costco uses free sampling throughout its stores. Whether a marketer's product is the first in a new product category, a new brand in an existing category, or simply an existing brand seeking customers, trial-inducing promotional efforts aim to make product trial convenient and low risk for potential customers.

15-3d Identify Prospects

Certain types of promotional efforts aim to identify customers who are interested in the firm's product and are likely potential buyers. Television advertisements may encourage the viewer to visit the company's website and share personal information in order to receive something of value from the company. Customers who respond to such a message usually have higher interest in the product, making them potential customers. The organization can respond with phone calls, e-mail, or personal contact by salespeople.

15-3e Retain Loyal Customers

Clearly, maintaining long-term customer relationships is a major goal of most marketers. Many companies, from fast-food companies such as Taco Bell to auto manufacturers such as BMW, know the long-term customer value for their products. Promotional efforts directed at customer retention can help an organization control its costs, because the costs of retaining customers are usually considerably lower than those of acquiring new ones. Frequent-user programs, such as those sponsored by airlines, car rental agencies, and hotels, aim to reward loyal customers and encourage them to remain loyal. Many supermarkets, such as Kroger and its affiliated brands, offer a loyalty program that gives $1.00 in fuel points for every dollar spent in the store. Discounts range from $0.10 to $1.00 off per gallon of fuel. Some organizations employ special offers that only their existing customers can use. To retain loyal customers, marketers not only advertise loyalty programs but also use reinforcement advertising, which assures current users they have made the right brand choice and tells them how to get the most satisfaction from the product.

15-3f Facilitate Reseller Support

Reseller support is a two-way street: producers generally want to provide support to resellers to assist in selling their products, and in turn they expect resellers to support their products. When a manufacturer, such as Procter & Gamble, advertises its home and health products to consumers, retailers and wholesalers should view this promotion as a form of strong manufacturer support. In some instances, a producer agrees to pay a certain proportion of retailers' advertising expenses for promoting its products. For example, when a manufacturer is introducing a new consumer brand in a highly competitive product category, it may be difficult to persuade supermarket managers to carry this brand. However, if the manufacturer promotes the new brand with free samples and coupon distribution in the retailer's area, a supermarket manager views these actions as strong support and is much more likely to carry the product. To encourage wholesalers and retailers to increase their inventories of its products, a manufacturer may provide them with special offers and buying allowances. In certain industries, a producer's salesperson may provide support to a wholesaler by working with the wholesaler's customers (retailers) in the presentation and promotion of the products. Strong relationships with resellers are important to a firm's ability to maintain a sustainable competitive advantage. The use of various promotional methods can help support sales growth.

15-3g Combat Competitive Promotional Efforts

At times, a marketer's objective in using promotion is to challenge a competitor's promotional or marketing programs. This reactive approach is to prevent a sales or market share loss. A combative promotional objective is used most often by firms in extremely competitive consumer markets, such as the fast-food, convenience store, and cable/Internet/cell phone markets. Stores that offer price-matching programs include Best Buy, Fry's Electronics, The Home Depot, Lowes, Target, Walmart, Staples, Office Depot, Office Max, and Toys "R" Us. It is not unusual for competitors to respond with a counter-pricing strategy or even match a competitor's pricing.

15-3h Reduce Sales Fluctuations

Product demand varies from one month to another because of such factors as climate, holidays, seasons, and the economy. A business, however, cannot operate at peak efficiency when sales fluctuate rapidly. Changes in sales volume translate into changes in production, inventory levels, personnel needs, and financial resources. When promotional techniques reduce fluctuations by generating sales during slow periods, a firm can use its resources more efficiently.

Promotional techniques are often designed to stimulate sales during sales slumps. For example, Snapper may offer sales prices on lawn mowers into the fall season to extend the selling season. During peak periods, a marketer may refrain from advertising to prevent stimulating sales to the point at which the firm cannot handle all of the demand. On occasion, a company advertises that customers can be better served by coming in on certain days. For example, in most states Logan's Road House allows kids 12 and under to receive one free kid's meal for each adult meal purchased.

To achieve the major objectives of promotion discussed here, companies must develop appropriate promotional programs. In the next section, we consider the basic components of such programs: the promotion mix elements.

|15-4 **THE PROMOTION MIX**

LO 15-4 Summarize the four variables of the promotion mix.

promotion mix A combination of promotional methods used to promote a specific product

Several promotional methods can be used to communicate with individuals, groups, and organizations. When an organization combines specific methods to manage the integrated marketing communications for a particular product, that combination is the product promotion mix. The four possible elements of a **promotion mix** are advertising, personal selling, public relations, and sales promotion (see Figure 15.3). For some products, firms use all four elements; for others, they use only two or three. In this section, we provide an overview of each promotion mix element; they are covered in greater detail in the next two chapters.

15-4a **Advertising**

Advertising is a paid nonpersonal communication about an organization and its products transmitted to a target audience through mass media, including television, radio, the Internet, newspapers, magazines, video games, direct mail, outdoor displays, and signs on mass transit vehicles. Advertising is changing as consumers' mass media consumption habits are changing. Companies are striving to maximize their presence and impact through digital media; ads are being designed that cater to smaller, more personalized audiences; and traditional media like newspapers are in a decline due to a drop in readership. Individuals and organizations use advertising to promote goods, services, ideas, issues, and people. Being highly flexible, advertising can reach an extremely large target audience or focus on a small, precisely defined segment. For instance, Subway's advertising focuses on a large audience of potential fast-food customers, ranging from children to adults, whereas advertising for Gulfstream jets aims at a much smaller and more specialized target market.

   Advertising offers several benefits. It is extremely cost-efficient when it reaches a vast number of people at a low cost per person. For example, the cost of a four-color, full-page advertisement in TIME magazine costs $366,600. With a circulation of 3 million, this makes the cost of reaching roughly a thousand subscribers $122.[10] Advertising also lets the source repeat the message several times. For example, Subway promotes a different 6-inch sub of the day for $3.50 in its "Life's Important Days" campaign, which relates significant life changes to the Subway Sub of the Day. Furthermore, advertising a product a certain way can add to the product's value, and the visibility an organization gains from advertising can

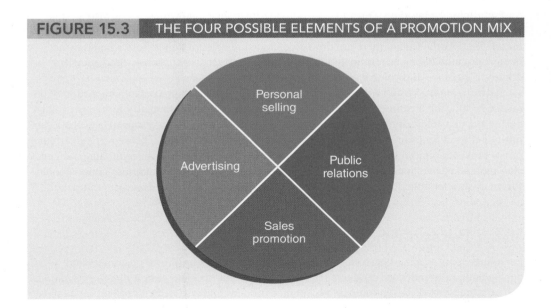

FIGURE 15.3   THE FOUR POSSIBLE ELEMENTS OF A PROMOTION MIX

SNAPSHOT

Marketing Expense Allocation

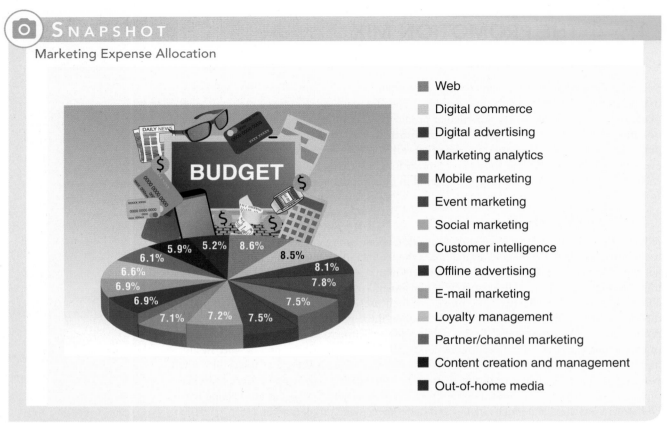

Legend:
- Web
- Digital commerce
- Digital advertising
- Marketing analytics
- Mobile marketing
- Event marketing
- Social marketing
- Customer intelligence
- Offline advertising
- E-mail marketing
- Loyalty management
- Partner/channel marketing
- Content creation and management
- Out-of-home media

Pie chart values: 8.6%, 8.5%, 8.1%, 7.8%, 7.5%, 7.5%, 7.2%, 7.1%, 6.9%, 6.9%, 6.6%, 6.1%, 5.9%, 5.2%

Note: *This research is based on Gartner's 2016–2017 CMO Spend Survey of 377 marketers in North America and the U.K. at companies with more than $250 million in annual revenue.*

Source: "Gartner CMO Spend Survey 2016–2017," *Gartner*, 2016, http://images.gartnerformarketers.com/Web/Gartner/%7B0cd7db62-e5cd-4599-9bae-9b68f9a6148d%7D_GML_144560_Spend_Ebook_R1c.pdf (accessed February 12, 2017).

enhance its image. For instance, incorporating touchable elements that generate positive sensory feedback in print advertising can be a positive persuasive tool.[11] At times, a firm tries to enhance its own or its product's image by including celebrity endorsers in advertisements. Peyton Manning, former quarterback for the Denver Broncos, does celebrity endorsements for Papa John's, Gatorade, DirecTV, Nationwide Insurance, and Buick. He is also a Papa John's franchisee in the Denver area and has a vested interest in supporting the Papa John's brand. On the other hand, there are downsides to using celebrity endorsers when they act inappropriately. Nike has terminated or suspended contracts with celebrity endorsers for domestic violence allegations.

Advertising has disadvantages as well. Even though the cost per person reached may be relatively low, the absolute dollar outlay can be extremely high, especially for commercials during popular television shows and those associated with popular websites. High costs can limit, and sometimes preclude, use of advertising in a promotion mix. Moreover, advertising rarely provides rapid feedback. Measuring its effect on sales is often difficult, and it is generally less persuasive than personal selling. There are online sources that house coupon codes for many retailers like RetailMeNot. The use of a coupon code allows retailers to track the use and appeal of varying promotional offers.

15-4b Personal Selling

Personal selling is a paid personal communication that seeks to inform customers and persuade them to purchase products in an exchange situation. The phrase *purchase products* is interpreted broadly to encompass acceptance of ideas and issues. Personal selling is most extensively used in the business-to-business market and also in the business-to-consumer market for high-end products such as homes, cars, electronics, and furniture.

Personal selling has both advantages and limitations when compared with advertising. Advertising is general communication aimed at a relatively large target audience, whereas personal selling involves more specific communication directed at one or several individuals. Reaching one person through personal selling costs considerably more than through advertising, but personal selling efforts often have greater impact on customers. Personal selling also provides immediate feedback, allowing marketers to adjust their messages to improve communication. Such interaction helps them determine and respond to customers' information needs.

When a salesperson and a customer meet face-to-face, they use several types of interpersonal communication. The predominant communication form is language, both spoken and written. A salesperson and customer frequently use **kinesic communication**, or communication through the movement of head, eyes, arms, hands, legs, or torso. Winking, head nodding, hand gestures, and arm motions are forms of kinesic communication. A good salesperson can often evaluate a prospect's interest in a product or presentation by noting eye contact and head nodding. **Proxemic communication**, a less obvious form of communication used in personal selling situations, occurs when either person varies the physical distance separating them. When a customer backs away from a salesperson, for example, he or she may be displaying a lack of interest in the product or expressing dislike for the salesperson. Touching, or **tactile communication**, is also a form of communication, although less popular in the United States than in many other countries. Handshaking is a common form of tactile communication both in the United States and elsewhere.

Sales managers need a variety of skills to oversee the sales force. These aptitudes include interpersonal, technical, and strategic skills. The importance of these different types of skills depends largely on level of management.[12] For instance, sales managers need strong leadership skills, and they must be able to use sales management technology to track and control sales strategies. A salesperson, however, needs extremely strong interpersonal skills and product knowledge, and needs to be likeable and responsive to customer needs.

15-4c **Public Relations**

Although many promotional activities focus on a firm's customers, other stakeholders—suppliers, employees, stockholders, the media, educators, potential investors, government officials, and society in general—are important to an organization as well. To communicate with customers and stakeholders, a company employs public relations. Public relations is a broad set of communication efforts used to create and maintain favorable relationships between an organization and its stakeholders. Maintaining a positive relationship with one or more stakeholders can affect a firm's current sales and profits, as well as its long-term survival. When United Record Pressing LLC announced their expansion in Nashville, it sent many signals for the company, which produces 30 to 40 percent of all vinyl records available in stores. This signaled a resurgence in the sales of vinyl record albums to consumers, a strengthening business model and growth mode for this privately held company, and a commitment to the rich history, dating back to 1949, to retain the original building on Chestnut Street as "an important place in musical history."[13]

Public relations uses a variety of tools, including annual reports, brochures, event sponsorship, and support of socially responsible programs aimed at protecting the environment or helping disadvantaged individuals. The goal of public relations is to create and enhance a positive image of the organization. Increasingly, marketers are going directly to consumers with their public relations efforts through social media. Pampered Chef places content on YouTube that shows consumers how to make certain recipes. This content familiarizes consumers with Pampered Chef and positions the organization as an aid in the kitchen.[14]

Other tools arise from the use of publicity, which is a component of public relations. Publicity is nonpersonal communication in news-story form about an organization or its products, or both, transmitted through a mass medium at no charge. A few examples of

kinesic communication
Communicating through the movement of head, eyes, arms, hands, legs, or torso

proxemic communication
Communicating by varying the physical distance in face-to-face interactions

tactile communication
Communicating through touching

publicity-based public relations tools are news releases, press conferences, feature articles, and social media sites such as YouTube and Twitter. For example, General Motors made headlines as the first automaker to broadcast on Facebook Live when they gave their Facebook fans an up-close look at a new car model.[15] To generate publicity, companies sometimes give away products to celebrities in the hope that the celebrities will be seen and photographed with the product, and those photos will stimulate awareness and product trial among their fans. Grammy nominees receive a gift bag known as the "Swag Bag." These bags can be worth around $30,000 and can consist of luxury products such as a 10-year supply of Oxygentix Breathable Foundation and Oxygenated Moisturizer worth up to $13,400, a week-long trip to the Golden Door spa, worth $8,850, as well as other high-end products and services. Donors of the gifts count on the publicity to create awareness of their products and also hope high visibility entertainers will use their products.[16] Public relations efforts may be the responsibility of an individual or of a department within the organization, or the organization may hire an external public relations firm.

Unpleasant situations and negative events, such as product tampering or an environmental disaster, may generate unfavorable public relations for an organization. Subway gained significant negative press for employing spokesperson Jared Fogle who lost around 200 pounds eating Subway sandwiches. Although making millions from the Subway role, the company had to sever ties with Fogle when he was charged with the possession and distribution of child pornography as well as other charges and was sentenced to 16 years in prison for his misconduct.[17] To minimize the damaging effects of unfavorable coverage, effective marketers have policies and procedures in place to help manage public relations problems. Often these plans are called crisis management plans and attempt to anticipate what can go wrong and how to respond.

Coupons as Sales Promotion
Boots Retail uses couponing to support product trial use and to support retail partners, such as Target.

Public relations should not be viewed as a set of tools to be used only during crises. An organization should have someone responsible for public relations either internally or externally and should have an ongoing public relations program.

15-4d Sales Promotion

Sales promotion is an activity or material that acts as a direct inducement, offering added value or incentive for the product to resellers, salespeople, or consumers. Examples include free samples, games, rebates, sweepstakes, contests, premiums, and coupons. *Sales promotion* should not be confused with *promotion;* sales promotion is just one part of the comprehensive area of promotion. Marketers spend more on sales promotion than on advertising, and sales promotion appears to be a faster-growing area than advertising. Coupons and coupon codes are important to retailers and manufacturers. Manufacturers such as Boots Retail use coupons to promote their products as shown in the No7 Lift & Illuminate Triple Action Serum ad. The ad encourages consumers to try the product with a $5.00 off coupon and lets them know that the product is available at Target, supporting one of their channels of distribution.

Generally, when companies employ advertising or personal selling, they depend on these activities continuously or cyclically. However, a marketer's use of sales promotion tends to be less consistent. Many products are seasonal. Toys may be discounted in January after the holiday selling season to move excess inventory. Marketers frequently rely on sales promotion to improve the effectiveness of other promotion elements, especially advertising and personal selling.

Coupons appear to be more effective for food and packaged goods marketers. Nine out of ten millennials use coupons, using coupon code websites such as coupon.com, Ebates, and traditional paper coupons.[18] Mobile devices are a personal technology, so they pose an unusual opportunity to reach consumers wherever they go. It is estimated that mobile Internet usage will soon surpass desktop usage. Mobile apps are used as tools to engage the consumer through sales promotion items such as coupons in close proximity to the consumer and retailer.

An effective promotion mix requires the right combination of elements. To see how such a mix is created, we now examine the factors and conditions affecting the selection of promotional methods that an organization uses for a particular product.

15-5 SELECTING PROMOTION MIX ELEMENTS

LO 15-5 Explain the factors that are used to determine a product's promotion mix.

Marketers vary the composition of promotion mixes for many reasons. Although a promotion mix can include all four elements, frequently, a marketer selects fewer than four. Many firms that market multiple product lines use several promotion mixes simultaneously.

15-5a Promotional Resources, Objectives, and Policies

The size of an organization's promotional budget affects the number and relative intensity of promotional methods included in a promotion mix. If a company's promotional budget is extremely limited, the firm is likely to rely on personal selling because it is easier to measure a salesperson's contribution to sales than to measure the sales effectiveness of advertising. Businesses must have significant promotional budgets to use regional or national advertising. Companies like Procter & Gamble, Unilever, General Motors, and Coca-Cola are among the leaders in worldwide media spending. Organizations with extensive promotional resources generally include more elements in their promotion mixes, but having more promotional dollars to spend does not necessarily mean using more promotional methods. Researchers have found that resources spent on promotion activities have a positive influence on shareholder value.

An organization's promotional objectives and policies also influence the types of promotion selected. If a company's objective is to create mass awareness of a new convenience good, such as a breakfast cereal, its promotion mix probably leans heavily toward advertising, sales promotion, and possibly public relations. If a company hopes to educate consumers about the features of a durable good, such as a home appliance, its promotion mix may combine a moderate amount of advertising, possibly some sales promotion designed to attract customers to retail stores, and a great deal of personal selling, because this method is an efficient way to inform customers about such products. If a firm's objective is to produce immediate sales of nondurable services, the promotion mix will probably stress advertising and sales promotion. For example, dry cleaners and carpet-cleaning firms are more likely to use advertising with a coupon or discount rather than personal selling.

15-5b Characteristics of the Target Market

Size, geographic distribution, sociocultural, and demographic characteristics of an organization's target market help dictate the methods to include in a product's promotion mix. To some degree, market size and diversity determine composition of the mix. If the size is limited, the promotion mix will probably use a more targeted form of marketing like personal selling, which can be very effective for reaching small numbers of people. With the low cost of social media, it is increasingly effective for small, niche markets. Organizations

ENTREPRENEURSHIP IN MARKETING

Dollar Shave Club's Razor-Sharp Marketing

The idea for Dollar Shave Club (DSC) emerged from a conversation entrepreneur Michael Dubin was having with his co-founder about the annoyances of shaving. They found it inconvenient and costly to have to purchase brand-name blades each month. They decided to create DSC, a subscription-based service headquartered in Venice, California. Consumers who become members of DSC are mailed razors for as little as $1 per month.

The entrepreneurs had to find a low-cost way of communicating with customers. For $4,500 Michael Dubin developed and starred in a humorous video marketing the benefits of Dollar Shave razors, while poking fun at the extra bells-and-whistles that come with brand-name razors. The video was posted on YouTube, where it went viral. Sales for DSC's subscription service soared.

Today, the firm is estimated to have $200 million in revenues. DSC communicates with customers frequently to measure customer satisfaction, and it continues to utilize promotional strategies through press releases and low-cost videos on YouTube. DSC's success eventually caught the attention of Unilever, which purchased DSC for $1 billion.[a]

selling to industrial markets and firms marketing products through only a few wholesalers frequently make personal selling the major component of their promotion mixes. When a product's market consists of millions of customers, organizations rely on mass marketing through advertising and sales promotion, because these methods reach large groups at a low cost per person. When the population density is uneven around the country, marketers may use regional advertising to target smaller markets.

Geographic distribution of a firm's customers also affects the choice of promotional methods. Personal selling is more feasible if a company's customers are concentrated in a small area than if they are dispersed across a vast region. When the company's customers are numerous and dispersed, regional or national advertising may be more practical.

Distribution of a target market's demographic characteristics, such as age, income, or education, may affect the types of promotional techniques a marketer selects, as well as the messages and images employed. According to the U.S. Census Bureau, the percentage of children living in families with two parents is 69, down from 88 in 1960.[19] To reach the households consisting of single parents, unmarried couples, singles, and "empty nesters" (whose grown children have left home), more companies are modifying the images used in their promotions and marketing channels.

15-5c Characteristics of the Product

Generally, promotion mixes for business products concentrate on personal selling, whereas advertising plays a major role in promoting consumer goods. This generalization should be treated cautiously, however. Marketers of business products use some advertising to promote products. Advertisements for computers, road-building equipment, and aircrafts are fairly common, and some sales promotion is also used occasionally to promote business products. Personal selling is used extensively for consumer durables, such as home appliances, automobiles, and houses, whereas consumer convenience items are promoted mainly through advertising and sales promotion. Public relations appears in promotion mixes for both business and consumer products.

Marketers of seasonal products often emphasize advertising—and sometimes sales promotion as well—because off-season sales generally will not support an extensive year-round sales force. Most lawn care companies, such as John Deere, Snapper, and Honda, have a sales force that sells to retailers such as The Home Depot, Lowe's, and Ace Hardware. In addition, these companies rely heavily on advertising and sales promotion to promote their products to a variety of retailers and distributors.

A product's price also influences the composition of the promotion mix. High-priced products call for personal selling, because consumers associate greater risk with the purchase of such products and usually want specific and comparative information from a salesperson. For low-priced convenience items, such as paper towels and deli meats, marketers use advertising rather than personal selling. When products are marketed through intensive distribution, firms depend strongly on advertising and sales promotion. Many convenience products like lotions, cereals, and coffee are promoted through samples, coupons, and rebates. When marketers choose selective distribution, a form of distribution that is between intensive and exclusive, promotion mixes vary considerably. Items handled through exclusive distribution—such as expensive watches, high-end electronics, and high-quality furniture—typically require a significant amount of personal selling.

A product's use also affects the combination of promotional methods. Manufacturers of highly personal products, such as laxatives, nonprescription contraceptives, and feminine hygiene products, depend on advertising because many customers do not want to talk with salespeople about these products. Service businesses often use tangible products to promote their intangible services. As a service business, Penske focuses on how certainty and reliability are key to their success in truck leasing and logistics. In this ad, they characterize the importance of transporting a food product, such as grapes, in a timely and anticipated manner to avoid their deterioration.

Portraying Characteristics of Service Products
Penske solves truck leasing and logistics problems for companies, assuring that their shipments arrive in excellent condition.

15-5d Costs and Availability of Promotional Methods

Costs of promotional methods are major factors to analyze when developing a promotion mix. National advertising and sales promotion require large expenditures. However, if these efforts succeed in reaching extremely large audiences, the cost per individual reached may be quite small, possibly a few pennies. Some forms of advertising are relatively inexpensive. Many small, local businesses advertise products through local newspapers, magazines, radio and television stations, outdoor boards, Internet ads, and signs on mass-transit vehicles.

Another consideration that marketers explore when formulating a promotion mix is availability of promotional techniques. Despite the tremendous number of media vehicles in the United States, a firm may find that no available advertising medium effectively reaches a certain target market. The problem of media availability becomes more pronounced when marketers advertise in foreign countries. Some media, such as television, simply may not be available, or advertising on television may be highly regulated. For example, Sweden has some of the strictest controls for food advertising to children. Marketers have agreed to not target children 16 and under with unhealthy food or drink messages.[20] In some countries, advertisers are forbidden to make brand comparisons on television. Other promotional methods also may have limitations. For instance, a firm may wish to increase its sales force but be unable to find qualified personnel.

15-5e Push and Pull Channel Policies

Another element that marketers consider when planning a promotion mix is whether to use a push policy or a pull policy. With a **push policy**, the producer promotes the product only to the next institution down the marketing channel. In a marketing channel with wholesalers

push policy Promoting a product only to the next institution down the marketing channel

pull policy Promoting a product directly to consumers to develop strong consumer demand that pulls products through a marketing channel

word-of-mouth communication Personal informal exchanges of communication that customers share with one another about products, brands, and companies

and retailers, the producer promotes to the wholesaler because, in this case, the wholesaler is the channel member just below the producer (see Figure 15.4). Each channel member in turn promotes to the next channel member. A push policy normally stresses personal selling. Sometimes sales promotion and advertising are used in conjunction with personal selling to push the products down through the channel.

As Figure 15.4 shows, a firm that uses a **pull policy** promotes directly to consumers to develop strong consumer demand for its products. It does so primarily through advertising and sales promotion. Because consumers are persuaded to seek the products in retail stores, retailers in turn go to wholesalers or the producers to buy the products. This policy is intended to pull the goods down through the channel by creating demand at the consumer level. Consumers are told that if the stores do not have the product, they should request that the stores begin carrying it. Push and pull policies are not mutually exclusive. At times, an organization uses both simultaneously.

15-6 THE GROWING IMPORTANCE OF WORD-OF-MOUTH COMMUNICATIONS

LO 15-6 Describe how word-of-mouth communication affects promotion.

When making decisions about the composition of promotion mixes, marketers should recognize that commercial messages, whether from advertising, personal selling, sales promotion, or public relations, are limited in the extent to which they can inform and persuade customers and move them closer to making purchases. Depending on the type of customers and the products involved, buyers to some extent rely on word-of-mouth communication from personal sources, such as family members and friends. **Word-of-mouth communication** is personal, informal exchanges of communication that customers share with one another either verbally or through social media about products, brands, and companies. Most customers are likely to be influenced by friends and family members when they make purchases. In addition, customers are increasingly going online for information and opinions about goods and services as well as about the companies. Electronic word of mouth is

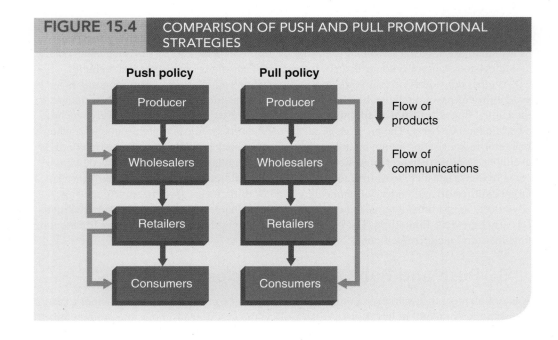

FIGURE 15.4   COMPARISON OF PUSH AND PULL PROMOTIONAL STRATEGIES

TABLE 15.3	CONSUMER TRUST IN BRANDS OR BRAND INFORMATION ON SOCIAL MEDIA CHANNELS	
Channel	**% of people who had little /notrust in 2014**	**% of people who have little /notrust in 2016**
Facebook	20	30
Twitter	15	25
Instagram	11	23
Pinterest	9	21
LinkedIn	8	20

Source: Sarah Vizard, "Consumer Trust in Brands on Social Media Falls as Line Between Marketing and Non-Commercial Blurs," Marketing Week, June 8, 2016, www.marketingweek.com/2016/06/08/consumer-trust-in-brands-on-social -media-falls-as-line-between-marketing-and-non-commercial-blurs/ (accessed February 17, 2017).

communicating about products through websites, blogs, e-mail, social networks, or online forums. Buyers can peruse Internet-based newsgroups, forums, and blogs to find word-of-mouth information. Users can go to a number of consumer-oriented websites, such as epinions.com and consumerreview.com, to learn about other consumers' feelings toward and experiences with specific products; some sites even encourage consumers to rate products they have tried. Users can also search within product categories and compare consumers' viewpoints on various brands and models. Not surprisingly, credibility has been identified as the most important attribute of a ratings website, and reducing risk and saving search effort were found to be the primary motives for using such sites.[21] As Table 15.3 shows, consumer confidence in social media as an authentic and credible source for brand information is declining. Companies that pay bloggers to post about their products have damaged the integrity of social media.

Personal and digital word-of-mouth communication are very important when people are selecting restaurants and entertainment along with automotive, medical, legal, banking, and personal services like hair care. Dollar Shave Club, recently acquired by Unilever, owes its success to word-of-mouth marketing. The YouTube video that made it famous has been viewed more than 22 million times, and it relies heavily on its 1.1 million members to refer their friends and family. The CEO reported 50,000 members refer a friend to the club each month.[22] Word-of-mouth communication is positively linked with new-customer acquisition when customer involvement and satisfaction exist.[23] For this reason, organizations should proactively manage their word-of-mouth communications.[24]

Hundreds of blogs and online news sites (such as Buzzfeed, TMZ, TechCrunch, Perez Hilton, and Engadget) play an essential role in propagating electronic word-of-mouth communications about everything from gossip to politics to consumer goods. They provide information on trends, reviews of products, and other information and have become so influential in introducing consumers to new products and shaping their views about them that marketers are increasingly monitoring them to identify new trends. Marketers must increasingly court bloggers, who wield growing influence over consumer perception of companies, goods, and services. Effective marketers who understand the importance of word-of-mouth communication attempt to identify opinion leaders and encourage them to try their products in the hope that they will spread favorable publicity about them. Apple, for example, has long relied on its nearly cult consumer following to spread by word of mouth their satisfaction with Apple products, such as MacBooks, iPods, iPhones, and iPads. The impact of consumer-generated communication—communication not made by companies—is powerful and is very effective compared to commercial messages. Celebrities who tweet about brands have source credibility if they have a large number of followers.

buzz marketing An attempt to incite publicity and public excitement surrounding a product through a creative event

viral marketing A strategy to get consumers to share a marketer's message, often through e-mail or online videos, in a way that spreads dramatically and quickly

Katy Perry and Justin Bieber have close to 100 million followers each. If followers have a social identification with the celebrity, they are more likely to engage in product involvement.[25] Interestingly, women—unlike men—are more likely to share negative word of mouth with those they have strong social ties with rather than those with whom they have weak social ties. In general, consumers are much more likely to complain of a bad experience versus sharing praise for a good experience. Cadbury's Alien ad was voted one of the best viral ads. This Canadian ad focused upon the experience aliens had consuming Cadbury chocolate left behind by American astronauts. The aliens engage in wild dance and excitement upon eating the chocolate.[26]

Buzz marketing is an attempt to incite publicity and public excitement surrounding a product through a creative event. Event attendance has a positive effect on brand equity.[27] Some marketers are piggybacking off the events of other companies, using long lines for an event or product launch as marketing opportunities. As long lines waited for the newest iPhones outside Apple's London store, a British apple juice brand carried a placard advertising "the latest in apple technology."[28] Buzz marketing can be an effective way of allowing a company to stand out from competing brands. Red Bull is another brand that excels at buzz marketing.

Buzz marketing works best as a part of an integrated marketing communication program that also uses advertising, personal selling, sales promotion, and publicity. However, marketers should also take care that buzz marketing campaigns do not violate any laws or have the potential to be misconstrued and cause undue alarm. For instance, stenciling a brand's name or logo on the sidewalk might be an effective buzz marketing technique but can also be viewed as illegal graffiti by city authorities.

Viral marketing is a strategy to get consumers to share a marketer's message, often through e-mail or online video such as YouTube, in a way that spreads dramatically and quickly. Blendtec, the powerful kitchen blender, developed videos showing its blender pulverizing everything from rakes to marbles and even Apple iPads. The "Will It Blend" videos have been viewed by over 50 million people and have attracted 1 million subscribers. Humor and the unexpected are key contributors to viral marketing success.[29] Interestingly, viral marketing appears to be more effective for products that are less utilitarian

EMERGING TRENDS IN MARKETING

Picture This: The Success of Product Placement

Watch a movie or television show carefully and you will likely identify several familiar product brands. These products are not there by accident. In fact, master of product placement Ruben Igielko-Herrlich of Propaganda Global Entertainment Marketing (GEM) makes it his business to help companies place their products in such media. Nokia's phones in The Matrix, the Audi R8 in the movie Iron Man, and the BMW in Mission Impossible are all a result of his company's efforts.

With the inundation of advertising consumers encounter on everything from television to social networking sites, it is becoming easier for them to ignore or skip over ads. Product placement provides marketers with the opportunity to present products to viewers as part of the show or movie without appearing too intrusive. It is a growing business estimated to surpass $11 billion in 2019.

Product placement is not limited to television and videos. The Kluger Agency focuses on promoting brands in music. Familiar brands from Subway, Coca-Cola, and Pizza Hut have appeared in virtual worlds and video games. Product placement is also gaining popularity internationally. For instance, East Asian brands have been featured more in box-office movies. A Chinese firm even acquired Propaganda GEM, showing the growing interest of marketers in China toward product placement as a marketing channel.[b]

(practical and functional) in nature. Promoting utilitarian products through social sharing mechanisms such as Facebook may actually be disadvantageous for practical no-frills products.[30]

Word of mouth, no matter how it is transmitted, is not effective in all product categories. It seems to be most effective for new-to-market and more expensive products. Despite the obvious benefits of positive word of mouth, marketers must also recognize the potential dangers of negative word of mouth. This is particularly important in dealing with online platforms that can reach more people and encourage consumers to "gang up" on a company or product.

product placement The strategic location of products or product promotions within entertainment media content to reach the product's target market

| 15-7 PRODUCT PLACEMENT

LO 15-7 Discuss how product placement impacts promotion.

A growing technique for reaching consumers is the selective placement of products within the context of television programs and movies viewed by the target market. **Product placement** is a form of advertising that strategically locates products or product promotions within entertainment media to reach the product's target markets. *The Lego Movie* represented perhaps the ultimate brand placement. Warner Bros. paid a licensing fee to Lego to use its brand to create the lead roles of Lego characters.[31] Not only was the movie successful, but Lego also went on to surpass Mattel as the world's largest toymaker. Such product placement on TV has become more important due to the increasing fragmentation of television viewers who have ever-expanding viewing options and technology that can screen advertisements (e.g., digital video recorders). A study found that 60 percent of respondents download or use digital video recorders so they can skip over the commercials.[32]

In-program product placements have been successful in reaching consumers as they are being entertained. Research demonstrates how the influence of TV series impacts consumers' intentions to purchase brands placed in those TV shows. Of course, individual traits, such as consumer sensitivity to social influences, may increase or decrease intentions to purchase a specific brand.[33] Televisions shows, such as *Nashville*, use product placements that attempt to fit into the story line. Lead character, Deacon Claybourne, has driven Ford trucks and unloaded equipment for concerts from the truck bed.

Reality programming in particular has been a natural fit for product placements because of the close interchange between the participants and the product (*Tiny House* has partnered with many advertisers including 3M's Command brand of reusable wall hooks). Global spending for product placements is now over $10.5 billion and growing.[34]

Product placement is not limited to U.S. movies and television shows. The European Parliament green-lighted limited use of product placement, only during certain types of programs and only if consumers were informed at the beginning of the segment that companies had paid to have their products displayed. In general, the notion of product placement has not been favorably viewed in Europe and has been particularly controversial in the United Kingdom. However, new legislation has legalized product placement in U.K. television programs.[35] Supporting the use of product placement are findings that product placement can promote pro-social behavior such as healthy eating habits. For example, product placements are effective in promoting the consumption of fruits and vegetables among children.[36]

Product Placement
The TV show *Nashville* uses a number of product placements, including Ford trucks.

Frederick M. Brown/Getty Images

15-8 CRITICISMS AND DEFENSES OF PROMOTION

LO 15-8 List major criticisms and defenses of promotion.

Even though promotional activities can help customers make informed purchasing decisions, consumer groups, government agencies, and members of society in general have long criticized promotion. There are two main reasons for such criticism: promotion does have flaws, and it is a highly visible business activity that pervades our daily lives. Although complaints about too much promotional activity are almost universal, a number of more specific criticisms have been lodged. Table 15.4 discusses these criticisms in more detail.

TABLE 15.4	CRITICISMS AND DEFENSES OF PROMOTION
Issue	**Discussion**
Is promotion deceptive?	Laws, government regulations, and industry self-regulation have helped to decrease most intentionally deceptive promotion; customers may be unintentionally misled because some words have diverse meanings. The vast majority of promotion is not deceptive.
Does promotion increase prices?	When promotion stimulates demand, higher production levels may result in lower per-unit production costs, which keeps prices lower; when demand is not stimulated, however, prices increase owing to the added costs of promotion; promotion fuels price competition, which helps keep prices lower.
Does promotion create needs?	Many marketers capitalize on people's needs by basing their promotional appeals on these needs; however, marketers do not actually create these needs; if there were no promotion, people would still have basic needs such as food, clothing, transportation, social, and physiological needs.
Does promotion encourage materialism?	Because promotion creates awareness and visibility for products, it may contribute to materialism in the same way that movies, sports, theater, art, and literature may contribute to materialism; if there were not promotion, it is likely that there would still be materialism among some groups, as evidenced by the existence of materialism among some ancient groups of people.
Does promotion help customers without costing too much?	Customers learn about products through promotion, allowing them to gain product information and make more intelligent buying decisions. Promotion helps create competition.
Should potentially harmful products be advertised?	Some critics suggest that promotion of possibly unhealthy products should not be allowed at all; others argue that as long as it is legal to sell such products, promoting those products should be allowed. In a society with commercial freedom of speech, there will always be diverse opinions.

Chapter Review

15-1 Define integrated marketing communications.

Integrated marketing communications is the coordination of promotion and other marketing efforts to ensure maximum informational and persuasive impact on customers.

15-2 Describe the steps of the communication process.

Communication is a sharing of meaning. The communication process involves several steps. First, the source translates meaning into code, a process known as coding or encoding. The source should employ signs or symbols familiar to the receiver or audience. The coded message is sent through a communications channel to the receiver or audience. The receiver or audience then decodes the message and usually supplies feedback to the source. When the decoded message differs from the encoded one, a condition called noise exists.

15-3 Recognize the definition and objectives of promotion.

Promotion is communication to build and maintain relationships by informing and persuading one or more audiences. Although promotional objectives vary from one organization to another and within organizations over time, ten primary objectives underlie many promotional programs. Promotion aims to create awareness of a new product, a new brand, or an existing product; to stimulate primary and selective demand; to encourage product trial through the use of free samples, coupons, limited free-use offers, contests, and games; to identify prospects; to stimulate word of mouth; to retain loyal customers; to facilitate reseller support; to combat competitive promotional efforts; to reduce sales fluctuations; and to generate positive social media posts.

15-4 Summarize the four variables of the promotion mix.

The promotion mix for a product may include four major promotional methods: advertising, personal selling, public relations, and sales promotion. Advertising is paid non-personal communication about an organization and its products transmitted to a target audience through a mass medium. Personal selling is paid personal communication that attempts to inform customers and persuade them to purchase products in an exchange situation. Public relations is a broad set of communication efforts used to create and maintain favorable relationships between an organization and its stakeholders. Sales promotion is an activity or material that acts as a direct inducement, offering added value or incentive for the product, to resellers, salespeople, or consumers.

15-5 Explain the factors that are used to determine a product's promotion mix.

The promotional methods used in a product's promotion mix are determined by the organization's promotional resources, objectives, and policies; characteristics of the target market; characteristics of the product; and cost and availability of promotional methods. Marketers also consider whether to use a push policy or a pull policy. With a push policy, the producer promotes the product only to the next institution down the marketing channel. Normally, a push policy stresses personal selling. Firms that use a pull policy promote directly to consumers, with the intention of developing strong consumer demand for the products. Once consumers are persuaded to seek the products in retail stores, retailers go to wholesalers or the producer to buy the products.

15-6 Describe how word-of-mouth communication affects promotion.

Most customers are likely to be influenced by friends and family members when making purchases. Word-of-mouth communication is personal, informal exchanges of communication that customers share with one another about products, brands, and companies. Customers may also choose to go online to find electronic word of mouth about products or companies. Buzz marketing is an attempt to incite publicity and public excitement surrounding a product through a creative event. Viral marketing is a strategy to get consumers to share a marketer's message, often through e-mail or online videos, in a way that spreads dramatically and quickly.

15-7 Discuss how product placement impacts promotion.

Product placement is the strategic location of products or product promotions within entertainment media content to reach the product's target market. In-program product placements have been successful in reaching consumers as they are being entertained rather than in the competitive commercial break time periods.

15-8 List major criticisms and defenses of promotion.

Promotional activities can help consumers make informed purchasing decisions, but they have also evoked much criticism. Promotion has been accused of deception. Although some deceiving or misleading promotions do exist, laws, government regulation, and industry self-regulation minimize deceptive promotion. Promotion has been blamed for increasing prices, but it usually tends to lower them. When demand is high, production and marketing costs decrease, which can result in lower prices. Moreover, promotion helps keep prices lower by facilitating price competition. Other criticisms of promotional activity are that it manipulates consumers into buying products they do not need, that it leads to a more materialistic society, and that consumers do not benefit sufficiently from promotional activity to justify its high cost. Finally, some critics of promotion suggest that potentially harmful products, especially those associated with violence, sex, and unhealthy activities, should not be promoted at all.

Go to www.cengagebrain.com for resources to help you master the content in this chapter as well as for materials that will expand your marketing knowledge!

Developing Your Marketing Plan

A vital component of a successful marketing strategy is the company's plan for communication to its stakeholders. One segment of the communication plan is included in the marketing mix as the promotional element. A clear understanding of the role that promotion plays, as well as the various methods of promotion, is important in developing the promotional plan. The following questions should assist you in relating the information in this chapter to several decisions in your marketing plan.

1. Review the communication process in Figure 15.1. Identify the various players in the communication process for promotion of your product.

2. What are your objectives for promotion? Use Table 15.2 as a guide in answering this question.
3. Which of the four elements of the promotional mix are most appropriate for accomplishing your objectives? Discuss the advantages and disadvantages of each.
4. What role should word-of-mouth communications, buzz marketing, or product placement play in your promotional plan?

Key Concepts

integrated marketing communications 394
communication 395
source 395
receiver 395
coding process 396
communications channel 397

decoding process 397
noise 397
feedback 397
channel capacity 398
promotion 398
primary demand 400
new introductory promotion 400
selective demand 400

promotion mix 403
kinesic communication 405
proxemic communication 405
tactile communication 405
push policy 409
pull policy 410

word-of-mouth communication 410
buzz marketing 412
viral marketing 412
product placement 413

Issues for Discussion and Review

1. What does the term *integrated marketing communications* mean?
2. Define *communication* and describe the communication process. Is it possible to communicate without using all the elements in the communication process? If so, which elements can be omitted?
3. Identify several causes of noise. How can a source reduce noise?
4. What is the major task of promotion? Do firms ever use promotion to accomplish this task and fail? If so, give several examples.
5. Describe the possible objectives of promotion and discuss the circumstances under which each objective might be used.
6. Identify and briefly describe the four promotional methods an organization can use in its promotion mix.
7. What forms of interpersonal communication besides language can be used in personal selling?
8. How do target-market characteristics determine which promotional methods to include in a promotion mix?

Assume a company is planning to promote a cereal to both adults and children. Along what major dimensions would these two promotional efforts have to differ from each other?
9. How can a product's characteristics affect the composition of its promotion mix?
10. Evaluate the following statement: "Appropriate advertising media are always available if a company can afford them."
11. Explain the difference between a pull policy and a push policy. Under what conditions should each policy be used?
12. In which ways can word-of-mouth communication influence the effectiveness of a promotion mix for a product?
13. Which criticisms of promotion do you believe are the most valid? Why?
14. Should organizations be allowed to promote offensive, violent, sexual, or unhealthy products that can be legally sold and purchased? Support your answer.

VIDEO CASE 15
Frank Pepe's Pizzeria Napoletana Uses Positive Word of Mouth to Remain a Premiere Pizzeria

Frank Pepe's Pizzeria Napoletana has opened one of the most recognizable pizzerias in the United States using word of mouth. After returning from World War I, Frank Pepe initially began with making bread during the week and pizzas on the weekend. After seeing a demand for his product, he utilized his entrepreneurial spirit and focused solely on pizza. Frank Pepe founded Pepe's Pizzeria in 1925, with a heavy influence from his Italian culture, in New Haven, CT.

Frank Pepe developed the New Haven-style thin crust pizza that earned him a reputation as owner of one of the country's premiere pizzerias. Many people began referring to Frank Pepe as "Old Reliable," which continued to generate positive feedback throughout different communities. Pepe's signature pizza, the White Clam Pizza, has been the most notable recipe since its development in the mid-1960s.

Since the beginning, Pepe's has been a family-run business. Frank's wife and children all worked in the original store and after retiring, they passed the business to their children, who still have a stake in the business today. Through the transition between generations, Pepe's has always aimed to deliver a premium product that is consistent and meets customer standards. As people come into the store, Pepe's employees engage in personal selling by communicating various menu items.

Current CEO Ken Berry places a high emphasis upon delivering the promise and guarantee of quality within their product every day. As chief executive operator, he sees the challenge of delivering this promise as a duty that helps protect and build the brand, which the Pepe family initially built. He strives to retain brand equity and rely upon feedback from loyal customers as the company continues to grow.

Including the first and flagship store, there are currently eight pizzerias within Connecticut and New York, with additional plans to expand into Boston. With each new store came the difficult task of maintaining the original experience for new, prospective, and loyal customers. When Pepe's began to consistently pursue expansion tactics, some customers appeared dismayed. There were protests and boycotts occurring on opening days, as other happy customers waited in long lines to test the reputation of the premiere pizza.

To ensure customer satisfaction at the new locations, Ken Berry discussed the critical nature of replicating every aspect of the original idea. Everything from the recipes being virtually unchanged to the layout and colors of the stores needed to be congruent to ensure success. He describes Pepe's as an experience that allows customers to step back in time with a handcrafted product.

Another aspect of developing demand for the company in new locations was the advertising tactics used. As Pepe's has always done, they relied upon word of mouth to retain and gain new customers. They place emphasis upon the experience and listen to customer feedback on whether they are delivering a quality product. At times they use direct mail, which can be an effective form of advertising, and they engage with consumers on Twitter and Facebook to remain connected with them. This is sometimes called electronic word of mouth. A major form of promotion comes in the form of free pizza, which is sales promotion. Generally, the week before a grand opening Pepe's will offer free pizza for a week at that location to allow new ovens to be broken in and workers to understand Pepe's culture, and to showcase the confidence that Pepe's has in their product to the local community.

For the public relations side of the company, Pepe's has a donation request option on their website, where customers are welcome to fill out an application to receive primarily gift cards from the company. They also hold a good neighbor night, which allows an organization to hold a fundraiser at any location. Fifteen percent of proceeds made that night is given to the organization. While Pepe's loses out on some of the proceeds, these events create quality relationships in the community as well as generating a potentially new customer base. They also donate gift cards to nonprofit organizations for fundraising purposes.

Throughout the years Pepe's has strived to deliver a promise to customers by staying true to the original product. They have maintained their brand equity through their dedication and standards set by customers, family members, and all stakeholders associated with the product. For Pepe's, it is clear that through positive word-of-mouth, advertising does not always need to be a costly expense.[37]

Questions for Discussion

1. What are the various promotion elements that Pepe's uses to communicate with customers?
2. What role does word of mouth play in Pepe's integrated marketing communications?
3. Evaluate free pizza as a form of sales promotion in Pepe's success.

chapter 16

Advertising and Public Relations

RADIO
TELEVISION
NEWSPAPERS
MAGAZINES
INTERNET

MEDIA

Olivier Le Moal/Shutterstock.com

LEARNING OBJECTIVES

16-1 Describe advertising and its different types.

16-2 Summarize the eight major steps in developing an advertising campaign.

16-3 Identify who is responsible for developing advertising campaigns.

16-4 Describe the different tools of public relations.

16-5 Analyze how public relations is used and evaluated.

Beloved Spokescharacters Imbue Brands with Personalities

Flo from Progressive, the Pine-Sol Lady, the GEICO gecko—these spokescharacters have become indelibly linked to their brands. Companies develop spokescharacters because they help consumers remember their brands. This can significantly impact brand awareness, especially for new customers. Studies have shown that spokescharacters lead to more favorable attitudes among consumers who have little familiarity with the brand than those who are highly familiar with it.

Spokescharacters also assist brands by providing them with a personality to which consumers can relate. Consider Ethel (played by actress Jean Hamilton), the spokescharacter for Frank's RedHot sauce. The elderly spokeswoman has become famous for her catchphrase: "Frank's RedHot. I put that s*** on everything." Consumers responded positively to the plucky 93-year-old, and Frank's RedHot maintains that its sales growth is double that of the competition.

Another successful spokesperson is the Trivago Guy. German Internet travel and hospitality firm Trivago hired Houston-born Tim Williams to be its spokesman. Americans seemed to find this scruffy-looking character highly relatable, so much so that Trivago's advertising awareness shot past competitors Orbitz and Expedia. Trivago recently introduced a female spokesperson to the mix, Australian-born Gabrielle Miller. Miller's campaign marks another success for Trivago, generating more digital actions, from searches to social media posts, than previous campaigns.

While it is clear that spokescharacters increase brand awareness, does this actually result in increased sales? Just because consumers know about a brand does not mean they will necessarily purchase it. However, brand awareness does have a major impact in placing the brand into the consumer's consideration set. Brands in the initial consideration set are three times more likely to be purchased than those that are not. Perhaps this is why competitors such as Priceline announced they would increase their advertising expenditures after the Trivago Guy became such a success.[1]

Progressive Casualty Insurance Company

advertising Paid non-personal communication about an organization and its products transmitted to a target audience through mass media

institutional advertising Advertising that promotes organizational images, ideas, and political issues

Both large organizations and small companies use conventional and online promotional efforts like advertising to change their corporate images, build brand equity, launch new products, or promote current brands. In this chapter, we explore many dimensions of advertising and public relations. First, we focus on the nature and types of advertising. Next, we examine the major steps in developing an advertising campaign and describe who is responsible for developing the campaigns. We then discuss public relations and how it is used. Finally, we examine various public relations tools and ways to evaluate the effectiveness of public relations.

16-1 THE NATURE AND TYPES OF ADVERTISING

LO 16-1 Describe advertising and its different types.

Advertising permeates our daily lives. At times, we view it positively; at other times, we feel bombarded and try to avoid it. Some advertising informs, persuades, or entertains us; some bores, annoys, or even offends us.

As mentioned in Chapter 15, **advertising** is a paid form of nonpersonal communication that is transmitted to a target audience through mass media, such as television, radio, the Internet, newspapers, magazines, direct mail, outdoor displays, and signs or wraps on vehicles. Advertising can have a profound impact on how consumers view certain products. One example is the promotion of locally grown and organic produce. Consumers are likely to view locally grown and organic produce as healthier even though there is no evidence to support this view—although the produce itself is fresher. Whole Foods and other supermarkets promote locally grown food as being more sustainable since it eliminates emissions from transporting food long distances and supports local farmers. Advertisements even influence how a brand's own sales force views company products. Salesperson perception of brand advertising is positively related to effort and performance because it influences how the salesperson identifies with the brand.[2] Organizations use advertising to reach a variety of audiences ranging from small, specific groups, such as coin collectors in Wyoming, to extremely large groups, such as all athletic-shoe buyers in the United States.

When asked to name major advertisers, most people immediately mention business organizations. However, many nonbusiness organizations—including governments, churches, universities, and charitable organizations—employ advertising to communicate with stakeholders. Each year, the U.S. government spends hundreds of millions of dollars in advertising to advise and influence the behavior of its citizens. Although this chapter analyzes advertising in the context of business organizations, much of the following concepts apply to all types of organizations, including nonprofits.

Advertising is used to promote goods, services, ideas, images, issues, people, and anything else advertisers want to publicize or encourage. Depending on what is being promoted, advertising can be classified as institutional or product advertising. Institutional advertising promotes organizational images, ideas, and political issues. Institutional advertisements may deal with broad image issues, such as organizational strengths or the friendliness of employees. They may also aim to create a more favorable view of the organization in the eyes of noncustomer groups, such as shareholders, consumer advocacy groups, potential shareholders, or the general public. Institutional advertising can be proactive to create a favorable view of the organization or its industry or, in contrast, reactive, in response to something that may negatively impact an organization's reputation. For example, Wells Fargo created an incentive system for its sales force that resulted in many new, unauthorized accounts being opened for customers. In response to the negative news stories on the company's behavior, Wells Fargo ran an ad promoting their focus on customer relationships. The goal was to improve overall brand image in a time of extremely negative news.

When a company promotes its position on a public issue—for instance, a tax increase, sustainability, regulations, or international trade coalitions—institutional advertising is referred to as **advocacy advertising**. Such advertising may be used to promote socially approved behavior, such as recycling or moderation in consuming alcoholic beverages. Philip Morris, for example, has run television advertisements encouraging parents to talk to their children about not smoking. Effectively communicating with teens about the health risks associated with smoking is critical because nearly 90 percent of smokers have their first cigarette before the age of 18.[3] This type of advertising not only has social benefits but also helps build an organization's image.

Product advertising promotes the uses, features, and benefits of products. AfterShokz Trekz Titanium can use advertising to promote its unique headphones. The headphones are not in or over the ear; instead, they transmit sound waves through the bones in your temples. This leaves your ears uncovered and improves safety when enjoying sound outdoors and during workouts. There are two types of product advertising: pioneer and competitive. **Pioneer advertising** focuses on stimulating demand for a product category (rather than a specific brand) by informing potential customers about the product's features, uses, and benefits. Product advertising that focuses on products before they are available tends to cause people to think about the product more and evaluate it more positively.[4] Pioneer advertising is also employed when the product is in the introductory stage of the product life cycle. When Tesla introduced a software update, version 7.0, referred to as "autopilot," to its cars with a sophisticated technology and camera package, the cars could perform tasks that normal automobiles could not. These Tesla vehicles could prevent drivers from being in accidents as well as steer, change lanes, adjust speed, and park. The early pioneers in this category had to educate consumers about the products and their benefits. **Competitive advertising** attempts to stimulate demand for a specific brand by promoting the brand's features, uses, and advantages through indirect or direct comparisons with competing brands. Cable, satellite, and streaming Internet television service providers use competitive advertising to position their brands such as Comcast, AT&T, DirecTV, and Sling TV. Advertising effects on sales must reflect competitors' advertising activities. The type and intensity of the competitive environment will determine the most effective approach.

To make direct product comparisons, marketers use a form of competitive advertising called **comparative advertising**, which compares the sponsored brand with one or more identified competing brands on the basis of one or more product characteristics. Surveys show that top creative advertising practitioners view comparative advertising favorably when it clearly identifies the competition.[5] Often, the brands that are promoted through comparative advertisements have low market shares and are compared with competitors that have the highest market shares in the product category. For example, Yoplait released an advertisement campaign called "The Yoplait Greek Taste Off" that directly compared its Greek yogurt with rival Chobani's. Yoplait, after its relatively

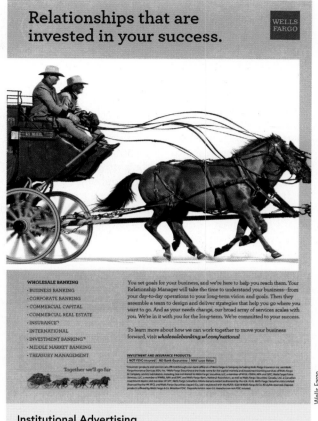

Institutional Advertising
Wells Fargo uses institutional advertising to promote its image of investing in and caring about its relationship with customers.

advocacy advertising
Advertising that promotes a company's position on a public issue

product advertising
Advertising that promotes the uses, features, and benefits of products

pioneer advertising
Advertising that tries to stimulate demand for a product category rather than a specific brand by informing potential buyers about the product

competitive advertising
Advertising that tries to stimulate demand for a specific brand by promoting its features, uses, and advantages relative to competing brands

EMERGING TRENDS IN MARKETING

The Rise of Native Advertising

Digital native advertising is online advertising that matches the appearance and purpose of the content in which it is embedded. For example, the wedding website The Knot may feature sponsored articles about wedding gowns that consumers can purchase through the website. Consumers find this advertising useful because the content is likely to follow the website's topics and style. Nearly 73 percent of Internet users familiar with native advertising believe it is equally or more effective than non-sponsored ads.

The effectiveness of this type of digital advertising is causing marketers to take notice. For instance, the marketing agency of *The Wall Street Journal* partnered with Starz to develop an article—complete with video clips and an interactive timeline—that features the economics of romantic

relationships throughout history. The sponsored content helped market Starz's show *The Girlfriend Experience*, while the focus on economics was meant to interest the *The Wall Street Journal's* business-savvy target market.

However, because the advertisements are meant to resemble the surrounding content, consumers might not always recognize that an article or advertisement is sponsored. One report claims that 71 percent of native advertising lacks sufficient transparency. The FTC maintains that advertising must be distinguished from editorial content, but this line becomes blurred when the advertising resembles the content so closely. Industry self-regulatory guidelines are encouraging advertisers to label native ads as sponsored content to avoid confusion.[a]

---

comparative advertising
Advertising that compares the sponsored brand with one or more identified brands on the basis of one or more product characteristics

reminder advertising
Advertising used to remind consumers about an established brand's uses, characteristics, and benefits

reinforcement advertising
Advertising that assures users they chose the right brand and tells them how to get the most satisfaction from it

native advertising Digital advertising that matches the appearance and the purpose of the content in which it is embedded

late start in the Greek yogurt industry, is trying to catch up to market leader Chobani.[6] Product categories that commonly use comparative advertising include soft drinks, toothpaste, pain relievers, foods, tires, automobiles, and detergents. Under the provisions of the 1988 Trademark Law Revision Act, marketers using comparative advertisements in the United States must not misrepresent the qualities or characteristics of competing products.

Other forms of competitive advertising include reminder and reinforcement advertising. **Reminder advertising** tells customers that an established brand is still around and still offers certain characteristics, uses, and advantages. Clorox, for example, reminds customers about the many advantages of its bleach products, such as their ability to kill germs, whiten clothes, and remove stains. **Reinforcement advertising** assures current users that they have made the right brand choice and tells them how to get the most satisfaction from that brand. Insurance companies like GEICO encourage potential new customers to spend 15 minutes on the phone getting an insurance quote and save 15 percent or more on their policy. Value propositions can provide reinforcement to consumers that they are making a good decision as a new or current customer.

One growing trend among marketers has been the use of **native advertising**, or digital advertising that matches the appearance and purpose of the content in which it is embedded. The word "native" refers to the fact that this form of advertising is meant to resemble the content itself. Native advertising has been associated with improved brand perception, awareness, and engagement over standard banner ads. Native advertising is expected to account for 74 percent of ad revenue by 2021.[7] In a world inundated with advertisements, native advertising offers marketers the opportunity to reach consumers in new and innovative ways. It also increases advertising revenue for the sites that host them. On the other hand, native advertising is potentially misleading when consumers do not realize that a video or post is sponsored by an organization. One survey revealed that over 50 percent of consumers felt deceived upon realizing that an article or video was sponsored content.[8] To avoid deception and possible legal repercussions, brands should clearly identify sponsored content on digital media sites.

16-2 DEVELOPING AN ADVERTISING CAMPAIGN

LO 16-2 Summarize the eight major steps in developing an advertising campaign.

An **advertising campaign** involves designing a series of advertisements and placing them in various advertising media to reach a particular target audience. As Figure 16.1 shows, the major steps in creating an advertising campaign are (1) identifying and analyzing the target audience, (2) defining the advertising objectives, (3) creating the advertising platform, (4) determining the advertising appropriation, (5) developing the media plan, (6) creating the advertising message, (7) executing the campaign, and (8) evaluating advertising effectiveness. The number of steps and the exact order in which they are carried out may vary according to the organization's resources, the nature of its product, and the type of target audience to be reached. Nevertheless, these general guidelines for developing an advertising campaign are appropriate for all types of organizations.

16-2a Identifying and Analyzing the Target Audience

The **target audience** is the group of people at whom advertisements are aimed. Advertisements for the Dyson vacuum cleaner target more affluent home owners, whereas the Dirt Devil targets lower- to middle-income households. Identifying and analyzing the target audience are critical processes; the information yielded helps determine other steps in developing the campaign. The target audience may include everyone in the firm's target market. Marketers may, however, direct a campaign at only a portion of the target market. For instance, until recently, the upscale yoga apparel organization Lululemon Athletica focused mainly on women. However, the firm is extending its focus to men interested in fitness with new lines of menswear. It is estimated that nearly 30 percent of Americans practicing yoga are men. That number has doubled in the last four years, representing a rapidly growing market. Proactive companies like Lululemon Athletica are taking advantage of shifting demographics in this market.[9] Starbucks is well known for their retail coffee experience and ambiance. Grocery stores now carry chilled, ready-to-drink Starbucks iced coffees and espressos.

advertising campaign The creation and execution of a series of advertisements to communicate with a particular target audience

target audience The group of people at whom advertisements are aimed

FIGURE 16.1   GENERAL STEPS IN DEVELOPING AND IMPLEMENTING AN ADVERTISING CAMPAIGN

8 Evaluate advertising effectiveness
7 Execute campaign
6 Create advertising message
5 Develop media plan
4 Determine advertising appropriation
3 Create advertising platform
2 Define advertising objectives
1 Identify and analyze target audience

Targeting Different Markets
Starbucks provides ready-to-drink coffee products in grocery stores at a higher price point than Nescafé's instant coffee, Taster's Choice.

The market for Starbucks products is a more affluent target market than the market for Nescafé Taster's Choice instant coffee. Starbucks' coffee is now sold, prepared and sitting on a traditional grocery store shelf.

Advertisers research and analyze advertising targets to establish an information base for a campaign. Information commonly needed includes location and geographic distribution of the target group; the distribution of demographic factors, such as age, income, race, gender, and education; lifestyle information; and consumer attitudes regarding purchase and use of both the advertiser's products and competing products. The exact kinds of information an organization finds useful depend on the type of product being advertised, the characteristics of the target audience, and the type and amount of competition. Advertisers' goal is to create a campaign that will resonate with the target market. For example, privacy concerns and irritating ads lead to avoidance, but when digital media and direct-mail advertising personalizes the information, acceptance of ads tends to increase.[10] Generally, the more an advertiser knows about the target audience, the more likely the firm is to develop an effective advertising campaign. When the advertising target is not well understood and differentiated, the campaign is more likely to fail.

16-2b **Defining the Advertising Objectives**

The advertiser's next step is to determine what the firm hopes to accomplish with the campaign. Because advertising objectives guide campaign development, advertisers should define objectives carefully. Advertising objectives should be stated clearly, precisely, and in measurable terms. Quantifiable metrics allow advertisers to evaluate advertising success at the end of the campaign in terms of whether objectives have been met. To provide precision and measurability, advertising objectives should contain benchmarks and indicate what the advertiser hopes to accomplish. If the goal is to increase sales, the advertiser should state the current sales level (the benchmark) and the amount of sales increase sought through advertising. An advertising objective should also specify a time frame so that advertisers know exactly how long they have to accomplish the objective. An advertiser with average monthly sales of $450,000 (the benchmark) might set the following objective: "Our primary advertising objective is to increase average monthly sales from $450,000 to $540,000 (20%) within 12 months."

If an advertiser defines objectives on the basis of sales, the objectives focus on increasing absolute dollar sales or unit sales, increasing sales by a certain percentage, or increasing the firm's market share. Even though an advertiser's long-run goal is to increase sales, not all campaigns are designed to produce immediate sales. Some campaigns aim to increase product or brand awareness, make consumers' attitudes more favorable, heighten consumers' knowledge of product features, or create awareness of positive, healthy consumer behavior, such as a healthy lifestyle and diet. If the goal is to increase product awareness, the objectives are stated in terms of communication. A specific communication objective might be to increase new product awareness, such as knowing that Southwest Rapid Rewards Premier Visa card offers 2 points for every dollar spent on Southwest flights and with travel partners.

16-2c Creating the Advertising Platform

Before launching a political campaign, party leaders develop a political platform stating major issues that are the basis of the campaign. Like a political platform, an **advertising platform** consists of the basic issues or selling points that an advertiser wishes to include in the advertising campaign. For example, McDonald's advertises all-day breakfasts as part of its advertising platform for its restaurants. A single advertisement in an advertising campaign may contain one or several issues from the platform. Although the platform sets forth the basic issues, it does not indicate how to present them.

An advertising platform should consist of issues important to customers. One of the best ways to determine those issues is to survey customers about what they consider most important in the selection and use of the product involved. Hulu surveyed their consumer panel, called the "Hulu Brain Trust" consisting of 500 members, and asked for some "true confessions" about the craziest places they have watched Hulu. The top five places include the bathroom, in a meeting, at a red light, wedding, and funeral. Hulu can use these interesting locations in digital media and other forms of advertising to better relate to its users.[11] Selling features must not only be important to customers; they should also be strongly competitive features of the advertised brand. For example, Southwest Airlines has a great sales proposition versus many of its competitors in promoting that "bags fly free," whereas many other airlines charge for checked luggage. Although research is the most effective method for determining what issues to include in an advertising platform, customer research can be expensive. Often a competitor and market analysis can expose attractive selling features.

Because the advertising platform is a base on which to build the advertising message, marketers should analyze this stage carefully. It has been found that, if the message is viewed as useful, it will create greater brand trust.[12] A campaign can be perfect in terms of selection and analysis of its target audience, statement of its objectives, media strategy, and the form of its message and delivery. On the other hand, campaigns will ultimately fail if the advertisements communicate information that consumers do not deem important when selecting and using the product. A Netflix ad was pulled from an outdoor board in Germany as it was deemed to have gone "a little too far." Netflix was using humor to promote their zombie comedy series *Santa Clarita Diet* and showed a billboard with a human finger sliced and seasoned as a special dish with a fork sticking out of it. Adolescents and children were particularly offended by the ads and many were disgusted and nauseated by the graphic. The ad may have backfired, but significant publicity was achieved through the controversy.[13]

advertising platform
Basic issues or selling points to be included in an advertising campaign

advertising appropriation
The advertising budget for
a specific time period

**objective-and-task
approach** Budgeting for
an advertising campaign by
first determining its objectives and then calculating
the cost of all the tasks
needed to attain them

**percent-of-sales
approach** Budgeting for
an advertising campaign
by multiplying the firm's
past and expected sales
by a standard percentage

16-2d Determining the Advertising Appropriation

The **advertising appropriation** is the total amount of money a marketer allocates for advertising for a specific time period. GEICO is a leading television advertiser in the United States, outspending Verizon, Progressive, Ford, Lionsgate, T Mobile and AT&T in the same period.[14] Many factors affect a firm's decision about how much to appropriate for advertising. Geographic size of the market and the distribution of buyers within the market have a great bearing on this decision. Both the type of product advertised and the firm's sales volume relative to competitors' sales volumes also play roles in determining what proportion of revenue to spend on advertising. Advertising appropriations for business products are usually quite small relative to product sales, whereas consumer convenience items, such as the cosmetics sold by Maybelline, generally have large advertising expenditures relative to sales. Retailers like Walmart usually have a much lower percent of sales spent on advertising. Figure 16.2 shows how advertising has grown throughout the years.

Of the many techniques used to determine the advertising appropriation, one of the most logical is the **objective-and-task approach**. Using this approach, marketers determine the objectives a campaign is to achieve and then attempt to list the tasks required to accomplish them. The costs of the tasks are calculated and added to arrive at the total appropriation. This approach has one main problem: marketers sometimes have trouble accurately estimating the level of effort needed to attain certain objectives. A chain of retail donut shops, for example, may find it extremely difficult to determine how much of an increase in national television advertising is needed to raise a brand's market share from 8 to 10 percent.

In the more widely used **percent-of-sales approach**, marketers simply multiply the firm's past sales, plus a factor for planned sales growth or decline, by a standard percentage based on both what the firm traditionally spends on advertising and the industry average. This approach, too, has a major flaw: it is based on the incorrect assumption that sales create advertising rather than the reverse. A marketer using this approach during declining sales

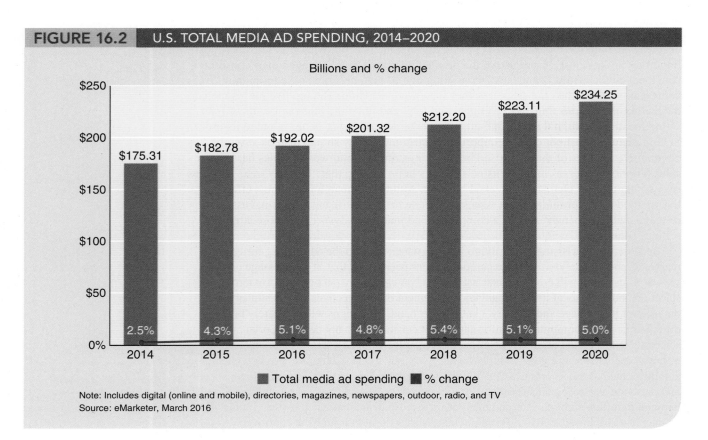

FIGURE 16.2   U.S. TOTAL MEDIA AD SPENDING, 2014–2020

Billions and % change

	2014	2015	2016	2017	2018	2019	2020
Total media ad spending	$175.31	$182.78	$192.02	$201.32	$212.20	$223.11	$234.25
% change	2.5%	4.3%	5.1%	4.8%	5.4%	5.1%	5.0%

■ Total media ad spending   ■ % change

Note: Includes digital (online and mobile), directories, magazines, newspapers, outdoor, radio, and TV
Source: eMarketer, March 2016

will reduce the amount spent on advertising, but such a reduction may further diminish sales. Though illogical, this technique has been favored because it is easy to implement.

Another way to determine advertising appropriation is the **competition-matching approach**. Marketers following this approach try to match their major competitors' appropriations in absolute dollars or to allocate the same percentage of sales for advertising that their competitors do. Although a marketer should be aware of what competitors spend on advertising, this technique should not be used alone because the firm's competitors probably have different advertising objectives and different resources available for advertising. Many companies and advertising agencies review competitive spending on a quarterly basis, comparing competitors' dollar expenditures on print, radio, and television with their own spending levels. Competitive tracking of this nature occurs at both the national and regional levels.

At times, marketers use the **arbitrary approach**, which usually means a high-level executive in the firm states how much to spend on advertising for a certain period. The arbitrary approach often leads to underspending or overspending. Although hardly a scientific budgeting technique, it is expedient. In general, the corporate culture will drive advertising budget decisions and is often not as profit-maximizing. However, budgeting is more complicated than relying on "rules of thumb."[15] A recent study showed that there is a need for unified measurement of consumers' consumption of traditional media and digital media to allow marketers to properly allocate and optimize the effectiveness of their advertising spending.[16] It is challenging to know how much to spend and how to measure advertising effectiveness.

16-2e Developing the Media Plan

Advertisers spend tremendous amounts on advertising media. These amounts have grown rapidly during the past two decades. Figure 16.3 shows the share of time people spend with different media categories. While print advertising is decreasing, online and television are popular advertising venues. To derive maximum results from media expenditures, marketers must develop effective media plans. A **media plan** sets forth the exact media vehicles to be used (specific magazines, television stations, social media, newspapers, and so forth) and the dates and times the advertisements will appear. The plan determines how many people

competition-matching approach Determining an advertising budget by trying to match competitors' advertising outlays

arbitrary approach Budgeting for an advertising campaign as specified by a high-level executive in the firm

media plan A plan that specifies the media vehicles to be used and the schedule for running advertisements

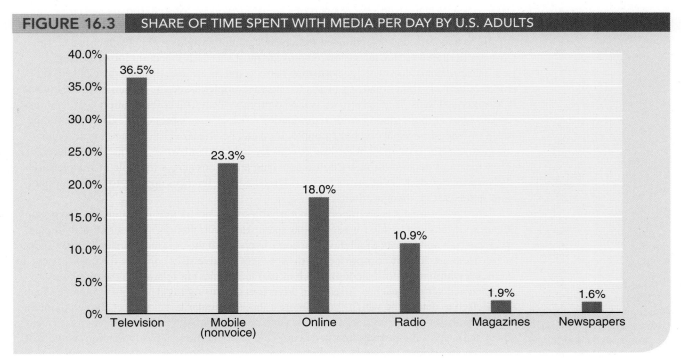

FIGURE 16.3 | SHARE OF TIME SPENT WITH MEDIA PER DAY BY U.S. ADULTS

- Television: 36.5%
- Mobile (nonvoice): 23.3%
- Online: 18.0%
- Radio: 10.9%
- Magazines: 1.9%
- Newspapers: 1.6%

Source: eMarketer, April 2014

in the target audience will be exposed to the message. The method also determines, to some degree, the effects of the message on those specific target markets. Media planning is a complex task requiring thorough analysis of the target audience. Sophisticated computer models have been developed to attempt to maximize the effectiveness of media plans.

To formulate a media plan, the planners select the media for the campaign and prepare a time schedule for each medium. The media planner's primary goal is to reach the largest number of people in the advertising target that the budget will allow. A secondary goal is to achieve the appropriate message reach and frequency for the target audience while staying within budget. *Reach* refers to the percentage of consumers in the target audience actually exposed to a particular advertisement in a stated period. *Frequency* is the number of times these targeted consumers are exposed to the advertisement.

Media planners begin with broad decisions but eventually make very specific ones. They first decide which kinds of media to use: radio, television, newspapers, digital or online advertising, magazines, direct mail, outdoor displays, or signs on mass-transit vehicles. Digital marketing in particular is growing, with spending on online and mobile advertising accounting for more than 38 percent of advertising dollars.[17] In fact, digital advertising sales have surpassed linear TV ad sales by more than $3 billion. The gap is expected to widen, with digital ad sales projected to increase to $80 billion as offline media sales decline.[18] Media planners assess different formats and approaches to determine which are most effective. Some media plans are highly focused and use just one medium. Others can be quite complex and dynamic.

Media planners take many factors into account when devising a media plan. They analyze location and demographic characteristics of consumers in the target audience, because people's tastes in media differ according to demographic groups and locations. Media planners also consider the sizes and types of audiences that specific media reach. For instance, *National Geographic* reaches relatively well-educated consumers who are often highly influential decision makers. The magazine has 28 million readers in the United States alone.[19] Many marketers of vehicles, nonprofit organizations, and electronics would consider this an attractive demographic. Declining broadcast television ratings and newspaper and magazine readership have led many companies to explore alternative media, including not only cable television and digital advertising but also ads on cell phones and product placements in video games. New media like social networking sites and mobile advertising are also attracting advertisers due to their large reach. When advertising is a part of a social networking site, consumers need to see the advertising as beneficial, or it may lead them to abandon the site.[20] Advertisers are using social media as a tool for understanding customers and gaining insights.[21] On the other hand, even in this age of digital media, television remains the most successful medium for advertising.[22]

The content of the message sometimes affects media choice. Print media can be used more effectively than broadcast media to present complex issues or numerous details in single advertisements. If an advertiser wants to promote beautiful colors, patterns, or textures, media offering high-quality color reproduction, such as magazines or television, should be used instead of newspapers. For example, food can be effectively promoted in full-color magazine advertisements but far less effectively in black-and-white media. Decisions are also made in selection for non-English speaking audiences across multiple media platforms. Advertisers' evaluation of distinct cultural traits and preferences appears to be more important in the case of diverse ethnic cultures.

The cost of media is an important but troublesome consideration. Planners try to obtain the best coverage possible for each dollar spent. However, there is no accurate way to compare the cost and impact of a television commercial with the cost and impact of a newspaper advertisement. A **cost comparison indicator** lets an advertiser compare the costs of several vehicles within a specific medium (such as two magazines) in relation to the number of people each vehicle reaches. Streaming advertisers are using big data from companies such as Nielsen to determine which shows interest their particular target market. Targeted, interactive ad technology has been available for years, but by finding out how campaigns perform on specific apps and devices, marketers are able to select the less costly medium while still reaching their target market.[23] Another common metric is *cost per thousand impressions (CPM)*, which is the cost comparison indicator for magazines; it shows the cost of exposing

cost comparison indicator
A means of comparing the costs of advertising vehicles in a specific medium in relation to the number of people reached

1,000 people to one advertisement. Media are selected by weighing the various advantages and disadvantages of each (see Table 16.1).

Like media selection decisions, media scheduling decisions are affected by numerous factors, such as target audience characteristics, product attributes, product seasonality, customer media behavior, and size of the advertising budget. There are three general types of media schedules: continuous, flighting, and pulsing. When a *continuous* schedule is used, advertising runs at a constant level with little variation throughout the campaign period. McDonald's is an example of a company that uses a continuous schedule. With a *flighting* schedule, advertisements run for set periods of time, alternating with periods in which no ads run. For example, an advertising campaign might have an ad run for two weeks, then suspend it for two weeks, and then run it again for two weeks. Companies like Hallmark, John Deere, and Ray-Ban use a flighting schedule. A *pulsing* schedule combines continuous and flighting schedules: during the entire campaign, a certain portion of advertising runs continuously, and during specific time periods of the campaign, additional advertising is used to intensify the level of communication with the target audience.

TABLE 16.1   ADVANTAGES AND DISADVANTAGES OF MAJOR MEDIA CLASSES

Medium	Advantages	Disadvantages
Newspapers	Reaches large audience; purchased to be read; geographic flexibility; short lead time; frequent publication; favorable for cooperative advertising; merchandising services	Not selective for socioeconomic groups or target market; short life; limited reproduction capabilities; large advertising volume limits exposure to any one advertisement
Magazines	Demographic selectivity; good reproduction; long life; prestige; geographic selectivity when regional issues are available; read in leisurely manner	High costs; 30- to 90-day average lead time; high level of competition; limited reach; communicates less frequently
Direct mail	Little wasted circulation; highly selective; circulation controlled by advertiser; few distractions; personal; stimulates actions; use of novelty; relatively easy to measure performance; hidden from competitors	Very expensive; lacks editorial content to attract readers; often thrown away unread as junk mail; criticized as invasion of privacy; consumers must choose to read the ad
Radio	Reaches 95 percent of consumers; highly mobile and flexible; very low relative costs; ad can be changed quickly; high level of geographic and demographic selectivity; encourages use of imagination	Lacks visual imagery; short life of message; listeners' attention limited because of other activities; market fragmentation; difficult buying procedures; limited media and audience research
Television	Reaches large audiences; high frequency available; dual impact of audio and video; highly visible; high prestige; geographic and demographic selectivity; difficult to ignore; on-demand capabilities	Very expensive; highly perishable message; size of audience not guaranteed; amount of prime time limited; lack of selectivity in target market
Digital media	Immediate response; potential to reach a precisely targeted audience; ability to track customers and build databases; highly interactive medium; real-time analytics	Costs of precise targeting are high; inappropriate ad placement; effects difficult to measure; concerns about security and privacy
Outdoor	Allows for frequent repetition; low cost; message can be placed close to point of sale; geographic selectivity; operable 24 hours a day; high creativity and effectiveness	Message must be short and simple; no demographic selectivity; seldom attracts readers' full attention; criticized as traffic hazard and blight on countryside; much wasted coverage; limited capabilities

Sources: Adapted from William F. Arens and Michael F. Weigold, *Contemporary Advertising* (Burr Ridge, IL: Irwin/McGraw-Hill, 2017); George E. Belch and Michael A. Belch, *Advertising and Promotion* (Burr Ridge, IL: Irwin/McGraw-Hill, 2015).

16-2f **Creating the Advertising Message**

The basic content and form of an advertising message are a function of several factors. A product's features, uses, and benefits affect the content of the message. The intensity of the advertising can also have an impact. For instance, push advertising on digital devices refers to advertising that is not requested by the user. While push advertising might alienate some consumers, younger consumers are more accepting of push advertising if the source is trusted, permission has been given, and the messages are relevant or entertaining.[24] Advertising that pushes too hard to the point that consumers feel uncomfortable may cause consumers to consider the product negatively. With the increase in digital technology, the cost of advertising for marketers is decreasing and advertising is becoming more frequent in venues such as mobile games and social media. As advertising becomes more embedded in our lives, advertisers must strive to not offend consumers by being too prevalent, obvious, or invasive.

Additionally, characteristics of the people in the target audience—gender, age, education, race, income, occupation, lifestyle, life stage, and other attributes—influence both content and form. For instance, gender affects how people respond to advertising claims that use hedging words like *may* and *probably* and pledging words, such as *definitely* and *absolutely.*

Researchers have found that women respond negatively to both types of claims, but pledging claims have little effect on men.[25] When Procter & Gamble promotes Crest toothpaste to children, the company emphasizes daily brushing and cavity control, focusing on fun and good flavors like bubblegum. When marketing Crest to adults, P&G focuses on functionality, stressing whitening, enamel protection, breath enhancement, and tartar and plaque control. To communicate effectively, advertisers use words, symbols, and illustrations that are meaningful, familiar, and appealing to people in the target audience.

Another controversy for advertisers is whether to advertise to children. Many countries have restrictions on advertising to this demographic. Sweden and Norway ban advertising directed at children, and Great Britain limits the advertising of foods high in fat, salt, or sugar on television and radio to children under 16. Many firms in the European Union and the United States are attempting self-regulation, developing codes of conduct regarding this type of advertising. Coca-Cola, Unilever, Dannon, and General Mills are just a few examples of brands that have pledged under the Children's Food & Beverage Advertising Initiative to not target advertising toward children under 12 years old.[26]

An advertising campaign's objectives and platform also affect the content and form of its messages. If a firm's advertising objectives involve large sales increases, the message may include hard-hitting, high-impact language, symbols, and messages. Slogans such as Home Depot's basic message, "More saving. More doing." can aid in brand recall. When designing slogans, marketers should make them short, retain them for a long period of time, and provide large marketing budgets to make the slogan memorable.[27] The use of spokescharacters or design elements can also be highly effective. Keebler uses elves as spokescharacters for its cookies. Viewers have come to associate these spokescharacters with the company. In the advertisement,

Spokescharacter
Keebler uses elves to promote the taste and quality of its cookies.

jif.com

Keebler uses the elves to show the "elfin magic" that goes into making cookies so tasty. The spokescharacter can provide a personality and improve brand equity by directly and indirectly enhancing excitement, sincerity, and trust.[28] Thus, the advertising platform is the foundation on which campaign messages are built.

Choice of media obviously influences the content and form of the message. Effective outdoor displays and short broadcast spot announcements require concise, simple messages. Magazine and newspaper advertisements can include considerable detail and long explanations. Because several kinds of media offer geographic selectivity, a precise message can be tailored to a particular geographic section of the target audience. Some magazine publishers produce **regional issues**, in which advertisements and editorial content of copies appearing in one geographic area differ from those appearing in other areas. A company may also choose to advertise in only one region. Such geographic selectivity lets a firm use the same message in different regions at different times.

Copy

Copy is the verbal portion of an advertisement and may include headlines, subheadlines, body copy, and a signature. Not all advertising contains all of these copy elements. Even handwritten notes on direct-mail advertising that say "Try this. It works!" seem to increase requests for free samples.[29] The headline is critical because often it is the only part of the copy that people read. It should attract readers' attention and create enough interest to make them want to read the body copy or visit the website. The subheadline, if there is one, links the headline to the body copy and sometimes serves to explain the headline.

Body copy for most advertisements consists of an introductory statement or paragraph, several explanatory paragraphs, and a closing paragraph. Some copywriters have adopted guidelines for developing body copy systematically: (1) identify a specific desire or problem, (2) recommend the product as the best way to satisfy that desire or solve that problem,

regional issues Versions of a magazine that differ across geographic regions

copy The verbal portion of advertisements

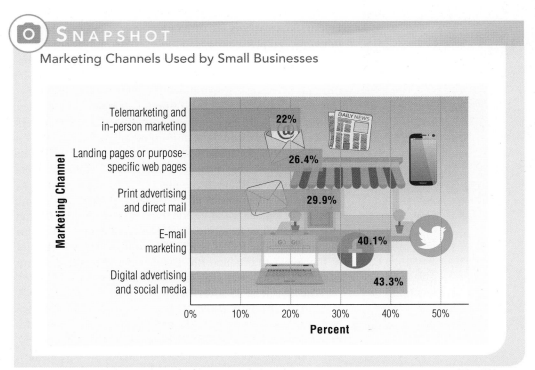

SNAPSHOT

Marketing Channels Used by Small Businesses

Source: Lead Pages, "2016 Small Business Marketing Trends Report," http://leadpages.s3.amazonaws.com/2016%20 Small%20Business%20Marketing%20Trends%20Report.pdf (accessed April 5, 2017).

storyboard A blueprint that combines copy and visual material to show the sequence of major scenes in a commercial

artwork An advertisement's illustrations and layout

illustrations Photos, drawings, graphs, charts, and tables used to spark audience interest in an advertisement

layout The physical arrangement of an advertisement's illustration and copy

(3) state product benefits and indicate why the product is best for the buyer's particular situation, (4) substantiate advertising claims, and (5) ask the buyer to take action. When substantiating claims, it is important to present the substantiation in a credible manner. The proof of claims should help strengthen both the image of the product and company integrity. A shortcut explanation of what much advertising is designed to accomplish is the AIDA model. Advertising should create *awareness,* produce *interest,* create *desire,* and ultimately result in a purchase (*action*). Typeface selection can help advertisers create a desired impression using fonts that are engaging, reassuring, or very prominent.[30]

The signature identifies the advertisement's sponsor. It may contain several elements, including the firm's trademark, logo, name, and address. The signature should be attractive, legible, distinctive, and easy to identify in a variety of sizes.

Often, because radio listeners are not fully "tuned in" mentally to what they are hearing, radio copy should be informal and conversational to attract listeners' attention. Radio messages are highly perishable and should consist of short, familiar terms, which increase their impact. The length should not require a rate of speech exceeding approximately 2.5 words per second.

In television copy, the audio material must not overpower the visual material, and vice versa. However, a television message should make optimal use of its visual portion, which can be very effective for product use, applications, and demonstrations. Copy for a television commercial is sometimes initially written in parallel script form. Video is described in the left column and audio in the right. When the parallel script is approved, the copywriter and artist combine copy with visual material by using a **storyboard**, which depicts a series of miniature television screens showing the sequence of major scenes in the commercial. Beneath each screen is a description of the audio portion to be used with that video segment. Technical personnel use the storyboard as a blueprint when producing the commercial.

Artwork

Artwork consists of an advertisement's illustrations and layout. **Illustrations** are often photographs but can also be drawings, graphs, charts, and tables. Illustrations are used to draw attention, encourage audiences to read or listen to the copy, communicate an idea quickly, or convey ideas that are difficult to express. Illustrations can be more important in capturing attention than text or brand elements, independent of size.[31] They are especially important, because consumers tend to recall the visual portions of advertisements better than the verbal portions. Advertisers use a variety of illustration techniques. They may show the product alone, in a setting or in use, or show the results of the product's use. For example, Systane, in this advertisement, shows a close-up of an eye to emphasize the importance of providing protection and comfort. The headline, "Your Eyes Take in a Lot," and the tagline, "The Relief is Real," both illustrate the benefits of this eye care product. Illustrations can also take the form of comparisons, contrasts, diagrams, and testimonials.

The **layout** of an advertisement is the physical arrangement of the illustration and the copy (headline, subheadline, body copy, and signature). These elements can be arranged in many ways. The final layout is the result of several stages of layout preparation. As it moves through these stages, the layout promotes an exchange of ideas among people developing the advertising campaign and provides instructions for production personnel.

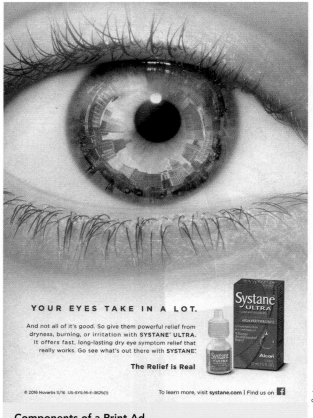

Components of a Print Ad
This Systane advertisement contains components of a print as, a headline, subheadline or tagline, body copy, and illustration.

16-2g Executing the Campaign

Execution of an advertising campaign requires extensive planning and coordination, because many tasks must be completed on time and several people and firms are involved. Production companies, research organizations, media firms, printers, and commercial artists are just a few of the people and firms contributing to a campaign.

Implementation requires detailed schedules to ensure that various phases of the work are done on time. Advertising management personnel must evaluate the quality of the work and take corrective action when necessary. In some instances, changes are made during the campaign so it meets objectives more effectively. For example, an auto company focusing on fuel efficiency may need to add more information relative to the competition to achieve its objectives.

16-2h Evaluating Advertising Effectiveness

A variety of ways exist to test the effectiveness of advertising. They include measuring achievement of advertising objectives; assessing effectiveness of copy, illustrations, or layouts; and evaluating certain media.

Advertising can be evaluated before, during, and after the campaign. An evaluation performed before the campaign begins is called a **pretest**. A pretest usually attempts to evaluate the effectiveness of one or more elements of the message. To pretest advertisements, marketers sometimes use a **consumer jury**, a panel of existing or potential buyers of the advertised product. Jurors judge one or several dimensions of two or more advertisements. Such tests are based on the belief that consumers are more likely than advertising experts to know what influences them. Companies can also solicit the assistance of marketing research firms, such as Information Resources Inc. (IRI), to help assess ads.

To measure advertising effectiveness during a campaign, marketers usually rely on "inquiries" or responses. In a campaign's initial stages, an advertiser may use several advertisements simultaneously, each containing a coupon, form, toll-free phone number, QR code, social media site, or website through which potential customers can request information. The advertiser records the number of inquiries or responses returned from each type of advertisement. If an advertiser receives 78,528 inquiries from advertisement A, 37,072 from advertisement B, and 47,932 from advertisement C, advertisement A is judged superior to advertisements B and C. Internet advertisers can also assess how many people "clicked" on an ad to obtain more product information. For the outdoor advertising industry, its independent auditor developed an "out-of-home" ratings system to determine the audiences likely to see an advertisement. Previous measurement systems used "Daily Effective Circulation," which essentially evolved around traffic counts, not on interested audiences. The industry has modified its rating system to account for new information, including vehicle speed and traffic congestion.[32]

Evaluation of advertising effectiveness after the campaign is called a **posttest**. Advertising objectives often determine what kind of posttest is appropriate. If the objectives' focus is on communication—to increase awareness of product features or brands or to create more favorable customer attitudes—the posttest should measure changes in these dimensions. Advertisers sometimes use consumer surveys or experiments to evaluate a campaign based on communication objectives. These methods are costly, however. In posttests, generalizations can be made about why advertising is failing or why media vehicles are not delivering the desired results.

For campaign objectives stated in terms of sales, advertisers should determine the change in sales or market share attributable to the campaign. However, changes in sales or market share brought about by advertising cannot be measured precisely; many factors independent of advertisements affect a firm's sales and market share. Competitors' actions, regulatory actions, and changes in consumer preferences, weather, and economic conditions are only a few factors that might enhance or diminish a company's sales or market share. For example, the statewide economic downturn in New Mexico has affected the state's ability to fund its

pretest Evaluation of advertisements performed before a campaign begins

consumer jury A panel of a product's existing or potential buyers who pretest ads

posttest Evaluation of advertising effectiveness after the campaign

very popular "New Mexico True" campaign. The campaign has successfully promoted the state's culture, people, and natural resources. However, the budget shortfall will not allow them to invest the $3.5 million needed to enter new markets like San Francisco.[33] By using data about past and current sales and advertising expenditures, advertisers can make gross estimates of the effects of a campaign on sales or market share.

Because it is difficult to determine the direct effects of advertising on sales, many advertisers evaluate print advertisements according to how well consumers can remember them. As more advertisers turn to mobile technology, total spending is estimated at $32 billion. Consumers are now dividing their attention between devices more than ever, with 36 percent of Americans using more than one device simultaneously, from smartphones and tablets to computers and smartwatches, so it's important to spend ad dollars wisely.[34] Researchers have found that ads that play on the theme of social desirability are more memorable when viewed in the presence of other people.

Posttest methods based on memory include recognition and recall tests. Such tests are usually performed by research organizations through surveys. In a **recognition test**, respondents are shown the actual advertisement and asked whether they recognize it. If they do, the interviewer asks additional questions to determine how much of the advertisement each respondent read. When recall is evaluated, respondents are not shown the actual advertisement but instead are asked about what they have seen or heard recently. For Internet advertising, research suggests that the longer a person is exposed to a website containing a banner advertisement, the more likely he or she is to recall the ad.[35]

Recall can be measured through either unaided or aided recall methods. In an **unaided recall test**, respondents identify advertisements they have seen recently but are not shown any clues to help them remember. A similar procedure is used with an **aided recall test**, but respondents are shown a list of products, brands, company names, or trademarks to jog their memories. Many successful marketers have worked with advertising agencies to create catchy jingles to help consumers recall ads. Campbell soup's "Mmm Mmm Good," McDonald's "You deserve a break today," and Coca-Cola's "I'd Like to Teach the World to Sing" are all iconic jingles. Jingles are making a comeback. Working with Bacardi, iHeartMedia came up with a jingle "Drink Bacardi tonight." The campaign increased purchase intent by 54 percent.[36] However, targeted advertising can be viewed negatively by both consumers and regulators, and it is recommended that free websites that generate revenues through advertising remind consumers about the benefits their websites offer as they ask permission to display advertisements.[37]

The major justification for using recognition and recall methods is that people are more likely to buy a product if they can remember an advertisement about it than if they cannot. However, recalling an advertisement does not necessarily lead to buying the product or brand advertised. Researchers also use a sophisticated technique called *single-source data* to help evaluate advertisements. With this technique, individuals' behaviors are tracked from television sets to checkout counters. Monitors are placed in preselected homes, and microcomputers record when the television set is on and which station is being viewed. At the supermarket checkout, the individual in the sample household presents an identification card. Checkers then record the purchases by scanner, and data are sent to the research facility. Some single-source data companies provide sample households with scanning equipment for use at home to record purchases after returning from shopping trips. Single-source data supplies information that links exposure to advertisements with purchase behavior.

16-3 WHO DEVELOPS THE ADVERTISING CAMPAIGN?

LO 16-3 Identify who is responsible for developing advertising campaigns.

An advertising campaign may be handled by an individual, a few people within a firm, a firm's own advertising department, or an advertising agency. In very small firms, one or two individuals are responsible for advertising (and for many other activities as well). Usually, these individuals depend heavily on local media (TV, radio, and newspaper) for copywriting, artwork, and advice about scheduling media.

In certain large businesses, especially large retail organizations, advertising departments or advertising agencies create and implement advertising campaigns. Depending on the size of the advertising program, an advertising department may consist of a few multi-skilled individuals or a sizable number of specialists, including copywriters, artists, social media experts, media buyers, and technical production coordinators. Advertising departments sometimes obtain the services of independent research organizations and hire freelance specialists when a particular project requires it.

Public Relations
Duncan Aldred, Vice President of Global Buick and GMC Sales, Service and Marketing, reveals the Buick Avista Concept on the eve of the 2016 North American International Auto Show.

Most large corporations employ an advertising agency to develop advertising campaigns. When an organization uses an advertising agency, the firm and the agency usually develop the advertising campaign jointly. How much each participates in the campaign's total development depends on the working relationship between the firm and the agency. Ordinarily, a firm relies on the agency for copywriting, artwork, technical production, and formulation of the media plan.

Advertising agencies assist businesses in several ways. An agency, especially a large one, can supply the services of highly skilled specialists—not only copywriters, artists, and production coordinators but also media experts, researchers, and legal advisers. Agency personnel often have broad advertising experience and are usually more objective than a firm's employees about the organization's products.

Because an agency traditionally receives most of its compensation from a 15 percent commission paid by the media from which it makes purchases, firms can obtain some agency services at low or moderate costs. If an agency contracts for $400,000 of television time for a firm, it receives a commission of $60,000 from the television station. Although the traditional compensation method for agencies is changing and now includes other factors, media commissions still offset some costs of using an agency. Like advertising, public relations can be a vital element in a promotion mix. We turn to this topic next.

16-4 PUBLIC RELATIONS TOOLS

LO 16-4 Describe the different tools of public relations.

Public relations is a broad set of communication efforts used to create and maintain favorable relationships between an organization and its stakeholders. An organization communicates with various stakeholders, both internal and external, and public relations efforts can be directed toward any and all of them. A firm's stakeholders can include customers, suppliers, employees, shareholders, the media, educators, potential investors, government officials, and society in general. The response to a negative event is also important. Managers spend more resources understanding and responding to negative word of mouth than they do to the promotion of positive word of mouth.[38] Organizations that delay their response or that are dishonest with stakeholders are likely to make a bad situation worse. For this reason, whenever there is an accident at its parks, Disney issues press releases immediately to inform the public about the incident. Being honest with consumers and responsive to their needs develops a foundation for open communication and trust in the long run.

Public relations can be used to promote people, places, ideas, activities, and even countries. It is often used by nonprofit organizations to achieve their goals. Public relations focuses on enhancing the image of the total organization. Assessing public attitudes and

public relations Communication efforts used to create and maintain favorable relations between an organization and its stakeholders

TABLE 16.2	TOP TEN PUBLIC RELATIONS FIRMS

Rank	PR Agency
1	Edelman
2	Weber Shandwick
3	FleishmanHillard
4	Ketchum
5	Burson-Marsteller
6	MSL Group
7	Hill+Knowlton Strategies
8	Ogilvy PR
9	BlueFocus
10	Golin

Source: "Top 10 Global PR Agency Ranking 2016," *The Holmes Report*, www.holmesreport.com/ranking-and-data/global-communications-report/2016-pr-agency-rankings/top-10 (accessed April 5, 2017).

creating a favorable image are no less important than direct promotion of the organization's products. Because the public's attitudes toward a firm are likely to affect the sales of its products, it is very important for firms to maintain positive public perceptions. In addition, employee morale is strengthened if the public perceives the firm positively.[39] Although public relations can make people aware of a company's products, brands, or activities, it can also create specific company images, such as innovativeness or dependability. By getting the media to report on a firm's accomplishments, public relations helps the company maintain positive public visibility. Some firms use public relations for a single purpose; others use it for several purposes. Table 16.2 lists the top ten public relations firms.

16-4a Public Relations Tools

Companies use a variety of public relations tools to convey messages and create images. Public relations professionals prepare written materials and use digital media to deliver brochures, newsletters, company magazines, news releases, blogs, managed social media sites, and annual reports that reach and influence their various stakeholders. Sometimes, organizations use less conventional tools in their public relations campaigns. AT&T, for example, holds an "It Can Wait" campaign to spread awareness about the dangers of texting and driving. Not only did it hold a pledge drive, but it also partnered with advertising agency BBDO to develop a documentary and held 400 local events to show individuals the impact their texting can have on their driving.[40] AT&T introduced the DriveMode app to silence incoming text messages while driving at 15 mph or faster. The campaign has resulted in more than 5 million app downloads and 14 million pledges.[41]

Public relations personnel also create corporate identity materials—such as logos, business cards, stationery, signs, and promotional materials—that make firms immediately recognizable. Speeches are another public relations tool. Because what a company executive says publicly at meetings or to the media can affect the organization's image, the speech must convey the desired message clearly. Event sponsorship, in which a company pays for part or all of a special event, like a benefit concert or a tennis tournament, is another public-relations tool. In order to appeal to Millennials, Budweiser has announced plans to sponsor more food events. Half of consumers between the ages of 21 and 27 years old identify themselves as foodies.[42] Sponsoring special events can be an effective means of increasing company or brand recognition with relatively minimal investment. Event sponsorship can gain companies considerable amounts of free media coverage. An organization tries to ensure that its product and the sponsored event target a similar audience and that the two are easily associated in customers' minds. Many companies as well as individuals assist in their charitable giving. Bill Daniels, the founder of Cablevision who passed away in 2000, set up a fund supported with more than a billion dollars to provide financial support for many causes, including business ethics.

Publicity is a part of public relations. **Publicity** is communication in news-story form about the organization, its products, or both, transmitted through a mass medium at no charge. For instance, each time Apple CEO Tim Cook announces that the company will introduce a new model of the iPhone and iPad, the story is covered in newspapers and television news shows throughout the world for months afterward. Although public relations has a larger, more comprehensive communication function than publicity, publicity is a very important aspect of public relations. Publicity can be used to provide information about goods or services; to announce expansions or contractions, acquisitions, research, or new-product launches; or to enhance a company's image.

publicity A news story type of communication about an organization and/or its products transmitted through a mass medium at no charge

GOING GREEN

Patagonia Advertising: Don't Buy This Jacket

One of apparel store Patagonia's most popular advertisements features its popular R2 coat with the headline: "Don't Buy This Jacket." In the copy, the advertisement explains that although the R2 uses recycled materials, it is still harmful to the environment. Patagonia advocates for decreased consumption where consumers purchase less (also termed green demarketing).

Patagonia was founded upon environmental principles with a three-part mission: sell quality products, cause no unnecessary harm, and find business solutions to environmental issues. Because excessive consumption generates waste, encouraging consumers to purchase less demonstrates Patagonia's environmental commitment. Patagonia wants consumers to purchase apparel only as needed.

Patagonia has incorporated public relations activities into its campaign as well. For instance, it developed a film showing fans wearing old Patagonia clothing held together by duct tape, demonstrating the value of less consumption. Patagonia also announced it would donate 100 percent of proceeds from sales generated on the day after Thanksgiving to environmental causes.

Because Patagonia clothing lasts a long time, its marketing indirectly promotes its own products as a solution to the constant need to replace worn-out apparel. The company even urges consumers to return worn out merchandise so Patagonia can recycle it into something else. This approach resonates with consumers as sustainable consumption becomes an important sociocultural value. Patagonia's sales increased 40 percent two years after it started the campaign.[b]

The most common publicity-based public relations tool is the **news release**, sometimes called a *press release*, which is usually a single page of typewritten copy containing fewer than 300 words and describing a company event or product. A news release gives the firm's or agency's name, address, phone number, and contact person. Companies sometimes use news releases when introducing new products or making significant announcements. Dozens of organizations, including Nike, Starbucks, and clean-energy companies, are partnering to create awareness of the economic benefits of national climate and energy legislation through press releases and other media. As Table 16.3 shows, news releases tackle a multitude of specific issues. A **feature article** is a manuscript of up to 3,000 words prepared for a specific publication. A **captioned photograph** is a photograph with a brief description explaining its contents. Captioned photographs are effective for illustrating new or improved products with highly visible features.

There are several other kinds of publicity-based public relations tools. For example, a **press conference** is a meeting called to announce major news events. Media personnel are invited to a press conference and are usually supplied with various written materials and photographs. Letters to the editor and editorials are sometimes prepared and sent to newspapers and magazines. Videos may be made available to broadcasters in the hope that they will be aired.

Publicity-based public relations tools offer several advantages, including credibility, news value, significant word-of-mouth communications, and a perception of media endorsement. The public may consider news coverage more truthful and credible than an advertisement because news media are not paid to provide the information. In addition, stories regarding a new-product introduction or a new environmentally responsible company policy, for example, are handled as news items and are likely to receive notice. Finally, the cost of publicity is low compared with the cost of advertising.[43]

Publicity-based public relations tools have some limitations. Media personnel must judge company messages to be newsworthy if the messages are to be published or broadcast at all. Consequently, messages must be timely, interesting, accurate, and in the public interest.

news release A short piece of copy publicizing an event or a product

feature article A manuscript of up to 3,000 words prepared for a specific publication

captioned photograph A photograph with a brief description of its contents

press conference A meeting used to announce major news events

TABLE 16.3	POSSIBLE ISSUES FOR PUBLICITY RELEASES
Support of a social cause	New products
Improved warranties	New slogan
Reports on industry conditions	Research developments
New uses for established products	Company's milestones and anniversaries
Product endorsements	Employment, production, and sales changes
Quality awards	Award of contracts
Company name changes	Opening of new markets
Interviews with company officials	Improvements in financial position
Improved distribution policies	Opening of an exhibit
International business efforts	History of a brand
Athletic event sponsorship	Winners of company contests
Visits by celebrities	Logo changes
Reports on new discoveries	Speeches of top management
Innovative business practices	Merit awards
Economic forecasts	Acquisitions and partnerships

It may take a great deal of time and effort to convince media personnel of the news value of publicity releases, and many communications fail to qualify. Although public relations personnel usually encourage the media to air publicity releases at certain times, they control neither the content nor the timing of the communication. Media personnel alter length and content of publicity releases to fit publishers' or broadcasters' requirements and may even delete the parts of messages that company personnel view as most important. Furthermore, media personnel use publicity releases in time slots or positions most convenient for them. Other outside public relations messages can be picked up during slow news times. Thus, messages sometimes appear in locations or at times that may not reach the firm's target audiences. Although these limitations can be frustrating, properly managed publicity-based public relations tools offer an organization substantial benefits.

16-5 EVALUATING PUBLIC RELATIONS EFFECTIVENESS

LO 16-5 Analyze how public relations is used and evaluated.

Because of the potential benefits of good public relations, it is essential that organizations evaluate the effectiveness of their public relations campaigns. Research can be conducted to determine how well a firm is communicating its messages or image to its target audiences. *Environmental monitoring* identifies changes in public opinion affecting an organization. A *public relations audit* is used to assess an organization's image among the public or to evaluate the effect of a specific public relations program. A *communications audit* may include a content analysis of messages, a readability study, or a readership survey. If an organization wants to measure the extent to which stakeholders view it as being socially responsible, it can conduct a *social audit.*

One approach to measuring the effectiveness of publicity-based public relations is to count the number of exposures in the media. To determine which releases are published in print media and how often, an organization can hire a clipping service, a firm that clips and sends news releases to client companies. To measure the effectiveness of television coverage, a firm can enclose a card with its publicity releases requesting that the television station record its name and the dates when the news item is broadcast (although station personnel do not always comply). Some multimedia tracking services exist, but they are quite costly.

Counting the number of media exposures does not reveal how many people have actually read or heard the company's message or what they thought about the message afterward. However, measuring changes in product awareness, knowledge, and attitudes resulting from the publicity campaign helps yield this information. To assess these changes, companies must measure these levels before and after public relations campaigns. Although precise measures are difficult to obtain, a firm's marketers should attempt to assess the impact of public relations efforts on the organization's sales. For example, critics' reviews of films can affect the films' box office performance. Interestingly, negative reviews (publicity) harm revenue more than positive reviews help revenue in the early weeks of a film's release.[44]

Chapter Review

16-1 Describe advertising and its different types.

Advertising is a paid form of nonpersonal communication transmitted to consumers through mass media, such as television, radio, the Internet, newspapers, magazines, direct mail, outdoor displays, and signs on mass-transit vehicles. Both business and nonbusiness organizations use advertising. Institutional advertising promotes organizational images, ideas, and political issues. When a company promotes its position on a public issue such as taxation, institutional advertising is referred to as advocacy advertising. Product advertising promotes uses, features, and benefits of products. The two types of product advertising are pioneer advertising, which focuses on stimulating demand for a product category rather than a specific brand, and competitive advertising, which attempts to stimulate demand for a specific brand by indicating the brand's features, uses, and advantages. To make direct product comparisons, marketers use comparative advertising, which compares two or more brands. Two other forms of competitive advertising are reminder advertising, which reminds customers about an established brand's uses, characteristics, and benefits, and reinforcement advertising, which assures current users they have made the right brand choice.

16-2 Summarize the eight major steps in developing an advertising campaign.

Although marketers may vary in how they develop advertising campaigns, they should follow a general pattern. First, they must identify and analyze the target audience, the group of people at whom advertisements are aimed. Second, they should establish what they want the campaign to accomplish by defining advertising objectives.

Objectives should be clear, precise, and presented in measurable terms. Third, marketers must create the advertising platform, which contains basic issues to be presented in the campaign. Advertising platforms should consist of issues important to consumers. Fourth, advertisers must decide how much money to spend on the campaign; they arrive at this decision through the objective-and-task approach, percent-of-sales approach, competition-matching approach, or arbitrary approach.

Advertisers must then develop a media plan, their fifth step, by selecting and scheduling media to use in the campaign. Some factors affecting the media plan are location and demographic characteristics of the target audience, content of the message, and cost of the various media. Sixth, the advertising message is created. The basic content and form of the advertising message are affected by product features, uses, and benefits; characteristics of the people in the target audience; the campaign's objectives and platform; and the choice of media. Advertisers use copy and artwork to create the message. Step seven, the execution of an advertising campaign requires extensive planning and coordination.

Finally, advertisers must devise one or more methods for evaluating advertisement effectiveness. Pretests are evaluations performed before the campaign begins; posttests are conducted after the campaign. Two types of posttests are a recognition test, in which respondents are shown the actual advertisement and asked whether they recognize it, and a recall test. In aided recall tests, respondents are shown a list of products, brands, company names, or trademarks to jog their memories. In unaided tests, no clues are given.

16-3 Identify who is responsible for developing advertising campaigns.

Advertising campaigns can be developed by personnel within the firm or in conjunction with advertising agencies.

A campaign created by the firm's personnel may be developed by one or more individuals or by an advertising department within the firm. Use of an advertising agency may be advantageous because an agency provides highly skilled, objective specialists with broad experience in advertising at low to moderate costs to the firm.

16-4 Describe the different tools of public relations.

Public relations is a broad set of communication efforts used to create and maintain favorable relationships between an organization and its stakeholders. Public relations can be used to promote people, places, ideas, activities, and countries, and to create and maintain a positive company image. Some firms use public relations for a single purpose; others use it for several purposes. Public relations tools include written materials, such as brochures, newsletters, and annual reports; corporate identity materials, such as business cards and signs; speeches; event sponsorships; and special events. Publicity is communication in news-story form about an organization, its products, or both, transmitted through a mass medium at no charge. Publicity-based public relations tools include news releases, feature articles, captioned photographs, and press conferences. Problems that organizations confront in using publicity-based public relations include reluctance of media personnel to print or air releases and lack of control over timing and content of messages.

16-5 Analyze how public relations is used and evaluated.

To evaluate the effectiveness of their public relations programs, companies conduct research to determine how well their messages are reaching their audiences. Environmental monitoring, public relations audits, and counting the number of media exposures are all means of evaluating public relations effectiveness. Organizations should avoid negative public relations by taking steps to prevent negative events that result in unfavorable publicity. To diminish the impact of unfavorable public relations, organizations should institute policies and procedures for dealing with news personnel and the public when negative events occur.

 Go to www.cengagebrain.com for resources to help you master the content in this chapter as well as for materials that will expand your marketing knowledge!

Developing Your Marketing Plan

Determining the message that advertising is to communicate to the customer is an important part of developing a marketing strategy. A sound understanding of the various types of advertising and different forms of media is essential in selecting the appropriate methods for communicating the message. These decisions form a critical segment of the marketing plan. To assist you in relating the information in this chapter to the development of your marketing plan, consider the following issues:

1. What class and type of advertising would be most appropriate for your product?
2. Discuss the different methods for determining the advertising appropriation.
3. Using Table 16.1 as a guide, evaluate the different types of media and determine which would be most effective in meeting your promotional objectives (from Chapter 15).
4. What methods would you use to evaluate the effectiveness of your advertising campaign?
5. Review Table 16.3 and discuss possible uses for publicity in your promotional plan.

Key Concepts

advertising 420
institutional advertising 420
advocacy advertising 421
product advertising 421
pioneer advertising 421

competitive advertising 421
comparative advertising 421
reminder advertising 422
reinforcement advertising 422

native advertising 422
advertising campaign 423
target audience 423
advertising platform 425
advertising appropriation 426

objective-and-task approach 426
percent-of-sales approach 426
competition-matching approach 427
arbitrary approach 427
media plan 427

Issues for Discussion and Review

1. What is the difference between institutional and product advertising?
2. What is the difference between competitive advertising and comparative advertising?
3. What are the major steps in creating an advertising campaign?
4. What is a target audience? How does a marketer analyze the target audience after identifying it?
5. Why is it necessary to define advertising objectives?
6. What is an advertising platform, and how is it used?
7. What factors affect the size of an advertising budget? What techniques are used to determine an advertising budget?
8. Describe the steps in developing a media plan.
9. What is the function of copy in an advertising message?
10. Discuss several ways to posttest the effectiveness of advertising.
11. What role does an advertising agency play in developing an advertising campaign?
12. What is public relations? Whom can an organization reach through public relations?
13. How do organizations use public relations tools? Give several examples you have observed recently.
14. Explain the problems and limitations associated with publicity-based public relations.
15. In what ways is the effectiveness of public relations evaluated?
16. What are some sources of negative public relations? How should an organization deal with unfavorable public relations?

VIDEO CASE 16
Scripps Networks Interactive: An Expert at Connecting Advertisers with Programming

Television advertisers have faced challenges in the past several years. People tend to watch fewer television shows at the time of airing or choose to watch them on Internet platforms such as Netflix or Hulu. The use of digital video recorders (DVR) has also contributed to this challenge as viewers can fast forward through commercials while watching their favorite shows. Scripps Networks Interactive, parent company to Food Network, HGTV, Travel Channel, DIY Network, Cooking Channel, and Great American Country, has found a way around this issue through product placement and integration, use of social media platforms, and promotion.

Scripps Networks Interactive is unique in that their programming appeals to similar target markets with similar interests. The director of Digital Media and Database Marketing for Scripps Networks Interactive states, "Our programming lends itself so well to speaking to lifestyle and what people are passionate and interested in, and I think our marketing communications strategy is a natural extension

of that." This presents a strong opportunity for gaining real results through advertising. At the same time, these promotional initiatives do not always seem like advertising to viewers. One way this is accomplished is through cross-promotional activities across networks. For example, while watching an episode of *Paula's Home Cooking* on the Food Network, viewers would see a commercial for a *Design Star* episode on HGTV featuring Paula Deen. (In 2013, Paula Deen's contract was not renewed after a racial slur controversy, demonstrating the downside of using celebrity advertisers for spokespeople.) These marketing promotions appear to be natural extensions of the show rather than advertising that is deemed intrusive.

Product placement and integration works well with the lifestyle content of the company's programming because viewers are interested in the content being provided. In most cases, "our audiences … actually look to our advertisers' products for ideas and as resources," states the Senior Vice President of Interactive Ad Sales Marketing for Scripps.

This creates an opportunity for the company to build strong relationships with advertisers. Advertisers seek out Scripps Networks not only for placement in their shows but also for integration into their social media space. The integration of television product placement and social media advertising has been a benefit for both parties. The Senior Vice President of Interactive Ad Sales Marketing explains, "If we tie a specific advertiser to *Iron Chef* or to *Chopped*, then there's opportunities for them to be driven from on-air to say 'check out the recipes from this specific episode online at foodnetwork.com'." Despite the culinary nature of these shows, the advertising platform Scripps has established attracts other vendors, including automobile manufacturers. Lexus, for example, was featured as the car driven by *Restaurant Impossible's* host Robert Irvine. These clips were then shown on the show's webpage, packaged as a Lexus advertisement.

Scripps has also found a way to integrate product placement into brick-and-mortar locations as well as on digital space. After Food Network host Guy Fieri won recognition as "The Next Food Network Star," he partnered with TGI Fridays in an endorsement agreement. Fieri hosted a recipe showdown on the Food Network, and TGI Fridays promoted these recipes in their restaurants. Partnerships between chefs and brands have also been developed to create co-branded products. Alex Guarnaschelli, a judge on *Chopped*, was approached by Fisher Nuts to share recipes containing their product. These advertisements were shown on both the Food Network and the Cooking Channel.

Another benefit of this integration is that the company and the advertiser become cooperative marketing partners, where both are working from different directions to promote both the show and the product simultaneously. The General Manager of New Business for the Food Network explains an example of this kind of relationship with Kohl's and *Worst Cooks in America*: "Kohl's is advertising in it—they are sponsoring it. They are putting things on Pinterest or tweeting. We are doing the same thing in the context of the character, so you get both this top-down and bottom-up thing coming together."

Promotions also work well on this platform. A digital marketer for Scripps Networks describes the effectiveness of promotions. "What makes it more than just a giveaway for money is tying in hooks that engage people to not only sign up to a sweepstakes to win a trip ... but making it part of the entertainment experience." For example, the Food Network ran a promotion for its show *The Great Food Truck Race*, where people were asked to go to the Facebook page and nominate or vote for their favorite local food truck. The winners would then be featured on the show's website. This event generated buzz and brought attention to the food trucks around the country that were being nominated. The nominees were featured on commercials aired during the show, where they asked viewers to vote for them online. The fans, businesses, and the show were all involved in generating buzz and promoting one another, creating an effect that is advantageous to all parties.[45]

Questions for Discussion

1. Why is the Food Network such an important venue for many advertisers?
2. Describe some of the ways that Scripps uses product placement on the Food Network.
3. Why do you think even non-food advertisers are attracted to the Food Network?

chapter 17

Personal Selling and Sales Promotion

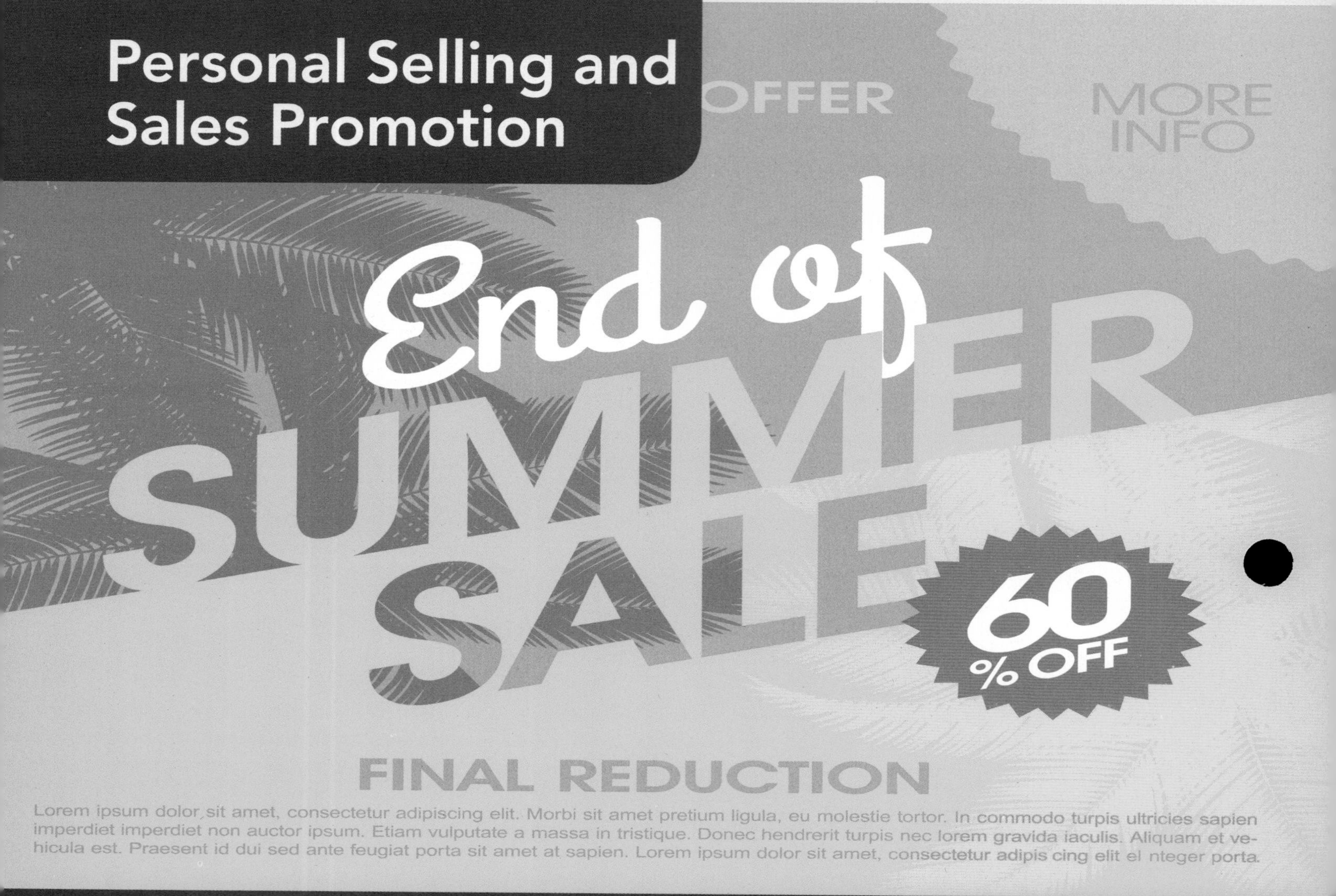

OFFER
MORE INFO
End of
SUMMER
SALE
60 % OFF
FINAL REDUCTION
Lorem ipsum dolor sit amet, consectetur adipiscing elit. Morbi sit amet pretium ligula, eu molestie tortor. In commodo turpis ultricies sapien imperdiet imperdiet non auctor ipsum. Etiam vulputate a massa in tristique. Donec hendrerit turpis nec lorem gravida iaculis. Aliquam et vehicula est. Praesent id dui sed ante feugiat porta sit amet at sapien. Lorem ipsum dolor sit amet, consectetur adipis cing elit el nteger porta.

Alhovik/Shutterstock.com

LEARNING OBJECTIVES

17-1 Describe the major purposes of personal selling.

17-2 Summarize the seven basic steps in the personal-selling process.

17-3 Identify the types of sales-force personnel.

17-4 Define team selling and relationship selling.

17-5 Discuss eight major decisions in sales management.

17-6 Describe sales-promotion activities and their use.

17-7 Review specific consumer-sales-promotion methods.

17-8 Investigate trade-sales-promotion methods.

Salesforce.com Sold on Stakeholder Satisfaction

Salesforce.com strives to create mutually beneficial relationships with all of its stakeholders, including customers, employees, and communities. Salesforce.com is a customer relationship management (CRM) vendor that provides a cloud-computing model to enable businesses to manage relationships with their customers. Because it can be difficult to manage the sales process, Salesforce.com also offers additional services for companies, such as social-media analytics. Users obtain the company's software through a subscription and download it directly onto their computers. The massive growth of the company in recent years indicates that customers are happy with Salesforce.com's CRM solutions. It earns $4.1 billion in annual revenues and is one of the fastest growing software companies in the world.

Salesforce.com is also beloved by its employees and communities. The firm provides large bonuses and allows some of its employees to own stock in the company. Salesforce.com's 1/1/1 Model—which stands for 1 percent time (employees are given 1 percent time to volunteer), 1 percent equity (1 percent of its capital is given to the Salesforce Foundation), and 1 percent product (1 percent of its products are donated or discounted to organizations such as nonprofits)—has been recognized by top institutions for philanthropy, such as Fortune's "50 Best Workplaces for Giving Back." Salesforce.com has donated more than 1.3 million employee hours to community causes, has donated or discounted licenses for its software to over 29,000 nonprofit organizations, and has awarded over $100 million in grants. By selling quality CRM products and valuing its relationships with stakeholders, Salesforce.com has achieved both high growth and a positive reputation.[1]

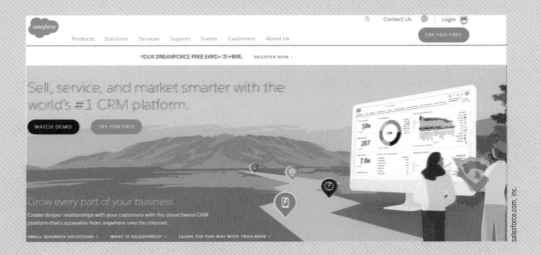

salesforce.com, inc.

For many organizations, targeting customers with appropriate personal selling techniques and messages can play a major role in maintaining long-term, satisfying customer relationships, which in turn contribute to company success. Marketing-strategy development should involve the sales organization during all stages of development and implementation. Top management needs extensive feedback from the sales force to better understand customers. Managers should strive to use sales-data analytics to provide information for both the sales force and strategic decision. Sales managers should communicate marketing strategy in a language with which salespeople feel comfortable.[2] As we saw in Chapter 15, personal selling and sales promotion are two important elements in a promotion mix. Personal selling is sometimes a company's sole promotional tool, and it is becoming increasingly professional and sophisticated, with sales personnel acting more as consultants, advisors, and sometimes as partners.

In this chapter, we focus on personal selling and sales promotion. We first consider the purposes of personal selling and then examine its basic steps. Next, we look at types of salespeople and how they are selected. After taking a look at several new types of personal selling, we discuss major sales-force-management decisions, including setting objectives for the sales force and determining its size; recruiting, selecting, training, compensating, and motivating salespeople; managing sales territories; and controlling and evaluating sales force performance. Then we examine several characteristics of sales promotion, reasons for using sales promotion, and sales-promotion methods available for use in a promotion mix.

| 17-1 THE NATURE OF PERSONAL SELLING

LO 17-1 Describe the major purposes of personal selling.

Personal selling is paid personal communication that attempts to inform customers and persuade them to purchase products in an exchange situation. For example, an HP salesperson describing the benefits of the company's servers, PCs, and printers to a small-business customer is engaging in personal selling. Likewise, a member of the American Marketing Association (AMA) manning a table at an event engages in personal selling to inform interested parties about the benefits of joining the AMA. Personal selling gives marketers the greatest freedom to adjust a message to satisfy customers' information needs. It is the most precise of all promotion methods, enabling marketers to focus on the most promising sales prospects. Personal selling is also the most effective way to form relationships with customers.
It is perhaps most critical with business-to-business transactions involving the purchase of expensive products. Because of the high-risk factors involved, personal selling is often necessary to assure prospective customers about the quality of the product and answer any questions.[3] Despite these benefits, personal selling is generally the most expensive element in the promotion mix. The average cost of a sales call for business-to-business sales is anywhere from $215 to $400.[4]

Millions of people earn their living through personal selling. Sales careers can offer high income, a great deal of freedom, a high level of training, and a high degree of job satisfaction. Although the public may harbor negative perceptions of personal selling, unfavorable stereotypes of salespeople are changing thanks to the efforts of major corporations, professional sales associations, and academic institutions. Personal selling will continue to gain respect as professional sales associations develop and enforce ethical codes of conduct.[5] Developing ongoing customer relationships today requires sales personnel with high levels of professionalism as well as technical and interpersonal skills.[6]

Personal selling goals vary from one firm to another. However, they usually involve finding prospects, determining their needs, persuading prospects to buy, following up on the sale, and keeping customers satisfied. Identifying potential buyers interested in the organization's products is critical. Because most potential buyers seek information before making purchases, salespeople can ascertain prospects' informational needs and then provide relevant information. To do so, sales personnel must be well trained regarding both their products and the selling process in general.

personal selling Paid personal communication that attempts to inform customers and persuade them to buy products in an exchange situation

Salespeople must be aware of their competitors. They must monitor the development of new products and keep abreast of competitors' sales efforts in their sales territories, how often and when the competition calls on their accounts, and what the competition is saying about their product in relation to its own. Salespeople must emphasize the benefits their products provide, especially when competitors' products do not offer those specific benefits. Salespeople often function as knowledge experts for the firm and provide key information for marketing decisions.[7]

Personal selling is changing today based on new technology, how customers gain information about products, and the way customers make purchase decisions. Customer information sharing through social media, mobile and Web applications, and electronic sales presentations are impacting the nature of personal selling. Technology and social media provide an unprecedented level of transparency and communication between salesperson and customers.[8] Many firms are using social media technology to reach business customers as well. "Social CRM" (customer relationship management) provides opportunities to manage data in discovering and engaging customers.[9] For instance, the cloud-computing models provided by Salesforce.com to enable firms to manage relationships with their customers can assist in personal-selling sales management. Digital technology has become such an important part of our lives that it is common for salespersons to access their CRM systems through their smartphones. Internal consumer data can help salespersons understand and collaborate with customers in ways that did not exist in the past.

Few businesses survive solely on profits from one-time customers. For long-run survival, most marketers depend on repeat sales and thus need to keep their customers satisfied. In addition, satisfied customers provide favorable word-of-mouth and other communications, thereby attracting new customers. Although the whole organization is responsible for achieving customer satisfaction, much of the burden falls on salespeople, because they are almost always closer to customers than anyone else in the company and often provide buyers with information and service after the sale. Indeed, a firm's market orientation has a positive influence on salespeople's attitudes, commitment, and influence on customer purchasing intentions.[10] Additionally, collaboration between sales and other marketing areas is positively related to market orientation that puts customers first, which positively impacts organizational performance.[11] Such contact gives salespeople an opportunity to generate additional sales and offers them a good vantage point for evaluating the strengths and weaknesses of the company's products and other marketing-mix components. Their observations help develop and maintain a marketing mix that better satisfies both the firm and its customers. Sales is no longer an isolated function in a global business world. The sales function is becoming part of a cross-functional strategic solution to customer management. This requires salespersons with both managerial and strategic skills.[12]

17-2 STEPS OF THE PERSONAL SELLING PROCESS

LO 17-2 Summarize the seven basic steps in the personal selling process.

The specific activities involved in the selling process vary among salespeople, selling situations, and cultures. No two salespeople use exactly the same selling methods. Nonetheless, many salespeople move through a general selling process. This process consists of seven

Prospecting
Companies often engage in prospecting at trade shows, which allow representatives to demonstrate the latest company products and collect information on consumers who might be interested in the preapproach and approach steps of personal selling.

Adriano Castelli/Shutterstock.com

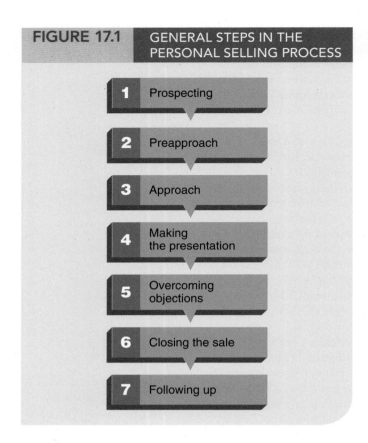

FIGURE 17.1   GENERAL STEPS IN THE PERSONAL SELLING PROCESS

1. Prospecting
2. Preapproach
3. Approach
4. Making the presentation
5. Overcoming objections
6. Closing the sale
7. Following up

steps, outlined in Figure 17.1: prospecting, preapproach, approach, making the presentation, overcoming objections, closing the sale, and following up.

17-2a **Prospecting**

Developing a database of potential customers is called **prospecting**. Salespeople seek names of prospects from company sales records, trade shows, commercial databases, newspaper announcements (of marriages, births, deaths, and so on), public records, trade association directories, and many other sources. Sales personnel also use responses to traditional and online advertisements that encourage interested persons to send in information request forms. Seminars and meetings targeted at particular types of clients, such as attorneys or accountants, may also produce leads.

Most salespeople prefer to use referrals—recommendations from current customers—to find prospects. For example, salespeople for Cutco Cutlery, which sells high-quality knives and kitchen cutlery, first make sales calls to their friends and families and then use referrals from them to seek out new prospects. Obtaining referrals requires that the salesperson have a good relationship with the current customer and therefore must have performed well before asking the customer for help. As might be expected, a customer's trust in and satisfaction with a salesperson influences his or her willingness to provide referrals. Research shows that one referral is as valuable as 12 cold calls.[13] Also, 80 percent of clients are willing to give referrals, but only 20 percent are ever asked. Among the advantages of using referrals are more highly qualified sales leads, greater sales rates, and larger initial transactions. Some companies even award discounts off future purchases to customers who refer new prospects to their salespeople. Consistent activity is critical to successful prospecting. Salespeople must actively search the customer base for qualified prospects that fit the target market profile. After developing the prospect list, a salesperson evaluates whether each prospect is able, willing, and authorized to buy the product. Based on this evaluation, prospects are ranked according to desirability or potential.

17-2b **Preapproach**

Before contacting acceptable prospects, a salesperson finds and analyzes information about each prospect's specific product needs, current use of brands, feelings about available brands, and personal characteristics. In short, salespeople need to know what potential buyers and decision makers consider most important and why they need a specific product. The most successful salespeople are thorough in their *preapproach,* which involves identifying key decision makers, reviewing account histories and problems, contacting other clients for information, assessing credit histories and problems, preparing sales presentations, identifying product needs, and obtaining relevant literature. Marketers are increasingly using marketing analytics and customer relationship management systems to comb through databases and thus identify their most profitable products and customers. CRM systems can also help sales departments manage leads, track customers, forecast sales, and assess performance. A salesperson with a lot of information about a prospect is better equipped to develop a presentation that precisely communicates with that prospect.

prospecting Developing a database of potential customers

17-2c **Approach**

The **approach**—the manner in which a salesperson contacts a potential customer—is a critical step in the sales process. In more than 80 percent of initial sales calls, the purpose is to gather information about the buyer's needs and objectives. Creating a favorable impression and building rapport with prospective clients are important tasks in the approach because the prospect's first impressions of the salesperson are usually lasting ones. During the initial visit, the salesperson strives to develop a relationship rather than just push a product. Indeed, coming across as a "salesperson" may not be the best approach because some people are put off by strong selling tactics. The salesperson may have to call on a prospect several times before the product is considered. The approach must be designed to deliver value to targeted customers. If the sales approach is inappropriate, the salesperson's efforts are likely to have poor results.

One type of approach is based on referrals, as discussed in the section on prospecting. The salesperson who uses the "cold canvass" approach calls on potential customers without prior consent. This approach is decreasing. Social media is becoming more typical in gaining the initial contact with a prospect. Repeat contact is another common approach: when making the contact, the salesperson mentions a previous meeting. The exact type of approach depends on the salesperson's knowledge and preferences, the product being sold, the firm's resources, and the prospect's characteristics.

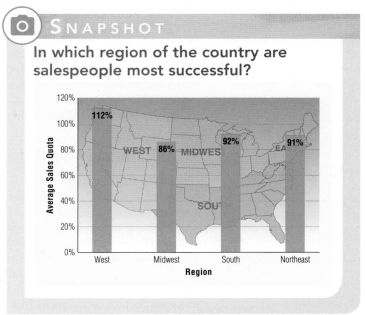

SNAPSHOT

In which region of the country are salespeople most successful?

Note: Based on a 2015 survey of more than 250 B2B salespeople.
Source: Steve W. Martin, "Salespeople Work Differently in Different Parts of the U.S., in 6 Charts," *Harvard Business Review*, December 13, 2016, https://hbr.org/2016/12/salespeople-work-differently-in-different-parts-of-the-u-s-in-6-charts (accessed April 3, 2017).

17-2d **Making the Presentation**

During the sales presentation, the salesperson must attract and hold the prospect's attention, stimulate interest, and spark a desire for the product. Salespeople who carefully monitor the selling situation and adapt their presentations to meet the needs of prospects are associated with effective sales performance.[14] Salespeople should match their influencing tactics—such as information exchange, recommendations, deadlines, promises, ingratiation, and inspirational appeals—to their prospects. Different types of buyers respond to different tactics, but most respond well to information exchange and recommendations, and virtually no prospects respond to threats.[15] If possible, the salesperson should demonstrate the product or invite the prospect to use it, if possible. If the customer is in a positive mood, suspicion will be eliminated and the presentation will gain strength.[16]

During the presentation, the salesperson must not only talk, but also listen. Listening is half of the communication process and is often the most important part for a salesperson. Nonverbal modes of communication are especially beneficial in building trust during the presentation.[17] Nonverbal signals provide a deeper understanding. The sales presentation gives the salesperson the greatest opportunity to determine the prospect's specific needs by listening to questions and comments and observing responses. For example, it has been found that complimenting the buyer on his or her questions adds to incremental sales.[18] Even though the salesperson plans the presentation in advance, she or he must be able to adjust the message to meet the prospect's informational needs. Adapting the message in response to the customer's needs generally enhances performance, particularly in new-task or modified rebuy purchase situations.[19]

approach The manner in which a salesperson contacts a potential customer

closing The stage in the personal selling process when the salesperson asks the prospect to buy the product

17-2e Overcoming Objections

An effective salesperson usually seeks out a prospect's objections in order to address them. If the objections are not apparent, the salesperson cannot deal with them, and the prospect may not buy. One of the best ways to overcome objections is to anticipate and counter them before the prospect raises them. However, this approach can be risky, because the salesperson may mention objections that the prospect would not have raised. If possible, the salesperson should handle objections as they arise. They can also be addressed at the end of the presentation.

17-2f Closing the Sale

Closing is the stage in the personal selling process when the salesperson asks the prospect to buy the product. During the presentation, the salesperson may use a *trial close* by asking questions that assume the prospect will buy. The salesperson might ask the potential customer about financial terms, desired colors or sizes, or delivery arrangements. Reactions to such questions usually indicate how close the prospect is to buying. Properly asked questions may allow prospects to uncover their own problems and identify solutions themselves. One questioning approach uses broad questions *(what, how, why)* to probe or gather information and focused questions *(who, when, where)* to clarify and close the sale. A trial close allows prospects to indicate indirectly that they will buy the product without having to say those sometimes difficult words: "I'll take it."

A salesperson should try to close at several points during the presentation because the prospect may be ready to buy. An attempt to close the sale may result in objections. Thus, closing can uncover hidden objections, which the salesperson can then address. One closing strategy involves asking the potential customer to place a low-risk, trial order.

17-2g Following Up

After a successful closing, the salesperson must follow up the sale. In the follow-up stage, the salesperson determines whether the order was delivered on time and installed properly, if installation was required. If the product is a service, it is important to determine if there are any concerns or if improvements can be made in the experience. He or she should contact the customer to learn if any problems or questions regarding the product have arisen. The follow-up stage is also used to determine customers' future product needs.

Outside Sales
Outside salespersons often engage in personal selling through face-to-face interactions. They are required to recognize potential buyers' needs and give them necessary information.

Monkey Business Images/Shutterstock.com

17-3 TYPES OF SALESPEOPLE

LO 17-3 Identify the types of sales force personnel.

To develop a sales force, a marketing manager decides what kind of salesperson will sell the firm's products most effectively. Most business organizations use several different kinds of sales personnel. Based on the functions performed, salespeople can be classified into different groups. One salesperson can, and often does, perform multiple functions.

17-3a Sales Structure

Most companies have an inside sales force. Inside salespeople support personnel or take orders, follow up on deliveries, and provide technical information. An outside sales force is also important. Usually sales calls outside the firm are more consultative and are built on developing long-term relationships. Using both inside and outside salespersons to manage accounts is very typical. This task is sometimes called *creative selling.* It requires that salespeople recognize potential buyers' needs and give them necessary information. Increasingly, inside salespersons manage the digital approaches to sales and outside salespersons are more face-to-face and relationship-oriented.

support personnel Sales staff members who facilitate selling but usually are not involved solely with making sales

missionary salespeople Support salespeople, usually employed by a manufacturer, who assist the producer's customers in selling to their own customers

Current-Customer Sales

Sales personnel who concentrate on current customers call on people and organizations that have purchased products from the firm before. These salespeople seek more sales from existing customers by following up on previous sales. Current customers can also be sources of leads for new prospects.

New-Business Sales

Business organizations depend to some degree on sales to new customers. New-business sales personnel locate prospects and convert them into buyers. Salespeople help generate new business in many organizations, but even more so in organizations that sell real estate, insurance, appliances, automobiles, and business-to-business supplies and services. These organizations depend in large part on new-customer sales.

17-3b **Support Personnel**

Support personnel facilitate selling but usually are not involved solely with making sales. They engage primarily in marketing industrial products, locating prospects, educating customers, building goodwill, and providing service after the sale. There are many kinds of sales support personnel; the three most common are missionary, trade, and technical salespeople.

Missionary Salespeople

Missionary salespeople, usually employed by manufacturers, assist the producer's customers in selling to their own customers. Missionary salespeople may call on retailers to inform and persuade them to buy the manufacturer's products. When they succeed, retailers

ENTREPRENEURSHIP IN MARKETING

Tastefully Simple: Taking a Bigger Bite into Family Meal Planning

Jill Blashack Strahan, founder and CEO of Tastefully Simple, is recognized for her entrepreneurial leadership that created a multi-million-dollar company. Before starting Tastefully Simple, Strahan had a small gift-basket business. However, when the gourmet foods she provided with her baskets proved more profitable than the baskets themselves, she shifted focus. In 1995 Tastefully Simple was conceived with the idea of providing easy-to-prepare foods with a gourmet twist. The company's products are offered through independent sales consultants across the United States. Since its founding, the

company's revenue has risen to between $50 and $100 million a year.

Consultants can earn 30 percent commissions for products, as well as other bonuses and incentives. It received recognition for being ranked in the top 5 percent of companies nationwide in employee satisfaction for seven years running. Although the firm has had to lay off some employees in a restructuring effort, Strahan believes the change will help it focus more on strategic growth. The empowering vision Strahan has provided for potential entrepreneurs has made it a favorite among those with an interest in entrepreneurship.[a]

trade salespeople Salespeople involved mainly in helping a producer's customers promote a product

technical salespeople Support salespeople who give technical assistance to a firm's current customers

team selling The use of a team of experts from all functional areas of a firm, led by a salesperson, to conduct the personal selling process

purchase products from wholesalers, which are the producer's customers. Manufacturers of medical supplies and pharmaceuticals often use missionary salespeople, called *detail reps,* to promote their products to physicians, hospitals, and pharmacists.

Trade Salespeople

Trade salespeople are not strictly support personnel, because they usually take orders as well. However, they direct much effort toward helping customers—especially retail stores—promote the product. They are likely to restock shelves, obtain more shelf space, set up displays, provide in-store demonstrations, and distribute samples to store customers. Food producers and processors commonly employ trade salespeople.

Technical Salespeople

Technical salespeople give technical assistance to the organization's current customers, advising them on product characteristics and applications, system designs, and installation procedures. Because this job is often highly technical, the salesperson usually has formal training in one of the physical sciences, information technology, or in engineering. Technical sales personnel often sell technical industrial products, such as computers, heavy equipment, and steel.

When hiring sales personnel, marketers seldom restrict themselves to a single category, because most firms require different types of salespeople. Several factors dictate how many of each type a particular company should have. Product use, characteristics, complexity, and price influence the kind of sales personnel used, as do the number and characteristics of customers. The types of marketing channels and the intensity and type of advertising also affect the composition of a sales force.

| 17-4 TEAM AND RELATIONSHIP SELLING

LO 17-4 Define *team selling* and *relationship selling.*

Personal selling has become an increasingly complex process due in large part to rapid technological innovation. Most important, the focus of personal selling is shifting from selling a specific product to building long-term relationships with customers by finding solutions to their needs, problems, and challenges. As a result, the roles of salespeople are changing. Among the newer philosophies for personal selling are team selling and relationship selling.

17-4a Team Selling

Many products, particularly expensive high-tech business products, have become so complex that a single salesperson can no longer be an expert in every aspect of the product and purchase process. **Team selling,** which involves the salesperson joining with people from the firm's financial, engineering, and other functional areas, is appropriate for such products. The salesperson takes the lead in the personal selling process, but other members of the team bring their unique skills, knowledge, and resources to the process to help customers find solutions to their own business challenges. Selling teams may be created to address a particular short-term situation, or they may be formal, ongoing teams. Team selling is advantageous in situations calling for detailed knowledge of new, complex,

Team Selling
Team selling is becoming popular, especially in companies where the selling process is complex and requires a variety of specialized skills.

Monkey Business Images/Shutterstock.com

and dynamic technologies like jet aircraft and medical equipment. It is also used to engage clients in construction, consulting, and other professional services. It can be difficult, however, for highly competitive salespersons to adapt to a team selling environment.

17-4b Relationship Selling

Relationship selling, also known as consultative selling, involves building mutually beneficial long-term associations with a customer through regular communications over prolonged periods of time. Like team selling, it is especially used in business-to-business marketing. Relationship selling involves finding solutions to customers' needs by listening to them, gaining a detailed understanding of their organizations, understanding and caring about their needs and challenges, and providing support after the sale. Sales representatives from organizations such as Eli Lilly have begun to change their sales tactics to focus on building relationships. Rather than spending large amounts of time describing the benefits of their products, high-quality medicines, Eli Lilly sales representatives are spending more time listening to the doctors. This sales tactic, known as soft selling, has often led to higher sales from customers who do not feel overly pressured to purchase a product they know little about.[20] Sales relationships are also built on being able to recover when customers are concerned about services.

Being proactive in identifying the need for recovery behaviors is a major part of relationship selling.[21] For example, contacting the customer if delivery time is longer than expected as well as explaining what happened and when the product will be delivered is important.

Relationship selling has significant implications for the seller. Studies show that firms spend six times longer on finding new customers than in keeping current customers.[22] Thus, relationship selling that generates loyal long-term customers is likely to be extremely profitable for the firm both in repeat sales as well as the money saved in trying to find new customers. Finally, as the personal-selling industry becomes increasingly competitive, relationship selling is one way that companies can differentiate themselves from rivals to create competitive advantages.[23]

17-5 MANAGING THE SALES FORCE

LO 17-5 Discuss eight major decisions in sales management.

The sales force is directly responsible for generating one of an organization's primary inputs: sales revenue. Without adequate sales revenue, businesses cannot survive. In addition, a firm's reputation is often determined by the ethical conduct of its sales force. Indeed, a positive ethical climate, one component of corporate culture, has been linked with decreased role stress and turnover intention and improved job attitudes and job performance in sales.[24] Research has demonstrated that a negative ethical climate will trigger higher-performing salespeople to leave a company at a higher rate than those in a company perceived to be ethical.[25] The morale and ultimately the success of a firm's sales force depend in large part on adequate compensation, room for advancement, sufficient training, and management support—all key areas of sales management. Salespeople who are not satisfied with these elements may leave. Evaluating the input of salespeople is an important part of sales force management because of its strong bearing on a firm's success. Empowering leadership that makes salespeople feel like important contributors positively impacts how a sales team spreads knowledge among its customers.[26] Additionally, sales environments that stress creativity appear to place greater significance on the selection and placement of salespeople, sales-force training, performance appraisals, and compensation systems.[27] Table 17.1 provides recommendations on how to attract and retain a top-quality sales force.

We explore eight general areas of sales management: establishing sales-force objectives, determining sales-force size, recruiting and selecting salespeople, training sales personnel,

relationship selling The building of mutually beneficial long-term associations with a customer through regular communications over prolonged periods of time

TABLE 17.1	SUGGESTIONS FOR ATTRACTING AND RETAINING A TOP SALES FORCE
Training and development	• On-the-job training • Online individual instruction • Seminars • On-site classroom instruction
Compensation	• Make sure pay mix isn't too risky (high commission, low base) for sales role • Mix base salary with commission, bonus, or both • Base bonuses/commission on reaching sales goals rather than on individual sales dollars • Maintain competitive benefits and expense reimbursement practices
Work/life autonomy	• Offer flexible hours • Consider telecommuting/work-at-home options
Product quality and service	• Ensure products meet customer needs • Provide the appropriate service after the sale

Source: "Attracting & Retaining a Top Sales Force," Where Great Workplaces Start, http://greatworkplace.wordpress.com/2010/02/10/attracting-retaining-a-top-sales-force/ (accessed March 29, 2017).

compensating salespeople, motivating salespeople, managing sales territories, and controlling and evaluating sales-force performance.

17-5a Establishing Sales-Force Objectives

To manage a sales force effectively, sales managers must develop sales objectives. Sales objectives tell salespeople what they are expected to accomplish during a specified time period. They give the sales force direction and purpose and serve as standards for evaluating and controlling the performance of sales personnel. Sales objectives should be stated in precise, measurable terms; specify the time period and geographic areas involved; and be achievable.

Sales objectives are usually developed for both the total sales force and individual salespeople. Objectives for the entire force are normally stated in terms of sales volume, market share, or profit. Volume objectives refer to dollar or unit sales. For example, the objective for an electric drill producer's sales force might be to sell $18 million worth of drills, or 600,000 drills annually. When sales goals are stated in terms of market share, they usually call for an increase in the proportion of the firm's sales relative to the total number of products sold by all businesses in that industry. When sales objectives are based on profit, they are generally stated in terms of dollar amounts or return on investment.

Sales objectives, or quotas, for individual salespeople are commonly stated in terms of dollar or unit sales volume. Other bases used for individual sales objectives include average order size, average number of calls per time period, and ratio of orders to calls.

17-5b Determining Sales-Force Size

Sales-force size is important, because it influences the company's ability to generate sales and profits. Moreover, size of the sales force affects the compensation methods used, salespeople's morale, and overall sales-force management. Sales-force size must be adjusted periodically, because a firm's marketing plans change along with markets and forces in the marketing environment. One danger in cutting back the size of the sales force to increase profits is that the sales organization may lose strength and resiliency, preventing it from rebounding when growth occurs or better market conditions prevail.

Several analytical methods can help determine optimal sales force size. One method involves determining how many sales calls per year are necessary for the organization to serve customers effectively and then dividing this total by the average number of sales calls a salesperson makes annually. A second method is based on marginal analysis, in which additional salespeople are added to the sales force until the cost of an additional salesperson equals the additional sales generated by that person. Although marketing managers may use one or several analytical methods, they normally temper decisions with subjective judgments.

recruiting Developing a list of qualified applicants for sales positions

17-5c Recruiting and Selecting Salespeople

To create and maintain an effective sales force, sales managers must recruit the right type of salespeople. In **recruiting**, the sales manager develops a list of qualified applicants for sales positions. Effective recruiting efforts are a vital part of implementing the strategic sales-force plan and can help assure successful organizational performance. The costs of hiring and training a salesperson increase as product knowledge, service requirements, and technical skills are required. Thus, recruiting errors are expensive.

To ensure that the recruiting process results in a pool of qualified applicants, a sales manager establishes a set of qualifications before beginning to recruit. Although marketers have tried for years to identify a set of traits characterizing effective salespeople, no set of generally accepted characteristics exists yet. Experts agree that good salespeople exhibit optimism, flexibility, self-motivation, good time-management skills, empathy, and the ability to network and maintain long-term customer relationships. Today, companies are increasingly seeking applicants capable of employing relationship-building and consultative approaches as well as the ability to work effectively in team selling efforts.

A sales manager generally recruits applicants from several sources: departments within the firm, other firms, employment agencies, educational institutions, respondents to advertisements, websites (like Monster.com), and individuals recommended by current employees. The specific sources depend on the type of salesperson required and the manager's experiences and successes with particular recruiting tactics.

The process of recruiting and selecting salespeople varies considerably from one company to another. Companies intent on reducing sales-force turnover are likely to have strict recruiting and selection procedures. Sales management should design a selection procedure that satisfies the company's specific needs. Some organizations use the specialized services

GOING GREEN

Virtual Savings: The Growth of Digital Coupons

Marketers are experiencing low redemption rates with print coupons in newspapers and magazines. The average redemption rate for these coupons during a six-month period was 0.34 percent. During times of prosperity, consumers are less likely to take the time to search for deals. However, there is potentially another explanation that marketers should consider: consumers' increased preference for convenience and their familiarity with the digital realm.

During this six-month period, only 0.6 percent of coupons distributed were digital. Yet the redemption rate for these coupons was 6.7 percent, much higher than traditional coupons. Digital coupons are more convenient for consumers because

they can pull up the coupons on their phones in-store. Websites such as RetailMeNot allow for consumers to search for coupons they want at their leisure. More than half of consumers in a study remarked they would use more coupons if they were placed online.

Digital coupons also allow marketers to target markets more precisely. Through the use of apps, marketers can send mobile codes or coupons to consumers as they approach nearby stores. In fact, it is estimated that 10 percent of coupons sent through text messages are used. Marketers who use coupons as a form of sales promotion would do well to pay attention to this growing consumer interest in digital sales promotion.[b]

of other companies to hire sales personnel. The process should include steps that yield the information required to make accurate selection decisions. However, because each step incurs a certain amount of expense, there should be no more steps than necessary. Stages of the selection process should be sequenced so that the more expensive steps, such as a physical examination, occur near the end. Fewer people will then move through higher-cost stages. Recruitment should not be sporadic; it should be a continuous activity aimed at reaching the best applicants. The selection process should systematically and effectively match applicants' characteristics and needs with the requirements of specific selling tasks. Finally, the selection process should ensure that new sales personnel are available where and when needed.

17-5d **Training Sales Personnel**

Many organizations have formal training programs; others depend on informal, on-the-job training. Some systematic training programs are quite extensive, whereas others are rather short and rudimentary. Whether the training program is complex or simple, developers must consider what to teach, whom to train, and how to train them.

A sales training program can concentrate on the company, its products, or selling methods. Training programs often cover all three. Such programs can be aimed at newly-hired salespeople, experienced salespeople, or both. The type of leadership is especially important for new salespeople who are just getting familiar with the selling process. Transformational leadership has proven highly effective in training new hires when sales managers encourage them to make errors during customer interactions and learn from them. This reduces feelings of helplessness among new salespeople when they encounter difficulties in the process.[28]

Sales Training
The Container Store provides 263 hours of training to its retail employees because they are the key to maintaining satisfied customers.

Training for experienced company salespeople usually emphasizes product information or the use of new technology, although salespeople must also be informed about new selling techniques and changes in company plans, policies, and procedures. Indian firm Infosys, for instance, partnered with three training firms to train its sales team concerning how to describe its cutting-edge technology and solutions. As part of its effort to reconfigure its sales training initiatives, the firm also adopted a more reliable form of measuring performance instead of the "bell curve" they had used before.[29] Sales managers should also use ethics training to institutionalize an ethical climate, improve employee satisfaction, and help prevent misconduct. Empowering the sales force through comprehensive training increases their effectiveness. The most successful sales forces tend to be those that clearly define the steps of the sales process, spend time each month on managing their sales representatives' pipelines, and train sales managers on how to manage efficiently.[30] Ordinarily, new sales personnel require comprehensive training, whereas experienced personnel need both refresher courses on established products and training regarding new-product information and technology changes. At the Container Store, new full-time store employees are given 263 hours of training. Because retail-store employees will be interacting with customers on a consistent basis, the organization believes extensive training will increase employees' personal-selling skills and help them form relationships with customers. As the advertisement indicates, the Container Store places great emphasis on its employees' happiness.

Sales training may be done in the field, at educational institutions, in company facilities, and/or online using web-based technology. For many companies, online training saves time and money and helps salespeople learn about new products quickly. Sales managers might even choose to use online platforms from companies such as GoToMeeting to interact with their sales force face-to-face. GoToMeeting provides an online platform so that sales training and meetings can be conducted face-to-face in HD video. The advertisement emphasizes that its technology works on computers, smartphones, and tablets. Some firms train new employees before assigning them to a specific sales position. Others put them into the field immediately, providing formal training only after they have gained some experience. Training programs for new personnel can be as short as several days or as long as three years; some are even longer. Sales training for experienced personnel is often scheduled when sales activities are not too demanding. Because experienced salespeople usually need periodic retraining, a firm's sales management must determine the frequency, sequencing, and duration of these efforts.

Virtual Sales Training
Video conferencing tools provide a virtual way to participate in sales training and meetings through face-to-face, high-definition video accessible through computers, tablets, and smartphones.

Sales managers, as well as other salespeople, also engage in sales training, whether daily on the job or periodically during sales meetings. In addition, a number of outside companies specialize in providing sales training programs. Materials for sales training programs range from videos, texts, online materials, manuals, and cases to programmed learning devices and digital media. Lectures, demonstrations, simulation exercises, role-plays, and on-the-job training can all be effective training methods. Self-directed learning to supplement traditional sales training has the potential to improve sales performance. The choice of methods and materials for a particular sales training program depends on type and number of trainees, program content and complexity, length and location, size of the training budget, number of trainers, and a trainer's expertise.

17-5e Compensating Salespeople

To develop and maintain a highly productive sales force, an organization must formulate and administer a compensation plan that attracts, motivates, and retains the most effective individuals. The plan should give sales management the desired level of control and provide sales personnel with acceptable levels of income, freedom, and incentive. It should be flexible, equitable, easy to administer, and easy to understand. Good compensation programs facilitate and encourage proper treatment of customers. Obviously, it is quite difficult to incorporate all of these requirements into a single program. Figure 17.2 shows the average salaries for sales representatives.

Developers of compensation programs must determine the general level of compensation required and the most desirable method of calculating it. In analyzing the required compensation plan, sales management must ascertain a salesperson's value to the company on the basis of the tasks and responsibilities associated with the sales position. Sales managers may consider a number of factors, including salaries of other types of personnel in the firm, competitors' compensation plans, costs of sales force turnover, and non-salary selling expenses. The national average for sales representatives is $52,000 (including commissions and bonuses).[31] Salespersons' compensation varies by industry and is often based on skills or knowledge needed to relate to customers. A high-level, high-performing salesperson or sales manager can make hundreds of thousands a year.

Sales compensation programs usually reimburse salespeople for selling expenses, provide some fringe benefits, and deliver the required compensation level. To achieve this,

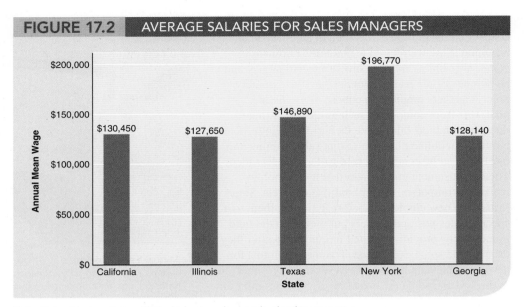

FIGURE 17.2   AVERAGE SALARIES FOR SALES MANAGERS

Note: States listed are those with the highest employment level in this occupation.

Source: Bureau of Labor Statistics, "Occupational Employment and Wages, May 2016," www.bls.gov/oes/current/oes112022.htm (accessed April 5, 2017).

a firm may use one or more of three basic compensation methods: straight salary, straight commission, or a combination of the two. Table 17.2 lists the major characteristics, advantages, and disadvantages of each method. In a **straight salary compensation plan**, salespeople are paid a specified amount per time period, regardless of selling effort. This sum remains the same until they receive a pay increase or decrease. Although this method is easy to administer and affords salespeople financial security, it provides little incentive for them to boost selling efforts. In a **straight commission compensation plan**, salespeople's compensation is determined solely by sales for a given period. A commission may be based on a single percentage of sales or on a sliding scale involving several sales levels and percentage rates (e.g., sales under $500,000 a quarter would receive a smaller commission than sales over $500,000 each quarter). Although this method motivates sales personnel to escalate their selling efforts, it offers them little financial security, and it can be difficult for sales managers to maintain control over the sales force. Many new salespeople indicate a reluctance to accept the risks associated with straight commission. However, more experienced salespeople know this option can provide the greatest income potential. For these reasons, many firms offer a **combination compensation plan** in which salespeople receive a fixed salary plus a commission based on sales volume. Some combination programs require that a salesperson exceed a certain sales level before earning a commission; others offer commissions for any level of sales.

When selecting a compensation method, sales management weighs the advantages and disadvantages listed in the table. Researchers have found that higher commissions are the most preferred reward, followed by pay increases. However, preferences on pay tend to vary, depending upon the industry.[32] Supermarket chain Trader Joe's pays its full-time staff starting salaries of between $40,000 and $60,000. This investment in employees has resulted in lower turnover for the company than at rival chains.[33]

17-5f **Motivating Salespeople**

Although financial compensation is an important incentive, additional programs are necessary for motivating sales personnel. The nature of the jobs, job security, and pay are considered to be the most important factors for the college student going into the sales area today.[34] A sales manager should develop a systematic approach for motivating salespeople to be

straight salary compensation plan Paying salespeople a specific amount per time period, regardless of selling effort

straight commission compensation plan Paying salespeople according to the amount of their sales in a given period

combination compensation plan Paying salespeople a fixed salary plus a commission based on sales volume

TABLE 17.2	CHARACTERISTICS OF SALES FORCE COMPENSATION METHODS		
Compensation Method	When Especially Useful	Advantages	Disadvantages
Straight salary	Compensating new salespeople; firm moves into new sales territories that require developmental work; sales requiring lengthy presale and postsale services	Gives salespeople security; gives sales managers control over salespeople; easy to administer; yields more predictable selling expenses	Provides no incentive; necessitates closer supervision of salespeople; during sales declines, selling expenses remain constant
Straight commission	Highly aggressive selling is required; nonselling tasks are minimized; company uses contractors and part-timers	Provides maximum amount of incentive; by increasing commission rate, sales managers can encourage salespeople to sell certain items; selling expenses relate directly to sales resources	Salespeople have little financial security; sales managers have minimum control over sales force; may cause salespeople to give inadequate service to smaller accounts; selling expenses less predictable
Combination	Sales territories have relatively similar sales potential; firm wishes to provide incentive but still control sales-force activities	Provides certain level of financial security; provides some incentive; can move sales-force efforts in profitable direction	Selling expenses less predictable; may be difficult to administer

Source: Charles Futrell, *Sales Management*, http://people.tamu.edu/~c-futrell/436/sm_home.html (accessed April 1, 2017).

productive. Effective sales-force motivation is achieved through an organized set of activities performed continuously by the company's sales management.

Sales personnel, like other people, join organizations to satisfy personal needs and achieve personal goals. Sales managers must identify those needs and goals and strive to create an organizational climate that allows each salesperson to fulfill them. Enjoyable working conditions, power and authority, job security, and opportunity to excel are effective motivators, as are company efforts to make sales jobs more productive and efficient. Convenience store QuikTrip, for example, invests in 24 hours of training each year for regular full-time salaried employees and 30 hours each year for regular full-time hourly employees.[35] This is significantly more than comparable convenience stores offer.[36] A strong positive corporate culture leads to higher levels of job satisfaction and organizational commitment and lower levels of job stress.[37]

Sales contests and other incentive programs can also be effective motivators. These can motivate salespeople to increase sales or add new accounts, promote special items, achieve greater volume per sales call, and cover territories more thoroughly. However, companies need to understand salespersons' preferences when designing contests in order to make them effective in increasing sales. Some companies find such contests powerful tools for motivating sales personnel to achieve company goals. Managers should be careful to craft sales contests that support a strong customer orientation as well as motivate salespeople. In smaller firms lacking the resources for a formal incentive program, a simple but public "thank you" and the recognition from management at a sales meeting, along with a small-denomination gift card, can be very rewarding.

Properly designed incentive programs pay for themselves many times over, and sales managers are relying on incentives more than ever. Recognition programs that acknowledge outstanding performance with symbolic awards, such as plaques, can be very effective when carried out in a peer setting. The most common incentive offered by companies is cash, followed by gift cards and travel.[38] Travel reward programs can confer a high-profile honor, provide a unique experience that makes recipients feel special, and build camaraderie among award-winning salespeople. However, some recipients of travel awards may feel they already travel too much on the job. Limited travel packages might also be a turn off. In one study, 70 percent of participants claimed they would be more motivated if they had more choices in travel destinations.[39] Cash rewards are easy to administer, are always appreciated by recipients, and appeal to all demographic groups. However, cash has no visible "trophy" value and provides few "bragging rights." The benefits of awarding merchandise are that the items have visible trophy value. In addition, recipients who are allowed to select the merchandise experience a sense of control, and merchandise awards can help build momentum for the sales force. The disadvantages of using merchandise are that employees may have lower perceived value of the merchandise and the company may experience greater administrative problems. Some companies outsource their incentive programs to companies that specialize in the creation and management of such programs.

17-5g Managing Sales Territories

The effectiveness of a sales force that must travel to customers is somewhat influenced by management's decisions regarding sales territories. When deciding on territories, sales managers must consider size, geographic shape, routing, and scheduling.

Several factors enter into the design of a sales territory's size and geographic shape. First, sales managers must construct territories that allow sales potential to be measured. Sales territories often consist of several geographic units, such as census tracts, cities, counties, or states, for which market data are obtainable. Sales managers usually try to create territories with similar sales potential, or requiring about the same amount of work. If territories have equal sales potential, they will almost always be unequal in geographic size. Salespeople with larger territories have to work longer and harder to generate a certain sales volume. Conversely, if sales territories requiring equal amounts of work are created, sales potential for those territories will often vary. Think about the effort required to sell in New York and Connecticut versus the sales effort required in a larger, less populated area like Montana and Wyoming. If sales personnel are partially or fully compensated through commissions, they will have unequal income potential. Many sales managers try to balance territorial workloads and earning potential by using differential commission rates. At times, sales managers use commercial programs to help them balance sales territories. Although a sales manager seeks equity when developing and maintaining sales territories, some inequities always prevail. A territory's size and geographical shape should also help the sales force provide the best possible customer coverage and minimize selling costs. Customer density and distribution are important factors. It is important for territories to be designed so that salespersons contact customers with the frequency and consistency that feels ideal.[40]

The geographic size and shape of a sales territory are the most important factors affecting the routing and scheduling of sales calls. Next in importance is the number and distribution of customers within the territory, followed by sales call frequency and duration. Those in charge of routing and scheduling must consider the sequence in which customers are called on, specific roads or transportation schedules to be used, number of calls to be made in a given period, and time of day the calls will occur. In some firms, salespeople plan their own routes and schedules with little or no assistance from the sales manager. In others, the sales manager maintains significant responsibility. No matter who plans

Managing Sales Territories
When considering business travel, sales managers must consider ways to maximize selling time and minimize nonselling time.

GaudiLab/Shutterstock.com

the routing and scheduling, the major goals should be to minimize salespeople's nonselling time (time spent traveling and waiting) and maximize their selling time.

17-5h Controlling and Evaluating Sales-Force Performance

To control and evaluate sales-force performance properly, sales management needs information. A sales manager cannot observe the field sales force daily and, thus, relies on salespeople's call reports, customer feedback, contracts, and invoices. Call reports identify the customers called on and present detailed information about interactions with those clients. Sales personnel must often file work schedules indicating where they plan to be during specific time periods. Data about a salesperson's interactions with customers and prospects can be included in the company's customer relationship management system. This information provides insights about the salesperson's performance. Companies such as SAS provide analytical capabilities that decipher big data to discover opportunities and deploy sales-force resources for optimal impact.

Evaluating Sales Performance
It's important for companies to analyze big data to evaluate the effectiveness of their sales forces.

Dimensions used to measure a salesperson's performance are determined largely by sales objectives, normally set by the sales manager. If an individual's sales objective is stated in terms of sales volume, that person should be evaluated on the basis of sales volume generated. Even if a salesperson is assigned a major objective, he or she is ordinarily expected to achieve several related objectives as well. Thus, salespeople are often judged along several dimensions. Sales managers evaluate many performance indicators, including average number of calls per day, average sales per customer, actual sales relative to sales potential, number of new-customer orders, average cost per call, and average gross profit per customer.

To evaluate a salesperson, a sales manager may compare one or more of these dimensions with predetermined performance standards. However, sales managers commonly compare a salesperson's performance with that of other employees operating under similar selling conditions or the salesperson's current performance with past performance. Sometimes, management judges factors that have less direct bearing on sales performance, such as personal appearance, product knowledge, and ethical standards. One concern is the tendency to reprimand top sellers less severely than poor performers for engaging in unethical selling practices.

After evaluating salespeople, sales managers take any needed corrective action to improve sales-force performance. They may adjust performance standards, provide additional training, or try other motivational methods. Corrective action may demand comprehensive changes in the sales force.

17-6 THE NATURE OF SALES PROMOTION

LO 17-6 Describe sales-promotion activities and their use.

Sales promotion is an activity or material, or both, that acts as a direct inducement, offering added value or incentive for the product to resellers, salespeople, or consumers. It encompasses all promotional activities and materials other than personal selling, advertising, and public relations. Retailers often offer buy-one-get-one-free sales, a sales-promotion tactic known as a bonus or premium. In competitive markets, where products are very similar, sales promotion provides additional inducements that encourage product

sales promotion An activity and/or material intended to induce resellers or salespeople to sell a product or consumers to buy it

trial and purchase. Supermarkets such as Whole Foods provide food samples to encourage purchases.

Marketers often use sales promotion to facilitate personal selling, advertising, or both. Companies also employ advertising and personal selling to support sales-promotion activities. For example, marketers frequently use advertising to promote contests, free samples, and premiums. The most effective sales-promotion efforts are highly interrelated with other promotional activities. Decisions regarding sales promotion often affect advertising and personal-selling decisions, and vice versa.

Sales promotion can increase sales by providing extra purchasing incentives. Many opportunities exist to motivate consumers, resellers, and salespeople to take desired actions. Some kinds of sales promotion are designed specifically to stimulate resellers' demand and effectiveness, some are directed at increasing consumer demand, and some focus on both consumers and resellers. Regardless of the purpose, marketers must ensure that sales-promotion objectives are consistent with the organization's overall objectives, as well as with its marketing and promotion objectives.

When deciding which sales-promotion methods to use, marketers must consider several factors, particularly product characteristics (price, size, weight, costs, durability, uses, features, and hazards) and target-market characteristics (age, gender, income, location, population density, usage rate, and shopping patterns). How products are distributed and the number and types of resellers may determine the type of method used. The competitive and legal environments may also influence the choice.

The use of sales promotion has increased dramatically over the past 30 years, primarily at the expense of advertising. This shift in how promotional dollars are used has occurred for several reasons. Heightened concerns about value have made customers more responsive to promotional offers, especially price discounts and point-of-purchase displays. Thanks to their size and access to checkout scanner data, retailers have gained considerable power in the supply chain and are demanding greater promotional efforts from manufacturers to boost retail profits. Declines in brand loyalty have produced an environment in which sales promotions aimed at persuading customers to switch brands are more effective. In addition, competition from online retailers including Amazon have pushed retailers to use more sales-promotion incentives. Finally, a stronger emphasis placed on improving short-term performance calls for greater use of sales-promotion methods that yield quick (although perhaps short-lived) sales increases.[41]

In the remainder of this chapter, we examine several consumer and trade sales-promotion methods, including what they entail and what goals they can help marketers achieve.

17-7 CONSUMER-SALES-PROMOTION METHODS

LO 17-7 Review specific consumer-sales-promotion methods.

consumer-sales-promotion methods Sales-promotion techniques that encourage consumers to patronize specific stores or try particular products

coupons Written price reductions used to encourage consumers to buy a specific product

Consumer-sales-promotion methods encourage or stimulate consumers to patronize specific retail stores or try particular products. Online sales promotion can create a higher level of product and brand recall.[42] Consumer-sales-promotion methods initiated by retailers often aim to attract customers to specific locations, whereas those used by manufacturers generally introduce new products or promote established brands. In this section, we discuss coupons, cents-off offers, money refunds and rebates, frequent-user incentives, point-of-purchase displays, demonstrations, free samples, premiums, consumer contests and games, and consumer sweepstakes.

17-7a Coupons and Cents-Off Offers

Coupons reduce a product's price and aim to prompt customers to try new or established products, increase sales volume quickly, attract repeat purchasers, or introduce new package sizes or features. Savings are deducted from the purchase price. Coupons are the most widely used consumer sales-promotion technique. Although part of the reason is greater spending power, consumers have indicated that a primary reason for not using coupons is they cannot find coupons for what they want to buy.[43] Digital coupons via websites and mobile apps are also becoming popular. Social deal sites like Groupon, LivingSocial, and CrowdCut, while not exactly in the coupon area, are encouraging consumers to look for deals or better prices. Bed Bath & Beyond frequently sends 20 percent off coupons to consumers through the mail. However, these coupons are becoming so common that some analysts believe it could hurt Bed Bath & Beyond because consumers are so used to getting coupons that they will not shop without them.[44] Despite the growth in digital coupons, there are still plenty of people who are willing to clip coupons from printed sources. It is estimated that more than 90 percent of coupons come from free-standing inserts in booklets. Even Millennials use print coupons over digital, although they are likely to use digital coupons more than any other age group. As a result, companies such as General Mills consider couponing to be a profitable sales promotion and will often increase its distribution of coupons close to major holidays.[45] To take advantage of renewed consumer interest in coupons, digital marketing—including mobile, social, and other platforms—is being used for couponing.

Print Coupons
Unilever has attached a manufacturer's coupon to an advertisement for its Caress Beauty Bar to encourage product purchase.

When deciding on the distribution method for coupons, marketers should consider strategies and objectives, redemption rates, availability, circulation, and exclusivity. The coupon distribution and redemption arena has become very competitive. To avoid losing customers, many grocery stores will redeem any coupons offered by competitors. Also, to draw customers to their stores, grocers double and sometimes even triple the value of customers' coupons.

Coupons offer several advantages. Print advertisements with coupons are often more effective at generating brand awareness than print ads without coupons. Generally, the larger the coupon's cash offer, the better the recognition generated. Coupons reward current product users, win back former users, and encourage purchases in larger quantities. Because they are returned, coupons also help a manufacturer determine whether it reached the intended target market. The advantages of using electronic coupons over paper coupons include lower cost per redemption, greater targeting ability, improved data-gathering capabilities, and greater experimentation capabilities to determine optimal face values and expiration cycles.[46]

Drawbacks of coupon use include fraud and misredemption, which can be expensive for manufacturers. Coupon fraud—including counterfeit Internet coupons as well as coupons cashed in under false retailer names—costs manufacturers hundreds of millions in losses each year.[47] Another disadvantage, according to some experts, is that coupons are losing their value; because so many manufacturers offer them, consumers have learned not to buy without some incentive, whether that pertains to a coupon, a rebate, or a refund. Furthermore, brand loyalty among heavy coupon users has increased as many consumers redeem coupons only for products they normally buy. It is believed that about three-fourths of coupons are redeemed by people already using the brand on the coupon. Thus, coupons have questionable success as an incentive for consumers to try a new brand or product. An additional problem with coupons is that stores often do not have enough of the coupon item in stock. This situation generates ill will toward both the store and the product.

THE ULTIMATE OFF-ROAD ADVENTURE!

Book Now and Grab 30% Off!

Catch Waterfall Resort's most affordable
two-night package and save. Contact us for details.

800.544.5125

GuestServices@WaterfallResort.com
www.WaterfallResort.com/Automotive

Valid on two night packages only, select dates. Cannot be combined with other offers.

Legendary Sport Fishing

Waterfall Resort

Cents-Off Offer
Waterfall Resort Alaska offers a 30 percent discount for consumers who book their reservations during a certain period of time.

cents-off offers Promotions that allow buyers to pay less than the regular price to encourage purchase

money refunds Sales-promotion techniques that offer consumers a specified amount of money when they mail in a proof of purchase, usually for multiple product purchases

rebates Sales-promotion techniques in which a consumer receives a specified amount of money for making a single product purchase

With **cents-off offers**, buyers pay a certain amount less than the regular price shown on the label or package. Like coupons, this method can serve as a strong incentive for trying new or unfamiliar products and is commonly used in product introductions. Hello Fresh and Blue Apron, two popular meal delivery services, often entice new customers by offering a price reduction on a subscriber's first box. Cents-off offers can stimulate product sales or multiple purchases, yield short-lived sales increases, and promote products during off-seasons. Grocery stores often promote food items with cents-off reductions at the point of purchase.

Cents-off offers are easy to control and are often used for specific purposes. If used on an ongoing basis, however, they reduce the price for customers who would buy at the regular price and may also cheapen a product's image. In addition, the method often requires special handling by retailers who are responsible for giving the discount at the point of sale.

17-7b Money Refunds and Rebates

With **money refunds**, consumers submit proof of purchase and are mailed a specific amount of money. Usually, manufacturers demand multiple product purchases before consumers qualify for money refunds. Marketers employ money refunds as an alternative to coupons to stimulate sales. Money refunds, used primarily to promote trial use of a product, are relatively low in cost. However, they sometimes generate a low response rate and, thus, have limited impact on sales.

With **rebates**, the consumer is sent a specified amount of money for making a single product purchase. Rebates are generally given on more expensive products than money refunds and are used to encourage customers. Marketers also use rebates to reinforce brand loyalty and encourage product purchase. On larger items, such as cars, rebates are often given at the point of sale. Most rebates, however, especially on smaller items, are given after the sale, usually through a mail-in process. Research suggests that these mail-in rebates are most effective in situations where consumers require a reason to purchase an item. On the other hand, rebates for products that provide instant gratification are more effective if provided at the point of purchase.[48]

One problem with money refunds and rebates is that many people perceive the redemption process as too complicated. According to one estimate, at least 40 percent of consumers do not get their money back, because they fail to meet the requirements. To eliminate these complications, many marketers allow customers to apply for a rebate online, which eliminates the need for forms that may confuse customers and frustrate retailers. Consumers might also have negative perceptions of manufacturers' reasons for offering rebates. They may believe the products are untested or have not sold well. If these perceptions are not changed, rebate offers may actually degrade product image and desirability.

17-7c Shopper Loyalty and Frequent-User Incentives

Various incentives exist for frequent product users and loyal customers. Organizations such as supermarkets often provide users with loyalty or shopper cards that allow them to track customer purchases while providing periodic discounts to shoppers for continued purchases. Shopper cards tend to have an impact on brand loyalty purchases for secondary brands, but not brands where there is strong brand performance.[49] A key purpose of shopper and frequent-user cards is to encourage continued loyalty. Cosmetics company Sephora has a rewards program called the Beauty Insider Program. Customers are provided with a loyalty card and are awarded points for every purchase. After reaching a certain number of points, the customers become eligible for rewards of free cosmetics.[50]

Many firms have similar incentives for rewarding customers who engage in repeat (frequent) purchases. For instance, major airlines offer frequent-flyer programs that reward customers who have flown a specified number of miles with free tickets for additional travel. Frequent-user incentives foster customer loyalty to a specific company or group of cooperating companies. They are favored by service businesses, such as airlines, auto rental agencies, hotels, and local coffee shops. Frequent-user programs not only reward loyal customers but also generate data that can contribute significant information about customers that helps marketers foster desirable customer relationships.

17-7d **Point-of-Purchase Materials and Demonstrations**

Point-of-purchase (POP) materials include outdoor signs, window displays, counter pieces, display racks, and self-service cartons. Innovations in POP displays include sniff-teasers, which give off a product's aroma in the store as consumers walk within a radius of four feet, and computerized interactive displays. These items, often supplied by producers, attract attention, inform customers, and encourage retailers to carry particular products. Retailers have also begun experimenting with new forms of POP technology, such as interactive kiosks allowing shoppers to browse through products. A retailer is likely to use point-of-purchase materials if they are attractive, informative, well-constructed, and in harmony with the store's image.

Demonstrations are excellent attention-getters. Manufacturers offer them temporarily to encourage trial use and purchase of a product or to show how a product works. Because labor costs can be extremely high, demonstrations are not used widely. They can be highly effective for promoting certain types of products, such as appliances, cosmetics, and cleaning supplies.

Even automobiles can be demonstrated, not only by a salesperson but also by the prospective buyer during a test drive. Cosmetics marketers, such as Estée Lauder and Clinique, sometimes offer potential customers "makeovers" to demonstrate product benefits and proper application.

17-7e **Free Samples and Premiums**

Marketers use **free samples** to stimulate trial of a product, increase sales volume in the early stages of a product's life cycle, and obtain desirable distribution. Trader Joe's gives out free samples of its coffee hoping to entice buyers to make a purchase. Sampling is the most expensive sales-promotion method because production and distribution—at local events, by mail or door-to-door delivery, online, in stores, and on packages—entail high costs. However, it can also be one of the most effective sales-promotion methods. In one survey, 92 percent of respondents said they would purchase a product if they liked it after getting a free sample. Samples eliminate the risk of trying a new product and allow consumers to feel as if they are getting something for free.[51] Other studies reveal that sampling can lead to repeat purchases as well as purchases of other products under the same brand name.[52] Despite high costs, use of sampling is increasing. In a given year, almost three-fourths of consumer-products companies may use sampling. Starbucks often provides free samples of its new drinks to try to stimulate interest in the new products.[53]

Premiums are items offered free or at a minimal cost as a bonus for purchasing a product. Cracker Jack, introduced in 1896 as the first junk food, had a prize of trivial value inside. Now it has a QR code to download a baseball game. Premiums are used to attract competitors' customers, introduce different sizes of established products, add variety to other promotional efforts, and stimulate consumer loyalty. Consumers appear to prefer premiums to discounts on products due to the perception that they are receiving something "free."[54] Creativity is essential when using premiums; to stand out and achieve a significant number of redemptions, the premium must match both the target audience and the brand's image. Premiums must also be easily recognizable and desirable. Consumers are more favorable toward a premium when the brand has

point-of-purchase (POP) materials Signs, window displays, display racks, and similar devices used to attract customers

demonstrations Sales-promotion methods a manufacturer uses temporarily to encourage trial use and purchase of a product or to show how a product works

free samples Samples of a product given out to encourage trial and purchase

premiums Items offered free or at a minimal cost as a bonus for purchasing a product

Source: Wal-Mart Stores, Inc.

Premium
Walmart offers a premium of free movie credits as a bonus for purchasing packages of Kleenex from the store.

high equity and there is a good fit between the product and the premium.[55] Premiums are placed on or inside packages and can also be distributed by retailers or through the mail. Examples include a service station giving a free car wash with a fill-up, a free shaving cream with the purchase of a razor, and a free plastic storage box with the purchase of Kraft Cheese Singles. The Walmart advertisement for Kleenex rewards consumers who purchase specially marked packages of Kleenex from Walmart with a $4 Vudu movie credit.

17-7f Consumer Contests, Consumer Games, and Sweepstakes

In **consumer contests**, individuals compete for prizes based on their analytical or creative skills. This method can be used to generate retail traffic and frequency of exposure to promotional messages. Contestants are usually more highly involved in consumer contests than in games or sweepstakes, even though total participation may be lower. Contests may also be used in conjunction with other sales-promotion methods, such as coupons. Oreo created a contest, the Oreo Dunk Challenge, where consumers can submit photos or videos dunking Oreos in milk on Facebook, Instagram, and Twitter. The winners win a VIP experience to meet one of the celebrities involved in the campaign, namely Christina Aguilera, Shaquille O'Neal, or Neymar da Silva Santos Júnior, plus $2,000.[56]

In **consumer games**, individuals compete for prizes based primarily on chance—often by collecting game pieces like bottle caps or a sticker on a carton of french fries. Because collecting multiple pieces may be necessary to win or increase an individual's chances of winning, the game stimulates repeated business. Development and management of consumer games is often outsourced to an independent public-relations firm, which can help marketers navigate federal and state laws that regulate games. Although games may stimulate sales temporarily, there is no evidence to suggest that they affect a company's long-term sales.

Entrants in a **consumer sweepstakes** submit their names for inclusion in a drawing for prizes. Sweepstakes are employed more often than consumer contests and tend to attract a greater number of participants. However, contestants are usually more involved in consumer contests and games than in sweepstakes, even though total participation may be lower. Contests, games, and sweepstakes may be used in conjunction with other sales-promotion methods like coupons.

consumer contests Sales-promotion methods in which individuals compete for prizes based on their analytical or creative skills

consumer games Sales-promotion methods in which individuals compete for prizes based primarily on chance

consumer sweepstakes A sales promotion in which entrants submit their names for inclusion in a drawing for prizes

trade-sales-promotion methods Methods intended to persuade wholesalers and retailers to carry a producer's products and market them aggressively

17-8 TRADE-SALES-PROMOTION METHODS

LO 17-8 Investigate trade-sales-promotion methods.

To encourage resellers, especially retailers, to carry their products and promote them effectively, producers use trade-sales-promotion methods. **Trade-sales-promotion methods** attempt to persuade wholesalers and retailers to carry a producer's products and market them more aggressively. Marketers use trade sales methods for many reasons, including countering the effect of lower-priced store brands, passing along a discount to a price-sensitive market segment, boosting brand exposure among target consumers, or providing additional incentives to move excess inventory or counteract competitors. These methods include buying allowances, buy-back allowances, scan-back allowances, merchandise allowances, cooperative advertising, dealer listings, free merchandise, dealer loaders, premium or push money, and sales contests.

17-8a Trade Allowances

Many manufacturers offer trade allowances to encourage resellers to carry a product or stock more of it. One such trade allowance is a **buying allowance**, a temporary price reduction offered to resellers for purchasing specified quantities of a product. A paper supplier could offer an office supply store $3.00 off every case of paper purchased. Such offers provide an incentive for resellers to handle new products, achieve temporary price reductions, or stimulate purchase of items in larger-than-normal quantities. The buying allowance, which takes the form of money, yields profits to resellers and is simple and straightforward. There are no restrictions on how resellers use the money, which increases the method's

Consumer Game
McDonald's Monopoly is a popular consumer game that gives customers the opportunity to win prizes with the purchase of McDonald's products.

effectiveness. One drawback of buying allowances is that customers may buy "forward"— that is, buy large amounts that keep them supplied for many months. Another problem is that competitors may match (or beat) the reduced price, which can lower profits for all sellers.

A **buy-back allowance** is a sum of money that a producer gives to a reseller for each unit the reseller buys after an initial promotional deal is over. This method is a secondary incentive in which the total amount of money resellers receive is proportional to their purchases during an initial consumer promotion, such as a coupon offer. Buy-back allowances foster cooperation during an initial sales-promotion effort and stimulate repurchase afterward. If the retailer's inventory becomes low after the initial promotion, the buy-back allowance helps the retailer restock the inventory. This is often offered for bread and other perishable products. The main disadvantage of this method is expense.

A **scan-back allowance** is a manufacturer's reward to retailers based on the number of pieces moved through the retailers' scanners during a specific time period. To participate in scan-back programs, retailers are usually expected to pass along savings to consumers through special pricing. Scan-backs are becoming widely used by manufacturers because they link trade spending directly to product movement at the retail level.

A **merchandise allowance** is a manufacturer's agreement to pay resellers certain amounts of money for providing promotional efforts like advertising or point-of-purchase displays. This method is best suited to high-volume, high-profit, easily handled products. A drawback is that some retailers perform activities at a minimally acceptable level simply to obtain allowances. Before paying retailers, manufacturers usually verify their performance. Manufacturers hope that retailers' additional promotional efforts will yield substantial sales increases.

17-8b Cooperative Advertising and Dealer Listings

Cooperative advertising is an arrangement in which a manufacturer agrees to pay a certain amount of a retailer's media costs for advertising the manufacturer's products. The amount allowed is usually based on the quantities purchased. As with merchandise allowances, a retailer must show proof that advertisements did appear before the manufacturer pays the agreed-upon portion of the advertising costs. These payments give retailers additional funds for advertising. Some retailers exploit cooperative-advertising agreements by crowding too many products into one advertisement. Not all available cooperative-advertising dollars are used. Some retailers cannot afford to advertise, while others can afford it but

buying allowance A temporary price reduction to resellers purchasing specified quantities of a product

buy-back allowance A sum of money given to a reseller for each unit bought after an initial promotion deal is over

scan-back allowance A manufacturer's reward to retailers based on the number of pieces scanned

merchandise allowance A manufacturer's agreement to pay resellers certain amounts of money for providing special promotional efforts, such as setting up and maintaining a display

cooperative advertising An arrangement in which a manufacturer agrees to pay a certain amount of a retailer's media costs for advertising the manufacturer's products

dealer listings Advertisements that promote a product and identify the names of participating retailers that sell the product

free merchandise A manufacturer's reward given to resellers that purchase a stated quantity of products

dealer loader A gift, often part of a display, given to a retailer that purchases a specified quantity of merchandise

premium money (push money) Extra compensation to salespeople for pushing a line of goods

sales contest A sales-promotion method used to motivate distributors, retailers, and sales personnel through recognition of outstanding achievements

do not want to advertise. A large proportion of all cooperative-advertising dollars is spent on newspaper advertisements.

Dealer listings are advertisements promoting a product and identifying participating retailers that sell the product. Dealer listings can influence retailers to carry the product, build traffic at the retail level, and encourage consumers to buy the product at participating dealers.

17-8c Free Merchandise and Gifts

Manufacturers sometimes offer free merchandise to resellers that purchase a stated quantity of products. Occasionally, free merchandise is used as payment for allowances provided through other sales-promotion methods. To avoid handling and bookkeeping problems, the "free" merchandise usually takes the form of a reduced invoice.

A dealer loader is a gift to a retailer that purchases a specified quantity of merchandise. Dealer loaders are often used to obtain special display efforts from retailers by offering essential display parts as premiums. For example, New Belgium Brewing can provide a Fat Tire bicycle to hang in a pub. Marketers use dealer loaders to obtain new distributors and push larger quantities of goods.

17-8d Premium Money

Premium money (push money) is additional compensation offered by the manufacturer to salespeople as an incentive to push a line of goods. This method is appropriate when personal selling is an important part of the marketing effort; it is not effective for promoting products sold through self-service. Premium money often helps a manufacturer obtain a commitment from the sales force, but it can be very expensive. The use of this incentive must be in compliance with retailers' policies as well as state and local laws.

17-8e Sales Contest

A sales contest is designed to motivate distributors, retailers, and sales personnel by recognizing outstanding achievements. To be effective, this method must be equitable for all individuals involved. One advantage is that it can achieve participation at all distribution levels. Positive effects may be temporary, however, and prizes are usually expensive.

Chapter Review

17-1 Describe the major purposes of personal selling.

Personal selling is the process of informing customers and persuading them to purchase products through paid personal communication in an exchange situation. The three general purposes of personal selling are finding prospects, persuading them to buy, and keeping customers satisfied.

17-2 Summarize the seven basic steps in the personal-selling process.

Many salespeople, either consciously or unconsciously, move through a general selling process as they sell

products. In prospecting, the salesperson develops a database of potential customers. Before contacting prospects, the salesperson conducts a preapproach that involves finding and analyzing information about prospects and their needs. The approach is the manner in which the salesperson contacts potential customers. During the sales presentation, the salesperson must attract and hold the prospect's attention to stimulate interest and desire for the product. If possible, the salesperson should handle objections as they arise. During the closing, the salesperson asks the prospect to buy the product or products. After a successful closing, the salesperson must follow up the sale.

17-3 Identify the types of sales-force personnel.

In developing a sales force, marketing managers consider which types of salespeople will sell the firm's products most effectively. The sales structure consists of the inside sales force and the outside sales force. The sales function focuses on both selling to current customers and generating new business sales. Sales support personnel facilitate selling, but their duties usually extend beyond making sales. The three types of support personnel are missionary, trade, and technical salespeople.

17-4 Define team selling and relationship selling.

The roles of salespeople are changing, resulting in an increased focus on team selling and relationship selling. Team selling involves the salesperson joining with people from the firm's financial, engineering, and other functional areas. Relationship selling involves building mutually beneficial long-term associations with a customer through regular communications over prolonged periods of time.

17-5 Discuss eight major decisions in sales management.

Sales-force management is an important determinant of a firm's success because the sales force is directly responsible for generating the organization's sales revenue. Major decision areas and activities are establishing sales-force objectives; determining sales-force size; recruiting, selecting, training, compensating, and motivating salespeople; managing sales territories; and controlling and evaluating sales-force performance.

Sales objectives should be stated in precise, measurable terms and specify the time period and geographic areas involved. The size of the sales force must be adjusted occasionally because a firm's marketing plans change along with markets and forces in the marketing environment.

Recruiting and selecting salespeople involve attracting and choosing the right type of salesperson to maintain an effective sales force. When developing a training program, managers must consider a variety of dimensions, such as who should be trained, what should be taught, and how training should occur. Compensation of salespeople involves formulating and administering a compensation plan that attracts, motivates, and retains the right types of salespeople. Motivated salespeople should translate into high productivity. Managing sales territories focuses on such factors as size, shape, routing, and scheduling. To control and evaluate sales-force performance, sales managers use information obtained through salespeople's call reports, customer feedback, and invoices.

17-6 Describe sales-promotion activities and their use.

Sales promotion is an activity or a material (or both) that acts as a direct inducement, offering added value or incentive for the product to resellers, salespeople, or consumers. Marketers use sales promotion to identify and attract new customers, introduce new products, and increase reseller inventories. Sales-promotion techniques fall into two general categories: consumer and trade.

17-7 Review specific consumer-sales-promotion-methods.

Consumer-sales-promotion methods encourage consumers to patronize specific stores or try a particular product. These sales-promotion methods include coupons; cents-off offers; money refunds and rebates; shopper, loyalty, and frequent-user incentives; point-of-purchase displays; demonstrations; free samples and premiums; and consumer contests, games, and sweepstakes.

17-8 Investigate trade-sales-promotion methods.

Trade-sales-promotion techniques can motivate resellers to handle a manufacturer's products and market them aggressively. These sales-promotion techniques include buying allowances, buy-back allowances, scan-back allowances, merchandise allowances, cooperative advertising, dealer listings, free merchandise, dealer loaders, premium (or push) money, and sales contests.

 Go to www.cengagebrain.com for resources to help you master the content in this chapter as well as for materials that will expand your marketing knowledge!

Developing Your Marketing Plan

When developing its marketing strategy, a company must consider the different forms of communication that are necessary to reach a variety of customers. Several types of promotion may be required. Knowledge of the advantages and disadvantages of each promotional element is necessary when developing the marketing plan. Consider the information in this chapter when evaluating your promotional mix:

1. Review the various types of salespeople described in this chapter. Given your promotional objectives (from

Chapter 15), do any of these types of salespeople have a place in your promotional plan?

2. Identify the resellers in your distribution channel. Discuss the role that trade-sales promotions to these resellers could play in the development of your promotional plan.

3. Evaluate each type of consumer-sales promotion as it relates to accomplishing your promotional objectives.

Key Concepts

personal selling 446
prospecting 448
approach 449
closing 450
support personnel 451
missionary salespeople 451
trade salespeople 452
technical salespeople 452
team selling 452
relationship selling 453

recruiting 455
straight salary compensation plan 458
straight commission compensation plan 458
combination compensation plan 458
sales promotion 461
consumer-sales-promotion methods 462
coupons 462
cents-off offers 464

money refunds 464
rebates 464
point-of-purchase (POP) materials 465
demonstrations 465
free samples 465
premiums 465
consumer contests 466
consumer games 466
consumer sweepstakes 466
trade-sales-promotion methods 466

buying allowance 467
buy-back allowance 467
scan-back allowance 467
merchandise allowance 467
cooperative advertising 467
dealer listings 468
free merchandise 468
dealer loader 468
premium money (push money) 468
sales contest 468

Issues for Discussion and Review

1. What is personal selling? How does personal selling differ from other types of promotional activities?
2. What are the primary purposes of personal selling?
3. Identify the elements of the personal-selling process. Must a salesperson include all these elements when selling a product to a customer? Why or why not?
4. How does a salesperson find and evaluate prospects? Do you consider any of these methods to be ethically questionable? Explain.
5. Describe the different types of support personnel.
6. Why are team selling and relationship selling becoming more prevalent?
7. Identify several characteristics of effective sales objectives.
8. How should a sales manager establish criteria for selecting sales personnel? What do you think are the general characteristics of a good salesperson?

9. What major issues or questions should management consider when developing a training program for the sales force?
10. Explain the major advantages and disadvantages of the three basic methods of compensating salespeople. In general, which method would you prefer? Why?
11. What major factors should be taken into account when designing the size and shape of a sales territory?
12. How does a sales manager, who cannot be with each salesperson in the field on a daily basis, control the performance of sales personnel?
13. What is sales promotion? Why is it used?
14. For each of the following, identify and describe three techniques and give several examples: (a) consumer-sales-promotion and (b) trade-sales-promotion methods.
15. What types of sales-promotion methods have you observed recently? Comment on their effectiveness.

VIDEO CASE 17
Nederlander Organization Rewards the Audience

The Nederlander Organization is in its 100th year of managing Broadway-type theaters in several states and the United Kingdom. It is a theatrical organization that owns concert venues and Broadway theaters. Nederlander describes itself as a lifestyle company, which puts them in a specific niche with a specific type of customer. Josh Lesnick, President and

CEO of Audience Rewards, explains, "I think with something like the arts, customers obviously want a good deal. They want a value-add, but it's really about the experience."

The organization engages in promotional activities for various concerts as well as production of Broadway shows. The success of such activities relies on building and maintaining strong relationships with the many theater owners and ticketing organizations. Nederlander Organization has leveraged these relationships with their Audience Rewards program, a type of sales promotion that has allowed them to build strong relationships with customers by enhancing their experience.

The unique nature of the industry and smaller size of their target market allows Nederlander to create a valuable experience for customers through personal selling and sales-promotion activities. Josh Lesnick describes Audience Rewards as similar to a frequent flyer program. Customers can become members for free and are entered into the ticketing system. When they buy tickets and go to shows, they collect points and are able to redeem them for free or discounted tickets and other rewards. The program was developed as an alternative to traditional discounting. "[It is] another way to incentivize customers to go to the theater more, to spend more money, to try out new art."

Nederlander's sales-promotion program strongly benefits smaller venues. The theater industry is composed of many small privately owned theaters, and each show is marketed individually. This can make it difficult and expensive for companies to advertise and promote their shows. Nederlander's Audience Rewards program helps ease this complexity because they work with many theater owners who support and take part in the program. Lesnick explains that it provides "a central platform to market across all the vendors and art."

The Audience Rewards program also depends on outside relationships with major companies who sponsor the rewards for the program. Acquiring such partnerships can be a challenge for most small companies; however, Nederlander's target market is an attractive opportunity for large companies. A market dominated by 30- to 59-year-old females with a high annual income of approximately $200,000 "appeals to our corporate partners because they want to get access to our customers," Lesnick explains. The program has also provided Nederlander with the opportunity to develop new products such as co-branded credit cards and Broadway-wide gift cards. With these new additions, customers and corporate partners are receiving valuable benefits.

Customers are not only able to receive free and discounted tickets, but they are also able to redeem their points to participate in special red carpet events and backstage passes to meet performers. Corporate partners receive the benefit of access to a more specific and profitable target market.

Before the institution of the Audience Rewards program, Nederlander was bringing in hundreds of thousands of dollars in ticket sales without the use of technology or innovative customer relationship management techniques. Sean Free, Vice President of Sales and Ticketing, comments on the types of technologies used by businesses for marketing and business strategies. He states that "e-mail blasts, and the retargeting efforts that people are now doing, and following people on the Internet through IP addresses ... is all very new ... and Broadway is usually one of the last industries to follow through with the latest technology." Despite the tendency for the industry's slow reaction, Nederlander's implementation of the Audience Rewards program has served as a catalytic innovation for the company. For example, six months before the premier of the Broadway show *Evita,* Nederlander, in conjunction with some of its partners, sent out five million promotional e-mails to over one million members over a 10-day period. Lesnick explains that the e-mails "created a sense of urgency and an incentive to buy early." This "generated in the pre-sale [revenue] of over $1 million ... which allowed the company to strategically realign their money to make other decisions."

In addition to the many benefits of this program, sales promotion has provided Nederlander Organization with a competitive advantage over other companies. Because this program relies on the relationships and support of the theater owners and outside companies with whom Nederlander has already solidified relationships, they have created a barrier to entry for other theater organizations due to their strong relationship marketing. This loyalty program has proven to be profitable and good for all partners and members involved with the company.[57]

Questions for Discussion

1. Why do you think more targeted promotional efforts such as personal selling and sales promotion are necessary for Nederlander's specific target market?
2. How does Nederlander's Audience Rewards program result in a competitive advantage?
3. Describe how Nederlander's strong customer relationship management results in increased loyalty to the organization.

endnotes

Chapter 1

[1]Marco della Cava, "Airbnb Pushes Itself Further and Farther," *USA Today*, August 20, 2015, 3B; Eric Newcomer, "Airbnb Overhauls Service for Business Travelers," *Bloomberg*, July 20, 2015, http://www.bloomberg.com /news/articles/2015-07-20/airbnb-overhauls -service-for-business-travelers (accessed December 3, 2016); Airbnb, "About Us," https://www.airbnb.com/about/about-us (accessed December 3, 2016); Tomio Geron, "Airbnb and the Unstoppable Rise of the Share Economy," *Forbes*, January 23, 2013, http:// www.forbes.com/sites/tomiogeron/2013/01/23 /airbnb-and-the-unstoppable-rise-of-the-share -economy/ (accessed December 3, 2016); Christine Lagorio-Chafkin, "Brian Chesky, Joe Gebbia, and Nathan Blecharczyk, Founders of Airbnb," *Inc.*, July 19, 2010, http://www.inc .com/30under30/2010/profile-brian-chesky -joe-gebbia-nathan-blecharczyk-airbnb.html (accessed December 3, 2016); Airbnbbusiness website, https://www.airbnb.com/business /signup (accessed December 3, 2016).

[2]"Definition of Marketing," American Market-ing Association, http://www.marketingpower .com/AboutAMA/Pages/DefinitionofMarketing .aspx (accessed July 7, 2010).

[3]Shwood website, https://www.shwoodshop .com/ (accessed December 26, 2016).

[4]Chrome Industries website, http://www .chromeindustries.com/our-story.html (accessed December 26, 2016).

[5]Kim Painter, "Shocking CDC Anti-Smoking Campaign Is Back with New Ads," *USA Today*, June 24, 2014, http://www.usatoday.com/story /news/nation/2014/06/24/cdc-smoking-ads -video/11306343/ (accessed November 12, 2014).

[6]"Top 15 Most Popular Recipe Websites," http://www.ebizmba.com/articles/recipe -websites (accessed December 27, 2016).

[7]Rajneesh Suri, Chiranjeev Kohli, and Kent B. Monroe, "The Effects of Perceived Scarcity on Consumers' Processing of Price Information," *Journal of the Academy of Marketing Science* 35, 1 (2007): 89–100.

[8]Natalie Mizik and Robert Jacobson, "Trading Off Between Value Creation and Value Appro-priation: The Financial Implications and Shifts in Strategic Emphasis," *Journal of Marketing* 67, 1 (January 2003): 63–76.

[9]Kasey Wehrum, "How May We Help You?" *Inc.*, March 2011, 63–68.

[10]O. C. Ferrell and Michael Hartline, *Market-ing Strategy* (Mason, OH: Cengage Learning, 2017), 108.

[11]Sara Leroi-Werelds, Sandra Streukens, Michael K. Brady, and Gilbert Swinnen, "Assessing the Value of Commonly Used Methods for Measuring Customer Value: A Multi-Setting Empirical Study," *Journal of the Academy of Marketing Science* 42, 4 (July 2014): 430–451.

[12]Randy Lewis, "Garth Brooks Unveils iTunes Alternative: GhostTunes," *Los Angeles Times,* September 4, 2014, http://www.latimes.com /entertainment/music/posts/la-et-ms-garth -brooks-ghost-tunes-itunes-alternative -competition-20140904-story.html (accessed November 12, 2014).

[13]Isabelle Maignan, Tracy Gonzalez-Padron, G. Tomas Hult, and O. C. Ferrell, "Stakeholder Orientation: Development and Testing of a Framework for Socially Responsible Market-ing," *Journal of Strategic Marketing* 19, 4 (2011): 313–338.

[14]Vijay K. Patel, Scott. C. Manley, O. C. Ferrell, Torsten M. Pieper, and Joseph F. Hair, Jr., "Stakeholder Orientation: Proactive and Responsive Components and Firm Performance," *European Management Journal* (2016): 1–11.

[15]Jack Ward, "Big Brands Boast Fake News Sites," *Wall Street Journal* (December 9, 2016): B1.

[16]Ajay K. Kohli and Bernard J. Jaworski, "Market Orientation: The Construct, Research Propositions, and Managerial Implications,"

Journal of Marketing 54, 2 (April 1990): 1–18; O. C. Ferrell, "Business Ethics and Customer Stakeholders," *Academy of Management Executive* 18, 2 (May 2004): 126–129.

[17]"Starbucks CEO Howard Schultz Is All Abuzz," *CBS News*, March 27, 2011, http:// www.cbsnews.com/stories/2011/03/27 /business/main20047618.shtml (accessed March 30, 2011).

[18]Eugene W. Anderson, Claes Fornell, and Sanal K. Mazvancheryl, "Customer Satisfac-tion and Shareholder Value," *Journal of Marketing* 68, 4 (October 2004): 172–185.

[19]Xeuming Luo and Christian Homburg, "Neglected Outcomes of Customer Satisfac-tion," *Journal of Marketing* 70, 2 (2007): 133–149.

[20]Kohli and Jaworski, "Market Orientation: The Construct, Research Propositions, and Managerial Implications."

[21]Kwaku Atuahene-Gima, "Resolving the Capability-Rigidity Paradox in New Product Innovation," *Journal of Marketing* 69, 4 (October 2005): 61–83.

[22]Gary F. Gebhardt, Gregory S. Carpenter, and John F. Sherry Jr., "Creating a Market Orienta-tion: A Longitudinal, Multifirm, Grounded Analysis of Cultural Transformation," *Journal of Marketing* 70, 4 (October 2006): 37–55.

[23]James D. Doyle and Anahit Armenakyan, "Value-creating Mechanisms within the Market Orientation—Performance Relationship: A Meta-analysis," *Journal of Strategic Marketing* 22, 3 (2014): 193–205.

[24]Sunil Gupta, Donald R. Lehmann, and Jennifer Ames Stuart, "Valuing Customers," *Journal of Marketing Research* 41, 1 (February 2004): 7–18.

[25]"Bazaarvoice Enables Rubbermaid to Listen, Learn, and Improve Products Based on Cus-tomer Conversations," *Business Wire*, January 21, 2010, http://www.businesswire.com/portal /site/home/permalink/?ndmViewId=news_view

&newsId=20100121005613&newsLang=en (accessed January 12, 2012); Tara DeMarco, "User-Generated R&D: Clay Shirky Explains How to Feed Innovation with Customer Insights," Bazaarvoice, May 3, 2011, http://www.bazaarvoice.com/blog/2011/05/03/user-generated-rd-clay-shirky-explains-how-to-feed-innovation-with-customer-insights/ (accessed December 1, 2014).

[26]Sarah Elbert, "Food for Thought: Interview with CEO Ken Powell," *Delta Sky Magazine* (December 2016): 66.

[27]Jacquelyn S. Thomas, Robert C. Blattberg, and Edward J. Fox, "Recapturing Lost Customers," *Journal of Marketing Research* 41, 1 (February 2004): 31–45.

[28]Jagdish N. Sheth and Rajendras Sisodia, "More Than Ever Before, Marketing Is Under Fire to Account for What It Spends," *Marketing Management* (Fall 1995): 13–14.

[29]Stephen L. Vargo and Robert F. Lusch, "Service-Dominant Logic: Continuing the Evolution," *Journal of the Academy of Marketing Science* 36, 1 (2008): 1–10.

[30]Southwest Airlines, "About Southwest," http://www.southwest.com/html/about-southwest/ (accessed November 12, 2014).

[31]Chezy Ofir and Itamar Simonson, "The Effect of Stating Expectations on Customer Satisfaction and Shopping Experience," *Journal of Marketing Research* 44, 1 (February 2007): 164–174.

[32]Robert W. Palmatier, Lisa K. Scheer, and Jan-Benedict E. M. Steenkamp, "Customer Loyalty to Whom? Managing the Benefits and Risks of Salesperson-Owned Loyalty," *Journal of Marketing Research* 44, 2 (May 2007): 185–199.

[33]Ruth M. Stock and Marei Bednareck, "As They Sow, So Shall They Reap: Customers' Influence on Customer Satisfaction at the Customer Interface," *Journal of the Academy of Marketing Science* 42, 4 (July 2014): 400–414.

[34]"The Riches in Returns: The Business of Reselling Returned Shop Items," *The Economist*, November 26, 2016, 12.

[35]Richard Waters and Hannah Kuchler, "Social Networks Now a Staple of Office Life," *Financial Times,* November 19, 2014, 15.

[36]Ibid.

[37]"Top Green Companies in the U.S. 2016," *Newsweek,* 2016, http://www.newsweek.com/green-2016/top-green-companies-us-2016 (accessed December 27, 2016).

[38]"Charitable Giving Statistics," *National Philanthropic Trust,* 2016, https://www.nptrust.org/philanthropic-resources/charitable-giving-statistics/ (accessed December 27, 2016).

[39]New Belgium website, http://www.newbelgium.com (accessed January 9, 2017); Brad Tuttle, "Craft Beer's Crazy Sales Rise is Starting to Go Flat," *Time*, June 28, 2016, http://time.com/money/4385458/craft-beer-sales-rise-peak (accessed January 9, 2017); Darren Dahl, "How New Belgium Brewing Has Found Sustainable Success," *Forbes*, January 27, 2016 http://www.forbes.com/sites/darrendahl/2016/01/27/how-new-belgium-brewing-has-found-sustainable-success (accessed January 9, 2017); "New Belgium Brewing: Ethical and Environmental Responsibility," in O. C. Ferrell, John Fraedrich, and Linda Ferrell, *Business Ethics: Ethical Decision Making and Cases*, 9th ed. (Mason, OH: Cengage Learning, 2013), 355–363; New Belgium, "The Tinkerer," YouTube, https://www.youtube.com/watch?v=8UfTzXhdz5Y (accessed March 27, 2012); Devin Leonard, "New Belgium and the Battle of the Microbrews," *Bloomberg Businessweek*, December 1, 2011, https://www.businessweek.com/magazine/new-belgium-and-the-battle-of-the-microbrews-12012011.html (accessed November 6, 2014); New Belgium, "Kim's Joy Ride: Fat Tire Ale," YouTube, https://www.youtube.com/watch?v=L94PE12VaFY (accessed March 27, 2012); "Case 15: New Belgium Brewing: Engaging in Sustainable Social Responsibility," in O. C. Ferrell, Debbie Thorne, and Linda Ferrell, *Business & Society: A Strategic Approach to Social Responsibility and Ethics*, 5th ed., (Chicago, IL: Chicago Business Press, 2016), 556–563.

FEATURE NOTES

[a]Jonathan Kauffmann, "Blue Bottle Coffee Faces Challenges as it Moves to New Ground," *San Francisco Chronicle*, October 8, 2016, http://www.sfchronicle.com/business/article/Blue-Bottle-Coffee-faces-challenges-as-it-moves-9952708.php (accessed December 3, 2016); Madeline Stone, "Why People Are Crazy about Blue Bottle, the Coffee Chain That Just Raised Another $70 Million from Tech Investors," *Business Insiders*, June 5, 2015, http://www.businessinsider.com/what-blue-bottle-coffee-is-like-2015-6/ (accessed December 3, 2016); "Blue Bottle Coffee: Palo Alto," https://bluebottlecoffee.com/cafes/palo-alto (accessed December 3, 2016); Danielle Sacks, "Brewing the Perfect Cup," *Fast Company*, September 2014, pp. 86–91; Richard Reynolds, "Coffee's Third Wave," *Imbibe*, http://imbibemagazine.com/coffee-s-third-wave/ (accessed December 3, 2016); Joel Stein, "Blue Bottle Coffee and the Next Wave of Artisanal Coffee Shops," *Bloomberg Businessweek*, May 1, 2014, https://www.bloomberg.com/news/articles/2014-05-01/blue-bottle-coffee-and-the-next-wave-of-artisanal-coffee-shops (accessed December 3, 2016).

[b]Leslie Eaton and David Cheesewright, "Wal-Mart and the Green Consumer," *The Wall Street Journal*, March 30, 2015, http://www.wsj.com/articles/wal-mart-and-the-green-consumer-1427770855 (accessed December 4, 2016); Associated Press, "Walmart Sets Plan as Customers Seek Green Items," *CBS DFW*, November 4, 2016, http://dfw.cbslocal.com/2016/11/04/walmart-sets-plan-as-customers-seek-green-items/ (accessed December 4, 2016); Phil Wahba, "Walmart: There's No Conflict Between Sustainability and Good Business," *Fortune*, September 29, 2015, http://fortune.com/2015/09/29/walmart-sustainability/ (accessed December 4, 2016); Walmart, "Sustainability Index," http://corporate.walmart.com/global-responsibility/environment-sustainability/sustainability-index-leaders-shop (accessed December 4, 2016).

Chapter 2

[1]Based on information in: Erin Griffin, "How Blue Apron Got It Right," *Fortune,* September 24, 2016, http://fortune.com/2016/09/24/how-blue-apron-got-it-right (accessed December 29, 2016); John Kell, "Discovering Luxury, Meals in the Mail: How Blue Apron Got Started and Where It's Headed," *Fortune,* September 12, 2016, http://fortune.com/2016/09/11/blue-apron-meal-delivery (accessed December 29, 2016); Sarah Halzack, "Why This Start-up Wants to Put Vegetables You've Never Heard of on Your Dinner Table," *Washington Post,* June 15, 2016, https://www.washingtonpost.com/news/wonk/wp/2016/06/15/why-this-start-up-wants-to-put-vegetables-youve-never-heard-of-on-your-dinner-table (accessed December 29, 2016).

[2]O. C. Ferrell and Michael Hartline, *Marketing Strategy,* 6th ed. (Mason, OH: Cengage Learning, 2014): 9.

[3]Christian Homburg, Karley Krohmer, and John P. Workman Jr., "A Strategy Implementation Perspective of Market Orientation," *Journal of Business Research* 57, 12 (2004): 1331–1340.

[4]Facebook, "Investor Relations: FAQ," https://investor.fb.com/resources/default.aspx (accessed January 13, 2017).

[5]Peter High, "Slack's CEO on the Future of the Fastest Growing Workplace Software Ever," *Forbes,* November 7, 2016, http://www.forbes.com/sites/peterhigh/2016/11/07/slacks-ceo-on-the-future-of-the-fastest-growing-workplace-software-ever/#53ea2e812641 (accessed January 13, 2017); Carrie Melissa Jones, "What a Mission-Driven Company Looks Like," *CMS Wire,* February 16, 2016, http://www.cmswire.com/social-business/what-a-mission-driven-company-looks-like/ (accessed January 13, 2017).

[6]Emile Rusch, "Re/Max Holdings Launching New Mortgage Business, Motto Mortgage," *The Denver Post,* October 25, 2016, http://www.denverpost.com/2016/10/25/remax-holdings-launching-new-mortgage-business-motto-mortgage/ (January 13, 2017).

[7]Stanley F. Slater, G. Tomas M. Hult, and Eric M. Olson, "On the Importance of Matching Strategic Behavior and Target Market Selection to Business Strategy in High-Tech Markets," *Journal of the Academy of Marketing Science* 35, 1 (2007): 5–17.

[8]"Latest Search Market Share Numbers: Google Search Up Across All Devices," *Search Engine Journal,* August 31, 2016, https://www.searchenginejournal.com/august-2016-search-market-share/172078/ (accessed January 13, 2017).

[9]Robert D. Buzzell, "The PIMS Program of Strategy Research: A Retrospective Appraisal," *Journal of Business Research* 57, 5 (2004): 478–483.

[10]"Amazon Is Gaining Ground in the Tablet Market," *Business Insider,* May 3, 2016, http://www.businessinsider.com/amazon-is-gaining-ground-in-the-tablet-market-2016-5 (accessed January 13, 2017).

[11]Alexander Coolidge, "P&G Profit Rises on Brand Sales, Cost-Cutting Continues," *Cincinnati Enquirer,* April 26, 2016, http://www.cincinnati.com/story/money/2016/04/26/pg-reports-28-billion-profit/83529032/ (accessed January 13, 2017).

[12]Mike Esterl, "'Share a Coke' Credited with a Pop in Sales," *The Wall Street Journal,* September 25, 2014, http://www.wsj.com/articles/share-a-coke-credited-with-a-pop-in-sales-1411661519 (accessed December 2, 2016); E. J. Schultz, "Coke Slaps More Than 70 Song Lyrics on Cans and Bottles," *AdAge,* March 31, 2016, http://adage.com/article/cmo-strategy/coke-slaps-70-song-lyrics-cans-bottles/303337/ (accessed December 2, 2016).

[13]Bruce Horovitz, "Coke Gets Moo Juice with Premium-Price Milk," *USA Today,* February 5, 2015, http://www.usatoday.com/story/money/2015/02/03/coca-cola-coke-fairlife-milk-premium-milk-dairy-nutrition/22798261/ (accessed December 5, 2016); Shruti Singh and Jennifer Kaplan, "Coke Thinks Designer Milk Could Be a Billion-Dollar Brand," *Business Week*, March 17, 2016, https://www.bloomberg.com/news/articles/2016-03-17/coke-thinks-designer-milk-could-be-a-billion-dollar-brand (accessed December 5, 2016).

[14]Nicole Lyn Pesce, "Whole Foods Enters the Meal-Kit Market Alongside Blue Apron, Plated," *New York Daily News,* November 4, 2016, http://www.nydailynews.com/life-style/eats/foods-enters-meal-kit-market-article-1.2858069 (accessed December 5, 2016).

[15]Derek F. Abell, "Strategic Windows," *Journal of Marketing* 42, 3 (1978): 21.

[16]Panos Mourdoukoutas, "By the Time Walmart Catches Up with Amazon, There Will Be No Neighborhood Stores," *Forbes,* August 13, 2016, http://www.forbes.com/sites/panosmourdoukoutas/2016/08/13/by-the-time-wal-mart-catches-up-with-amazon-there-will-be-no-neighborhood-stores/#13e557f7315f (accessed December 6, 2016).

[17]Robert F. Everett, "A Crack in the Foundation: Why SWOT Might Be Less Than Effective in Market Sensing Analysis," *Journal of Marketing and Management,* Special Issue 1, 1 (2014): 58–78.

[18]"Can Google Home Prove to Be Smarter than Amazon's Echo?," *Forbes*, May 24, 2016, http://www.forbes.com/sites/greatspeculations/2016/05/24/can-google-home-prove-to-be-smarter-than-amazons-echo/#1831c1d167a0 (accessed December 6, 2016).

[19]Jared M. Hansen, Robert E. McDonald, and Ronald K. Mitchell, "Competence Resource Specialization, Causal Ambiguity, and the Creation and Decay of Competitiveness: The Role of Marketing Strategy in New Product Performance and Shareholder Value," *Journal of the Academy of Marketing Science,* 41, 3 (2013): 300–319.

[20]Tilottama G. Chowdhury, Sreedhar Madhavarm, S. Ratneshwar, and Rhetta Standifer, "The Appropriateness of Different Modes of Strategy from a Product-Market Perspective," *Journal of Strategic Marketing,* 22, 5 (2014): 442–468.

[21]Dean Takahashi, "Mobile Games Hit $35.8B in 2015, Taking 85% of all App Revenues," *VentureBeat,* February 10, 2016, http://venturebeat.com/2016/02/10/mobile-games-hit-34-8b-in-2015-taking-85-of-all-app-revenues/ (accessed December 6, 2016).

[22]Myles Edwin Mangram, "The Globalization of Tesla Motors: A Strategic Marketing Plan Analysis," *Journal of Strategic Marketing,* 20, 4 (2012): 289–312.

[23]Kyle Stock, "Millennials Hit the Road in a Sleek New Generation of RVs," *Bloomberg,*

December 5, 2016, https://www.bloomberg .com/news/articles/2016-12-05/millennials -hit-the-road-in-a-sleek-new-generation-of-rvs (accessed December 6, 2016).

24Shikhar Sarin, Goutam Challagalla, and Ajay K. Kohli, "Implementing Changes in Marketing Strategy: The Role of Perceived Outcome- and Process-Oriented Supervisory Actions," *Journal of Marketing Research,* 49, 4 (2012): 564–580.

25Paul R. LaMonica, "McDonald's Sales Soar Thanks to All Day Breakfast," CNN Money, January 25, 2016, http://money.cnn .com/2016/01/25/investing/mcdonalds-earnings /index.html (accessed December 8, 2016).

26Michella Ore, "Polished Role Models: Helena Fogarty," *Polish Magazine,* July 1, 2014, http://www.polishmagazine.com; Bernadette Tansey, "Turning a Business into a

One-Way Ticket to Paradise," *CNBC.com,* July 2, 2012; Derek Thomas, "'How She Did It' Winner! Swimwear Company, Mi Ola," Balboa Capital, November 8, 2016, http://www .balboacapital.com/swimwear-company-mi -ola-contest-winner/ (accessed January 13, 2017); Mi Ola website, http://mi-ola.com; Cengage Learning, *Mi Ola Swimwear* video.

FEATURE NOTES

aBased on information in Sarah Very Bloomberg, "Procter & Gamble Under Pressure to Make a Deal as Eco-Friendly Products Surge," *St. Louis Post-Dispatch*, October 14, 2016, http://www.stltoday.com/business/local /procter-gamble-under-pressure-to-make-a -deal-as-eco/article_e36641d4-e907-5be0-88d2 -b815b869fdc0.html (accessed December 29, 2016); Erin Caproni, "P&G Launches New Tide Detergent," *Cincinnati Business Courier*, May 20, 2016, http://www.bizjournals.com /cincinnati/news/2016/05/20/p-g-launches -new-tide-detergent.html (accessed December

29, 2016); Beth Kowitt, "Seventh Generation CEO: Here's How the Unilever Deal Went Down," *Fortune,* September 20, 2016, http:// fortune.com/2016/09/20/seventh-generation -unilever-deal/ (accessed December 29, 2016).

bBased on information in Fabiola Cineas, "Philly Shark Tank Entrepreneurs: Where Are They Now?" *Philadelphia Magazine,* December 26, 2016, http://www.phillymag .com/business/2016/12/26/philly-shark-tank -entrepreneurs-where-are-they-now/ (accessed December 29, 2016); Kate Sinclair,

"Christopher Gray on How to Be a Social Entrepreneur," *New York Times,* November 4, 2016, http://www.nytimes.com/2016/11/06 /education/edlife/christopher-gray-on-how-to -be-a-social-entrepreneur.html?_r=1 (accessed December 29, 2016); Eric Weiner, "Christopher Gray's Scholly App Is Bringing Millions of Dollars to College Students in Need," *Smithsonian,* December 2016, http://www .smithsonianmag.com/innovation/financial -aide-christopher-gray-winner-smithsonian -ingenuity-awards-2016-youth-180961123 (accessed December 29, 2016).

Chapter 3

1Mike Montgomery, "What Entrepreneurs Can Learn from the Philanthropic Struggles of TOMS Shoes," *Forbes,* April 28, 2015, http:// www.forbes.com/sites/mikemontgomery /2015/04/28/how-entrepreneurs-can-avoid -the-philanthropy-pitfalls/#641123dc3ab6 (accessed December 14, 2016); TOMS, "Safe Births," http://www.toms.com/what -we-give-safe-births (accessed December 14, 2016); TOMS, "Coffee," http://www.toms. com/coffee (accessed December 14, 2016); Jeremy Quittner, "What the Founder of TOMS Shoes Is Doing Now," *Fortune,* September 8, 2016, http://fortune.com/2016/09/08/what -the-founder-of-toms-shoes-is-doing-now/ (accessed December 14, 2016); UNM Daniels Fund Ethics Initiative website, "TOMS: One for One Movement," https://danielsethics .mgt.unm.edu/pdf/toms%20case.pdf (accessed December 14, 2016); Booth Moore, "Toms Shoes' Model Is Sell a Pair, Give a Pair Away," *Los Angeles Times,* April 19, 2009, http:// www.latimes.com/fashion/alltherage

/la-ig-greentoms19-2009apr19-story.html (accessed December 14, 2016); Stacy Perman, "Making a Do-Gooder's Business Model Work," *Bloomberg Businessweek,* January 23, 2009, https://www.bloomberg.com/news /articles/2009-01-23/making-a-do-gooders -business-model-work (accessed December 14, 2016); "Tom's Sunglasses," *YouTube,* December 5, 2012, https://www.youtube.com /watch?v=FE-KVrILpOM (accessed December 14, 2016); Scott Gerber, "Exit Interview: Blake Mycoskie," *Inc.,* December 2014/January 2015, p. 144.

2Nathan Oliverez-Giles, "Facebook Messenger Brings Group Video Calling to Apps and Web," *Wall Street Journal*, December 19, 2016, http:// www.wsj.com/articles/facebook-messenger -brings-group-video-calling-to-apps-and-web -1482184260 (accessed December 28, 2016).

3P. Varadarajan, Terry Clark, and William M. Pride, "Controlling the Uncontrollable: Managing Your Market Environment," *Sloan

Management Review* 33, 2 (Winter 1992): 39–47.

4Peter Hartlaub, "Sweet! America's Top 10 Brands of Soda," *NBC News,* http://www. nbcnews.com/id/42255151/ns/business-us _business/t/sweet-americas-top-brands-soda/# .WHbiQrYrKV4 (accessed December 27, 2016).

5Ibid.

6Matt Southern, "Latest Search Market Share Number: Google Search Up Across All Devices," *Search Engine Journal*, August 31, 2016, https://www.searchenginejournal.com /august-2016-search-market-share/172078 / (accessed December 27, 2016).

7Economist staff, "Should Digital Monopolies Be Broken Up?" *The Economist,* November 29–December 5, 2014, 11.

8Ibid.

9Alice Holbrook, "Is There a Subprime Auto Loan Bubble?" *USA Today,* September 27, 2014, http://www.usatoday.com/story/money

/personalfinance/2014/09/27/subprime-auto
-loan/16272641/ (accessed November 14,
2014); Richard Davies, "Subprime Auto Loans
Help Fuel Auto Sales Boom," *ABC News,* October 2, 2014, http://abcnews.go.com/blogs
/business/2014/10/subprime-auto-loans-help-fuel
-auto-sales-boom/ (accessed November 14,
2014).

[10]Economist staff, "The World's Biggest
Economic Problem," *The Economist,*
October 25, 2014, 15.

[11]Joshua Gallu, "Dodd–Frank May Cost $6.5
Billion and 5,000 Workers," *Bloomberg,* February 14, 2011, http://www.bloomberg.com/
news/2011-02-14/dodd-frank-s-implementation
-calls-for-6-5-billion-5-000-staff-in-budget
.html (accessed February 22, 2011); Binya-
min Appelbaum and Brady Dennis, "Dodd's
Overhaul Goes Well Beyond Other Plans," *The
Washington Post,* November 11, 2009, http://
www.washingtonpost.com/wp-dyn/content/ar-
ticle/2009/11/09/AR2009110901935.html?hpi
d=topnews&sid=ST2009111003729 (accessed
February 22, 2011).

[12]"Wall Street Reform: Bureau of Consumer
Financial Protection (CFPB)," U.S. Treasury,
http://www.treasury.gov/initiatives/Pages/cfpb
.aspx (accessed February 22, 2011).

[13]"Campaign Finance," *The New York Times*,
October 8, 2010, http://topics.nytimes.com
/top/reference/timestopics/subjects/c/campaign
_finance/index.html (accessed January 24,
2011).

[14]Mike Snider, "AT&T 'Throttled' Data Speed,
Feds Say," *USA Today*, October 29, 2014, 1B.

[15]Samuel Rubenfeld and Austen Hufford,
"Teva Settles Foreign Corruption Probe for
$519 Million," *Wall Street Journal*, December
22, 2016, http://www.wsj.com/articles
/teva-settles-foreign-corruption-probe-for
-519-million-1482418901 (accessed December
28, 2016).

[16]Deitra Crawley, "How Company Size Influences FCPA Enforcement," *Inside Counsel*,
March 22, 2016, http://www.insidecounsel
.com/2016/03/22/how-company-size-influences
-fcpa-enforcement (accessed January 11,
2017); "Bribery Act Guidance," Serious Fraud
Office, https://www.sfo.gov.uk/publications
/guidance-policy-and-protocols/bribery-act
-guidance/ (accessed January 11, 2017).

[17]H. David Kotz, *Financial Regulation and
Compliance: How to Manage Competing and
Overlapping Regulatory Oversight,* (Hoboken,
NJ: John Wiley & Sons, Inc., 2015), 180.

[18]Michael J. Comer and Timothy E. Stephens,
Bribery and Corruption, (New York:
Routledge, 2016).

[19]Samuel Rubenfeld, "Lockheed Martin Gets
into Step with UK Bribery Act with New
Policy," *The Wall Street Journal,* June 8, 2011,
http://blogs.wsj.com/corruption-currents
/2011/06/08/lockheed-martin-gets-into
-step-with-uk-bribery-act-with-new-policy
/ (accessed November 14, 2014).

[20]"The New York State's Division of Consumer
Protection Warns New Yorkers about Military
Identity Theft," Department of State, Division
of Consumer Protection, http://www.dos.
ny.gov/press/2014/militaryidtheft716.html (accessed November 14, 2014).

[21]Anica Zeyen, Markus Beckmann, and Stella
Wolters, "Actor and Institutional Dynamics in
the Development of Multi-stakeholder Initiatives," *Journal of Business Ethics,* accepted
November 11, 2014, DOI 10.1007
/s10551-014-2468-1.

[22]"Council of Better Business Bureaus," Better
Business Bureau, http://www.bbb.org
/council/about/council-of-better-business
-bureaus/?id=184871 (accessed November 14,
2014); Associated Press, "BBB expels largest
bureau over pay-to-play charges," *Fox News,*
March 12, 2013, www.foxnews.com
/us/2013/03/12/bbb-expels-largest-bureau
-over-pay-to-play-charges/ (accessed
November 14, 2014).

[23]ASRC, "NAD Recommends Pursuit of
Research Discontinue All Challenged Claims
for Supplement Marketed as 'Cures' for Brain
Injury, ADHD, Autism," June 19, 2014, http://
www.asrcreviews.org/2014/06/nad-recommends
-pursuit-of-research-discontinue-all-challenged
-claims-for-supplement-marketed-as-cures-for
-brain-injury-adhd-autism/.

[24]"NARB Recommends Rust-Oleum Discontinue Use of 2X Ultra Cover Product Names,"
Coatings World, September 21, 2016, http://
www.coatingsworld.com/contents
/view_breaking-news/2016-09-21/narb
-recommends-rust-oleum-discontinue-use
-of-2x-ultra-cover-product-name (accessed
December 28, 2016).

[25]Kyle McGeeney, "Pew Research Center Will
Call 75% Cellphones for Surveys in 2016,"
Pew Research Center, January 5, 2016, http://
www.pewresearch.org/fact-tank/2016/01/05
/pew-research-center-will-call-75-cellphones
-for-surveys-in-2016/ (accessed December 28,
2016).

[26]"The World's Most Innovative Companies,"
Forbes, http://www.forbes.com/companies
/salesforce/ (accessed December 28, 2016).

[27]William M. Pride and O. C. Ferrell, *Marketing: Concepts and Strategies,* 12th ed. (Boston,
MA: Houghton Mifflin, 2003), 493.

[28]Economist staff, "Home, Hacked Home,"
*The Economist: Special Report on Cyber
-Security*, July 12, 2014, pp. 14–15; Economist
staff, "Prevention Is Better Than Cure," *The
Economist: Special Report on Cyber-Security*,
July 12, 2014, 16.

[29]Matt Hamblen, "Tablet Sales Growth Slows
Dramatically," *Computer World,* October 15,
2014, http://www.computerworld.com
/article/2834238/tablet-sales-growth-slows
-dramatically.html (accessed November 14,
2014).

[30] O.C. Ferrell, Debbie McAlister, and Linda
Ferrell, *Business and Society*, 5th ed. (Chicago,
IL: Chicago Business Press, 2016), 323.

[31]Alex Barinka and Doni Bloomfield, "Amid
Mobile-Pay Buzz, PayPal May Be Left Behind," *Boston Globe,* October 3, 2014, http://
www.bostonglobe.com/business
/2014/10/02/amid-mobile-pay-buzz-paypal-may
-left-behind/NjCWT3EgATzbGmhRSJkqDN
/story.html (accessed November 14, 2014).

[32] O.C. Ferrell, Debbie McAlister, and Linda
Ferrell, *Business and Society*, 5th ed. (Chicago,
IL: Chicago Business Press, 2016), 323.

[33]Wan He, Daniel Goodkind, and Paul Kowal,
"An Aging World: 2015," United States Census
Bureau, March 2016, https://www.census.gov
/content/dam/Census/library/publications
/2016/demo/p95-16-1.pdf (accessed December
28, 2016).

[34]Rich Miller, "Is Everybody Single? More
Than Half the U.S. Now, Up From 37% in
'76," *Bloomberg,* September 8, 2014, http://
www.bloomberg.com/news/2014-09-09/single
-americans-now-comprise-more-than-half-the
-u-s-population.html (accessed November 14,
2014).

[35]Kelvin Pollard and Paola Scommegna, "Just How Many Baby Boomers Are There?" *Population Reference Bureau,* April 2014, http://www.prb.org/Publications/Articles/2002/JustHowManyBabyBoomersAreThere.aspx (accessed November 14, 2014); MarketingCharts staff, "So How Many Millennials Are There in the US, Anyway? (Updated)," *MarketingCharts,* June 30, 2014, http://www.marketingcharts.com/traditional/so-how-many-millennials-are-there-in-the-us-anyway-30401/ (accessed November 14, 2014).

[36]Josh Zumbrun, "Behind the Ongoing U.S. Baby Bust, in 5 Charts," *The Wall Street Journal,* June 7, 2016, http://blogs.wsj.com/economics/2016/06/07/behind-the-ongoing-u-s-baby-bust-in-5-charts/ (accessed January 12, 2017).

[37]Neil Shah, "Baby Bust Threatens Growth," *The Wall Street Journal,* December 4, 2014, A3.

[38]U.S. Bureau of the Census, *Statistical Abstract of the United States, 2010,* 58; "U.S. and World Population Clock," http://www.census.gov/popclock/ (accessed November 14, 2014).

[39] "U.S. Foreign-Born Population Trends," *Pew Research Center,* September 28, 2015, http://www.pewhispanic.org/2015/09/28/chapter-5-u-s-foreign-born-population-trends/ (accessed January 12, 2017).

[40]Zeke J. Miller from Time, "Obama to Give Legal Status to Almost Five Million Undocumented Immigrants," *Fortune,* November 20, 2014, http://fortune.com/2014/11/20/obama-will-give-legal-status-to-almost-5-million-undocumented-immigrants/ (accessed December 9, 2014).

[41]"Modern Immigration Wave Brings 59 Million to U.S., Driving Population Growth and Change Through 2065," *Pew Research Center,* September 28, 2015, http://www.pewhispanic.org/2015/09/28/modern-immigration-wave-brings-59-million-to-u-s-driving-population-growth-and-change-through-2065/ (accessed January 12, 2017).

[42]"Google Seeks to Reach Hispanic Market with New Web Domain, .SOY," *Fox News Latino,* October 19, 2014, http://latino.foxnews.com/latino/money/2014/10/19/google-seeks-to-reach-hispanic-market-with-new-web-domain-soy/ (accessed November 14, 2014).

[43]Karsten Strauss, "The Companies with the Best CSR Reputations in the World in 2016," *Forbes,* September 15, 2016, http://www.forbes.com/sites/karstenstrauss/2016/09/15/the-companies-with-the-best-csr-reputations-in-the-world-in-2016/#36ebbeef7b83 (accessed January 12, 2017).

[44]The Xerox Foundation, https://www.xerox.com/en-us/about/corporate-citizenship/foundation (accessed January 12, 2017); "Xerox Maui Funds New Shelving Units at Maui Food Bank," *Maui Now,* April 25, 2016, http://mauinow.com/2016/04/25/xerox-maui-funds-new-shelving-units-at-maui-food-bank/ (accessed January 12, 2017).

[45]Debbie Thorne, O. C. Ferrell, and Linda Ferrell, *Business and Society,* 3rd ed. (New York: Houghton Mifflin, 2008), 48–50.

[46]O. C. Ferrell, "Business Ethics and Customer Stakeholders," *Academy of Management Executive* 18, 2 (May 2004): 126–129.

[47]"In the Community," *Panera Bread,* https://www.panerabread.com/en-us/en_us/community/community-giving.html (accessed December 26, 2016).

[48]Archie Carroll, "The Pyramid of Corporate Social Responsibility: Toward the Moral Management of Organizational Stakeholders," *Business Horizons* 34, 4 (July/August 1991): 42.

[49]"2016 Global Fraud Survey," http://www.acfe.com/rttn2016/docs/2016-report-to-the-nations.pdf (accessed December 28, 2016).

[50]Sundar Bharadwaj, "Do Firms Pay a Price for Deceptive Advertising?" *Knowledge@Emory,* October 15, 2009, http://knowledge.emory.edu/article.cfm?articleid=1275 (accessed November 3, 2009).

[51]Nathan Bomey, "Volkswagen Will Buy Back 20k More Polluting Diesel Cars," *USA Today,* December 20, 2016, http://www.usatoday.com/story/money/cars/2016/12/20/volkswagen-3-liter-diesel-settlement/95661794/ (accessed December 28, 2016).

[52]Jiyun Kang and Gwendolyn Hustvedt, "Building Trust Between Consumers and Corporations: The Role of Consumer Perceptions of Transparency and Social Responsibility," *Journal of Business Ethics* 125, 2 (2014): 253–265.

[53]Edelman Insights, *2016 Edelman Trust Barometer,* http://www.edelman.com/insights/intellectual-property/2016-edelman-trust-barometer/global-results/ (accessed January 12, 2017).

[54]HCL Technologies, "Life as an Ideapreneur," http://www.hcltech.com/careers/life-ideapreneur (accessed November 14, 2014).

[55]David Kesmodel, Jacob Bunge, and Betsy McKay, "Shoppers Push Meat Industry to Wean Itself Off Drugs," *The Wall Street Journal,* November 4, 2014, A1, A12.

[56]Tim Barnett and Sean Valentine, "Issue Contingencies and Marketers' Recognition of Ethical Issues, Ethical Judgments and Behavioral Intentions," *Journal of Business Research* 57, 4 (2004): 338–346.

[57]Laura Stampler, "What These Companies Did in the Wake of Hurricane Sandy Will Restore Your Faith in Big Business," Yahoo Finance! November 2, 2012, http://finance.yahoo.com/news/what-these-companies-did-in-the-wake-of-hurricane-sandy-will-restore-your-faith-in-big-business.html (accessed December 11, 2012).

[58]"BMW Ultimate Drive for the Cure," *National Capital Chapter BMW Car Club of America,* http://old.nccbmwcca.org/index.php?cure (accessed December 27, 2016).

[59]Christine Birkner, "Fully Engaged," *Marketing News,* September 2014, 8–10.

[60]Cone Communications, *2013 Cone Communications Social Impact Study,* http://www.conecomm.com/stuff/contentmgr/files/0/e3d2eec1e15e-858867a5c2b1a22c4cfb/files/2013_cone_comm_social_impact_study.pdf (accessed November 17, 2014).

[61]Douglas MacMillan, "Warby Parker Adds Storefronts to Its Sales Strategy," *The Wall Street Journal,* November 17, 2014, http://online.wsj.com/articles/warby-parker-adds-storefronts-to-its-sales-strategy-1416251866 (accessed November 17, 2014); Warby Parker, "Buy a Pair, Give a Pair," http://www.warbyparker.com/buy-a-pair-give-a-pair (accessed November 17, 2014).

[62]Simona Romani, Silvia Grappi, and Richard P. Bagozzi, "Corporate Socially Responsible Initiatives and Their Effects on Consumption of Green Products," *Journal of Business Ethics,* accepted November 19, 2014, DOI: 10.1007/s10551-014-2485-0.

[63]Forest Stewardship Council, "Kimberly-Clark Grows Its Commitment to FSC," *Newsletter Stories,* January 23, 2014, https://us.fsc.org

/newsletter.239.809.htm (accessed November 17, 2014).

[64]Gergely Nyilasy, Harsha Gangadharbatla, and Angela Paladino, "Perceived Greenwashing: The Interactive Effects of Green Advertising and Corporate Environmental Performance on Consumer Reactions," *Journal of Business Ethics* 125, 4 (2014): 693–707.

[65]Jill Gabrielle Klein, N. Craig Smith, and Andrew John, "Why We Boycott: Consumer Motivations for Boycott Participation," *Journal of Marketing* 68, 3 (July 2004): 92–109.

[66]Muel Kaptein, "Toward Effective Codes: Testing the Relationship with Unethical Behavior," *Journal of Business Ethics* 99, 2 (2011): 233–251.

[67]Bruce R. Gaumnitz and John C. Lere, "Contents of Codes of Ethics of Professional Business Organizations in the United States," *Journal of Business Ethics* 35, 1 (2002): 35–49.

[68]"2010 World's Most Ethical Companies—Company Profile: Barrett-Jackson," *Ethisphere*, Q1, 32.

[69]Nobuyuki Fukawa and Sunil Erevelles, "Perceived Reasonableness and Morals in Service Encounters," *Journal of Business Ethics* 125, 3 (2014): 381–400.

[70]Anis Ben Brik, Belaid Rettab, and Kamel Mellahi, "Market Orientation, Corporate Social Responsibility, and Business Performance," *Journal of Business Ethics* 99, 3 (2011): 307–324.

[71]O. C. Ferrell and Michael Hartline, *Marketing Strategy*, 4th ed. (Mason, OH: Cengage Learning, 2008), 76–79.

[72]Marjorie Kelly, "Holy Grail Found: Absolute, Definitive Proof That Responsible Companies Perform Better Financially," *Business Ethics* 18, 4 (Winter 2005): 4–5; Xueming Luo and C. B. Bhattacharya, "Corporate Social Responsibility, Customer Satisfaction, and Market Value," *Journal of Marketing* 70, 4 (October 2006): 1–18; Isabelle Maignan, O. C. Ferrell, and Linda Ferrell, "A Stakeholder Model for Implementing Social Responsibility in Marketing," *European Journal of Marketing* 39, 9/10 (September/October 2005): 956–977.

[73]Cone Communications, *2013 Cone Communications Social Impact Study*, http://www.conecomm.com/stuff/contentmgr/files/0/e3d2eec1e15e-858867a5c2b1a22c4cfb/files/2013_cone_comm_social_impact_study.pdf (accessed November 17, 2014).

[74]Maignan, Ferrell, and Ferrell, "A Stakeholder Model for Implementing Social Responsibility in Marketing."

[75]Kurt Eichenwald, "The Great Smartphone War," *Vanity Fair*, June 2014, http://www.vanityfair.com/business/2014/06/applesamsung-smartphone-patent-war (accessed January 11, 2016); "Samsung Ordered to Pay Apple $120m for Patent Violation," *The Guardian*, May 2, 2014, http://www.theguardian.com/technology/2014/may/03/ samsung-ordered-to-pay-apple-120m-forpatent-violation?CMP5EMCNEWEML6619I2 (accessed January 11, 2016); Dan Levine, "Apple, Google Agree to Settle Lawsuit Alleging Hiring Conspiracy," *Reuters*, April 24, 2014, http://www.reuters.com/article/2014/04/24/ us-apple-google-settlement-idUSBREA3N1Y120140424 (accessed January 11, 2016); Ian Scerr, "Apple, Samsung Square off over Patent Damages," *The Wall Street Journal*, December 6, 2012, http://online.wsj.com/ article/SB10001424127887323501404578164021886466686.html?mod5WSJ_article_comments#articleTabs%3Darticle (accessed January 11, 2016); Evan Ramstad, "Award to Apple Isn't Raised," *The Wall Street Journal*, June 30, 2012, http://online.wsj.com/article/SB100014241278873243292045782728704322069736.html?KEYWORDS5apple1samsung KEYWORDS%3Dapple1samsung (accessed January 11, 2016); Dino Grandoni, "How the Apple Samsung Lawsuit Hurt Consumers," *The Huffington Post*, July 31, 2012, http://www.huffingtonpost.com/2012/07/31/apple-samsunglawsuit-consumers_n_1721623.html (accessed January 11, 2016); Paul Elias, "Apple's Samsung Verdict Nearly Cut in Half by Federal Judge," *The Huffington Post*, March 1, 2013, http://www.huffingtonpost.com/2013/03/01/ half-of-billion-apple-samsung-settlementinvalidated_n_2792624.html (accessed January 11, 2016); Scott Bicheno, "Global smartphone market Q3 2015—Samsung strikes back," *Telecoms*, October 29, 2015, http://telecoms. com/450101/global-smartphone-marketq3-2015-samsung-strikes-back/ (accessed January 11, 2016); based on a news clip from the BBC, May 2014, https://vimeo.com/ album/3731955/video/151163184.

FEATURE NOTES

[a]Andria Cheng, "'Fair Trade' Becomes a Fashion Trend," *The Wall Street Journal*, July 8, 2015, B7; Catherine Clifford, "First Coffee, Now Fashion: Apparel Brands Seek Fair Trade Certification Despite Challenges," *Entrepreneur*, October 17, 2013, http://www.entrepreneur.com/article/229444 (accessed December 3, 2016); Hayli Goode, "Ethical vs Fair Trade Fashion, Because the Difference Definitely Matters," *Bustle*, April 30, 2015, http://www.bustle.com/ articles/79529-ethical-vs-fair-trade-fashionbecause-the-difference-definitely-matters (accessed October 5, 2015); Andria Cheng, "'Fair Trade' Labeling Extends Beyond Coffee and Chocolate and Into the World of Fashion," *Market Watch*, July 7, 2015, http://www.marketwatch.com/story/fair-trade-labeling-extends-beyond-coffee-and-chocolate-and-into-the-world-of-fashion-2015-07-07 (accessed December 3, 2016).

[b] UNM Daniels Fund Ethics Initiative, "Harmless Harvest: First Fair Trade to Life Coconut Water," 2016, https://danielsethics.mgt.unm.edu/pdf/harmless-harvest.pdf (accessed December 17, 2016); Elaine Watson, "Harmless Harvest Raw Coconut Water: We're Not Competing with Vita Coco or Zico," *Food Navigator,* January 6, 2016, http://www.foodnavigator-usa.com/Manufacturers/Harmless-Harvest-raw-coconut-water-We-re-not-competing-with-Vita-Coco (accessed December 17, 2016); Liz Welch, "How These 2 Guys Are Winning the Hyper-Competitive Coconut Water Wars," *Inc.*, June 2016, http://www.inc.com/magazine/201606/liz-welch/harmless-harvest-coconut-water-sustainability.html (accessed December 17, 2016); Kat Odell, "Taste Test: The Best Coconut Water," *Eater.com,* March 18, 2016, http://www.eater

.com/drinks/2016/3/18/11222874/taste-test -coconut-water-best (accessed December 17, 2016); Quality Assurance & Food Safety,

"Harmless Harvest Takes 'Constructive Capitalism' Approach," August 16, 2016, http://www.qualityassurancemag.com/article

/harmless-harvest-takes-constructive -capitalism-approach/ (accessed December 17, 2016).

Chapter 4

[1]Hadley Malcolm, "Ikea Wants to Get a Little More Personal," *USA Today*, June 15, 2015, 6B (accessed December 11, 2015); Denise Lee Yohn, "How IKEA Designs Its Brand Success," *Forbes*, June 10, 2015, http://www.forbes.com /sites/deniselyohn/2015/06/10/how-ikea -designs-its-brand-success/#3bf5e07d3901 (accessed December 17, 2016); IKEA, Life at Home Report website, http://lifeathome.ikea. com (accessed December 17, 2016).

[2]Tripp Mickle and Valerie Bauerlein, "Nascar, Once a Cultural Icon, Hits the Skids," *The Wall Street Journal*, February 21, 2017, https://www.wsj.com/articles/long-in-victory -lane-nascar-hits-the-skids-1487686349?tesla=y (accessed March 12, 2017).

[3]Allison Enright, "Surviving 2010," *Marketing News,* February 28, 2010, 30–33.

[4]Jack Clark, "How to Manage Data Like Facebook," *Bloomberg Businessweek,* October 16, 2014, 35–36.

[5]Dhruv Grewal Parasuraman and R. Krishnan, *Marketing Research* (Boston: Houghton Mifflin, 2007).

[6]Barry Babin and William Zikmund, *Exploring Marketing Research* (Mason, OH: Cengage Learning, 2016), 113.

[7]John Webb, "Oracle Hosts PeopleSoft Customer Advisory Boards," Oracle, August 21, 2013, https://blogs.oracle.com/peoplesoft /entry/peoplesoft_customer_advisory_board (accessed November 19, 2017).

[8]Phil Wahba, "The Change Agent Inside CVS," *Fortune*, September 11, 2015, http://fortune .com/2015/09/11/cvs-health-helena-foulkes/ (accessed December 21, 2015).

[9]Christine Birkner, "Pint-Size Participants," *Marketing News,* June 2014, 8–9.

[10]Daniel Gross, "Lies, Damn Lies, and Focus Groups," *Slate*, October 10, 2003, http://www .slate.com/articles/business/moneybox/2003/10 /lies_damn_lies_and_focus_groups.html (accessed November 19, 2014).

[11]Barry Babin and William Zikmund, *Exploring Marketing Research* (Mason, OH: Cengage Learning, 2016), 113.

[12]Andreas Persson and Lynette Ryals, "Making Customer Relationship Decisions: Analytics v Rules of Thumb," *Journal of Business Research* 67, 8 (August 2014): 1725–1732.

[13]Donna F. Davis, Susan L. Golicic, Courtney N. Boerstler, Sunny Choi, and Hanmo Oh, "Does Marketing Research Suffer from Methods Myopia?" *Journal of Business Research* 66, 9 (2013): 1245–1250.

[14]Vikas Mittal and Wagner A. Kamakura, "Satisfaction, Repurchase Intent, and Repurchase Behavior: Investigating the Moderating Effects of Customer Characteristics," *Journal of Marketing Research* 38, 1 (February 2001): 131–142.

[15]Melinda F. Emerson, "Using Social Media to Test Your Idea Before You Try to Sell It," *The New York Times*, August 3, 2012, http:// boss.blogs.nytimes.com/2012/08/03/using -social-media-to-test-your-idea-before-you -try-to-sell-it/ (accessed November 19, 2014).

[16]Robert M. Graves, "Nonresponse Rate and Nonresponse Bias in Household Surveys," *Public Opinion Quarterly* 70, 5 (2006): 646–675.

[17]Brittany Wallman, "Rollout of Better Cellphone, Wireless Service Coming," *Sun Sentinel*, March 15, 2017, http://www.sun-sentinel.com/local /broward/fl-reg-cell-reception-microtowers -20170315-story.html (accessed March 18, 2017).

[18]Ray Poynter, "Mobile Market Research, 2014," *International Journal of Market Research* 56, 6 (2014): 705–707.

[19]Joshua Brustein, "How an Online Survey Company Joined the $1 Billion Club," *Bloomberg Businessweek,* September 24, 2014, http:// www.businessweek.com/articles/2014-09-24 /how-qualtrics-turned-online-surveys-into-a -1-billion-business (accessed December 16, 2014).

[20]"About Qualtrics," Qualtrics website, http:// www.qualtrics.com/about/ (accessed December 16, 2014); Joshua Brustein, "How an Online Survey Company Joined the $1 Billion Club," *Bloomberg Businessweek,* September 24, 2014, http://www.businessweek.com /articles/2014-09-24/how-qualtrics-turned -online-surveys-into-a-1-billion-business

(accessed December 16, 2014); "After Snap, Will One of These 12 Tech Companies Be the Next to IPO?" *Silicon Republic*, February 10, 2017, https://www.siliconrepublic.com /companies/snapchat-ipo-who-is-next (accessed March 17, 2017).

[21]Joshua Brustein, "How an Online Survey Company Joined the $1 Billion Club," *Bloomberg Businessweek,* September 24, 2014, http://www .businessweek.com/articles/2014-09-24/how -qualtrics-turned-online-surveys-into-a-1 -billion-business (accessed December 16, 2014).

[22]Molly Sloat, "Sphere of Influence," *Marketing News,* November 2014, 16–17.

[23]David Robertson, "Building Success: How Thinking 'Inside the Brick' Saved Lego," *Wired,* October 9, 2013, http://www.wired .co.uk/magazine/archive/2013/10/features /building-success (accessed November 19, 2014); Lego Ideas website, https://ideas.lego .com/ (accessed November 19, 2014).

[24]Amazon Mechanical Turk website, http://aws.amazon.com/mturk/ (accessed December 16, 2014).

[25]Michael Buhrmester, Tracy Kwang, and Samuel B. Gosling, "Amazon's Mechanical Turk: A New Source of Inexpensive, Yet High-Quality Data?" *Perspectives on Psychological Science* 6, 1 (2011): 3–5.

[26]James Vincent, "Amazon's Mechanical Turkers want to be recognized as 'actual human beings'," *The Verge*, December 4, 2014, http://www.theverge.com/2014/12/4/7331777 /amazon-mechanical-turk-workforce -digitallabor (accessed January 11, 2016); Utpal Dholakia, "My Experience as an Amazon Mechanical Turk (MTurk) Worker," July 20, 2015, https://www.linkedin.com /pulse/my-experience-amazon-mechanical -turk-mturk-worker-tpaldholakia (accessed January 11, 2016).

[27]Sue Shellenbarger, "A Few Bucks for Your Thoughts?" *The Wall Street Journal*, May 18, 2011, http://online.wsj.com/article/SB1000142 4052748703509104576329110724411724 .html (accessed November 19, 2014).

[28]Bas Donkers, Philip Hans Franses, and Peter C. Verhoef, "Selective Sampling for Binary Choice Models," *Journal of Marketing Research* 40 (November 2003): 492–497.

[29]Hsin-Hui Lin and Shu-Fei Yang, "An Eye Movement Study of Attribute Framing in Online Shopping," *Journal of Marketing Analytics,* 2(2), June 2014, 72–80.

[30]Charles Duhigg, "How Companies Learn Your Secrets," *The New York Times*, February 19, 2012, http://www.nytimes.com/2012/02/19/magazine/shopping-habits.html (accessed November 19, 2014).

[31]Piet Levy, "10 Minutes with…Gregory A. Reid," *Marketing News*, February 28, 2010, 34.

[32]Mike Deri Smith, "Fake Reviews Plague Consumer Websites," *The Guardian*, January 26, 2013, http://www.guardian.co.uk/money/2013/jan/26/fake-reviews-plague-consumer-websites (accessed November 19, 2014).

[33]David Aaker, V. Kumar, George Day, and Robert Lane, *Marketing Research*, 10th ed. (New York: Wiley & Sons, 2010).

[34]"BehaviorScan Rx," IRI, http://www.iriworldwide.com/default.aspx?TabId=159&productid=75 (accessed November 19, 2014).

[35]Douglas Laney, "The Importance of 'Big Data': A Definition," Gartner, June 2012.

[36]Peter Daboll, "5 Reasons Why Big Data Will Crush Big Research," *Forbes,* December 3, 2013, http://www.forbes.com/sites/onmarketing/2013/12/03/5-reasons-why-big-data-will-crush-big-research (accessed November 19, 2014).

[37]Danny Bradbury and Tim Anderson, "Big Data and Marketing: An Inevitable Partnership," *The Guardian,* October 16, 2013, http://www.theguardian.com/technology/2013/oct/16/big-data-and-marketing-an-inevitable-partnership (accessed November 19, 2014).

[38]Steven Norton, "Big Companies Rein In Data Sprawl," *The Wall Street Journal*, October 22, 2015, B4.

[39]Paula B. Goes, "Editor's Comments: Big Data and IS Research," *MIS Quarterly* 38, 3 (September 2014): iii–viii.

[40]Amrit Kirpalani, "What Marketing Executives REALLY Think of Big Data," *Direct Marketing News,* November 22, 2013, http://www.dmnews.com/what-marketing-executives-really-think-of-big-data/article/322236 (accessed November 19, 2014).

[41]Tyler Loechner, "Big Data Generating Big Results for Marketers, But Not All Have Adopted It," RTM Daily, October 24, 2013, http://www.mediapost.com/publications/article/212007/big-data-generating-big-results-for-marketers-but.html (accessed November 19, 2014).

[42]Bradbury and Anderson, "Big Data and Marketing: An Inevitable Partnership."

[43]Mehboob Feelani, "Watson, Come Here. I Want You," *Fortune,* October 27, 2014, 36.

[44]Kashmir Hill, "How Target Figured Out a Teen Girl Was Pregnant Before Dad Did," *Forbes,* February 16, 2012, http://www.forbes.com/sites/kashmirhill/2012/02/16/how-target-figured-out-a-teen-girl-was-pregnant-before-her-father-did (accessed November 19, 2014).

[45]SAS, "Big Data, Bigger Marketing," http://www.sas.com/software/customer-intelligence/big-data-marketing.html (accessed November 19, 2014).

[46]James Rubin, "Survey Demonstrates the Benefits of Big Data," *Forbes,* November 15, 2013, http://www.forbes.com/sites/forbesinsights/2013/11/15/survey-demonstrates-the-benefits-of-big-data (accessed November 19, 2014).

[47]Daboll, "5 Reasons Why Big Data Will Crush Big Research."

[48]Aamer Madhani, "White House Raises Concerns about 'Big Data'," *USA Today,* May 2, 2014, 5A; Melissa S. Barker, Donald I. Barker, Nicolas F. Bormann, Mary Lou Roberts, and Debra Zahay, Social Media Marketing (Mason, OH: Cengage Learning, 2016), 25–26.

[49]Jayson DeMers, "2014 Is the Year of Digital Marketing Analytics: What It Means for Your Company," *Forbes,* February 10, 2014, http://www.forbes.com/sites/jaysondemers/2014/02/10/2014-is-the-year-of-digital-marketing-analytics-what-it-means-for-your-company/ (accessed December 15, 2014).

[50]Marketing Science Institute, "MSI Closes Knowledge Gap on Marketers' Top Concerns," *Marketing Science Institute Review,* Fall 2014, 1–2.

[51]Elisabeth A. Sullivan, "Marketing Analytics," *Marketing News,* December 2014, 24–33.

[52]Regina Pefanis Schlee and Katrin R. Harich, "Teaching Students How to Integrate and Assess Social Networking Tools in Marketing Communications," *Marketing Education Review* 23, 3 (2013): 209–223.

[53]Elisabeth A. Sullivan, "Marketing Analytics," *Marketing News,* December 2014, 24–33.

[54]Doug Henschen, "Big Data Success: 3 Companies Share Secrets," *InformationWeek,* October 4, 2013, http://www.informationweek.com/big-data/big-data-analytics/big-data-success-3-companies-share-secrets/d/d-id/1111815? (accessed December 15, 2014).

[55]Frank Germann, Gary L. Lilien, and Arvind Rangaswamy, "Performance Implications of Deploying Marketing Analytics," *International Journal of Research in Marketing* 30, 2 (2013): 114–128.

[56]Chares Duhigg, "How Companies Learn Your Secrets," *The New York Times*, February 15, 2012, http://www.nytimes.com/2012/02/19/magazine/shopping-habits.html (accessed November 19, 2014).

[57]Emily Steel and Julia Angwin, "The Web's Cutting Edge, Anonymity in Name Only," *The Wall Street Journal*, August 4, 2010, http://online.wsj.com/article/SB10001424052748703294904575385532109190198.html (accessed November 19, 2014).

[58]Morgan Downs (Producer), *Inside the Mind of Google* [DVD], United States: CNBC Originals, 2010.

[59]"Top 25 Global Research Organizations," *Marketing News,* August 2014, 40.

[60]Reprinted with permission of The Marketing Research Association, P.O. Box 230, Rocky Hill, CT 06067-0230, 860-257-4008.

[61]Ellen Byron, "From Diapers to 'Depends': Marketers Discreetly Retool for Aging Boomers," The Wall Street Journal, February 5, 2011, http://online.wsj.com/article/SB10001424052748704013604576104394209062996.html (accessed March 30, 2012); Bruce Horovitz, "Big-Spending Baby Boomers Bend the Rules of Marketing," USA Today, November 16, 2010, http://www.usatoday.com/money/advertising/2010-H-16-1Aboomerbuyers16_CV_N.htm (accessed March 30, 2012); Mark Bradbury, "The 7 Incredible Facts about Boomers' Spending Power," The Huffington Post, March 17, 2015, http://www.huffingtonpost.com/mark-bradbury/the-7-incredible-facts-about-boomers-spending_b_6815876.html (accessed January 21, 2016); Synchrony Financial, "These findings about how millennials and baby boomers shop may surprise you," Business Insider, April 22, 2015, http://www.businessinsider.com/sc/how-millennials-and-baby-boomers-shop-2015-4 (accessed January 21, 2016).

FEATURE NOTES

[a]Geoffrey A. Fowler, "Strategies to Outfox Facebook's Tracking," *The Wall Street Journal*, August 6, 2014, D1; "If a Consumer Asked You, 'Why Is Tracking Good?' What Would You Say?" *Ad Exchanger*, October 28, 2011, https://adexchanger.com/online-advertising /why-is-tracking-good/ (accessed December 17, 2016); Ad Traders, "The Ethical Issues with 3rd Party Behavioral Strategy," *Ad Exchanger*, October 31, 2011, https:// adexchanger.com/the-debate/3rd-party -behavioral-tracking/ (accessed December 17, 2016); Nicholas Carr, "Tracking is an Assault on Liberty, with Real Dangers," *The Wall Street Journal*, August 6, 2010, http://www.wsj.com /articles/SB10001424052748703748904575 411682714389888 (accessed December 17, 2016); Tim Peterson, "Facebook Makes Opting Out of Behavioral Ad Targeting Easier," *AdvertisingAge*, September 15, 2015, http://adage .com/article/digital/facebook-makes-opting -ad-tracking-easier/300371/ (accessed December 17, 2016).

[b]Danny Bradbury, "Small Business, Big Data: How to Boost Your Marketing with Analytics," *Forbes*, June 5, 2015, http://www.forbes.com /sites/ramcommercial/2015/06/05/small-busi ness-big-data-how-to-boost-your-marketing -with-analytics/#66e9645c79b3 (accessed December 17, 2016); Kimberly A. Whitler, "How the Best Marketers Are Using Analytics to Create Competitive Advantage," *Forbes*, July 18, 2015, http://www.forbes.com/sites /kimberlywhitler/2015/07/19/how-some-of-the -best-marketers-are-using-analytics-to-create -a-competitive-advantage/#3dd8d4ce4870 (accessed December 17, 2016); Louis Columbus, "Roundup of Analytics, Big Data & Business Intelligence Forecasts and Market Estimates, 2015," *Forbes*, May 25, 2015, http://www.forbes.com/sites/louiscolumbus /2015/05/25/roundup-of-analytics-big-data -business-intelligence-forecasts-and-market -estimates-2015/#74fa33284869 (accessed December 17, 2016); Krystle Vermes, "84% of B2B Marketers Consider Analytics to Be Very Important to Success," *KoMarketing*, August 8, 2016, http://www.komarketingassociates.com /industry-news/report-84-b2b-marketers -consider-analytics-important-success-3172/ (accessed December 17, 2016).

Chapter 5

[1]Based on information in: Danny King, "Marriott Creates Division for Luxury Brands," *Travel Weekly*, December 5, 2016, http://www .travelweekly.com/Travel-News/Hotel-News /Marriott-creates-division-for-luxury-brands (accessed December 30, 2016); Nikki Ekstein, "Marriott and Starwood Reveal the Future of Their Luxury Brands," *Bloomberg*, November 28, 2016, https://www.bloomberg.com/news /articles/2016-11-28/marriott-and-starwood -reveal-future-of-their-luxury-brands (accessed December 30, 2016); Kathryn Luttner, "Marriott Launches Digital Magazine Targeting Millennials," *Campaign US*, November 7, 2016, http://www.campaignlive .com/article/marriott-launches-digital -magazine-targeting-millennials/1414642 (accessed December 30, 2016).

[2]Costanza Nosi, Carlo Alberto Pratesi, and Antonella D'Agostino, "A Benefit Segmentation of the Italian Market for Full Electric Vehicles," *Journal of Marketing Analytics*, 2, 2 (2014): 120–134.

[3]Tina Owen, "Recipe for a Successful Baking Company," *Wilmette University News*, December 6, 2016, http://willamette.edu/news /library/2016/12/happy-campers-gluten-free .html (accessed January 16, 2017).

[4]Aaron Ricadela and Michael Ross, "Adidas Is a Late Starter in the Race for the Women's Market," *Bloomberg*, March 1, 2016, https://www.bloomberg.com/news /articles/2016-03-01/adidas-makes-late-sprint -in-crowded-race-to-sell-women-sneakers (accessed January 16, 2017).

[5]Greg Petro, "How Under Armour and Forever 21 Are Winning with Millennials," *Forbes*, April 12, 2016, http://www.forbes.com/sites /gregpetro/2016/04/12/how-under-armour -and-forever-21-are-winning-with-millennials /#42370464a1ec (accessed January 16, 2017).

[6]Art Weinstein, "Target Market Selection in B2B Technology Markets," *Journal of Marketing Analytics*, 2, 1 (2014): 59–69.

[7]Richard Fry, "Millennials Overtake Baby Boomers as America's Largest Generation," Pew Research Center, April 25, 2016, http:// www.pewresearch.org/fact-tank/2016/04/25 /millennials-overtake-baby-boomers/ (accessed December 14, 2016).

[8]"Median Age of the Resident Population of the United States from 1960 to 2015," *Statista*, https://www.statista.com/statistics/241494 /median-age-of-the-us-population/ (accessed December 15, 2016).

[9]Mike Snider, "Women Get Their Own Beer; Will They Want It?," *USA Today*, May 28, 2016, http://www.usatoday.com/story /money/2016/05/21/women-get-but-they-want -their-own-beer/83857942/ (accessed December 15, 2016).

[10]"QuickFacts," United States Census Bureau, http://www.census.gov/quickfacts/table /PST045215/00 (accessed December 15, 2016).

[11]"Marketing to Women—Quick Facts," She-Conomy, http://she-conomy.com/report /marketing-to-women-quick-facts (accessed December 15, 2016).

[12]"About Iman," Iman Cosmetics, http://www .imancosmetics.com/aboutiman (accessed December 15, 2016).

[13]Molly Soat, "Inside the Mind of the Wedding Consumer," *Marketing News*, November 2015, https://www.ama.org/publications /MarketingNews/Pages/inside-mind-wedding -consumer.aspx (accessed December 16, 2016); Kathryn Vasel, "Couples Are Spending More than Ever to Get Hitched," CNN, April 6, 2016, http://money.cnn.com/2016/04/05/pf /average-wedding-costs/ (accessed December 16, 2016).

[14]"The American Family Today," *Pew Research Center*, December 17, 2015, http:// www.pewsocialtrends.org/2015/12/17/1-the -american-family-today/ (accessed December 19, 2016).

[15]Aaron Terrazos, "All Ages Welcome: Why Living Alone Isn't Just for America's Young

and Old Anymore," Zillow, June 28, 2016, http://www.zillow.com/research/americans -living-alone-12639/ (accessed December 19, 2016).

[16]"For Couples Skipping the Ring, It Pays to Plot Out Finances," NPR, April 17, 2016, http://www.npr.org/2016/04/17/473498335/for -couples-skipping-the-ring-it-pays-to-plot -out-finances (accessed December 19, 2016).

[17]"American Community Survey Data on Same Sex Couples," U.S. Census Bureau, https:// www.census.gov/hhes/samesex/data/acs.html (accessed December 19, 2016).

[18]Claritas PRIZM, https://segmentationsolutions .nielsen.com/mybestsegments/Default.jsp?ID=70 (accessed January 16, 2017).

[19]Alexandra Samuel, "Psychographics Are Just as Important for Marketers as Demographics," *Harvard Business Review*, March 11, 2016, https://hbr.org/2016/03/psychographics -are-just-as-important-for-marketers-as -demographics (accessed December 19, 2016).

[20]Joseph T. Plummer, "The Concept and Application of Life Style Segmentation," *Journal of Marketing*, 38, 1 (1974): 33.

[21]Claritas PRIZM, https://segmentationsolutions .nielsen.com/mybestsegments/Default.jsp? ID=70 (accessed January 16, 2017).

[22]Philip Kotler and Kevin Keller, *Marketing Management*, 15th ed. (Englewood Cliffs, NJ: Prentice Hall, 2016).

[23]Charles W. Chase Jr., "Selecting the Appropriate Forecasting Method," *Journal of Business Forecasting*, 16, 3 (1997): 2, 23, 28–29.

[24]Ed Thompson, "Striking a Balance between Sales and Operations in the Forecasting Process," *Journal of Business Forecasting*, 32, 4 (Winter 2013–2014): 29–31.

[25]Daniel P. Kline, "Doritos, Cheetos Moving Beyond Taco Bell, Burger King," *The Motley Fool*, December 19, 2016, http://www.fool .com/investing/2016/12/19/doritos-cheetos

-tacos-moving-beyond-taco-bell.aspx (accessed December 20, 2016).

[26]"Mike Boyle Strength & Conditioning Launches Global CFSC Certification," International Health, Racquet & Sportsclub Association, October 7, 2016, http://www .ihrsa.org/news/2016/10/7/mike-boyle -strength-conditioning-launches-global-cfsc -certif.html (accessed December 20, 2016); Caroline Earle, "Setting the Trend for the Future of Gyms with Boston-Based Strength Coach, Mike Boyle," *BostInno*, February 17, 2014, http://bostinno.streetwise.co/2014/02/17 /interview-with-boston-coach-mike-boyle / (accessed December 20, 2016); Jenni Whalen, "Q&A: Boston Trainer Mike Boyle," *Boston Magazine*, June 13, 2013, http://www.bostonmagazine.com/health /blog/2013/06/13/mike-boyle/ (accessed December 20, 2016); www.bodybyboyle.com; Cengage Learning, *Mike Boyle Strength and Conditioning* video.

FEATURE NOTES

[a]Based on information in Rob Marvin, "5 Ways @WalmartLabs Is Revolutionizing Mobile Retail," *PC Magazine*, March 23, 2016, http:// www.pcmag.com/article2/0,2817,2493418,00 .asp (accessed December 30, 2016); Sara Rush Wirth, "Next-Level Mobile Apps Drive Engage-ment," *Restaurant Business Online*, September 17, 2015, http://www.restaurantbusinessonline .com/operations/technology/next-level-mobile -apps-drive-engagement?page=0%2C3 (accessed December 30, 2016).

[b]Based on information in Artemis Berry, "A Quick 'Chat' with ReplyYes CEO Dave Cotter," *National Retail Federation*, September 23, 2016, https://medium.com /nrf-events/a-quick-chat-with-replyyes-ceo -dave-cotter-8a634e844452#.951u93cqh (accessed December 30, 2016); Dina Bass, "These Startups Are Selling Vinyl Records, Graphic Novels, and Indian Food via Text Message," *Bloomberg*, April 14, 2016, https://www.bloomberg.com/news

/articles/2016-04-14/these-startups-are-selling -vinyl-records-graphic-novels-and-indian -food-via-text-message (accessed December 30, 2016); Christopher Heine, "How a Chatbot Helped This Vinyl Records Startup Make $1 Million in 8 Months," *Billboard*, April 28, 2016, http://www.billboard.com/articles /business/7350110/chatbot-vinyl-records -startup-the-edit (accessed December 30, 2016).

Chapter 6

[1]Based on information in Yuyu Chen, "Frito-Lay CMO: 'Innovation Is More Important Than Ever'," *Digiday*, December 6, 2016, http:// digiday.com/brands/frito-lay-cmo-innovation -important-ever/ (accessed February 2, 2017); Robert Klara, "Q&A: Frito-Lay's New CMO on Why the Brand Is Making Doritos Out of Card-board," *Adweek*, October 2, 2016, http://www .adweek.com/brand-marketing/qa-frito -lay-s-new-cmo-why-brand-making-doritos -out-cardboard-173845/ (accessed February 2, 2017); Karlene Lukovitz, "Lay's Revives 'Do Us a Flavor,' With A Twist," *MediaPost*,

January 10, 2017, http://www.mediapost.com /publications/article/292571/lays-revives-do -us-a-flavor-with-a-twist.html (accessed February 2, 2017).

[2]Kathleen Mortimer and Andrew Pressey, "Customer Information Search and Credence Services: Implications for Service Providers," *Journal of Services Marketing*, 27, 1 (2013): 49–58.

[3]Björn Frank, Takao Enkawa, and Shane J. Schvaneveldt, "How Do the Success Factors Driving Repurchase Intent Differ between

Male and Female Customers?" *Journal of the Academy of Marketing Science*, 42, 2 (2014): 171–185.

[4]Athina Nella and Christou Evangelos, "Segmenting Wine Tourists on the Basis of Involvement with Wine," *Journal of Travel & Tourism Marketing*, 31, 7 (2014): 783–798.

[5]Russell W. Belk, "Situational Variables and Consumer Behavior," *Journal of Consumer Research* 2, 3 (1975): 157–164.

[6]Humayun Khan, "How Retailers Manipulate Sight, Smell, and Sound to Trigger Purchase

Behavior in Consumers," *Shopify,* April 25, 2016, https://www.shopify.com/retail/119926083-how-retailers-manipulate-sight-smell-and-sound-to-trigger-purchase-behavior-in-consumers (accessed on January 11, 2017).

7Tracey S. Dagger and Peter J. Danaher, "Comparing the Effect of Store Remodeling on New and Existing Customers," *Journal of Marketing,* 78, 3 (2014): 62–80.

8Ryan S. Elder and Ariadna Krishna, "The Effects of Advertising Copy on Sensory Thoughts and Perceived Taste," *Journal of Consumer Research* 36, 5 (2010): 748–756.

9George E. Newman, Margarita Gorlin, and Ravi Dhar, "When Going Green Backfires: How Firm Intentions Shape the Evaluation of Socially Beneficial Product Enhancements," *Journal of Consumer Research,* 41, 3 (2014): 823–839.

10Brendan Murphy and Emma DeFelice, "Permission to Connect: How 'Human Era' Brands Become More Likeable," *CampaignUS,* December 15, 2016, http://www.campaignlive.com/article/permission-connect-human-era-brands-become-likable/1418763 (accessed January 10, 2017).

11Barry J. Babin and Eric G. Harris, *CB5* (Mason, OH: Cengage Learning, 2014).

12Aric Rindfleisch, James E. Burroughs, and Nancy Wong, "The Safety of Objects: Materialism, Existential Insecurity, and Brand Connection," *Journal of Consumer Research* 36, 1 (June 2009): 1–16.

13Claritas PRIZM, https://segmentationsolutions.nielsen.com/mybestsegments/Default.jsp?ID=70&pageName=Learn%2BMore&menuOption=learnmore (accessed January 11, 2017).

14Harry L. Davis and Benny P. Rigaux, "Perception of Marital Roles in Decision Processes," Journal of Consumer Research 1, June 1974, pp. 5–14; Mandy Putnam and William R. Davidson, "Family Purchasing Behavior: 11 Family Roles by Product Category" (Columbus, Ohio: Management Horizons, Inc., A Division of Price Waterhouse, 1987).

15"Women Make Up 85% of All Consumer Purchases," *Bloomberg,* July 22, 2016, https://www.bloomberg.com/news/videos/b/9e28517f-8de1-4e59-bcda-ce536aa50bd6 (accessed January 12, 2017).

16William J. Qualls, "Household Decision Behavior: The Impact of Husbands' and Wives' Sex Role Orientation," Journal of Consumer Research 14, September 1987, pp. 264–279; Larry Neale, Renee Robbie, and Brett Martin, "Gender Identity and Brand Incongruence: When in Doubt, Pursue Masculinity," Journal of Strategic Marketing 23, May 2015, pp. 1–13.

17Paul A. Eisenstein, "A Minivan for Millennials? Is That, Like, Even Possible?" *NBC News,* January 5, 2017, http://www.nbcnews.com/business/autos/minivan-millennials-even-possible-n702641 (accessed January 9, 2017).

18"How Social Media Influences Shopping Behavior," eMarketer, March 17, 2016, https://www.emarketer.com/Article/How-Social-Media-Influences-Shopping-Behavior/1013718 (accessed January 12, 2017).

19Gavin O'Malley, "Women's Purchasing Influenced by Social Media," *Social Media Daily*, July 18, 2016, http://www.mediapost.com/publications/article/280569/womens-purchasing-influenced-by-social-media.html (accessed January 12, 2017).

20Kasey Lobaugh, "Digital Influence Report: Global Findings from Nine Countries," *Deloitte Digital*, February 24, 2016, http://www.deloittedigital.com/us/blog/digital-influence-report-global-findings-from-nine-countries (accessed January 12, 2017).

21Hayley FitzPatrick, "Target Announces Its Next Designer Collaboration: Victoria Beckham," Yahoo Style, October 20, 2016, https://www.yahoo.com/style/target-announces-its-next-designer-collaboration-135106778.html (accessed January 23, 2017).

22Sandra L. Colby and Jennifer M. Ortman, "Projections of the Size and Composition of U.S. Population: 2014 to 2060," United States Census Bureau, March 2015, https://www.census.gov/content/dam/Census/library/publications/2015/demo/p25-1143.pdf (accessed January 23, 2017).

23United States Census Bureau, "QuickFacts," https://www.census.gov/quickfacts/table/PST045216/00 (accessed January 23, 2017).

24David Love, "2016 Nielsen Report: Black Buying Power Has Reached Tipping Point, But How Will Black America Leverage It to Create Wealth?" *Atlanta Black Star,* February 4, 2016, http://atlantablackstar.com/2016/02/04/2016-nielsen-report-black-buying-power-reached-tipping-point-will-black-america-leverage-create-wealth/ (accessed January 23, 2017); Janie Boschma, "Black Consumers Have 'Unprecidented Impact' in 2015," *The Atlantic,* February 2, 2016, http://www.theatlantic.com/politics/archive/2016/02/black-consumers-have-unprecedented-impact-in-2015/433725/ (accessed January 23, 2017).

25"Allstate Black History Month Campaign Spotlights Modern African-American Inspirational Stories," Allstate, press release, February 1, 2016, http://finance.yahoo.com/news/allstate-black-history-month-campaign-140000349.html (accessed January 23, 2017).

26"Hispanic Influence Reaches New Heights in the U.S.," *Nielsen,* August 8, 2016, http://www.nielsen.com/us/en/insights/news/2016/hispanic-influence-reaches-new-heights-in-the-us.html (accessed January 24, 2017); United States Census Bureau, "QuickFacts."

27Cecilia M.O. Alvarez, Peter R. Dickson, and Gary K. Hunter, "The Four Faces of the Hispanic Consumer: An Acculturation-Based Segmentation," *Journal of Business Research,* 67, 2 (February 2014): 108–115.

28Annie Baxter, "Target Reaches Out to Latino Consumers," *Marketplace,* December 12, 2016, http://www.marketplace.org/2016/12/12/economy/target-reaches-out-latino-consumers (accessed January 24, 2017); Ashley Rodriguez, "Retailers Duke It Out for Hispanic Shoppers' Dollars," *Advertising Age,* April 6, 2015, http://adage.com/article/cmo-strategy/retailers-duke-hispanic-shoppers-dollars/297902/ (accessed January 24, 2017).

29Jessica Binns, "Macy's Latin Explosion," *The Robin Report,* July 18, 2016, http://www.therobinreport.com/macys-latin-explosion/ (accessed January 24, 2017); Rick Wartzman, "How Macy's Found Its Fit in the Hispanic Market," *Fortune,* April 17, 2015, http://fortune.com/2015/04/17/macys-diversity-hispanic-consumers/ (accessed January 24, 2017).

30Eli Bishop, "6 Brands That Succeed at Understanding Hispanic Marketing," *Business 2 Community,* October 7, 2014, http://www.business2community.com/marketing/6-brands-succeed-understanding-hispanic-marketing-01030311 (accessed January 24, 2017).

31"Asian-Americans Are Expanding Their Footprint in the U.S. and Making an Impact,"

Nielsen, May 19, 2016, http://www.nielsen .com/us/en/insights/news/2016/asian -americans-are-expanding-their-footprint-and -making-an-impact.html (accessed January 25, 2017); United States Census Bureau, "State & Country QuickFacts."

[32]"Asian-Americans Are Not One Big Group," *Washington Examiner,* March 16, 2015, http://www.washingtonexaminer.com/asian -americans-are-not-one-big-group/article /2561445 (accessed January 24, 2017).

[33]Alexia Fernandez Campbell, "The Over-looked Consumer with Billions to Spend," *The Atlantic,* August 24, 2016, http://www .theatlantic.com/business/archive/2016/08/the -overlooked-consumer-group-with-billions-to -spend/497105/ (accessed January 24, 2017).

[34]Amy Jo Coffey, "Understanding the Invisibility of the Asian-American Television Audience: Why Marketers Often Overlook an Audience of 'Model' Consumers," *Journal of Advertising Research,* 53 (January 2013): 101–118.

[35]Paul Lucas, "AIG Opens Office to Target Asian Americans," *Insurance Business,* November 7, 2016, http://www.ibamag.com /us/news/breaking-news/aig-opens-office-to

-target-asian-americans-40118.aspx (accessed January 25, 2017).

[36]Phil Wahba, "Shoplifting, Worker Theft Cost Retailers $32 Billion Last Year," *Fortune,* June 24, 2015, http://fortune.com/2015/06/24 /shoplifting-worker-theft-cost-retailers-32 -billion-in-2014/ (accessed January 25, 2017).

[37]Ana Serafin Smith, "Retailers See Increase in Organized Retail Crime," *National Retail Federation,* press release, October 18, 2016, https://nrf.com/media/press-releases/retailers -see-increase-organized-retail-crime (accessed January 25, 2017).

[38]Craig Guillot, "Omnichannel's Pervasiveness Requires an Efficient Strategy for Processing Returns," *Stores,* November 2016, https://nrf .com/news/omnichannels-pervasiveness -requires-efficient-strategy-processing-returns (accessed January 25, 2016).

[39]Don Reisinger, "Microsoft Touts Study Showing the Cost of Pirated Software," *CNET,* March 19, 2014, http://www.cnet.com/news /microsoft-touts-study-showing-the-cost-of -pirated-software/ (accessed January 25, 2017).

[40]Brielle Jaekel, "Ford Values Mobile with a New Subsidiary Focused on Innovation," Mobile Marketer, March 14, 2016, http://www

.mobilemarketer.com/cms/news/strategy/22431 .html (accessed January 26, 2017); "Ford's 'Futurist' Predicts Upcoming Trends," *CBS This Morning,* December 12, 2014, http://www .cbsnews.com/videos/fords-futurist -predicts-upcoming-trends (accessed January 26, 2017); Melissa Wylie, "What It Means to Be Ford's 'Futurist'—No Crystal Ball," *Business Journals,* December 14, 2015, http:// www.bizjournals.com/bizwomen/news/profiles -strategies/2015/12/what-it-means-to-be-fords -futurist-no-crystal-ball.html?page=all (accessed January 26, 2017); Dale Buss, "Ford Futurist Sheryl Connelly Issues 2016 Trends Report," *Brand Channel,* December 9, 2015, http://brandchannel.com/2015/12/09/ford -future-trends-sheryl-connelly-120915/ (accessed January 26, 2017); Michael Martinez, "Ford at CES: Dramatic Change on Way," *Detroit News,* January 5, 2016, http://www.detroitnews.com /story/business/autos/ford/2016/01/04/ford-tout -drones-driverless-cars-ces/78289104 (accessed January 26, 2017); Bradley Berman, "Big Auto Searches for Meaning Beyond Selling Cars," *MIT Technology Review,* January 21, 2016, http://www.technologyreview.com/s/545646 /big-auto-searches-for-meaning-beyond-selling -cars/ (accessed January 26, 2017).

FEATURE NOTES

[a]Based on information in Lauren Effron, "How Fashion Icon Eileen Fisher Brought Mindfulness into Business with Huge Success," *ABC News,* October 5, 2016, http://abcnews.go.com/Health /fashion-icon-eileen-fisher-brought-mindfulness -business-huge/story?id=42484462 (accessed February 3, 2017); Kate Hammarback, "Green Is the New Black," *University of Oregon, Lundquist College of Business Blog,* February 11, 2016, http://blogs.uoregon.edu/uobusiness/2016/02/11 /green-is-the-new-black/ (accessed February 3,

2017); http://www.greeneileen.org/ (accessed February 3 and 7, 2017).

[b]Based on information in John Kell, "Cover-Girl's First-Ever Male Model Is Genius Gen Z Marketing," *Fortune,* October 13, 2016, http:// fortune.com/2016/10/13/covergirl-male-model -gen-z-james-charles/ (accessed February 3, 2017); Ann-Christine Diaz, "Teen Makeup Star James Charles Is the First Male CoverGirl," *Advertising Age,* October 12, 2016, http://adage

.com/article/cmo-strategy/teen-makeup-star -james-charles-male-covergirl/306264/ (accessed February 3, 2017); "She's One of the New Faces of CoverGirl. And She's Wearing a Hijab," *Washington Post,* November 8, 2016, https:// www.washingtonpost.com/news/acts-of-faith /wp/2016/11/08/shes-one-of-the-new-faces-of -covergirl-and-shes-wearing-a-hijab/?utm _term=.73a401adae9f (accessed February 3, 2017).

Chapter 7

[1]Based on information in Shira Ovide, "Face-book Risks Breaking Its Perfect Business Model," *Bloomberg,* January 9, 2017, https://www .bloomberg.com/gadfly/articles/2017-01-09 /facebook-learns-to-share-but-may-break-its -perfect-business-model (accessed February 7, 2017); Ingrid Lunden, "Workplace by

Facebook Opens to Sell Enterprise Social Net-working to the Masses," *TechCrunch,* October 10, 2016, https://techcrunch.com/2016/10/10 /facebook-workplace/ (accessed February 7, 2017); Jessica Guynn, "Facebook Messenger: You've Got Ads," *USA Today,* November 8, 2016, http://www.usatoday.com/story/tech

/news/2016/11/08/facebook-messenger-advertising/93472936 (accessed February 7, 2017); Jack Marshall, "Shrugging off 'Atlas,' Facebook Continues Pivot from Ad Tech," *Wall Street Journal,* November 18, 2016, https:// www.wsj.com/articles/facebook-discontinues -atlas-ad-serving-tool-1479496840 (accessed

February 7, 2017); Jack Marshall, "Facebook Wants to Help Sell Every Ad on the Web," *Wall Street Journal,* May 27, 2016, https://www.wsj.com/articles/facebook-wants-to-help-sell-every-ad-on-the-web-1464321603 (accessed February 7, 2017); www.facebook.com.

[2]"Statistics of U.S. Businesses (SUSB) Main," all industries, U.S. Bureau of the Census, http://www.census.gov/data/tables/2014/econ/susb/2014-susb-annual.html (accessed January 27, 2017).

[3]"Statistics of U.S. Businesses (SUSB) Main," all industries, U.S. Bureau of the Census; Kimberly Amadeo, "U.S. Retail Sales Statistics and Trends," *The Balance,* January 13, 2017, https://www.thebalance.com/u-s-retail-sales-statistics-and-trends-3305717 (accessed January 27, 2017); Barbara Farfan, "2016 US Retail Industry Overview," *The Balance,* August 13, 2016, https://www.thebalance.com/us-retail-industry-overview-2892699 (accessed January 27, 2017).

[4]Deloitte, *Global Powers of Retailing 2017: The Art and Science of Customers,* January 2017, https://www2.deloitte.com/global/en/pages/consumer-business/articles/global-powers-of-retailing.html (accessed January 27, 2017).

[5]"What Is the Total Government Spending?" *US Government Spending,* http://www.usgovernmentspending.com/percent_gdp (accessed January 30, 2017).

[6]Aramark, "Aramark Named to Fortune Magazine's 2016 List of 'World's Most Admired Companies'," press release, February 19, 2016, http://www.aramark.com/about-us/news/aramark-general/fortune-2016-most-admired-companies.

[7]United States Department of Labor, "North American Industry Classification Systems (NAICS)," https://www.osha.gov/oshstats/naics-manual.html (accessed January 30, 2017).

[8]"Notable Contract Awards," Booz Allen Hamilton, www.boozallen.com/media-center/company-news/notable-contract-awards (accessed January 26, 2017).

[9]Christopher Harress, "Huntsville's Raytheon Signs Huge US Navy Missile Contract," *Alabama.com,* January 25, 2017, http://www.al.com/news/index.ssf/2017/01/huntsvilles_raytheon_signs_hug.html (accessed January 30, 2017).

[10]Kate Maddox, "Staples to Launch New Campaign Aimed at Small Businesses," *Advertising Age,* February 6, 2015, http://adage.com/article/btob/staples-launch-campaign-aimed-small-businesses/297043/ (accessed January 30, 2017).

[11]Anne Maarit Jalkala and Joona Keränen, "Brand Positioning Strategies for Industrial Firms Providing Customer Solutions," *Journal of Business & Industrial Marketing,* 29, 3 (2014): 253–264.

[12]Hannu Sakari Makkonen and Wesley J. Johnston, "Innovation Adoption and Diffusion in Business-to-Business Marketing," *Journal of Business & Industrial Marketing,* 29, 4 (2014): 324–331.

[13]Das Narayandas and V. Kasturi Rangan, "Building and Sustaining Buyer-Seller Relationships in Mature Industrial Markets," *Journal of Marketing* 68, 3 (2004): 63.

[14]"Food for Thought," Jet Blue, https://www.jetblue.com/green/food/ (accessed January 30, 2017).

[15]Bain & Company, "Service Design & Operations," http://www.bain.com/consulting-services/performance-improvement/service-operations.aspx (accessed January 30, 2017); Oliver Straehle, Michael Fuellemann, and Oliver Bendig, "Service Now! Time to Wake up the Sleeping Giant," November 27, 2012, http://www.bain.com/Images/Bain%20study_Service_Now.pdf.

[16]Elena Fraj, Eva Martinez, and Jorge Matute, "Green Marketing in B2B Organisations: An Empirical Analysis from the Natural-Resource-Based View of the Firm," *Journal of Business & Marketing,* 28, 5 (2013): 396–410.

[17]Ali Jahromi Tamaddoni, Stanislav Stakhovych, and Michael Ewing, "Managing B2B Customer Churn, Retention and Profitability," *Industrial Marketing Management,* 43, 7 (2014): 1258–1268.

[18]Frederick E. Webster Jr. and Yoram Wind, "A General Model for Understanding Organizational Buyer Behavior," *Journal of Marketing,* 36, 2 (1972): 12–19.

[19]Kate Maddox, "Cintas Launches First National Brand Campaign in Its 87-Year History," *Advertising Age,* January 26, 2016, http://adage.com/article/btob/cintas-launches-national-brand-campaign-history/302356/ (accessed January 31, 2017).

[20]Kunal Swani, Brian P. Brown, and George R. Milne, "Should Tweets Differ for B2B and B2C? An Analysis of Fortune 500 Companies' Twitter Communications," *Industrial Marketing Management,* 43, 4 (2014): 873–881.

[21]Michael Moores, "5 Lessons for Successful B2B eCommerce," Industry Week, June 9, 2016, http://www.industryweek.com/customer-relationships/5-lessons-successful-b2b-ecommerce (accessed January 31, 2017).

[22]Acquity Group, "2014 State of B2B Procurement Study: Uncovering the Shifting Landscape in B2B Commerce," https://www.accenture.com/us-en/insight-state-b2b-procurement-study-uncovering-shifting-landscape.aspx (accessed January 31, 2017).

[23]Nona Tepper, "Paddleboard Manufacturer Boga Makes a Splash Through E-commerce," Internet Retailer, March 9, 2015, https://www.internetretailer.com/2015/03/09/paddleboard-manufacturer-boga-makes-splash-through-e-commerce (accessed January 31, 2017).

[24]"About Us," Amazon Business, https://www.amazon.com/b2b/info/amazon-business?layout=landing (accessed January 31, 2017); Nandita Bose, "Amazon's Business Marketplace Hits $1 Billion in Sales," Reuters, May 4, 2016, http://www.reuters.com/article/us-amazon-com-business-idUSKCN0XV1J2 (accessed January 31, 2017).

[25]Paul Demery, "AutoWurld.com Launches as a Wholesale and Retail Marketplace," Internet Retailer, March 9, 2015, https://www.internetretailer.com/2015/03/09/autowurldcom-launches-wholesale-and-retail-marketplace (accessed January 31, 2017).

[26]"About Alibaba," Alibaba, http://activities.alibaba.com/alibaba/following-about-alibaba.php?spm=a2700.7848340.0.0.zec1aK (accessed January 31, 2017).

[27]"The Ultimate Guide to How and Where to Use Apple Pay," *MacWorld,* August 29, 2016, http://www.macworld.com/article/2834669/ios/the-ultimate-guide-on-how-and-where-to-use-apple-pay.html (accessed February 1, 2017); Menchie Mendoza, "Apple Pay Availability Tops 2 Million Locations, Soon Adding Chains Like Chick-Fil-A," *Tech Times,* February 4, 2016, http://www.techtimes.com/articles/130671/20160204/apple-pay-availability-tops-2-million-locations-soon-adding-chains-like-chick-fil-a.htm (accessed February 4, 2016); Caitlin McGarry, "Why Your Favorite Stores Still Don't Support Apple

Pay," *MacWorld,* June 5, 2015, http://www .macworld.com/article/2932356/ios/why-your -favorite-stores-still-dont-support-apple-pay .html (accessed February 4, 2016); James F. Peltz, "Mobile-Payment Systems Draw More Shoppers and Merchants," *Los Angeles Times,* January 18, 2016, http://www.latimes .com/business/la-fi-agenda-mobile-payments

-20160118-story.html (accessed February 4, 2016); Bill Snyder, "McDonald's CIO on Why It's Supporting Apple Pay on Launch Day," *CIO,* October 16, 2014, http://www.cio .com/article/2834502/consumer-technology /mcdonalds-cio-on-why-its-supporting-apple -pay-on-launch-day.html (accessed February 4, 2016); Sarah Perez, "Walgreens Becomes First

Retailer to Integrate Its Loyalty Program with Apple Pay," *Tech Crunch,* November 5, 2015, http://techcrunch.com/2015/11/05/walgreens -becomes-first-retailer-to-integrate-its-loyalty -program-with-apple-pay (accessed February 4, 2016).

FEATURE NOTES

[a]Based on information in Kevin Pang, "Milk Jumps onto the Small-Batch Bandwagon," *New York Times,* April 12, 2016, http://www .nytimes.com/2016/04/13/dining/milk-dairy -locavore.html (accessed February 6, 2017); Martha C. White, "The Latest Foodie Trend Is Small-Batch Milk for $14 a Gallon," *Time,* April 13, 2016, http://time.commoney /4291928/local-organic-milk-small-batch-trend/ (accessed February 6, 2017); Mary Ellen Shoup, "Creating 'Farmers by Proxy': 1871 Evokes Small-Batch Milk Nostalgia," *Dairy Reporter,* April 22, 2016, http://www.dairyreporter.com

/Retail-Shopper-Insights/1871-Dairy-aims -to-bring-back-nostalgia-of-small-batch-dairy (accessed February 6, 2017).

[b]Based on information in Sheila Shayon, "P&G Makes First Recyclable Shampoo Bottle from Beach Plastic," *Brand Channel,* January 25, 2017, http://www.brandchannel .com/2017/01/25/pg-recyclable-shampoo -bottle-012517/ (accessed February 6, 2017); Jason Blevins, "Through the Looking Glass, Some Envisioning Rebound," *The Denver Post,* April 22, 2016, http://www.denverpost .com/2016/04/22/through-the-looking-glass

-some-envisioning-rebound/ (accessed February 6, 2017); Jenna Swan, "New Business of the Year: Clean Conscience Recycling Recognized for Strong Start," *Sylvan Lake News (Alberta, Canada),* October 31, 2016, http://www .sylvanlakenews.com/news/399365711.html (accessed February 6, 2017); Tom Szaky, "Henkel's Adhesive Packaging Recycling Program Is a Game Changer," *Packaging Digest,* October 5, 2016, http://www.packagingdigest .com/sustainable-packaging/henkels-recycling -program-for-adhesive-packaging-is-a-game -changer-2016-10-05 (accessed February 6, 2017).

Chapter 8

[1]Emma S Hinchliffe, "On Obama's Cue, Netflix Launches in Cuba," *USA Today,* February 10, 2015, 1A; Sam Schechner, "Net-flix to Expand Into Italy, Portugal, Spain," *The Wall Street Journal,* June 8, 2015, B4; Carrie Khan, "Netflix Streams Its Way to Cuba–Slow-ly," *NPR,* February 14, 2015, http://www .npr.org/2015/02/14/386323314/netflix -streams-its-way-to-cuba-slowly (accessed December 17, 2016); Trefis Team, "China Makes Sense for Netflix, But It Won't Be Easy," *Trefis Team,* May 26, 2015, http://www .trefis. com/stock/nflx/articles/297718 /china-makes-sense-for-netflix-but-it -won't-be-easy/2015-05-26 (accessed October 7, 2015); Trefis Team, "A Closer Look at Netflix's Foray Into Japan," *Trefis,* February 18, 2015, http://www.trefis.com/stock/nflx/ articles/281080/a-closer-look-at-netflix's- foray-into-japan/2015-02-18 (accessed October 7, 2015); Charles Riley, "Netflix admits its plan for China has failed," *CNN,* October 18, 2016, http://money.cnn.com/2016/10/18/ technology/netflix-china/ (accessed December 17, 2016).

[2]"Percentage of Procter & Gamble's net sales worldwide in 2016, by region," Statista, https://www.statista.com/statistics/244122 /percentage-of-procter-and-gambles-net-sales -worldwide-by-region/ (accessed January 20, 2017).

[3]"Our Story," Walmart, http://corporate.walmart. com/our-story/ (accessed January 25, 2017); "Starbucks Coffee International," Starbucks, http://www.starbucks.com/business/international -stores (accessed January 25, 2017).

[4]Matthew Campbell, "Emirates Has Every Advantage an Airline Could Want. And It May Run Out of Sky," *Bloomberg Businessweek,* January 9–15, 2017, 36.

[5]"Export Assistance," Office of the United States Trade Representative, http://www.ustr .gov/trade-topics/trade-toolbox/export -assistance (accessed November 21, 2014).

[6]Gary A. Knight and S. Tamer Cavusgil, "In-novation, Organizational Capabilities, and the Born-Global Firm," *Journal of International Business Studies* (March 2004): 124–141.

[7]Kate Taylor, "Taco Bell Has Created a Wildly Popular Hit Overseas – But it Won't be Coming to America Anytime Soon," *Business Insider,* October 11, 2016, http://www.businessinsider .com/taco-bell-kimchi-quesadilla-thrives-in -korea-2016-10 (accessed January 31, 2017).

[8]Wayne Ma and Julie Jargon, "McDonalds Pulls Back in China with Deal," *The Wall Street Journal,* January 10, 2017, B1.

[9]Anton Piësch, "Speaking in Tongues," *Inc.* (June 2003), 50.

[10]Xiaoling Guo, "Living in a Global World: Influence of Consumer Global Orientation on Attitudes Toward Global Brands from Devel-oped Versus Emerging Countries," *Journal of International Marketing* 21, 1 (2013): 1–22.

[11]Sadrudin A. Ahmed and Alain D'Astous, "Moderating Effects of Nationality on Coun-try-of-Origin Perceptions: English-Speaking Thailand Versus French-Speaking Canada," *Journal of Business Research* 60 (March 2007): 240–248; George Balabanis and Ada-mantios Diamantopoulos, "Domestic Country Bias, Country-of-Origin Effects, and Consumer

Ethnocentrism: A Multidimensional Unfolding Approach," *Journal of the Academy of Marketing Science* (January 2004): 80–95; Harri T. Luomala, "Exploring the Role of Food Origin as a Source of Meanings for Consumers and as a Determinant of Consumers' Actual Food Choices," *Journal of Business Research* 60, 2 (2007): 122–129; Durdana Ozretic-Dosen, Vatroslav Skare, and Zoran Krupka, "Assessments of Country of Origin and Brand Cues in Evaluating a Croatian, Western and Eastern European Food Product," *Journal of Business Research* 60 (February 2007): 130–136.

12Chris Isidore, "Despite Trump's Latest Threat, BMW Won't Budge on Mexican Plant," CNN Money, January 16, 2017, http://money.cnn.com/2017/01/16/news/companies/trump-bmw-mexico/ (accessed January 25, 2016).

13Peter Evans and Caitlan Reeg, "Personal-Care Firms Uncover New Markets," *The Wall Street Journal*, May 20, 2014, B2.

14David A. Griffith, Goksel Yalcinkaya, and Gaia Rubera, "Country-Level Performance of New Experience Products in a Global Rollout: The Moderating Effects of Economic Wealth and National Culture," *Journal of International Marketing* 22, 4 (2014): 1–20.

15Philip Coggan, "Markets in a Muddle," *The Economist: The World in 2011 Special Edition*, 145.

16Lingling Wei, "China Pushed Yuan Lower," *The Wall Street Journal*, February 27, 2014, A1.

17Peter Coy, "Dollar So Ripped, it Might Actually Rip," *Bloomberg Businessweek*, January 9–15, 2017, 12.

18Ibid.

19The CIA, *The World Fact Book*, https://www.cia.gov/library/publications/the-world-factbook/rankorder/rankorderguide.html (accessed January 31, 2017).

20Ibid.

21Stephen A. Samaha, Joshua T. Beck, and Robert W. Palmatier, "The Role of Culture in International Relationship Marketing," *Journal of Marketing* 78 (September 2014): 78–98.

22"The Rise of Capitalism," *The Economist*, January 21, 2012, 11.

23"Men of Steel, House of Cards," *The Economist*, January 7, 2017, 11.

24"U.S. Trade Representative Announces Fiscal 2010 Tariff-Rate Quota Allocations for Raw Cane Sugar, Refined Specialty Sugar, Sugar Containing Products," October 1, 2009, http://www.highbeam.com/doc/1P3-1870093731.html (accessed November 26, 2014).

25U.S. Census Bureau, Foreign Trade Division, "U.S. International Trade in Goods and Services," January 6, 2017, https://www.census.gov/foreign-trade/Press-Release/current_press_release/exh2.pdf (accessed January 28, 2017).

26Charles R. Taylor, George R. Franke, and Michael L. Maynard, "Attitudes toward Direct Marketing and Its Regulation: A Comparison of the United States and Japan," *Journal of Public Policy & Marketing* (Fall 2000): 228–237.

27Tom Schoenberg and Matt Robinson, "Walmart Balks at Paying $600-Million-Plus in Bribery Case," Bloomberg Markets, October 6, 2016, https://www.bloomberg.com/news/articles/2016-10-06/wal-mart-said-to-balk-at-paying-600-million-plus-in-bribe-case (accessed January 17, 2017).

28Julius Melnitzer, "U.K. Enacts 'Far-Reaching' Anti-Bribery Act," *Law Times*, February 13, 2011, http://www.lawtimesnews.com/201102148245/Headline-News/UK-enacts-far-reaching-anti-bribery-act (accessed November 26, 2014).

29Bruce Einhorn, Isabel Reynolds, and Tm Schoenberg, "Japan Feels the Heat on Bribery," *Bloomberg Businessweek,* November 2014, 17–18.

30"Measuring the Magnitude of Global Counterfeiting," U.S. Chamber of Commerce's Global Intellectual Property Center, http://www.theglobalipcenter.com/wp-content/themes/gipc/map-index/assets/pdf/2016/GlobalCounterfeiting_Report.pdf (accessed January 28, 2017).

31Kathy Chu, "Alibaba to Act Faster Against Counterfeits," *The Wall Street Journal,* May 15, 2014, B1.

32Business for Social Responsibility website, www.bsr.org (accessed November 26, 2014).

33Casey Dunn, "Taking Sustainability to the Global Level," *Southwest Magazine,* December 2014, p. 158.

34Natalia Drozdiak and Sam Schechner, "EU Files Additional Formal Charges Against Google," *Wall Street Journal*, July 16, 2016, http://www.wsj.com/articles/google-set-to-face-more-eu-antitrust-charges-1468479516 (accessed January 17, 2017).

35"This Is Systembolaget," https://www.systembolaget.se/English/ (accessed November 26, 2014).

36CIA, *The World Fact Book*, https://www.cia.gov/library/publications/the-world-factbook/rankorder/rankorderguide.html (accessed January 31, 2017).

37Lev Grossman, "The Man Who Wired the World," *Time,* December 15, 2014, 30–40.

38Josh Constine, "Facebook Has Connected 40M People with Internet.org," *Tech Crunch*, November 2, 2016, https://techcrunch.com/2016/11/02/omnipresent/ (accessed January 31, 2017).

39Vivienne Walt, "Is Africa's Rise for Real This Time?" *Fortune,* September 18, 2014, 166–172; Charles Graeber, "Africa on Nothing But a Phone," *Bloomberg Businessweek,* June 5, 2014, http://www.businessweek.com/articles/2014-06-05/safaricoms-m-pesa-turns-kenya-into-a-mobile-payment-paradise (accessed November 26, 2014).

40Economist staff, "Special Report: The World Economy," *The Economist*, October 4, 2014, 1–18.

41Global Affairs Canada, "North American Free Trade Agreement (NAFTA)," http://www.international.gc.ca/trade-agreements-accords-commerciaux/agr-acc/nafta-alena/info.aspx?lang=eng (accessed January 28, 2017).

42"Population by Year, Province and Territory," *Statistics Canada*, September 28, 2016, http://www.statcan.gc.ca/tables-tableaux/sum-som/l01/cst01/demo02a-eng.htm (accessed January 28, 2017); "Canada GDP Per Capita," *Trading Economics*, http://www.tradingeconomics.com/canada/gdp-per-capita (accessed January 28, 2017); "Canada," Office of the United States Trade Representative, https://ustr.gov/countries-regions/americas/canada (accessed January 28, 2017).

43"Country Info," *EDC*, www.edc.ca/EN/Country-Info/Pages/Mexico.aspx (accessed November 21, 2014); Secretaria de Economia, "Why Mexican Products?" http://www.ottawa.economia.gob.mx/swb/swb/Ottawa/Importing_from_Mexico (accessed November 21, 2014).

44CIA, *The World Fact Book*, https://www.cia.gov/library/publications/the-world-factbook/rankorder/rankorderguide.html (accessed January 28, 2017).

45Office of the United States Trade Representative, "Mexico," May 1, 2014, http://www.ustr.gov/countries-regions/americas/mexico (accessed January 28, 2017).

46"Trade Agreements," Pro Mexico, http://www.promexico.gob.mx/en/mx/tratados-comerciales (accessed January 28, 2017); Joann Muller, "America's Next Car Capital Will Soon Be…Mexico," *Forbes,* September 8, 2014, 128–134; Tim Mullaney, "It's Small Cars, Not Auto Jobs, Making the Big U.S. Move to Mexico," CNBC, October 19, 2016, http://www.cnbc.com/2016/10/19/small-cars-not-us-manufacturing-jobs-are-moving-to-mexico.html (accessed January 28, 2017).

47"Special Report: Mexico," *The Economist*, November 24, 2012, 3–16.

48"CAFTA-DR (Dominican Republic-Central America FTA)," Office of the United States Trade Representative, www.ustr.gov/trade-agreements/free-trade-agreements/cafta-dr-dominican-republic-central-america-fta (accessed January 28, 2017).

49Economist staff, "Crisis Revisited," *Economist,* December 13, 2014, p. 17; "Euro Area," European Commission, https://ec.europa.eu/info/business-economy-euro/euro-area_en (accessed January 28, 2017).

50"Euro Area 1999–2015," *European Central Bank*, https://www.ecb.europa.eu/euro/intro/html/map.en.html (accessed January 28, 2017); "Europe in 12 Lessons," *Europa*, http://europa.eu/abc/12lessons/lesson_2/index_en.htm (accessed January 28, 2017).

51Mike Bird, "Fog Around Brexit Causes Pound to Fall," *Wall Street Journal*, January 10, 2017, B13.

52"Special Advertising Section: The European Union and the United States," *Foreign Policy*, January 2013, 1.

53Joanna Klonsky, Stephanie Hanson, and Brianna Lee, "Mercosur: South America's Fractious Trade Bloc," *Council on Foreign Relations*, July 31, 2012, http://www.cfr.org/trade/mercosur-south-americas-fractious-trade-bloc/p12762 (accessed January 14, 2015); "MERCOSUR," *Ministry of Foreign Affairs*, http://www.itamaraty.gov.br/en/politica-externa/integracao-regional/6347-mercosur-en (accessed January 31, 2017).

54"Agri-Food Regional Profile Common Market of the South (Mercosur)," Agriculture and Agrifood Canada, January 2011, www.ats.agr.gc.ca/lat/3947-eng.htm (accessed November 26, 2014); Joanna Klonsky, Stephanie Hanson, and Brianna Lee, "Mercosur: South America's Fractious Trade Bloc," Council on Foreign Relations, July 31, 2012, http://www.cfr.org/trade/mercosur-south-americas-fractious-trade-bloc/p12762 (accessed November 26, 2014).

55Michael Reid, "The Hangover: Latin America after the Commodity Boom," *The Economist,* The World in 2015 Edition, p. 57.

56Juan Forero, "Cuba's Private Sector Braces for Change," *The Wall Street Journal*, January 11, 2017, A18.

57Tim Padgett, "How Business Can Change Cuba," *Bloomberg Businessweek,* October 16, 2014, 8–9.

58"About APEC," http://www.apec.org/About-Us/About-APEC.aspx (accessed November 21, 2014); "U.S.-APEC Trade Facts," Office of the Unites States Trade Representative, https://ustr.gov/trade-agreements/other-initiatives/asia-pacific-economic-cooperation-apec/us-apec-trade-facts (accessed January 31, 2017).

59Asia-Pacific Economic Cooperation, *APEC Australia 2007, Forbes* Promotion, 1–6, http://www.forbesspecialsections.com/SectionPDFs/APECAustralia.pdf (accessed November 21, 2014); APEC Policy Support Unit, "APEC Region Trade Still Outperforms World," *Asia-Pacific Economic Cooperation,* September 7, 2012, http://www.apec.org/Press/News-Releases/2012/0907_trade.aspx (accessed November 21, 2014).

60"The People's Republic of China," Office of the United States Trade Representative, https://ustr.gov/countries-regions/china-mongolia-taiwan/peoples-republic-china (accessed January 28, 2017); "China GDP Annual Growth Rate," *Trading Economics*, http://www.tradingeconomics.com/china/gdp-growth-annual (accessed January 27, 2017).

61James Miles, "Ever More Muscle," *The Economist,* The World in 2015 Edition, p. 75.

62Vijay Vaitheeswaran, "China: A Hunger for Better Services," *The Economist,* November 20, 2014, The World in 2015 Edition, http://www.economist.com/news/21631946-middle-kingdom-meets-magic-kingdom-hunger-better-services (accessed January 5, 2015).

63Zheng Yangpeng, "China's Internet Users Grew in 2016 by the Size of Ukraine's Population to 731 Million," *South China Morning Post*, January 22, 2017, http://www.scmp.com/tech/china-tech/article/2064396/chinas-internet-users-grew-2016-size-ukraines-population-731-million (accessed January 28, 2017).

64Brendan Greeley, "Supercool South Korea!" *Bloomberg Businessweek,* August 10, 2014, p. 63.

65Associated Press, "Lands of Opportunity: Foreign Markets Fueling Growth of US Tech Trendsetters, Other Companies," *Fox Business*, July 28, 2014, http://www.foxbusiness.com/technology/2014/07/28/lands-opportunity-foreign-markets-fueling-growth-us-tech-trendsetters-other/ (accessed November 26, 2014).

66"Overview," Association of Southeast Asian Nations, http://www.asean.org/asean/about-asean/overview (accessed November 26, 2014).

67Parag Khanna, "ASEAN Is Key to 'Asian Century'," CNN, August 15, 2013, http://www.cnn.com/2013/08/14/opinion/asean-dream-khanna/ (accessed November 21, 2014).

68ASEAN website, http://www.asean.org/ (accessed November 26, 2014).

69Simon Long, "Safety in Numbers," *The Economist,* The World in 2015 Edition, p. 68.

70"FAQ – Free Trade Agreement," The Official Portal of Malaysia External Trade Development Corporation, http://www.matrade.gov.my/en/malaysian-exporters/going-global/understanding-free-trade-agreements/494-free-trade-agreement-faq (accessed January 23, 2012).

71Debbie Too, "Obstacles Hinder ASEAN Integration," *Brunei Times*, June 3, 2014, http://www.bt.com.bn/business-national/2014/06/03/obstacles-hinder-asean-integration-020614-aec (accessed November 26, 2014).

72Kathy Quiano, "ASEAN Summit Starts amid Cloud of Thai-Cambodia Border Row," CNN, May 7, 2011, http://articles.cnn.com/2011-05-07/world/asia.asean.summit_1_asean-leaders-asean-summit-southeast-asian-nations?

_s=PM:WORLD (accessed November 26, 2014).

[73]Eric Bellman, "Asia Seeks Integration Despite EU's Woes," *The Wall Street Journal*, July 22, 2011, A9.

[74]"Members and Observers," World Trade Organization, http://www.wto.org/english /thewto_e/whatis_e/tif_e/org6_e.htm (accessed November 21, 2014).

[75]"What Is the WTO?" World Trade Organization, www.wto.org/english/thewto_e/whatis_e /whatis_e.htm (accessed November 26, 2014).

[76]Reuters, "Indonesia Challenges EU over Anti-dumping on Biodiesel Imports – WTO," June 11, 2014, http://www.reuters.com/ article/2014/06/11/us-trade-biodiesel-idUSK-BN0EM14X20140611 (accessed November 26, 2014); European Commission, "EU to Impose Definitive Anti-Dumping Duties on Biodiesel from Argentina and Indonesia," November 21, 2013, http://europa.eu/rapid /press-release_IP-13-1140_en.htm (accessed November 26, 2014).

[77]Pradeep Tyagi, "Export Behavior of Small Business Firms in Developing Economies: Evidence from the Indian Market," *Marketing Management Journal* (Fall/Winter 2000): 12–20.

[78]Berrin Dosoglu-Guner, "How Do Exporters and Non-Exporters View Their 'Country of Origin' Image Abroad?" *Marketing Management Journal* (Fall/Winter 2000): 21–27.

[79]WTSC Industrial Group, http://www.wtsc.eu /index.shtml (accessed January 28, 2017).

[80]Farok J. Contractor and Sumit K. Kundu, "Franchising Versus Company-Run Operations: Model Choice in the Global Hotel Sector," *Journal of International Marketing* (November 1997): 28–53.

[81]Jennifer Alsever, "Smaller Businesses Struggle to Make It in the U.S.A.," *Fortune,* November 17, 2014, 29–32.

[82]Greg IP, "We Are Not the World," *The Wall Street Journal*, January 7–8, 2017, C1.

[83]"Suddenly, Made in USA Looks Like a Strategy," *Bloomberg Businessweek*, March 28, 2011, 57–58.

[84]Sky Team website, https://www.skyteam. com/About-us/Our-members/ (accessed November 26, 2014).

[85]Dana L. Alden, James B. Kelley, Petra Riefler, Julie A. Lee, and Geoffrey N. Soutar, "The Effect of Global Company Animosity on Global Brand Attitudes in Emerging and Developed Markets: Does Perceived Value Matter?" *Journal of International Marketing* 21 (2): 17–38.

[86]Deborah Owens, Timothy Wilkinson, and Bruce Keillor, "A Comparison of Product Attributes in a Cross-Cultural/Cross-National Context," *Marketing Management Journal* (Fall/Winter 2000): 1–11.

[87]Luciana Magalhaes, "Dunkin' Donuts Is Set for a Return to Brazil," *The Wall Street Journal,* September 12, 2014, B5.

[88]Larry Light, "How Organisations Manage Global Brands in an Increasingly Global World," *Journal of Brand Strategy* 2, 3 (2013): 228–235.

[89]Anil K. Gupta and Vijay Govindarajan, "Converting Global Presence into Global Competitive Advantage," *Academy of Management Executive* (May 2001): 45–58.

[90]Susanna Kim, "Alibaba: How Did the Chinese Company Gets Its Name?" ABC News, September 18, 2014, http://abcnews .go.com/Business/alibaba-chinese-company /story?id525591454 (accessed January 13, 2016); Leena Rao, "Disney Teams Up With Alibaba to Sell Movies, TV Shows in China," *Fortune*, December 15, 2015, http://fortune .com/2015/12/15/disney-alibaba/ (accessed January 13, 2016); Patrick Frater, "Alibaba Seeks International Expansion Hitches with 'Avengers' in China," *Variety*, May 14, 2015, http://variety.com/2015/biz/asia/alibabaseeks

-international-expansion-1201495896 / (accessed January 13, 2016); Bloomberg News, "Alibaba to Open Offices in Europe as U.S. Expansion Continues," *Bloomberg*, October 13, 2015, http://www.bloomberg.com /news/articles/2015-10-13/alibaba-to-open -offices-in-europe-as-u-s-expansion-continues (accessed January 13, 2016); Paul Mozur, "Alibaba Profit Surges, but a Revenue Gain of 40% Still Misses Forecasts," *The New York Times*, January 29, 2015, http://www.nytimes.com /2015/01/30/business/international/in-alibaba -earnings-revenue-falls-short.html (accessed January 13, 2016); Helen H. Wang, "Why Amazon Should Fear Alibaba," *Forbes*, July 8, 2015, http://www.forbes.com/sites/helenwang /2015/07/08/why-amazon-should-fear -alibaba/ (accessed January 13, 2016); John Watling, "China's Internet Giants Lead in Online Finance," *The Financialist*, February 14, 2014, https://www.thefinancialist.com/not -just-a-paypal-clone-chinas-internet -giants-chart-their-own-course/ (accessed January 13, 2016); Juro Osawa, Paul Mozur, and Rolfe Winkler, "Alibaba Flexes Muscles Before IPO," *The Wall Street Journal*, April 15, 2015, http://www.wsj .com/news/articles/SB100014240527 02303887804579501411932558776 (accessed January 13, 2016); Bloomberg News, "Alibaba's IPO Filing: Everything You Need to Know," *The Wall Street Journal*, May 6, 2014, http://blogs.wsj.com/digits/2014/05/06/alibabas -ipo-filing-everything-you-need-to-know / (accessed January 13, 2016); Gillian Wong, "Alibaba's Global Ambitions Face Counterfeit Challenge," *The Wall Street Journal*, November 10, 2015, http://www.wsj.com/articles/alibabas- global-ambitions-face-genuine-counterfeit- challenge-1447147654 (accessed January 13, 2016); Steven Davidoff Solomon, "Alibaba Investors Will Buy a Risky Corporate Structure," *The New York Times*, May 6, 2014, http://dealbook. nytimes.com/2014/05/06/i-p-o -revives-debate-over-a-chinese-structure/ (accessed January 13, 2016).

FEATURE NOTES

[a]Pete Engardio, "Cradle of a Green Revolution," *Businessweek*, November 2, 2009, 40-41; Bryan Walsh, "Electric Cars: China's Power Play," *Time*, August 31, 2009, http:// content.time.com/time/magazine

/article/0,9171,1917647,00.html (accessed December 17, 2016); Daniel K. Gardner, "Meet China's Green Crusader," *The New York Times*, November 1, 2009, http://www .nytimes.com/2009/02/11/opinion/11iht

-edgardner.1.20105872.html (accessed December 17, 2016); Adam Aston, "China's Surprising Clout in Cleantech," *Businessweek*, November 30, 2009, 56; Bloomberg News, "China to Slow Green Growth for First Time after Record Boom," *Bloomberg*, September 22, 2016, https://www.bloomberg.com/news/articles/2016-09-22/china-to-rein-in-green-growth-for-first-time-after-record-boom (accessed December 17, 2016); "Court in China Issues Record Pollution Fine," *BBC*, December 31, 2014, http://www.bbc.com/news/world-asia-china-30640385 (accessed December 17, 2016); Feng Hao, "China's EV Push Hurting Fuel Economy Standards," *China Dialogue*, November 21, 2016, https://www.chinadialogue.net/article/show/single/en

/9414-China-s-EV-push-hurting-fuel-economy-standards (accessed December 17, 2016).

[b]Alexandra Wexler, "'Africa's IKEA' Steinhoff to Buy Sleepy's Owner Mattress Firm for $2.4 Billion," *The Wall Street Journal,* August 7, 2016, http://www.wsj.com/articles/steinhoff-to-buy-mattress-firm-for-2-4-billion-1470599217 (accessed November 20, 2016); Mike Stone, "Steinhoff to Buy Mattress Firm for $3.8 Billion, Including Debt," *Reuters,* August 7, 2016, http://www.reuters.com/article/us-mattress-frm

-hldg-m-a-steinhoff-intern-idUSKCN10I0RA (accessed November 20, 2016); Janice Kew and Thomas Mulier, "Billionaire Weise Invests $1.8 Billion More in Steinhoff," *Bloomberg,* September 28, 2016, http://www.bloomberg.com/news/articles/2016-09-28/steinhoff-to-raise-up-to-2-4-billion-euros-in-share-sale (accessed November 20, 2016); "Who We Are," *Steinhoff,* http://www.steinhoffinternational.com/ (accessed November 20, 2016).

Chapter 9

[1]Geoff Weiss, "How Ipsy, Michelle Phan's Million-Member Sampling Service, Is Giving Birchbox a Run for Its Money," *Entrepreneur*, March 31, 2015, https://www.entrepreneur.com/article/244536 (accessed February 21, 2017); Erin Griffith, "YouTube Star Michelle Phan's Beauty Startup Ipsy Raises $100 Million," *Fortune*, September 14, 2015, http://fortune.com/2015/09/14/ipsy-glam-bag-michelle-phan-funding/ (accessed February 21, 2017); Khadeeja Safdar, "Birchbox, a Pioneer in Subscription Beauty Sales, Scales Back," June 15, 2016, http://www.wsj.com/articles/birchbox-retrenches-amid-rapid-rise-in-competition-cash-squeeze-1465983002 (accessed February 21, 2017); Tamar Anitai, "Makeup Tutorial: Learn How to Get Lady Gaga's Scary 'Bad Romance' Eyes," January 27, 2010, http://www.mtv.com/news/2295046/makeup-tutorial-learn-how-to-get-lady-gagas-scary-bad-romance-eyes/ (accessed February 21, 2017); Nicole Laporte, "How Ipsy Founder Michelle Phan is Using Influencers to Reinvent the Cosmetics Industry," Fast Company, January 11, 2016, https://www.fastcompany.com/3054926/behind-the-brand/how-ipsy-founder-michelle-phan-is-using-influencers-to-reinvent-the-cosmeti (accessed February 21, 2017).

[2]Lauren I. Labrecque, Jonas vor dem Esche, Charla Mathwick, Thomas P. Novak, and Charles F. Hofacker, "Consumer Power: Evolution in the Digital Age," *Journal of Interactive Marketing* 27, 4 (2013): 257–269.

[3]O.C. Ferrell, "Broadening Marketing's Contribution to Data Privacy," *Journal of the Academy of Marketing Science* 43, (March 2017).

[4]"Internet Users," Internet Live Stats, 2016, http://www.internetlivestats.com/internet-users/ (accessed February 21, 2017).

[5]Piet Levy, "The State of Digital Marketing," *Marketing News*, March 15, 2010, 20–21.

[6]Maria Teresa Pinheiro Melo Borges Tiago and José Manuel Cristóvão Veríssimo, "Digital Marketing and Social Media: Why Bother?" *Business Horizons* 57, 6 (2014): 703–708.

[7]Charisse Jones, "Department Stores Become Endangered," *USA Today*, January 6–8, 2017: 1A.

[8]Sanjit Kumar Roy and Gul T. Butaney, "Customer's Relative Loyalty: An Empirical Examination," *Journal of Strategic Marketing* 22, 3 (2014): 206–221.

[9]Melissa S. Barker, Donald I. Barker, Nicholas F. Bormann, Mary Lous Roberts, and Debra Zahay, *Social Media Marketing: A Strategic Approach*, 2nd ed. (Mason, OH: Cengage Learning, 2017).

[10]Ken Yeung, "Now with 2.5M Advertisers, Facebook Targets TV Budgets with New Ad-Buy Offering," *Venture Beat,* September 27, 2015, http://venturebeat.com/2015/09/27/now-with-2-5m-advertisers-facebook-targets-tv-budgets-with-new-ad-buying-offering/ (accessed March 2, 2017).

[11]Melissa S. Barker, Donald I. Barker, Nicholas F. Bormann, Mary Lous Roberts, and Debra Zahay, *Social Media Marketing: A Strategic Approach*, 2nd ed. (Mason, OH: Cengage Learning, 2017).

[12]Darius Fisher, "How to Handle Negative Yelp Reviews," *The Huffington Post*, June 7, 2016, http://www.huffingtonpost.com/darius-fisher

/how-to-handle-negative-ye_b_10324196.html (accessed March 2, 2017).

[13]"Dodge Brand Connecting With Its Fans by Inviting a Limited Number to the Hotly Anticipated Reveal of the All-New 2018 Dodge Challenger SRT Demon in NYC," *Yahoo! Finance*, February 22, 2017, http://finance.yahoo.com/news/dodge-brand-connecting-fans-inviting-130000410.html (accessed March 2, 2017).

[14]V. Kumar, Xi Zhang, and Anita Luo, "Modeling Customer Opt-In and Opt-Out in a Permission-Based Marketing Context," *Journal of Marketing Research* 51, 4 (2014): 403–419.

[15]Michael Durkheimer, "For Young Investors With At Least $50,000, Snapchat Usage Almost Ties Facebook," *Forbes*, March 5, 2017, https://www.forbes.com/sites/michaeldurkheimer/2017/03/05/for-young-investors-with-at-least-50000-snapchat-usage-almost-ties-facebook/#ea016564886d (accessed March 5, 2017).

[16]Christie Baraket, "QZone tops WeChat as China's Biggest Open-Platform Social Network," *Adweek*, March 12, 2014, http://www.adweek.com/digital/qzone-tops-wechat-chinas-biggest-open-platform-social-network/ (accessed March 5, 2017).

[17]Shannon Greenwood, Andrew Perrin, and Maeve Duggan, "Social Media Update 2016," *Pew Research Center*, November 11, 2016, http://www.pewinternet.org/2016/11/11/social-media-update-2016/ (accessed March 5, 2017).

[18]Maria Vernuccio, "Communicating Corporate Brands Through Social Media: An Exploratory

Study," *Journal of Business Communication* 51, 3 (2014): 211–233.

[19]Deepa Seetharaman, "Ad Push Props Facebook Revenue," *The Wall Street Journal*, February 2, 2017, B1.

[20]Ivy Guerrero, "5 Most Popular Facebook Ads," *Insider Monkey*, November 1, 2016, http://www.insidermonkey.com/blog/5-most-popular-facebook-ads-484062/4/ (accessed March 5, 2017).

[21]Anita Balakrishnan, "Facebook Ad Revenue Shoots Up 53%, Sending Shares Climbing Up," *CNBC*, February 1, 2017, http://www.cnbc.com/2017/02/01/facebook-earnings-q4-2016.html (accessed March 5, 2017).

[22]Amol Sharma, "NFL Throws in with Twitter," *The Wall Street Journal*, September 26, 2013, B2; Brad Stone, "Twitter Wants to Be Your TV," *Bloomberg Businessweek,* April 28–May 4, 2014, pp. 39–40.

[23]Nathan McAlone, "Investors Are Going Nuts for Snapchat — Here's How Snap Thinks It Can Turn a $500 Million Loss Into Profit," *Business Insider*, March 5, 2017, http://www.businessinsider.com/how-will-snapchat-make-money-2017-3 (accessed March 5, 2017).

[24]Haley Tsukayama, "Snapchat Files for its Initial Public Offering: Here are the 10 Most Interesting Things We've Learned so Far," *The Washington Post*, February 3, 2017, https://www.washingtonpost.com/news/the-switch/wp/2017/02/03/snapchat-files-for-its-initial-public-offering-here-are-the-10-most-interesting-things-weve-learned-so-far/?utm_term=.591d0ee20f98 (accessed March 5, 2017).

[25]Kathleen Chaykowski, "Snapchat's Big Weakness: The Olds," *Forbes*, March 1, 2017, https://www.forbes.com/sites/kathleenchaykowski/2017/03/01/snapchats-big-weakness-the-olds/#15eb5908230b (accessed March 5, 2017).

[26]Ryan Faughnder, "Is Snapchat a Media Company? Even Hollywood Can't Decide," *Los Angeles Times*, March 1, 2017, http://www.latimes.com/business/hollywood/la-fi-ct-snap-chat-studios-20170224-story.html (accessed March 5, 2017).

[27]Douglas A. McIntyre, "YouTube Viewership Hits a Billion Hours of Content a Day," *24/7 Wall St.*, February 27, 2017, http://247wallst.com/apps-software/2017/02/27/youtube-viewership-hits-100-billion-hours-of-content-a-day/ (accessed March 5, 2017).

[28]Rachel Strugatz, "Beauty's Battle for Views: Brands vs. Vloggers," *WWD*, February 23, 2017, http://wwd.com/beauty-industry-news/beauty-features/youtube-l2-beautys-battle-for-views-brands-vs-bloggers-10814639/ (access March 5, 2017).

[29]Mike Snider, "How YouTube TV compares to rivals Sling, PlayStation, DirecTV," *USA Today*, March 5, 2017, http://www.usatoday.com/story/tech/talkingtech/2017/03/05/how-youtube-tv-compares-rivals-sling-playstation-directv/98551276/ (accessed March 5, 2017).

[30]Sujan Patel, "How LinkedIn Uses LinkedIn for Marketing," *Forbes*, March 4, 2017, https://www.forbes.com/sites/sujanpatel/2017/03/04/how-linkedin-uses-linkedin-for-marketing/2/#3b96f9d3657f (accessed March 5, 2017).

[31]Amanda Walgrove, "5 B2B Brands that Rock LinkedIn Marketing," *Contently*, February 24, 2017, https://contently.com/strategist/2015/02/24/5-b2b-brands-that-rock-linkedin/ (accessed March 5, 2017).

[32]KBK Communications, "Social Media," 2013, http://www.kbkcommunications.com/ (accessed December 11, 2014).

[33]David Cohen, "Tumblr Will Be 10 Sunday, Causing David Karp to Reflect," *Adweek*, February 17, 2017, http://www.adweek.com/digital/tumblr-10-david-karp/ (accessed March 5, 2017).

[34]Dan Mitchell, "Why Mayer Chose Tumblr," *CNN Money,* May 20, 2013, http://tech.fortune.cnn.com/2013/05/20/why-mayer-chose-tumblr/ (accessed December 11, 2014); "About Tumblr," Tumblr, http://www.tumblr.com/about (accessed December 11, 2014); Stuart Dredge, "Tumblr Audience Up to 420m as Yahoo Predicts $100m Revenues in 2015," *The Guardian,* October 23, 2014, http://www.theguardian.com/technology/2014/oct/23/tumblr-yahoo-revenues-2015-ads-nsfw (accessed December 11, 2014).

[35]Easy Recipes for Real Life: Tastefully Simple blog, https://www.tastefullysimple.com/ (accessed December 11, 2014); Stacie Schaible, "Dunedin Woman Says 'Mommy' Blogs Hit the Target," *wfla*, December 10, 2013, http://www.wfla.com/story/24184742/mommy-blogs-hit-the-target (accessed December 11, 2014).

[36]"Wikipedia: Size Comparisons," *Wikipedia*, https://en.wikipedia.org/wiki/Wikipedia:Size_comparisons (accessed March 5, 2017).

[37]Charlene Li and Josh Bernoff, *Groundswell* (Boston, MA: Harvard Business Press, 2008), 24.

[38]Ibid., 25–26.

[39]Robert Wulff, "Why Aren't Fortunate 500 Companies Blogging?" Tribute Media, June 11, 2015, https://www.tributemedia.com/blog/why-arent-fortune-500-companies-blogging (accessed March 5, 2017).

[40]Yoni Heisler, "Once Mocked, Facebook's $1 Billion Acquisition of Instagram was a Stroke of Genius," *BGR*, December 29, 2016, http://bgr.com/2016/12/29/facebook-instagram-acquisition-1-billion-genius/ (accessed March 5, 2017).

[41]Bryan Clark, "Snapchat Growth Slowed Significantly After Launch of Instagram Stories," The Next Web, February 3, 2017, https://thenextweb.com/socialmedia/2017/02/03/snapchat-growth-slowed-significantly-after-the-launch-of-instagram-stories/ (accessed March 5, 2017).

[42]Scott Martin, "Action! Facebook Rolls Out Video Features," *USA Today*, June 21, 2013, B1; Victor Luckerson, "A Year Later, Instagram Hasn't Made a Dime. Was It Worth $1 Billion?" *Time,* April 9, 2013, http://business.time.com/2013/04/09/a-year-later-instagram-hasnt-made-a-dime-was-it-worth-1-billion/ (accessed December 11, 2014).

[43]Laura Schlereth, "Marketers' Interest in Pinterest," *Marketing News*, April 30, 2012, 8–9; The Creative Group, "Pinterest Interest: Survey: 17 Percent of Marketers Currently Using or Planning to Join Pinterest," August 22, 2012, www.sacbee.com/2012/08/22/4747399/pinterest-interest-survey-17-percent.html (accessed August 24, 2012); Jason Falls, "How Pinterest Is Becoming the Next Big Thing in Social Media for Business," *Entrepreneur,* February 7, 2012, www.entrepreneur.com/article/222740 (accessed December 10, 2014); Pinterest website, http://pinterest.com/ (accessed December 10, 2014); "Whole Planet Foundation," *Pinterest,* http://pinterest.com/wholefoods/whole-planet-foundation/ (accessed December 10, 2014).

[44]Jeff Bercovici, "Social Media's New Mad Men," *Forbes,* November 2014, pp. 71–82.

[45]Nicole Lee, "Pinterest Uses AI and Your Camera to Recommend Pins," *Engadget*, February 8, 2017, https://www.engadget.com/2017/02/08/pinterest-uses-ai-and-your-camera-to-recommend-pins/ (accessed March 5, 2017).

[46]Kelly Clay, "3 Things You Can Learn about Your Business with Instagram," *Forbes*, August 9, 2012, http://www.forbes.com/sites/kellyclay/2012/08/09/3-things-you-can-learn-about-your-business-with-instagram/ (accessed December 12, 2014).

[47]Zale Jewelers Pinterest page, https://www.pinterest.com/zalesjewelers/ (accessed December 9, 2014).

[48]Douglas MacMillan and Elizabeth Dwoskin, "Smile! Marketers Are Mining Selfies," *The Wall Street Journal,* October 10, 2014, B1–B2.

[49]Cari Sommer, "YouTube Sensation Bethany Mota on How to Use Your Platform for Good," *Forbes*, December 12, 2016, https://www.forbes.com/sites/carisommer/2016/12/12/how-youtube-sensation-bethany-mota-is-using-her-platform-for-good/#2a6d839c322c (accessed March 5, 2016); Emma Oulton, "Bethany Mota's Book 'Make Your Mind Up' Promised to be an Empowering Read," *Bustle*, October 17, 2016, https://www.bustle.com/articles/189997-bethany-motas-book-make-your-mind-up-promises-to-be-an-empowering-read (accessed March 5, 2017).

[50]Kate Rockwood, "Why Spending $1,000 on an Instagram Post Might Actually Be Worth It," *Inc.*, February 2017, http://www.inc.com/magazine/201702/kate-rockwood/tip-sheet-social-media-influencers.html (accessed March 5, 2017).

[51]"About Influenster," *Influenster*, https://www.influenster.com/about (accessed March 5, 2017).

[52]Ann Lukits, "Podcasts Send Shoppers to Omega-3s," *The Wall Street Journal,* December 9, 2014, D2.

[53]"Mobile Fact Sheet," *Pew Research Center*, January 12, 2017, http://www.pewinternet.org/fact-sheet/mobile/ (accessed March 5, 2017).

[54]Davey Alba, "Mary Meeker Says Advertisers Aren't Spending Enough on Mobile," *Wired*, June 1, 2016, https://www.wired.com/2016/06/mary-meeker-says-advertisers-arent-spending-enough-mobile/ (accessed March 5, 2017).

[55]Thomas Claburn, "Google Tells Businesses 'Fall In Love With Mobile'," *Information Week*, February 28, 2012, http://www.informationweek.com/news/mobility/business/232601587 (accessed December 12, 2014); Lauren Johnson, "Mobile Video Generates 58pc Brand Recall: Study," *Mobile Marketer,* November 12, 2012, http://www.mobilemarketer.com/cms/news/research/14222.html (accessed December 12, 2014).

[56]Mark Milian, "Why Text Messages Are Limited to 160 Characters," *Los Angeles Times*, May 3, 2009, http://latimesblogs.latimes.com/technology/2009/05/invented-text-messaging.html (accessed December 12, 2014); "Eight Reasons Why Your Business Should Use SMS Marketing," *Mobile Marketing Ratings*, http://www.mobilemarketingratings.com/eight-reasons-sms-marketing.html (accessed December 12, 2014).

[57]Sara Angeles, "How to Put Text Message Marketing to Work This Holiday Season," *Fox Business,* November 7, 2013, http://smallbusiness.foxbusiness.com/marketing-sales/2013/11/07/how-to-put-text-message-marketing-to-work-this-holiday-season/ (accessed December 12, 2014).

[58]Davey Alba, "Mary Meeker Says Advertisers Aren't Spending Enough on Mobile," *Wired*, June 1, 2016, https://www.wired.com/2016/06/mary-meeker-says-advertisers-arent-spending-enough-mobile/ (accessed March 5, 2017).

[59]Shawn Hessinger, "60 Percent of Online Traffic Now Comes from Mobile," July 8, 2014, *Small Biz Trends,* http://smallbiztrends.com/2014/07/online-traffic-report-mobile.html (accessed December 12, 2014).

[60]Anita Campbell, "What the Heck Is an App?" *Small Business Trends*, March 7, 2011, http://smallbiztrends.com/2011/03/what-is-an-app.html (accessed December 12, 2014).

[61]Kenneth Olmstead and Michelle Atkinson, "Chapter 1: The Majority of Smartphone Owners Download Apps," Pew Research Center, November 10, 2015, http://www.pewinternet.org/2015/11/10/the-majority-of-smartphone-owners-download-apps/ (accessed March 5, 2017).

[62]Olga Khariff and Leslie Patton, "Starbucks Takes its Pioneering Mobile-Phone App to Grande Level," *Bloomberg*, March 30, 2016, https://www.bloomberg.com/news/articles/2016-03-30/starbucks-takes-its-pioneering-mobile-phone-app-to-grande-level (accessed March 5, 2017).

[63]Umika Pidaparthy, "Marketers Embracing QR Codes, for Better or Worse," *CNN Tech*, March 28, 2011, http://articles.cnn.com/2011-03-28/tech/qr.codes.marketing_1_qr-smart-phone-users-symbian?_s=PM:TECH (accessed December 12, 2014).

[64]Brad Tuttle, "The Creepy New Way Macy's Tempts You to Make Impulse Purchases," *Time*, September 16, 2014, http://time.com/money/3432693/macys-shopkick-ibeacon/ (accessed April 1, 2017).

[65]Deanna Ting, "What Marriott Learned from Starwood's Loyalty and Digital Expertise," *Skift*, February 13, 2017, https://skift.com/2017/02/13/what-marriott-learned-from-starwoods-loyalty-and-digital-expertise/ (accessed April 1, 2017).

[66]Greg Sterling, "Beacon Marketers Have New Ways Around App Download Requirement," *Marketing Land*, April 19, 2016, http://marketingland.com/beacon-market-matures-marketers-drop-173651 (accessed April 1, 2017).

[67]Brad Stone and Olga Kharif, "Pay as You Go," *Bloomberg Businessweek*, July 18–July 24, 2011, 66–71.

[68]"Google Wallet," http://www.google.com/wallet/what-is-google-wallet.html (accessed December 10, 2014); Brett Molina and Marco della Cava, "CVS Says No Way to Apple Pay," *USA Today,* October 28, 2014, 2A–2B.

[69]Vangie Beal, "All About Widgets," *Webopedia™*, August 31, 2010, http://www.webopedia.com/DidYouKnow/Internet/2007/widgets.asp (accessed December 10, 2014).

[70]Rachael King, "Building a Brand with Widgets," *Bloomberg Businessweek*, March 3, 2008, http://www.businessweek.com/technology/content/feb2008/tc20080303_000743.htm (accessed December 12, 2014).

[71]TripAdvisor, "Welcome to TripAdvisor's Widget Center," http://www.tripadvisor.com/Widgets (accessed December 12, 2014).

[72]Melissa S. Barker, Donald I. Barker, Nicholas F. Bormann, Mary Lous Roberts, and Debra Zahay, *Social Media Marketing: A Strategic*

Approach, 2nd ed. (Mason, OH: Cengage Learning, 2017).

[73]Matt McGee, "As Google Analytics Turns 10, We Ask: How Many Websites Use It?" Marketing Land, November 12, 2015, http://marketingland.com/as-google-analytics-turns-10-we-ask-how-many-websites-use-it-151892 (accessed March 5, 2017).

[74]"By Tailoring the Features of Google Analytics, LunaMetrics Helps PBS Increase both Conversions and Visits by 30%," *Google Analytics*, https://static.googleusercontent.com/media/www.google.com/en//intl/pt_ALL/analytics/customers/pdfs/pbs.pdf (accessed March 24, 2017).

[75]Quentin Hardy, "Google Introduces Products that will Sharpen its Ad Focus," *The New York Times*, March 15, 2016, https://www.nytimes.com/2016/03/16/technology/google-introduces-products-that-will-sharpen-its-ad-focus.html (accessed March 24, 2017).

[76]Internet Live Stats, "Internet Users," http://www.internetlivestats.com/internet-users/ (accessed January 7, 2015).

[77]Sonja Gensler, Franziska Völckner, Yuping Liu-Thompkins, and Caroline Wiertz, "Managing Brands in the Social Environment," *Journal of Interactive Marketing* 27, 4 (2013): pp. 242–256.

[78]Emily Orofino, "Can This Genius Beauty Brand Crowdsource the Next Big Thing?" *POPSUGAR*, July 10, 2016, https://www.popsugar.com/beauty/Volition-Beauty-Custom-Made-Beauty-Products-41873521 (accessed March 25, 2017).

[79]Maghan McDowell, "More Merchants to Add 'Shop' Section on Facebook Page," *WWD*, April 14, 2016, http://wwd.com/business-news/media/more-merchants-to-add-shop-section-on-facebook-page-10410194/ (accessed March 25, 2017).

[80]Sarah Perez, "AmazonFresh Drops to $14.99 per Month for Prime Members," *TechCrunch*, October 6, 2016, https://techcrunch.com/2016/10/06/amazonfresh-drops-to-14-99-per-month-for-prime-members/ (accessed March 5, 2017).

[81]Mariam Gottfried, "Amazon Puts Groceries in Its Shopping Cart," *The Wall Street Journal*, October 28, 2013, C6; Amazon Fresh, https://fresh.amazon.com/help (accessed December 12, 2014); Marcus Wohlsen, "The Next Big Thing You Missed: Online Grocery Shopping Is Back, and This Time It'll Work," *Wired*, February 4, 2014, http://www.wired.com/2014/02/next-big-thing-missed-future-groceries-really-online/ (accessed December 12, 2014).

[82]Emma Sopadjieva, Utpal M. Dholakia, and Beth Benjamin, "A Study of 46,000 Shoppers Shows that Omnichannel Retailing Works," *Harvard Business Review*, January 3, 2017, https://hbr.org/2017/01/a-study-of-46000-shoppers-shows-that-omnichannel-retailing-works (accessed March 5, 2017).

[83]Cheryl Wischhover, "How ColourPop Became the Most Popular (and Most Mysterious) Beauty Brand on the Internet," *Fashionista*, January 22, 2016, http://fashionista.com/2016/01/colourpop-instagram-beauty (accessed March 5, 2017).

[84]Lindsay Kolowich, "14 of the Best Brands on Instagram Right Now," *HubSpot*, February 21, 2017, https://blog.hubspot.com/marketing/instagram-best-brands#sm.000009ty2hnlotct2w4p7tr8o6gpc (accessed April 1, 2017).

[85]Robert Hof, "Online Ad Revenues Blow Past Broadcast TV, Thanks to Mobile and Video," *Forbes*, April 10, 2014, http://www.forbes.com/sites/roberthof/2014/04/10/online-ad-revenues-blow-past-broadcast-tv-thanks-to-mobile-and-video/ (accessed January 7, 2015).

[86]Shawn D. Baron, Caryn Brouwer, and Amaya Garbayo, "A Model for Delivering Branding Value Through High-Impact Digital Advertising," *Journal of Advertising Research* 54 (3), September 2014, 286–291.

[87]Alistair Barr, "Google Earnings: What to Watch," *The Wall Street Journal*, April 16, 2014, http://blogs.wsj.com/digits/2014/04/16/google-earnings-what-to-watch-4/ (accessed January 7, 2015); Conor Dougherty, "Analysts Ask What's Next for Google?" *The New York Times*, October 16, 2014, http://www.nytimes.com/2014/10/17/technology/google-search-ad-growth-slows.html (accessed January 7, 2015).

[88]Cotton Delo, "Facebook Wants to Turn 25 Million Small Businesses into Advertisers," *Advertising Age*, April 7, 2014, http://adage.com/article/digital/facebook-turn-small-businesses-advertisers/292495/ (accessed January 7, 2015).

[89]"FTC Cracking Down on Social Influencers' Labeling of Paid Promotions," *AdAge*, August 5, 2016, http://adage.com/article/digital/ftc-cracking-social-influencers-labeling-promotions/305345/ (accessed March 5, 2017).

[90]Aruna Viswanatha and Robert McMillan, "Yahoo Faces SEC Probe Over Data Breaches," *The Wall Street Journal*, January 23, 2017, A1.

[91]O.C. Ferrell, "Broadening Marketing's Contribution to Data Privacy," *Journal of the Academy of Marketing Science* 43 (2) March 2017.

[92]Cecilia Kang, "Bill Would Curb Tracking of and Advertising to Children on Internet," *The Washington Post*, November 14, 2013, http://www.washingtonpost.com/business/technology/ bills-would-curb-tracking-of-and-advertising-to-children-on-internet/2013/11/14/dee03382- 4d58-11e3-ac54-aa84301ced81_story.html (accessed January 20, 2016); Anne Flaherty, "Senate Chairman Calls for 'Do Not Track' Bill," *Yahoo! News*, April 24, 2013, phys.org/ news/2013-04-senate-chairman-track-bill.html (accessed January 20, 2016).

[93]Jesse Brody, "Terms and Conditions," *Marketing News*, November 2014, 34–41.

[94]Will Bourne, "Birth of the Resistance," *Inc.*, July/August 2014, 24–32, 110.

[95]Jesse Brody, "Terms and Conditions," *Marketing News*, November 2014, 34–41.

[96]Elizabeth Weise, "Sony Hack Leaves Intriguing Clues," *USA Today*, December 4, 2014, 1B.

[97]Ben Rossen, "Ransomware – A Closer Look," *Federal Trade Commission*, November 10, 2016, https://www.ftc.gov/news-events/blogs/business-blog/2016/11/ransomware-closer-look (accessed March 25, 2017).

[98]Sarah Needleman, "Social-Media Con Game," *The Wall Street Journal*, October 12, 2009, http://online.wsj.com/article/SB100014240527487044715045744455502831219412.html (accessed December 12, 2014).

[99]Elizabeth Weise, "Consumers Have to Protect Themselves Online," *USA Today*, May 22, 2014, 1B.

[100]"Pirate Bay Sets Sail Again After Servers Raided in Sweden Are Migrated to New Base in Ukraine," *KOAM TV*, January 7, 2015, http://www.koamtv.com/story/27783382/pirate-bay

-sets-sail-again-after-servers-raided-in-sweden -are-migrated-to-new-base-in-ukraine (accessed January 7, 2015).

[101]Business Software Alliance, "Seizing Opportunity Through License Compliance," *BSA,* 2016, http://globalstudy.bsa.org/2016/ (accessed March 29, 2017).

[102]Aubry R. Fowler III, Barry J. Babin, and May K. Este, "Burning for Fun or Money: Illicit Consumer Behavior in a Contemporary Context," presented at the Academy of Marketing Science Annual Conference, May 27, 2005, Tampa, FL.

[103]Kevin Shanahan and Mike Hyman, "Motivators and Enablers of SCOURing: A Study of Online Piracy in the US and UK," *Journal of Business Research* 63 (2010): 1095–1102.

[104]Erica E. Phillips, "U.S. Officials Chase Counterfeit Goods Online," *The Wall Street Journal,* November 28, 2014, http://www.wsj .com/articles/u-s-officials-chase-counterfeit -goods-online-1417217763 (accessed December 10, 2014).

[105]Todd Wasserman, "Zappos Facebook Activity Over 2 Months Drives 85,000 Website Visits," *Mashable*, February 6, 2013, http:// mashable.com/2013/02/06/zappos-facebook -results/ (accessed December 12, 2014); Laura Stampler, "Why Zappos Sees Sponsored Posts on Facebook as 'A Necessary Evil'," *Business Insider*, February 6, 2013, http://www.busines-sinsider.com/zappos-on-facebook -and-social-media-2013-2 (accessed December 12, 2014); Mike Schoultz, "Zappos

Marketing Strategy…What Is Their Difference Maker?" *Digital Spark Marketing*, November 12, 2013, http://www .digitalsparkmarketing.com/creative-marketing /brand/zappos-marketing-strategy/ (accessed December 12, 2014); Amy Porterfield, "9 Companies Doing Social Media Right and Why," *Social Media Examiner*, April 12, 2011, http://www.socialmediaexaminer.com/9 -companies-doing-social-media-right -and-why/ (accessed December 12, 2014); Kenny Kline, "6 Companies that Prove the Power of Word-of-Mouth Marketing," *The Huffington Post*, March 20, 2017, http://www .huffingtonpost.com/entry/6-companies -that-prove-the-power-of-word-of-mouth -marketing_us_58d09600e4b0e0d348b3474a (accessed March 25, 2017).

FEATURE NOTES

[a]Mike Isaac, "Facebook Mounts Effort to Limit Tide of Fake News," *The New York Times,* December 15, 2016, http://www.nytimes. com/2016/12/15/technology/facebook-fake -news.html?_r=0 (accessed December 23, 2016); Andrew Higgins, Mike McIntire, and Gabriel J.X. Dance, "Inside a Fake News Sausage Factory: 'This Is All About Income'," *The New York Times,* November 25, 2016, http:// www.nytimes.com/2016/11/25/world /europe/fake-news-donald-trump-hillary -clinton-georgia.html (accessed December 23, 2016); David Pierson, "Facebook Bans Fake News From its Advertising Network—But Not its News Feed," *Los Angeles Times,* November 15, 2016, http://www.latimes.com/business

/la-fi-facebook-fake-news-20161115-story.html (accessed December 23, 2016).

[b]Greg Bensinger, "Rebuilding History's Biggest Dot-Com Bust," *The Wall Street Journal*, January 13, 2015, B1–B2; Farhad Manjoo, "Grocery Deliveries in Sharing Economy," *The New York Times*, May 21, 2015, http://www .nytimes.com/2014/05/22/technology /personaltech/online-grocery-start-up-takes -page-from-sharing-services.html (accessed October 5, 2015); Laura Entis, "After Many Strikeouts, a $44 Million Home Run," *Entrepreneur*, July 22, 2014, http://www .entrepreneur.com/article/235796 (accessed October 5, 2015); Hadley Malcolm, "Target

starts testing grocery delivery with Instacart," *USA Today*, September 15, 2015, http://www. usatoday.com/story/money/2015/09/15 /target-testing-grocery-delivery-with -instacart/72301440/ (accessed October 5, 2015); Ellen Huet, "Whole Foods Invests in Instacart at 2014 Valuation," *Bloomberg*, September 23, 2016, https://www.bloomberg.com /news/articles/2016-09-23/whole -foods-invests-in-instacart-at-2014-valuation (accessed December 3, 2016); Greg Bensinger, "Grocery-Delivery Startup Instacart Cuts Pay for Couriers," *The Wall Street Journal*, March 11, 2016, http://www.wsj.com/articles/grocery -delivery-startup-instacartcuts-pay-for-couriers -1457715105 (accessed December 3, 2016).

Chapter 10

[1]Based on information in Gabriel Goodwin, "Attention Local Audiophiles: Shinola Expands to Music," *Metro Times (Detroit),* November 15, 2016, http://www.metrotimes .com/the-scene/archives/2016/11/15/attention -local-audiophiles-shinola-expands-to-music (accessed February 20, 2017); Tom Perkins, "Adventures in Authenticity at Shinola," *Metro Times (Detroit),* August 17, 2016, http://www .metrotimes.com/detroit/adventures-in -authenticity-at-shinola (accessed February 20, 2017); Alexandra Gibbs, "Vinyl Fans Rejoice!

Panasonic, Sony Are Reviving the Turntable," *CNBC,* January 8, 2016, http://www.cnbc .com/2016/01/01/vinyl-fans-rejoice-panasonic -sony-are-reviving-the-turntable.html (accessed February 20, 2017); Robert Klara, "How Shinola Went From Shoe Polish to the Coolest Brand in America," *Adweek,* June 22, 2015, http://www.adweek.com/brand-marketing /how-shinola-went-shoe-polish-coolest-brand -america-165459/ (accessed February 20, 2017); Kristin Regan, "American Innovation: 5 Questions with Shinola CMO Bridget Russo,"

Brand Channel, October 27, 2016, http:// brandchannel.com/2016/10/27/5-questions -shinola-102716/ (accessed February 20, 2017).

[2]"Drury Hotels Is the Only Hotel to Receive 11 Consecutive J.D. Power Awards," Drury Hotels, press release, 2016, https://druryhotels .com/about/pressreleases/JDPower2016 (accessed February 6, 2017).

[3]Erica Shaffer, "McDonald's Making More Menu Changes," *Food Business News,* November

7, 2016, http://www.foodbusinessnews.net/articles/news_home/Business_News/2016/11/McDonalds_making_more_menu_cha.aspx?ID={7F1F4BA2-3429-4BF0-8A3F-8C84BE07B077} (accessed February 6, 2017); "Here's How McDonald's Is Now Seeking to Attract Millennials," *Forbes,* November 17, 2016, http://www.forbes.com/sites/greatspeculations/2016/11/17/heres-how-mcdonalds-is-now-seeking-to-attract-millennials/#1d1312862d09 (accessed February 6, 2017).

4He Huifeng, "The Asian Suppliers Behind Some of the iPhone 7's Key Components," *South China Morning Post,* September 8, 2016, http://www.scmp.com/business/article/2017678/asian-suppliers-behind-some-iphone-7s-key-components (accessed February 6, 2017).

5"Product Images & Info," Apple, http://www.apple.com/pr/products/ (accessed February 6, 2017).

6William P. Putsis Jr. and Barry L. Bayus, "An Empirical Analysis of Firms' Product Line Decisions," *Journal of Marketing Research* 38, 1 (2001): 110–118.

7"Agriculture," John Deere & Co. website, https://www.deere.com/en_US/industry/agriculture/agriculture.page (accessed February 6, 2017).

8Michael D. Johnson, Andreas Herrmann, and Frank Huber, "Evolution of Loyalty Intentions," *Journal of Marketing* 70, 2 (2006): 122–132.

9Tim Nudd, "Ad of the Day: Lil Buck Defies Gravity in Apple's First Big TV Spot for Its Airpods," *AdAge,* January 17, 2017, http://www.adweek.com/brand-marketing/ad-day-lil-buck-defies-gravity-apples-first-big-tv-spot-its-airpods-175581/ (accessed February 9, 2017).

10Richard L. Gruner, Christian Homburg, and Bryan A. Lukas, "Firm-Hosted Online Brand Communities and New Product Success," *Journal of the Academy of Marketing Science,* 42, 1 (2014): 29–48.

11Elaine Watson, "Why Do 85% of New CPG Products Fail within Two Years?" *Food Navigator,* July 31, 2014, http://www.foodnavigator-usa.com/Markets/Why-do-85-of-new-CPG-products-fail-within-two-years (accessed February 9, 2017); Joan Schneider and Julie Hall, "Why Most Product Launches Fail,"

Harvard Business Review, April 2011, https://hbr.org/2011/04/why-most-product-launches-fail (accessed February 9, 2017).

12Matt Timms, "Life in Plastic, Not so Fantastic; the Tale of Barbie's Decline," *The New Economy,* January 7, 2015, http://www.theneweconomy.com/home/life-in-plastic-not-so-fantastic-barbies-great-decline (accessed February 9, 2017).

13Beth Kowitt, "Stonyfield Gives Its Yogurt a Makeover," *Fortune,* February 13, 2017, http://fortune.com/2017/02/13/stonyfield-yogurt-sugar/ (accessed February 13, 2017).

14Adapted from Everett M. Rogers, *Diffusion of Innovations* (New York: Macmillan, 1962): 81–86.

15Arch G. Woodside and Wim Biemans, "Managing Relationships, Networks, and Complexity in Innovation, Diffusion, and Adoption Processes," *Business & Industrial Marketing* 20, 7 (2005): 335–338.

16Rogers, *Diffusion of Innovations,* 247–250.

17"Common Language in Marketing," American Marketing Association, http://www.marketing-dictionary.org/Brand (accessed February 3, 2017).

18Warren Church, "Investment in Brand Pays Large Dividends," *Marketing News*, November 15, 2006, p. 21.

19John Kell, "Miller Lite Tastes Success Again," *Fortune,* March 4, 2015, http://fortune.com/2015/03/04/miller-lite-new-success/ (accessed February 10, 2017).

20Rosellina Ferraro, Amna Kirmani, and Ted Matherly, "Look At Me! Look At Me! Conspicuous Brand Usage, Self-Brand Connection, and Dilution," *Journal of Marketing Research* 50, 4 (2013): 477–488.

21C. D. Simms and P. Trott, "The Perception of the BMW Mini Brand: The Importance of Historical Associations and the Development of a Model," *Journal of Product & Brand Management* 15, 4 (2006): 228–238.

22Douglas Holt, "Branding as Cultural Activism," from *How Brands Become Icons: The Principle of Cultural Branding* (Boston, MA: Harvard Business School Press, 2004).

23Nigel Hollis, "Branding Unmasked," *Marketing Research* 17, 3 (2005): 24–29.

24David A. Aaker, *Managing Brand Equity: Capitalizing on the Value of a Brand Name* (New York: Free Press, 1991): 16–17.

25Don E. Schulz, "The Loyalty Paradox: What Is Brand Loyalty after All?" *Marketing Management* 14, 5 (2005): 10–11.

26"2017 Brand Keys Customer Loyalty Engagement Index," Brand Keys, http://info.brandkeys.com/acton/attachment/943/f-0071/1/-/-/-/-/2017%20CLEI%20-%20Table%20of%20Categories%20and%20Winners.pdf (accessed February 10, 2017).

27Mitchell C. Olsen, Rebecca J. Slotegraaf, and Sandeep R. Chandukala, "Green Claims and Message Frames: How Green New Products Change Brand Attitude," *Journal of Marketing,* 78, 5 (2014): 119–137.

28"Consumer Reports' Best and Worst Car Brands," *Newsday,* December 7 2016, http://www.newsday.com/classifieds/cars/consumer-reports-best-and-worst-car-brands-in-2016-include-audi-subaru-and-lexus-1.11504841 (accessed February 10, 2017).

29Simone M. de Droog, Patti M. Valkenburg, and Moniek Buijzen, "Using Brand Characters to Promote Young Children's Liking of and Purchase Requests for Fruit," *Journal of Health Communication: International Perspectives* 26, 1 (2010): 79–89.

30"Market Profile," Private Label Manufacturers Association, http://plma.com/storeBrands/marketprofile14a.html (accessed February 3, 2017).

31Chiranjeev S. Kohli, Katrin R. Harich, and Lance Lethesser, "Creating Brand Identity: A Study of Evaluation of New Brand Names," *Journal of Business Research* 58, 11 (2005): 1506–1515.

32Richard R. Klink, and Gerard A. Athaide, "Creating Brand Personality with Brand Names," *Marketing Letters,* 23, 1 (2012): 109–117.

33Sophia Yan, "What's in a Brand Name? In China, Everything," *CNN Money,* September 7, 2015, http://money.cnn.com/2015/09/07/news/foreign-firms-china-branding/ (accessed February 10, 2017).

34Dorothy Cohen, "Trademark Strategy," *Journal of Marketing* 50, 1 (1986): 63.

35Chiranjeev Kohli and Rajheesh Suri, "Brand Names That Work: A Study of the Effectiveness of Different Brand Names," *Marketing Management Journal* 10, 2 (2000): 112–120.

36"Fact Sheets: Types of Protection—Trademarks vs. Generic Terms," International Trademark Association, http://www.inta.org/TrademarkBasics/FactSheets/Pages/TrademarksvsGenericTermsFactSheet.aspx (accessed February 19, 2015).

37"Global Trade in Fake Goods Worth Nearly Half a Trillion Dollars a Year—OECD and EUIPO," Organisation for Economic Co-operation and Development, April 18, 2016, http://www.oecd.org/industry/global-trade-in-fake-goods-worth-nearly-half-a-trillion-dollars-a-year.htm (accessed February 13, 2017); "Counterfeit Goods: How to Tell the Real from the Ripoff," *Consumer Reports,* May 28, 2015, http://www.consumerreports.org/cro/magazine/2015/05/counterfeit-goods-how-to-tell-real-from-ripoff/index.htm (accessed February 10, 2017).

38Suzanne Kapner, "West Elm to Launch Its Own Boutique Hotels," *Wall Street Journal,* September 26, 2016, https://www.wsj.com/articles/west-elm-to-launch-its-own-boutique-hotels-1474844931 (accessed February 13, 2017).

39Shantini Munthree, Geoff Bick, and Russell Abratt, "A Framework for Brand Revitalization," *Journal of Product & Brand Management* 15, 3 (2006): 157–167.

40Kaleel Rahman and Charles S. Areni, "Generic, Genuine, or Completely New? Branding Strategies to Leverage New Products," *Journal of Strategic Marketing,* 22, 1 (2014): 3–15.

41Chris Pullig, Carolyn J Simmons, and Richard G. Netemeyer, "Brand Dilution: When Do New Brands Hurt Existing Brands?" *Journal of Marketing* 70, 2 (2006): 52–66.

42"Kids' Room Color Coordinator," Target, http://www.target.com/spot/kids-room-color-coordinator/landing (accessed February 3, 2017).

43Deena Crawley and Steve McKee, "Twenty Co-Branding Examples," *Bloomberg*, January 23, 2015, http://www.bloomberg.com/ss/09/07/0710_cobranded/8.htm (accessed February 26, 2016); PR Newswire, "Best Western and Harley-Davidson Partnership Goes Global," press release, February 20, 2013, http://www.prnewswire.com/news-releases/best-western-and-harley-davidson-partnership-goes-global-192015471.html (accessed February 13, 2017).

44SC Johnson, "Minimizing Packaging," http://www.scjohnson.com/en/commitment/focus-on/lesswaste/minimizingpackaging.aspx (accessed February 13, 2017).

45Madeline Farber, "Tostitos New Chip Bag Will Tell You When You're Drunk," *Fortune,* January 26, 2017, http://fortune.com/2017/01/26/tostitos-chip-bag-super-bowl-drunk/ (accessed February 13, 2017).

46"Wild Planet Announces Packaging Redesign," *International Supermarket News,* February 4, 2017, http://www.internationalsupermarketnews.com/news/27574 (accessed February 13, 2017).

47"Laundry Detergent," Seventh Generation, http://www.seventhgeneration.com/laundry-detergent (accessed February 13, 2017).

48Barrett J. Brunsman, "P&G Redesigns Packaging, Launches New Ad Campaign As Poison Concerns Mount," *Cincinnati Business Courier,* April 21, 2016, http://www.bizjournals.com/cincinnati/news/2016/04/21/p-g-redesigns-packaging-launches-new-ad-campaign.html (accessed February 13, 2017);

Serena Ng, " P&G, Other Laundry Pod Makers Agree to New Safety Standards," *The Wall Street Journal,* September 4, 2015, http://www.wsj.com/articles/p-g-other-laundry-pod-makers-agree-to-new-safety-standard-1441397456 (accessed February 13, 2017).

49Stack Wine website, http://drinkstack.com/ (accessed February 13, 2017); Steve Ferree, "Take Stack Wine with You for International Picnic Day," *Examiner.com,* June 7, 2015, http://www.examiner.com/article/take-stack-wine-with-you-for-international-picnic-day (accessed February 26, 2016).

50Valerie Folkes and Shashi Matta, "The Effect of Package Shape on Consumers' Judgments of Product Volume: Attention as a Mental Contaminant," *Journal of Consumer Research,* 31, 2 (2004): 390.

51"Menu and Vending Machine Labeling Requirements," U.S. Food & Drug Administration, http://www.fda.gov/Food/IngredientsPackagingLabeling/LabelingNutrition/ucm217762.htm (accessed February 13, 2017).

52"Made in USA," Federal Trade Commission, https://www.ftc.gov/tips-advice/business-center/advertising-and-marketing/made-in-usa (accessed February 13, 2017).

53Curt Nickisch, "GaGa's for Lady Gaga? Coincidental Celebrity Lifts Local Brands," *WBUR radio (Boston)*, February 29, 2012, http://www.wbur.org/2012/02/29/gaga-for-gaga; GaGa website, http://gagagourmet.com/ (accessed February 20, 2015, February 24, 2017); "Going Goo Goo for GaGa," *Warwick Online (RI)*, May 12, 2011, http://warwickonline.com/stories/Going-goo-goo-for-GaGa,54475?print=1; "GaGa" Cengage video.

FEATURE NOTES

aBased on information in Jamie Condliffe, "What's Next for AI Home Assistants," *MIT Technology Review*, February 16, 2017, https://www.cnet.com/how-to/google-home-now-lets-you-shop-for-everyday-items-with-your-voice/ (accessed February 21, 2017); Tom Simonite, "Alexa Gives Amazon a Powerful Data Advantage," *Technology Review*, January 18, 2017, http://www.technologyreview.com

/s/603380/alexa-gives-amazon-a-powerful-data-advantage/ (accessed February 21, 2017); Lisa Eadicicco, "Amazon Is Already Winning the Next Big Arms Race in Tech," *Time*, January 5, 2017, http://time.com/4624067/amazon-echo-alexa-ces-2017 (accessed February 21, 2017); Karissa Bell, "Hey, Siri: How'd You and Every Other Digital Assistant Get Its Name?" *Mashable*, January 12, 2017,

http://mashable.com/2017/01/12/how-alexa-siri-got-names (accessed February 21, 2017).

bBased on information in Dan Solomon, "Thanks to Radiohead and Bon Iver, Apparently Vinyl Record Unboxing Videos Are a Thing," *Fast Company Create*, September 29, 2016, https://www.fastcocreate.com/3064211/thanks-to-radiohead-and-bon-iver-apparently

-vinyl-record-unboxing-videos-are-a-thing (accessed February 20, 2017); Yuyu Chen, "A YouTube Institution, 'Unboxing' Is Making

Its Way to Snapchat," Digiday, June 13, 2016, http://digiday.com/brands/youtube-institution

-unboxing-making-way-snapchat/ (accessed February 20, 2017).

Chapter 11

[1]Based on information in Kirsten Korosec, "Why Hyundai's New Hybrid Could Dethrone the Toyota Prius," *Fortune,* February 14, 2017, http://fortune.com/2017/02/14/hyundai-ioniq -hybrid (accessed February 23, 2017); David Undercoffler, "Hyunda-Kia: Finding Strength in Small Cars," *Automotive News,* February 1, 2017, http://www.autonews.com/article /20170201/RETAIL01/302019996/hyundai -kia%3A-finding-strength-in-small-cars (accessed February 23, 2017); Casey Williams, "Hyundai's Luxury Sub-brand, Genesis, Provides Premium Value," *Portland Press Herald,* February 19, 2017, http://www .pressherald.com/2017/02/19/hyundais-luxury -sub-brand-genesis-provides-premium-value/ (accessed February 23, 2017).

[2]James F. Peltz, "Why Americans Are Eating Less Cold Cereal for Breakfast," *Los Angeles Times,* October 10, 2016, http://www.latimes .com/business/la-fi-agenda-breakfast-cereals -20161010-snap-story.html (accessed February 14, 2017).

[3]Jonathan Maze, "McDonald's Looks to the Big Mac for Growth," *Nation's Restaurant News,* January 18, 2017, http://www.nrn.com /food-trends/mcdonald-s-looks-big-mac-sales -growth (accessed February 14, 2017).

[4]"Henry's Hard Soda Launches New Grape Flavor," *Brewbound,* January 31, 2017, http:// www.brewbound.com/news/henrys-hard-soda -launches-new-grape-flavor (accessed February 14, 2017).

[5]Robert E. Carter and David J. Curry, "Perceptions versus Performance When Managing Extensions: New Evidence about the Role of Fit between a Parent Brand and an Extension," *Journal of the Academy of Marketing Science*, 4, 2 (2013): 253–269.

[6]Jeff Daniels, "Food Companies Are Cooking Up New Recipes for Your Favorite Foods," *CNBC,* September 16, 2016, http://www.cnbc .com/2016/09/19/food-companies-are-cooking -up-new-recipes-for-your-favorite-foods.html (accessed February 15, 2017).

[7]Matthew Dolan, "Ford Redesigns Its Best-Selling F-150 Pickup for 2018," *USA Today*, January 8, 2017, http://www.usatoday.com /story/money/cars/2017/01/08/ford-redesigns -its-best-selling-f-150-pickup-2018/96311094/ (accessed February 15, 2017).

[8]Scott Anthony, "Kodak's Downfall Wasn't About Technology," *Harvard Business Review,* July 15, 2016, https://hbr.org/2016/07/kodaks -downfall-wasnt-about-technology (accessed February 15, 2017).

[9]Elizabeth Paton, "Dyson Wants to Create a Hair Dryer Revolution," *The New York Times,* April 27, 2016, http://www.nytimes .com/2016/04/28/fashion/dyson-hair-dryer.html (accessed February 15, 2017).

[10]"Brush. Whiten. Go." Colgate, http://www .colgateopticwhite.com/toothbrushes/whitening -pen-and-toothbrush (accessed February 15, 2017).

[11]Lanre Bakare, "The Best a Man Can Get? Dollar Shave Club, Harry's Lead Shaving's Young Turks," *The Guardian,* October 20, 2015, http://www.theguardian.com/fashion /2015/oct/20/dollar-shave-club-harrys-shaving -gillette-young-turks-razors (accessed February 15, 2017); Dollar Shave Club, https://www .dollarshaveclub.com/ (accessed February 15, 2017).

[12]Christoph Fuchs and Martin Schreier, "Customer Empowerment in New Product Development," *Journal of Product Innovation Management* 28, 1 (2011): 17–31.

[13]Arina Soukhoroukova, Martin Spann, and Bernd Skiera, "Sourcing, Filtering, and Evaluating New Product Ideas: An Empirical Exploration of the Performance of Idea Markets," *Journal of Product Innovation Management* 29, 1 (2012): 100–112.

[14]Fuchs and Schreier, "Customer Empowerment in New Product Development."

[15]Rakin Azfar, "Lay's Do Us a Flavor Contest Is Back, This Time with Snapchat Activation," *Mobile Marketing,* January 12, 2017, http:// www.mobilemarketer.com/cms/news/social

-networks/24301.html (accessed February 15, 2017).

[16]Procter & Gamble, Connect + Develop website, http://www.pgconnectdevelop.com/ (accessed February 14, 2017).

[17]Kaleidoscope, http://kascope.com/ (accessed February 14, 2017).

[18]Cherryh Cansier, "Pei Wei Test Kitchen Turns Up 'Priceless' ROI," *Fast Casual,* October 24, 2016, https://www.fastcasual.com/articles /pei-wei-test-kitchen-stirs-up-priceless-roi/ (accessed February 15, 2017).

[19]Chloe Sorvino, "Inside Billionaire James Dyson's Reinvention Factory: From Vacuums to Hair Dryers and Now Batteries," *Forbes,* August 24, 2016, http://www.forbes.com /sites/chloesorvino/2016/08/24/james-dyson -exclusive-top-secret-reinvention-factory -/#1172b604372c (accessed February 15, 2017).

[20]JoAndrea Hoegg and Joseph W. Alba, "Seeing Is Believing (Too Much): The Influence of Product Form on Perceptions of Functional Performance," *Journal of Product Innovation Management* 28, 3 (2011): 346–359.

[21]Sarah Whitten, "Fast-Food Menu Tests Suggest Upscale Items Could Be Coming to McDonald's, Wendy's," *CNBC,* September 19, 2016, http://www.cnbc.com/2016/09/19 /fast-food-menu-tests-suggest-upscale-items -could-be-coming-to-mcdonalds-wendys.html (accessed February 15, 2017).

[22]Roger J. Calantone and C. Anthony Di Benedetto, "The Role of Lean Launch Execution and Launch Timing on New Product Performance," *Journal of the Academy of Marketing Science* 40, 4 (2012): 526–538.

[23]"Personal Care and Cleaning Products Benchmarks by Industry," American Customer Satisfaction Index, http://www.theacsi.org /index.php?option=com_content&view=article &id=147&catid=&Itemid=212&i=Personal +Care+and+Cleaning+Products (accessed February 16, 2017).

[24]"Consumer Shipping Benchmarks by Industry," American Customer Satisfaction Index, http://www.theacsi.org/index.php?option

Endnotes content

=com_content&view=article&id=147&catid=&Itemid=212&i=Consumer+Shipping (accessed February 16, 2017).

25 Jeanne Bliss, "Trader Joe's Customer Experience Obsession," *1 to 1,* May 24, 2012, http://www.1to1media.com/weblog/2012/05/trader_joes_customer_experienc.html (accessed February 16, 2017); David DiSalvo, "What Trader Joe's Knows about Making Your Brain Happy," *Forbes,* February 19, 2015, http://www.forbes.com/sites/daviddisalvo/2015/02/19/what-trader-joes-knows-about-making-your-brain-happy/ (accessed February 16, 2017).

26 Marco Bertini, Elie Ofek, and Dan Ariely, "The Impact of Add-On Features on Consumer Product Evaluations," *Journal of Consumer Research* 36, 1 (2009): 17–28.

27 Neeru Paharia, Jill Avery, and Anat Keinen, "Positioning Brands against Large Competitors to Increase Sales," *Journal of Marketing Research* 51, 6 (2014): 647–656.

28 Deanna Ting, "Wyndham Is Repositioning All 16 of Its Brands to Appeal to Anyone and Everyone," *Skift,* June 8, 2016, https://skift.com/2016/06/08/wyndham-is-repositioning-all-16-of-its-brands-to-appeal-to-anyone-and-everyone/ (accessed February 16, 2017).

29 Phil W. Hudson, "Why Did Chick-fil-A Kill the Spicy Chicken Biscuit?" *Atlanta Business Chronicle,* July 28, 2016, http://www.bizjournals.com/atlanta/news/2016/07/28/why-did-chick-fil-a-kill-the-spicy-chicken-biscuit.html (accessed February 17, 2017).

30 Alexander Coolidge, "P&G Bids Beauty Care Adieu This Week," *Cincinnati.com,* September 24, 2016, http://www.cincinnati.com/story/money/2016/09/24/pg-bids-beauty-care-adieu-week/90408548/ (accessed February 17, 2017).

31 Haytham Sawalhy, "5 Reasons to Say Yes to Homesourcing with the Cloud Contact Center," *Orange Business Services,* May 8, 2014, http://www.orange-business.com/en/blogs/enterprising-business/crm/5-reasons-to-say-yes-to-homesourcing-with-the-cloud-contact-center (accessed February 17, 2017).

32 The information in this section is based on Hoffman and Bateson, *Services Marketing: Concepts, Strategies, and Cases* (Mason, OH: Cengage Learning, 2011): 57; Valarie A. Zeithaml, A. Parasuraman, and Leonard L. Berry, *Delivering Quality Service: Balancing Customer Perceptions and Expectations* (New York: Free Press, 1990).

33 K. Sivakumar, Mei Li, and Beibei Dong, "Service Quality: The Impact of Frequency, Timing, Proximity, and Sequence of Failures and Delights," *Journal of Marketing* 78, 1 (2014): 41–58.

34 J. Paul Peter and James H. Donnelly, *A Preface to Marketing Management* (Burr Ridge, IL: Irwin/McGraw-Hill, 2011).

35 "About Pinterest," https://help.pinterest.com/en/guide/all-about-pinterest (accessed February 17, 2017); Jess Collins, "Six Ways Businesses Should Be Using Pinterest to Drive Revenue," *The Guardian,* December 4, 2014, http://www.theguardian.com/media-network/2014/dec/04/business-pinterest-social-media-revenue (accessed February 17, 2017).

36 Michael Giebelhausen, Stacey G. Robinson, Nancy J. Sirianni, and Michael K. Brady, "Touch Versus Tech: When Technology Functions as a Barrier or a Benefit to Service Encounters," *Journal of Marketing* 78, 4 (2014): 113–124.

37 Michael D. Hartline and O. C. Ferrell, "Service Quality Implementation: The Effects of Organizational Socialization and Managerial Actions of Customer Contact Employee Behavior," *Marketing Science Institute Report,* no. 93–122 (Cambridge, MA: Marketing Science Institute, 1993).

38 Kare Anderson, "The Priceless Power of Socially Empowered Employees," *Forbes,* August 11, 2013, http://www.forbes.com/sites/kareanderson/2013/08/11/3000/ (accessed February 17, 2017).

39 Hoffman and Bateson, *Services Marketing: Concepts, Strategies, and Cases,* 69–70.

40 Hoffman and Bateson, *Services Marketing: Concepts, Strategies, and Cases,* 163.

41 Stephanie Clifford and Catherine Rampall, "Sometimes, We Want Prices to Fool Us," *The New York Times* April 13, 2013, http://www.nytimes.com/2013/04/14/business/for-penney-a-tough-lesson-in-shopper-psychology.html.

42 "Jets Raising Season Ticket Prices by Average of 4 Percent," *CBS New York,* March 1, 2016, http://newyork.cbslocal.com/2016/03/01/jets-raising-season-ticket-prices-metlife-stadium/ (accessed February 17, 2017).

43 Don Reisinger, "'A La Carte' TV Is Slowly Making Inroads," *Fortune,* March 15, 2016, http://fortune.com/2016/03/15/a-la-carte-tv/ (accessed February 17, 2017).

44 Danielle Muoio, "That Comcast Customer Service Rep Wasn't Going Rogue," *Bloomberg Businessweek,* July 18, 2014, http://www.businessweek.com/articles/2014-07-18/that-comcast-customer-service-rep-wasnt-going-rogue (accessed February 17, 2017); Thomas C. Frohlich, Evan Comen, and Samuel Stebbins, "Customer Service Hall of Shame," *24/7 Wall St.,* August 23, 2016, http://247wallst.com/special-report/2016/08/23/customer-service-hall-of-shame-4/6/ (accessed February 17, 2017).

45 Douglas J. Guth, "Restaurants Take a Chance on Tech-Based Food Delivery," *Crain's Cleveland Business,* March 5, 2016, http://www.crainscleveland.com/article/20160305/NEWS/160309902/restaurants-take-a-chance-on-tech-based-food-delivery (accessed February 17, 2017).

46 Ashley Rodriguez, "Chase Relaunches Website with Focus on Branded Content, Simplicity," *Advertising Age,* July 20, 2015, http://adage.com/article/cmo-strategy/chase-unveils-website-redesign-brings-branded-content-homepage/299542/ (accessed February 17, 2017).

47 Ellen Chisa, "Evolution of the Product Manager," *Communications of the ACM,* 57, 11 (2014) 48–52.

48 Based on information in Philippe Legrain, "Refugees Are a Great Investment," *Chicago Tribune,* February 3, 2017, http://www.chicagotribune.com/news/sns-wp-refugees-analysis-01747606-ea4f-11e6-bf6f-301b6b443624-20170203-story.html (accessed February 24, 2017); Robert Klara, "How Huy Fong Put Heat in a Bottle and Seared Sriracha into Our Lives," *Adweek,* January 25, 2016, http://www.adweek.com/news/advertising-branding/how-huy-fong-put-heat-bottle-and-seared-sriracha-our-lives-169131 (accessed February 17, 2017); David Pierson, "With No Trademark, Sriracha Name Is Showing Up Everywhere," *Los Angeles Times,* February 10, 2015, http://www.latimes.com/business/la-fi-sriracha-trademark-20150211-story.html (accessed February 17, 2017); Elizabeth Segran, "Hot Sauce, USA," *Fast Company,* November 2015, pp. 52–54; http://www.huyfong.com (accessed February 24, 2017).

FEATURE NOTES

[a]Based on information in Gregory Schmidt, "Challenges of Getting a Product Made in the U.S.A.," *New York Times*, July 27, 2016, https://www.nytimes.com/2016/07/28/business/smallbusiness/challenges-of-getting-a-product-made-in-the-usa.html (accessed February 23, 2017); Julio Ojeda-Zapata, "Local iPhone-case Maker: 'I Am About to Lose My Mind'," *Twin Cities Pioneer Press (Minnesota)*, September 9, 2016, http://www.twincities.com/2016/09/09/local-iphone-case-maker-im-about-to-lose-my-mind/ (accessed February 23, 2017); Julio Ojeda-Zapata, "Shop for Tech Gifts That Just Happen To Be Very, Very Minnesotan," *Twin Cities Pioneer Press (Minnesota)*, December 6, 2016, http://www.twincities.com/2016/12/06/shop-for-tech-gifts-that-just-happen-to-be-very-very-minnesotan/ (accessed February 23, 2017); www.padandquill.com.

[b]Based on information in "Starbucks Baristas Can't Keep Up with Mobile Orders," *Fortune*, January 27, 2017, http://fortune.com/2017/01/27/starbucks-mobile-orders-slowdown (accessed February 23, 2017); Sarah Perez, "Starbucks Unveils a Virtual Assistant That Takes Your Order via Messaging or Voice," *TechCrunch*, January 30, 2017, https://techcrunch.com/2017/01/30/starbucks-unveils-a-virtual-assistant-that-takes-your-order-via-messaging-or-voice/ (accessed February 23, 2017); Janet I. Tu, "Starbucks Rolls Out Mobile Pay App in China," *Seattle Times*, July 13, 2016, http://www.seattletimes.com/business/starbucks/starbucks-rolls-out-mobile-pay-app-in-china/ (accessed February 23, 2017).

Chapter 12

[1]Based on information in Robert Niles, "After Latest Ticket Price Increase, Is Disneyland Still a Good Value?" *Orange County Register,* February 16, 2017, http://www.ocregister.com/articles/disney-744224-disneyland-prices.html (accessed March 22, 2017); Brad Tuttle, "Disney Quietly Raises Theme Park Admission Prices Again," *Time,* February 13, 2017, http://time.com/money/4668833/disney-theme-park-prices-universal/ (accessed March 22, 2017); Brooks Barnes, "Disney Introduces Demand-Based Pricing at Theme Parks," *New York Times,* February 27, 2016, https://www.nytimes.com/2016/02/28/business/disney-introduces-demand-based-pricing-at-theme-parks.html?mcubz=1 (accessed March 22, 2017); Robert Niles, "Ticket Prices Are Going Up at Disneyland, Walt Disney World," *Theme Park Insider,* February 11, 2017, http://www.themeparkinsider.com/flume/201702/5446/ (accessed March 22, 2017).

[2]"Walmart's Price Matching Policy," Walmart, http://help.walmart.com/app/answers/detail/a_id/31/~/walmarts-price-matching-policy (accessed February 20, 2017).

[3]Phil Wahba, "Procter & Gamble Is Shaving the Price of Its Gillette Razors," *Fortune,* February 23, 2017, http://fortune.com/2017/02/23/procter-gamble-razor/ (accessed February 24, 2017).

[4]"The Profit Impact of Market Strategies (PIMS) Overview," The Strategic Planning Institute, http://pimsonline.com/about_pims_db.htm (accessed February 20, 2017).

[5]"20 Outrageously Priced Products, and How to Save on Them," *MSN.com,* September 11, 2015, http://www.msn.com/en-us/money/spendingandborrowing/20-outrageously-priced-products-and-how-to-save-on-them/ss-AAebfaz (accessed February 21, 2017).

[6]*Dictionary of Marketing Terms*, American Marketing Association, https://www.ama.org/resources/Pages/Dictionary.aspx (accessed February 21, 2017).

[7]Alexander Rusetski, Jonlee Andrews, and Daniel C. Smith, "Unjustified Prices: Environmental Drivers of Managers' Propensity to Overprice," *Journal of the Academy of Marketing Science* 42, 4 (2014): 452–469.

[8]Amy Livingston, "Is a Warehouse Store (Costco, Sam's Club, BJ's) Worth It? Costs, Pros, & Cons," *Money Crashers*, June 10, 2015, http://www.moneycrashers.com/warehouse-store-costco-samsclub-bjs-membership-worth-it/ (accessed February 21, 207).

[9]"Twins Single Game Tickets Go on Sale February 25," *KSFY,* February 21, 2017, http://www.ksfy.com/content/sports/Twins-Single-Game-Tickets-go-on-Sale-February-25--414404873.html (accessed March 27, 2017).

[10]"What Is Dynamic Pricing?" Uber, https://help.uber.com/h/34212e8b-d69a-4d8a-a923-095d3075b487 (accessed March 27, 2017).

[11]Bill Snyder, "Report Analyzes Amazon's Dynamic Pricing Strategy," *CIO,* January 16, 2015, http://www.cio.com/article/2870961/consumer-technology/report-analyzes-amazons-dynamic-pricing-strategy.html (accessed February 28, 2017).

[12]Jan Wieseke, Sascha Alavi, and Johannes Habel, "Willing to Pay More, Eager to Pay Less: The Role of Customer Loyalty in Price Negotiations," *Journal of Marketing* 78, 6 (2014): 17–37.

[13]Shu-Hao Chang and Kai-Yu Wang, "Investigating the Antecedents and Consequences of an Overall Store Price Image in Retail Settings," *Journal of Marketing* 22, 3 (2014): 299–314.

[14]Shai Danziger, Liat Hadar, and Vicki G. Morwitz, "Retailer Pricing Strategy and Consumer Choice Under Price Uncertainty," *Journal of Consumer Research* 41 (2014): 761–774.

[15]Sy Mukherjee, "Johnson & Johnson Is Dialing Down Crazy Drug Price Hikes," *Fortune,* February 27, 2017, http://fortune.com/2017/02/27/pharma-drug-price-hikes/ (accessed February 28, 2017).

[16]Based on information in "How Warby Parker Successfully Disrupted the Eyewear Monopoly," *CBS News,* February 8, 2017, http://www.cbsnews.com/news/warby-parker-cofounders-neil-blumenthal-dave-gilboa-affordable-eyewear-philanthropy/ (accessed March 22, 2017); Richard Benson, "Warby Parker Is Bringing Affordable Eyewear to the Developing World," *Wired UK,* June 1, 2016, http://www.wired.co.uk/article/warby-parker-glasses-profit-purpose; Farnoosh Torabi, "Warby

Parker: How to Limit Risk When You Try to Double Your Size," *CNBC,* May 3, 2016, http://www.cnbc.com/2016/05/03/warby-parker-how-to-limit-risk-when-you-try-to-double-your-size.html; Ginia Bellafante, "At Warby Parker, a Sense of Exclusion in a Low Price,"

New York Times, May 20, 2016, http://www.nytimes.com/2016/05/22/nyregion/at-warby-parker-a-sense-of-exclusion-in-a-low-price.html; Courtney Rubin, "Smile! Photo Booths Prove You're a Happy Customer," *New York Times,* October 6, 2015, http://www.nytimes

.com/2015/10/08/fashion/photo-booths-warby-parker-topshop.html; *Innovation Agents: Dave Gilboa, co-founder, Warby Parker,* http://www.youtube.com/watch?v=jJSKGUPou8w; www.warbyparker.com.

FEATURE NOTES

[a]Based on information in Rosemary Feitelberg, "Fashion Designers and Retailers Are Upgrading Their Plus-Size Offerings," *Los Angeles Times,* March 14, 2017, http://www.latimes.com/fashion/la-ig-wwd-plus-size-offerings-20170314-story.html (accessed March 22, 2017); Teresa Novellino, "Gwynnie Bee Founder Is Living the 'Project Runway: Fashion Startup' Dream," *New York Business Journal,* October 31, 2016, http://www.bizjournals.com/newyork/news/2016/10/31/gwynnie-bee-founder-

project-runway-fashion-startup.html (accessed March 22, 2017); "Gwynnie Bee," *Columbus CEO (OH),* October 10, 2016, http://www.columbusceo.com/content/stories/2016/10/columbus-region-gwynnie-bee.html (accessed March 22, 2017).

[b]Based on information in Sy Mukherjee, "Mylan's EpiPen Is Bleeding Market Share to Its Rivals," *Fortune,* March 6, 2017, http://fortune.com/2017/03/06/mylan-epipen-competitors-surge/ (accessed March 22,

2017); Jonathan D. Rockoff, "Rival to EpiPen Allergy Treatment to Return to Market," *Wall Street Journal,* January 19, 2017, https://www.wsj.com/articles/rival-to-epipen-allergy-treatment-to-return-to-market-1484855236 (accessed March 22, 2017); Anne Steele, "Mylan Launches Cheaper Generic EpiPen Alternative," *Wall Street Journal,* December 16, 2016, https://www.wsj.com/articles/mylan-launches-cheaper-generic-epipen-alternative-1481896300 (accessed March 22, 2017).

Chapter 13

[1]Based on information in Ebon Novy-Williams, "Sports Champion T-Shirts, Delivered Just After the Buzzer," *Bloomberg,* March 15, 2017, https://www.bloomberg.com/news/articles/2017-03-15/sports-champion-t-shirts-delivered-just-after-the-buzzer (accessed March 22, 2017); Danny Ecker, "Retailers Prepare for Late-Night Cubs Frenzy," *Chicago Business,* November 2, 2016, http://www.chicagobusiness.com/article/20161102/BLOGS04/161109958/retailers-prepare-for-late-night-cubs-frenzy (accessed March 22, 2017); Tamara Chuang, "Prepping for Super Bowl Victory Means Weighing Economics of Losing," *Denver Post,* February 4, 2016, http://www.denverpost.com/2016/02/04/prepping-for-super-bowl-victory-means-weighing-economics-of-losing (accessed March 22, 2017).

[2]Ricky W. Griffin, *Fundamentals of Management,* 8th ed. (Mason, OH: Cengage Learning, 2016): 18.

[3]Dan Gilmore, "State of the Logistics Union 2016," *Supply Chain Digest,* June 23, 2016, http://www.scdigest.com/firstthoughts/16-06-23.php?cid=10867 (accessed March 2, 2017).

[4]UltraShipTMS, http://www.ultrashiptms.com/about-ultra/ (accessed March 3, 2017).

[5]YAHOO Finance! "Industry Center—Industrial Equipment Wholesale—Applied Industrial Technologies, Inc. Company Profile," https://biz.yahoo.com/ic/10/10192.html (accessed March 3, 2017).

[6]Phil Wahba, "The Amazon Vs. Target Battle Is Moving to College Campuses," *Fortune,* October 12, 2016, http://fortune.com/2016/10/12/amazon-target-barnes-and-noble-college/ (accessed March 3, 2017).

[7]Leo Aspinwall, "The Marketing Characteristics of Goods," in *Four Marketing Theories* (Boulder, CO: University of Colorado Press, 1961): 27–32.

[8]"2016 Global Manufacturing Competitiveness Index," Deloitte, https://www2.deloitte.com/global/en/pages/manufacturing/articles/global-manufacturing-competitiveness-index.html (accessed March 3, 2017).

[9]Andrew Khouri and James F. Peltz, "Hanjin Bankruptcy Disrupts Shipping at L.A. and Long Beach Ports," *The Los Angeles Times,* September 1, 2016, http://www.latimes.com/business/la-fi-hanjin-bankruptcy

-20160901-snap-story.html (accessed March 3, 2017).

[10]Suppliers Partnership for the Environment, www.supplierspartnership.org/ (accessed March 3, 2017).

[11]IGA website, www.iga.com/about.aspx (accessed March 3, 2017).

[12]Wroe Alderson, *Dynamic Marketing Behavior* (Homewood, IL: Irwin, 1965), 239.

[13]Adam Rapp, Lauren Skinner Beitelspacher, Dhruv Grewal, and Douglas E. Hughes, "Understanding Social Media Effects across Seller, Retailer, and Consumer Interactions," *Journal of the Academy of Marketing Science* 41, 31 (2013): 547–566.

[14]M. Kelly Cunningham, "Reducing Channel Conflict," *Journal of Marketing Development & Competitiveness* 7, 1 (2013): 78–83.

[15]"Keeping It Under Your Hat," *The Economist,* April 16, 2016, http://www.economist.com/news/business-and-finance/21696911-tech-fashion-old-management-idea-back-vogue-vertical-integration-gets-new (accessed March 3, 2017); "Tesla Will Start Charging Money to Use Its Supercharging Stations," *The Los*

Angeles Times, November 7, 2016, http://www.latimes.com/business/autos/la-fi-hy-tesla-charging-20161107-story.html (accessed March 3, 2017).

[16]"Inditex Press Dossier," Inditex, https://www.inditex.com/documents/10279/225503/inditex_eng_low.pdf/198427c0-f4ce-4330-8209-2aed01fe8b53 (accessed March 3, 2017), p. 6.

[17]Clare O'Connor, "How Ace Hardware Turned Corner Stores into a \$4.7 Billion Co-op," *Forbes,* March 2, 2015, http://www.forbes.com/sites/clareoconnor/2015/02/11/how-ace-hardware-turned-corner-stores-into-a-4-7-billion-co-op/ (accessed March 3, 2017).

[18]"Sherwin Williams to Buy Valspar for \$11.3 Billion," *Fortune,* March 20, 2016, http://fortune.com/2016/03/20/sherwin-williams-valspar/ (accessed March 3, 2017).

[19]Karen M. Kroll, "3PLs Up the Ante," *Inbound Logistics,* January 2017, http://www.inboundlogistics.com/cms/article/3pls-up-the-ante/ (accessed March 6, 2017).

[20]Sarwant Singh, "Future of Logistics: Five Technologies that Will Self-Orchestrate the Supply Chain" *Forbes,* September 22, 2016, https://www.forbes.com/sites/sarwantsingh/2016/09/22/future-of-logistics-5-technologies-that-will-self-orchestrate-the-supply-chain/#965b60b1d2b1 (accessed March 6, 2017).

[21]Adam Lashinsky, "The Cutting Edge of Care," *Fortune,* March 9, 2015, http://fortune.com/2015/03/09/dollar-shave-club/ (accessed March 6, 2017); Darren Dahl, "Riding the Momentum Created by a Cheeky Video" *The New York Times,* April 11, 2013, http://www.nytimes.com/2013/04/11/business/smallbusiness/dollar-shave-club-from-viral-video-to-real-business.html (accessed May 6, 2017).

[22]Mark B. Solomon, "Hospital Chain Trinity Health, XPO Partner to Take Supply Chain in House," *DC Velocity,* March 9, 2016, http://www.dcvelocity.com/articles/20160309-hospital-chain-trinity-health-xpo-partner-to-take-supply-chain-in-house/ (accessed March 6, 2017).

[23]Christopher Bjork, "Zara Builds Its Business around RFID," *The Wall Street Journal,* September 16, 2014, http://www.wsj.com/articles/at-zara-fast-fashion-meets-smarter-inventory-1410884519?autologin=y (accessed March 6, 2017); "RFID Talking Blog," *RFID 24-7,* March 17, 2016, http://rfid24-7.com/2016/03/17/inditex-continues-rfid-rollout-to-2000-zara-locations/ (accessed March 6, 2017).

[24]Distribution Unlimited Inc., http://www.distributionunlimited.com/ (accessed March 6, 2017).

[25]Angel González, "Amazon's Robot Army Grows by 50 Percent," *The Seattle Times,* December 28, 2016, http://www.seattletimes.com/business/amazon/amazons-robot-army-grows/?utm_source=twitter&utm_medium=social&utm_campaign=article_left_1.1 (accessed March 6, 2017); Marcus Wohlsen, "A Rare Peek Inside Amazon's Massive-Wish Fulfilling Machine," *Wired,* June 16, 2014, http://www.wired.com/2014/06/inside-amazon-warehouse/ (accessed March 6, 2017).

[26]"Supply Chain Graphic of the Week; US Logistics Cost Breakdown 2015," *Supply Chain Digest,* June 30, 2016, http://www.scdigest.com/ontarget/16-06-30-2.php?cid=10904 (accessed March 6, 2017).

[27]David Hummels and Georg Schaur, "Time as a Trade Barrier," *National Bureau of Economic Research,* January 2012, No. 17758, http://papers.nber.org/papers/w17758#fromrss (accessed March 6, 2017).

[28]"About Us," Expeditors International, https://www.expeditors.com/about-us/company (accessed March 6, 2017).

[29]Douglas Yu, "Taza Reduces Dark Chocolate Bitterness Through Stone Grinding Process," *Confectionery News,* March 6, 2017, http://www.confectionerynews.com/Manufacturers/Taza-reduces-dark-chocolate-bitterness-through-stone-grinding-process (accessed March 22, 2017); Alina Dizik, "Stone-Ground Chocolate Gets Hate Mail and Lots of Love," *Wall Street Journal,* January 13, 2015, http://www.wsj.com/articles/stone-ground-chocolate-gets-hate-mail-and-lots-of-love-1421191491 (accessed March 6, 2017); "Taza Chocolate and Drink Craft Beer Prove That Beer and Chocolate Make a Perfect Pair," *Boston Globe,* February 13, 2012, http://www.boston.com/lifestyle/blogs/thenextgreatgeneration/2012/02/taza_chocolate_and_drink_craft.html (accessed March 6, 2017); Rachel Leah Blumenthal, "A Tour of the Taza Chocolate Factory," *CBS Local News (Boston),* October 26, 2011, http://boston.cbslocal.com/2011/10/26/a-tour-of-the-taza-chocolate-factory/ (accessed March 6, 2017); Ariel Shearer, "Review: Taza Chocolate," *Boston Phoenix,* October 31, 2011, http://thephoenix.com/Boston/food/128984-review-taza-chocolate/ (accessed March 6, 2017); Courtney Holland, "Sweet Batches of Local Flavor," *Boston Globe,* August 18, 2010, http://www.boston.com/lifestyle/food/articles/2010/08/18/batch_ice_cream_is_big_on_local_flavor/ (accessed February 25, 2015); Kerry J. Byrne, "Festival of Food Trucks," *Boston Herald,* August 6, 2010, http://www.bostonherald.com/entertainment/food_dining/dining_news/2010/08/festival_food_trucks (accessed February 25, 2015); Stephanie Larason, "Taza Chocolate to Showcase Three New Amaze Bars at 2016 Summer Fancy Food Show," Specialty Food Association, June 6, 2016, https://www.specialtyfood.com/news/article/taza-chocolate-to-showcase-three-new-amaze-bars-at-2016-summer-fancy-food-show-booth-4408-june-26-28-2016-123612/ (accessed March 6, 2017); Interviews with company staff and video, "Taza Cultivates Channel Relationships with Chocolate"; Taza company website, www.tazachocolate.com (accessed March 6, 2017).

FEATURE NOTES

[a]Based on information in Kurt Schlosser, "REI Sees 36 percent Spike in Online Traffic as Millions Decided to #OptOutside on Black Friday," *Geek Wire,* December 5, 2016, http://www.geekwire.com/2016/rei-sees-36-percent-spike-online-traffic-millions-decided-optoutside-black-friday/ (accessed March 22, 2017); John Kell, "Why REI Is Opting Out of Black Friday Again This Year," *Fortune,* October 24, 2016, http://fortune.com/2016/10/24/rei-closing-black-friday-again/ (accessed March 22, 2017); Patrick Coffee, "How One Brave Idea Drove REI's Award-Winning #OptOutside Campaign," *Adweek,* June 28, 2016, http://www.adweek.

com/brand-marketing/how-one-brave-idea-drove-reis-award-winning-optoutside-campaign-172273/ (accessed March 22, 2017).

ᵇBased on information in Keith Nelson Jr., "Flip, a Mobile Sneaker Resale App, Will Pay You for Sneakers No One Wants," *Digital Trends,* March 8, 2016, http://www.digitaltrends.com/mobile/flip-sneaker

-resale-marketplace/ (accessed March 22, 2017); Abigail Tracy, "Flip Wants to Make It Yeezy for Sneakerheads to Buy and Sell Collectible Kicks," *Forbes,* March 4, 2016, https://www.forbes.com/sites/abigailtracy/2016/03/04/sneakerheads-ebay-flip-stockx-air-jordans-nike-secondary-market-sneakers-kanye-west-yeezy-adidas/#4971013162b0

(accessed March 22, 2017); Malika Renee Butss, "Flip Is the Sneaker Retailing Application for the Snapchat Generation," *Trend Hunter,* March 8, 2016, www.trendhunter.com/trends/sneakerselling-app (accessed March 22, 2017).

Chapter 14

¹Based on information in Hannah Madans, "As Part of $7 Billion Makeover, Troubled Target Remodeling Orange Store, Opening 2 New Locations," *Orange County Register,* February 28, 2017, http://www.ocregister.com/articles/target-745252-stores-orange.html (accessed March 23, 2017); Phil Wahba, "Target's New Manhattan Location Is a Big Test for Its Smaller-Store Strategy," *Fortune,* October 4, 2016, http://fortune.com/2016/10/05/target-manhattan-smaller-store (accessed March 23, 2017); Jonathan Berr, "Target Has High Hopes for Its New Tiny Stores," *CBS News,* November 18, 2016, http://www.cbsnews.com/news/target-has-high-hopes-for-its-new-tiny-stores/ (accessed March 23, 2017).

²"Retail's Impact," National Retail Foundation, https://nrf.com/sites/default/files/Documents/The%20Economic%20Impact%20of%20the%20US%20Retail%20Industry%20REV.pdf (accessed March 7, 2017).

³Vicky Huang, "Tesla to Become Latest American Company to Target India's Monstrous Growth," *The Street,* February 11, 2017, https://www.thestreet.com/story/13994605/1/tesla-to-become-the-latest-american-company-to-target-india-s-monstrous-growth.html (accessed March 7, 2017).

⁴"2017 Top 250 Global Powers of Retailing," National Retail Federation, https://nrf.com/news/2017-top-250-global-powers-of-retailing (accessed March 7, 2017).

⁵"About NACS," The Association for Convenience and Petroleum Retailing, http://www.nacsonline.com/NACS/About_NACS/Pages/default.aspx (accessed March 6, 2017).

⁶"Company Facts," Sam's Club, http://corporate.samsclub.com/our-story/company-facts (accessed March 7, 2017); "Why Become a Member," Costco, http://www

.costco.com/membership-information.html (accessed March 7, 2017).

⁷James F. Peltz and Samantha Masunaga, "Why Sporting Goods Retailers Are Fumbling," *Los Angeles Times,* April 19, 2016, http://www.latimes.com/business/la-fi-sport-chalet-problems-20160419-story.html (accessed March 7, 2017).

⁸Hayley Peterson, "Macy's Shoppers Developed a Habit During the Recession—and Its Haunting the Brand to This Day," *Business Insider,* November 15, 2016, http://www.businessinsider.com/macys-is-adding-backstage-outlets-to-its-stores-2016-11 (accessed March 7, 2017).

⁹Mall of America, www.mallofamerica.com (accessed March 8, 2017).

¹⁰"ICSC Shopping Center Definitions," International Council of Shopping Centers, http://www.icsc.org/uploads/research/general/US_CENTER_CLASSIFICATION.pdf (accessed March 8, 2017).

¹¹Jeanne W. Ross, Cynthia M. Beath, and Ina Sebastian, "Why Nordstrom's Digital Strategy Works (and Yours Probably Doesn't)," *Harvard Business Review,* January 14, 2015, https://hbr.org/2015/01/why-nordstroms-digital-strategy-works-and-yours-probably-doesnt (accessed March 8, 2017).

¹²Olga Kharif, "After Retail Stumble, Beacons Shine from Banks to Sports Arenas," *Bloomberg,* December 5, 2016, https://www.bloomberg.com/news/articles/2016-12-05/after-retail-stumble-beacons-shine-from-banks-to-sports-arenas (accessed March 8, 2017).

¹³Matthew Townsend, "'Smart Mirrors' Come to the Dressing Room," *Bloomberg Businessweek,* February 16, 2017, https://www.bloomberg.com/news/articles/2017-02-16

/-smart-mirrors-come-to-the-fitting-room (accessed March 8, 2017).

¹⁴Sara Halzack, "5 New Technologies that may Change How You Shop," *The Washington Post,* January 14, 2015, http://www.washingtonpost.com/news/business/wp/2015/01/14/5-new-technologies-that-may-change-how-you-shop/ (accessed March 8, 2017).

¹⁵Elizabeth Weise, "How Amazon's Line-less Grocery Service Might Really Work," *USA Today,* December 6, 2016, http://www.usatoday.com/story/tech/news/2016/12/06/amazon-go-surveillance-cameras-shopping-grocery-supermarket/95055200/ (accessed March 8, 2017).

¹⁶Rollo A. S. Grayson and Lisa S. McNeill, "Using Atmospheric Elements in Service Retailing: Understanding the Bar Environment," *Journal of Services Marketing* 23, 7 (2009): 517–527.

¹⁷Andreas Herrmann, Manja Zidansek, David E. Sprott, and Eric R. Spangenberg, "The Power of Simplicity: Processing Fluency and the Effects of Olfactory Cues on Retail Sales," *Journal of Retailing* 89, 1 (2013): 30–43.

¹⁸Charles Dennis, J. Brakus, and Eleftherios Alamanos, "The Wallpaper Matters: Digital Signage as Customer-Experience Provider at the Harrods (London, U.K.) Department Store," *Journal of Marketing Management* 29, 3/4 (2013): 338–355.

¹⁹The Category Management Association, http://catman.global/ (accessed March 9, 2017).

²⁰Ashley Littles, "The Benefits of Direct Marketing," Humboldt Merchant Services, May 13, 2016 http://www.hbms.com/resources/the-benefits-of-direct-marketing (accessed March 9, 2017).

[21]Stefany Zaroban, "US e-Commerce Sales Grow 15.6% in 2016," *Internet Retailer,* February 17, 2017, https://www.digitalcommerce360.com/2017/02/17/us-e-commerce-sales-grow-156-2016/ (accessed March 9, 2017).

[22]Khadeeja Safdar, "Why Wayfair Thinks It Can Be the Amazon of Furniture," *The Wall Street Journal,* October 2, 2016, http://www.wsj.com/articles/why-wayfair-inc-thinks-it-can-be-the-amazon-of-furniture-1475460361 Wall Street Journal, (accessed March 9, 2017).

[23]Do Not Call, www.donotcall.gov (accessed March 9, 2017); Natalie Olivo, "FTC Reaches Settlement with Alleged Illegal Telemarketers," *Law360,* November 2, 2016, https://www.law360.com/articles/858243/ftc-reaches-settlement-with-alleged-illegal-telemarketers (accessed March 9, 2017).

[24]"2016 DSN Global 100 List," *Direct Selling News*, June 1, 2016, http://directsellingnews.com/index.php/view/2016_dsn_global_100_list#.WMLYhfnsKUk (accessed March 10, 2017).

[25]"Industry Fact Sheets," Direct Selling Association, http://www.dsa.org/benefits/research/factsheets (accessed March 10, 2017); "Global Statistics," World Federation of Direct Selling Associations, http://wfdsa.org/global-statistics/ (accessed March 10, 2017).

[26]"25 Vending Machines You Won't Believe Exist," *MSN*, July 28, 2016, http://www.msn.com/en-in/money/gadgets/25-vending-machines-you-wont-believe-exist/ss-AA7zV4r (accessed March 10, 2017); Seth Fiegerman, "Snapchat Unveils Strange Vending Machine for Its Sunglasses," *CNN Money*, November 10, 2016, http://money.cnn.com/2016/11/10/technology/snapchat-vending-machine/ (accessed March 10, 2017).

[27]"2017 Franchise Business Economic Outlook," International Franchise Association Education Foundation, January 2017, http://franchise.org/sites/default/files/Franchise_Business_Outlook_Jan_2017.pdf (accessed March 10, 2017).

[28]"Statistics of U.S. Business Number of Firms, Number of Establishments, Employment, Annual Payroll, and Estimated Receipts by Enterprise Employment Size for the United States, All Industries," Statistics of U.S. Businesses (SUSB) Main, Bureau of the Census, September 29, 2016 release, https://www2.census.gov/programs-surveys/susb/tables/2014/us_6digitnaics_2014.xlsx (accessed March 10, 2017).

[29]The National Association of Wholesaler-Distributors, http://www.naw.org/busservices/bindex.php (accessed March 10, 2017).

[30]Macdonalds Consolidated, http://macdonaldsconsolidated.ca/ (accessed March 10, 2017).

[31]"About Us," AmerisourceBergen, http://www.amerisourcebergen.com/abcnew/about.aspx (accessed March 10, 2017).

[32]Nina Godlewski, "Sephora App Update Lets Users Virtually Try on Makeup," *International Business Times*, March 16, 2017, http://www.ibtimes.com/sephora-app-update-lets-users-virtually-try-makeup-2510021 (accessed March 23, 2017); Jason Trout, "5 Excellent Examples of Omnichannel Retailing Done Right," *Multichannel Merchant,* February 2, 2017, http://multichannelmerchant.com/must-reads/5-excellent-examples-omnichannel-retailing-done-right-02022017/ (accessed March 23, 2017); Barbara Thau, "Inside Three Retail Innovation Labs," *Retail Dive,* January 28, 2016, Retail Dive, http://www.retaildive.com/news/inside-three-retail-innovation-labs/411810/ (accessed March 23, 2017); LVMH website (https://www.lvmh.com/houses/selective-retailing/sephora/).

FEATURE NOTES

[a]Based on information in Korri Kezar, "JCPenney has five initiatives to increase in-store sales, profits," *Dallas Business Journal,* February 27, 2017, http://www.bizjournals.com/dallas/news/2017/02/27/j-c-penney-has-five-initiatives-to-increase-in.html (accessed March 23, 2017); Tim Denman and Jamie Grill-Goodman, "5 Retailers That Matter," *Retail Info Systems,* March 22, 2017, https://risnews.com/5-retailers-that-matter (accessed March 23, 2017); Hannah Madans, "Store-within-a-Store: Chains Co-opt Small Retailers to Lure More Customers," *Orange County Register,* December 27, 2016, http://www.ocregister.com/articles/store-739409-stores-bloomingdale.html.

[b]Based on information in Michelle Fox, "After Betting Big on Digital, Domino's Pizza Is Now Eyeing Voice Technology," *CNBC,* March 16, 2017, http://www.cnbc.com/2017/03/16/after-betting-big-on-digital-dominos-pizza-is-now-eyeing-voice-technology.html (accessed March 23, 2017); Susan Berfield, "Domino's Atoned for Its Sins Against Pizza and Built a $9 Billion Empire," *Bloomberg Businessweek,* March 15, 2017, https://www.bloomberg.com/features/2017-dominos-pizza-empire/ (accessed March 23, 2017); Ileana Najarro, "Domino's Opens Facebook Ordering to All Customers in Time for Super Bowl," *Houston Chronicle,* February 1, 2017, http://www.chron.com/business/bizfeed/article/All-Houston-Domino-s-customers-can-now-order-10900010.php (accessed March 23, 2017).

Chapter 15

[1]"Outsell and Agency Partner Saatchi & Saatchi's Integrated Marketing Campaign for Toyota North America Receives Top Industry Accolades," Yahoo! Finance, April 13, 2016, http://finance.yahoo.com/news/outsell-agency-partner-saatchi-saatchis-130000225.html (accessed December 24, 2016); "Campaign: 2015 Toyota Camry Launch," Outsell, http://www.outsellauto.com/files/saatchi/CamryAward2015/ (accessed December 24, 2016); "IAC Award," Internet Advertising Competition, http://www.iacaward.org/iac/winner/16084/outsell-and-saatchi--saatchi-wins-2016-webaward-for-2015-toyota-camry-launch.html (accessed December 26, 2016).

2Patrick Coffee, "Star Wars' Adam Driver Lands Lead Role in Snickers' Super Bowl LI Ad," January 11, 2017, http://www.adweek.com/news/advertising-branding/star-wars-adam-driver-lands-lead-role-snickers-super-bowl-li-ad-175504 (accessed January 27, 2017); James Miller, "Case Study: How Fame Made Snickers' 'You're Not You When You're Hungry' Campaign a Success," October 26, 2016, http://www.campaignlive.co.uk/article/case-study-fame-made-snickers-youre-not-when-youre-hungry-campaign-success/1410807 (accessed January 26, 2017).

3Jerrid Grimm, "The 10 Best Branded Content Partnerships of 2016," *Advertising Age*, http://adage.com/article/agency-viewpoint/10-branded-content-partnerships-2016/307284/ (accessed January 26, 2017).

4Chris Leone, "How Much Should You Budget for Marketing in 2017?" *Web Strategies*, October 20, 2016, http://www.webstrategiesinc.com/blog/how-much-budget-for-online-marketing-in-2017 (accessed January 26, 2017).

5George Slefo, "40% of Marketers Say They Plan Facebook Audits," *Advertising Age*, January 19, 2017, http://adage.com/article/digital/marketers-facebook-audits-digital-ad-trust/307539/ (accessed January 26, 2017).

6Pierre Berthon, Karen Robson, and Leyland Pitt, "The Theory and Practice of Advertising: Counting the Cost to the Consumer," *Journal of Advertising Research* 53, 3 (2013): 244–246.

7"How Americans Get Their News," *American Press Institute*, March 17, 2014, http://www.americanpressinstitute.org/publications/reports/survey-research/how-americans-get-news/ (accessed December 18, 2014).

8E.J. Schultz, Jack Neff, Jessica Wohl, Adrianne Pasquarelli, "Lowdown: First Reviews Are in on Bud Light's New Campaign," *Advertising Age*, January 25, 2017, http://adage.com/article/cmo-strategy/lowdown-reviews-bud-light-s-campaign/307693/ (accessed January 26, 2017).

9Lindsay Friedman, "The 12 Worst Social-Media Fails of 2016," *Entrepreneur*, September 22, 2016, https://www.entrepreneur.com/slideshow/272286 (accessed January 31, 2017).

10Time Media Kit, *Advertising Rates,* http://www.timemediakit.com/2016-advertising-rates/ (accessed February 12, 2017).

11Joann Peck and Jennifer Wiggins, "It Just Feels Good: Customers' Affective Response to Touch and Its Influence in Persuasion," *Journal of Marketing* 70(October 2006): 56–69.

12Thomas L. Powers, J'Aime C. Jennings, and Thomas E. DeCarlo, "An Assessment of Needed Sales Management Skills," *Journal of Personal Selling & Sales Management* 34, 3 (Summer 2014): 206–222.

13Ryan Burleson, "Vinyl Record Manufacturer in Nashville Is Said to Be Expanding," *New York Times,* December 25, 2016, https://www.nytimes.com/2016/12/25/arts/music/vinyl-record-manufacturer-in-nashville-is-said-to-be-expanding.html?_r=0 (accessed February 12, 2017).

14Pampered Chef YouTube Channel, http://www.youtube.com/user/PamperedChefVideo (accessed January 6, 2015).

15Joel Comm, "What GM's Live Video Says about Content Marketing Strategy In 2017," *Forbes*, February 14, 2017, http://www.forbes.com/sites/forbescoaches-council/2017/02/14/what-gms-live-video-says-about-content-marketing-strategy-in-2017/#24e70273cdac (accessed February 15, 2017).

16Meghan Friedman, "Here's What's Inside the $30,000 Swag Bags at this Year's Grammys," *Harper's Bazaar*, February 7, 2017, http://www.harpersbazaar.com/culture/art-books-music/news/a20473/grammys-gift-bag-2017-distinctive-assets/ (accessed February 12, 2017).

17Mallory Schlossberg, "Brands are Playing a 'Deadly Game of Russian Roulette' with Celebrities That's Costing Them Millions," *Business Insider,* August 27, 2016, http://www.businessinsider.com/celebrity-endorsements-can-be-dangerous-2016-8 (accessed January 12, 2017).

18Polly Mosendz, "Penny-Pinching Millennials Are Keeping the Coupon Alive," *Bloomberg*, June 16, 2016, https://www.bloomberg.com/features/2016-millennials-coupons/ (accessed February 12, 2017).

19"The Majority of Children Live with Two Parents, Census Bureau Reports," United States Census Bureau, November 17, 2016, http://www.census.gov/newsroom/press-releases/2016/cb16-192.html (accessed February 19, 2017).

20"Restrictions of Food Marketing and Advertisements Aimed at Children," *Food Directions LLC.*, February 6, 2017, http://fooddirection-sllc.com/2017/02/06/restrictions-of-food-marketing-and-advertisements-aimed-at-children/ (accessed February 17, 2017).

21Pratibha A. Dabholkar, "Factors Influencing Consumer Choice of a 'Rating Web Site': An Experimental Investigation of an Online Interactive Decision Aid," *Journal of Marketing Theory and Practice* 14 (Fall 2006): 259–273.

22Ramona Sukhraj, "How Dollar Shave Club Grew from Viral Video to $1 Billion Acquisition," *Impact Branding & Design*, July 21, 2016, https://www.impactbnd.com/blog/how-dollar-shave-club-grew-from-just-a-viral-video-to-a-615m-valuation-brand (accessed February 19, 2017).

23Tomás Bayón, "The Chain from Customer Satisfaction via Word-of-Mouth Referrals to New Customer Acquisition," *Journal of the Academy of Marketing Science* 35, 2 (June 2007): 233–249.

24Rodolfo Vázquez-Casielles, Leticia Suárez-Álvarez, and Ana-Belén Del Río-Lanza, "The Word of Mouth Dynamic: How Positive (and Negative) WOM Drives Purchase Probability: An Analysis of Interpersonal and Non-Interpersonal Factors," *Journal of Advertising Research* 53, 1 (2013): 43–60.

25Seung-A Annie Jin and Joe Phua, "Following Celebrities' Tweets About Brands: The Impact of Twitter-Based Electronic Word-of-Mouth on Consumers' Source Credibility Perception, Buying Intention, and Social Identification with Celebrities," *Journal of Advertising* 43, 2 (2014): 181–195.

26Dominic Powell, "The Top 10 Most Viral Advertisements of 2016 Revealed," December 12, 2016, http://www.smartcompany.com.au/marketing/advertising/79989-top-10-viral-advertisements-2016-revealed/ (accessed February 17, 2017).

27Lia Zarantonello and Bernd H. Schmitt, "The Impact of Event Marketing on Brand Equity: The Mediating Roles of Brand Experience and Brand Attitude," *International Journal of Advertising* 32, 2 (2013): 255–280.

28Simon Zekaria, "Apple's Crowds Draw a Crowd of Guerilla Marketers," *The Wall Street Journal,* September 19, 2014, http://blogs.wsj.com/digits/2014/09/19/apples-crowds-draw

-a-crowd-of-guerrilla-marketers/ (accessed January 9, 2015).

[29]"Blendtec Celebrates 10 Years of Viral Marketing Success," *Nasdaq GlobeNewswire*, November 7, 2016, https://globenewswire.com/news-release/2016/11/07/887174/10165944/en/Blendtec-Celebrates-10-Years-of-Viral-Marketing-Success.html (accessed February 17, 2017).

[30]Christian Schulze, Lisa Schöler, and Bernd Skiera, "Not All Fun and Games: Viral Marketing for Utilitarian Products," *Journal of Marketing* 78, 1 (January 2014): 1–19.

[31]Suzanne Vranica, "The Best and Worst of Marketing in 2014," *The Wall Street Journal,* December 29, 2014, B1, B4.

[32]Alan Wolk, "Time is Running Out for the 30-Second TV Commercial," *The Guardian,*

June 22, 2015, https://www.theguardian.com/media-network/2015/jun/22/30-second-commercial-advertising-outdated (accessed February 19, 2016).

[33]Valeria Noguti and Cristel Antonia Russell, "Normative Influences on Product Placement Effects: Alcohol Brands in Television Series and the Influence of Presumed Influence," *Journal of Advertising* 43, 1 (2014): 2014, 46–62.

[34]"Global Product Placement Spending 2012–2019," https://www.statista.com/statistics/261454/global-product-placement-spending/ (accessed February 17, 2017).

[35]Lilly Vitorovich, "Product Placement to Be Allowed in U.K. TV Programs," *Wall Street Journal*, December 21, 2010, B5.

[36]Karine M. Charry, "Product Placement and the Promotion of Healthy Food to Preadolescents—When Popular TV Series Make Carrots Look Cool," *International Journal of Advertising* 33, 3 (2014): 599–616.

[37]Pepe's Pizzeria website, http://www.pepespizzeria.com/ (accessed January 9, 2015); Kara Baskin, "The Fireplace to Stay in Brookline Home; Pepe's Pizzeria Won't Move In," *Boston Globe,* September 18, 2014, http://www.bostonglobe.com/lifestyle/food-dining/2014/09/18/the-fireplace-stay-brookline-home-pepe-pizzeria-won-move/Bz2r5AdCR9jI1dNMH3eVkM/story.html (accessed January 9, 2015); "Good Neighbor Night: Avon Walk for Breast Cancer," http://pepespizzeria.com/pizza/category/pepes-pizza-good-neighbor-nights/ (accessed January 9, 2015).

FEATURE NOTES

[a]Serena Ng and Paul Ziobro, "Razor Sales Move Online, Away From Gillette," *The Wall Street Journal*, June 23, 2015, B1; "How YouTube Crashed Our Website—And Why We Loved It," *Inc.*, July/August 2015, 98–100; Adam Lashinsky, "The Cutting Edge of Care," *Fortune*, March 15, 2015, 61–62; Dollar Shave Club website, http://www.dollarshaveclub.com/ (accessed July 14, 2015); Paresh Dave, "Up to 2 million members, Dollar Shave Club worth $615 million, investors say," *Los Angeles Times*, June 22, 2015, http://www.latimes.com/business/technology/la-fi-tn-dollar-shave-club-investment-20150622-story.html (accessed July 14, 2015); "Meet the 2015 CNBC Disruptor 50 Companies," *CNBC*, May 12, 2015, http://www.cnbc.com/2015/05/12/dollar-shave-club-disruptor-50.html (accessed July 14, 2015); Dollar Shave Club, "DollarShaveClub.com – Our Blades Are F***ing Great," YouTube, March 6, 2012, https://www.youtube.com/watch?v=ZUG9qYTJMsI (accessed July 14, 2015); Dollar Shave Club, "Let's Talk About #2," YouTube, June 4, 2013, https://www.youtube.com/watch?v=3FOae1V1-Xg (accessed July 14, 2015);

"Pay Up – TV Commercial," YouTube, November 10, 2014, https://www.youtube.com/watch?v=5Ds-82SYmLs&feature=iv&src_vid=JbsJPO-ZreM&annotation_id=annotation_2355018053 (accessed July 14, 2015); Dollar Shave Club, "Tranq Dart – TV Commercial," YouTube, November 10, 2014, https://www.youtube.com/watch?v=PWPkZH_UicU (accessed July 14, 2015); Mike Isaac and Michael J. de la Merced, "Dollar Shave Club Sells to Unilever for $1 Billion," *The New York Times*, July 20, 2016, http://www.nytimes.com/2016/07/20/business/dealbook/unilever-dollar-shave-club.html?_r=0 (accessed November 12, 2016); Sean Czarnecki, "7 Questions for Dollar Shave Club's Kristina Levsky," *PR Week*, August 22, 2016, http://www.prweek.com/article/1406314/7-questions-dollar-shave-clubs-kristina-levsky (accessed December 26, 2016).

[b]Ronald Grover, "I Can Make Your Product a Star," *Businessweek*, July 13–20, 2009, pp. 68–69; Propaganda GEM website, http://www.propagandagem.com/ (accessed December 23, 2016); Fast Company, "Why You Bought Those

Reese's Pieces: A History of Product Placement in Movies," YouTube, March 19, 2015, https://www.youtube.com/watch?v=tGOeM4nB1Ys (accessed December 23, 2016); Abe Sauer, "China Product Placement: Q&A with Ruben Igielko-Herrlich, Propaganda GEM," *Brand Channel*, May 19, 2016, https://www.youtube.com/watch?v=tGOeM4nB1Ys (accessed December 23, 2016); Laurent Muzellec, "James Bond, Dunder Mifflin, and the Future of Product Placement," *Harvard Business Review*, June 23, 2016, https://hbr.org/2016/06/james-bond-dunder-mifflin-and-the-future-of-product-placement (accessed December 23, 2016); The Kluger Agency website, http://www.klugeragency.com/ (accessed December 23, 2016); Will Freeman, "Six of the best product placements in video games," *The Guardian*, July 13, 2014, https://www.theguardian.com/technology/2014/jul/03/six-of-the-best-product-placement-video-games (accessed December 23, 2016).

Chapter 16

[1]David Court, Dave Elzinga, Susan Mulder, and Ole Jørgen Vetvik, "The Consumer Decision Journey," *McKinsey Quarterly*, June 2009,

http://www.mckinsey.com/business-functions/marketing-and-sales/our-insights/the-consumer-decision-journey (accessed

December 29, 2016); CBS Sunday Morning, "TV Commercial Spokespeople Tell All," YouTube, April 10, 2016, https://www.youtube

.com/watch?v=Zx_2vm7NV8A (accessed December 29, 2016); Judith A. Garretson and Ronald W. Niedrich, "Spokes-Characters: Creating Character Trust and Positive Brand Attitudes," *Journal of Advertising* 33(2), 2004: 25–36; Steven Perlberg, "People Are Oddly Mesmerized by the 'Trivago Guy'—and Now It's Helping Their Brand," *The Wall Street Journal*, August 11, 2014, http://blogs.wsj.com/cmo/2014/08/11/trivago-guy-ads/ (accessed December 29, 2016); Felix Gillette, "Branded for Life," *Bloomberg*, September 27, 2012, https://www.bloomberg.com/news/articles/2012-09-27/branded-for-life (accessed December 29, 2016); Dennis Schaal, "Did the Trivago Guy Just Lose His TV Gig?" *Skift*, April 19, 2017, https://skift.com/2017/04/19/did-the-trivago-guy-just-lose-his-tv-gig/ (accessed May 23, 2017).

[2]Douglas E. Hughes, "This Ad's for You: The Indirect Effect of Advertising Perceptions on Salesperson Effort and Performance," *Journal of the Academy of Marketing Science* 41, 1 (2013): 1–18.

[3]Ashton Goodell, "Shock Value in Anti-Smoking Ads Effective, Teens Say," *Fox 13 News*, February 4, 2014, http://fox13now.com/2014/02/04/shock-value-in-anti-smoking-ads-effective-teens-say/ (accessed February 25, 2017).

[4]Micael Dahlén, Helge Thorbjørnsen, and Henrik Sjödin, "A Taste of 'Nextopia'," *Journal of Advertising* 40, 1 (Winter 2011): 33–44.

[5]Fred K. Beard, "Practitioner Views of Comparative Advertising: How Practices Have Changed in Two Decades," *Journal of Advertising Research* 53, 3 (2013): 313–323.

[6]E.J. Schultz, "Yoplait Calls Out Chobani by Name in Greek Yogurt Taste Test Campaign," *Advertising Age,* January 19, 2014, http://adage.com/article/news/yoplait-calls-chobani-greek-taste-test-ads/291188/ (accessed November 10, 2014).

[7]Ben Plomion, "Three Predictions For Native Advertising In 2017," *Forbes*, January 10, 2017, https://www.forbes.com/sites/forbescommunicationscouncil/2017/01/10/three-predictions-for-native-advertising-in-2017/#7fb5c1e6677e (accessed February 25, 2017).

[8]Joe Lazauskas, "3 Ways Brands Can Make Native Advertising More Effective in 2017,"

Contently, January 4, 2017, https://contently.com/strategist/2017/01/04/better-native-advertising-2017/ (accessed February 25, 2017).

[9]Marlynn Wei, "New Survey Reveals the Rapid Rise of Yoga and Why Some People Still Haven't Tried It," *Harvard Health Publications*, June 15, 2016, http://www.health.harvard.edu/blog/new-survey-reveals-the-rapid-rise-of-yoga-and-why-some-people-still-havent-tried-it-201603079179 (accessed February 25, 2017).

[10]Tae Hyun Baek and Mariko Morimoto, "Stay Away from Me," *Journal of Advertising* 41, 1 (Spring 2012): 59–76.

[11]Sami Main, "Hulu Users Reveal the Weirdest Places They've Watched TV," *Adweek*, February 24, 2017, http://www.adweek.com/tv-video/hulu-users-reveal-the-weirdest-places-theyve-watched-tv/ (accessed February 25, 2017).

[12]Daniel A. Sheinin, Sajeev Varki, and Christy Ashley, "The Differential Effect of Ad Novelty and Message Usefulness on Brand Judgments," *Journal of Advertising* 40, 3 (Fall 2011): 5–17.

[13]Tim Nudd, "Netflix's Ads for Santa Clarita Diet are Good Gross Fun, but One Went a Little Too Far," February 22, 2017, http://www.adweek.com/creativity/netflixs-ads-for-santa-clarita-diet-are-good-gross-fun-but-one-went-a-little-too-far/ (accessed February 25, 2017).

[14]"Leading TV Advertisers in the United States from February 17 to 23, 2017, by Weekly Advertising Spending (in million U.S. dollars)," Statista, https://www.statista.com/statistics/384835/estimated-tv-ad-spend-us-companies/ (accessed February 26, 2017).

[15]Douglas West, John B. Ford, and Paul W. Farris, "How Corporate Cultures Drive Advertising and Promotion Budgets: Best Practices Combine Heuristics and Algorithmic Tools," *Journal of Advertising Research* (June 2014): 149–162.

[16]Amy Mitchell, "How Bad Data Can Blindside Your Marketing Analytics," *Adweek*, http://www.adweek.com/sponsored/where-data-projects-fall-short/ (accessed February 26, 2017).

[17]"Digital Ad Spending to Surpass TV Next Year," *eMarketer*, March 8, 2016, https://www.emarketer.com/Article/Digital-Ad-Spending

-Surpass-TV-Next-Year/1013671 (accessed March 12, 2017).

[18]Jeanine Poggi, "Digital Advertising Tops TV in the U.S. for the First Time," *AdvertisingAge*, March 29, 2017, http://adage.com/article/advertising/magna-u-s-digital-ad-sales-top-tv-time-2016/308468/ (accessed April 5, 2017).

[19]"National Geographic Media Kit," *National Geographic*, http://www.nationalgeographic.com/mediakit/pdf/ng-magazine/NGM_Media_Kit_2017.pdf (accessed March 12, 2017).

[20]David G. Taylor, Jeffrey E. Lewin, and David Strutton, "Friends, Fans, and Followers: Do Ads Work on Social Networks? How Gender and Age Shape Receptivity," *Journal of Advertising Research* 51, 1 (2011): 258–275.

[21]Sonia Dickinson-Delaporte and Gayle Kerr, "Agency-Generated Research of Consumer-Generated Content: The Risks, Best Practices, and Ethics," *Journal of Advertising Research* 54, 4 (December 2014): 469–478.

[22]Geoffrey Precourt, "What We Know about TV Today (and Tomorrow)," *Journal of Advertising Research* 53, 1 (2013): 3–4.

[23]Mike Shields, "Advertising on Streaming TV Devices Is About to Get More Targeted," *The Wall Street Journal*, February 27, 2017, https://www.wsj.com/articles/advertising-on-streaming-tv-devices-is-about-to-get-more-targeted-1488193202 (accessed March 12, 2017).

[24]Shintaro Okazaki and Patrick Barwise, "Has the Time Finally Come for the Medium of the Future? Research on Mobile Advertising," 50th Anniversary Supplement, *Journal of Advertising Research* 51, 1 (2011): 59–71.

[25]Ilona A. Berney-Reddish and Charles S. Areni, "Sex Differences in Responses to Probability Markers in Advertising Claims," *Journal of Advertising* 35 (Summer 2006): 7–17.

[26]Better Business Bureaus, "Children's Food & Beverage Advertising Initiative," http://www.bbb.org/council/the-national-partner-program/national-advertising-review-services/childrens-food-and-beverage-advertising-initiative/ (accessed April 5, 2017).

[27]Chiranjeev Kohli, Sunil Thomas, and Rajneesh Suri, "Are You in Good Hands? Slogan Recall: What Really Matters," *Journal of Advertising Research* 53, 1 (2013): 31–42.

[28]Judith Anne Garretson Folse, Richard G. Netemeyer, and Scot Burton, "Spokescharacters," *Journal of Advertising* 41, 1 (Spring 2012): 17–32.

[29]Daniel J. Howard and Roger A. Kerin, "The Effects of Personalized Product Recommendations on Advertisement Response Rates: The 'Try This. It Works!' Technique," *Journal of Consumer Psychology* 14, 3 (2004): 271–279.

[30]Pamela W. Henderson, Joan L. Giese, and Joseph A. Cote, "Impression Management Using Typeface Design," *Journal of Marketing* 68 (October 2004): 60–72.

[31]Rik Pieters and Michel Wedel, "Attention Capture and Transfer in Advertising: Brand, Pictorial, and Text-Size Effects," *Journal of Marketing* 68 (April 2004): 36–50.

[32]Nathalie Tadena, "What Traffic Congestion, Car Speeds Mean for Outdoor Ads," *The Wall Street Journal,* June 17, 2014, http://blogs.wsj.com/cmo/2014/06/17/measuring-the-other-type-of-on-the-go-ads/ (accessed January 20, 2015).

[33]Bruce Krasnow, "New Mexico Tourism Chief: No Funds to Grow Ad Campaign," *Taos News*, January 29, 2017, http://www.taosnews.com/stories/new-mexico-tourism-chief-no-funds-to-grow-ad-campaign,38564 (accessed April 5, 2017).

[34]Marissa Delisle, "Mobile Marketing Trends 2017," *Digital Turbine*, January 6, 2017, https://www.digitalturbine.com/blog/mobile-marketing-trends-2017/ (accessed April 5, 2017).

[35]Peter J. Danaher and Guy W. Mullarkey, "Factors Affecting Online Advertising Recall: A Study of Students," *Journal of Advertising Research* 43 (2003): 252–267.

[36]"The Power of the Jingle," *AdvertisingAge*, February 8, 2017, http://adage.com/article/iheart-media/power-jingle/307801/ (accessed April 5, 2017).

[37]Jan H. Schumann, Florian von Wangenheim, and Nicole Groene, "Targeted Online Advertising: Using Reciprocity Appeals to Increase Acceptance Among Users of Free Web Services," *Journal of Marketing* 78 (January 2014): 59–75.

[38]Martin Williams and Francis Buttle, "Managing Negative Word-of-mouth: An Exploratory Study," *Journal of Marketing Management* 30, 13/14 (2014): 1423–1447.

[39]George E. Belch and Michael A. Belch, *Advertising and Promotion* (Burr Ridge, IL: Irwin/McGraw-Hill, 2008), 570.

[40]"AT&T: It Can Wait: The Power of Movement," *PR Week Awards,* http://fleishmanhillard.com/work/att-can-wait-power-movement/ (accessed January 21, 2015).

[41]Carmen Gonzalez Caldwell, "AT&T Campaign: When Driving, Texting and Other Smartphone Activities Can Wait," *Miami Herald*, April 5, 2017, http://www.miamiherald.com/news/local/crime/article142979794.html (accessed April 5, 2017).

[42]Tripp Mickle, "Budweiser Unhitches the Clydesdales," *The Wall Street Journal,* November 24, 2014, B2, B4.

[43]Belch and Belch, *Advertising and Promotion*, 580–581.

[44]Suman Basuroy, Subimal Chatterjee, and S. Abraham Ravid, "How Critical Are Critical Reviews? The Box Office Effects of Film Critics, Star Power, and Budgets," *Journal of Marketing* 67 (October 2003): 103–117.

[45]Brian Steinberg, "Food Net's Endorsements Are Woven Inconspicuously Into Its Programming Mix," *Variety*, November 5, 2013, http://variety.com/2013/tv/features/food-net-brand-tie-ins-that-sizzle-but-dont-burn-1200796087/ (accessed November 13, 2014); Carey Polis, "'From Scratch' Goes Behind the Scenes at the Food Network," *The Huffington Post*, October 1, 2013, http://www.huffingtonpost.com/2013/10/01/from-scratch-food-network_n_3984233.html (accessed November 13, 2014); Stuart Elliot, "Two Media Mainstays Expand Their Video Presence," *The New York Times*, October 2, 2013, http://www.nytimes.com/2013/10/03/business/media/two-media-mainstays-expand-their-video-presence.html (accessed November 13, 2014); John Moulding, "Scripps Network Hails the Impact of Dynamic Advertising Insertion," *Videonet*, October 31, 2013, http://www.v-net.tv/scripps-networks-hails-the-impact-of-dynamic-advertising-insertion/ (accessed November 13, 2014).

FEATURE NOTES

[a]Mike Shields, "Publishers Worry that Native Ads Are Vulnerable to Blocking," *The Wall Street Journal*, October 5, 2015, http://www.wsj.com/articles/publishers-worry-that-native-ads-are-vulnerable-to-ad-blocking-1444039200 (accessed October 12, 2015); Lin Grensing-Pophal, "Consumers Coming to Accept Native Advertising Done Right," *EContent Magazine*, July/August 2014, 8–10; Molly Soat, "The Native Frontier," *Marketing News*, May 2015, 34–43; Suzanne Vranica, "Majority of Native Ads Lack Transparency," *The Wall Street Journal*, August 3, 2016, http://www.wsj.com/articles/majority-of-native-ads-lack-transparency-1470218409 (accessed December 23, 2016); Christine Birkner,

"Why WSJ's Sponsored Content Features the Economics of Sex and Drugs," *AdWeek*, April 7, 2016, http://www.adweek.com/news/advertising-branding/why-wsjs-sponsored-content-features-economics-sex-and-drugs-170666 (accessed December 23, 2016).

[b]Tim Nudd, "Ad of the Day: Patagonia," *Ad Week*, November 28, 2011, http://www.adweek.com/news/advertising-branding/ad-day-patagonia-136745 (accessed December 28, 2016); Kyle Stock, "Patagonia's Confusing and Effective Campaign to Grudgingly Sell Stuff," *Bloomberg*, November 25, 2013, https://www.bloomberg.com/news/articles/2013-11-25/patagonias-confusing

-and-effective-campaign-to-grudgingly-sell-stuff (accessed December 28, 2016); Andrew Cave, "'Don't Buy This Racket': Patagonia to Give Away All Retail Revenues on Black Friday," *Forbes*, November 21, 2016, http://www.forbes.com/sites/andrewcave/2016/11/21/dont-buy-this-racket-patagonia-to-give-away-all-retail-revenues-on-black-friday/#1ea56050230c (accessed December 28, 2016); Brandon J. Reich and Catherine A. Armstrong Soule, "Green Demarketing in Advertisements: Comparing 'Buy Green' and 'Buy Less' Appeals in Product and Institutional Advertising Contexts," *Journal of Advertising* 45, 4 (2016): 441–458.

Chapter 17

1. Salesforce.com, "Join the Power of Us Program," http://www.salesforce.org/nonprofit/power-of-us/ (accessed December 26, 2016); Fortune, "100 Best Companies to Work For: Salesforce.com," 2016, http://fortune.com/best-companies/salesforce-23/ (accessed December 26, 2016); Salesforce.com, "Recognition," 2016, http://www.salesforce.com/company/awards/company.jsp (accessed December 26, 2016); Milton Moskowitz and Charles Kapelke, "25 Top-Paying Companies," *CNNMoney*, January 26, 2011, http://money.cnn.com/galleries/2011/pf/jobs/1101/gallery.best_companies_top_paying.fortune/index.html (accessed December 26, 2016); Salesforce.com, "Salesforce.org's 1-1-1 integrated philosophy," http://www.salesforce.org/ (accessed December 26, 2016); Chris Kanaracus, "Salesforce.com's Marc Bernioff Talks Growth, Microsoft," *InfoWorld*, June 6, 2011, http://www.infoworld.com/article/2621807/applications/salesforce-com-ceo-benioff-talks-growth--analytics--and-microsoft.html (accessed December 26, 2016); Steve D. Jones, "Salesforce.com Shares Weaken on Concern about Billings Growth," *The Wall Street Journal*, November 18, 2011, https://www.wsj.com/articles/BT-CO-20111118-712216 (accessed December 13, 2011); Salesforce.com, "Salesforce.com Named to Ethisphere's 'World's Most Ethical Companies' List for Fifth Consecutive Year," April 27, 2011, http://www.salesforce.com/company/news-press/press-releases/2011/04/110427.jsp (accessed December 26, 2016).

2. Avinash Malshe and Avipreet Sohi, "What Makes Strategy Making across the Sales-Marketing Interface More Successful?" *Journal of the Academy of Marketing Science* 37, 4 (Winter 2009): 400–421.

3. "Advantages of Personal Selling," KnowThis.com, www.knowthis.com/principles-of-marketing-tutorials/personal-selling/advantages-of-personal-selling/ (accessed April 2, 2012).

4. Kim Zimmerman, "B2B Inside Sales Teams Leverage Social, Video and Data to Reach Top Prospects," *Demand Gen Report*, January 20, 2016, http://www.demandgenreport.com/features/industry-insights/b2b-inside-sales-teams-leverage-social-video-and-data-to-reach-top-prospects (accessed March 29, 2017).

5. Jon M. Hawes, Anne K. Rich, and Scott M. Widmier, "Assessing the Development of the Sales Profession," *Journal of Personal Selling & Sales Management* 24 (Winter 2004): 27–37.

6. Dawn R. Deeter-Schmelz and Karen Norman Kennedy, "A Global Perspective on the Current State of Sales Education in the College Curriculum," *Journal of Personal Selling & Sales Management* 31, 1 (Winter 2011): 55–76.

7. Willem Verbeke, Bart Dietz, and Ernst Verwaal, "Drivers of Sales Performance: A Contemporary Meta-Analysis. Have Salespeople Become Knowledge Brokers?" *Journal of the Academy of Marketing Science* 39 (2011): 407–428.

8. Lisa Terry, "Customer Service," *Inbound Logistics,* December 2014, 33–36.

9. Michael Rodriguez and Robert M. Peterson, "Generating Leads via Social CRM: Early Best Practices for B2B Sales," abstract in Concha Allen (ed.), "Special Abstract Section: 2011 National Conference in Sales Management," *Journal of Personal Selling* 31, 4 (Fall 2011): 457–458.

10. Eli Jones, Paul Busch, and Peter Dacin, "Firm Market Orientation and Salesperson Customer Orientation: Interpersonal and Intrapersonal Influence on Customer Service and Retention in Business-to-Business Buyer–Seller Relationships," *Journal of Business Research* 56 (2003): 323–340.

11. Kenneth Le Meunier-FitzHugh and Nigel F. Piercy, "Exploring the Relationship Between Market Orientation and Sales and Marketing Collaboration," *Journal of Personal Selling & Sales Management* 31, 3 (Summer 2011): 287–296.

12. Kaj Storbacka, Pia Polsa, and Maria Sääksjärvi, "Management Practices in Solution Sales—A Multilevel and Cross-Functional Framework," *Journal of Personal Selling & Sales Management* 31, 1 (Winter 2011): 35–54.

13. Julie T. Johnson, Hiram C. Barksdale Jr., and James S. Boles, "Factors Associated with Customer Willingness to Refer Leads to Salespeople," *Journal of Business Research* 56 (2003): 257–263.

14. Ralph W. Giacobbe, Donald W. Jackson Jr., Lawrence A. Crosby, and Claudia M. Bridges, "A Contingency Approach to Adaptive Selling Behavior and Sales Performance: Selling Situations and Salesperson Characteristics," *Journal of Personal Selling & Sales Management* 26 (Spring 2006): 115–142.

15. Richard G. McFarland, Goutam N. Challagalla, and Tasadduq A. Shervani, "Influence Tactics for Effective Adaptive Selling," *Journal of Marketing* 70 (October 2006).

16. Thomas E. DeCarlo and Michael J. Barone, "The Interactive Effects of Sales Presentation, Suspicion, and Positive Mood on Salesperson Evaluations and Purchase Intentions," *Journal of Personal Selling & Sales Management* 33 (1), Winter 2013, 53–66.

17. John Andy Wood, "NLP Revisited: Nonverbal Communications and Signals of Trustworthiness," *Journal of Personal Selling & Sales Management* 26 (Spring 2006), 198–204.

18. John Dunyon, Valerie Gossling, Sarah Willden, and John S. Seiter, "Compliments and Purchasing Behavior in Telephone Sales Interactions," abstract in Dawn R. Deeter-Schmelz (ed.), "Personal Selling & Sales Management Abstracts," *Journal of Personal Selling & Sales Management* 31, 2 (Spring 2011): 186.

19. Stephen S. Porter, Joshua L. Wiener, and Gary L. Frankwick, "The Moderating Effect of Selling Situation on the Adaptive Selling Strategy—Selling Effectiveness Relationship," *Journal of Business Research* 56 (2003): 275–281.

20. Jonathon D. Rockoff, "Drug Sales Reps Try a Softer Pitch," *The Wall Street Journal*, January 10, 2012, B1–B2; J.K. Wall, "Lilly's Latest Sales Strategy: The Soft Sell," IBJ.com, http://www.ibj.com/articles/47717-lilly-s-latest-sales-strategy-the-soft-sell (accessed January 21, 2015).

21. Gabriel R. Gonzalez, K. Douglas Hoffman, Thomas N. Ingram, and Raymond W. LaForge, "Sales Organization Recovery Management and Relationship Selling: A Conceptual Model and Empirical Test," *Journal of Personal Selling & Sales Management* 30, 3 (Summer 2010): 223–238.

22. "The Right Questions and Attitudes Can Beef Up Your Sales, Improve Customer Retention," *Sell!ng* (June 2001): 3.

23. Eli Jones, Steven P. Brown, Andris A. Zoltners, and Barton A. Weitz, "The Changing

Environment of Selling and Sales Management," *Journal of Personal Selling & Sales Management* 25, 2 (Spring 2005): 105–111.

[24]Fernando Jaramillo, Jay Prakash Mulki, and Paul Solomon, "The Role of Ethical Climate on Salesperson's Role Stress, Job Attitudes, Turnover Intention, and Job Performance," *Journal of Personal Selling & Sales Management* 26 (Summer 2006): 272–282.

[25]Christophe Fournier, John F. Tanner Jr., Lawrence B. Chonko, and Chris Manolis, "The Moderating Role of Ethical Climate on Salesperson Propensity to Leave," *Journal of Personal Selling & Sales Management* 3, 1 (Winter 2009–2010): 7–22.

[26]Bulent Menguc, Seigyoung Auh, and Aypar Uslu, "Customer Knowledge Creation Capability and Performance in Sales Teams," *Journal of the Academy of Marketing Science* 41 (2013), 19–39.

[27]Leonidas A. Zampetakis, "Sales Force Management Practices in Organizations with a Supportive Climate towards Creativity," *Journal of Strategic Marketing* 22 (1), 2014, 59–72.

[28]Jeffrey P. Boichuk, Willy Bolander, Zachary R. Hall, Michael Ahearne, William J. Zahn, and Melissa Nieves, "Learned Helplessness among Newly Hired Salespeople and the Influence of Leadership," *Journal of Marketing* 78 (January 2014), 95–111.

[29]"Infosys Working to Improve Sales Team's Efficiency, Revamps Training," *The Economic Times,* December 19, 2014, http://articles .economictimes.indiatimes.com/2014-12-29 /news/57494843_1_basab-pradhan-vishal -sikka-sales-engine (accessed January 22, 2015).

[30]Jason Jordan and Robert Kelly, "Companies with a Formal Sales Process Generate More Revenue," *Harvard Business Review,* January 21, 2015, https://hbr.org/2015/01 /companies-with-a-formal-sales-process -generate-more-revenue (accessed January 22, 2015).

[31]Glassdoor, "Sales Salaries," March 24, 2017, https://www.glassdoor.com/Salaries/sales-salary -SRCH_KO0,5.htm (accessed March 29, 2017).

[32]Tara Burnthorne Lopez, Christopher D. Hopkins, and Mary Anne Raymond, "Reward Preferences of Salespeople: How Do Commissions Rate?" *Journal of Personal Selling & Sales Management* 26 (Fall 2006): 381–390.

[33]Jolie Lee, "Container Store pays workers on average $50,000," *USA Today,* October 17, 2014, http://www.usatoday.com/story/money /business/2014/10/17/container-store-salaries -retail/17426865/ (accessed January 23, 2015).

[34]Denny Bristow, Douglas Amyx, Stephen B. Castleberry, and James J. Cochran, "A Cross-Generational Comparison of Motivational Factors in a Sales Career Among Gen-X and Gen-Y College Students," *Journal of Personal Selling & Sales Management* 31, 1 (Winter 2011): 35–54.

[35]"Best Companies 2014," *Fortune,* http:// fortune.com/best-companies/quiktrip-48/ (accessed January 23, 2015).

[36]Lee, "Container Store pays workers on average $50,000."

[37]John W. Barnes, Donald W. Jackson Jr., Michael D. Hutt, and Ajith Kumar, "The Role of Culture Strength in Shaping Salesforce Outcomes," *Journal of Personal Selling & Sales Management* 26 (Summer 2006): 255–270.

[38]Patricia Odell, "Motivating the Masses," *Promo,* September 1, 2005, http://promomaga-zine.com/research/pitrends/marketing _motivating_masses/ (accessed April 20, 2011).

[39]Anne Hamilton, "Incentive Travel That Pays," *Direct Selling News* 10 (8), August 2014, 60–61.

[40]G. Alexander Hamwi, Brian N. Rutherford, Hiram C. Barksdale, Jr., and Julie T. Johnson, "Ideal Versus Actual Number of Sales Calls: An Application of Disconfirmation Theory," *Journal of Personal Selling & Sales Management* 33 (3), Summer 2013, 307–318.

[41]George E. Belch and Michael A. Belch, *Advertising and Promotion* (Burr Ridge, IL: Irwin/McGraw-Hill, 2004), 514–522.

[42]Esmeralda Crespo-Almendros and Salvador Del Barrio-Garcia, "The Quality of Internet-User Recall: A Comparative Analysis by Online Sales-Promotion Types," *Journal of Advertising Research* 54 (1), March 2014, 46–60.

[43]Brad Tuttle, "Why Americans Are Cutting Coupons out of Their Lives," *Time,* February 28, 2013, http://business.time.com/2013/02/28/ why-americans-are-cutting-coupons-out-of-their-lives (accessed February 11, 2016).

[44]Sarah Halzack, "The Trouble with Those 20 Percent Off Coupons from Bed, Bath &

Beyond," *The Washington Post,* https://www .washingtonpost.com/news/business/ wp/2015/09/30/the-trouble-with-those-20-percent-off-coupons-from-bed-bath-beyond/ (accessed February 12, 2016).

[45]Venessa Wong, "Clipping Forever: Why the Humble Coupon Isn't Going Away," *Bloom-berg Businessweek,* November 7, 2014, http:// www.businessweek.com/articles/2014-11-07/ clipping-forever-why-the-humble-coupon-isnt -going-away (accessed January 23, 2015).

[46]Arthur L. Porter, "Direct Mail's Lessons for Electronic Couponers," *Marketing Management Journal* (Spring/Summer 2000): 107–115.

[47]Coupon Information Corporation, http://www .cents-off.com/faq.php?st=1fe91 (accessed February 5, 2011).

[48]John T. Gourville and Dilip Soman, "The Consumer Psychology of Mail-in Rebates," *Journal of Product & Brand Management,* 20(2), 2011, 147–157.

[49]Don E. Schultz and Martin P. Block, "Sales Promotion Influencing Consumer Brand Preferences/Purchases," *Journal of Consumer Marketing* 31 (3), 212–217.

[50]Sephora, "Beauty Insider Program & Rewards," http://www.sephora.com /customerService/customerServiceTemplate. jsp?mediaId=10800052#100Point (accessed January 23, 2015).

[51]Jeana Delano, "The Power of Product Samples," *Global Cosmetic Industry,* November 2014, 46–48.

[52]Kenneth Hein, "Sampling Inspires Repeat Purchases," *Adweek,* August 4, 2009, http:// www.adweek.com/news/advertising-branding /sampling-inspires-repeat-purchases-99961 (accessed January 24, 2013).

[53]Bruce Horovitz, "Social Media Drives Week of Freebies," *USA Today,* July 11, 2012, 1B.

[54]Katherine Hobson, "A Sales Promotion That Works for Shoes May Not for Chocolate," *The Wall Street Journal,* February 8, 2011, http://blogs.wsj.com/health/2011/02/08/a -sales-promotion-that-works-for-shoes -may-not-for-chocolate/ (accessed April 3, 2012).

[55]Teresa Montaner, Leslie de Chernatony, and Isabel Buil, "Consumer Response to Gift Promotions," *Journal of Product & Brand Management* 20, 2 (2011): 101–110.

[56]Jessica Wohl, "Oreo Enlists Celebs to Demonstrate the Perfect Dunk in Latest Global Push," *AdvertisingAge*, February 8, 2017, http://adage.com/article/cmo-strategy /oreo/307896/ (accessed April 1, 2017).

[57]Kenneth Jones, "Broadway's Major Producers Join with Regional Presenters for Audience Rewards Program," *Playbill*, June 28, 2007, http://www.playbill.com/news/article /109186-Broadways-Major-Producers-Join -With-Regional-Presenters-for-Audience -Rewards-Program (accessed December 11, 2013); Nederlander Organization - Announcements, "Audience Rewards Hits 1 Million Members," August 25, 2012, http://www .nederlander.com/press_03.html (accessed December 11, 2013); Audience Rewards, "Our History," https://www.audiencerewards .com/redeemcenter/infopage=.cfm?id=25 (accessed December 11, 2013).

FEATURE NOTES

[a]"Tastefully Simple Founder and Founding Partner Recognized," *Echo Press*, October 19, 2012, http://dev1.echopress.com/event/article /id/98803/ (accessed January 16, 2014); Beth Douglass Silcox and Barbara Seale, "The Most Influential Women in Direct Selling," *Direct Selling News,* October 2012, 58–59; Tastefully Simple website, https://www.tastefullysimple. com/ (accessed December 26, 2016); "DSN Global 100: The Top Direct Selling Companies in the World," *Direct Selling News,* June 1, 2012, http://directsellingnews.com/index.php /view/dsn_global_100_the_top_direct_selling _companies_in_the_world/P7#.UIGz-EPUmx8F (accessed December 26, 2016); "DSN Global 100," *Direct Selling News,* June 1, 2014, http://directsellingnews.com /index.php/view/the_2013_dsn_global_100 _list?popup=yes#.UthLx_XLQ4k (accessed December 26, 2016); BestCompany.com, "Tastefully Simple," 2016, https://bestcompany .com/mlm/company/tastefully-simple/ (accessed December 26, 2016); Tastefully Simple, "Awards & Recognition," https://www .tastefullysimple.com/about-us/awards -recognition (accessed December 26, 2016); "Tastefully Simple Streamlines Operations," *Voice of Alexandria,* November 9, 2016, http:// www.voiceofalexandria.com/news/local _business_news/tastefully-simple-streamlines -operations/article_933bbc28-a6bd-11e6-b33e -8fb44a689e7d.html (accessed December 26, 2016).

[b]AJ Agrawal, "7 Ways to Boost Your Revenue with Digital Coupon Marketing," *Forbes*, May 31, 2016, http://www.forbes.com/sites /ajagrawal/2016/05/31/7-ways-to -boost-your-revenue-with-digital-coupon -marketing/#3d58be375570 (accessed December 26, 2016); Globe Newswire, "Improving Economy, Increasing Shopper Demand for Digital Offers Impacting Coupon Use," *Nasdaq Global Newswire*, February 1, 2016, https://globenewswire.com/news -release/2016/02/01/806336/10159649/en /Improving-Economy-Increasing-Shopper-Demand-for-Digital-Offers-Impacting-Coupon-Use.html (accessed December 26, 2016); Inmar, "Traditional Paper Coupons Continue to Dominate in Terms of Distribution Despite Data Showing Digital Coupons Driving Exponential Redemption Relative to Distribution Volume," August 4, 2016, https://www.inmar. com/press-release/promotion-industry -analysis-by-inmar-finds-significant -coupon-gap-between-marketers-current -offerings-and-shoppers-demands/ (accessed December 26, 2016); Inmar, "Analysis of 2015 Promotion Sector Activity Finds Easing of Home-Budget Pressures and Increasing Shopper Reluctance To Work For Deals Contributing to Overall Decline in Coupon Redemption—Despite Marked Redemption Growth Among Some Promotion Methods," February 1, 2016, https://www.inmar.com/press-release/ improving-economy-increasing-shopper-demand-for-digital-offers-impacting-coupon-use/ (accessed December 26, 2016).

glossary

accessory equipment Equipment that does not become part of the final physical product but is used in production or office activities

advertising Paid nonpersonal communication about an organization and its products transmitted to a target audience through mass media

advertising appropriation The advertising budget for a specific time period

advertising campaign The creation and execution of a series of advertisements to communicate with a particular target audience

advertising platform Basic issues or selling points to be included in an advertising campaign

advocacy advertising Advertising that promotes a company's position on a public issue

aesthetic modifications Changes to the sensory appeal of a product

agents Intermediaries that represent either buyers or sellers on a permanent basis

aided recall test A posttest that asks respondents to identify recent ads and provides clues to jog their memories

approach The manner in which a salesperson contacts a potential customer

arbitrary approach Budgeting for an advertising campaign as specified by a high-level executive in the firm

artwork An advertisement's illustrations and layout

Asia-Pacific Economic Cooperation (APEC) An alliance that promotes open trade and economic and technical cooperation among member nations throughout the world

Association of Southeast Asian Nations (ASEAN) An alliance that promotes trade and economic integration among member nations in Southeast Asia

atmospherics The physical elements in a store's design that appeal to consumers' emotions and encourage buying

attitude An individual's enduring evaluation of feelings about and behavioral tendencies toward an object or idea

attitude scale A means of measuring consumer attitudes by gauging the intensity of individuals' reactions to adjectives, phrases, or sentences about an object

automatic vending The use of machines to dispense products

average fixed cost The fixed cost per unit produced

average total cost The sum of the average fixed cost and the average variable cost

average variable cost The variable cost per unit produced

balance of trade The difference in value between a nation's exports and its imports

benefit segmentation The division of a market according to benefits that consumers want from the product

Better Business Bureau A local, nongovernmental regulatory agency, supported by local businesses, that helps settle problems between customers and specific business firms

big data Massive data files that can be obtained from both structured and unstructured databases

blogs Web-based journals (short for "weblogs") in which writers editorialize and interact with other Internet users

brand A name, term, design, symbol, or any other feature that identifies one marketer's product as distinct from those of other marketers

brand competitors Firms that market products with similar features and benefits to the same customers at similar prices

brand equity The marketing and financial value associated with a brand's strength in a market

brand extension Using an existing brand to brand a new product in a different product category

brand insistence The degree of brand loyalty in which a customer strongly prefers a specific brand and will accept no substitute

brand licensing An agreement whereby a company permits another organization to use its brand on other products for a licensing fee

brand loyalty A customer's favorable attitude toward a specific brand

brand manager The person responsible for a single brand

brand mark The part of a brand not made up of words

brand name The part of a brand that can be spoken

brand preference The degree of brand loyalty in which a customer prefers one brand over competitive offerings

brand recognition A customer's awareness that the brand exists and is an alternative purchase

breakdown approach Measuring company sales potential based on a general economic forecast for a specific period and the market potential derived from it

break-even point The point at which the costs of producing a product equal the revenue made from selling the product

brokers Intermediaries that bring buyers and sellers together temporarily

buildup approach Measuring company sales potential by estimating how much of a product a potential buyer in a specific geographic area will purchase in a given period, multiplying the estimate by the number of potential buyers, and adding the totals of all the geographic areas considered

bundle pricing Packaging together two or more complementary products and selling them for a single price

business analysis Evaluating the potential contribution of a product idea to the firm's sales, costs, and profits

B2B E-commerce sites Online marketplaces where buyers and sellers from around the world can exchange information, goods, services, ideas, and payments

business (organizational) buying behavior The purchase behavior of producers, government units, institutions, and resellers

business cycle A pattern of economic fluctuations that has four stages: prosperity, recession, depression, and recovery

business market Individuals or groups that purchase a specific kind of product for resale, direct use in producing other products, or use in general daily operations

business products Products bought to use in an organization's operations, to resell, or to make other products

business services The intangible products that many organizations use in their operations

buy-back allowance A sum of money given to a reseller for each unit bought after an initial promotion deal is over

buying allowance A temporary price reduction to resellers purchasing specified quantities of a product

buying behavior The decision processes and actions of people involved in buying and using products

buying center The people within an organization who make business purchase decisions

buying power Resources—such as money, goods, and services—that can be traded in an exchange

buzz marketing An attempt to incite publicity and public excitement surrounding a product through a creative event

captioned photograph A photograph with a brief description of its contents

captive pricing Pricing the basic product in a product line low, but pricing related items at a higher level

cash-and-carry wholesalers Limited-service wholesalers whose customers pay cash and furnish transportation

catalog marketing A type of marketing in which an organization provides a catalog from which customers make selections and place orders by mail, telephone, or the Internet

category killer A very large specialty store that concentrates on a major product category and competes on the basis of low prices and product availability

category management A retail strategy of managing groups of similar, often substitutable products produced by different manufacturers

centralized organization A structure in which top-level managers delegate little authority to lower levels

cents-off offers Promotions that allow buyers to pay less than the regular price to encourage purchase

channel capacity The limit on the volume of information a communication channel can handle effectively

channel captain The dominant leader of a marketing channel or a supply channel

channel power The ability of one channel member to influence another member's goal achievement

client-based relationships Interactions that result in satisfied customers who use a service repeatedly over time

closing The stage in the personal selling process when the salesperson asks the prospect to buy the product

co-branding Using two or more brands on one product

codes of conduct Formalized rules and standards that describe what a company expects of its employees

coding process Converting meaning into a series of signs or symbols

cognitive dissonance A buyer's doubts shortly after a purchase about whether the decision was the right one

combination compensation plan Paying salespeople a fixed salary plus a commission based on sales volume

commercialization Deciding on full-scale manufacturing and marketing plans and preparing budgets

commission merchants Agents that receive goods on consignment from local sellers and negotiate sales in large, central markets

communication A sharing of meaning through the transmission of information

communications channel The medium of transmission that carries the coded message from the source to the receiver

community shopping centers A type of shopping center with one or two department stores, some specialty stores, and convenience stores

company sales potential The maximum percentage of market potential that an individual firm within an industry can expect to obtain for a specific product

comparative advertising Advertising that compares the sponsored brand with one or more identified brands on the basis of one or more product characteristics

comparison discounting Setting a price at a specific level and comparing it with a higher price

competition Other firms that market products that are similar to or can be substituted for a firm's products in the same geographic area

competition-based pricing Pricing influenced primarily by competitor's prices

competition-matching approach Determining an advertising budget by trying to match competitors' advertising outlays

competitive advantage The result of a company matching a core competency to opportunities it has discovered in the marketplace

competitive advertising Advertising that tries to stimulate demand for a specific brand by promoting its features, uses, and advantages relative to competing brands

component parts Items that become part of the physical product and are either finished items ready for assembly or products that need little processing before assembly

concentrated targeting strategy A market segmentation strategy in which an organization targets a single market segment using one marketing mix

concept testing Seeking potential buyers' responses to a product idea

conclusive research Research designed to verify insights through objective procedures and to help marketers in making decisions

consideration set A group of brands within a product category that a buyer views as alternatives for possible purchase

consistency of quality The degree to which a product has the same level of quality over time

consumer buying behavior The decision processes and purchasing activities of people who purchase products for personal or household use and not for business purposes

consumer buying decision process A five-stage purchase decision process that includes problem recognition, information search, evaluation of alternatives, purchase, and postpurchase evaluation

consumer contests Sales promotion methods in which individuals compete for prizes based on their analytical or creative skills

consumer games Sales promotion methods in which individuals compete for prizes based primarily on chance

consumer jury A panel of a product's existing or potential buyers who pretest ads

consumer market Purchasers and household members who intend to consume or benefit from the purchased products and do not buy products to make profits or serve an organizational need

consumer misbehavior Behavior that violates generally accepted norms of a particular society

consumer products Products purchased to satisfy personal and family needs

consumer-sales promotion methods Sales promotion techniques that encourage consumers to patronize specific stores or try particular products

consumer socialization The process through which a person acquires the knowledge and skills to function as a consumer

consumer sweepstakes A sales promotion in which entrants submit their names for inclusion in a drawing for prizes

contract manufacturing The practice of hiring a foreign firm to produce a designated volume of the domestic firm's product or a component of it to specification; the final product carries the domestic firm's name

convenience products Relatively inexpensive, frequently purchased items for which buyers exert minimal purchasing effort

convenience store A small, self-service store that is open long hours and carries a narrow assortment of products, usually convenience items

cooperative advertising An arrangement in which a manufacturer agrees to pay a certain amount of a retailer's media costs for advertising the manufacturer's products

copy The verbal portion of advertisements

core competencies Things a company does extremely well, which sometimes give it an advantage over its competition

corporate strategy A strategy that determines the means for utilizing resources in the various functional areas to reach the organization's goals

cost comparison indicator A means of comparing the costs of advertising vehicles in a specific medium in relation to the number of people reached

cost-based pricing To establish the price, a percentage of the cost is added to the cost

cost-plus pricing Adding a specified dollar amount or percentage to the buyer's cost to establish the selling price

coupons Written price reductions used to encourage consumers to buy a specific product

crowdsourcing Combines the words *crowd* and *outsourcing* and calls for taking tasks usually performed by a marketer or researcher and outsourcing them to a crowd, or potential market, through an open call

cultural relativism The concept that morality varies from one culture to another and that business practices are therefore differentially defined as right or wrong by particular cultures

culture The accumulation of values, knowledge, beliefs, customs, objects, and concepts that a society uses to cope with its environment and passes on to future generations

customary pricing Pricing on the basis of tradition

customer advisory boards Small groups of actual customers who serve as sounding boards for new-product ideas and offer insights into their feelings and attitudes toward a firm's products and other elements of its marketing strategy

customer contact The level of interaction between provider and customer needed to deliver the service

customer forecasting survey A survey of customers regarding the types and quantities of products they intend to buy during a specific period

customer relationship management (CRM) Using information about customers to create marketing strategies that develop and sustain desirable customer relationships

customer services Human or mechanical efforts or activities that add value to a product

customers The purchasers of organizations' products; the focal point of all marketing activities

cycle analysis An analysis of sales figures for a three- to five-year period to ascertain whether sales fluctuate in a consistent, periodic manner

cycle time The time needed to complete a process

database A collection of information arranged for easy access and retrieval

dealer listings Advertisements that promote a product and identify the names of participating retailers that sell the product

dealer loader A gift, often part of a display, given to a retailer that purchases a specified quantity of merchandise

decentralized organization A structure in which decision-making authority is delegated as far down the chain of command as possible

decline stage The stage of a product's life cycle when sales fall rapidly

decoding process Converting signs or symbols into concepts and ideas

Delphi technique A procedure in which experts create initial forecasts, submit them to the company for averaging, and then refine the forecasts

demand curve A graph of the quantity of products a firm expects to sell at various prices if other factors remain constant

demand-based pricing Pricing based on the level of demand for the product

demonstrations Sales promotion methods a manufacturer uses temporarily to encourage trial use and purchase of a product or to show how a product works

department stores Large retail organizations characterized by a wide product mix and organized into separate departments to facilitate marketing efforts and internal management

depth of product mix The average number of different product items offered in each product line

derived demand Demand for business products that stems from demand for consumer products

descriptive research Research conducted to clarify the characteristics of certain phenomena to solve a particular problem

differential pricing Charging different prices to different buyers for the same quality and quantity of product

differentiated targeting strategy A strategy in which an organization targets two or more segments by developing a marketing mix for each segment

digital distribution Delivering content through the Internet to a computer or other device

digital marketing Uses all digital media, including the Internet and mobile and interactive channels, to develop communication and exchanges with customers

digital media Electronic media that function using digital codes; when we refer to digital media, we are referring to media available via computers, cellular phones, smartphones, and other digital devices that have been released in recent years

direct marketing The use of the telephone, Internet, and nonpersonal media to introduce products to customers, who can then purchase them via mail, telephone, or the Internet

direct ownership A situation in which a company owns subsidiaries or other facilities overseas

direct selling Marketing products to ultimate consumers through face-to-face sales presentations at home or in the workplace

direct-response marketing A type of marketing in which a retailer advertises a product and makes it available through mail or telephone orders

discount A deduction from the price of an item

discount stores Self-service, general-merchandise stores that offer brand-name and private-brand products at low prices

discretionary income Disposable income available for spending and saving after an individual has purchased the basic necessities of food, clothing, and shelter

disposable income After-tax income

disruptive innovation Identifies old technologies that can be exploited in new ways or develops new business models to give customers more than they've come to expect from current products in a specific market

distribution The decisions and activities that make products available to customers when and where they want to purchase them

distribution centers Large, centralized warehouses that focus on moving rather than storing goods

drop shippers Limited-service wholesalers that take title to goods and negotiate sales but never actually take possession of products

dumping Selling products at unfairly low prices

early adopters Careful choosers of new products

early majority Those adopting new products just before the average person

electronic data interchange (EDI) A computerized means of integrating order processing with production, inventory, accounting, and transportation

electronic marketing (e-marketing) The strategic process of pricing, distributing, and promoting products, and discovering the desires of customers using digital media and digital marketing

embargo A government's suspension of trade in a particular product or with a given country

environmental analysis The process of assessing and interpreting information gathered through environmental scanning

environmental scanning The process of collecting information about forces in the marketing environment

European Union (EU) An alliance that promotes trade among its member countries in Europe

evaluative criteria Objective and subjective product characteristics that are important to a buyer

everyday low prices (EDLPs) Setting a low price for products on a consistent basis

exchange The provision or transfer of goods, services, or ideas in return for something of value

exchange controls Government restrictions on the amount of a particular currency that can be bought or sold

exclusive dealing A situation in which a manufacturer forbids an intermediary from carrying products of competing manufacturers

exclusive distribution Using a single outlet in a fairly large geographic area to distribute a product

executive judgment A sales forecasting method based on the intuition of one or more executives

experimental research Research that allows marketers to make causal inferences about relationships

expert forecasting survey Sales forecasts prepared by experts outside the firm, such as economists, management consultants, advertising executives, or college professors

exploratory research Research conducted to gather more information about a problem or to make a tentative hypothesis more specific

exporting The sale of products to foreign markets

extended decision making A consumer problem-solving process employed when purchasing unfamiliar, expensive, or infrequently bought products

external search An information search in which buyers seek information from sources other than their memories

extreme-value stores Retailers that are a fraction of the size of conventional discount stores and typically offer very low prices on smaller size name-brand nonperishable household items

family branding Branding all of a firm's products with the same name

family packaging Using similar packaging for all of a firm's products or packaging that has one common design element

feature article A manuscript of up to 3,000 words prepared for a specific publication

Federal Trade Commission (FTC) An agency that regulates a variety of business practices and curbs false advertising, misleading pricing, and deceptive packaging and labeling

feedback The receiver's response to a decoded message

first-mover advantage The ability of a company to achieve long-term competitive advantages by being the first to offer an innovative product in the marketplace

fixed costs Costs that do not vary with changes in the number of units produced or sold

focus group An interview that is often conducted informally, without a structured questionnaire, in small groups of 8 to 12 people, to observe interaction when members are exposed to an idea

franchising An arrangement in which a supplier (franchiser) grants a dealer (franchisee) the right to sell products in exchange for some type of consideration

free merchandise A manufacturer's reward given to resellers that purchase a stated quantity of products

free samples Samples of a product given out to encourage trial and purchase

freight forwarders Organizations that consolidate shipments from several firms into efficient lot sizes

full-service wholesalers Merchant wholesalers that perform the widest range of wholesaling functions

functional modifications Changes affecting a product's versatility, effectiveness, convenience, or safety

General Agreement on Tariffs and Trade (GATT) An agreement among nations to reduce worldwide tariffs and increase international trade

general-merchandise retailer A retail establishment that offers a variety of product lines that are stocked in considerable depth

general-merchandise wholesalers Full-service wholesalers with a wide product mix but limited depth within product lines

generic brands Brands indicating only the product category

geodemographic segmentation A method of market segmentation that clusters people in zip code areas and smaller neighborhood units based on lifestyle and demographic information

geographic pricing Reductions for transportation and other costs related to the physical distance between buyer and seller

globalization The development of marketing strategies that treat the entire world (or its major regions) as a single entity

good A tangible physical entity

government markets Federal, state, county, or local governments that buy goods and services to support their internal operations and provide products to their constituencies

green marketing A strategic process involving stakeholder assessment to create meaningful, long-term relationships with customers while maintaining, supporting, and enhancing the natural environment

gross domestic product (GDP) The market value of a nation's total output of goods and services for a given period; an overall measure of economic standing

growth stage The stage of a product's life cycle when sales rise rapidly and profits reach a peak and then start to decline

heterogeneity Variation in quality

heterogeneous market A market made up of individuals or organizations with diverse needs for products in a specific product class

homesourcing A practice in which customer-contact jobs, especially at call centers, are outsourced into the homes of workers

homogeneous market A market in which a large proportion of customers have similar needs for a product

horizontal channel integration Combining organizations at the same level of operation under one management

hypermarkets Stores that combine supermarket and discount store shopping in one location

hypothesis An informed guess or assumption about a certain problem or set of circumstances

idea A concept, philosophy, image, or issue

idea generation Seeking product ideas that will help organizations to achieve objectives

illustrations Photos, drawings, graphs, charts, and tables used to spark audience interest in an advertisement

import tariff A duty levied by a nation on goods bought outside its borders and brought into the country

importing The purchase of products from a foreign source

impulse buying An unplanned buying behavior resulting from a powerful urge to buy something immediately

individual branding A policy of naming each product differently

industrial distributor An independent business organization that takes title to industrial products and carries inventories

inelastic demand Demand that is not significantly altered by a price increase or decrease

information inputs Sensations received through sight, taste, hearing, smell, and touch

in-home (door-to-door) interview A personal interview that takes place in the respondent's home

innovators First adopters of new products

inseparability Being produced and consumed at the same time

installations Facilities and nonportable major equipment

institutional advertising Advertising that promotes organizational images, ideas, and political issues

institutional markets Organizations with charitable, educational, community, or other nonbusiness goals

intangibility A service is not physical and therefore cannot be touched

integrated marketing communications Coordination of promotion and other marketing efforts for maximum informational and persuasive impact

intensive distribution Using all available outlets to distribute a product

intermodal transportation Two or more transportation modes used in combination

internal search An information search in which buyers search their memories for information about products that might solve their problem

international marketing Developing and performing marketing activities across national boundaries

introduction stage The initial stage of a product's life cycle—its first appearance in the marketplace—when sales start at zero and profits are negative

inventory management Developing and maintaining adequate assortments of products to meet customers' needs

joint demand Demand involving the use of two or more items in combination to produce a product

joint venture A partnership between a domestic firm and a foreign firm or government

just-in-time (JIT) An inventory-management approach in which supplies arrive just when needed for production or resale

kinesic communication Communicating through the movement of head, eyes, arms, hands, legs, or torso

labeling Providing identifying, promotional, or other information on package labels

laggards The last adopters, who distrust new products

late majority Skeptics who adopt new products when they feel it is necessary

late-mover advantage The ability of later market entrants to achieve long-term competitive advantages by not being the first to offer a product in a marketplace

layout The physical arrangement of an advertisement's illustration and copy

learning Changes in an individual's thought processes and behavior caused by information and experience

level of involvement An individual's degree of interest in a product and the importance of the product for that person

level of quality The amount of quality a product possesses

licensing An alternative to direct investment that requires a licensee to pay commissions or royalties on sales or supplies used in manufacturing

lifestyle An individual's pattern of living expressed through activities, interests, and opinions

lifestyle shopping center A type of shopping center that is typically open air and features upscale specialty, dining, and entertainment stores

limited decision making A consumer problem-solving process used when purchasing products occasionally or needing information about an unfamiliar brand in a familiar product category

limited-line wholesalers Full-service wholesalers that carry only a few product lines but many products within those lines

limited-service wholesalers Merchant wholesalers that provide some services and specialize in a few functions

line extension Development of a product closely related to one or more products in the existing product line but designed specifically to meet somewhat different customer needs

logistics management Planning, implementing, and controlling the efficient and effective flow and storage of products and information from the point of origin to consumption in order to meet customers' needs and wants

mail survey A research method in which respondents answer a questionnaire sent through the mail

mail-order wholesalers Limited-service wholesalers that sell products through catalogs

manufacturer brands Brands initiated by producers

manufacturers' agents Independent intermediaries that represent two or more sellers and usually offer customers complete product lines

marginal cost (MC) The extra cost incurred by producing one more unit of a product

marginal revenue (MR) The change in total revenue resulting from the sale of an additional unit of a product

market A group of individuals and/or organizations that have needs for products in a product class and have the ability, willingness, and authority to purchase those products

market density The number of potential customers within a unit of land area

market growth/market share matrix A helpful business tool based on the philosophy that a product's market growth rate and its market share are important considerations in determining its marketing strategy

market opportunity A combination of circumstances and timing that permits an organization to take action to reach a particular target market

market orientation An organizationwide commitment to researching and responding to customer needs

market potential The total amount of a product that customers will purchase within a specified period at a specific level of industry-wide marketing activity

market segment Individuals, groups, or organizations sharing one or more similar characteristics that cause them to have similar product needs

market segmentation The process of dividing a total market into groups with relatively similar product needs to design a marketing mix that matches those needs

market share The percentage of a market that actually buys a specific product from a particular company

market test Making a product available to buyers in one or more test areas and measuring purchases and consumer responses to marketing efforts

marketing The process of creating, pricing, distributing, and promoting goods, services, and ideas to facilitate satisfying exchange relationships with customers and to develop and maintain favorable relationships with stakeholders in a dynamic environment

marketing analytics Uses tools and methods to measure and interpret the effectiveness of a firm's marketing activities

marketing channel A group of individuals and organizations that direct the flow of products from producers to customers within the supply chain

marketing citizenship The adoption of a strategic focus for fulfilling the economic, legal, ethical, and philanthropic social responsibilities expected by stakeholders

marketing concept A managerial philosophy that an organization should try to satisfy customers' needs through a coordinated set of activities that also allows the organization to achieve its goals

marketing cost analysis Analysis of costs to determine which are associated with specific marketing efforts

marketing environment The competitive, economic, political, legal and regulatory, technological, and sociocultural forces that surround the customer and affect the marketing mix

marketing implementation The process of putting marketing strategies into action

marketing information system (MIS) A framework for managing and structuring information gathered regularly from sources inside and outside the organization

marketing intermediaries Middlemen that link producers to other intermediaries or ultimate consumers through contractual arrangements or through the purchase and resale of products

marketing mix Four marketing variables—product, pricing, distribution, and promotion—that a firm controls to meet the needs of customers within its target market

marketing objective A statement of what is to be accomplished through marketing activities

marketing plan A written document that specifies the activities to be performed to implement and control the organization's marketing activities

marketing research The systematic design, collection, interpretation, and reporting of information to help marketers solve specific marketing problems or take advantage of marketing opportunities

marketing strategy A plan of action for identifying and analyzing a target market and developing a marketing mix to meet the needs of that market

markup pricing Adding to the cost of the product a predetermined percentage of that cost

Maslow's hierarchy of needs The five levels of needs that humans seek to satisfy, from most to least important

materials handling Physical handling of tangible goods, supplies, and resources

maturity stage The stage of a product's life cycle when the sales curve peaks and starts to decline as profits continue to fall

media plan A plan that specifies the media vehicles to be used and the schedule for running advertisements

megacarriers Freight transportation firms that provide several modes of shipment

merchandise allowance A manufacturer's agreement to pay resellers certain amounts of money for providing special promotional efforts, such as setting up and maintaining a display

merchant wholesalers Independently owned businesses that take title to goods, assume ownership risks, and buy and resell products to other wholesalers, business customers, or retailers

micromarketing An approach to market segmentation in which organizations focus precise marketing efforts on very small geographic markets

mission statement A long-term view, or vision, of what the organization wants to become

missionary salespeople Support salespeople, usually employed by a manufacturer, who assist the producer's customers in selling to their own customers

mobile application A software program that runs on mobile devices and gives users access to certain content

modified rebuy purchase A new-task purchase that is changed on subsequent orders or when the requirements of a straight rebuy purchase are modified

money refunds Sales promotion techniques that offer consumers a specified amount of money when they mail in a proof of purchase, usually for multiple product purchases

monopolistic competition A competitive structure in which a firm has many potential competitors and tries to develop a marketing strategy to differentiate its product

monopoly A competitive structure in which an organization offers a product that has no close substitutes, making that organization the sole source of supply

motive An internal energizing force that directs a person's behavior toward satisfying needs or achieving goals

MRO supplies Maintenance, repair, and operating items that facilitate production and operations but do not become part of the finished product

multichannel distribution   The use of a variety of marketing channels to ensure maximum distribution

multichannel retailing   Employing multiple distribution channels that complement brick-and-mortar stores with websites, catalogs, and apps where consumers can research products, read other buyers' reviews, and make actual purchases

multinational enterprise   A firm that has operations or subsidiaries in many countries

multiple sourcing   An organization's decision to use several suppliers

multiple-unit pricing   The strategy of setting a single price for two or more units

National Advertising Review Board (NARB)   A self-regulatory unit that considers challenges to issues raised by the National Advertising Division (an arm of the Council of Better Business Bureaus) about an advertisement

native advertising   Digital advertising that matches the appearance and the purpose of the content in which it is embedded

negotiated pricing   Establishing a final price through bargaining between seller and customer

neighborhood shopping centers   A type of shopping center usually consisting of several small convenience and specialty stores

new introductory promotion   Promotion that informs consumers about a new product

new-product development process   A seven-phase process for introducing products

news release   A short piece of copy publicizing an event or a product

new-task purchase   An organization's initial purchase of an item to be used to perform a new job or solve a new problem

noise   Anything that reduces a communication's clarity and accuracy

non-price competition   Emphasizes factors other than price to distinguish a product from competing brands

nonprobability sampling   A sampling technique in which there is no way to calculate the likelihood that a specific element of the population being studied will be chosen

nonstore retailing   The selling of products outside the confines of a retail facility

North American Free Trade Agreement (NAFTA)   An alliance that merges Canada, Mexico, and the United States into a single market

North American Industry Classification System (NAICS)   An industry classification system that generates comparable statistics among the United States, Canada, and Mexico

objective-and-task approach   Budgeting for an advertising campaign by first determining its objectives and then calculating the cost of all the tasks needed to attain them

odd-number pricing   The strategy of setting prices using odd numbers that are slightly below whole-dollar amounts

off-peak pricing   The practice of reducing prices of services used during slow periods in order to boost demand

off-price retailers   Stores that buy manufacturers' seconds, overruns, returns, and off-season merchandise for resale to consumers at deep discounts

offshore outsourcing   The practice of contracting with an organization to perform some or all business functions in a country other than the country in which the product will be sold

offshoring   The practice of moving a business process that was done domestically at the local factory to a foreign country, regardless of whether the production accomplished in the foreign country is performed by the local company (e.g., in a wholly owned subsidiary) or a third party (e.g., subcontractor)

oligopoly   A competitive structure in which a few sellers control the supply of a large proportion of a product

omni-channel retailing   Retailing where retailers offer a seamless experience on mobile, desktop, or traditional retail spaces

online fraud   Any attempt to conduct fraudulent activities online, including deceiving consumers into releasing personal information

online retailing   Retailing that makes products available to buyers through Internet connections

online survey   A research method in which respondents answer a questionnaire via e-mail or on a website

on-site computer interview   A variation of the shopping mall intercept interview in which respondents complete a self-administered questionnaire displayed on a computer monitor

operations management   The total set of managerial activities used by an organization to transform resource inputs into goods, services, or both

opinion leader   A member of an informal group who provides information about a specific topic to other group members

order processing   The receipt and transmission of sales order information

outsourcing   The practice of contracting noncore operations with an organization that specializes in that operation

patronage motives   Motives that influence where a person purchases products on a regular basis

penetration pricing   Setting prices below those of competing brands to penetrate a market and gain a significant market share quickly

percent-of-sales approach   Budgeting for an advertising campaign by multiplying the firm's past and expected sales by a standard percentage

perception   The process of selecting, organizing, and interpreting information inputs to produce meaning

performance standard   An expected level of performance against which actual performance can be compared

periodic discounting   Temporary reduction of prices on a patterned or systematic basis

perishability   The inability of unused service capacity to be stored for future use

personal interview survey   A research method in which participants respond to survey questions face-to-face

personal selling   Paid personal communication that attempts to inform customers and persuade them to buy products in an exchange situation

personality   A set of internal traits and distinct behavioral tendencies that result in consistent patterns of behavior in certain situations

physical distribution   Activities used to move products from producers to consumers and other end users

pioneer advertising   Advertising that tries to stimulate demand for a product category rather than a specific brand by informing potential buyers about the product

podcast   Audio or video file that can be downloaded from the Internet with a subscription that automatically delivers new content to listening devices or personal computers; podcasts offer the benefit of convenience, giving users the ability to listen to or view content when and where they choose

point-of-purchase (POP) materials   Signs, window displays, display racks, and similar devices used to attract customers

population   All the elements, units, or individuals of interest to researchers for a specific study

posttest Evaluation of advertising effectiveness after the campaign

power shopping center A type of shopping center that combines off-price stores with category killers

premium money (push money) Extra compensation to salespeople for pushing a line of goods

premium pricing Pricing the highest-quality or most versatile products higher than other models in the product line

premiums Items offered free or at a minimal cost as a bonus for purchasing a product

press conference A meeting used to announce major news events

pretest Evaluation of advertisements performed before a campaign begins

price competition Emphasizes price as an issue and matching or beating competitors' prices

price elasticity of demand A measure of the sensitivity of demand to changes in price

price leaders Products priced below the usual markup, near cost, or below cost

price lining The strategy of selling goods only at certain predetermined prices that reflect definite price breaks

price skimming Charging the highest possible price that buyers who most desire the product will pay

pricing objectives Goals that describe what a firm wants to achieve through pricing

primary data Data observed and recorded or collected directly from respondents

primary demand Demand for a product category rather than for a specific brand

private distributor brands Brands initiated and owned by resellers

private warehouses Company-operated facilities for storing and shipping products

probability sampling A type of sampling in which every element in the population being studied has a known chance of being selected for study

process materials Materials that are used directly in the production of other products but are not readily identifiable

producer markets Individuals and business organizations that purchase products to make profits by using them to produce other products or using them in their operations

product A good, a service, or an idea

product adoption process The stages buyers go through in accepting a product

product advertising Advertising that promotes the uses, features, and benefits of products

product competitors Firms that compete in the same product class but market products with different features, benefits, and prices

product deletion Eliminating a product from the product mix

product design How a product is conceived, planned, and produced

product development Determining if producing a product is technically feasible and cost effective

product differentiation Creating and designing products so that customers perceive them as different from competing products

product features Specific design characteristics that allow a product to perform certain tasks

product item A specific version of a product that can be designated as a distinct offering among a firm's products

product life cycle The progression of a product through four stages: introduction, growth, maturity, and decline

product line A group of closely related product items viewed as a unit because of marketing, technical, or end-use considerations

product manager The person within an organization responsible for a product, a product line, or several distinct products that make up a group

product mix The total group of products that an organization makes available to customers

product modification Change in one or more characteristics of a product

product placement The strategic location of products or product promotions within entertainment media content to reach the product's target market

product positioning Creating and maintaining a certain concept of a product in customers' minds

product specifications Written statements describing a product's necessary characteristics, standards of quality, and other information essential to identifying the best supplier for the needed product

promotion Communication to build and maintain relationships by informing and persuading one or more audiences

promotion mix A combination of promotional methods used to promote a specific product

prospecting Developing a database of potential customers

proxemic communication Communicating by varying the physical distance in face-to-face interactions

psychological influences Factors that in part determine people's general behavior, thus influencing their behavior as consumers

psychological pricing Strategies that encourage purchases based on consumers' emotional responses, rather than on economically rational ones

public relations Communication efforts used to create and maintain favorable relations between an organization and its stakeholders

public warehouses Storage space and related physical distribution facilities that can be leased by companies

publicity A news story type of communication about an organization and/or its products transmitted through a mass medium at no charge

pull policy Promoting a product directly to consumers to develop strong consumer demand that pulls products through a marketing channel

pure competition A market structure characterized by an extremely large number of sellers, none strong enough to significantly influence price or supply

push policy Promoting a product only to the next institution down the marketing channel

quality Characteristics of a product that allow it to perform as expected in satisfying customer needs

quality modifications Changes relating to a product's dependability and durability

quota A limit on the amount of goods an importing country will accept for certain product categories in a specific period of time

quota sampling A nonprobability sampling technique in which researchers divide the population into groups and then arbitrarily choose participants from each group

rack jobbers Full-service, specialty-line wholesalers that own and maintain display racks in stores

radio frequency identification (RFID) Using radio waves to identify and track materials tagged with special microchips

random discounting Temporary reduction of prices on an unsystematic basis

random factor analysis An analysis attempting to attribute erratic sales variations to random, nonrecurrent events

random sampling A form of probability sampling in which all units in a population have an equal chance of appearing in the sample, and the various events that can occur have an equal or known chance of taking place

raw materials Basic natural materials that become part of a physical product

rebates Sales promotion techniques in which a consumer receives a specified amount of money for making a single product purchase

receiver The individual, group, or organization that decodes a coded message

reciprocity An arrangement unique to business marketing in which two organizations agree to buy from each other

recognition test A posttest in which respondents are shown the actual ad and are asked if they recognize it

recruiting Developing a list of qualified applicants for sales positions

reference group A group that a person identifies with so strongly that he or she adopts the values, attitudes, and behavior of group members

reference pricing Pricing a product at a moderate level and positioning it next to a more expensive model or brand

regional issues Versions of a magazine that differ across geographic regions

regional shopping centers A type of shopping center with the largest department stores, widest product mixes, and deepest product lines of all shopping centers

regression analysis A method of predicting sales based on finding a relationship between past sales and one or more independent variables, such as population or income

reinforcement advertising Advertising that assures users they chose the right brand and tells them how to get the most satisfaction from it

relationship marketing Establishing long-term, mutually satisfying buyer-seller relationships

relationship selling The building of mutually beneficial long-term associations with a customer through regular communications over prolonged periods of time

reliability A condition that exists when a research technique produces almost identical results in repeated trials

reminder advertising Advertising used to remind consumers about an established brand's uses, characteristics, and benefits

research design An overall plan for obtaining the information needed to address a research problem or issue

reseller markets Intermediaries that buy finished products and resell them for a profit

retail positioning Identifying an unserved or underserved market segment and serving it through a strategy that distinguishes the retailer from others in the minds of consumers in that segment

retailer An organization that purchases products for the purpose of reselling them to ultimate consumers

retailing All transactions in which the buyer intends to consume the product through personal, family, or household use

roles Actions and activities that a person in a particular position is supposed to perform based on expectations of the individual and surrounding persons

routinized response behavior A consumer problem-solving process used when buying frequently purchased, low-cost items that require very little search-and-decision effort

sales analysis Analysis of sales figures to evaluate a firm's performance

sales branches Manufacturer-owned intermediaries that sell products and provide support services to the manufacturer's sales force

sales contest A sales promotion method used to motivate distributors, retailers, and sales personnel through recognition of outstanding achievements

sales-force forecasting survey A survey of a firm's sales force regarding anticipated sales in their territories for a specified period

sales forecast The amount of a product a company expects to sell during a specific period at a specified level of marketing activities

sales offices Manufacturer-owned operations that provide services normally associated with agents

sales promotion An activity and/or material intended to induce resellers or salespeople to sell a product or consumers to buy it

sample A limited number of units chosen to represent the characteristics of a total population

sampling The process of selecting representative units from a total population

scan-back allowance A manufacturer's reward to retailers based on the number of pieces scanned

screening Choosing the most promising ideas for further review

seasonal analysis An analysis of daily, weekly, or monthly sales figures to evaluate the degree to which seasonal factors influence sales

secondary data Data compiled both inside and outside the organization for some purpose other than the current investigation

secondary-market pricing Setting one price for the primary target market and a different price for another market

segmentation variables Characteristics of individuals, groups, or organizations used to divide a market into segments

selective demand Demand for a specific brand

selective distortion An individual's changing or twisting of information that is inconsistent with personal feelings or beliefs

selective distribution Using only some available outlets in an area to distribute a product

selective exposure The process by which some inputs are selected to reach awareness and others are not

selective retention Remembering information inputs that support personal feelings and beliefs and forgetting inputs that do not

self-concept A perception or view of oneself

selling agents Intermediaries that market a whole product line or a manufacturer's entire output

service An intangible result of the application of human and mechanical efforts to people or objects

shopping mall intercept interviews A research method that involves interviewing a percentage of individuals passing by "intercept" points in a mall

shopping products Items for which buyers are willing to expend considerable effort in planning and making purchases

single-source data Information provided by a single marketing research firm

situational influences Influences that result from circumstances, time, and location that affect the consumer buying decision process

social class An open group of individuals with similar social rank

social influences The forces other people exert on one's buying behavior

social network A website where users can create a profile and interact with other users, post information, and engage in other forms of Web-based communication

social responsibility An organization's obligation to maximize its positive impact and minimize its negative impact on society

sociocultural forces The influences in a society and its culture(s) that change people's attitudes, beliefs, norms, customs, and lifestyles

sole sourcing An organization's decision to use only one supplier

source A person, group, or organization with a meaning it tries to share with a receiver or an audience

Southern Common Market (MERCOSUR) An alliance that promotes the free circulation of goods, services, and production factors, and has a common external tariff and commercial policy among member nations in South America

special-event pricing Advertised sales or price cutting linked to a holiday, season, or event

specialty products Items with unique characteristics that buyers are willing to expend considerable effort to obtain

specialty-line wholesalers Full-service wholesalers that carry only a single product line or a few items within a product line

stakeholders Constituents who have a "stake," or claim, in some aspect of a company's products, operations, markets, industry, and outcomes

statistical interpretation Analysis of what is typical and what deviates from the average

storyboard A blueprint that combines copy and visual material to show the sequence of major scenes in a commercial

straight commission compensation plan Paying salespeople according to the amount of their sales in a given period

straight rebuy purchase A routine purchase of the same products under approximately the same terms of sale by a business buyer

straight salary compensation plan Paying salespeople a specific amount per time period, regardless of selling effort

strategic alliance A partnership that is formed to create a competitive advantage on a worldwide basis

strategic business unit (SBU) A division, product line, or other profit center within the parent company

strategic channel alliance An agreement whereby the products of one organization are distributed through the marketing channels of another

strategic marketing management The process of planning, implementing, and evaluating the performance of marketing activities and strategies, both effectively and efficiently

strategic performance evaluation Establishing performance standards, measuring actual performance, comparing actual performance with established standards, and modifying the marketing strategy, if needed

strategic planning The process of establishing an organizational mission and formulating goals, corporate strategy, marketing objectives, marketing strategy, and a marketing plan

strategic windows Temporary periods of optimal fit between the key requirements of a market and the particular capabilities of a company competing in that market

stratified sampling A type of probability sampling in which the population is divided into groups with a common attribute and a random sample is chosen within each group

styling The physical appearance of a product

subculture A group of individuals whose characteristics, values, and behavioral patterns are similar within the group and different from those of people in the surrounding culture

supermarkets Large, self-service stores that carry a complete line of food products, along with some nonfood products

superregional shopping centers A type of shopping center with the widest and deepest product mixes that attracts customers from many miles away

superstores Giant retail outlets that carry food and nonfood products found in supermarkets, as well as most routinely purchased consumer products

supply chain All the organizations and activities involved with the flow and transformation of products from raw materials through to the end customer

supply-chain management (SCM) The coordination of all the activities involved with the flow and transformation of supplies, products, and information throughout the supply chain to the ultimate consumer

supply management In its broadest form, refers to the processes that enable the progress of value from raw material to final customer and back to redesign and final disposition

support personnel Sales staff members who facilitate selling but usually are not involved solely with making sales

sustainable competitive advantage An advantage that the competition cannot copy

SWOT analysis Assessment of an organization's strengths, weaknesses, opportunities, and threats

tactile communication Communicating through touching

target audience The group of people at whom advertisements are aimed

target market A specific group of customers on whom an organization focuses its marketing efforts

team selling The use of a team of experts from all functional areas of a firm, led by a salesperson, to conduct the personal selling process

technical salespeople Support salespeople who give technical assistance to a firm's current customers

technology The application of knowledge and tools to solve problems and perform tasks more efficiently

telemarketing The performance of marketing-related activities by telephone

telephone depth interview An interview that combines the traditional focus group's ability to probe with the confidentiality provided by telephone surveys

telephone survey A research method in which respondents' answers to a questionnaire are recorded by an interviewer on the phone

television home shopping A form of selling in which products are presented to television viewers, who can buy them by calling a toll-free number and paying with a credit card

test marketing Introducing a product on a limited basis to measure the extent to which potential customers will actually buy it

third-party logistics (3PL) firms Firms that have special expertise in core physical distribution activities such as warehousing, transportation, inventory management, and information technology and can often perform these activities more efficiently

time series analysis A forecasting method that uses historical sales data to discover patterns in the firm's sales over time and generally involves trend, cycle, seasonal, and random factor analyses

total budget competitors Firms that compete for the limited financial resources of the same customers

total cost The sum of average fixed and average variable costs times the quantity produced

trade name Full legal name of an organization

trade sales promotion methods Methods intended to persuade wholesalers and retailers to carry a producer's products and market them aggressively

trade salespeople Salespeople involved mainly in helping a producer's customers promote a product

trademark A legal designation of exclusive use of a brand

trading company A company that links buyers and sellers in different countries

traditional specialty retailers Stores that carry a narrow product mix with deep product lines

transfer pricing Prices charged in sales between an organization's units

transportation The movement of products from where they are made to intermediaries and end users

trend analysis An analysis that focuses on aggregate sales data over a period of many years to determine general trends in annual sales

truck wholesalers Limited-service wholesalers that transport products directly to customers for inspection and selection

tying agreement An agreement in which a supplier furnishes a product to a channel member with the stipulation that the channel member must purchase other products as well

unaided recall test A posttest in which respondents are asked to identify advertisements they have seen recently but are not given any recall clues

undifferentiated targeting strategy A strategy in which an organization designs a single marketing mix and directs it at the entire market for a particular product

unsought products Products purchased to solve a sudden problem, products of which customers are unaware, and products that people do not necessarily think about buying

validity A condition that exists when a research method measures what it is supposed to measure

value A customer's subjective assessment of benefits relative to costs in determining the worth of a product

value analysis An evaluation of each component of a potential purchase

variable costs Costs that vary directly with changes in the number of units produced or sold

vendor analysis A formal, systematic evaluation of current and potential vendors

venture team A cross-functional group that creates entirely new products that may be aimed at new markets

vertical channel integration Combining two or more stages of the marketing channel under one management

vertical marketing system (VMS) A marketing channel managed by a single channel member to achieve efficient, low-cost distribution aimed at satisfying target market customers

viral marketing A strategy to get consumers to share a marketer's message, often through e-mail or online videos, in a way that spreads dramatically and quickly

warehouse clubs Large-scale, members-only establishments that combine features of cash-and-carry wholesaling with discount retailing

warehouse showrooms Retail facilities in large, low-cost buildings with large, on-premises inventories and minimal services

warehousing The design and operation of facilities for storing and moving goods

wholesaler An individual or organization that sells products that are bought for resale, for making other products, or for general business operations

wholesaling Transactions in which products are bought for resale, for making other products, or for general business operations

widgets Small bits of software on a website, desktop, or mobile device that enable users to interface with the application and operating system

width of product mix The number of product lines a company offers

wiki Type of software that creates an interface that enables users to add or edit the content of some types of websites

willingness to spend An inclination to buy because of expected satisfaction from a product, influenced by the ability to buy and numerous psychological and social forces

word-of-mouth communication Personal informal exchanges of communication that customers share with one another about products, brands, and companies

World Trade Organization (WTO) An entity that promotes free trade among member nations by eliminating trade barriers and educating individuals, companies, and governments about trade rules around the world

name index

Nelson, Keith, 344
Netemeyer, Richard, 431
Netemeyer, Richard G., 261
Newell, Keemer, 344
Newman, George E., 142
Ng, Serena, 265, 408
Nickisch, Curt, 269
Niedrich, Ronald W., 419
Nieves, Melissa, 456
Niles, Robert, 301
Noguti, Valeria, 413
Norton, Steven, 98
Nosi, Costanza, 112
Novak, Thomas P., 214
Novelino, Teresa, 306
Novy-Williams, Ebon, 331
Nudd, Tim, 250, 437
Nyilasy, Gergely, 70

O

O'Connor, Clare, 348
Odell, Kat, 71
Odell, Patricia, 459
Ofek, Elie, 283
Ofir, Xhezy, 16
Oh, Hammo, 86
Ojeda-Zapta, Julio, 280
Okazaki, Shintaro, 430
Oliverez-Giles, Nathan, 50
Olivo, Natalie, 378
Olmstead, Kenneth, 224
Olsen, Mitchell C., 256
Olson, Eric M., 29
O'Malley, Gavin, 150
Ore, Michella, 47
Ore, Michella Caproni, 40
Orofino, Emily, 228, 229
Ortman, Jennifer, 153
Osawa, Juro, 210
Oulton, Emma, 223
Ovide, Shira, 161
Owen, Tina, 112
Owens, Deborah, 207
Ozretic-Dosen, Durdana, 188

P

Padgett, Tim, 199
Paharia, Neeru, 285
Painter, Kim, 8
Paladino, Angela, 70
Palmatier, Robert W., 16, 189
Pang, Kevin, 164
Parasuraman, Dhruv Grewal, 84
Pasquarelli, Adrianne, 399
Patel, Sujan, 220
Patel, Vijay K., 11
Paton, Elizabeth, 274
Patton, Leslie, 225
Peck, Joann, 404
Pekham, Vicoria, 151
Pelberg, Steven, 419
Peltz, James, 272
Peltz, James F., 183, 345, 370

Perez, Sarah, 230, 283
Perkins, Tom, 241
Perman, Stacy, 49
Perrin, Andrew, 218
Persson, Andreas, 85
Pesce, Nicole Lyn, 32
Peter, Paul, 290
Peters, Rik, 432
Peterson, Hayley, 370
Peterson, Robert M., 447
Peterson, Tim, 93
Petro, Greg, 113
Pham, D. J. Amy, 151
Phan, Michelle, 213, 223
Phillips, Erica E., 234
Phua, Joe, 412
Pidaparthy, Umika, 225
Pieper, Torsten M., 11
Piercy, Nigel F., 447
Pierson, David, 221, 299
Piësch, Anton, 187
Pinheiro, Maria Teresa, 215
Pitt, Leyland, 396
Plomion, Ben, 422
Plummer, Joseph T., 119
Poggi, Jeanine, 428
Polis, Carey, 442
Pollard, Kelvin, 64
Polsa, Pia, 447
Porter, Arthur L., 463
Porter, Stephen S., 449
Powell, Dominic, 412
Powers, Thomas L., 405
Poynter, Ray, 92
Pratesi, Carlo Alberto, 112
Pressey, Andrew, 136
Pride, William M., 51, 62
Pullig, Chris, 261
Putnam, Mandy, 148
Putsis, William P., 248
Pyykkonen, Travis, 164

Q

Qualls. William J., 149
Quiano, Kathy, 200
Quittner, Jeremy, 49

R

Rahman, Kaleel, 261
Raider, Jeff, 327
Rampall, Catherine, 293
Ramstad, Evan, 77
Rangan, Kasturi, 169
Rangaswamy, Arvind, 100
Rao, Leena, 210
Rapp, Adam, 347
Rateneshwar, S., 35
Ravid, S. Abraham, 439
Raymond, Mary Anne, 458
Reeg, Caitlan, 188
Regan, Kristin, 241
Reich, Brandon J., 437
Reid, Michael, 199

Reifler, Petra, 207
Reisinger, Don, 155, 294
Rettan, Belaid, 73
Reynolds, Isabel, 192
Reynolds, Richard, 14
Riboud, Douglas, 71
Ricadela, Aaron, 112
Rich, Anne K., 446
Rigaux, Benny P., 148
Riley, Charles, 185
Rindfleisch, Aric, 147
Robbie, Renee, 149
Roberts, Mary Lou, 99, 217, 226, 227
Robertson, David, 93
Robinson, Matt, 192
Robinson, Stacey G., 291
Robson, Karen, 396
Rockoff, D., 321
Rockoff, Jonathan D., 453
Rockwood, Kate, 223
Rodriguez, Ashley, 154, 295
Rodriguez, Michael, 447
Rogers, Everett M., 253, 254
Romani, Simona, 70
Ross, Jeanne W., 373
Ross, Michael, 112
Rossen, Ben, 234
Roy, Sanjit Kumar, 216
Rubenfeld, Samuel, 60
Rubera, Gaia, 188
Rubin, Courtney, 327
Rubin, James, 99
Rusch, Emile, 29
Rusetski, Alexander, 313
Russell, Cristel Antonia, 413
Rutherford, Brian N., 460
Ryals, Lynette, 85

S

Sääksjärvi, Maria, 447
Sacks, Danielle, 14
Safdar, Khadeeja, 213, 377
Salzberg, Matt, 25
Samaha, Stephen A., 189
Samuel, Alexandra, 119
Sarin, Shikhar, 36
Sauer, Abe, 412
Sawalhy, Haytham, 288
Scerr, Ian, 77
Schaal, Dennis, 419
Schaible, Stacie, 221
Schaur, Georg, 355
Schechner, Sam, 185, 195
Scheer, Lisa K., 16
Schlee, Regina Pefanis, 100
Schlereth, Laura, 222
Schlossberg, Mallory, 406
Schmidt, Gregory, 280
Schmitt, Bernd H., 412
Schneider, Joan, 250
Schoenberg, Tom, 192
Schöler, Lisa, 413
Schoultz, Mike, 238

Schreier, Martin, 275, 276
Schultz, Don E., 464
Schultz, E. J., 399, 422
Schultz, Howard, 283
Schultz, Nich, A1
Schulze, Christian, 413
Schumann, Jan H., 434
Schvaneveldt, Shane J., 137
Scommegna, Paola, 64
Seale, Barbara, 451
Sebastian, Ina, 373
Seetharaman, Deepa, 219
Segran, Elizabeth, 299
Seiter, John S., 449
Shaffer, Erica, 244
Shah, Neil, 64
Shanahan, Kevin, 234
Sharma, Amol, 219
Sheinin, Daniel A., 425
Shellenbarger, Sue, 94
Sherry, John F. Jr., 15
Shervani, Tasadduq A., 449
Sheth, Jagdish N., 16
Shields, Mike, 422, 428
Shlosser, Kurt, 337
Shoup, Mary Ellen, 164
Shultz, E. J., 31
Shultz, Howard, 13
Shulz, Don E., 256
Silcox, Beth Douglass, 451
Simmons, Carolyn J., 261
Simms, C. D., 255
Simonite, Tom, 243
Simonson, Itamar, 16
Sinclair, Kate, 40
Singerman, Seth, 379
Singh, Sarwant, 348, 349
Singh, Shruti, 31
Sirianni, Nancy, 291
Sisodia, Rajendras, 16
Sivakumar, K., 288
Skare, Vatroslav, 188
Skiera, Bernd, 275, 413
Slater, Stanley F., 29
Slefo, George, 395
Sloat, Molly, 92
Slotegraaf, Rebecca J., 256
Smith, Ana Serafin, 155
Smith, Daniel C., 313
Smith, Mike Deri, 96
Smith, N. Craig, 71
Snider, Mike, 114, 220
Snyder, Bill, 183, 315
Soat, Molly, 116
Solomon, Dan, 263
Solomon, Mark B., 352
Solomon, Paul, 453
Solomon, Steven Davidoff, 210
Sommer, Cari, 223
Sopadjieva, Emma, 230
Sorvino, Chloe, 277
Soukhoroukova, Arina, 275
Soule, Catherine A. Armstrong, 437
Soutar, Geoffrey N., 207

company index

subject index